Lee I. Levine, editor of the volume, is a member of the Institute of Archaeology of the Hebrew University of Jerusalem.

JERUSALEM

ITS SANCTITY

AND CENTRALITY

TO JUDAISM,

CHRISTIANITY,

AND ISLAM

✦ ✦ ✦

JERUSALEM

ITS SANCTITY

AND CENTRALITY

TO JUDAISM,

CHRISTIANITY,

AND ISLAM

✦ ✦ ✦

Edited by Lee I. Levine

CONTINUUM ✦ NEW YORK

1999
The Continuum Publishing Company
370 Lexington Avenue
New York, NY 10017

Printed in the United States of America

Library of Congress Cataloging-in-Publication Data

Jerusalem : its sanctity and centrality to Judaism, Christianity, and
    Islam / edited by Lee I. Levine.
        p.   cm.
    Includes bibliographical references and index.
    ISBN 0-8264-1024-3
    1. Jerusalem—History. 2. Jerusalem in Judaism. 2. Jerusalem in
Christianity. 2. Jerusalem in Islam. I. Levine, Lee I.
DS109.9.J4576   1998   98-15267
956.94'42—dc21   CIP

ITEM CHARGED

P.Barcode:

Due Date: 7/9/2019 10:30 PM

Title: Jerusalem : its sanctity and
              centrality to Judaism, Christianity,
              and Islam / edited by Lee I.
              Levine
Author:
CallNo.:   DS109.9 .J4576 1999
Enum.:
Chron.:
Copy: 1
I.Barcode:

*Non-reserve items can be renewed by logging
into your library account at www.jkmlibrary.org.
All library materials are subject to recall.*

In memory of the untimely passing
of an esteemed colleague and conference participant,
Hava Lazarus-Yafeh

Contents

VI. JERUSALEM IN THE LATE MIDDLE AGES AND MODERN ERA

Preface

On June 23–28, 1996, forty internationally-renowned scholars convened in Jerusalem for deliberations on *The Sanctity and Centrality of Jerusalem to Judaism, Christianity and Islam.* The conference was under the auspices of four academic institutions: The Jewish Theological Seminary of America (the Louis Finkelstein Institute for Religious and Social Studies); The Seminary of Judaic Studies (recently renamed The Schechter Institute of Judaic Studies); The Hebrew University of Jerusalem; and Tantur Ecumenical Institute for Theological Studies. They were joined by eleven co-sponsoring institutions: The American Jewish Congress; Bethlehem University; Boston College; Brandeis University; The Israel Academy of Sciences and Humanities; The National Association of Arab Americans, Notre Dame University; Tel-Aviv University; Union Theological Seminary; Yad Izhak Ben-Zvi; and Yale University. This volume includes the presentations delivered during that week-long conference.

We wish to acknowledge a number of key persons whose commitment to the idea of such a scholarly gathering was crucial to its realization and success. Chancellor I. Schorsch of The Jewish Theological Seminary offered his enthusiastic support from the outset, as did the chairman of The Seminary of Judaic Studies International Board, Professor J. Fleishman. Father T. Stransky, Director of the Tantur Ecumenical Institute, was a full partner in the planning of the conference; he graciously placed at our disposal the beautiful premises of his institution in southern Jerusalem as the primary site for our proceedings. Other venues for conference sessions included The Seminary of Judaic Studies, the Hebrew University, and Bethlehem University. Special thanks are due Professor Y. Nini of Tel-Aviv University, Dr. Z. Zameret of Yad Izhak Ben-Zvi, and Dr. M. Hassassian of Bethlehem University, each of whom hosted an evening of public lectures presented by conference participants.

I would like to thank H. Davis for her efforts in organizing the conference, coordinating its schedule, and preparing the abstract booklet, conference program, and other materials. She was likewise instrumental in editing and preparing this volume for publication.

Finally, our gratitude to Continuum Publishing Company of New York for its cooperation in publishing these proceedings.

THE EDITOR

Introduction

A city will inevitably adopt many of the characteristics and forms regnant in any given age. When that city is not just another urban center, but possesses a spiritual and religious dimension as well, the reshaping of its urban terrain might indeed be extensive and reflect ideas and practices which find literary and religious expression as well.

The study of Jerusalem offers a unique opportunity to examine the impact of a dominant culture on a city. Each time Jerusalem was conquered and ruled by a different group, the city's physical appearance was inevitably reshaped, including its size, population, leadership, public buildings, and governing institutions. Moreover, given the differing traditions, other aspects of urban life were lifewise affected. New religious edifices were built and given special prominence, and the yearly calendar was altered and new holidays celebrated, both publicly and privately. Under these circumstances, the newly dominant culture would quickly reshape the city's landscape in accordance with its particular traditions. Thus, the politics and religious life of a city such as Jerusalem, including varied cultural creations and archeological remains, are inextricably intertwined, and each component reflects in one way or another the ideals and worldviews of the ruling power.

What uniquely characterizes Jerusalem is the religious value it holds for each of the three major religions of the western world. Dominated over the centuries by a variety of cultures and traditions, Jerusalem bears the stamp of each in its physical and spiritual legacies. It is therefore fascinating not only to study how each tradition totally redefined this urban setting to suit its own political, social, and religious agendas, but also to compare the similarities and differences between them. The following types of questions were addressed throughout the conference:

- How did the Jews, Christians, and Muslims each reshape the city during their political hegemony? How did the city-plan, as well as the organization and location of public buldings, reflect the character of the ruling power? In what ways do the art and architecture of each period represent the ideas and values propagated by the various regimes?

• What political and social institutions were created by each tradition, and how did these institutions promote the particular agenda of each? Who constituted the leadership elite in the city, and how did it evolve over time in response to changing political and religious contexts?

• How was the religious life of the city expressed in each era, in its material, institutional, and spiritual realms? It what ways was the religious ambience of the city affected by its political and social contexts? Were the forms and practices developed in Jerusalem by each tradition reflective of practices elsewhere? To what degree did the city develop its own distinct ideas and religious forms, and to what degree was it receptive to outside influences?

✦ ✦ ✦

The articles in this volume have been organized chronologically, commencing with the biblical tradition. Japhet offers a broad sweep of the development of Jerusalem as a chosen city. Beginning with the pre-Israelite era, she traces the city's gradual evolution toward a status of uncontested preeminence in Jewish life, carefully noting the various political, social, and religious factors impacting on this development from one era to the next. The other articles in this section focus on what are undoubtedly two of the most momentous events in the First Temple period. Zakovitch hones in on the Davidic traditions, and Hallo on the era of Hezekiah. Their analyses provide an illuminating study of contrasts.

Zakovitch offers an insightful literary approach, focusing on the sources as evidence as to how David, his contemporaries, and the events associated with them were understood and depicted by later tradition. The specific historical implications are downplayed, but the relationship between these literary traditions and their ideological projections is meticulously scrutinized.

Hallo, for his part, draws heavily on Assyriological sources in an effort to reconstruct the events surrounding Sennacherib's siege of 701 B.C.E. and Jerusalem's escape from destruction. The extent to which external sources can illuminate and corroborate the biblical historical narrative is cogently argued, as are the implications for contemporary controversies regarding the historical reliability of the biblical narrative. Specifically, Hallo takes sharp issue with those scholars who would deny any value both to the Bible as an historical record and to related archeological evidence for the reconstruction (however partial) of the First Temple period.

The articles which address aspects of the Second Temple period concentrate on the last part of this 600-year era, i.e., the Hasmonean and, more particularly, Herodian eras. Influenced by the dominant culture symbolized by the Greek *polis*, Jerusalem's status as the "mother" city of the Jews gained in importance. My article argues that by the early Roman period the city had become ever-more Jewish in many of its practices and observances. At the same time, however, it had also become a cosmopolitan city replete with institutions, languages, material culture, social patterns, and religious practices, many of which were adopted and adapted from the Greco-Roman world. Jerusalem was, at one and the same time, the most Jewish and most cosmopolitan of cities in Roman Palestine. The tensions and creativity resulting from these diverse and, at times, conflicting tendencies were a hallmark of the city's landscape during these centuries.

Goodman argues that pilgrimage, especially from the Diaspora, was a product of Herod's vision and initiative. The encouragement of Diaspora involvement in the city was important to this king for political, cultural, and especially economic reasons. The Temple played a crucial role in this scenario, constituting an engaging focus for visitors from abroad and thus attracting considerable funds which spurred the economy of the city as a whole, its environs, and Judaea generally. Goodman's linking of Judaean developments to wider phenomena in the Roman world adds an important dimension to his analysis.

Several articles focus on the extent to which the city played a role in messianic movements of the later Second Temple period. Baumgarten offers a multifaceted view of messianism in the era, a view that has become widely accepted of late. Many differing messianic ideologies were to be found in Judaean society, some purely ideational in nature, others more practically oriented; some apocalyptic, others with specific political goals; some based on a crystallized philosophy, others revolving around a charismatic individual; some which place Jerusalem at its center, others seemingly oblivious to the city. While Baumgarten focuses on several non-Jerusalem-oriented messianic phenomena, particularly that of John the Baptist, Sanders discusses the role Jerusalem and its Temple played in the life of Jesus, in Acts, and especially in the writings of Paul. While not a central theme in any of the above, the significance of the city and Temple, both historical and symbolic, found expression in each and every case.

Alexander focuses on the book of Jubilee's reference to Jerusalem as the navel of the universe and on the city's geographical centrality as reflected in the description of the Table of Nations (Genesis 10). Claiming that neither earlier biblical nor Near Eastern models can fully account for this motif, Alexander looks to Greek models and finds the characterization of certain Greek religious centers as *omphaloi* (e.g., Delphi), as well as to the Ionic cartographic tradition, as the probable sources of Jubilees' description. He places these ideas in the context of the newly-expanding Hasmonean state, with its center in Jerusalem, and views them as an attempt to legitimize Hasmonean territorial expansion. Alexander also discusses the thirteenth-century Hereford map of the world, which probably derived from at least a fifth-century original. Reflecting a "symbolic and mythological geography" within Christianity, this map may have in some way been drawn from the Jubilees cartographic tradition. Finally, recalling a number of rabbinic statements on the centrality of Jerusalem, as well as the claim that the Temple contained the Foundation Stone for the entire universe, Alexander suggests that such a tradition may be polemical, intended either to counter Rome's claim of centrality, or perhaps a less-centripetal, Diaspora-oriented, Jewish view.

Finally, Shinan analyzes the names for Jerusalem which appear in several rabbinic traditions. Some lists include ten names, and others seventy. He emphasizes the uniqueness of such lists in that they include negative as well as positive appellations and that they reflect the rabbinic memories of Jerusalem—her failings as well as her glory. Moreover, Shinan notes third- and fourth-century Samaritan parallels to such listings and suggests that these Jewish traditions may also stem from polemical concerns.

A major focus of the conference was Byzantine Jerusalem (324–638 C.E.). Tsafrir opens this section by offering a comprehensive account of the transformation of the city into a hub of Christian activity, commencing in the days of Constantine and continuing through the sixth century, with the flurry of building activity associated with Justinian. A Christian stamp was thus imprinted on the city, and the Church, through its various buildings and institutions, quickly came to dominate urban affairs, much as the Temple authorities had done earlier.

While also affecting other parts of Palestine, the Constantinian revolution was primarily aimed at Jerusalem and its environs. From a backwater town named Aelia Capitolina, the city was now thrust into the forefront of religious and political prominence. Christian clergy, monks, and pilgrims filled its streets, and the city's ecclesiastical leadership strove for ever-greater political and religious prominence and recognition in the Byzantine world.

Rubin deftly traces the attempts of Jerusalem bishops to promote their city's cause by claiming that it is both the site of holy places where relics were found and where holy signs occur—in the present no less than in the past.

Pilgrimage became a widespread and significant phenomenon in Byzantine Palestine, much as it had been earlier, at the end of the Second Temple period. Bowman's study of the first such pilgrim itinerary (that of the Bordeaux Pilgrim, ca. 333) offers an original interpretation to what has generally been regarded as a dry listing of places and distances. He contends that the biblical associations (both of the Hebrew Bible and the New Testament) conjured up at these different sites may be understood as conveying a profound religious message for the Christian pilgrim.

The phenomenon of pilgrimage is taken up by Bitton-Ashkelony from an entirely different perspective. She discusses the more reserved attitudes of the fourth- to fifth-century church fathers Augustine and Gregory of Nyssa which range from downplaying the religious value of pilgrimage to Jerusalem (Augustine) to outright opposition to the phenomenon (Gregory). She firmly argues that these reservations were not directed against pilgrimage as a religious value per se, but rather against the need for fulfilling this ideal specifically in Jerusalem; local pilgrimage to holy places and to tombs of martyrs and saints was of equal, if not superior, value.

Irshai discusses the Jewish dimension of the Jerusalem Church. Beginning with the primitive church in the first century, whose Jewish roots are self-evident, he points out aspects of the Aelia church which bore Jewish traits, not the least of which was the apparent presence in the city of a number of Jewish-Christian synagogues. Even in the fourth century, Jews appeared as significant figures in some of the writings of Cyril of Jerusalem, in his letter to Emperor Constantius II and especially in his fifteenth catechetical lecture, which Irshai suggests was reworked to include references to Julian's abortive attempt to rebuilt the Jerusalem Temple.

Perrone tackles the intriguing question of the interrelationship between historical-earthly Jerusalem on the one hand, and the symbolic-heavenly one on the other. After tracing this dichotomy from New Testament times through the Ebionites, Justin, the gnostics, Irenaeus, Tertullian, Origen, and various chiliast ideologies down to the fourth century, he notes the divergent attitudes of Eusebius and Cyril. The focus of Perrone's study, however, is the varying attitudes toward Jerusalem espoused by Jerome in his different writings, with a particular emphasis on his famous *Epistle* 46—from the enthusiastic embrace of the earthly "Constantinian" Jerusalem by a pilgrim to the denial of any unique status of the city. What is unusual about *Epistle* 46 is that it grapples with these two polarities in an attempt to reconcile between them. Perrone accounts for these differences by attempting to reconstruct the *Sitz im Leben* of each within Jerome's career.

Wilken focuses on the Byzantine tradition, which was fully committed to earthly Jerusalem as the gateway to heaven. It was only in this city that the true message of Jesus and the New Testament could be fully received, understood, and internalized, and it is only by living where Jesus lived, seeing what he saw, and touching what he touched that one could experience the fullest spiritual life. The bearers of this message were the monks of Jerusalem's Judaean Desert who propagated an all-encompassing love for the earthly city. Wilken incorporates into his discussion Sabas' and Theodosius' well-known petition to the emperor Anastasius, as well as the emotional laments of the sixth-century monks, Strategius and Sophronius, as they witnessed the capture of Jerusalem by the Persians and Muslims respectively.

Bradshaw takes up the fascinating question of the influence of Jerusalem on Christian liturgy. Following an overview of the *status questionis*, he notes the many ways that this liturgy was assumed to have developed within the context of the city's rituals and was disseminated throughout the Christian world by returning pilgrims. Without totally denying the cogency of this view, Bradshaw, however, seeks to fine-tune it, suggesting, for one, that even when Jerusalem practices were imitated, it was often a very selective process and may have taken place only after a long interval. Moreover, some of the so-called Jerusalem rituals may have in fact been introduced into the city by visiting pilgrims; in other words, the city imported traditions and not only exported them. Finally, Bradshaw notes that a number of liturgical traditions usually associated with Jerusalem were, in reality, of foreign vintage, often differing significantly from those of Jerusalem itself.

Stemberger completes the section on Byzantine Jerusalem with a discussion of Christian and Jewish sources which respond to the Persian and Muslim conquests of the city in the early seventh century. These conquests, especially the former, unleashed a wide range of religious responses, from dirges over the city's grim fate to ecstatic eschatological visions of messianic proportions. The relevant writings of Strategius, Sophronius, and Pseudo Methodius are noted from the Christian side, as are the apocalyptic Sefer Zerubbabel, the *piyyutim* of Qallir and several midrashim from the Jewish.

A fourth focus of the volume addresses the early Middle Ages, when Jerusalem came under Muslim rule. Grabar's keynote address at the conference offered a panoramic overview of medieval Jerusalem (with a retrospective glance beginning with Aelia Capitolina) and thus opens this section. Grabar deftly surveys the development of sacred space in the city from one period to the next, noting that each successive regnant religious tradition added its own unique stamp to the city while incorporating earlier ones as well. The rich tapestry of early medieval Jerusalem, with its Christian and Jewish communities living beside the dominant Muslim population, is captured through Grabar's description of the evolution of holy sites and what he terms the "petrification" of memories, in this case from biblical and New Testament sources as well as from late traditions associated with the prophet Muḥammad himself. Once again, we see that Jerusalem absorbed different religious traditions while providing the setting for the emergence of new forms and patterns.

Whatever Jerusalem's importance in Islamic tradition, there is no gainsaying that Mecca remained its supreme religious center. The contrast between the place of Mecca in Islam and that of Jerusalem in Judaism is skillfully drawn by Lazarus-Yafeh. Beginning with a number of similarities between each holy city (its prehistory, the dissemination of holiness from one particular sacred spot to an entire city, and the phenomenon of pilgrimage), her discussion then focuses on three significant differences: (1) memories of the destruction of the Temple and their impact on the eschatological hopes within Judaism (not to be found in Islam); (2) the competition between Mecca and Medina (with no similar phenomenon in Judaism); and (3) the symbolism surrounding Jerusalem (with nothing comparable with respect to Mecca). These differences are explained not merely as a result of different historical circumstances, but indeed as a reflection of the very essence of each religious tradition.

Elad traces the beginning of Muslim worship at the Ḥaram el-Sharif (the Muslim term for the area of the Temple Mount) and the practice of pilgrimage to Jerusalem as encouraged by the ruling Umayyads. He analyzes the religious ceremonies involved in such visits and attempts to reconstruct the motivations for such pilgrimages, as well as the routes taken by pilgrims and the specific places visited both in the Ḥaram and throughout the city.

Neuwirth discusses the early religious development of Islam, when the new faith transcended its pagan roots, Medina-based setting, and Jerusalem orientation and proceeded to develop a character and symbolism of its own. Despite the hostility toward the Jews of Medina when they failed to accept Muḥammad, many elements of Judaism did, in fact, penetrate early Muslim worship, such as the focus on sacred space, praying in its direction, and the use of Scriptures as an integral part of the ritual ceremony. Neuwirth argues that the "exodus" to Medina stimulated the search for a scriptural substitute for former ritual patterns and accorded a universal dimension to the new community and its message.

Rosen-Ayalon's article concludes this section by comparing descriptions of the city of Jerusalem by a Muslim, Jew, and Christian, all of whom visited Jerusalem in the eighth decade of the twelfth century. As might have been expected, each dwells on his own religious community, Al-Harawi on the Muslim, Benjamin of Tudela on the Jewish, and Theoderic on the Christian. Nevertheless, in a number of instances they each relate to the buildings and monuments of the "others," and a comparison of these descriptions and the organization of their respective material is most instructive. None of these authors, however, relates in a meaningful way to the city's population as a whole, or to its institutions and ruling authorities. This introspective focus appears to have been characteristic of medieval (and, for that matter, modern) Jerusalem society.

A further focus of the conference—and the present volume—was the place of Jerusalem in medieval Jewish and Christian traditions. Stroumsa's contribution continues a theme noted with respect to the Byzantine period, i.e., the tension between the notions of earthly and heavenly Jerusalem, which is now further sharpened by the preeminence attained by the city in the Byzantine period. Stroumsa studies these two contrasting yet interrelated dimensions in the Middle Ages. On the one hand, the upsurge of interest in earthly Jerusalem, sparked by the same religious currents which eventually led to the Crusades, was often expressed in the building of local imitations of Jerusalem *loca sacra*, e.g., churches which resembled the Holy Sepulchre, mounds reminiscent of the Golgotha, and monasteries which were often referred to as Jerusalem. Attempts to actually create a replica of Jerusalem are also known and are referred to by the author as an early example of EuroDisney. Concomitant to this tendency, which generally languished after the failure of the Crusades, was the contrasting development of a mystical, spiritual Jerusalem, which could be realized within one's own soul. Building on traditions articulated by Augustine and John Cassian, multiple levels of meaning were assigned to Jerusalem which could be realized through spiritual exercises and mystical contemplation. Going to Jerusalem came to be associated with leading a life of true spirituality and virtue.

Constable's investigation focuses on the symbol of the cross in medieval Europe, describing its alleged power in the religious and political spheres during the ninth to twelfth centuries. More specifically, the cross was associated with Jerusalem in the various ceremonies and celebrations throughout the Christian liturgical year. The Crusades provided the opportunity for the identification of this effort with the symbol of the cross, and according to tradition Pope Urban II ordered all crusaders to wear a cross insignia on their outer garments; some even had it branded on their foreheads. The cross was also associated with other crusades (e.g., in Spain), and was used by pilgrims as well. Thus, by the twelfth century the cross had become a symbol of "Christian power and of individual salvation."

That the crusades highlighted the centrality of Jerusalem is well known; Chazan, however, goes one step further and focuses on Jewish awareness of this phenomenon among their Christian oppressors. In describing crusading efforts, the Hebrew chronicles, particularly the Mainz Anonymous, use biblical terminology which is laden with messianic meaning and often associated with Jerusalem (e.g., Isa. 40). Of more import, however, are the responses of the Jewish community, not only in the well-known martyrological sphere, thereby reflecting the religious fervor of the crusaders themselves, but also in the fact that the sacrifices being offered by Jewish martyrdom were reminiscent of Temple sacrifices and even more desired by God than the sacrifice of Jesus.

This latter sacrifice, the very core of Chrisitan faith, paled—in Jewish eyes at least—before the slaughter of Jewish men, women, and children on the altar of their faith during the crusades. Moreover, just as Christianity had appropriated the biblical imagery of Abraham's readiness to sacrifice his son for its theological agenda, so, too, did Ashkenazic Jewry in the way it carried out this martyrdom. The Hebrew chronicles often invoke the image of the 'Aqedah when describing these events.

Linder deals with medieval Christian liturgical reaction to the collapse of crusader efforts, particularly defeat at the hands of Saladin in 1187. Liturgical expression varied in extent and content. Individual prayers, a single Mass, and even a full week's liturgical cycle were instituted in the coming years and decades to commemorate this and subsequent crusading events. Some of these responses were of short duration, others struck deeper roots and continued to be recited for centuries. The geographical distribution of these prayers was wide, with a particular concentration in France and England. Beginning with concerns such as the crusading efforts and Jerusalem, some of these prayers eventually came to include other issues as well, such as prayers for the welfare of the king and his realm.

The many and varied ways that the memory of Jerusalem has been perpetuated in Jewish tradition is the subject of Golinkin's broad investigation. He divides these traditions into three categories: (1) the various customs attributed to Second Temple Jerusalem; (2) post-destruction ceremonies intended to preserve the city's memory; and (3) unique customs of Jerusalem which evolved over the last two millennia. Spanning the realms of prayer, days of mourning, wedding and funeral customs, and others, these customs on occasion continue those practiced during Second Temple times.

Turning to Jewish liturgy, Reif has plotted the use of the theme of Jerusalem during the formative period of Jewish liturgy, i.e., the first millennium C.E. Noting the various prayers and prayer-settings in which Jerusalem is mentioned (whether in a historical or eschatological mode), Reif then discusses the various motifs associated with the city and the broader religious ideas behind them. Finally, he offers an overview as to how Jerusalem was viewed historically at various stages in this period.

Visotzky relates to three midrashim which he dates to about the ninth century—Midrash Mishle, Tanna d'be Eliyahu and Pirqe de-Rabbi Eliʿezer—and notes the references to Jerusalem in each. Whereas the city is rarely mentioned in Midrash Mishle, it plays a more prominent role in Tanna d'be Eliyahu, where it is noted several dozen times. However, Jerusalem is most prominently featured in a wide range of contexts in Pirqei de-Rabbi Eliʿezer. Anti-Samaritan (regarding the priority of Jerusalem over Mount Gerizim) and anti-Karaite passages are especially noted, and the question is raised as to whether the editor of this midrash might have, in fact, lived in the city.

Ben-Shammai addresses a field which is now being inundated with new primary material as a result of access to Russian libraries and archives over the last decade. Once published and digested, these medievel exegetical texts, both Rabbanite and Karaite, will undoubtedly enrich our knowledge of Jewish cultural and religious life. In what he describes as preliminary remarks, Ben-Shammai declares his "aim of putting the subject on the agenda" by focusing on the names given to Jerusalem by these exegetes in their translations and commentaries. The biblical term is almost universally preserved, and the word used more and more by the Muslims, al-Quds, was likewise used by Arabic-speaking Jews when referring to the Temple and its precincts. Ben-Shammai suggests that the emphasis on the city may stem not only from the biblical text itself, but from a more contemporary agenda as well. From his survey of this material, he raises the following questions: could the Muslim conquest and shaping of the city have increased messianic expectations among the Jews, and not only among the Karaite population where it was clearly a central factor? Might the newly-claimed status of Baghdad as a "City of Peace" have caused Jewish exegetes to reemphasize the centrality and sanctity of Jerusalem? Or might this Rabbanite emphasis have been a response to internal Jewish polemics, particularly with regard to the Karaites?

Our volume concludes with two articles that take us into the late Middle Ages and modern period respectively. Each deals with a particular Christian community in Jerusalem. O'Mahony addresses the oft-neglected Ethiopian church prior to 1650. Garnering scraps of information from a wide variety of sources, he skillfully traces a series of events which point to the struggles and intrigues surrounding this community's quest for recognition and legitimation in the holy city. Roussos' presentation has a more contemporary ring as he addresses the frictions between local churches as their sponsoring countries, i.e., the European powers of the nineteenth and twentieth centuries, vied for positions of power in the city. Issues of the city's internationalization and extraterritoriality, well known from twentieth-century diplomacy, had already surfaced in the nineteenth century, and were exploited by the different countries and churches in the course of promoting their own particular agendas.

✦ ✦ ✦

While it is the written version of the formal presentations that ultimately finds expression in this volume, many of the most riveting moments of the conference were during the discussions and exchanges which took place after each paper. As is customary in delivering scholarly papers, most speakers focused on specific topics within well-defined historical contexts. In the less formal exchanges, however, participants felt freer to make wide-ranging diachronic and synchronic comparisons.

Many commented on the fascinating changes in Jerusalem's evolving urban landscape from one period to the next. As the city encompassed two parallel north-south ridges, the focus of Jerusalem's urban plan as represented by its holiest buildings shifted from one to the other in successive eras. Under Jewish sovereignty (and under earlier Jebusite rule as well), the Temple was located on the eastern ridge: broad streets, bridges, and monumental staircases all connected various parts of the Herodian city with the Temple Mount. However, for a variety of reasons, one of which was their declared aim of replacing the Jewish memory of the city, the Christians of the fourth century and later shifted the religious focus of the city to its western ridge. There they erected not only a new temple in the form of the Constantinian Church of the Holy Sepulchre, but many other churches and monasteries as well, including Justinian's massive Nea Church at the southern end of the city's main north-south street (*cardo*), near Mount Zion. Other clusters of sacred institutions were to be found on Mount Zion itself, as well as on the slopes and crest of the Mount of Olives. The Temple Mount was deliberately ignored and left desolate.

The Muslims, however, reversed this process and built their central mosques on the Jewish holy site along the eastern ridge. This move not only constituted an explicit architectural challenge to Christianity's heretofore preeminence in the city, but also allowed for the utilization of a large, available tract of land which also happened to be be associated with a sacred past honored by Islam as well. In addition, we can detect an interesting development within the Muslim tradition itself. At first, the Temple Mount's surroundings were used for large palaces, and remains of a number of them have been found near the Mount's southwestern corner. As time went on, however, two significant changes took place: more and more buildings bearing a religious character—prayer halls, monasteries, schools, and hospices—were erected adjacent to the Mount's northern and western perimeters; these buildings were raised in order to put them as close as possible to the Ḥaram's entrances. This necessitated the building of high-vaulted substructures to allow for their significant elevation.

Common to Jerusalem in each successive period was the prominence of religious institutions and their leadership in civic affairs. With the exception of Herod's thirty-three year rule, Jerusalem for centuries was principally under the sway of high priests. Other religious groups such as the priestly Sadducees and the Pharisees likewise constituted influential bodies in the latter part of the Second Temple period. In a similar vein, Byzantine Jerusalem saw the local clergy rise to prominence, as bishops, priests, and monks assumed a central role in the city's daily affairs. The same appears to have held true for the Muslim period as well.

As might be expected, many expressions of religious piety were similar from one tradition to the next. Thus, large-scale gatherings of the faithful in the Temple, churches, or mosques were regular occurrences. The presence in the city of not only the official clergy, but of a wide spectrum of holy men, was a familiar phenomenon. Egeria's account of her experiences in Jerusalem is a vivid statement of the aura of sanctity that pervaded the city and its population at certain holy moments throughout the year. Pilgrimage to Jerusalem was a common phenomenon in every age and, as a result, the ambience in Jerusalem always had an international, cosmopolitan dimension.

Nevertheless, there were also some notable differences between the various traditions and how each related to Jerusalem. For Christians and Muslims, Jerusalem was in essence a holy city, and its importance was due solely to the religious traditions associated with it. For both Christianity and Islam, there were other cities which functioned either as a political capital or religious center, comparable, if not surpassing, the sanctity of Jerusalem (e.g., Rome and Constantinople with regard to Christianity; Mecca, Medina, and Baghdad in Islam). For the Jews, however, Jerusalem was both a political capital and an exclusive religious center. It was a home both in a secular and religious sense. Not only was the Temple located there, but so, too, were royal palaces, civic and social institutions, as well as entertainment facilities (the gymnasium, theater, amphitheater, and hippodrome). As a result, the loss of Jerusalem in 70 was a far more crushing blow for Judaism than its loss for Christians in 638 C.E., or for Muslims in 1099 C.E.

Similarities and differences were likewise evident in the ways each religious tradition treated "the other." Second Temple Jerusalem knew of very few non-Jewish residents (the Herodian court being a major exception). What the status of non-Jews might have been we do not know, although it is quite certain that no outward pagan worship would have been tolerated. Christians, for their part, banned Jews from living in the city and allowed them to be present only on specific occasions. In contrast, the Muslims appear to have adopted a policy which accorded a place—albeit inferior—to Christian and Jew alike.

Finally, the loss or absence of Jerusalem, whether due to conquest or sheer distance, aroused profound religious stirrings within each of the three religious traditions. Whether in the form of poetry or prayer, customs or ceremonies, or in the use of Jerusalem-related names for buildings and institutions found elsewhere, each tradition reflects a deep attachment to the city and a profound acknowledgment of its centrality and sanctity.

June, 1998   Lee Levine
Jerusalem

Abbreviations

AB	Anchor Bible
ACO	*Acta conciliorum oecumenicorum*
AnBoll	*Analecta Bollandiana*
Ant.	Josephus, *Jewish Antiquities*
ARN	Avot de-Rabbi Nathan
B	Babylonian Talmud (Bavli)
b.	ben, bar (son of)
BA	*Biblical Archaeologist*
BAR	*Biblical Archaeology Review*
BASOR	*Bulletin of the American Schools of Oriental Research*
BDB	F. Brown, S. R. Driver, and C. A. Briggs, *A Hebrew and English Lexicon of the Old Testament*
BGA	Bibliotheca Geographorum Arabicorum
BSOAS	*Bulletin of the School of Oriental and African Studies*
CBQ	*Catholic Biblical Quarterly*
CCSL	*Corpus Christianorum, Series Latina*
CP	*Classical Philology*
CSCO	*Corpus Scriptorum Christianorum Orientalium*
CSEL	*Corpus Scriptorum Ecclesiasticorum Latinorum*
CSHB	*Corpus Scriptorum Historiae Byzantinae*
DOP	*Dumbarton Oaks Papers*
EI	*Eretz-Israel* (Israel Exploration Society)
EJ	*Encyclopaedia Judaica*
ESI	*Excavations and Surveys in Israel*
GCS	*Die griechischen christlichen Schriftsteller der ersten drei Jahrhunderte*
HTR	*Harvard Theological Review*
HUCA	*Hebrew Union College Annual*
ICC	International Critical Commentary
IEJ	*Israel Exploration Journal*
J	Jerusalem Talmud (Yerushalmi)
JAOS	*Journal of the American Oriental Society*

JbAC	*Jahrbuch für Antike und Christentum*, Münster
JBL	*Journal of Biblical Literature*
JJS	*Journal of Jewish Studies*
JNES	*Journal of Near Eastern Studies*
JPOS	*Journal of the Palestine Oriental Society*
JQR	*Jewish Quarterly Review*
JRS	*Journal of Roman Studies*
JSOT	*Journal for the Study of the Old Testament*
JSS	*Journal of Semitic Studies*
JTS	*Journal of Theological Studies*
LA	*Liber Annuus*
LCC	Loeb Classical Library
M	Mishnah
MGH	Monumenta Germaniae Historica
MGWJ	*Monatsschrift für Geschichte und Wissenschaft des Judentums*
NEAEHL	*New Encyclopaedia of Archaeological Excavations in the Holy Land* (ed. E. Stern)
NTS	*New Testament Studies*
OC	*Oriens Christianus*
OCP	*Orientalia Christiana Periodica*
OrChr	*Oriens Christianus*
PAAJR	*Proceedings of the American Academy for Jewish Research*
PBSR	*Papers of the British School at Rome*
PEFQSt	*Palestine Exploration Fund Quarterly Statement*
PEQ	*Palestine Exploration Quarterly*
PG	*Patrologiae cursus completus, Series Graeca* (J.-P. Migne)
PL	*Patrologiae cursus completus, Series Latina* (J.-P. Migne)
PO	*Patrologia Orientalis*
POC	*Proche-Orient Chrétien*
PPTS	Palestine Pilgrims' Text Society
PRK	Pesiqta de-Rav Kahana
QDAP	*Quarterly of the Department of Antiquities of Palestine*
RAC	*Reallexikon für Antike und Christentum*
RB	*Revue Biblique*
REA	*Revue des Etudes Arméniennes*
REAN	*Revue des Etudes Anciennes*
REJ	*Revue des Etudes Juives*
RHPhR	*Revue d'histoire et de philosophie religieuses*
RHR	*Revue de l'histoire des religions*

ROC	*Revue de l'Orient Chrétien*
RQ	*Revue de Qumran*
RSR	*Recherches de science religieuse*
SC	*Sources chrétiennes*
SCI	*Scripta Classica Israelica*
SH	Scripta Hierosolymitana
StTh	*Studia Theologica* (Lund)
T	Tosefta
TDNT	*Theological Dictionary of the New Testament*
TDOT	*Theological Dictionary of the Old Testament*
TRE	*Theologische Realenzyklopädie*
TU	*Texte und Untersuchungen zur Geschichte der altchristlichen Literatur*
TZ	*Theologische Zeitschrift*
VC	*Vigiliae Christianae*
ZDPV	*Zeitschrift des deutschen Palästina Vereins*
ZKG	*Zeitschrift für Kirchengeschichte*

· I ·

JERUSALEM
IN BIBLICAL
TRADITION

1

From the King's Sanctuary to the Chosen City

SARA JAPHET

Towards the end of the First Commonwealth, in the seventh century B.C.E., a new concept was introduced into several biblical works— the concept of the "chosen place/city." This concept is most prominent in Deuteronomy, where it is one of the most important innovations—some would say, *the* most important innovation in the book. We find there the commandment that when the people of Israel enter the land, conquer it, and settle in it, and when God grants them safety from all their enemies (Deut. 12:10), they should restrict the worship of the Lord to one place, "the site that the Lord your God will choose amidst all your tribes as His habitation, to establish His name there" (ibid., 12:5).[1]

In addition to Deuteronomy, the concept appears in the Deuteronomistic sections of the Former Prophets, for some of which there are parallels in Chronicles,[2] in two psalms (78:68; 132:13), in the prophecy of Zechariah,[3] and lastly, in Chronicles, aside from the parallel sections.[4] However, there is a difference between the formulation of this concept in Deuteronomy and in all the other sources. In spite of the importance of this concept, the name of the "place" is not given in Deuteronomy; "the place which the Lord will choose" remains anonymous throughout the book. In all the other sources, "the place" is unequivocally Jerusalem, "the city the Lord *had* chosen out of all the tribes of Israel to establish His name there" (I Kgs. 14:21).

Nonetheless, Deuteronomy and almost all the other sources are silent regarding the mode of this "choosing": how will the Lord, or how did the Lord, choose the "place?" This total silence seems to be intentional and eloquent, in itself an aspect of Deuteronomy's overall philosophy. The absolute denunciation of all earlier places of worship also involves the rejection of all earlier forms of consecration. No actual act of "choosing" is suggested.

This complex of ideas requires some further clarification. Ancient Israel knew many "holy places," sites dedicated to the God of Israel, where sacrifices and worship were conducted. This was indeed the prevalent practice in Israel described by the biblical narratives, established by the law, and confirmed by archeological excavations.[5] The manner in which these places were consecrated may be learned from various biblical stories, a good example of which is the story of Jacob in Beth-el. Jacob "came upon a certain place and stopped there for the night, for the sun had set" (Gen. 28:11). During his sleep he had a dream, in which God revealed himself to him: "And the Lord was standing beside him and He said: 'I am the Lord, the God of your father Abraham . . .'." (ibid., 28:13). Jacob awoke from his sleep and exclaimed: "Surely the Lord is present in this place, and I did not know it!" (ibid., 28:16). He then consecrated the stone on which he slept by pouring oil on it, and dedicated the place to God (ibid., 28:18–22).

Similar biblical texts make it clear that it is the divine revelation—in various forms and on various occasions—which designates a place as holy: "And he built an altar there to the Lord who had appeared to him" (ibid., 12:7; also 35:1). The same idea is expressed normatively in a legal injunction in Exodus: "in every place where I pronounce My name (בכל המקום אשר אזכיר את שמי)[6] I will come to you and bless you" (Ex. 20:21), God's "pronouncing his name" being his self-introduction in revelation.

Viewed from the perspective of the norm and practice prevalent in ancient Israel for a long time, the demand expressed in Deuteronomy may be regarded as no less than a revolution, for in Deuteronomy worship is not merely central, but absolutely exclusive: there is only one place "chosen" by God.[7] Any worship outside this one place is viewed as a severe transgression of the Lord's commandment, comparable to the worst practices of the surrounding Canaanites.

This "choosing" of "the place" was not enacted by God's revelation. According to Deuteronomy there was only one revelation, the one-time theophany in Sinai, and no other. Even the Sinaitic revelation did not include seeing, only hearing: "you heard the sound of words but perceived no shape—nothing but a voice" (Deut. 4:12; "since you saw no shape when the Lord your God spoke to you at Horeb out of the fire"—v. 15; see also vv. 33, 36; 5:26). This is no doubt another aspect of Deuteronomy's polemic against earlier and contemporary views of God's revelation to his people. According to Deuteronomy, after Sinai, God will transmit his will to the people through the agency of the prophets and through them alone (18:15–18). However, choosing the place is attributed to God himself and not to any prophet, and no form of this "choosing" is specified.

The book of Kings continues in the footsteps of Deuteronomy and nowhere refers to the question of how the Lord chose Jerusalem among all the other places on earth.[8] Jerusalem is simply described as the "place which the Lord had chosen." The issue remains an enigma: how will the place be chosen, or how was the place chosen?

When we look at the history of Jerusalem as depicted in the Bible, it becomes clear that the concept of "chosenness" was not a complete innovation at the time, when it suddenly occupied the center of religious thought. It was the end product of a long process to which historical circumstances and religious beliefs and practices contributed their part. Could we, then, begin from the point where Deuteronomy left off and answer the question of how Jerusalem became "the chosen city"? We should say from the outset that the attempt to answer this question is not new, and certainly not modern. It was already done in the Bible, in the late book of Chronicles, which demonstrates that the question mark left by Deuteronomy already bothered ancient generations. I prefer, however, to leave the Chronicler's answer to the end of my article, and turn now to the perspective of the modern historian.

◆ ◆ ◆

The beginning of the process is marked by the astonishing awareness of Jerusalem's foreignness. It remains outside the earliest traditions of Israel and carries no historical or religious memories. The biblical traditions of Israel's prehistory—formulated in the Bible as the period of the Patriarchs—present Jerusalem as a Canaanite city. While in itself a historical fact, suggested by Egyptian sources,[9] its presentation in Genesis deviates from the practice of the book regarding other places and sites. We learn from Genesis that Abraham, Isaac, and Jacob roamed through the land then occupied by the Canaanites and built altars in the Lord's honor in all the places that God appeared to them.[10] Jerusalem, however, is not included among them. It appears explicitly in Gen. 14, where its ruler at the time of Abraham is the Canaanite Melchizedek, described as holding the dual position of king and priest: "And Melchizedek, king of Salem,[11] brought out bread and wine; he was a priest of God Most High. He blessed him, saying: 'Blessed be Abram of God Most High . . . and blessed be God Most High who has delivered your foes into you hand'. And [Abram] gave him a tenth of everything" (Gen. 14:18–20). Jerusalem lay outside the purview of the most ancient religious traditions of Israel.[12]

The foreignness of Jerusalem is revealed even more strongly for the period of the Judges by three explicit statements:

1. *Josh. 15:63*: "But the Judites could not dispossess the Jebusites, the inhabitants of Jerusalem; so the Judites dwell with the Jebusites in Jerusalem to this day."

2. *Judg. 1:21*: "The Benjaminites did not dispossess the Jebusite inhabitants of Jerusalem; so the Jebusites have dwelt with the Benjaminites in Jerusalem to this day."

3. *Judg. 19:10–12*: in the story of the concubine, the foreignness of Jerusalem is presented as a matter of fact and common knowledge: "But the man refused to stay for the night. He set out and traveled as far as the vicinity of Jebus—that is, Jerusalem. . . . Since they were close to Jebus, and the day was very far spent, the attendant said to his master: 'Let us turn aside to this town of the Jebusites and spend the night in it'. But his master said to him: 'We will not turn aside to a town of aliens who are not of Israel, but will continue to Gibeah'."

Jerusalem was not part of the Israelite territory after the conquest.[13]

✦ ✦ ✦

The history of Jerusalem as an Israelite city begins with David, who conquered it in one of his first campaigns after he became king of both Judah and Israel:

> All the elders of Israel came to the king at Hebron, and King David made a pact with them in Hebron before the Lord. And they anointed David king over Israel. . . . The king and his men set out for Jerusalem against the Jebusites who inhabited the region. . . . David captured the stronghold of Zion; it is now the City of David (II Sam. 5:3–7).

After he conquered the city, David undertook four steps: restoration and rebuilding of the city (ibid., 5:9); establishment of Jerusalem as his capital (ibid., 5:11); bringing the ark of the Lord up to Jerusalem and providing a sanctuary for it (ibid., 6:2–19); and beginning preparations for building the Temple (ibid., 7; I Chron. 21–29). David's considerations in undertaking these measures, as well as their meaning and implications, have been discussed by many scholars,[14] and I will refer to them only briefly.

David's major political consideration seems to have been his wish to loosen the fetters of tribal ties. As long as he was king of the tribe of Judah alone, perhaps under the patronage of the Philistines, his capital was in Hebron, the southern city which was very conspicuously connected with the tribe of Judah (II Sam. 2:1–4). Moving to Jerusalem—which did not, in fact, belong to any of the tribes—signaled the weakening of his ties with the tribe of Judah and the beginning of a new era. There were also geographical and strategic considerations. Jerusalem was conveniently located in the center of the hill-country, on the intersections of roads from north to south and east to west. It was strategically positioned on a hill, surrounded on three sides by deep valleys, and had a dependable supply of water.[15] Moreover, since it had been in the hands of the Jebusites up to this point, David could claim it as his own property. He actually calls it "the City of David."

While the establishment of a new capital at a major historical and political turning point is a well known phenomenon in political history, David's second step was less common and reveals his true genius. As already noted, Jerusalem was not connected with the ancient traditions of Israel and carried no venerated historical memories. David undertook to change this situation by turning Jerusalem not merely into an Israelite city, but also into a holy city. The tactic he chose to employ was the transfer of the ark to Jerusalem.

The ark was the most sacred cultic object in the history of Israel. It was not associated with any tribe in particular, but rather with the people as a whole, and its origin was traditionally associated with the people's wanderings in the wilderness (Ex. 25:10–22; Deut. 10:1–5).[16] It was the most important concrete symbol of God's presence amidst his people; by means of the ark God led them safely through the wilderness.[17] After the conquest of the land, the ark found its final abode in Shiloh (I Sam. 3:3), but as a result of the war against the Philistines (ibid., 4–6), it was stored in the city of Kiriath-jearim (ibid., 7:1–2) and practically forgotten.

David brings the ark to Jerusalem in an elaborate and magnificent procession. He does not despair, even after the first failure (II Sam. 6:6–10), and finally establishes a sanctuary for the ark in the traditional way, in a tent. By the very presence of the ark in Jerusalem, the city becomes holy, the unifying religious center of all Israel. At the time this was, of course, a contrived sanctification, which was even publicly mocked by Michal, Saul's daughter (ibid., 6:20–21). In time, however, this situation changed. The foundations laid by David were built upon by Solomon, who erected the Temple as a magnificent building and brought the ark of the Lord from its tent to the "holy of holies" inside the Temple (I Kgs. 8:1–10).[18] At this time the Temple was, in fact, the king's chapel, part of the grand building complex in Jerusalem. However, time on the one hand, and the experience of pilgrimage on the other, had their impact, and the status of the Temple, as well as the sanctity of Jerusalem, were eventually absorbed into the people's collective consciousness.

After Solomon's death, the people of northern Israel parted ways with the House of David and anointed their own king, Jeroboam. This king's greatest effort, according to the biblical story, was directed toward this matter: to disconnect the ties of the people with Jerusalem:

> Jeroboam said to himself: "Now the kingdom may well return to the House of David. If these people still go up to offer sacrifices at the House of the Lord in Jerusalem, the heart of these people will turn

back to their master King Rehoboam of Judah; they will kill me and go back to King Rehoboam of Judah." So the king took counsel and made two golden calves. He said to the people: "You have been going up to Jerusalem long enough. This is your God, O Israel, who brought you up from the land of Egypt!" He set up one in Beth-el and placed the other in Dan (ibid., 12:26–29).

Thus, Jerusalem's position had been established in the people's mind. Jeroboam was not afraid of the political power of Judah, nor of the attraction of the House of David, but of the religious attraction of Jerusalem.

✦ ✦ ✦

The next crucial point in the history of Jerusalem occurred two hundred years later, during the reign of Hezekiah, at the end of the eighth century B.C.E. At his time, the Assyrian king Sennacherib undertook a military campaign against the kingdom of Judah, during which he took hold of all the fortified cities of Judah except Jerusalem. Jerusalem withstood the long and severe siege (II Kgs. 18:13), and then, for one reason or another, the siege was lifted and Sennacherib returned to his country. Jerusalem was saved (ibid., 19:7, 35).[19]

The historical and political significance of these events cannot be overestimated; after the conquest of northern Israel about twenty years earlier (722 B.C.E.), the conquest of Jerusalem would have meant the end of Judah, and with it the end of the national entity called "Israel." However, the deliverance of Jerusalem also had far-reaching and long-lasting theological ramifications in connection with our topic. In the general context of biblical historical philosophy, this deliverance automatically meant that Jerusalem was protected by God. However, the "self-evident" theological interpretation became sharply focused and greatly highlighted in conjunction with the prophecy of Isaiah which preceded the deliverance.

Throughout the Assyrian siege, Isaiah demonstrated a position of complete spiritual confidence. He proclaimed that the Assyrian campaign was indeed a deserved, albeit temporary, punishment for Judah. Jerusalem would not be conquered (see, e.g., ibid., 19:28, 34). The withdrawal of Sennacherib not only confirmed Isaiah's farsightedness, but turned his words into a theological maxim: Jerusalem had a unique position in the earthly world. It was indestructible, for the Lord's presence and special grace protected it from all evil.

The deliverance of Jerusalem from the Assyrian threat in the days of Hezekiah, and the contrast between its survival and the destruction of the kingdom of Israel, may be seen as the seed which would grow and flourish in later generations into a new theology of election. The full bloom of this theology is found about a hundred years later, in the reign of Josiah, at the end of the seventh century.

✦ ✦ ✦

King Josiah (640–609 B.C.E.) was one of the last kings of Judah and its last great ruler. Josiah took advantage of the decline of Assyrian power, using this short interval of independence as an opportunity for change and expansion. The biblical story of Josiah's activity centers upon his religious actions and his most important undertaking in this area: a comprehensive cultic reform, in the eighteenth year of his rule (622 B.C.E.; ibid., 22–23; II Chron. 34–35).[20]

The reform had two major objectives: to remove from the land every form of idolatry (an understandable step, with which I will not deal in this context) and to abolish all the sanctuaries to the Lord throughout the land, in both Judah and Israel—except the central Temple in Jerusalem. Josiah proceeds differently in each of the various religious centers: he deals most severely and cruelly with the sanctuaries of the northern territories which had belonged to the kingdom of Israel (II Kgs. 23.15–16, 19–20), but much more mildly with the shrines of Judah. Nevertheless, he defiles these shrines as well, discharges the priests and other attendants of the sanctuaries, and brings them all to Jerusalem:

> He brought all the priests from the towns of Judah [to Jerusalem], and defiled the shrines where the priests had been making offerings—from Geba to Beer-sheba. He also demolished the shrines of the gates, . . . The priests of the shrines, however, did not ascend the altar of the Lord in Jerusalem, but they ate unleavened bread along with their kinsmen (ibid., 23:8–9).

Josiah followed the religious philosophy of Deuteronomy to the letter: worship of the God of Israel is exclusive and can be conducted only in Jerusalem! Thus, in the century between Hezekiah and Josiah a new religious philosophy evolved and a vigorous and energetic king came on the scene to implement it.

The underlying motives of this theology, and of Josiah's actions, are not made fully clear in the biblical story. Deuteronomy explains the commandment by the wish to distance the people of Israel from the forms of worship of the other nations: "Do not worship the Lord your God in like manner" (Deut. 12:4), but it does not clarify why one should abolish the sanctuaries to the God of Israel for that purpose. Scholars have tried to explain it in their own terms. Some would explain the Deuteronomistic philosophy as a corollary of the monotheistic idea: that *one God* should *have one place* of worship; that the existence of many shrines might be interpreted by the people as an admission of the existence of various forms of this deity, and therefore tend to polytheism.[21] Some would explain it in more practical religious terms: that the forms of worship developed in the provincial shrines could be affected by popular beliefs and customs, which the more sophisticated priests in Jerusalem could not accept. Other scholars would explain the emergence of this philosophy and reform on political grounds: it was one aspect of the king's attempt to centralize his rule, to annex to his kingdom the territories which were formerly under Assyrian rule, and to create an absolutely unified kingdom. The aim was political, but the means were religious.[22]

Whatever the reasons that brought about this religious revolution (and they should be viewed as a complex rather than as single and unidimensional), the effects of this reform were enormous. Although such a system may seem to the observer totally inviable, contrary to human nature and man's need for God's nearness and presence, in the long run the reform did prevail. This was not the result of the religious logic of the reform or of Josiah's power, but of the concrete historical circumstances and their religious interpretation. Thirty-six years after the reform, and twenty-two years after Josiah's death, Jerusalem was conquered by the Babylonians, the land of Judah was destroyed, the Temple was burned to ashes, and many of the people were exiled. A spirit of repentance swept the people and turned the Deuteronomistic philosophy of history into a major religious force. When the fortunes of the people eventually changed, and the Persian kings allowed the people of Judah to restore their religious life, only one sanctuary was built in the land of Judah—the Temple of Jerusalem.[23]

✦ ✦ ✦

Very little is known about the history of Israel at the beginning of the Second Temple period under Persian rule, and our views are colored by the picture portrayed in the book of Ezra-Nehemiah. Although Ezra-Nehemiah does not abound in the Deuteronomistic terminology of "choosing,"[24] the exclusivity of Jerusalem seems self-evident for this book. There is complete identification between the God of Israel and Jerusalem; He is defined as "the God that is in Jerusalem" (Ezra 1:3).

It seems, however, that this picture does not fully represent the historical reality, and that at least at the beginning of that period matters were more complicated. It is doubtful that Jerusalem was, in fact, the only sanctuary for the Lord, and that worship of the God of Israel was not performed in other places as well, either in the land of Israel or abroad.[25] Against this historical background, the idea of "the chosen place" developed in two opposing directions. One direction was a continuous effort to strengthen the idea of Jerusalem's exclusivity. This was done by broadening the theological basis of the "choice" and founding it on explicit traditions and additional religious concepts. The opposite direction also propagated the idea of "chosenness and exclusivity," but focused on denying that chosenness to Jerusalem. A forceful propagator of the first direction is the book of Chronicles. The propagators of the opposite view are the Samaritans, for whom it is a most important religious tenet: there is indeed a "chosen place"; this place is not Jerusalem, but rather Shechem. The two opposing currents center on one aspect of the idea of "chosenness," which was either neglected or intentionally avoided by Deuteronomy: the circumstances in which the choice was originally made. Both sources provide answers to the question left open in Deuteronomy: how and when did God choose the "chosen place?"

Chronicles insists on the election of Jerusalem in all contexts which relate to the building of the Temple, starting with the time of David. In all the parallel sections in this pericope, which the Chronicler takes from the books of Samuel-Kings, he adds phrases and passages which explicitly relate how Jerusalem was actually chosen. I Chron. 21 borrows the story of the threshing floor of Araunah from II Sam. 24, but ends it very differently. Among the additions to the story we find that God confirmed by fire His pleasure with the altar built by David. To the words taken from II Sam. 24:25: "And David built there an altar to the Lord and sacrificed burnt offerings and offerings of well being," repeated verbatim in I Chron. 21:26, Chronicles adds the words: "He invoked the Lord, who answered him with fire from heaven on the altar of burnt offerings." The Chronicler ends the passage with a proclamation by David: "Here will be the House of the Lord and here the altar of burnt offerings for Israel" (ibid., 22:1). The place was chosen and consecrated by God's revelation in fire, and was publicly announced by David's proclamation.

The Chronicler also introduces a few changes into the story of the building of the Temple, some of which are clearly related to our topic. In his introduction to these chapters, the Chronicler adds a clear description of the Temple's location, which is absent from Kings:

> Then Solomon began to build the House of the Lord in Jerusalem on Mount Moriah, where [the Lord] had appeared to his father David, at the place which David had designated, at the threshing floor of Ornan the Jebusite (II Chron. 3:1).

According to this view, the place of the Temple was chosen by God's revelation to David, but it is also the place called "Mount Moriah," connected to the period of the patriarchs, to the binding of Isaac.

Then, when Solomon dedicated the altar and the Temple, the Chronicler adds to the story of I Kings that:

> When Solomon finished praying, fire descended from heaven and consumed the burnt offering and the sacrifices, and the glory of the Lord filled the house. . . . All the Israelites witnessed (lit., saw) the descent of fire and the glory of the Lord on the House (II Chr. 7:1–3).

The question of how the Lord chose Jerusalem receives in Chronicles an unequivocal answer: God already chose Jerusalem in the time of David, when He revealed Himself to David by the fire on the altar. It was then reaffirmed for all the people of Israel in the time of Solomon, when God's fire descended from heaven to the altar, and His glory filled the Temple!

The borrowing of motifs from the Sinai theophany (Ex. 19) and from the dedication of the Tabernacle (ibid., 40:34–38) is unmistakable; the Jerusalem Temple is the successor of the Tabernacle, the place chosen by God as His one and only abode, as the only place of worship. According to Chronicles, the exclusivity of Jerusalem as the place of worship was a binding principle and a historical fact throughout the monarchical period.[26]

The Samaritans, too, take the idea of "the chosen place" for granted: there is only one place of worship of the God of Israel. Their answer, however, is diametrically opposed to that of the Chronicler. God chose "the place" at the very outset of Israel's existence, when he made the binding covenant between Himself and the people of Israel, at the revelation at Sinai. The Samaritans introduce the choice of place into the most venerated text of God's revelation: the ten commandments. In the Samaritan Bible, the tenth commandment reads as follows:

> So, when the Lord your God has brought you into the land of the Canaanites which you are about to invade and occupy, you shall set up large stones, coat them with plaster and inscribe upon them all the words of this Teaching. When you cross the Jordan you shall set up these stones, about which I charge you this day, on Mount Garizim. There, too, you shall build an altar to the Lord your God . . . that mountain on the other side of the Jordan, beyond the west road which is in the land of the Canaanites who dwell in the Arabah, near Gilgal by the terebinths of Moreh, near Shechem (Ex. 20, after verse 14).[27]

According to the Samaritans, the mountain of Garizim was chosen by God in His self-revelation to the people of Israel at Sinai. Following this view, the

Samaritan Pentateuch systematically changes the Deuteronomic statements regarding "the place that the Lord your God will choose": in place of the MT "will choose" (יבחר) the Samaritans have "has chosen" (בחר).

The Samaritans' answer to the question of "chosenness" demonstrates very clearly that by the time of the schism, the idea of exclusivity was fully rooted in the people's minds.[28] The rivalry between Jerusalem and Shechem had to lead to a schism because it was transferred from the political realm to the religious one: theologically speaking, it was an either-or situation—either Jerusalem or Shechem.

The concept of the "chosen place"—election which means cultic exclusivity—had enormous political and religious effects, in its time and for the future, for Judaism and for the religions that developed from it. All these, however, lie outside the scope of this paper, which here comes to its end.

Notes

1. Biblical quotations follow the version of the New Jewish Publication Society (NJPS) unless otherwise stated. "The site that the Lord will choose" is mentioned twenty times in Deuteronomy, with variations. See also 12:11, 14, 18, 21, 26; 14:23, 24, 25; 15:20; 16:2, 6, 7, 11, 15, 16; 17:8, 10; 26:2; 31:11.

2. Josh. 9:27; I Kgs. 8:16, 44, 48; 11:13; 32, 36; 14:21; II Kgs. 21:7; 23:27; II Chron. 6:5, 34, 38; 12:13; 33:7.

3. In Zech. 1:17; 2:16 as a prophecy for the future, in 3:2 as God's epithet: "the Lord who has chosen Jerusalem."

4. II Chron. 6:6; 7:12, 16.

5. The narratives refer, on the one hand, to the period of the Patriarchs and, on the other, to the history of the people of Israel after the conquest. Of the latter we may mention the following examples: (1) Josh. 24:25–26, also verse 1: a sanctuary (מקדש ה') in Shechem; (2) Josh. 8:30–31: an altar on Mount Ebal (3) Judg. 6:24: Gideon's altar in Ophra; (4) I Sam. 1–4: a central sanctuary in Shiloh; (5) I Sam. 7:5–12; 8:25: a place of worship in Mitzpah; (6) I Sam. 7:17; 9:12, 22–25: a place of worship in Ramah; (7) I Sam. 11:15: in Gilgal; (8) I Sam. 10:3: a place of pilgrimage "to God at Beth-el"; (9) I Sam. 21:5, 7, 10; 22:11–19: a sanctuary, with many priests, in Nob; (10) I Kgs. 3:4: "the largest shrine" in Gibeon; (11) I Kgs. 18:18–38; also 19:14—Elijah's altar on Mount Carmel; (12) Amos 7:13: "it is the king's sanctuary and a royal palace"—about Beth-el. Regarding the laws, see below Ex. 20:22–26; the laws of pilgrimage in Ex. 23:17 and 34:23, and perhaps also Lev. 17. Archaeological excavations have brought to light several sanctuaries and altars; one may mention the sanctuaries of Arad and Beer-sheba as examples.

6. The translation follows the common meaning of זכ"ר in the Hiph'il (see, for instance, *Thesaurus of the Language of the Bible*, III [Jerusalem, 1968], 35, entry זכ"ר hiph'il 3). The translations (and the dictionaries), including the NJPS, ascribe this one verse a different meaning, which is not confirmed elsewhere. The NJPS translates here: "in every place where I cause My name to be mentioned."

7. It is interesting that this one place is not defined in Deuteronomy as "holy" (קדוש), but as "chosen." Although the term "holy" is found in several places in Deuteronomy, in particular in reference to the people (עם קדוש), it never applies to the place of worship. Only God's abode in heaven is described as holy: השקיפה ממעון קדשך מן השמים (Deut. 26:15). The absence of the term "holy" characterizes also the revelation stories in Genesis and in Joshua-Kings; by contrast, in the P section of the Pentateuch it applies, inter alia, to the Tabernacle.

8. The absence of any *hieros logos* for the Jerusalem Temple in the Deuteronomistic history (that is, Joshua-Kings) is therefore no coincidence. Although one may regard II Sam. 24 as having been originally such a story, no connection is made in either Samuel or Kings between the "threshing floor" of Araunah and the Temple site. For the book of Chronicles, see below.

9. Jerusalem is mentioned already in the Execration Texts of the nineteenth–eighteenth centuries B.C.E., while correspondence with Jerusalem is included in the el-Amarna letters (of the fourteenth century B.C.E.), from which we also learn the name of its king, Abed-Heppa. These letters provide information about some of the historical circumstances and the relations of Jerusalem with the Egyptian authorities (see S. Abramsky and M. Avi-Yonah, "Jerusalem [Names and History]," *EJ*, IX [Jerusalem, 1971], 1379–80).

10. Abraham is connected particularly with the Negeb in the south of the country, with the names of Hebron and Beer-Sheba, but also with Beth-el and Shechem in the central hill-country (Gen. 13:18: "the terebinths of Mamre which are in Hebron"; 14:13; 18:1; 21:31; 22: 19; 23; ibid., 12:6, 8, 13:3–4). Isaac is connected with the land of the Philistines and the Negeb (ibid., 26:1–22, 23–33; 28:10), while Jacob is connected more with the north, and particularly with Shechem and Beth-el (ibid., 28:19; 33:18; 35:1–15). Some other names are also mentioned (ibid., 32:3: Mahanaim; ibid., 32:31: Peniel).

11. For "Salem" (שלם) as an epithet of Jerusalem, see Ps. 76:3.

12. Later tradition, starting with II Chron. 3:1, identified "the land of Moriah," the place of the binding of Isaac (Gen. 22:2), with Jerusalem. This is not the case in Genesis itself. The story does not mention a specific place-name, but speaks very generally about "the land of" Moriah; moreover, no connection is made between Moriah and Jerusalem. This is also true regarding II Sam. 24, which may be viewed to some extent as the *hagios logos* of the Temple. Cf. below.

13. Although we do hear that the Israelites fought against Jerusalem, and perhaps also had the upper hand in some of these battles (Josh. 10:23–27; 12:10; Judg. 1:8). Geographically, it was located on the border between Benjamin and Judah (Josh. 15:8; 18:16); nominally, it probably belonged to the tribe of Benjamin (Deut. 32:12), but neither of these tribes succeeded in conquering the city.

14. See B. Mazar, "Jerusalem—'Royal Sanctuary' and Seat of the Monarchy," *Biblical Israel, State and People*, ed. S. Ahituv (Jerusalem, 1992), 88–99.

15. See: E. Efrat, "Jerusalem (Geography)," *EJ*, IX (above, note 9), 1514–16.

16. Although the traditions about the ark differ in many details, the basic tenet of the tradition—the origin of the ark in the wandering period—is common to all. On the origin, history, and meaning of the ark, see H. J. Zobel, "ארון," *TDOT*, I, eds. G. J. Botterweck and H. Ringgren, trans. J. T. Willis (Grand Rapids, 1974), 363–74.

17. Num. 10:33–36: "They marched from the mountain of the Lord a distance of three days. The Ark of the Covenant of the Lord traveled in front of them on the three days' journey to seek out a resting place for them; and the Lord's cloud kept above them by day, as they moved on from camp. When the Ark was to set out, Moses would say: 'Advance, O Lord! May Your enemies be scattered and may Your foes flee before You!' And when it halted, he would say: 'Return, O Lord, You who are Israel's myriad of thousands' " (see also Josh. 3–4).

18. One of the epithets of the Temple is indeed: "a resting-place for the Ark of the Covenant of the Lord . . . the foot stool of our God" (I Chron. 28:2; also 22:19; cf. Ps. 132).

19. For a discussion of this campaign, see M. Cogan and H. Tadmor, *II Kings*, Anchor Bible (New York, 1988), 223–51. See also the article by W. Hallo in this volume.

20. M. Weinfeld, *From Joshua to Josiah: Turning Points in the History of Israel from the Conquest of the Land until the Fall of Judah* (Jerusalem, 1992), 163–79 (Hebrew).

21. See, for example, A. Rofé, *Introduction to the Composition of the Pentateuch* (Jerusalem, 1994), 42 (Hebrew).

22. See: S. Zmirin, *Josiah and his Time*² (Jerusalem, 1977) (Hebrew).

23. This fact is strongly emphasized by Y. Kaufmann (*The History of the Religion of Israel*⁴, I [Jerusalem and Tel Aviv, 1960], 90–94) (Hebrew). On the building of the Second Temple and its early history, see S. Japhet, "The Temple in the Restoration Period: Reality and Ideology," *Union Seminary Quarterly Review* 43 (1991), 191–251.

24. "The place where I have chosen to establish My name" is found only once, in Nehemiah's prayer (1:9), which abounds in Deuteronomistic phraseology. The root בח"ר; (choose) appears only once more in the book (referring to the election of Abraham), in Neh. 9:7.

25. Most known are the sanctuaries in Egypt, first in Elephantine and later the temple of Honio in Leontopolis (on these sanctuaries, see briefly M. Haran, *Temples and Temple Worship in Ancient Israel* [Oxford, 1978], 46–48). In the Land of Israel stood the Samaritan temple in Shechem, and perhaps also the sanctuary in Beth-el (II Kgs. 17:28–33). See the interesting views of H. Eshel, "The Historical Background of Building Temples for the God of Israel in Bethel and Samaria following the Destruction of the First Temple," Masters thesis (Hebrew University of Jerusalem, 1988) (Hebrew). Most interesting is the text of Mal. 1: 10–11, which refers to the offering of "incense and oblation" to the Lord "everywhere": "If only you would lock My doors, and not kindle fire on My altar to no purpose! I take no pleasure in you—said the Lord of Hosts—and I will accept no offering from you. For from where the sun rises to where it sets, My name is honored among the nations and everywhere incense and pure oblation are offered to My name: for My name is honored among the nations—said the Lord of Hosts."

26. On this feature in the Chronicler's view of history, see S. Japhet, *The Ideology of the Book of Chronicles and its Place in Biblical Thought*² (Frankfurt, Bern, New York and Paris, 1997), 202–47.

27. This text is a compilation of various biblical texts, particularly Deut. 27:2ff. (also Ex. 13:5; Deut. 4:5; 11:30). The dependence is well known, but so, too, are the differences between these texts, and there is no need to elaborate.

28. The date of the schism is much debated among scholars. For a summary of the views, see L. L. Grabbe, *Judaism from Cyrus to Hadrian*, 2 vols. (Minneapolis, 1992), II, 503–507. Eshel regards the development of the Samaritans' belief in the sanctity of Mount Garizim, and consequently of the emergence of Samaritanism, as rather late. See H. Eshel, "The Samaritans in the Persian and Hellenistic Periods: The Origins of Samaritanism," Ph.D. dissertation (Hebrew University of Jerusalem, 1994), esp. pp. 216–26 (Hebrew, with English summary).

2

The First Stages of Jerusalem's Sanctification under David: A Literary and Ideological Analysis

YAIR ZAKOVITCH *

God's twofold election of David and his line and of Jerusalem—appears in Ps. 78; it tells of God's disillusionment with the temple in Shiloh and the line of Ephraim, and how religious hegemony was transferred to Jerusalem and the Davidic dynasty:

> He did choose the tribe of Judah, Mount Zion, which He Loved. He built His Sanctuary like the heavens, like the earth that He established forever. He chose David, His servant, and took him from the sheepfolds. He brought him from minding the nursing ewes to tend His people Jacob, Israel, His very own. He tended them with blameless heart; with skillful hands he led them (vv. 61–72).[1]

In the course of ascertaining the status of Jerusalem in the history and consciousness of the nation in the biblical period, we find that the city was eclipsed by other, more ancient and venerable ones that enjoyed a greater degree of sanctity. The stories of the patriarchs as recounted in Genesis establish the dominance of other sites of cult worship: Abraham's first stop in Canaan was in Shechem, and "he built an altar there to the Lord (Gen. 12:6–7); Jacob, too, returning from Paddan-aram, camped in Shechem and bought a parcel of land there; he, too, erected an altar in Shechem (ibid., 33:18–20). Indeed, it seems that it was incumbent upon all who entered the Land of Canaan to first camp in Shechem and erect an altar: Joshua, leading the Israelites to the land, also erected an altar in Shechem (Josh. 8:30–35), in compliance with Moses' injunction (Deut. 27).

16

Beth-el was also an extremely important place of cult worship; Abraham made it the second camp of his journey and built another altar there (Gen. 12:8). Jacob underwent significant experiences in Beth-el on his way to Paddan-aram (ibid., 28) as well as on his return journey (ibid., 35).

Abraham had a special affinity to the site of the terebinths of Mamre in Hebron. It is here that he settled (ibid., 13:18), had a divine revelation, and received tidings of the imminent birth of his son (ibid., 18). He bought a parcel of land—the cave of Machpelah—as the burial place for Sarah (ibid., 23) and where, in time, other patriarchs and matriarchs would be buried as well.

Jerusalem is never mentioned by this name, neither in Genesis nor in the rest of the Pentateuch. Its secondary status in patriarchal traditions is to be attributed to the fact that the city was conquered only in the time of David, where it subsequently became known as the City of David (II Sam. 5:6–9). Prior to that, the so-called Jebusites, the ruling tribe in the city, called it Jebus. Jerusalem was clearly an alien city in the time of the judges, as is evident from the story of the concubine at Gibeah which mentions Jerusalem only in passing; the concubine's husband refuses to stay in the city for the night, as it is not an Israelite city:

> Since they were very close to Jebus, and the day was very far spent, the attendant said to his master: "Let us turn aside to this town of the Jebusites and spend the night in it." But his master said to him: "We will not turn aside to a town of aliens who are not of Israel, but will continue to Gibeah" (Judg. 19:11–17) [2]

The above account, however, seems to contradict the rendering of the conquest and settlement of the land as it appears at the beginning of Judges: "The Judites attacked Jerusalem and captured it; they put it to the sword and set the city on fire" (ibid., 1:8). Later in the same chapter we find a different account: "The Benjaminites did not dispossess the Jebusite inhabitants of Jerusalem; so the Jebusites have dwelt with the Benjaminites in Jerusalem to this day" (ibid., 1:21). To complicate matters even further, an almost identical verse in the book of Joshua reads: "But the Judites could not dispossess the Jebusites, the inhabitants of Jerusalem; so the Judites dwell with the Jebusites in Jerusalem to this day" (15:63). The key to this quandary lies in the bias that guided the author of both verses in Judg. 1: the entire passage (up to 2: 5) is a clear pro-Judite account, in which Judah is the first to dispossess the inhabitants of the land, as God had commanded; he is highly successful while the other tribes are castigated for their failure. The verse from Josh. 15 thus underlies both biased verses in Judg. 1: according to the book of Joshua, Judah failed to conquer Jerusalem; in Judg. 1, he is successful while the tribe of Benjamin fails. We can therefore glean nothing from Judg. 1 that would undermine the view that Jerusalem had no role in Israelite history prior to the time of David.[3]

After having united the Israelite tribes under his rule and having filled his Philistine enemies with terror, David continues his drive to conquer the Jebusite city that refuses to regard him and his army with due respect. The complacent Jebusites are confident that the protection provided by the blind and the lame will suffice to overcome the upstart and repel David's efforts to conquer the fortress. They boast that "Even the blind and the lame will turn you back" (II Sam. 5:6), but David overcomes them, takes the fortress, names it the City of David (v. 9), and declares it his capital.[4] Since the City of David, or Jerusalem, had been neutral in the nation's historical consciousness, and no single Israelite tribe could claim it as its own, David's move was calculated so as not to spark accusations of favoritism toward any particular tribe.[5]

The timing seemed auspicious for David and his kingdom; it was the opportune moment to bring the Ark to Jerusalem for the nation, city, and king alike. The Ark, ancient symbol of the unity of the people and of God's choice to call them His own, had accompanied the Israelites since their wanderings in the desert.[6] The Ark had misguidedly been taken by the Israelites into battle against the Philistines. It was captured and taken to Philistia, and then to Beth-shemesh and to Kiriath-jearim, where it remained for twenty years in the house of Abinadab. Thus, it was only fitting that the Ark reside in Jerusalem and endow the city with a religio-political dimension.

The long years of the ark's residence in the house of Abinadab apparently dulled the justified awe of its holiness, and David would pay dearly for his callousness during his first attempt to bring the Ark to his city. David hitherto had nothing but success in his undertakings and now wished to celebrate the arrival of the Ark in Jerusalem in great pomp: "David again assembled all the picked men of Israel, thirty thousand strong" (II Sam. 6:10). Accompanying "the Ark of God to which the Name was attached, the name Lord of Hosts Enthroned on the Cherubim" (ibid., 6:2), then, was a bold display of youthful strength and military might. This appellation of the Ark indicates that God was its source of power and recalls the first, abortive, attempt to enlist its power in the battle against the Philistines: "So the troops sent men to Shiloh; . . . and brought down from there the Ark of the Covenant of the Lord of Hosts Enthroned on the Cherubim" (I Sam. 4:4). Could this repetition of the same appellation hint, perhaps, at David's repetition of the sin previously committed by the Israelites? David does as he sees fit with the Ark of God, using it as if it were an object at the command of men; he does not request

God's permission for his actions.[7] The author introduces subtle irony by contrasting the Divine presence and the Ark with the attitude exhibited toward them by the people: God is the "Enthroned on the Cherubim" (ישב הכרובים); they serve as his chariot, while David and his men "loaded (וירכבו) the Ark of God onto a new cart" (II Sam. 6:3). The allusion to their lack of understanding is temporarily lost amid the riot of the revelers: "David and all the House of Israel danced before the Lord [to the sound of] all kinds of cypress wood [instruments], with lyres, harps, timbrels, sustrums, and cymbals" (ibid., 6:5). It was no longer a celebration of young men alone, but of the entire House of Israel.

The celebrations were abruptly terminated by the fatal act of Uzzah, son of Abinadab: "But when they came to the threshing floor of Nacon, Uzzah reached out for the Ark of God and grasped it, for the oxen had stumbled. The Lord was incensed at Uzzah. And God struck him down on the spot for his indiscretion, and he died there beside the Ark of God" (ibid., 6:6–7). The account in I Chronicles is clearer: ". . . and struck him down, because he raised a hand against the Ark" (13:10). Uzzah's gesture of reaching out to touch the Ark is construed as having had harmful intent. The same collocation is used in the verses "Do not raise your hand against the boy . . ." (Gen. 22:12) and "But when the angel raised its hand upon Jerusalem to destroy it . . ." (II Sam. 24:16). History repeats itself because people fail to learn the lessons of the past: Uzzah's intentions were good and proper, as had been those of the people of Beth-shemesh who rejoiced at seeing the Ark of God.[8] Moreover, Uzzah hastened to prevent the Ark from falling off the cart. However, this act stresses his profound incomprehension, shared by the general public and David as well, of God's ability to ensure the well-being of His Ark. God had "single-handedly" smitten the Philistines by means of the Ark, freed it from captivity, and returned it to the Israelites; is this not a sure sign that God could prevent its fall as well? It seems more than likely that God purposely caused the oxen to stumble, to instill in King David the awareness that the Ark is deserving of the same respect due God Himself, and anyone who mistakenly distinguishes between the two forfeits his life.

God had now aborted the festivities; the mighty troops and the House of Israel were nowhere to be seen. David's reaction indicates that he had not grasped the lesson, and he countered the wrath of God with his own fury: "David was distressed because the Lord had inflicted a breach upon Uzzah; and that place was named Perez-uzzah" (ibid., 6:8). When God enabled David, descendant of Perez (Ruth 4:8–22), to win a victory over his enemies, David triumphantly renamed the site Baal-perazim, saying "the Lord has broken through my enemies before me, as waters break through a dam" (ibid., 5:20).

However, when God struck down Uzzah, David's emissary, David expressed his anger by renaming the site Perez-uzzah. David remained unaware that his victory in battle at Baal-perazim was his reward for asking God if he should go to war against the Philistines (ibid., 5:19), while the tragedy at Perez-uzzah was his punishment for failing to consult God's will.[9]

David was frightened as well as irate: "David was afraid of the Lord that day; he said, 'How can I let the Ark of the Lord come to me?' " (ibid., 6:9). Note the king's humiliation here; the words "to me" indicate that he took personal umbrage at the incident. David's reaction is remarkably similar to that of the inhabitants of Beth-shemesh, even to the same mistaken lesson derived from the event—the removal of the Ark elsewhere: "So David would not bring the Ark to his place in the City of David; instead, he diverted it to the house of Obed-edom the Gittite" (ibid., 6:10). Does David's decision reflect some unspoken wish on his part to punish God? David took the Ark from the Israelites and brought it to the home of an idol-worshipper, a Philistine from Gath.

This was not the first encounter between the Ark and the city of Gath: when the Ark was seized by the Philistines, it brought a scourge upon Ashdod, and the victims sent out messengers to ask: "What shall we do with the Ark of the God of Israel?," and the reply was: "Let the Ark of the God of Israel be removed to Gath" (I Sam. 5:8), hoping that a change in location would bring them respite. David's decision to remove the Ark to the home of a dweller in Gath is no wiser than the decisions of the Philistines or the inhabitants of Beth-shemesh.

Just as the blow God dealt to Beth-shemesh was followed by a lengthy period of calm during the long years in which the Ark remained in Kiriath-jearim, so, too, was the home of Obed-edom the Gittite blessed in the wake of the tragedy at Perez-uzzah: "The Ark of the Lord remained in the house of Obed-edom the Gittite three months, and the Lord blessed Obed-edom and his whole household" (II Sam. 6:11). Were it not for the Ark's munificence, it would have remained in the house of Obed-edom in Gath longer still, but God was seeking to spur David to action: "It was reported to King David that 'the Lord has blessed Obed-edom's house and all that belongs to him because of the Ark of God'. Thereupon David went and brought up the Ark of God from the house of Obed-edom to the City of David, amid rejoicing (ibid., 6: 12). LXX (the Lucianic version) adds: "And David said, 'I will return the blessing to my house',," as if his reasons for bringing the Ark to the city were wholly personal.[10] Would David's house truly be blessed once more?

David was warier this time, fearing perhaps that the Ark would strike again. "When the bearers of the Ark of the Lord had moved forward six paces, he sacrificed an ox and a fatling" (ibid., 6:13). David was ecstatic: "David whirled with all his might before the Lord" (ibid., 6:14), and the people rejoiced with him: "Thus David and all the House of Israel brought up the Ark of the Lord with shouts and with blasts of the horn" (ibid., 6:15). Compare this to Ps. 47:6: "God ascends midst acclamation, the Lord, to the blasts of the horn." The Ark remained quiescent this time, wreaking no havoc, and the procession seems to have gone well. Was David's caution sufficient, however, to ensure that the Ark would shower blessings upon the king and the people of Israel? Could David have once again repeated his mistake of failing to consult God's will regarding the transfer of the Ark to Jerusalem? In any event, just at their peak, the festivities became clouded over: "Michal daughter of Saul looked out of the window and saw King David leaping and whirling before the Lord; and she despised him for it" (II Sam. 6:16).[11] Unseen, Michal watched David from the window as he set the Ark in the tent he pitched for it and made sacrifices and offerings (v. 18). David renders to God what is God's and to the people what is the people's. God had blessed the house of Obed-edom, whereas David blessed the entire people "in the name of the Lord of Hosts" (v. 18) and adds from his own bounty: "And he distributed among the people—the entire multitude of Israel, man and woman alike—to each a loaf of bread, a cake made in a pan, and a raisin cake" (ibid., 6:19). With this largesse the public festivities were concluded: "Then all the people left for their homes" (ibid.); all left and the stage was cleared for a conclusion typical of biblical stories.[12] David's plan had indeed come to a satisfactory end: the Ark arrived at the destination David had wished, the City of David, thus putting an end to the peregrinations that began when it left the temple at Shiloh. But the reader is still in for a surprise: the story was not yet over, and it is far from clear that all will end on a happy note.

Silence now replaced the tumult, and the personal aspect superseded the public one; David "went back to bless his household" (ibid., 6:20), and, recalling the LXX version for v. 12, we realize once more that David expected God to bless his own household. The reader accompanies David on his way home with some trepidation, having already seen what the king has not: the chilling scorn of Michal, watching David from the window.

When Michal went to greet her husband, she showed her contempt for him. LXX pauses in the narrative at this point to emphasize the queen's bitter invective, by the addition of the words "she blessed him" before reporting Michal's speech to the king.[13] She counteracted his wish for a blessing for his household by blessing him with a greeting that was nothing but a curse, as is evident from her ironic rhetorical question: "Didn't the king of Israel do himself honor today?" (ibid., 6:20), an innuendo that it was not honorable behavior at all; on the contrary, it was pathetic and despicable. She greeted her husband David by his title, "King of Israel," as a king whose behavior was not worthy of a sovereign, "exposing himself today in the sight of the slavegirls of his subjects as one of the riffraff might expose himself!" (ibid., 6:20).

Michal was well aware that David was frolicking "before the Lord" to glorify Him, but in seeking to denigrate him she charged him with exposing himself before the slavegirls. The king retorted with biting words: "It was before the Lord who chose me instead of your father and all his family and appointed me ruler over the Lord's people Israel! I will dance before the Lord" (ibid., 6: 21). The beginning of this verse is clearer in the LXX version: "I dance before God, blessed be He, who has chosen. . . ."[14] David had not sought to display himself before the women, but rather before God, in gratitude for what God had done for him. Michal, his wife, as member of the House of David, was not worthy of blessing, but David will bless God for having chosen him. David was aware that Michal, as "daughter of Saul," had been condescending to him, and he reminded her that God was displeased with her father and chose David instead. The reader is reminded of the words spoken by the people when David was anointed king: "Long before now, when Saul was king over us, it was you who led Israel to war; and the Lord said to you: 'you shall shepherd my people Israel, you shall be ruler of Israel' " (ibid., 5:2).

David dared not deny the accusations Michal leveled at him. Furthermore, wishing to show respect for God, he cared nothing for how Michal perceived him: "I will dance before the Lord and dishonor myself even more, and be low in my own esteem"—LXX reads "in your esteem."[15] David did not consider his honor compromised by dancing before common women: "but among the slavegirls that you speak of I will be honored" (ibid., 6:22); had Michal been scrupulously honest with herself, she would have admitted that she was not of noble blood either. True, she was the daughter of one king and the wife of another, but her father was not born to royalty—he was a simple peasant who ventured out to look for asses and found the kingship in their stead.

The incident of bringing the Ark to Jerusalem concludes in the dry, laconic tone of a chronicle: "So to her dying day Michal daughter of Saul had no children" (ibid., 6:23). The narrator does not explicitly state that this was God's punishment for her pride, but the perceptive reader can immediately grasp that the woman who initially appeared high up at the window as "the daughter of Saul" had been judged accordingly by the divine power, sharing the fate of the waning House of Saul.

Michal was dealt a punishing blow, but David did not escape unscathed from the incident either; true, the king had succeeded in bringing the Ark of

God to Jerusalem, his capital, and the people all witnessed his joy. But there was still no peace within the privacy of his own home.

David had to subject his actions to careful scrutiny in order to fathom why the mission had not been entirely successful, why his joy was imperfect. David had assumed that he had the authority to determine where the Ark of God was to reside and that he alone could decide when to ask for a blessing for his house; he ultimately learned that both of these were to be left to God's judgment alone. Later on, David did not dare build a shrine for the Ark without consulting Nathan the prophet first: "Here I am dwelling in a house of cedar, while the Ark of the Lord abides in a tent" (ibid., 7:2). At the end of chapter 7, God promised David that his line will last forever, and David made a request of God: "Be pleased, therefore, to bless Your servant's house, that it abide before you forever, for You, O Lord God, have spoken. May Your servant's house be blessed forever by Your blessing" (ibid., 7:29).[16]

The book of Chronicles contains a different, later, redaction of the story of how the Ark was brought to Jerusalem (I Chron. 13–16). According to this account, David admitted that he abused the Ark by moving it from Kiriath-jearim: "Because you were not there the first time, the Lord our God burst out against us, for we did not show due regard for Him" (ibid., 15:13) and he was now assiduous in adhering to the stricture of the Law: "The priests and the Levites sanctified themselves in order to bring up the Ark of the Lord God of Israel. The Levites carried the Ark of God by means of poles on their shoulders, as Moses had commanded in accordance with the word of the Lord" (ibid., 15:14–15, and see also vv. 20, 27, and compare with Deut. 10:8: "At that time the Lord set apart the tribe of Levi to carry the Ark of the Lord's Covenant").[17]

According to the Chronicler, the liturgy that accompanied the Ark on its way to Jerusalem—the arrangement of verses from Ps. 105, 96, 107, and 106 (in that order) and the hymns of praise and thanksgiving recited by the Levites Assaf and his brothers—merit great importance. This privileged status of the liturgy corresponds with the prevailing view at the time of the Chronicler, according to which the psalms recited in the Temple were David's inspiration and creation.[18]

The act of bringing the Ark to Jerusalem points to David's political wisdom; however, there is no clear-cut, definitive indication that God chose the site. A veritable miracle—and incontrovertible proof of the sanctity of Jerusalem for the people and the faith of Israel—appears in the concluding chapter of II Samuel, which tells of the census David conducted among the people, the ensuing pestilence, and how it was arrested finally at "the threshing floor of Araunah the Jebusite" (II Sam. 24).

This chapter was not penned as a single unit, and the concept of the sanctity of Jerusalem was initially foreign to it. A close reading of the chapter shows that it contains contradictory verses: the pestilence, which was punishment for the census that David conducted, was to have lasted three days: "shall there be three days of pestilence in your land?" (v. 13), and, indeed, it does last that long: "the Lord sent a pestilence upon Israel from morning until the set time" (v. 15). However, in verse 16, the text weaves mention of Jerusalem into the fabric of the story, and at some point God retracts his intention of sending a pestilence: "But when the angel raised his hand against Jerusalem to destroy it, the Lord renounced further punishment and said to the angel who was destroying the people: 'Enough! Stay your hand!' The angel of the Lord was then by the threshing floor of Araunah the Jebusite." Moreover, this same verse does not jibe with the concluding verse of the chapter (v. 25): "The Lord responded to the plea for the land; and the plague against Israel was checked"—for God had already stopped the destructive angel![19]

The original narrative of the chapter, then, would include verses 1–15 and 25[b] alone: the pestilence endured until the "set time," as David had been forewarned, and at that time God stopped it and "responded to the plea for the land."

What was the function of the original narrative? The story shares several points of similarity with the episode of David and the wife of Uriah the Hittite (ibid., 12). The root *ḥrh*, indicating God's rage toward Israel over the census (ibid., 24:1), is used in the story of Bath-sheba, wherein David raged against the rich man who stole the pauper's lamb, i.e., against himself: "David flew into a rage against the man" (ibid., 12:5). When David discovered that he himself was the culprit, he asked for forgiveness: "And David said to Nathan: 'I stand guilty before the Lord' " (v. 13), and in the census: "And David said to the Lord: 'I have sinned grievously in what I have done'." And, just as God assents and forgives him in the incident of Bath-sheba ("The Lord has remitted your sin; you shall not die"—ibid., 12:13), he requests here, too: "Please, O Lord, remit the guilt of your servant, for I have acted foolishly" (ibid., 24:10).

Moreover, it was these similarities that impelled the redactor of the appendix to II Samuel to affix the last story in the book to the list of David's warriors; Uriah the Hittite was the last among them (ibid., 23:39). It is understood that the king's sin against Uriah prolonged God's rage toward Israel. This reading is corroborated by the absence of the census story in the parallel accounts appearing in I Chron. 11 and elsewhere; neither does the list of warriors in I Chronicles end with the mention of Uriah the Hittite (ibid., 11:41[a]), but continues with vv. 41ᵇ–47. The list in I Chronicles would appear to preserve an original passage that was intentionally omitted from the masoretic text in order to create a meaningful juxtaposition.[20]

If we are correct in establishing this link between the story of the census and the incident of David and Bath-sheba, we must try to understand why God raged against Israel. Should he not rather have raged against David? I believe that the verse originally read: "The anger of the Lord again flared up against David and He incited David against the people." Only upon the addition of a new element to the story, namely, its reuse as part of a polemic on the sanctity of Jerusalem, was the first verse amended accordingly.

The original story addressed another sin committed by David in addition to the incident with Bath-sheba—the sin of the census-taking. David is required to choose an appropriate punishment for himself: "Shall a seven-year[21] famine come upon you on the land, or shall you be in flight from your adversaries for three months while they pursue you, or shall there be three days of pestilence in your land?" (II Sam. 24:13). David avoided assuming responsibility; instead of choosing the punishment that would inflict personal injury on him—flight from his pursuing enemies—he opted for a collective punishment. His eloquent response conceals his selfishness: "I am in great distress. Let us fall into the hands of the Lord, for his compassion is great; and let me not fall into the hands of men" (ibid., 24:14). Following upon his decision, a terrible plague killed seventy thousand people.

It emerges that the original narrative sought to denounce David by heaping sins upon him, and we must ask who would be likely to wish this. In order to reply conclusively, we must analyze the points of similarity and divergence between the original layer of the census story (ibid., 24) and another one appearing in the appendix to II Sam: the impaling of seven sons of the House of Saul by the Gibeonites (21:1–14). The following are the points of similarity between the two accounts:

1. Both episodes deal with a sin committed by a king: Saul breaking his oath to the Gibeonites (chapter 21) and David's sin (chapter 24);
2. Saul's sin generated the punishment of a three-year famine: "There was a famine during the reign of David, year after year for three years" (v. 1), and David was granted the option of choosing between three alternatives for punishment, one of them being "a three-year famine" (the proximity to the story in chapter 21 is another reason to prefer the reading of "three" to "seven"—v. 13);
3. Chapter 21 speaks of both Israel and Judah: "and Saul had tried to wipe them out in his zeal for the people of Israel and Judah" (v. 2); likewise,

in chapter 24, the opening verse reads "Go and number Israel and Judah";

4. The two stories end on a similar note: "God responded to the plea of
the land thereafter" (ibid., 21:14); "The Lord responded to the plea for
the land, and the plague against Israel was checked" (ibid., 24:25).

The story in chapter 21 is thus an anti-Saul text which purports to justify
David for having seven sons of the House of Saul killed;[22] chapter 24, then,
is the anti-Davidic response of the House of Saul: David's sin is no less severe
than the one committed by Saul. The redactor of the chapter accuses David
of hypocrisy: is his act of handing over seven males of Saul's line to the Gibeonites indeed only a desperate attempt to stop the three-year famine? David
is clearly unfazed by the prospect of a three-year famine; were he concerned
about it, and had he been less selfish, he would have chosen the punishment
of pursuit by his enemies, sparing the people of both a three-year famine and
a three-day pestilence.

Therefore, the opening of the anti-Davidic story was changed with the
intention of softening its acerbic tone, and the second layer, comprising verses
16–25, was added. The sin becomes a vague wrongdoing perpetrated by the
people, for which God incites David to punish them (v. 1). The new insertion
concentrates on the sanctity conferred on Jerusalem and the process of its
becoming a center of cult worship for the entire people of Israel.

✦   ✦   ✦

In its present formulation, chapter 24 of II Samuel bears an affinity to two
patriarchal traditions and to a brief episode in I Kings, all dealing with the
acquisition of land in Israel. It is only those accounts telling of landowners
selling parcels of land to the Israelites of their own accord, explicitly stating
that the transaction was carried out in the presence of witnesses and for the
full price, that furnish proof of the ownership of the land by the people of
Israel. As the Bible cannot report the purchase of every parcel of land, it tells
only of those central figures in the history of the nation who bought tracts of
land that became sites of great import for the history of the land and the
historical consciousness of its people. The four stories tell of such acquisitions:
the cave of Machpelah in Hebron (Gen. 23:8–20); Shechem (Gen. 33:19);
the threshing floor of Araunah in Jerusalem (II Sam. 24:21–24; I Chron. 21:
22–28); and Samaria (I Kgs. 16:24). The purpose of buying land was either
to erect an altar, as in Shechem and Jerusalem, or for burial (Hebron, as well
as Shechem, as Joseph is brought there for burial—Josh. 24:32).

The four stories revolve around capital cities in the biblical land of Israel.

Two were capitals of the kingdom of Judah: Hebron was David's first capital during his reign over Judah alone, and Jerusalem was the capital of his united monarchy; and two were capital cities of the northern kingdom: Shechem was the first capital of the north after the division of the kingship, and Samaria was the capital of the dynasty of Omri and continued to serve as capital of the northern kingdom until its destruction.

The reader is aware that the stories about the acquisition of the capital cities of the kingdom of Judah are replete with allusions to the patriarch Abraham, who bought Hebron, and the burial of the patriarchs there; and to King David, founder of the royal dynasty, who bought Jerusalem. The same is true about the acquisition of the capital cities of the northern kingdom; Shechem figures prominently in the life of the patriarch Jacob, and the short account about Samaria tells of Omri, founder of the major royal dynasty in the north. Three of these cities also appear in the Bible in the context of conquest—Shechem (Gen. 48:22), Hebron (Judg. 1:10), and Jerusalem (II Sam. 5:6–8). The traditions about the acquisition of these places legitimizes their ownership by the people of Israel.

Only two of the four abovementioned accounts, those of Hebron and Jerusalem, the two capitals of the kingdom of Judah, go into much detail. The capital cities of the northern kingdom receive only brief mention. This bias is obviously due to the dominant role of the authors from Judah in the redaction of the biblical narrative.

The story of David's acquisition of Jerusalem is identical in many respects to the account of Abraham's purchase of Hebron; Araunah was willing to give David the threshing floor gratis, but David declined the offer and insisted on paying for it. Both the name of the owner and the amount he received for the land, fifty sheqalim, are stated. The similarity between the story of Araunah's threshing floor and the account of the cave of Machpelah was obvious to the redactor of the story of the threshing floor in I Chron. 21, where the similarity is stressed even further. While David, in II Samuel, wished to buy the threshing floor at "a price," in I Chron. 21:24 he insisted on paying the "full price," the very expression employed in Gen. 21:9. In general, the root *qnh* that is used to describe David's act in II Sam. 24:21–24 is replaced in I Chronicles twice by the root *ntn* (vv. 22, 25) so as to emphasize the link to the Genesis episode. In Chronicles, the root *qnh* appears only once (v. 24) and reappears in Gen. 23:18. I Chronicles also mentions the presence of witnesses, the sons of Ornan, at the transaction.[23]

The account of the acquisition of Jerusalem is first and foremost a claim for the legitimation of the site's sanctification and its transformation into a center for the entire people of Israel. The purpose of the story, namely, to present Jerusalem as the center for both factions, Judah and Israel, is evident already in the story of the census of Judah and Israel which preceded the plague: "all the tribes of Israel, from Dan to Beer-sheba" (II Sam. 24:2). The pestilence—which was the punishment for the census-taking—also afflicted the entire people: "70,000 of the people died, from Dan to Beer-sheba" (ibid., 24:15). However, it is in Jerusalem that God halts the destroying angel from his task: "But when the angel raised his hand over Jerusalem to destroy it, the Lord renounced further punishment and said to the angel who was destroying the people, 'Enough! Stay your hand!' The angel of the Lord was then by the threshing floor of Araunah the Jebusite" (ibid., 24:16). The story informs us, then, that God chose the site, and Gad the seer, in fact, instructs David to build an altar on the threshing floor of Araunah (v. 18). David builds an altar and offers sacrifices (v. 25); the story concludes with the words "The Lord responded to the plea for the land, and the plague against Israel was checked" (ibid., 24:28).

The validity of this version of the sanctification of Jerusalem was sustained as long as the unified monarchy stood firm, but the rift in the kingdom created a new situation. I Kings was redacted with a bias in favor of the kingdom of Judah and the House of David, denouncing Jeroboam for choosing Beth-el and Dan and wishing to isolate the northern tribes from Jerusalem: "If these people still go up to offer sacrifices at the House of the Lord in Jerusalem, the heart of these people will turn back to their master, King Rehoboam of Judah; they will kill me and go back to King Rehoboam of Judah." So the king seeks counsel and fashions two golden calves, and addresses the people: " 'You have been going up to Jerusalem long enough. This is your God, O Israel, who brought you up from the land of Egypt!' He set one up in Beth-el and placed the other in Dan" (I Kgs. 12:27–29). It is noteworthy that Jeroboam to some degree remains true to traditional practice by resuming Israelite worship of God in the ancient cult sites of Beth-el dating from the time of the patriarchs, and Dan, a place of cult worship dating from the time of the Judges (Judg. 18).[24]

When the northern tribes seceded from the House of David, claiming "We have no portion in David, no share in Jesse's son! To your tents, O Israel! Now look to your own House, O David" (I Kgs. 12:16), the story of the hallowing of Jerusalem in the time of David lacked the power to instill in the northern tribes a sense of belonging to the city. In order to make the northern tribes accept the centrality of Jerusalem and convince them of its sanctity, it had to be affiliated with a figure accepted by all the factions of the people, namely, Abraham. Thus, attention was diverted temporarily from the first king to the first patriarch.

Two passages in Genesis associate the sanctity of Jerusalem with Abraham. The first (Gen. 14:18–20) recounts the story of Melchizedek of Salem. These three verses were inserted into the narrative telling of the war of the four kings against the five kings, and interrupt the flow of the story.[25] "When he returned from defeating Chedorlaomer and the kings with him, the king of Sodom came out to meet him in the Valley of Shaveh, which is the Valley of the King" (v. 17); "Then the king of Sodom said to Abraham, 'Give me the persons, and take the possessions for yourself' " (v. 21). The three verses which interrupt the meeting between the king of Sodom and Abraham were incorporated smoothly and skillfully into the body of the narrative. The word "king" appears in v. 17, although the king referred to in vv. 18–20 is a different king altogether: "King Melchizedek of Salem." Verse 20 tells of Abraham giving something to Melchizedek: "And [Abram] gave him. . . ."; in v. 21 the king of Sodom tells Abraham: "Give me the persons. . . ." Moreover, Melchizedek mentions God, "Creator of heaven and earth," in his blessing (v. 19)—a phrase which recurs in Abraham's oath: "I swear to the Lord, God Most High, Creator of heaven and earth" (v. 22). This serves to identify God Most High as the God of Israel, Creator of heaven and earth.

The incorporation of the encounter between Abraham and Melchizedek into Gen. 14 serves, then, to link Abraham and Salem, i.e., Jerusalem, as we read in Ps. 76:3: "Salem became His abode; Zion, His den." The story recognizes that Jerusalem is occupied by a foreign, Canaanite power, and was not conquered by Abraham, but this is not due to any weakness on his part; the narrative portrays Abraham as a hero, and the king of Salem blesses him with a reference to "God Most High, Who has delivered your foes into your hand" (ibid., 14:20). However, it is stated that the sanctity of Jerusalem predates the settlement of the Israelites in the city. The Canaanite inhabitants of the city worshipped God Most High, Creator of Heaven and Earth, identified with Yahweh.

Melchizedek concedes the supremacy of Abraham: "And King Melchizedek of Salem brought out bread and wine" (v. 18). Abraham, for his part, acknowledges the sanctity of the site and gives the priest of God Most High "a tenth of everything" (v. 20) to express his gratitude for his victory and triumph.

The name Melchizedek, king of Jerusalem, is also the name of the king of Zion in Ps. 110 (v. 4: "You are a priest forever, a rightful king by My decree" [Melchizedek: lit., "rightful king"]). Moreover, the element zedek is inextricably bound with Jerusalem from time immemorial and evokes the image of Adonizedek, king of Jerusalem in the time of Joshua (Josh. 10:1); it relates also to Zadok, the founder of the priestly dynasty in Jerusalem and priest in the Temple of Solomon.[26]

A second account in Genesis dates the hallowing of Jerusalem to the time of Abraham in the story of the binding of Isaac (Gen. 22), in which God put Abraham to a test "on one of the heights" in "the land of Moriah" (v. 2). In this story, one verse alone bears the burden of acting as a connective device: "And Abraham named the site Adonai-yireh, whence the present saying 'On the mount of the Lord there is vision'." This verse disrupts the narrative flow of verses 13 to 15.[27] The term "Mount of the Lord" that appears in the intervening verses (see, for example, Isa. 2:3; 30:29) could not have been formulated before the establishment of the Temple on that site (see Ibn Ezra's commentary to Deut. 1:1). Here, too, this addition, serving to anchor the events in Jerusalem, is skillfully incorporated into the narrative: the root *r'h* appears in verses 4 and 13; compare especially "God will see to the sheep for His burnt offering" (v. 8) with "Adonai-yireh" (v. 14). The root *r'h* alliterates with the sound of the name Moriah. Indeed, several ancient translations of the Bible translated Moriah as stemming from vision, sight.

It is noteworthy that the story of the binding of Isaac (Gen. 22), which incorporates an allusion to the hallowing of Jerusalem, bears several similarities to the story of the hallowing of the city in the time of David (II Sam. 24). Both stories contain a severe threat to the continuity of the line of Abraham: the demand to sacrifice Isaac and the plague; in both, respite is granted after a substitute is sacrificed on the altar; in the story of the binding of Isaac, God stops Abraham with the injunction: "Do not raise your hand against the boy" (Gen. 22:12), and in the story of the census and the plague, God stops the angel with the words: "Stay your hand!" (II Sam. 24:16); Abraham equips himself with all the implements needed for the sacrifice of Isaac (Gen. 22:6), and David, in the threshing floor incident, buys from Araunah the implements he needs to offer sacrifices (II Sam. 24:24). The author of I Chronicles depicts the angel as holding a drawn sword in his hand (21:16), just as Abraham held the firestone and the knife (Gen. 22:6); in the Chronicles version, David is put to the test, like Abraham (Gen. 22:1): "Satan arose against Israel and incited David to number Israel" (I Chron. 21:1)—and we are well aware of Satan's role in putting righteous men to the test from the book of Job.[28]

The Chronicler adds an important and dramatic element to the story of the hallowing of Jerusalem, that of divine fire which descends from the heavens, confirming God's choice of the act and the place: "And David built there an altar to the Lord and sacrificed there burnt offerings and offerings of well-being. He invoked the Lord, who answered him with fire from heaven on the altar of burnt offerings" (ibid., 21:26). This element accords with the tone of the consecration of the Temple of the Wilderness in Sinai: "And the Presence of the Lord appeared to all the people. Fire came forth and consumed the burnt offering and the fat parts on the altar. And all the people saw, and shouted, and fell on their faces" (Lev. 9:23–24). Chronicles includes a similar miracle in the story of the consecration of the Temple of Solomon: "When Solomon finished praying, fire descended from heaven and consumed the burnt offering and the sacrifices, and the glory of the Lord filled the House" (II Chron. 7:1). It is no coincidence that the author of Chronicles chose to insert miracles precisely at these two junctures: the story of the threshing floor appears in the book of Chronicles at the beginning of the section dealing with David's preparations for the building of the Temple (I Chron. 22–29), while II Chron. 1–6 depict Solomon's role in completing the endeavor undertaken by his father. The miracle in the time of Solomon thus concludes the segment that opened with a similar miracle experienced by his father.[29]

Yet another verse was inserted in the narrative of the story of the threshing floor in I Chronicles: "David said: 'Here will be the House of the Lord and here the altar of burnt offerings for Israel' " (22:1). The language is reminiscent of Jacob's reaction after his dream in Beth-el: "Shaken, he said . . . 'This is none other than the abode of God, and this is the gateway to heaven' " (Gen. 28:17). In both stories, the speaker is moved by awe and fear, as evidenced by Jacob's words: "How awesome is this place!" (ibid.) and by the description of David as "terrified by the sword of the angel of the Lord" (I Chron. 21:30). The Chronicler seems to have consciously adopted the spirit of his predecessor in Genesis as his underlying bias, expressing a wish to conflate the various places of cult worship into one site—Jerusalem.

The Mount of Moriah is first mentioned by that name in the description in II Chronicles of the building of the Temple of Solomon; note that this name does not appear in the story of the binding of Isaac; there the site is called "one of the heights in the land of Moriah." The Chronicler explains the name and identifies the mount with the site of the Temple: "Then Solomon began to build the House of the Lord in Jerusalem on Mount Moriah, where [the Lord] had appeared to his father David, which he made ready in the place that David had appointed, at the threshing floor of Ornan the Jebusite" (II Chron. 3:1). Perhaps the correct reading should follow the ancient translations: "in the place where David had designated, at the threshing floor. . . ." LXX reads: "on the Mount of Moriah where God had appeared to his father David," thus further reinforcing the allusion to the story of the binding of Isaac.[30]

Abraham is conspicuously absent from this story, and the explanation of the name Moriah, from the root r'h of which the author of Gen. 22 is so fond, is associated here with David. This chapter, then, was redacted in light of the opposite principle to the one we have seen above; after the division of the kingdom, the sanctity of Jerusalem was associated with Abraham, to raise its status for all the tribes, and for this reason the story of the binding of Isaac was glossed with the addition that it took place in Jerusalem. In Chronicles, however, composed in the period of the Return to Zion, it was David whom the authors sought to set up as the first to sanctify Jerusalem. This is because at this time the returning exiles evinced separatist tendencies and were unwilling to include others in the project of building the Temple. The returning exiles of the tribe of Judah set themselves apart from the Samaritans, who had remained in Israel and had not been exiled,[31] telling them: "It is not for you and us to build a House to our God, but we alone will build it to the Lord God of Israel" (Ezra 4:3). In order to dissuade the Samaritans from seeking to participate in building the Temple, they must be made to forget that Jerusalem was holy to the patriarchs, since they considered themselves descendants of Abraham. The sanctity of Jerusalem had to be reestablished as stemming from David of Judah, who was not a figure of special consequence for the northern tribes or the Samaritans.

At the time of the return of the exiles, there was a need for complete identity between "one of the heights" and the Mount of the Lord in Jerusalem, because the Samaritans, who had been excluded by the tribe of Judah, identified "one of the heights" with Mount Gerizim in Shechem. According to the Samaritans, Mount Gerizim has thirteen names, among them Beth-el, the gateway to heaven, Luzia, "one of the heights," and Adonai-yireh. The Samaritans employed the same tactic as the Chronicler: the latter identified Beth-el and the Mount of Moriah with Jerusalem, as the Samaritans had previously identified the same sites with Shechem.[32] The Samaritan identification of Moriah with Shechem is aided, of course, by the resemblance between the names Moriah and the "terebinth of Moreh," the name of the cult site in Shechem (Gen. 12:6).

In conclusion, let us recapitulate the main points of our discussion. Jerusalem was not a holy city to the Israelites in the pre-Davidic period (the time of the Judges, Samuel, and Saul), when God was worshipped in Shechem, Beth-el, Hebron, and Dan, and the sanctity of these sites was associated with the era of the patriarchs. After David made the neutral, newly-conquered site of Jerusalem his capital, and after Solomon built his Temple there, the sanctity of the city was associated with bringing the Ark, symbol of the unity of Israel and the Divine presence, to Jerusalem. The holiness of the city was especially bolstered by a story that contained an element of the sanctity of Jerusalem only at a secondary stage: the salvation of the entire people of Israel from the pestilence in the time of David, who then built an altar there. The insertion of the story of the threshing floor of Arauna in its present place, at the end of the book of Samuel, serves as a link to the story of the building of the

Temple of Solomon in the book of Kings and is designed to inform the reader how the altar in Jerusalem came to be built. The altar is mentioned in the next chapter (I Kgs. 1:50–53) and is the same altar to which Adonijah and Joab son of Zeruiah fled for protection (ibid., 2:28–34).

Upon the division of the kingdom, when the northern tribes resumed their cultic practices, despite denunciations by the House of David, traditions surrounding the sanctification of Jerusalem in the time of Abraham were formed in Judah. The status of Abraham as the forefather of the entire people was utilized by means of interspersing allusions to him in existing stories that originally had nothing to do with Jerusalem. When the exiles returned, they attributed the sanctity of Jerusalem to David, due both to their wish to be set apart from the Samaritans and to their desire to show that Moriah signified the place of cult worship in Jerusalem and not in Shechem.

Notes

*Translated from the Hebrew by Ms. Sara Friedman.

1. On the date and intent of Ps. 78, see recently Y. Zakovitch, " 'Give Ear, My People, to My Teachings'—Psalm 78—Source, Structure, Message," *David King of Israel Alive and Enduring?*, ed. O. Lifshitz (Jerusalem, 1997), 117–202 (Hebrew).

2. On the program of the story of the concubine at Gibeah, see the classic article by M. Gudemann, "Tendenz und Abfassungszeit der letzten Capitel des Buches der Richter," *MGWJ* 18 (1869), 357–68.

3. On the pro-Judite bias of Judg. 1, see, for instance, M. H. Segal, *Introduction to the Bible*, I (Jerusalem, 1967), 165ff.

4. On the conquest of the city, see Y. Yadin, "The Blind and the Lame and the Conquest of Jerusalem," *Proceedings of the First World Congress of Jewish Studies* (Jerusalem, 1952), 222–25 (Hebrew).

5. On the reasons for the choice of Jerusalem as capital, see A. Alt, *Old Testament History and Religion* (Garden City, 1966), 283.

6. On the traditions of the Ark in the book of Samuel and how they related to each other, see L. Rost, *The Succession to the Throne of David* (Sheffield, 1982), 6–34; G. W. Ahlstrom, "The Travels of the Ark—A Religio-Historical Composition," *JNES* 34 (1984), 141–49.

7. This understanding of David's sin differs from that proposed by S. Gelander (*David and His God* [Jerusalem, 1991], 42), who assumes that the author is unwilling to hint at David's error. David's failure to consult God before taking such a momentous step is a repeat performance of his previous sin: the decision to flee to King Achish (I Sam. 21:11–16) without consulting God; see Y. Zakovitch, " 'Is David also among the Prophets?' 1 Sam. 21:11–16 in Circles of Inner-Biblical Interpretation," *Shnaton, An Annual for Biblical and Ancient Near Eastern Studies* 11 (1997), 114–30 (Hebrew).

8. The affinity between the Beth-shemesh and Perez-uzzah incidents was noted by N. J. Tur Sinai, *The Language and the Book: Belief and Doctrine* (Jerusalem, 1955), 87–95 (Hebrew).

9. M. Garsiel (*Biblical Names, a Literary Study of Midrashic Derivations and Puns* [Ramat-Gan, 1991], 188–89) has noted only the associative link between the *midrashim* of the name Baal-perazim and Perez-uzzah, but not the significance of the juxtaposition of the two stories.

10. The rendition of LXX is not the result of additions by commentators or of an organic element that was lost. See, for instance, H. P. Smith, *The Books of Samuel*, ICC (Edinburgh, 1899), 295.

11. On the link between Michal's two scenes and the shattering of David's hopes of receiving a blessing for his household, see Gelander (above, note 7), 45–53. Michal's role is discussed from other perspectives in D. J. A. Clines and T. Eshkenazi (eds.), *Telling Queen Michal's Story*, JSOT Supplement Series 119 (Sheffield, 1991).

12. See I. L. Seeligmann, "Hebrew Literature and Biblical Historiography," *Studies in Biblical Literature*, eds. A. Hurvitz et al. (Jerusalem, 1992), 47–50 (Hebrew).

13. See P. Kyle McCarter, Jr. (*II Samuel*, AB 9 [Garden City, 1984], 186), who asserts that these words were an organic part of LXX and were then lost in the scribal process.

14. S. R. Driver, *Notes on the Hebrew Text and the Topography of the Book of Samuel* (Oxford, 1913), 273.

15. LXX reads: "in your esteem"; ibid.

16. The repetition of the formula for blessing the household attests to deliberate juxtaposition. On juxtaposition in biblical narrative, see Y. Zakovitch, *Introduction to Inner-Biblical Interpretation* (Even-Yehuda, 1992), 35–41 (Hebrew).

17. See S. Japhet, *The Ideology of the Books of Chronicles and its Place in Biblical Thought* (Frankfurt-am-Main, 1989), 238.

18. Ibid., 382.

19. The problematics of the structure of this chapter and the suggested solutions are admirably presented by A. Rofé, *Israelite Belief in Angels in the Pre-Exilic Period as Evidenced by Biblical Traditions* (Jerusalem, 1979), 185–86.

20. The compilers of the midrash in Pesiqta Rabbati sensed the reason for the juxtaposition of the passages and saw that some names had been omitted from the list appearing in I Chronicles. See Zakovitch (above, note 16), 40–44.

21. This should read "three-year," following I Chronicles and in keeping with the sliding scale in the text, from three years to three months, then three days; see, for e.g., Driver (above, note 14), 376.

22. This is part of a marked program in the book of Samuel to emphasize that David had nothing to do with the fall of the House of Saul: when Saul and his three sons were killed in battle with the Philistines, David mourned for them in the moving elegy for Saul and Jonathan (II Sam. 1); after Joab son of Zeruiah killed Abner son of Ner, David gave vent to his rage in an elegy (ibid., 3); Saul's remaining son, Ish-bosheth, is also murdered, and once more David rages and retaliates by killing the murderers (ibid., 4). Only Mephibosheth, Jonathan's crippled son, who was unfit for the kingship, was shown signs of affection by David (ibid., 8).

23. On the process whereby two similar stories are made even more similar by assimilation, see my "Assimilation in Biblical Narrative," *Empirical Models for Biblical Criticism*, ed. J. Tigay (Philadelphia, 1985), 175–96.

24. The present version of the establishment of the temple at Dan (Judg. 17–18) derides the circumstances that led to its establishment and the worship conducted there; see, for instance, S. Talmon, *King, Cult and Calendar in Ancient Israel* (Jerusalem, 1986), 39–52.

25. On these verses as a later addition, see, for instance, J. Skinner, *Genesis*, ICC (Edinburgh, 1919), 269.

26. On the place of the Melchizedek tradition in the early kingdom, see, for instance, J. Leaver, "Melchizedek," *Biblical Encyclopaedia*, IV (Jerusalem, 1962), 1156 (Hebrew).

27. See H. Gunkel, *Genesis* (Göttingen, 1966), 176.

28. Here, too, the influence of assimilation may be discerned (see above, note 23).

29. See Japhet (above, note 17), 83–84.

30. The LXX version is preferable; see, for instance, E. L. Curtis, *The Books of Chronicles*, ICC (Edinburgh, 1919), 325.

31. The Samaritans consider themselves descendants of the tribes of the northern kingdom who were not exiled; the returning exiles, by contrast, claimed that the Samaritans were new-comers who were brought to Samaria by the king of Assyria in order to replace the northern tribes that were exiled to Assyria (II Kgs. 17:24–27); see S. Talmon, *Literary Studies in the Hebrew Bible* (Jerusalem, 1993), 134–59.

32. On the Samaritan identification of Moriah with Mount Gerizim, see J. A. Montgomery, *The Samaritans* (New York, 1968), 237.

3

Jerusalem under Hezekiah: an Assyriological Perspective

WILLIAM W. HALLO

Jerusalem 735–701 B.C.E.

As we gather here to observe the thirtieth centennial, more or less, of the capture of Jerusalem from the Jebusites by King David, there are those who question the validity of the disciplines of biblical archaeology[1] and even of biblical history,[2] or at least of their traditional designations. Today I would like to defend the case for "biblical history" by testing it against a single illustrative reign, that of Hezekiah. The choice is easy enough for an Assyriologist, for it is exclusively during this reign that Jerusalem is mentioned by name in cuneiform documents from Mesopotamia (as against those from Egypt in the Amarna period). The reason why it did not appear earlier is not far to seek: Judah had been beyond the interest of the Assyrians (let alone the Babylonians) until 735 or 734 B.C.E., when it was besieged by the northern kingdom of Israel under Pekah and his ally, Rezin of Damascus, in an anti-Assyrian move designed, perhaps, to substitute a more tractable king in Judah for Ahaz who, according to one view, had just assumed the coregency of that land.[3] But this father and immediate predecessor of Hezekiah held staunchly to his pro-Assyrian policy; in a move typical for the period,[4] he appealed for help to Tiglath-Pileser III, with fateful consequences for both Israel, which was shorn of half of its possessions, and Judah, which was reduced to vassalage.[5]

The incorporation of Israel into the Assyrian empire was consummated by its next two kings, Salmaneser V and Sargon II, with the capture of Samaria in 722 B.C.E., a feat variously credited to either king in the different cuneiform sources,[6] and even regarded as two separate events in some modern treatments.[7] Two years later, Sargon returned to the west and referred to himself, apparently in that connection, as *mušakniš māt Iauda*, "the subduer of the land of Judah,"[8] but to him it was still a land "which is far away."[9] There is no indication that he invaded Judah either in 720[10]or 712 B.C.E. when he, or rather his *turtānu*, returned once more to the western front to deal with the Philistine city-state of Ashdod. Throughout that time Ahaz remained a loyal vassal, deaf to the incitements of the rebels, mindful that he now bordered on Assyrian provinces both to the west (Ashdod) and to the north (Israel), and perhaps encouraged by prophecies like Isa. 20.[11]

The same was true even of Hezekiah in the first decade of his reign, according to some.[12] It was not until the death of Sargon in battle in 705 B.C.E., and the general rebellion that greeted this unique event and the succession of his son Sennacherib, that Hezekiah demonstrably joined the rebellion. Indeed, he became the leader of its western wing and received the embassy of Merodach-baladan, leader of its eastern wing, some time between 705 and 702 B.C.E., i.e., during the latter's exile and second tenure, according to one view.[13] It was only after this that Sennacherib, seeking to maintain the expansionist policy of his predecessors and to deal with rebellion in the decisive manner that had become traditional with them, turned his attention to Jerusalem. He thus confronted Hezekiah, whose reign had begun twenty-two years before his own (727 B.C.E.) according to some scholars,[14] or ten (715 B.C.E.) according to others.[15]

All told, Hezekiah's reign has numerous points of contact with extra-biblical sources. At first glance, it might seem that the last word or at least the latest word had been said about these, for even in the short time since I accepted my assignment for this conference, excellent articles have appeared on the subject by N. Na'aman[16] and O. Borowski,[17] both scholars with an exemplary first-hand knowledge of the material, and it is barely a decade since it was surveyed by H. Tadmor, the acknowledged master of the field.[18] As Tadmor points out, the campaign of Sennacherib against Judah and Jerusalem in the reign of Hezekiah is the longest account in the Bible of any encounter between Israel and Assyria, and at one and the same time the most detailed description of an Assyrian campaign to the west in the cuneiform sources.[19] If, nevertheless, I am prepared to review the ground once more, it is at least partly because some aspects of it still deserve another look in the light of recent research. More generally, the extra-biblical sources can be used to illustrate and evaluate the divergent methodologies currently competing in biblical historiography.

I shall concentrate first on some objective facts and leave the Jerusalem of ideology to the conclusion. For biblical historians, nothing is more objective than an inscription, and in Hezekiah's case this has long been available in the form of the inscription commemorating the completion of "the tunnel on the eastern side of the City of David which carries the water of the Gihon spring to a pool at its southern end"[20]—surely the same Gihon mentioned in connection with Hezekiah's hydraulic accomplishments in II Chron. 32:30. Although no royal name is mentioned in it, the paleography points to an eighth century date and makes the association of the feat with that mentioned in Chronicles (cf. also II Kgs. 20:20)[21] highly probable, if not universally accepted.[22] The geologist D. Gill has shown that the tunnel made extensive use of a preexisting natural fissure in the rock,[23] and in his new edition of the inscription, K. Lawson Younger, Jr. has identified this fissure with the ZDH, which remains its main crux.[24] Meantime, the original—which was cut out of the rock by vandals, recovered from a Jerusalem antiquities dealer by the Ottoman authorities, and removed to Istanbul in 1880—remains there to this day despite all efforts to negotiate for its return.[25]

Jerusalem in 701 B.C.E.

The biblical account describes Hezekiah's waterworks as part of his preparation for the impending Assyrian invasion. In effect, he is quoted as saying "why should the kings of Assyria come and find much water?" (II Chron. 32:4). So we now turn to the question: when in the reign of Hezekiah did the Assyrians invade Judah? For a long time the so-called two-campaign theory held sway, based on the apparently irreconcilable discrepancies between the biblical account of Sennacherib's invasion and the Assyrian king's own version of the event as preserved in three copies of his annals (one of which is now right here in Jerusalem)[26] as well as its imaginative recasting by Herodotus.[27] But it has become increasingly clear that the minimalist demand for extra-biblical verification of biblical historiography cannot be met in any mechanical way. Neither source is so objective as to be free of the biases imposed by its own ideological agendas. The miraculous deliverance of Jerusalem according to the book of Kings (and Isaiah) can be reconciled with the limited victory claimed by the Assyrians if these biases are taken into account.

Na'aman has shown how the genuine disaster suffered by Judah as a whole could have been subordinated to the overriding recollection of the sparing of Jerusalem in the memory of the Deuteronomistic historian of II Kings.[28] Tadmor in particular has analyzed the official Assyrian version of events to show, point by point, how each of its elements fits into the wider context of the official ideology.[29] Analogous differences appear between the cuneiform sources themselves when they happen to report on the same event from different vantage-points, as is best illustrated by the battle of Der twenty years earlier (722 B.C.E.).[30] Today, only one or two defendants of the two-campaign theory remain;[31] unless we accept the startling hypothesis proposed by B.

Becking, that Sennacherib as crown prince "holding a high military rank" campaigned against Jerusalem in 715 B.C.E. on behalf of his father Sargon II,[32] we can safely date the one campaign of Sennacherib against Judah, the third campaign of his reign, in his fourth year, i.e., 701 B.C.E.[33]

There can also be little doubt that the ultimate goal of Sennacherib's campaign was Jerusalem. But even the Assyrian war machine could not venture an assault against so great a redoubt without first neutralizing the approaches to it. Hence, the brunt of the Assyrian attack was borne by the fortress of Lachish, which in its day—like Latrun in 1948 C.E.—guarded the approaches to the capital[34] and indeed was a kind of second capital itself.[35] Perhaps because the fall of Lachish was a major success of Sennacherib's campaign, it received a disproportionate share of attention not only in his annals but also in the reliefs decorating the "Palace without a rival" which he reconstructed in Nineveh.[36] Between them they illustrate Assyrian siege techniques in an unmatched fashion and, as Tadmor indicates,[37] the reliefs in particular occupy a central position in Sennacherib's new palace. Borowski has used the reliefs, with their depiction of incense stands being carried off as booty, to suggest that Hezekiah's reforms did not go so far as to abolish all offerings to local shrines.[38]

An equally fascinating discovery was made long ago by R. D. Barnett, who identified the peculiar "uniforms" worn by the male deportees from Lachish with those of Sennacherib's troops appearing in other reliefs, and drew from there the conclusion that some contingents of exiles from Lachish were quickly incorporated into the Assyrian army and thus formed the first "Jewish regiment" in history.[39]

The fate of Lachish was shared by many other towns and garrisons in Judah, if not necessarily precisely the forty-six "fortified walled cities and surrounding small towns, which were without number"[40] that Sennacherib in his annals claims to have besieged.[41] Nor is the figure of 200,150 people exiled from them to Assyria exempt from the stereotyped exaggerations of the Assyrian chancery, as newly investigated by M. de Odorico, who described this figure as a " 'high-exact' number."[42] His study cites[43] an earlier one by S. Stohlmann, according to whom this "exile of 701" was every bit as shattering as the more famous exiles of 722 and 586.[44] If it did not have the same impact on its contemporaries, this may be because it did not serve as an object-lesson to the prophets of the time. Rather, it represents a significant convergence of biblical and Assyrian testimony.

Jerusalem itself was, of course, spared, and it was this event that burned itself into Judahite consciousness and later memory. Sennacherib could claim no more than that he had shut up Hezekiah in the city like a bird in his cage, and even this claim was little more than a metaphor borrowed from an inscription of Tiglath-pileser III, as Tadmor has shown.[45] The same scholar has made a strong case for suggesting that the Assyrian king did not even try to throw a true siege against the city;[46] the siege of Lachish and the other towns had drained his strength[47] and though he had the means to press a siege if he had chosen to, he was preoccupied with matters closer to home: his great building projects in Nineveh and his "Babylonian problem."[48] He contented himself with exacting heavy tribute, with the liberation of Padi[49] from imprisonment in Jerusalem, his restoration to the throne of Eqron,[50] and the transfer of part of western Judah to Philistine rule (Mic. 1:10–16).[51] The account in II Kgs. 19:35 and Isa. 37:36 attributes Sennacherib's retreat to the angel of the Lord who struck down 185,000 men—a figure uncannily close to the 200,150 exiles of Sennacherib's annals—while Herodotus weighs in with a garbled version of matters that recalls a plague of mice sending the Assyrian army packing. The figures for the size of Hezekiah's tribute in the biblical account (300 talents of silver and 30 talents of gold, not including the metals from the Temple doors) are also noticeably similar to those in the Assyrian annals (800 talents of silver and 30 talents of gold), as has often been remarked.[52]

The Aftermath of the Invasion

What is worth more than passing notice, being a relatively new addition to the roster of extra-biblical verifications, is the denouement of the invasion. According to the next two verses in II Kgs. 19:36–37 and Isa. 37:37–38, Sennacherib, at some point after his return to Nineveh and while sacrificing to his god Nisroch, was murdered by his sons Adramelech and Sharezer, who then fled to Ararat (Urartu), leaving the field to Esarhaddon. This notice has long been met with skepticism by biblical historians. While the assassination of the Assyrian monarch was well established in the cuneiform sources, the identity of the assassins and their subsequent fate apparently was not. In fact, however, it was! Hidden in a letter to Esarhaddon, that had been published already in 1911,[53] was a report on the intrigues surrounding the assassination. It took a 1980 study by S. Parpola to ferret out the true import of this letter and identify one of the assassins in it as Arad-Mullissu, son of the king.[54] From here it is only a relatively small step to the Adramelech of the Bible—even if we do not choose to follow Parpola's further proposal, that the king was crushed alive under one of the colossi guarding the entrance to the Temple where, according to a misinterpretation of the annals of his grandson Assurbanipal[55] or W. von Soden's reading of other Assyrian evidence on the event,[56] the murder took place. As to the flight to Urartu, given the constant warfare between Assyria and Urartu in the first millennium, it remains distinctly plausible that Urartu would have been eager to shelter a rebel against the king of Assyria. M. Garsiel adds to all this the interpretation put on the very name of Sennacherib, or what he calls its "Midrashic Name derivation" (MND), which links it to the Hebrew roots for "destroy" (ḤRB) and "shame" (ḤRP) in defiance of its plain Akkadian etymology (II Kgs. 19:16–17, 24 = Isa. 37:17–18, 25).[57]

On the Judahite side, too, the abortive invasion had an aftermath, at least in the narrative as arranged in II Kings and Isaiah. Hezekiah fell ill immediately after or, according to Na'aman,[58] immediately before the siege, and though the king recovered, he associated (or was required to associate)[59] his son Manasseh with him as coregent for most of the remaining fifteen years of his reign, according to one theory, waiting only until the latter was old enough—twelve according to E. Thiele—to take on the duties of the office. This solution solves a knotty problem of biblical chronology.[60]

The pericope on Hezekiah's illness has an almost folkloristic character, but at least three of its four discrete parts can be paralleled from extra-biblical sources. I have no comparative data for therapy by fig cake or fig paste[61]—ďvelet ťēnīm—of II Kgs. 20:7 (= Isa. 38:21) which many commentators regard as extraneous to the pericope.[62] Even here, however, I may call attention to the existence of an equivalent concoction called—in the plural—kamānāte ša titti in Akkadian[63] and gideśta in Sumerian, though in the latter case decorated with dates or date syrup rather than figs.[64] Isaiah's initial prediction "For thou shalt die, and not live" (38:1)[65] echoes "he (she) shall die, he (she) shall not live" of the Laws of Eshnunna,[66] of a medical text, and of the hemerologies of Mesopotamia, as seen by M. Stol.[67] The divine reversal of this prediction is accompanied by an assurance of divine protection for Jerusalem (38:6), at least for the time being.[68]

Unlike his father Ahaz, Hezekiah had appealed for *divine* help in the face of Jerusalem's siege,[69] and the response had come together with this first and most explicit biblical allusion to the (temporary) inviolability of the city as demonstrated by a divine sign (ôt). In the words of Isaiah, " 'I am going to make the shadow on the steps, which has descended on the dial (Heb. 'steps')[70] of Ahaz because of the sun, recede ten steps'. And the sun('s shadow) receded ten steps, the same steps it had descended" (38:8). Without going into the scientific problems raised by this sign, it is well to recall Y. Yadin's discussion of an Egyptian sundial or rather sun-staircase of the type alluded to here.[71] It is preserved in a model in the Cairo Museum and catches the shadow of the sun, not like a sundial where it is cast by a pole on a semicircular surface, but rather by two walls on two flights of steps. With the help of an improved reading of the biblical passage provided by the Isaiah Scroll from Qumran, as read by S. Iwry,[72] it is thus possible to preserve the "sun-staircase" of the tradition, even if the "sundial" has to go.[73]

But most important for me personally is the new light still being shed on the psalm of individual thanksgiving, which in the version in Isaiah is attributed to Hezekiah after his recovery. Such attributions are familiar, for instance, from the prayers of Hannah and Jonah, and in a recent study J. Watts tends to dismiss them as created or positioned *ad rem*, though rendering a useful service in treating it in the context of the entire genre of what he calls "insert hymns in Hebrew narrative."[74] The general question of the relationship of narrative and poetic versions of given biblical pericopes is a complicated one.[75] The case of Hezekiah's prayer is distinguished by the fact that it is described as a "writing" or even a "letter" (*mikhtav*). I have therefore long tried to connect it with the *mikhtam* genre in the Psalter on the one hand, and with the cuneiform literary genre which I have identified as the "letter-prayer" on the other.[76]

In particular, I called attention to the emergence of the *royal* letter-prayer as a means for appealing to the deity in matters affecting the health of the king or the welfare of his kingdom.[77] Admittedly, the genre flourished more than a thousand years before Isaiah, but it did not die out then. At least one of the prototypes dating to the nineteenth century B.C.E. survived in recognizable form into the seventh! This was already indicated in my edition of the original Sumerian text[78] and has more recently been confirmed in R. Borger's edition of the late bilingual Sumero-Akkadian version.[79] While this is not enough in and of itself to date the prayer of Hezekiah or to derive its generic inspiration from cuneiform models, it at least has served to remove a weighty chronological argument against the juxtaposition of the two genres. Moreover, a native Assyrian genre of letters to the god Assur had developed in the meantime for public proclamation after major triumphs such as the eighth campaign of Sargon. It is even possible that the third campaign of Sennacherib was so commemorated in the form of the so-called Azeka inscription as originally interpreted by Na'aman.[80]

If the biblical historians and prophets adopted the motifs and sometimes even the idioms of the Assyrian royal chancery, as has been argued, for example, by H. L. Ginsberg[81] and S. Paul,[82] they must have been equally capable of deliberately turning the tables on Sennacherib and treating his death as a punishment for his sins against God and Jerusalem.[83] It thus appears within the realm of possibility that they similarly adapted the genre of the royal letter-prayer for the story of Hezekiah and the rescue of Jerusalem.

With the death of Hezekiah in 698 (Tadmor) or 687 (Thiele), the name of Jerusalem again disappears entirely from the cuneiform records of Babylonia and Assyria, as is easily demonstrated thanks to the work of S. Parpola[84] and R. Zadok.[85] When the Babylonian Chronicle (5 rev. 12) reports on the first siege of Nebuchadnezzar II in 597 B.C.E., it says simply that the king "pitched his camp in front of the city of Judaea."[86]

Jerusalem in Ideology

A few speculative remarks may be ventured on the Jerusalem of ideology, a central theme of this conference. I have nothing to contribute to the question of its sanctity, except perhaps to recall the etymology—whether real or popular—most often offered for its name, i.e., City of Shalim, a deity with ample connections not only to Ugarit but to "the earliest Semitic pantheon" of Mesopotamia, as presented by J. J. M. Roberts.[87] This etymology is usually buttressed by appeal to the name of the city in the shortened form Shalem found in the Bible in connection with Melkizedek[88] or in parallelism with Zion.[89]

Perhaps a contextual light can be thrown on the concept of the city's centrality—the background, as it were—of its later reputation as the *omphalos*, the navel of the earth. The concept has had both defenders, beginning with W. Roscher[90] and A. J. Wensinck,[91] and critics, notably S. Talmon who prefers to regard the term *tābōr hā'āretz*[92] as a purely topographical feature.[93] We know little of the systematic geographical insights of the biblical writers beyond such texts as the Table of Nations in Gen. 10, whereas we are quite well informed about the geographic and even the cartographic attainments of the Mesopotamians, which were considerable.[94] An insightful study by P. Michalowski has taught us to pay attention in the Mesopotamian case to what he calls "mental maps and ideology."[95] He was particularly concerned with the ideological role of the early Mesopotamian designations of foreign and distant lands such as Aratta in the east, Dilmun in the south, and especially Subartu in the north. But his insights can equally well be applied to the case of a native city at the very heart of a culture and its beliefs,[96] and they can be paralleled by the later case of the famous Babylonian *mappa mundi*, last edited by W. Horowitz and discussed by M. Stol, where Babylon occupies a central position in the top of the circle representing the known world.[97]

Thus, we are led to a related point: the city's inviolability. I have already alluded to this ideological component of the biblical narratives.[98] It is expressed once implicitly, by the juxtaposition of Sennacherib's siege and his assassination as if to say *post hoc ergo propter hoc*, and once explicitly, when the prophet conveys the divine promise of protection for the city. In the older view of, for instance, J. Hayes, "the tradition of Zion's inviolability" and invulnerability goes back to pre-Hezekian and even to pre-Davidic and pre-Israelite times,"[99] while in the classic treatment by B. Childs, this "Zion tradition" starts and ends with "Isaiah and the Assyrian crisis."[100] What, then, is the comparative evidence? Clearly, only one city in the Mesopotamian experience is a candidate for a comparable status: Babylon. Its inviolability is implied by the respect it was accorded by the Assyrians, the long-time rivals of the Babylonians, yet also their debtors in matters religious and cultural. Only two Assyrian kings ventured to destroy the city, and both paid a heavy price. The first was Tukulti-Ninurta I in the thirteenth century B.C.E., who ended his days in a fiery death besieged in his own capital that he had newly built and named after himself. The second was Sennacherib—and if the biblical historian and prophet had no trouble in seeing his assassination as retribution for the abortive siege of Jerusalem, neither did the court scribes of Nabonidus in treating it as fit retribution for his consummated destruction of Babylon, as noted by J. J. M. Roberts[101] and, once more, by H. Tadmor.[102] B. Porter, in her study of Esar-haddon's Babylonian policy, has shown how Sennacherib's son and successor marshalled all the physical and spiritual resources of the empire to reverse the effects of his father's depredations.[103] P.-A. Beaulieu goes even further. According to him, both the founder of the Chaldaean dynasty, Nabopolassar, and its last king, Nabonidus, believed that Marduk himself had caused the assassination of Sennacherib, the destruction of Assyria, and the restoration of Babylon and its cult.[104] The analogy goes a long way toward explaining the tremendous role played by the siege of Jerusalem in the consciousness of biblical prophets and historians, and the gap between their view of the event and that of the Assyrians.[105]

Methodological Conclusions

What, then, is the general methodological lesson we can learn from the case of Jerusalem under Hezekiah? The simple test of the minimalists, that the biblical version of events must have extra-biblical, preferably contemporaneous, verification before it can be regarded as historical, is an impossible demand even in the best of circumstances as here, where the events loom so large in Assyrian royal inscriptions and art, but are presented in such a widely divergent manner. However, the maximalist willingness to accept the biblical version until falsified by extra-biblical sources, preferably contemporaneous and bearing on the same matters,[106] also lacks a rational basis, given the randomness of these sources and their accidental discovery. Because Mesopotamian references to Jerusalem by name were confined to the single reign of Sennacherib and his contemporary Hezekiah, we cannot treat the absence of conflicting sources about Jerusalem in other periods as confirmation of every biblical statement about the city. The task of the biblical historian thus remains as before: to weigh the comparative evidence point by point in order to discover, if possible, the nature of its convergence with the biblical data and the reasons for its divergence.[107]

Notes

1. W. Dever as reported by H. Shanks, "Should the term 'Biblical Archaeology' be abandoned?," *BAR* 7/3 (1981), 54–57.

2. K. W. Whitelam at the joint meetings of the Society of Biblical Literature and the American Schools of Oriental Research, Philadelphia, November 1995. See now idem, *The Invention of Ancient Israel: the Silencing of Palestinian History* (London and New York, 1996). Cf. also H. Shanks, " 'Annual Miracle' Visits Philadelphia," *BAR* 22/2 (1996), 52–56, 69.

3. E. Thiele, *A Chronology of the Hebrew Kings* (Grand Rapids, 1977), 46–51; idem, *The Mysterious Numbers of the Hebrew Kings*[2] (Grand Rapids, 1983), 129–34.

4. M. Liverani, "Kitru, kataru," *Mesopotamia* 17 (1982), 43–66; N. Na'aman, "Hezekiah and the Kings of Assyria," *Tel Aviv* 21 (1994): 239 and note 5; M. Cogan and H. Tadmor, *II Kings*, AB 11 (Garden City, NY, 1988), 184–94; S. B. Parker, "Appeals for Military Intervention: Stories from Zinjirli and the Bible," *BA* 59 (1996), 213–24.

5. For the possible parallel to the virtually simultaneous appeal by Nabonassar of Babylon for Tiglath-pileser's help against the Aramaeans and Chaldaeans, see most recently W. Hallo, "The Nabonassar Era and other epochs in Mesopotamian Chronology and Chronography," *A Scientific Humanist: Studies in Memory of Abraham Sachs*, eds. E. Leichty et al., Occasional Publications of the Samuel Noah Kramer Fund 9 (Philadelphia, 1988), 189f

6. B. Becking, *The Fall of Samaria: an Historical and Archaeological Study*, Studies in the History of the Ancient Near East 2 (Leiden, 1992)—based on his thesis, *De Ondergang van Samaria* (Meppel, 1985).

7. H. Winckler, *Alttestamentliche Untersuchungen* (Leipzig, 1892), 15–20, H. Tadmor, "The Campaigns of Sargon II," *Journal of Cuneiform Studies* 12 (1958), 34–39, and especially Becking (above, note 6), 34–45.

8. Becking (ibid., 54–55) wants to associate this claim with the alleged campaign of 715.

9. Na'aman (above, note 4), 235.

10. Let alone in 715: Becking (above, note 6), 54 and note 30.

11. Na'aman (above, note 4), 239f., 243, 247f.; G. L. Mattingly, "An Archaeological Analysis of Sargon's Campaign against Ashdod," *Near Eastern Archaeological Society Bulletin* 17 (1981), 47–64. Cf. the situation of the northern kingdom in the time of Tiglath-pileser III, when Israel "became a much smaller state surrounded by three Assyrian provinces on its former territory"; Becking (above, note 6), 1.

12. Na'aman (above, note 4).

13. J. A. Brinkman, "Merodachbaladan," *Studies Presented to A. Leo Oppenheim*, eds. R. D. Biggs and J. A. Brinkman (Chicago, 1964), 31–33. Cf. Na'aman (above, note 4), 244, with prior literature. Differently H. Tadmor and M. Cogan, "Hezekiah's Fourteenth Year: the King's Illness and the Babylonian Embassy," *EI*, XVI (Jerusalem, 1982), 198–201 (Hebrew; Eng. summary, 258–59).

14. E.g., Cogan and Tadmor (above, note 4), 15 and 228, based on II Kgs. 18:1 and 9f. Becking ([above, note 6], 53) even argues for a coregency with Ahaz in the preceding year.

15. Thiele, *Chronology* (above, note 3), 52–54, idem, *Mysterious Numbers* (above, note 3), 174–76, followed among many others by Na'aman (above, note 4), 236–38. See now especially A. F. Rainey, "review of J. A. Soggin, *An Introduction to the History of Israel and Judah,*" *JAOS* 116 (1996), 546–48. I also follow Thiele; see already W. W. Hallo, "From Qarqar to Carchemish: Assyria and Israel in the Light of New Discoveries," *BA* 23 (1960), 35, 55; idem and W. K. Simpson, *The Ancient Near East: a History* (New York, 1971), 140 (2nd ed., Fort Worth, TX, 1998), 136. Note especially the extension of the Passover to the north in Hezekiah's first year (II Chron. 30), for which see H. Haag, "Das Mazzenfest des Hiskia," *Wort und Geschichte: Festschrift für K. Elliger,* eds. H. Gese and H. P. Rüger, AOAT 18 (Kevelär, 1973), 87–94.

16. N. Na'aman, "Ahaz's and Hezekiah's Policy toward Assyria in the days of Sargon and Sennacherib's Early Years," *Zion* 59 (1994), 5–30 (Hebrew; English summary, p. v); idem (above, note 4).

17. O. Borowski, "Hezekiah's Reforms and the Revolt against Assyria," *BA* 58 (1995), 148–55.

18. H. Tadmor, "Sennacherib's Campaign to Judah: Historical and Historiographic Considerations," *Zion* 50 (1985), 65–80 (Hebrew; English summary, p. x).

19. Ibid., 66.

20. Borowski (above, note 17), 153.

21. On this verse see most recently Cogan and Tadmor (above, note 4), 221f., 260, with previous literature.

22. A contrary conclusion has now been arrived at by J. Rogerson and P. R. Davies, "Was the Siloam tunnel built by Hezekiah?" *BA* 59 (1996), 138–49. But see now R. S. Hendel, "The Date of the Siloam Inscription: a Rejoinder to Rogerson and Davies," *BA* 59 (1996), 233–37; J. M. Cahill, "A Rejoinder to 'Was the Siloam Tunnel Built by Hezekiah?',", *BA* 60 (1997), 184–85; J. A. Hacket et al., "Defusing Pseudo-scholarship: the Siloam Inscription Ain't Hasmonaean," *BAR* 23/2 (March/April 1997), 41–50, 68.

23. D. Gill, "How They Met—Geology Solves Longstanding Mystery of Hezekiah's Tunnelers," *BAR* 20/4 (1994), 20–33, 64; cf. J. N. Wilford, "Biblical Puzzle Solved: Jerusalem Tunnel is a Product of Nature," *New York Times* (August 9, 1994), C 1, 8.

24. K. Lawson Younger, Jr., "The Siloam Tunnel Inscription," *Ugarit-Forschungen* 26 (1994), 543–56.

25. H. Shanks, "Returning Cultural Artifacts—Turkey is all take, no give," *BAR* 17/3 (1991), 12; idem, "Please return the Siloam Inscription to Jerusalem," ibid., 58–60.

26. P. Ling-Israel, "The Sennacherib Prism in the Israel Museum—Jerusalem," *Bar-Ilan Studies in Assyriology Dedicated to Pinhas Artzi,* eds. J. Klein and A. Skaist (Ramat Gan, 1990), 213–48 and Pls. i–xvi.

27. For a representative statement, see E. Nicholson, "The Centralisation of the Cult in Deuteronomy," *VT* 13 (1963), 380–89. It is no longer found in idem, *Deuteronomy and Tradition* (Philadelphia, 1967).

28. Na'aman (above, note 4), 247–50.

29. Tadmor (above, note 18).

30. Hallo (above, note 15), 53, 59.

31. Notably W. H. Shea, "One Invasion or two?" *Ministry* (March, 1980), 26–28; idem, "Sennacherib's Second Palestinian Campaign," *JBL* 104 (1985), 401–18; cf. on this Hallo and Simpson (above, note 15), 142 (2nd ed., 138); W. Hallo, "The Expansion of Cuneiform Literature," *PAAJR* 46–47 (1980), 316f. and note 43; S. Stohlmann, "The Judean Exile after

701 B.C.E.," *Scripture in Context II: More Essays on the Comparative Method*, eds. W. W. Hallo, J. C. Moyer and L. G. Perdue (Winona Lake, 1983), 158f., note 37. For others, see P. Dion, "Sennacherib's Expedition to Palestine," *Eglise et Théologie* 20 (1989), 5–25.

32. Becking (above, note 6), 54f. and note 35.

33. See in detail Cogan and Tadmor (above, note 4), 245–51.

34. D. Ussishkin, "Lachish," *Anchor Bible Dictionary*, IV (New York, 1992), 121–23.

35. B. Mazar *apud* Tadmor (above, note 18), 77, note 32.

36. D. Ussishkin, *The Conquest of Lachish by Sennacherib* (Tel-Aviv, 1982); idem (above, note 34), 123f.; Cf. J. M. Russell, *Sennacherib's Palace without Rival at Nineveh* (Chicago, 1991).

37. Tadmor (above, note 18), 76–77.

38. Borowski (above, note 17).

39. R. D. Barnett ("The Siege of Lachish," *IEJ* 8 [1958], 161–64) cited Hallo (above, note 15), 59; cf. ibid., 39, Fig. 2; and 45, Fig. 3. For a more nuanced assessment, see Stohlmann (above, note 31), 162–64.

40. Cogan and Tadmor (above, note 4), 246.

41. 46 URU.MEŠ-*šú dan-nu-ti* É.BÀD.MEŠ *ù* URU.MEŠ TUR.MEŠ *ša li-me-ti-šú-nu* (Chicago Prism iii, 19f.).

42. M. de Odorico, *The Use of Numbers and Quantifications in the Assyrian Royal Inscriptions*, State Archives of Assyria Supplements 3 (Helsinki, 1995), 114. On p. 171 he lists it among the " 'very high-exact' numbers" or the "round numbers exacted." For an earlier assessment of the figures, see H. Sauren, "Sennacherib, les arabes, les déportés juifs," *Die Welt des Orients* 16 (1985), 80–99. For a reading of the comparable figures in the census totals of Num. 1 and 26, see W. Hallo, *The Book of the People*, Brown Judaic Studies 225 (Atlanta, 1991), 82f.

43. De Odorico (above, note 42), 114, note 305. Cf. also A. R. Millard, "Large Numbers in the Assyrian Royal Inscriptions," *Ah, Assyria: Studies in Assyrian History and Ancient Near Eastern Historiography Presented to Hayim Tadmor*, eds. M. Cogan and I. Eph'al, SH 33 (Jerusalem, 1991), 213–22; D. M. Fouts, "Another Look at Large Numbers in Assyrian Royal Inscriptions," *JNES* 53 (1994), 205–11.

44. Stohlmann (above, note 31), esp. pp. 174–75.

45. Tadmor (above, note 18), 75; cf. now idem, *The Inscriptions of Tiglath-pileser III King of Assyria* (Jerusalem, 1994), 78f.

46. Tadmor (above, note 18), 75.

47. Ibid., 78.

48. Ibid., 69–70, 77.

49. The recent discovery of a sixth-century inscription mentioning the building of a temple in Eqron by Padi not only clinches the identification of Tell Miqne with the ancient Philistine city, but also confirms that Padi was a dynastic name there.

50. The event could hardly have taken place any sooner. Its placement in the Assyrian annals illustrates their tendency to rearrange chronology to suit structural requirements of the inscription; see Tadmor (above, note 18), 74.

51. See New Jewish Publication Society version (NJV) ad loc.; for the broader significance, see W. Hallo, "Scurrilous Etymologies," *Pomegranates and Golden Bells: Studies in Honor of Jacob Milgrom*, eds. D. P. Wright et al. (Winona Lake, 1995), 771. Cf. also A. Demsky, "The Houses of Achzib: a Critical Note on Mica 1:14b," *IEJ* 16 (1966), 211–15.

52. E.g., Cogan and Tadmor (above, note 4), 229 *ad* II Kgs. 18:14 (not in Isaiah).

53. R. F. Harper, *Assyrian and Babylonian Letters*, XI (Chicago, 1911), no. 1091.

54. S. Parpola, "The Murderer of Sennacherib," *Death in Mesopotamia* (Copenhagen, 1980), 171–82. Cf. also S. Zawadzki, "Oriental and Greek Tradition about the Death of Sennacherib," *State Archives of Assyria Bulletin* 4 (1990), 69–72.

55. Cogan and Tadmor (above, note 4), 240; W. Hallo, "The Death of Kings: Traditional Historiography in Contextual Perspective," *Ah, Assyria . . .* (above, note 43), 162f.

56. W. von Soden, "Gibt es Hinweise auf die Ermordung Sanheribs im Ninurta-Tempel (wohl) in Kalah in Texten aus Assyrien?," *N.A.B.U.* (1990), 16–17, no. 22; cf. Hallo (above, note 51), 774 and note 58.

57. M. Garsiel, *Midrashic Name Derivation in the Bible* (Ramat Gan, 1987), 32–33 (Hebrew); idem, *Biblical Names: a Literary Study of Midrashic Derivations and Puns* (Ramat Gan, 1991), 46–48; Hallo (above, note 51), 773, note 47.

58. Na'aman (above, note 4), 236–38, 244.

59. As suggested by Na'aman (ibid, 239 and note 3).

60. Thiele, *Chronology* (above, note 3), 27–28, 66; idem, *Mysterious Numbers* (above, note 3), 64, 173–78.

61. So J. Watts, *Psalm and Story: Insert Hymns in Hebrew Narrative*, JSOT Supplement Series 139 (Sheffield, 1992), 119.

62. Cogan and Tadmor (above, note 4), 255–57.

63. C. H. W. Johns, *Assyrian Deeds and Documents* (Cambridge, 1898), no. 1095:8, cited by von Soden, *Akkadisches Handwörterbuch* ((Wiesbaden, 1966–), 430a, s.v. *kamānu*, and edited by J. N. Postgate, *Taxation and Conscription in the Assyrian Empire*, Studia Pohl Series Maior 3 (Rome, 1974), 336 (cf. ibid., 70–71, 84–85, 221–22); F. M. Fales and J. N. Postgate, *Imperial Administrative Records, Part II*, State Archives of Assyria 11 (Helsinki, 1995), n. 28. On *kamānu* and its possible Hebrew cognate *kawwan*, "sacrificial cake in the shape of a vagina," in Jer. 44: 19, and even possibly the *kiyyun* (sacrificial cake?) of the enigmatic passage Amos 5:26, see W. Hallo, "New Moons and Sabbaths: a Case Study in the Contrastive Approach," *HUCA* 48 (1977), 15. On Amos 5:26, see also idem, "Cult Statue and Divine Image: a Preliminary Study," *Scripture in Context II* (above, note 31), 15, note 114; S. Paul, "Hosea 8:8–10 and Ancient Near Eastern Royal Epithets," *Studies in Bible*, ed. S. Japhet, SH 31 (Jerusalem, 1986), 196 and elsewhere.

64. W. Hallo, "Lugalbanda Excavated," *JAOS* 103 (1983), 174–75, l. 291; translation based on the variant, which B. Alster ("Ur 3 Texts in Danish Private Collections," *Oriens Antiquus* 26 [1987], 6 and n. 4) prefers to restore as *làl-zú-lum-ma* and translates "date syrup."

65. *Kî mēt attā welō* transl. follows old Jewish Publication Society version (= Authorized Version). NJV has "For you are going to die; you will not get well."

66. *Imât ul iballuṭ* in paragraphs 12, 13, and 28. Latest translation by M. Roth, *Law Collections from Mesopotamia and Asia Minor*, Writings from the Ancient World 6 (Atlanta, 1995), 60–61, 63.

67. M. Stol, "Diagnosis and Therapy in Babylonian Medicine," *Jaarbericht . . . van het Vooraziatisch-Egyptisch Genootschap "Ex Oriente Lux"* 32 (1993), 53 and notes 61–62.

68. Watts (above, note 61), 121–22 and p. 122, note 1.

69. Cf. esp. II Kgs. 19:15–19 = Isa. 37:15–20. For other contrasts with the siege under Ahaz, see C. R. Seitz, "Account A and the Annals of Sennacherib: a Reassessment," *JSOT* 58 (1993), 54–56.

70. *ma'alot.*

71. Y. Yadin, "The Dial of Ahaz," *EI*, V (Jerusalem, 1958), 91–96 and Pl. 10 (Hebrew; Eng. Summary, 88*f.).

72. S. Iwry, "The Qumran Isaiah and the End of the Dial of Ahaz," *BASOR* 147 (1957), 27–33.

73. Ibid.; W. Hallo, *Origins: the Ancient Near Eastern Background of Some Modern Western Institutions*, Studies in the History of the Ancient Near East 6 (Leiden, 1996), 123.

74. Watts (above, note 61), 118–31; cf. H. P. Mathys (*Dichter und Beter: Theologen aus*

spätalttestamentlicher Zeit [Freiburg, 1994]; ref. courtesy R. R. Wilson) who, however, does not include Hezekiah's psalm in his survey, presumably regarding it as earlier than his other examples.

75. See previous note and cf. K. Lawson Younger, Jr., "Heads! Tails! or the Whole Coin?! Contextual Method and Intertextual Analysis: Judges 4 and 5," *The Biblical Canon in Comparative Perspective: Scripture in Context IV*, Ancient Near Eastern Texts and Studies 11 (Lewiston, NY, 1991), 109–46.

76. W. Hallo, "Individual Prayer in Sumerian: the Continuity of a Tradition, *JAOS* 88 (1968), 71–89.

77. Idem, "The Royal Correspondence of Larsa: I. A Sumerian Prototype for the Prayer of Hezekiah?" *Kramer Anniversary Volume: Cuneiform Studies in Honor of Samuel Noah Kramer*, ed. B. L. Eichler, Alter Orient und Altes Testament 25 (Neukirchen-Vluyn, 1976) 209–24.

78. Idem, "The Royal Correspondence of Larsa: II. The Appeal to Utu," *ZIKIR ŠUMIM: Assyriological Studies Presented to F.R. Kraus*, eds. G. van Driel et al. (Leiden, 1982), 95–109; previously idem, "Letters, Prayers and Letter-Prayers," *Proceedings of the Seventh World Congress of Jewish Studies: Studies in the Bible and the Ancient Near East* (Jerusalem, 1981).

79. R. Borger, *Ein Brief Sin-idinnams von Larsa an den Sonnengott*, Nachrichten der Akademie der Wissenschaften in Göttingen, I. Phil.-hist. Klasse 2 (Göttingen, 1991). The intervening stage of the composition has meantime been identified at Emar; see M. Civil, "Sin-iddinam in Emar and SU.A=Simeški," *N.A.B.U.* 1996, 36-37.

80. N. Na'aman, "Sennacherib's 'Letter to God' on his Campaign to Judah," *BASOR* 214 (1974), 25–39; idem (above, note 4), 245–47. Becking ([above, note 6], 3, note 8, and 54, note 50) dates the text(s) to 715 B.C.E.!

81. H.L. Ginsberg, "Reflexes of Sargon in Isaiah after 715 B.C.E.," *JAOS* 88 (1968), 47–53.

82. S. Paul, "Deutero-Isaiah and Cuneiform Royal Inscriptions," *JAOS* 88 (1968), 180–86; idem, "Sargon's Administrative Diction in II Kings 17:27," *JBL* 88 (1969), 73–74; idem (above, note 63).

83. Tadmor (above, note 18), 78.

84. S. Parpola, *Neo-Assyrian Toponyms*, Alter Orient und Altes Testament 6 (Neukirchen-Vluyn, 1970).

85. R. Zadok, *Geographical Names according to New- and Late-Babylonian Texts*, Repertoire Géographique des Textes Cunéiformes 8 (Wiesbaden, 1985).

86. URU *Ia-a-hu-du*. A. K. Grayson, *Assyrian and Babylonian Chronicles*, Texts from Cuneiform Sources 5 (Glückstadt, 1975), 102; cf. W. Hallo, "Nebukadnezar Comes to Jerusalem," *Through the Sound of Many Voices: Writings (for) W. Gunther Plaut*, ed. J. V. Plaut (Toronto, 1982) 40–57.

87. J. J. M. Roberts, *The Earliest Semitic Pantheon*, The Johns Hopkins Near Eastern Studies 2 (Baltimore and London, 1972), 65 and 113, notes 414–18.

88. Gen. 14:18.

89. Ps. 76:3.

90. W. H. Roscher, *Omphalos* (Leipzig, 1913); idem, *Neue Omphalosstudien* (Leipzig, 1915); idem, *Der Omphalosgedanke* (Leipzig, 1918).

91. A. J. Wensinck, *The Idea of the Western Semites Concerning the Navel of the Earth*, Verhandelingen der koninklijke Akademie der Wetenschappen, Afd. Letterkunde, nieuwe reeks 17/1 (Amsterdam, 1916).

92. Judg. 9:36–37; Ezek. 38:11–12.

93. S. Talmon, "The 'Navel of the Earth' and the Comparative Method," *Scripture in History and Theology: Essays in Honor of J. Coert Rylaarsdam*, eds. A. L. Merrill and T. W.

Overholt Pittsburgh Theological Monograph Series 17 (Pittsburgh, 1977) 243–68; reprinted in idem, *Literary Studies in the Hebrew Bible: Form and Content* (Jerusalem and Leiden, 1993), 50–75.

94. W. Hallo, "The Road to Emar," *Journal of Cuneiform Studies* 18 (1964), 57–88; idem (above, note 73), 78–97.

95. P. Michalowski, "Mental Maps and Ideology: Reflections on Subartu," *The Origins of Cities in Dry-Farming Syria and Mesopotamia in the Third Millennium B.C.*, ed. H. Weiss (Guilford, CT, ;1986), 129–56.

96. I may illustrate this with the case of the spring Gihon which played such a major role in supplying the city with water, and hence in allowing a city to rise on this otherwise forbidding site in the first place. That spring has a name reminiscent of the second of the four rivers of paradise according to Gen. 4:13. The first is Pishon and the other two are the familiar Tigris and Euphrates. Did the first two names simply mean something like Gusher and Bubbler respectively (Speiser) and therefore represent familiar, almost general hydronyms? Or did the biblical author deliberately insert the name of Jerusalem's spring into his version of the Eden tradition in order to suggest that Jerusalem partook of a touch of Paradise? We can see a hint of a tradition of what could be interpreted as four rivers around a central area among the designs incised on the reverse of very early schooltexts from Fara (Shuruppak) and Abu Salabikh in Mesopotamia and Ebla in Syria (Hallo [above, note 73], 81f.). My thanks to Larry Stager for a helpful discussion on these points.

97. W. Horowitz, "The Babylonian *mappa mundi*," *Iraq* 50 (1988), 147–66; M. Stol, "De babylonische wereldkaart," *Phoenix* 34/2 (1988–89), 29–35.

98. Above, notes 68–69.

99. J. H. Hayes, "The Tradition of Zion's Involability," *JBL* 82 (1963), 419–26.

100. B. S. Childs, *Isaiah and the Assyrian Crisis* (Naperville, IL, 1967).

101. J. J. M. Roberts, "Myth versus History," *CBQ* 38 (1976), 10.

102. Tadmor (above, note 18), 79 and note 40.

103. B. N. Porter, *Images, Power, and Politics: Figurative Aspects of Esarhaddon's Babylonian Policy* (Philadelphia, 1993).

104. P.-A. Beaulieu, *The Reign of Nabonidus King of Babylon 556–539 B.C.*, Yale Near Eastern Researches 10 (New Haven and London, 1989), 105–106, 115.

105. See already the classic statement by Childs (above, note 100). Cf. now M. Weinfeld ("Jerusalem—a Political and Spiritual Capital" [in press]), who dates the earliest messianic expectations to Hezekiah's reign.

106. Stated with unusual candor by Becking ([above, note 6], 52): "the dates in the Book of Kings can only be considered as untrustworthy when they can be falsified by contemporaneous evidence."

107. A similar point is made, if briefly, by Seitz (above, note 69).

· II ·

JERUSALEM
IN THE
SECOND TEMPLE
PERIOD

4

Second Temple Jerusalem:
A Jewish City in the Greco-Roman Orbit

LEE I. LEVINE

Introduction

By the end of the Second Temple period, in 70 C.E., Jerusalem had been under Jewish hegemony for almost one thousand years. The city had come to be regarded, by Jew and non-Jew alike, as a quintessentially Jewish city. Jerusalem's population was overwhelmingly Jewish, as were its leadership, calendar, and public institutions, first and foremost of which was the Temple.

In the course of the First and Second Temple periods, Jerusalem had evolved into the central sacred site of the Jewish people. This status was not achieved overnight, but was the result of an ongoing process spanning many centuries. Beginning with David's decision to conquer the city and transform it into his political and religious capital, it reached a peak in the First Temple period with Josiah's decision to centralize Jewish sacrificial cult in the city. Whereas beforehand it had been permissible to offer sacrifices to the God of Israel anywhere in the country, now only those sacrifices brought to the Jerusalem Temple were recognized as legitimate and sanctioned.

However, the centrality of the city became even more pronounced in the ensuing Second Temple period. Cyrus' recognition of Jerusalem by virtue of its holy Temple was to be repeated later on by Hellenistic and Roman conquerors, and Antiochus III's edict on behalf of Jerusalem upon its capture ca. 200 B.C.E. is clear testimony of this status (*Ant.* 12, 138–44). Moreover, the transformation of the city into the capital of a substantial political kingdom, first in the days of the Hasmoneans and later under Herod, further imbued Jerusalem with a status and importance heretofore unmatched.

Parallel to this enhanced political status, Jerusalem also enjoyed a heightened religious standing. Isaiah had already envisioned the city as a spiritual focus for all nations (2:1–4), and in the aftermath of the destruction Ezekiel describes the city as the center of the world and its name as "the Lord is there" (5:5, 48:35), while II Chronicles refers to the Lord as "the God of Jerusalem" (32:19). As has been noted in previous articles in this volume, the author of Chronicles emphasizes God's choice of Jerusalem by relating that a fire descended from heaven onto the altar David built there (I Chron. 21:26; cf. II Sam. 24:25) and by explicitly identifying Moriah of the *'Aqedah* story with the Temple Mount (II Chron. 3:1). Deutero-Isaiah (48:2, 52:1) and Nehemiah (11:1) extend the realm of holiness beyond the Temple (Isa. 27:13; Jer. 31:22) to embrace all of Jerusalem, while Zechariah takes this one step further and includes all of Judaea as well (2:14–17). Centuries later, these ideas were elaborated in the *Letter of Aristeas* (83), *Jubilees* (8:17–19), as well as by Josephus (*War* 3, 52) and Philo (*Embassy* 37, 281). During the Second Temple period, the twin concepts of an eschatological and heavenly Jerusalem made their appearance (*Enoch* 85–90) and became even more prominent in the generation following the destruction of the Second Temple (*IV Ezra; II Baruch;* cf. also Rev. 21–22; Heb. 12).

The Jewish Dimension of Jerusalem in the Hellenistic-Hasmonean Period

The Second Temple period witnessed a series of efforts aimed at defining Jerusalem as the quintessential Jewish city by emphasizing its uniqueness and particularity. Ezra and Nehemiah's attempts to separate the city and its population from the surrounding regions and peoples was a religious policy which reflected Judaea's geographical and political isolation; this policy would be advocated by other authors and sects down to the end of the Second Temple era. We have the testimonies of a number of Greek writers from the early Hellenistic period indicating the relative success of this policy. Hecataeus of Abdera, for instance, describes the uniqueness of Jerusalem, its Temple, and people, as well as the success of Jewish society in preserving its ancestral traditions. Ben Sira advocates a similar posture, and the agenda of the second-century Hasidim seems to have had an intensive Jewish focus.[1]

Moreover, during these three centuries, between Ezra and Nehemiah on the one hand and the Hasmoneans on the other, a number of practices and literary works evolved which clearly expressed a particularistic social and religious thrust. This proclivity was expressed early on in a variety of ways, from banning foreign merchants on the Sabbath, emphasizing the use of Hebrew, to driving out foreign wives.[2] The division of the Jewish population into priestly *mishmarot* and lay *ma'amadot*, each with semi-annual obligations in the Temple, also seems to have evolved at this time, as did a series of halakhic requirements, such as spending the "second tithe" in the city four times every seven years.[3] The emergence of apocalyptic literature in the third and second centuries is a further expression of Jewish particularism, as was the newly-established centrality of the Torah in Jewish religious life, a centrality which found expression in Sabbath and festival communal-reading frameworks that crystallized during this period.[4]

This introversive focus on the Jewish body polity was given a dramatic boost in the mid-second century B.C.E., with the ascendance of the Hasmoneans and the establishment of a sovereign state boasting ambitious territorial designs. Among the most prominent changes effected, the following may be noted:

1. The Hasmoneans radically altered the geographical concept of Eretz-Israel to include almost all of the territory west of the Jordan River and large tracts to its east; for the 400-or-so years beforehand, Jewish Judaea included only the region around Jerusalem, which was more or less contiguous with the Persian administrative region, Yehud.

2. Concomitant with the successful conquests, there crystallized an ideology that the Jews under Hasmonean hegemony were, in fact, reclaiming their ancestral homeland and, in fact, were obliged to eliminate all pagan worship. This led to the destruction of pagan shrines and, at times, to the death or exile of native populations (e.g., I Macc. 13:43–53). Ironically, it was precisely at this time that the institution of conversion first made its appearance in a Jewish context, as the Hasmoneans forced conversion upon the Idumeans in the south and the Itureans in the north (*Ant.* 13, 257–58, 318).

3. The Hasmonean era witnessed an enhanced prominence of the Temple in Jewish life. The Hasmoneans rose to power as defenders of the Temple and its purity from foreign cults, and this achievement played a central role in their court propaganda, as indicated by II Maccabees and the letters prefacing that book. Brief references in I Maccabees and Josephus indicate that each and every Hasmonean ruler devoted energy and funds to improving and strengthening the Temple and its surroundings.

4. Together with the above campaigns to ban idolatry and reemphasize the Temple's prominence came a greater emphasis on matters of ritual purity within Jewish society. This new focus found expression in many of the halakhic decisions ascribed in our sources to the early Pharisees and the Qumran community. In the material culture, this emphasis is evident in the appearance of ritual baths (*miqva'ot*), and this tendency is further

underscored by the almost exclusive use of local (as against imported) ware and by the more frequent recourse to using the ashes of a red heifer, intended for purification from corpse impurity. This rare sacrifice was reportedly offered seven times (five, according to another tradition) from the Hasmonean period onward, i.e., in the last two hundred years of the Second Temple period. Only two cases are noted for the previous millennium (M Parah 3:5).

5. Jewish art underwent a radical change at this time, and was now characterized by the studious avoidance of any figural representation, either human or animal. Up to this point, such depictions were not uncommon in Jewish circles, from the cherubs over the holy ark and the lions of Solomon's throne, to the figurines found in Israelite settlements and the human and animal images on Yehud coins from Persian and Hellenistic Jerusalem. The magnificent Tobiad palace in 'Iraq el-Emir (between Jericho and Amman), dating from the early second century B.C.E., is adorned with majestic figures of eagles and lions carved in stone. However, commencing under the Hasmoneans and continuing for some three centuries, human and animal representations were not to be found in Judaea. Exceptions to this rule exist, but they are few and far between.[5]

6. Finally, the emergence of Jewish sects—e.g., Pharisees, Sadducees, and Essenes (including the Qumran community as well), each with its own particular religious agenda—is a further indication of a more concerted Jewish emphasis at this time, at least within certain circles.

The Hellenistic Dimension of Hasmonean Jerusalem

Understanding the Jewish component of Second Temple Jerusalem is necessary for an understanding of the city and and its workings—necessary but not sufficient in and of itself. Another force at work in the wake of, and even before, Alexander's conquests of the East was Hellenistic culture, and this dimension was to shape the city profoundly. The social and cultural message of the Hellenistic world was radically different from the Jerusalem of Ezra and Nehemiah. Alexander had married a Persian princess and compelled his officers and soldiers to wed Persian women. The message here was loud and clear: isolation, insulation, and estrangement were to be rejected; a meeting of cultures—symbiosis, synthesis, and even syncretism—were the order of the day. This, of course, is a far cry from the mass-divorce from non-Jewish spouses by members of the Jerusalem aristocracy that was advocated by Ezra and Nehemiah.

Moreover, what had been of marginal significance before Alexander became much more central after his conquest. The impact of Hellenism on the Near East in general, and on Judaea and Jerusalem in particular, was considerable. From the very beginning of this era, there are indications of Jerusalem's participation in the life of the wider Hellenistic world, such as its diplomatic relations with Sparta, which developed in the third and second centuries B.C.E. or its use of imported Rhodian wine, as attested by the discovery of hundreds of stamped amphora handles dating from the mid-third to the late second centuries B.C.E. Several books written or edited in the third century B.C.E., e.g., Ecclesiastes (*Qohelet*) and the Song of Songs, appear to reflect either Hellenistic genres (in the case of the latter) or the questioning of traditional Jewish values resulting, inter alia, from the impact of Hellenistic culture (in the case of the former). Contrastingly, a number of other books written at about this time express opposition to certain hellenizing tendencies, as, for example, *Ben Sira* and *Jubilees*, although even these exhibit a certain measure of outside influence.[6]

The pièce de résistance of Hellenization in Judaea, occurred in 175 B.C.E., when the high priest Jason converted Jerusalem into a Greek *polis* replete with *gymnasium* and *ephebium* (II Macc. 4). Whether this step represents the culmination of a 150-year process of Hellenization in Jerusalem, or whether it was the initiative of only a small coterie of Jerusalem priests with no wider cultural or social ramifications, has been debated for decades.[7] The answer may well lie somewhere between these two polar positions. In any event, Jason's move constituted a bold step in the city's adaptation to the wider world, a process which would be interrupted—albeit only temporarily—by the persecutions of Antiochus IV and the resultant Maccabean revolt.

A further stage in the Hellenization process took place under Hasmonean rule. The motivation of the Hasmonean revolt has often been misunderstood. It has been contended that this revolt came in protest to the process and progress of Hellenization in Judaea, but this is patently not the case. The Maccabees revolted in response to the persecutions imposed by the king—a most exceptional policy for an enlightened Hellenistic king. It was an extreme measure and was undoubtedly motivated by the most unusual of circumstances, although there is little scholarly agreement as to precisely what these were.[8] Following their victory, the Hasmoneans themselves quickly adopted Hellenistic mores; they instituted holidays celebrating military victories (Nicanor Day on the 13th of Adar), as did the Greeks; they signed treaties with Rome and forged close alliances with the upper strata of Jerusalem society, whose hellenized proclivities are attested by names such as Alexander, Diodorus, Apollonius, Eupolemus, Antiochus, Numenius, Antiochus, Jason, Antipater, and Aeneas.[9]

Under Hasmonean rule (141–63 B.C.E.), instances of Hellenization within Jerusalem became more commonplace. The document in I Macc. 14, recording the public appointment of Simon as leader, high priest, and *strategos*, is written in a style strikingly reminiscent of documents from the Hellenistic world. The structure of this declaration, the claims put forward to justify and explain this appointment, the use of purple robes and gold ornaments by the Hasmoneans, the dating of an era commencing with Simon's appointment, and, finally, recording the text of this document on bronze tablets and placing them in a prominent place in the Temple area and in the (Temple?) treasury are well-known Hellenistic practices.

Beginning with the second generation, the Hasmoneans began adopting Greek names in addition to their Hebrew ones: John Hyrcanus I (134–104 B.C.E.), Aristobulus I (104–103 B.C.E.), Alexander Jannaeus (103–76 B.C.E.), Salome Alexandra (76–67 B.C.E.), Aristobolus II (67–63 B.C.E.), Hyrcanus II (63–40 B.C.E.), and, finally, Antigonus (40–37 B.C.E.). Hellenization in the Hasmonean court is likewise reflected by the hiring of foreign mercenaries and, more poignantly, by the assumption of royalty by Aristobolus I, Alexander Jannaeus, and Aristobolus II. No less telling in this regard is the sole rule of a queen, Salome Alexandra. Her smooth and unchallenged succession may well have been facilitated by contemporary Ptolemaic practice.

Several burial monuments and graves discovered in Hasmonean Jerusalem similarly reflect a significant appropriation of Hellenistic forms. The two principal remains of such funerary monuments, the priestly Bnei Hezir tomb from the Qidron Valley to the east of the city and Jason's tomb (also probably belonging to a priestly family) to the west (in today's Rehavia neighborhood), were both built in typical Hellenistic fashion—the former with its facade in classic Doric style (columns, pilasters, and frieze), the latter with its single Doric column and pyramid-like monument. Both tombs feature *kukhim* (or loculi, rectangular niches cut perpendicularly into the tomb's wall for primary burials), a burial arrangement which reached Judaea from Alexandria and Palestine's southern coastal region (e.g., Marisa). The tomb of Jason features scenes of merchant- and warships, a gazelle, as well as a series of menorah graffiti. Both of these tombs feature a variety of inscriptions, one in Hebrew in the Bnei Hezir tomb, and Greek and Aramaic ones in Jason's tomb.[10]

The tiny bronze coins minted by the Hasmoneans are a fascinating example of the cultural synthesis of Hellenistic and Jewish traditions. The very issuance of coins for economic and political purposes clearly reflects contemporary practice of both established kingdoms and newly-founded political entities seeking recognition and legitimacy. While only inscriptions in ancient Hebrew script (the First Temple precursor of the Aramaic square script introduced into Jewish society in the Persian period) appear on the coinage of Hyrcanus I and

Aristobolus I, Greek inscriptions appear under Alexander Jannaeus. These inscriptions bear the Greek name of the ruler as well as his Greek title, i.e., βασιλεύς; the Hebrew inscriptions, by contrast, bear the ruler's Hebrew name (Yoḥanan, Judah, Jonathan, Mattathias) as well as the title "high priest" or "king." On occasion, these bilingual inscriptions appear on either side of the same coin.[11]

Moreover, the symbols appearing on these coins were, with rare exception, borrowed from the surrounding Hellenistic world: anchors, cornucopiae, a wheel or star design, and floral representations. However, in this regard the Hasmonean rulers introduced one very unique element: no images of living beings—neither animal nor human—appear on any of their coins. Thus, the artistic and epigraphical components of the coins minted in Jerusalem under Hasmonean auspices reveal a fascinating symbiosis of Jewish and Hellenistic elements, reflecting the desire of the Hasmoneans to live comfortably in both the Hellenistic and Jewish worlds; this is the message they wished to convey via one of the most public vehicles at their disposal. In a similar vein, contemporary Phoenician coins exhibited native symbols together with Phoenician and Greek legends. Hasmonean numismatic evidence is thus significant on two counts: it reflects the vision and policy of those who ruled, while the message contained therein was aimed at the population at large for whom these coins were made.

Other evidence from Hasmonean society, though limited, likewise points in the direction of Jewish and Hellenistic symbiosis. This thrust is reflected, for example, in the archeological finds from the Hasmonean palaces at Jericho. There we find, side by side with the large swimming pool and pavilion, the latter in Doric style and following Hellenistic aristocratic tastes, a series of ritual baths (*miqva'ot*) reflecting the Hasmoneans' priestly commitment to maintain their ritual purity with regularity. Even a book as hostile to the Jewish Hellenizers and their reforms as II Maccabees, written toward the end of the second century B.C.E., reflects a certain ambivalence. II Maccabees was the first to use the terms "Judaism" (2:21; 8:1; 14:38) and "Hellenism" (4:13) as contrasting values and clashing cultural forces. Yet, the book itself was written in Greek, patterned in the tradition of Greek "pathetic" historiography, while borrowing Greek literary motifs in its narratives. This was not the only such case in the literary sphere. At about the same time, the Greek translation of the book of Esther utilized the finest of Greek linguistic and stylistic techniques, especially in the additions to the Hebrew text which focused on particularistic values, emphasizing the chasm between Greek and Jew (i.e., between Haman and Mordecai). It is explicitly stated that this Greek translation was carried out in Jerusalem.

Thus, far from stifling Hellenistic influence, Hasmonean rule was actually catalytic. To maintain diplomatic relations, support a bureaucracy, build a military force, create a kingdom, and develop its capital, Greek language and ways had to be learned. As Bickerman has aptly remarked with regard to a number of Hellenistic native rulers who took over in the wake of the Seleucid collapse: "Cosmopolitanism was the price of independence."[12]

Herodian Jerusalem and the Process of Hellenization

With the Roman conquest of the East and the subsequent ascension of Herod as king of Judaea, a new era opened for Jerusalem that was marked by a far greater intensity of contact with, and integration into, the surrounding culture. The reasons for this increased contact are threefold. First and foremost was Rome's establishment of an empire whose borders embraced the entire *oikumene*. With control of these areas firmly secured, Rome justifiably boasted of a *pax Romana*, an era which allowed for freedom and security of movement. Internal boundaries essentially disappeared and the flow of traffic, be it of a commercial, social, religious or cultural nature, now became commonplace. As a result, Jerusalem was linked more firmly than ever to a network of urban centers in the Roman East.[13]

A second factor behind Jerusalem's increased international contacts relates to Herod himself. Without a doubt, the most fundamental operative principle of Herod's public policy was the integration of his Judaean kingdom into the warp and woof of the Roman world. Herod's ability to maintain and strengthen political connections was proven time and again in the course of his 33-year reign.[14] His political loyalty was matched by a fascination with the cultural and social world of his time, both in its Hellenistic and Roman versions. As has been well documented archeologically over the last generation, Herod directed much of his enormous energies to promoting Hellenistic-Roman civilization, in its many ramifications, throughout his kingdom and beyond.

Finally, a third factor which had considerable influence on the cultural milieu of Herodian Jerusalem was linked to the dramatically-expanding Jewish Diaspora.[15] With rare exception, these communities were highly acculturated socially and culturally. Herod actively encouraged the involvement of Diaspora Jewry in the life of Jerusalem. He took the initiative by bringing a number of priestly families to Jerusalem from Egypt and Babylonia. Moreover, his rebuilding of the Jerusalem Temple on a monumental scale served not only as a source of inspiration for Jews everywhere, but also as an inducement and attraction for many to visit the city, primarily in the framework of the pilgrimage festivals. Jews from throughout the Diaspora were among the multitudes streaming into the city in the course of the year. One has only to read Acts 2:9–11 to realize the extent of their presence: therein appears a list of places whose languages could be heard on the streets of the city during a festival. The gatherings of pilgrims in Jerusalem appear to have represented a microcosm of the entire Roman world, bringing a wide range of cultures into the city.

Of no less significance to our discussion is the fact that permanent communities of Diaspora Jews were likewise to be found in Jerusalem. The existence of such communities is attested in three sources: rabbinic literature, which takes note of a synagogue of Alexandrians in Jerusalem (T Megillah 2: 17); the Theodotus inscription, which speaks of a Jerusalem synagogue founded by Jews from Rome;[16] and Acts 6:9, which lists a series of Diaspora synagogues in the city established by Jews from Alexandria, Cyrene, Asia, Cilicia, and a synagogue of freedman. The extent of this permanent form of Diaspora presence in the city is unknown but, together with the constant stream of visitors from abroad, their influence on city life and affairs was undoubtedly considerable.

How did the above-noted developments impact on the city, and what impressions might a visitor to Jerusalem have had? Even before entering it walls, one could not help but be struck by the many funerary monuments surrounding the city.[17] As was the case with the earlier Hasmonean period, burial remains from the first centuries B.C.E. and C.E. offer clear evidence of Hellenistic influence. The monuments in the Qidron Valley (the so-called Absalom and Zechariah tombs) are typical Hellenistic monuments that could be found throughout the Roman East. Wealthy Jerusalemites copied the finest examples of Hellenistic architecture when building those tombs, which featured solid square bases, columns, capitals, architraves, and cornices, all conforming to regnant Hellenistic styles. Often these monuments were capped with a *tholos* or pyramid, both ubiquitous architectural elements throughout the East.

Diaspora Jews as well seem to have expended sizable sums of money on funerary monuments in Jerusalem. Nicanor of Alexandria, who contributed a magnificent gate to the Temple, also erected an impressive tomb on the crest of today's Mount Scopus. But what may have been the most magnificent tomb of all was that of Queen Helena of Adiabene and her royal family to the north of the city. Pausanias takes note of this tomb together with that of King Mausolus of Halicarnassus whose mausoleum became one of the seven wonders of the world: "I know many wonderful graves and will mention two of them, the one at Halicarnassus, and one in the land of the Hebrews."[18]

Furthermore, the use of stone chests (ossuaries) for secondary burial of bones first appears in the time of Herod and quickly became the dominant form of secondary burial down to the time of the city's destruction. Why such a practice crystallized in Jerusalem at this time has been a subject of considerable speculation.[19] However, it would appear most plausible, given the date of their appearance and the fact that their use declined precipitously following the year 70, that the use of ossuaries was a product of Roman influence. Romans likewise used small stone boxes, along with the better-known urns, for gathering their ashes following cremation. Although the adoption of such ossuaries by Jews would have required a large measure of adaptation, viewing this Roman practice as the inspiration for the use of ossuaries can best explain the dating of this Jerusalem burial custom. As it first appeared in the Herodian era, it reflects the profound impact Rome was having on the city. It would also explain the timing of this custom's disappearance. Once the city was destroyed, the social and cultural matrix which supported it also disappeared, and the practice then began to sink into oblivion. If this line of reasoning is to be accepted, then the introduction of ossuaries may be construed less as a statement of particular Jewish religious beliefs than as a social convention which the relatively affluent Jerusalemites borrowed from the Romans.

Once in the city itself, our visitor would undoubtedly have been struck by the many similarities between Jerusalem and other Greco-Roman urban centers. The three towers to the north of Herod's palace, the Antonia fortress north of the Temple, public buildings such as the *bouleuterion*, agora, Xystus, as well as the palaces and residences of the wealthy classes in the Upper City, almost always followed Hellenistic-Roman styles.[20]

Excavations of the city's Jewish Quarter after 1967 offer remarkable evidence of the extent to which this wealthy, oft-priestly, stratum of Jerusalem society imported and adopted the regnant artistic styles and material goods from the surrounding world. Among the most relevant finds in this regard are mosaic floors featuring geometric and floral designs, frescoes often similar to those found at Pompeii (emphasizing architectural designs, colored panels, imitation marble, and architectural and floral motifs), a glass decanter from Sidon, imported western and eastern terra sigillata, fine (or thin-walled) ware, Pompeian red ware, Italian amphorae, and perfume bottles. Herodian society, and this includes the remains from Jericho and Herod's desert fortresses, as well as Jerusalem, was strikingly different from its Hasmonean predecessor in the quantity and quality of imported wares imported into the country. Whereas Hasmonean society had relied primarily on local ware, the Herodian upper classes utilized foreign-made ceramics to a far greater extent. Thus, from this aspect as well, the wealthy residential neighborhoods of the Upper City of Jerusalem and elsewhere were well ensconced in the wider Greco-Roman material culture.[21]

Three major structures in and around the city were erected by Herod as entertainment institutions. In a relatively detailed account, Josephus records the functions of these buildings during the games organized by the king (*Ant.* 15, 267–79). The theater was the setting for dramatic and musical performances, the amphitheater for bloody spectacles between gladiators or animals, or between gladiators and animals, while the hippodrome featured chariot and perhaps foot races. Herod constructed these buildings with the intention of introducing well-known and widespread Greco-Roman institutions into his capital, thereby placing Jerusalem in the cultural forefront along with other major urban centers of the East. No sizable Roman city with any modicum of civic pride would do without one or more of these institutions, much as any respectable modern city would do without a center for the performing arts, museums, or major sports facilities. However, Herod was not content with simply erecting these structures; he also allocated considerable sums of money to promote quadrennial spectacles, to which he invited the foremost athletes and performers of the time.

The pièce de résistance of Herod's building projects in the city was the rebuilding of the Temple. The king's munificence in this regard knew few bounds. He doubled the size of the Temple Mount area, creating the largest *temenos* (sacred precinct) known in the ancient world. Around three sides of this *temenos* he built porticoes, and along the fourth a monumental basilica (royal stoa) measuring well over 250 meters. This basilica was the largest-known building of its kind at the time. In the overall plan of this complex, Herod utilized a recognized Hellenistic model. Similar *temenoi*, with their artificial platforms, porticoes, basilicas, and temples, are known from North Africa, Syria, and Asia Minor, and this type of building, referred to as a *caesareum*, is described by Philo and other Greco-Roman authors of this period. Herod thus adopted this overall model and its components with regard to his showcase Temple.[22]

Other aspects of the Temple complex likewise reflect Hellenistic influence. The architectural components of some of these buildings discovered in archeological excavations conform to regnant Greek traditions; the columns, capitals, basilical plan, lintels, etc. all follow Hellenistic architectural models. There should be nothing particularly revolutionary in such a realization. As noted, Jews have never possessed an architectural tradition of their own, and their buildings borrowed heavily from the architectural and artistic styles in vogue in contemporary society. Solomon's Temple itself had been patterned after a typical Phoenician temple plan.[23]

In moving from place to place within Jerusalem, our imaginary visitor would have been struck by his or her ability to communicate linguistically in all parts of the city.[24] Although Latin and Hebrew might have been heard at times, these languages were spoken by only a small minority of the population, the former only by visiting Roman officials and soldiers. Almost everyone in the city spoke either Aramaic or Greek (or both). The latter appears in about 37% of the city's inscriptions and was certainly the preferred language of the city's Diaspora population. The monumental Theodotus inscription from a Jerusalem synagogue, as well as Acts' description of the Hellenist wing of the early church (the term "Hellenist" probably referring to the language of these people as well as their origin), attests to the use of Greek by the foreign-born. Aramaic is evidenced not only in the phrases ascribed to Jesus in the gospels, but also by a series of documents dating from this period (letters, the marriage document [*ketubah*], and several literary works).

Tertullian once asked: "*Quid Athenis et Hierosolymis?*" ("What has Athens in common with Jerusalem?"). On the basis of our examination of the city, its practices, composition, and institutions at the end of the Second Temple period, we would have to answer: a great deal! Jerusalem was affected by Hellenistic and Roman culture as was Athens.

Nevertheless, as in the earlier Hasmonean period, our presumed visitor to the city could not help but be struck at the same time by some significant differences between Jerusalem and other Roman cities. Perhaps one of the most immediate realizations was in the public realm. In contrast to other urban landscapes, Jerusalem was bereft of any figural art.[25] The ubiquitous statues of deities, emperors, prominent citizens, and animals which might have graced the streets, plazas and public buildings elsewhere were not to be seen. Although the Jews were not adverse to figural representations in other periods of their history, during these particular centuries, as noted above, there was a general consensus that such depictions were to be eschewed.

The Temple was the one institution which, more than any other, bestowed upon the entire city a distinct Jewish ambience. Not only were its holidays, rituals, and leadership determined by Jewish tradition, but the rhythm of daily life was dictated by the Jewish cycle of holy days and holidays, all of which were focused on the Temple Mount. Symbolic of this preeminence was a stone found at the southwestern corner of the Temple Mount with the inscription בית התקיעה—a place of trumpeting.[26] This discovery jibes well with Josephus' account that a priest would announce the onset and conclusion of Sabbaths and holidays by sounding a trumpet from the walls of the Temple Mount (*War* 4, 582). Moreover, leaders of almost all the major sects of first-century Jewish society were wont to meet their students and conduct other affairs in the Temple Mount area.

But the presence of the Temple as a unique Jewish institution was felt on an even wider scale. Given the requirement of ritual purity for everything connected with its precincts, this concern became part of everyday life for much of the population. One of most salient expressions of this concern was the emergence of a vigorous stone vessel industry. A wide range of everyday utensils (including tables) were created in stone.[27] Stone became the preferred medium as it is not susceptible to impurity as is ceramic ware, for example. Although such vessels have been found in almost all Jewish settlements, the largest quantity has turned up in and around Jerusalem. The ever-increasing use of ritual baths (*miqva'ot*) at this time further emphasizes this concern for purity. Not only were such baths located near the entrances to the Temple for those about to enter its precincts, but they became a regular feature among certain sects (e.g., the Essenes), among the priests living in the Upper City, and even in many agricultural installations throughout Judaea whose produce might find its way to the Temple.[28] Certain practices that were widespread in the Hellenistic and early Hasmonean periods, such as importing foreign wines, had now disappeared. Almost no Rhodian jar handles have been found in Herodian and post-Herodian Jerusalem.

Conclusion

In measuring the urban dimensions of this interplay between Judaism and Hellenism[29]—from the material culture, to the institutions, languages, and diverse social and religious practices—the impact of the latter on Jerusalem must be judged as most significant. Indeed, Jerusalem had a great deal in common with its pagan neighbors of the first century. Nevertheless, within the context of this extensive influence, there were many instances when a foreign influence was seriously altered in the process of adaptation to Jewish practice, or were even rejected entirely because they offended Jewish sensibilities. Moreover, as we have seen, there were numerous instances in which strong Hellenistic proclivities existed side by side with distinctly Jewish behavior. Thus, the hippodrome seems to have been located not far from the Temple, and most homes of the wealthy in Jerusalem's Upper City included Hellenistic-Roman decorations alongside their ritual baths. Even Herod himself was careful to avoid figural representations in his palaces and public buildings (at least in Judaea), and he likewise demanded circumcision before allowing female members of his family to marry non-Jews. All these nuances were at play in the city at one and the same time, and in a wide variety of areas in city life. It is thus important to underscore the need for a balanced picture in order to appreciate the totality of this phenomenon.

In short, Jerusalem occupied a most unusual position within Jewish Palestine. On the one hand, it was the most Jewish of all cities, given the presence of the Temple, the priesthood, and the leadership of almost all sects and religious groups, not to speak of the many religious observances associated specifically with this city. On the other hand, Jerusalem was also the most hellenized of Jewish cities, both in terms of its population, languages, institutions, and general cultural ambience. Jerusalem's Janus-type posture made it a truly remarkable city, for Jewish society in particular and within the larger Roman world in general.

Notes

1. *Hecataeus*: M. Stern, *Greek and Latin Authors on Jews and Judaism*, 3 vols. (Jerusalem, 1974–84), I, 20–44; Ben-Sira 1:1 and throughout; *Hasidim*: I Macc. 2:42; 7: 12–17.

2. Ezra 9–10; Neh. 13.

3. M Ta'anit 4:2–3; S. Safrai, "Religion in Everyday Life," *The Jewish People in the First Century*, eds. S. Safrai and M. Stern, 2 vols. (Philadelphia, 1974–76), II, 817–28.

4. *Apocalyptic literature*: M. Stone, *Scriptures, Sects and Visions* (Cleveland, 1980), 27–35; *Torah-reading*: L. Levine, "The Nature and Origin of the Palestinian Synagogue Reconsidered," *JBL* 115 (1996), 438–41.

5. N. Avigad, *Beth She'arim*, III (New Brunswick: Rutgers, 1976), 277–78. Moreover, it appears that the terms *Ioudaios* and *Yehudi*, which before the Hasmonean period bore a geographical meaning (i.e., "Judean"), now acquired a cultural and religious connotation as well, which would become predominant in the subsequent Roman era. See S. J. D. Cohen, "Religion, Ethnicity, and 'Hellenism' in the Emergence of Jewish Identity in Maccabean Palestine," *Religion and Religious Practice in the Seleucid Kingdom*, eds. P. Bilde et al. (Aarhus, 1990), 204–23; idem, "*Ioudaios to genos* and Related Expressions in Josephus," *Josephus and the History of the Greco-Roman Period: Essays in Memory of Morton Smith*, eds. F. Parente and J. Sievers (Leiden, 1994), 23–28; idem, "Ioudaios: 'Judaean' and 'Jew' in Susanna, First Maccabees, and Second Maccabees," *Geschichte-Tradition-Reflexion: Festschrift für Martin Hengel zum 70. Geburtstag*, I: *Judentum*, ed. P. Schäfer (Tübingen, 1996), 211–20.

6. M. Hengel, *Judaism and Hellenism*, 2 vols. (Philadelphia, 1974), I, 107ff.

7. For different views on this question, see E. Bickerman, *From Ezra to the Last of the Maccabees* (New York, 1962), 93–111; V. Tcherikover, *Hellenistic Civilization and the Jews* (Philadelphia, 1961), 117–203.

8. In addition to Bickerman (above, note 7), see Hengel, *Judaism and Hellenism* (above, note 6), 255–309.

9. See, for example, I Macc. 8:17; 12:16, 14:22, 24; Josephus, *Ant.* 13, 260; 14, 146.

10. E. Goodenough, *Jewish Symbols in the Greco-Roman Period*, 13 vols. (New York, 1953–68), I, 79–84.

11. Y. Meshorer, *Ancient Jewish Coinage*, 2 vols. (Dix Hills, N.Y., 1982), I, 35–98.

12. E. Bickerman, *The Jews in the Greek Age* (Cambridge, 1988), 302.

13. F. Millar, *The Roman East, 31 BC–AD 337* (Cambridge, 1993), 1–23.

14. A. Schalit, *King Herod* (Jerusalem, 1960), 240–73 (Hebrew); M. Stern, *The Kingdom of Herod* (Tel-Aviv, 1992), 25–46; L. I. Levine, "Herod, the King and His Era," *King Herod and His Era*, Edan 5, ed. M. Naor (Jerusalem, 1985), 2–10 (Hebrew); Meshorer (above, note 11), II, 5–30.

15. E. Schürer, *The History of the Jewish People in the Age of Jesus Christ (175 B.C.–A.D. 135)*, rev. ed.; 3 vols. (Edinburgh, 1973–87), III, pp. 1–76; M. Stern, "The Jewish Diaspora," *The Jewish People in the First Century* (above, note 3), I, 117–83.

16. R. Riesner, "Synagogues in Jerusalem," *The Book of Acts in its Palestinian Setting*, ed., R. Bauckham (Grand Rapids, 1995), 192–200.

17. For a summary of these finds, see H. Geva, "Jerusalem," *NEAEHL*, II, 747–57; N. Avigad, "The Rock-Carved Facades of the Jerusalem Necropolis," *IEJ* 1 (1950–51), 96–106; L. Y. Rahmani, *A Catalogue of Jewish Ossuaries in the Collections of the State of Israel* (Jerusalem, 1994), 264–80. See also A. Kloner, "The Necropolis of Jerusalem in the Second Temple Period," Ph.D. dissertation (Hebrew University of Jerusalem, 1980) (Hebrew).

18. *Description of Greece* 7, 16, 4–5, M. Stern, *Greek and Latin Authors on Jews and Judaism*, 3 vols. (Jerusalem, 1974–84), II, 196.

19. See, for example, Kloner (above, note 17), 250–53; E. M. Meyers, *Jewish Ossuaries: Reburial and Rebirth* (Rome, 1971); L. Y. Rahmani, "Ancient Jerusalem's Funerary Customs and Tombs I–IV," *BA* 44 (1981), 171–77, 229–35; 45 (1981): 43–53; 45 (1982): 109–19; idem (above, note 17), 53–59; idem, "Ossuaries and Ossilegium (Bone-Gathering) in the Late Second Temple Period," *Ancient Jerusalem Revealed*, ed. H. Geva (Jerusalem, 1994), 191–206; N. Rubin, "Secondary Burials in the Mishnaic and Talmudic Periods: A Proposed Model of the Relationship of Social Structure to Burial Practice," *Graves and Burial Practices in Israel in the Ancient Period*, ed. I. Singer (Jerusalem, 1994), 248–69 (Hebrew).

20. M. Avi-Yonah, "Jerusalem in the Hellenistic and Roman Periods," *The World History of the Jewish People—The Herodian Period*, ed. M. Avi-Yonah (Jerusalem, 1975), 235–49.

21. N. Avigad, *Discovering Jerusalem* (Jerusalem, 1980), 81–202.

22. Avi-Yonah (above, note 20), 212–19; B. Mazar, "The Archaeological Excavations near the Temple Mount," *Jerusalem Revealed: Archaeology in the Holy City, 1968–1974*, ed. Y. Yadin (New Haven, 1976), 25–40; M. Ben-Dov, *In the Shadow of the Temple: The Discovery of Ancient Jerusalem* (Jerusalem, 1985), 73–147; *NEAEHL*, II, 736–44. On the Hellenistic *temenos* as a model for Herod's Temple Mount, see E. Sjøqvist, "Kaisareion," *OR* 1 (1954): 86–108; J. B. Ward-Perkins, "The Caesareum at Cyrene," *PBSR* 26 (1958), 175–86; G. Foerster, "Art and Architecture in Palestine," *The Jewish People in the First Century* (above, note 3), II, 980.

23. For other instances of foreign influences on Temple practice, see S. Lieberman, *Hellenism in Jewish Palestine* (New York, 1962), 144–46, 164–79; J. L. Rubenstein, *The History of Sukkot in the Second Temple and Rabbinic Periods* (Atlanta, 1995), 145–48.

24. On the languages of first century Jerusalem, see, for example, J. A. Fitzmyer, "Languages of Palestine in the First Century A.D.," *CBQ* 32 (1970), 501–31; J. N. Sevenster, *Do You Know Greek? How Much Greek Could the First Jewish Christians Have Known?* (Leiden, 1968); K. Treu, "Die Bedeutung des Griechischen für die Juden im römischen Reich," *Kairos* 15 (1973), 123–44; Ch. Rabin, "Hebrew and Aramaic in the First Century," *The Jewish People in the First Century* (above, note 3), 1007–39; G. Mussies, "Greek in Palestine and the Diaspora," ibid., II, 1040–64; T. Rajak, *Josephus: The Historian and His Society* (Philadelphia, 1984), 46–58; idem, "The Location of Cultures in Second Temple Palestine: The Evidence of Josephus," *The Book of Acts in its Palestinian Setting* (above, note 16), 1–14; M. Hengel, *The 'Hellenization' of Judaea in the First Century after Christ* (London, 1989), 7–18;

25. Avi-Yonah, "Jewish Art and Architecture," *World History of the Jewish People* (above, note 20), 250–63; R. Hachlili, *Ancient Jewish Art and Archaeology in the Land of Israel* (Leiden, 1988), 65–119.

26. *NEAEHL*, II, 740.

27. Y. Magen, "Jerusalem as a Center of the Stone Vessel Industry during the Second

Temple Period," *Ancient Jerusalem Revealed* (above, note 19), 244–56; (= "The Stone Vessel Industry During the Second Temple Period," *'Purity Broke Out in Israel' (Tractate Shabbat 13b): Stone Vessels in the Late Second Temple Period*, ed. O. Rimon [Haifa, 1994], 7–27).

28. D. Amit, "Ritual Baths in Har Hebron—Points of Reference for Reconstructing Jewish Settlement in the Second Temple Period," *Studies on Judaea and Samaria: Proceedings of the Third Congress—1993*, eds. Z. Erlich and Y. Eshel (Qedumim, 1994), 157–89 (Hebrew); idem, " 'Jerusalem' Ritual Baths from the Second Temple Period in Har Hebron," *Studies on the Land: Festschrift in Honor of Y. Felix*, eds. Z. Safrai et al. (Ramat Gan, 1997), 35–48 (Hebrew).

29. This subject is presented more elaborately in my *Judaism and Hellenism in Antiquity: Conflict or Confluence?* (Seattle, 1998), Chap. II.

5

The Pilgrimage Economy of Jerusalem in the Second Temple Period

MARTIN GOODMAN

There have been many general studies of the economy of Jerusalem in the late Second Temple period.[1] It is clear that, despite social tensions engendered by the inequitable distribution of wealth, this was an exceptionally prosperous society.[2] The basis of such prosperity can hardly have been the exploitation of the agrarian hinterland in the Judaean hills which, despite the panegyrical remarks of Josephus (*War* 3, 49–50), was too poor and too far from the coast for the encouragement of cash crops for interregional trade. Jerusalem did not lie on any important trade route. Nor was prosperity a product of the political role of the city in the Herodian period and under Roman procuratorial rule, for the government of Judaea was often based elsewhere than Jerusalem and, in marked context to Ptolemaic Alexandria, Jerusalem never developed a society and economy based around a royal court. The wealth of Jerusalem derived in one form or another from its sanctity. It is a truism that without its religious role Jerusalem would never have become a major city; specifically, although by the end of the Second Temple period the city may have attracted wealthy visitors to study or to settle in an exciting international atmosphere, the main cause of prosperity was the presence of the Temple. The aim of this paper will be to explore the role in the economy of mass pilgrimage and, in particular, the significance of pilgrimage from abroad.

In theory, the economic impact of pilgrimage should have been immense. According to the Torah (Ex. 23:17; Deut. 16:16), every adult Jewish male was required to visit the Temple three times each year, and although the total size of the Jewish population in this period is unknown, it was undoubtedly very large indeed.[3] Comparison with the history of Mecca in more recent times encourages speculation that much of Jerusalem's society might have been bound up in the service industries required by pilgrims, so that the periodic pilgrim festivals might have become the "harvest" of the city,[4] although since Jerusalem did at least have *some* indigenous economic base, the city would not have been as totally dependent on visitors as Mecca became.[5]

Some aspects of the pilgrimage process and its importance in later Second Temple Judaism can be derived from explicit evidence in the ancient sources, particularly the writings of Josephus and early rabbinic texts.[6] Visitors might use tents (*Ant.* 17, 213–17) but often they needed to be given accommodation by institutions[7] or individuals (Mark 11:11), for which they might pay in cash or in kind (as envisaged in T Maʿaser Sheni 1:12). They needed food, drink, luxuries, and souvenirs, and it is reasonable to assume that the craftsmen of the city, who greeted the pilgrims on arrival according to M Bikkurim 3:3, took advantage of the market for their goods. Pilgrims tended to stay not just for the minimum period required, but for the whole festival period, often bringing with them their wives and children, even though the latter were under no obligation to visit the Temple at all.[8] Proper performance of pilgrimage without considerable expenditure was more or less impossible, however cheaply the pilgrim tried to live, since, according to early rabbinic texts, there was a requirement for the money earned in exchange for the second tithe (Deut. 14:26) to be spent by the pilgrim while within the boundaries of the city.[9]

It is unlikely that every adult male Jew visited Jerusalem at the same time, but ancient comments on the impact of pilgrimage in the first century C.E. make it clear that the festivals were very crowded. The interest of the sources lies naturally not in economics but in the political volatility which resulted from the presence of huge numbers of people (*War* 2, 224 and elsewhere). Passover was apparently a particularly popular pilgrimage time (*Ant.* 17, 214), but the Pentecost and Tabernacles festivals were also well attended. Numbers in ancient texts are always hard to evaluate, but Josephus clearly intended to impress his readers when he gave the figure of 2,700,000 male pilgrims who came to Jerusalem for the Passover in 66 C.E (*War* 6, 425); the size of the city's normal population is unknown, but even the highest estimate is under a quarter of a million.[10]

As Philo remarked with pride, these pilgrims came from all over the Jewish world: they were "thousands of men from thousands of cities" (*Special Laws* 1, 69). Such mass international pilgrimage is not attested for any other cult in the Roman empire, for the simple reason that only Jews insisted (at least in theory) both that only one Temple was a valid place for sacrifices and that all adult male devotees of the cult were duty bound to make regular obeisance there. Other shrines, like the sanctuary of Asclepius at Pergamum or Artemis at Perge, also hosted regular large gatherings,[11] but these festivals were essentially local affairs for the surrounding region. A devotee of Asclepius in Italy would usually visit a shrine to the god closer to home than Pergamum, and would see no value in the long trek to Asia Minor; pagan pilgrims who embarked on long journeys were the exception, not the rule.[12]

It seems clear that mass international pilgrimage was a feature of Judaism which distinguished it from other religions, thus explaining the nervousness of the Roman authorities at the potentiality for political unrest among such huge crowds. It is worth comparing the caution of Trajan when asked by Pliny the Younger about setting up a fire brigade in Nicomedia in Bithynia (*Letters* 10, 33–34). It is also likely (if unprovable) that such pilgrimage was to prove an important element in the prosperity of the city in the last century of its existence. Below I shall investigate a question which, I think, has not been previously asked by scholars: when did such mass international pilgrimage start?

It has been noted before that no reference to international pilgrimage can be found in any source referring to the period before Herod.[13] I would like to suggest that this silence may not be accidental. It seems to me significant that nothing about such pilgrimage can be found in the glowing description of Jerusalem found in *Ps. Aristeas to Philocrates* 83–120, a text composed probably in the mid-second century B.C.E., or in the writings of any of the Greek and Latin gentile authors who wrote about Jews before the mid-first century B.C.E.[14]—despite the fact that mass movements across international borders would have been very noticeable in the late Hellenistic period, with Jews coming from Alexandria (in Ptolemaic territory until 31 B.C.E.) or Babylonia (in Parthian territory). Both Jewish and non-Jewish writers referred quite frequently to the transfer of money from the Diaspora to the Temple. This was the theme of Cicero (*On Behalf of Flaccus* 28), Josephus described it as an ancient custom (*Ant.*14, 185–267; 16, 160–78), and according to Bar. 1: 10–14 Babylonian Jews sent money (rather than themselves) to Jerusalem for offerings and prayers to be made on their behalf in the holy city on the feast days. None of these sources, however, refers to Diaspora pilgrimage. It seems likely that the pilgrimage feasts before Herod's time involved essentially only local Jews from the land of Israel; the vastly expanded Temple court which Herod was to build would eventually be filled to overflowing, but no source suggests a problem with lack of space in the Temple before then.

If mass pilgrimage began in Herod's reign, how did it come about? By chance, perhaps. It is notoriously hard to gauge the intentions of individuals from their actions. But it seems to me more likely that the prime motivator was Herod himself. Herod was a remarkable businessman, speculator, and entrepreneur,[15] and had initiated numerous complex financial schemes.[16] It is hard to believe that he was unaware of the economic consequences of the upsurge in the number of visitors to Jerusalem during his rule, especially when his own expenditure did so much to support it (see below). It was unlikely that Diaspora pilgrimage would have become popular unless it was encouraged. Diaspora Jews were not tied into the Temple service by the close links of the *ma'amad* system, which apparently applied only to inhabitants of the land of Israel.[17] It is possible that the loyalty to Jerusalem of the huge Jewish population of Egypt (and especially Alexandria) was threatened by the competing attractions of the shrine at Leontopolis, although concern about such competition cannot be proved. Josephus even hints that pilgrims were only expected to go up to Jerusalem "from the ends of the land which the Hebrews shall conquer" (*Ant.* 4, 203). It was a product not of a change of halakha from the biblical requirement, but of custom, that Diaspora Jews had come to assume that they were not required to visit the Temple three times a year. If their custom was to alter, they would have to wish to go.

Herod had good economic reasons to encourage pilgrimage from the Diaspora. The kingdom of Judaea, granted to him and captured for him by the Roman state,[18] lacked more than a few capital assets. There was a limit to the wealth to be derived from natural resources such as the balsam groves of 'En Gedi, and Judaea was not well suited to bring in a large income from agricultural exports. The only real asset of the kingdom to be exploited was the status of Jerusalem as a religious center, and that is what Herod set out to do.

The time was propitious for the venture. The *pax Romana* permitted freedom of movement throughout much of the world inhabited by Jews, particularly after the suppression of Mediterranean piracy by Pompey in 67 B.C.E.[19] After 31 B.C.E., the huge Alexandrian Jewish community was, like Judaea, integrated into the Roman empire; the Jews of Syria and Asia Minor had been incorporated within the empire earlier. The Babylonian community remained under Parthian rule at this time, but trading contacts between the empires multiplied, as is evident from the sudden prosperity of the caravan city of Palmyra,[20] which facilitated communications of other kinds. In any event, the brief episode of Parthian control over Judaea in 40–37 B.C.E.[21] initiated far closer relations between Palestinian and Babylonian Jews than had been known for many centuries.[22] Even if Herod's Hasmonaean predecessors thought of encouraging mass pilgrimage (which is unknown, although many of them invested in the repair of the Temple itself), political instability would have made it difficult.[23] By contrast, Herod chose the right time.

The economic advantages brought by such pilgrims were multifarious. Pilgrims helped to protect delivery of the offerings sent to the Temple, even by those who did not themselves go up to worship (cf. *Ant.* 17, 312–13, on the caravans which came from Babylon); according to T Sheqalim 2:3, which may or may not be based on anything more than speculation, the offerings from remote lands were a rich source of Temple income. Jews from the Mediterranean Diaspora seem to have picked up from their gentile compatriots the practice of euergetism, apparently uncommon among Judaean Jews outside the Herodian family. Thus, the gates of the Temple were plated with gold by Alexander the Alabarch, who came from Alexandria (*War* 5, 201–206), and there are other examples of such conspicuous expenditure by individuals in search of prestige.[24] Visitors were bound to spend money on the purchase of souvenirs,[25] and although it is impossible to tell precisely when the non-biblical requirement to spend all second tithe money in Jerusalem became current,[26] it is probable that it was in operation in Herod's time.

How could Herod set about attracting Diaspora pilgrims to the holy city? The dictatorial methods he used in the administration of Judaea[27] would hardly work in this case, since he lacked any formal powers outside his kingdom, but he was an expert at diplomacy, as shown by his ability to prosper through the Roman civil wars. The examples of the capitalist schemes of the Ptolemies in Egypt and the radical reorganization of Rome by Augustus after Actium undoubtedly influenced his general policies, but in this case only indirectly.

Some methods of encouragement were simply practical. Herod protected the pilgrimage route from Babylonia by installing a military colony in Batanaea (*Ant.* 17, 29–31), although there is no evidence that he encouraged a network of protected pilgrimage routes for the Mediterranean Jews; on the contrary, arrival at his new port city of Caesarea would have presented a disconcerting first view of the holy land for pious Jews, since the temple of Rome and Augustus dominated the harbor.[28] The Temple provided, either through its own staff or by leasing space to entrepreneurs, good facilities for the exchange of foreign currencies (M Sheqalim 2:1, 4), but Herod's only obvious contribution to this service was the building of the great basilica in which it was probably housed.

More significant, perhaps, were Herod's efforts to alter Diaspora attitudes to the Temple to make Diaspora Jews feel that pilgrimage would be worthwhile. Among more blatant moves was the appointment of high priests from the principal Diaspora communities, such as the Babylonian Hananel, and Jesus b. Phiabi and Boethus, both from Egypt. This preference for non-Judaean priests as incumbents of the highest office has often been discussed as part of the suppression of the local Jewish elite,[29] but it is reasonable also to emphasize its effect in raising the profile of Diaspora Jews in Jerusalem. Herod in any case maintained contact with many Diaspora communities, portraying himself as their protector throughout the Roman empire, much as

Hyrcanus had done before him; in this case, his patronage may have bought the king prestige in the eyes of his Roman masters by showing him to be a ruler with a constituency wider than just Judaea, and the promotion of pilgrimage may only have been a secondary motive.[30]

It is plausible to postulate a similar dual motive for the single action by Herod most likely to have stimulated pilgrimage—the rebuilding of the Temple. Rebuilding began in 20/19 B.C.E. and was basically completed by ca.12 B.C.E., although work on the building continued fairly constantly until 64 C.E., since the edifice needed frequent repair.[31] Herod himself explained his massive expenditure as a product of his piety and wealth, according to Josephus, whose report probably derived from Nicolaus of Damascus (*Ant.* 15, 380–90), and the new edifice was doubtless intended to reflect the glory of his rule, much as Augustus tried to enhance his own image by the rebuilding of the city of Rome. The initial completion of the Temple project was celebrated on the anniversary of Herod's accession to power (ibid., 15, 421–31). Like Augustus in contemporary Rome, Herod enhanced public space by enlarging the hillside through the use of an artificial platform built on arches. It is less likely that Herod's main hope was to win popularity with his Jewish subjects, who were apparently nervous about the whole project and the possibility that it might prove sacrilegious (ibid., 15, 385); like Augustus, Herod's main hope may have been to ensure his reputation for posterity.

At the same time, it is a reasonable assumption that Herod believed that his rebuilding made economic sense and that it was more than simply a heavy financial drain. It is hard to doubt Josephus' insistence (ibid., 15, 380; 17, 162) that Herod paid for the initial construction out of his own pocket, but the continuing work on the site, not completed until more than three-quarters of a century later, was financed from Temple money and the grandiose project may have served a useful purpose in releasing into the economy sacred funds otherwise kept idle in the Temple treasury.[32] In practice, the building project stimulated the entire economic life of the kingdom.[33] Despite the behavior of Agrippa II in seeking alternative jobs for the workmen after the Temple was finally completed in 64 C.E. (ibid., 20, 219–22), it is implausible to see the provision of employment as a prime aim of Herod. Equally implausible is the picture of Herod's finances given by Josephus (*Ant.* 16,150–55), where he described Herod's munificence as the product of a passion for honor which blinded him to the economic consequences of his generosity. According to Josephus, it was only after prolonged famine that Herod's expenditure on urban reconstruction led him into difficulties in feeding his subjects from his own resources (ibid., 15, 302–16). The whole thrust of this paper is to encourage the view that Herod's expenditure was really a capital investment expected to pay off in time in the promotion of tourism. Pilgrimage to the great new sanctuary, one of the wonders of the Roman world, built on a massive scale with meticulous care, became an enjoyable and awe-inspiring experience, such that Diaspora Jews would be willing to undergo the inevitable discomforts of the journey and, on arrival, would spend their money in the holy city.

It takes time for investment in infrastructure to pay off, and it is unlikely that Herod's own finances benefited greatly from the influx of tourists he encouraged. His own income derived from direct and indirect taxation in Judaea (benefiting in the latter case from the increase in interregional trade) and by the profit from tax concessions in various parts of the empire leased to him by the Roman state. It also remained true, even in the very last days of the Temple, that the great majority of pilgrims still seems to have come from the land of Israel. There is no evidence that a Diaspora Jew like Philo went up more than once to Jerusalem (*On Provid.* 2, 64), and it is a surprising fact that non-local coin issues have rarely turned up in the archaeology of the city.[34] Nonetheless, by the mid-first century C.E., many Jews from many different places could be found in the vicinity of the Temple (Acts 2: 9–11; 6:9), and Jerusalem was, in the eyes of Pliny the Elder, one of the great cities of his time (*Nat. Hist.* 5, 14).

Notes

1. For example, J. Jeremias, *Jerusalem in the Time of Jesus* (London, 1969).

2. M. Goodman, *The Ruling Class of Judaea: the Origins of the Jewish Revolt against Rome A.D. 66–70* (Cambridge, 1987), 51–75.

3. For estimates of the size of the Jewish population, see L. H. Feldman, *Jew and Gentile in the Ancient World* (Princeton, 1993), 293, 555–56.

4. M. N. Pearson, *Pious Passengers: the Hajj in Earlier Times* (London, 1994), 172–87.

5. F. E. Peters, *Jerusalem and Mecca: the Typology of the Holy City in the Near East* (New York and London, 1986).

6. See especially S. Safrai, *Pilgrimage in the Time of the Second Temple*[2] (Jerusalem, 1985) (Hebrew). See also J. Feldman, "La circulation de la Tora: les pèlerinages au second Temple," *La Société juive à travers l'histoire*, IV, ed. S. Trigano (Paris, 1992–93), 161–78.

7. J.-B. Frey, *Corpus Inscriptionum Judaicarum*, II (Rome, 1952), no. 1404.

8. Safrai (above, note 6), chapter 6.

9. E. P. Sanders, *Judaism: Practice and Belief* (London, 1992), 128–29.

10. See the figures quoted by Feldman (above, note 3).

11. R. MacMullen, *Paganism in the Roman Empire* (New Haven, 1981), 25–26.

12. Ibid., 29.

13. Safrai (above, note 6), 55.

14. See the authors cited in volume I of M. Stern, *Greek and Latin Authors on Jews and Judaism* (Jerusalem, 1974).

15. M. Grant, *Herod the Great* (London, 1971), 173.

16. See especially E. Gabba, "The Finances of King Herod," *Greece and Rome in Eretz Israel: Collected Essays*, eds. A. Kasher et al. (Jerusalem, 1990), 160–68.

17. On the *ma'amad*, see M Ta'anit 4:2–3.

18. On Herod's accession to power, see Josephus, *Ant.* 14, 381–93.

19. See P. Greenhalgh, *Pompey: the Roman Alexander* (London, 1980), 91–100.

20. On Palmyra, see J. Starcky and M. Gawlikowski, *Palmyra²* (Paris, 1985), 36–42; E. Will, *Les Palmyréniens: la venise des sables* (Paris, 1992), 33–46.

21. E. Schürer, *The History of the Jewish People in the Age of Jesus Christ*, eds. G. Vermes et al., 3 vols. (Edinburgh, 1973–87), I, 278–83.

22. On Herod and the Jews of Babylonia, see J. Neusner, *A History of the Jews of Babylonia*, I: *The Parthian Period*, rev. ed. (Leiden, 1969), 34–39.

23. I owe this observation to Ed Sanders.

24. On the inscription near the Temple by a Jew from Rhodes, see B. Isaac, "A Donation for Herod's Temple in Jerusalem," *IEJ* 33 (1983), 86–92.

25. See M. Del Verme, *Giudaismo e Nuovo Testamento: il caso delle Decime* (Naples, 1989), 194–97.

26. J. Jeremias, *Jerusalem in the Time of Jesus* (London, 1969), 9.

27. A. Schalit, *König Herodes: der Mann und sein Werk* (Berlin, 1969).

28. On the buildings of Caesarea, see K. G. Holum and R. L. Hohlfelder (eds.), *King Herod's Dream: Caesarea on the Sea* (London and New York, 1988), 72–105.

29. See especially M. Stern, "Social and Political Realignments in Herodian Judaea," *The Jerusalem Cathedra*, III, ed. L. I. Levine (Jerusalem, 1982), 40–62.

30. Josephus, *Ant.* 16, 27–65; cf. Schürer (above, note 21), I, 319.

31. Ibid., I, 292, note 12, on the chronology.

32. Gabba (above, note 16), 166–68.

33. Ibid., 166.

34. Z. Safrai, "Jerusalem as an Economic Center during the Roman-Byzantine Period," *Recent Innovations in the Study of Jerusalem*, eds. Z. Safrai and A. Faust (Ramat Gan, 1996), 29 (Hebrew).

6

The Role of Jerusalem
and the Temple in
"End of Days" Speculation
in the Second Temple Period

ALBERT I. BAUMGARTEN

Variety of Messianic Scenarios

Morton Smith published a brief article entitled, "What is Implied by the Variety of Messianic Figures," where, like in so many of his other contributions at that time,[1] he posed a question and proposed an answer that served as an impetus for much scholarly discussion to follow. He attempted to make better sense of the data accumulating from Dead Sea scrolls and other sources concerning messianic[2] and other eschatological scenarios, while facing the common conclusion that Judaism and Christianity went their separate ways as a result of a disagreement concerning the messianic status of Jesus. Smith noted that the variety of messianic figures in Second Temple Judaism, *a variety often to be found in the very same text*, was so great that messianic eschatology could not have been the cause of the emergence of different groups. As Smith wrote:

> If a group had no single eschatological myth, it cannot have been or-
> ganized as a community of believers in the myth it did not have. . . .
> If the variety of eschatological prediction is any evidence, eschatology
> was, for the members of these groups, a comparatively arbitrary and
> individual matter. . . . Such an arbitrary and individual matter can
> hardly have been the basis of group organization and practice.[3]

Smith, therefore, proposed to turn in other directions in the search to understand why groups arose and split off from each other, but this aspect of his insight is not my concern in this article.[4] Rather, I would like to take up Smith's central thesis: the variety of messianic and other eschatological expectations, and the fact that Jews did not have a standard checklist of events which were to occur at the time of the redemption, which would prove that the end was at hand. This conclusion has been basic to several attempts to assess ancient Jewish scenarios for the end of the world, as already implied in the title of the collection edited by J. Neusner, W. Green, and E. Frerichs, *Judaisms and their Messiahs* (Cambridge, 1987), or reflected in many of the contributions to J. Charlesworth's *The Messiah: Developments in Earliest Judaism and Christianity* (Minneapolis, 1992). As stated explicitly by J. J. Collins, at the outset of his recent comprehensive study of ancient Jewish messianism, the assumption among scholars used to be that ancient Jewish messianism was both ubiquitous and consistent. Recent discussions of the matter, however, based in large part on the Dead Sea scrolls, have yielded a "sweeping reaction" and a "dramatic shift" against that synthesis. It is the newly-recognized variety which Collins intends to describe, even while arguing that perhaps the pendulum of scholarly opinion has shifted too far.[5]

How is this variety of eschatological vision, messianic and non-messianic, to be explained? Sometimes, consideration of the social, economic, political, or religious situation of the author of a particular scenario is helpful: eschatological expectations, one may argue, were tailor-made to suit the circumstances of those who believed in them. Thus, for example, I suggest it is no accident that in Ben-Sira's formulation of his hopes for the punishment of the nations and vindication of Zion (36:1–17), he did not indicate any desire for a new or rebuilt Temple, despite the fact that hopes for a new or rebuilt Temple were fairly widespread in eschatological scenarios of other Jews of the Second Temple era.[6] This cannot be an accident. When one remembers, however, that any hint that the end of time will bring a new Temple is inevitable criticism of the existing one as inferior by comparison, Ben Sira's omission becomes more comprehensible. Ben Sira was a firm supporter of the then current order, viewing it as the fulfillment of all his dreams.[7] When expressing his prayers for the future, he asked for the continuation of the prevailing situation forever, beseeching God, according to the Hebrew version:

> May His love abide upon Simon, and may He keep in him the covenant
> of Phinehas; may one never be cut off from Him; and as for His off-
> spring, (may it be) as (enduring as) the days of heaven (50:24).

The author of these lines had no reason to include a new Temple in his aspirations for the end of days.

On the other hand, explaining a particular scenario on the basis of the social, economic, political, or religious commitments of its author does not always yield useful insights. Reality is often too disorderly to be so easily understood: class interests and cultural commitment, for example, do not always concur. Think, in the contemporary world, of phenomena such as "radical chic" or of middle class socialists. Incoherence and inconsistency, especially when viewed by the standards of our logic, as well as "inelegant landings"—combinations of positions whose congruity we may find difficult to grasp—should not be surprising.[8] The historian's task is to explain as best as possible what is known, while recognizing that there are limits to both our knowledge and understanding. Sometimes we may ask better questions than the available evidence or our ability to comprehend allows us to answer, but even these questions have value.

Jerusalem in the Careers of the Sign Prophets

The account of Jesus, as told in the gospels, creates a certain bias in favor of seeing Jerusalem as the inevitable last stop of a Jewish messianic movement. After a career as preacher, miracle worker, and healer in the Galilee, Jesus' story reached its inevitable climax, as foretold in the Scriptures (Matt. 16:21–23, 17:22, 20:17–19 and parallels), in Jerusalem. There he was accused, tried, crucified, buried, and resurrected. In light of Smith's thesis, as summarized above, one must ask: was Jerusalem always the last stop in ancient Jewish scenarios of the end of days, and if not, why not?

Evidence exists for a number of movements led by sign prophets which flourished in Judaea in the last century before the destruction of the Temple.[9] The principal witness to these activities was Josephus, with some additional light thrown on the subject by the New Testament. Josephus' testimony on these matters was not entirely objective, as he seems to have played down the eschatological side of Judaism in general, as, for example, in his discussion of the prophecies of Daniel (*Ant.* 10, 210).[10] The modern reader must therefore supplement Josephus' information, adding the messianic dimension to the understanding of what these figures were doing. Indeed, in all the cases to be discussed below, the reader must add the eschatological aspect to Josephus' bare details.[11] Nevertheless, the role of Jerusalem in these scenarios of redemption is not as obvious as might be thought, hence worth careful analysis.

Aside from Jesus, there were two other groups for whom the culmination of human history was to take place in Jerusalem. Josephus mentions the anonymous Egyptian prophet who promised his followers that he would lead a military assault on Jerusalem from the Mount of Olives (*War* 2, 261). In the parallel report in *Ant.* 20, 169–72, the victory to come was more miraculous in nature: the walls of Jerusalem would fall down.[12] According to both versions, the result was the same: Felix led out his troops who slaughtered the followers, while the Egyptian himself escaped and disappeared. Jerusalem was also the venue of deliverance promised by yet another anonymous prophet of the revolt era who led 6,000 poor women and children, and a mixed multitude of males, to expect redemption in the Temple on the eve of its fall (*War* 6, 283–85). All these people perished in the capture and destruction of the Temple by the Roman army.[13] The first of these events in particular testifies to the centrality of Jerusalem in scenarios of the end of days. Unlike the local women, children, and mixed multitude in the summer of 70 C.E.—not to be taken seriously in any case, by ancient standards, because of their age, sex, and social standing, and inevitably devoted to Jerusalem as they lived there and feared for the future of its Temple—the Egyptian prophet came from the Diaspora to play out his part in the drama of the end of days at the place where he believed its most decisive moments would occur.

In contrast to these are the prophetic figures in whose careers Jerusalem did not have a role. First among them is Theudas, who persuaded his followers to take their possessions and cross the Jordan. The waters would then part at his command. As usual in such events, his followers were captured and Theudas himself beheaded (*Ant.* 20, 97–99). Much is unclear or unspecified in this story, such as in what direction Theudas and his disciples were crossing the Jordan, from which side to which? What did they hope to achieve by this action, other than perhaps on the symbolic level, if they were crossing the Jordan from east to west and thus reenacting the opening moments of the conquest of the land?[14] In any case, Jerusalem plays no part whatsoever in this drama.

Next are figures, again anonymous, at the time of Felix. We are told that they took people *out of Jerusalem to the desert* and promised to show them there miracles of freedom or liberation in harmony with God's design. These activities were taken seriously enough by Felix to order his troops to slaughter these "madmen" (*War* 2, 258–60; *Ant.* 20, 167–68). The place of Jerusalem in this scenario is explicitly different from its role in the "standard" one based on the Christian model. One must leave Jerusalem for the desert in order to witness and participate in the finale of God's design for the world. Were these Jews who left Jerusalem for the desert promised that they would ever return and, if so, what might happen then? Josephus, our only witness to these events, did not tell.

According to Josephus, an anonymous figure at the time of Festus persuaded some to follow him into the wilderness, where they would find salvation and rest from troubles. Following the usual pattern, they, too, were massacred by the Roman troops (ibid., 20, 188). Where these people came from, and where they were to go, is not mentioned explicitly. Nevertheless, the absence of any role assigned to Jerusalem is notable.

Finally, there is the case of Jonathan the Sicarius, who promised his followers signs in the desert outside Cyrene (*War* 7, 437–50; *Life* 424–25). Jonathan was a refugee from Jerusalem in the years after the end of the revolt. Nevertheless, the venue for his signs was in far-off Cyrene, and Jerusalem had no part in the expectations aroused by this figure. On being captured, Jonathan accused many of the leading Jews of Cyrene, and Josephus as well, of having supported his efforts. Ultimately, many of the leading Jews of Cyrene were executed, while Josephus continued to enjoy the trust of the Flavian house. Thus, the consequences of this episode were limited to the Jewish community of Cyrene.

The conclusion to be drawn from these examples is straightforward: as one might expect on the basis of Smith's thesis, among the varieties of Jewish messianic expectation were ones which included Jerusalem as the last stop, and ones which did not.

John the Baptist

This conclusion has important implications for understanding the reports of the career of John the Baptist, of whose activities we learn from the gospels and from Josephus, *Ant.* 18, 116–19. Recently, scholars have insisted more effectively against a simplistic harmonization of the various accounts.[15] For example, the eschatological side of John's activities—so central to the gospel version—was not explicitly noted by Josephus. At best, one might argue that it was implicit in John's call for repentance, culminating in baptism—a sign of readiness to be accepted into the kingdom of heaven which was soon to unfold. With this understanding, John appears to be another instance of Josephus' tendency to play down or remove the messianic aspect of the work of figures he portrayed. Josephus' evidence should therefore be supplemented, and his John should be understood in an eschatological context, even if we had no other evidence on John from the gospels.

In comparing the versions, however, one detail illuminated by the above analysis has been overlooked. Josephus' John was active in the Peraea, and Jerusalem is never mentioned. Appropriately, the king who acted against John was Herod Antipas, whose domain extended to the Peraea and who was concerned about John's growing influence among his subjects, lest it should lead to sedition. Congruent with this context, John was executed at Machaerus.

Some of these basic facts remain the same in the story of John told in the gospels: Herod Antipas was still the king who executed John at a prison in his realm (Mark 6:14–29 and parallels; Machaerus is not explicitly named in the gospels). Apparently that part of the story was too fixed to be liable to change, but much of the rest has been recast. In the gospel versions, John is much more explicitly a figure with an eschatological message, the forerunner of the Messiah, Jesus. In these accounts, the residents of *Judaea and Jerusalem* were attracted by his teachings (ibid., 1:5//Matt. 3:5). Matthew adds the inhabitants of the region around the Jordan to the list of those fascinated by John's preaching. Next, while we are never told where Josephus' John baptized (did he use whatever ritual baths were available, or streams in the Peraea, or perhaps the Jordan?), John of the gospels baptized in the Jordan, nowhere else, and it was there that he baptized Jesus (Mark 1:9 and parallels). Consistent with this picture of John is the family background attributed to him: he was the son of the priest Zachariah, of the priestly course of Abijah, who served in the Temple and lived in the hill country of Judaea (Luke 1:8–23, 39).

All this, however, created a problem: if John attracted residents of Judaea, Jerusalem, and perhaps the area around Jericho, and baptized in the Jordan, how is it that he was sentenced and executed by Herod Antipas? Even by the wildest stretch of the imagination, John of the gospels posed no political threat to Herod Antipas' rule, of the sort described by Josephus. While Herod Antipas had a palace in Jerusalem, where he spent festivals (ibid., 23:7) and pursued other interests, his kingdom did not include Judaea, which was subject to direct Roman rule by officials such as Pontius Pilate. How and why, then, did Herod Antipas come to play the part in John's death which was a fixed component of the story?

The gospels therefore changed the reason for John's execution, from Herod Antipas' suspicions of John's growing power into a dispute of a personal origin. John criticized Herod's marriage with Herodias, his brother's wife, leading Herodias to hate John, so that she incited her daughter Salome to ask Herod Antipas for the head of John the Baptist (Mark 6:14–29 and parallels). Explaining a clash as a confrontation with a personal basis is a standard tactic in popular storytelling, ancient and modern (as is explaining success or cooperation as due to good personal relations, or "chemistry").[16] I propose that with the change of venue of John's activity to Judaea and Jerusalem, and with no political motive for Herod Antipas to be concerned with the actions of a prophet/preacher working there, the gospel authors had no choice but to tell a slightly different story and provide an alternate cause for Herod Antipas to execute John.

Josephus' connection to John the Baptist was much less charged than that of the gospel authors: neither Josephus nor any figure he venerated had been baptized by John, thus possibly acknowledging John's seniority. Josephus did not relegate John to the role of a forerunner of the figure he believed to be messiah: Josephus did not have John himself concede that he was not fit to tie the sandals of the one who was still to come (ibid., 1:4–8 and parallels). Josephus did not write from the perspective of a movement which regarded the followers of John the Baptist as potential members of their own group, who (merely?) needed to be convinced to switch their loyalty from John to some other messianic figure (Matt. 11:11–15//Luke 7:28, 16:16), as had been the case with Apollos of Alexandria. Apollos only knew the baptism of John at first, and preached it boldly in the synagogue, but being fervent in spirit he had already seen that it culminated in Jesus' career. All he needed was to be taught the "more correct" way of God by Priscilla and Aquila at Ephesus, and then he became a most effective preacher for the Christian cause (Acts 18:24–28). Josephus did not believe that disciples of John, such as those whom Paul met in Ephesus, only required to be told that John's mission on earth was pointing to the higher status of Jesus, and then they would become Christian (ibid., 19:1–7). Josephus did not have to argue that a new message was appropriate after John (Matt. 11:13//Luke 16:16). Whatever John the Baptist did, Josephus' version of his career therefore seems less tendentious than the Christian accounts. Attention should first focus on the deviations of the gospel versions from that of Josephus, rather than the other way round.[17]

The historical John, I suggest, was therefore active in the Peraea, and not in Judaea and Jerusalem. As such, he quite naturally came into conflict with Herod Antipas, who feared his growing influence. John's was a messianic scenario in which Jerusalem did not play a part. The gospel authors, however, considered John a forerunner of Jesus, whose messianic career had reached its climax in Jerusalem. Under those circumstances, it was virtually obligatory that the forerunner preach to the same audience, in Judaea and Jerusalem. Hence, the gospel version of John's career was transposed to Judaea and Jerusalem, and he became a messianic figure in whose scenario of redemption Jerusalem played a key role.

Historical Interpretation

Why was Jerusalem a crucial element in some scenarios, but apparently missing in others? One line of explanation would focus on the places of origin of the central figures: those not themselves from the Jerusalem vicinity placed less importance on the city's role in the end of days. This sort of explanation will not help much, however, as it cannot explain Josephus' Egyptian, who promised the conquest of Jerusalem by natural or miraculous means.

Alternately, we should not underestimate the attractions of a desert location

for the decisive acts of the redemption of the world. The desert was traditionally the refuge for those on the lam, in some degree of tension with authorities.[18] As eschatological dramas are based on the hope for change and thus are
inevitably revolutionary in some sense, a desert location may be appropriate.
Furthermore, the sense that the crucial first moments of the finale of human
history should take place in the desert may have been reinforced by aspects of
the biblical tradition, from the crossing of the Jordan as the beginning of the
conquest of the land, to the verse in Isa. 40:3, in which the prophet cries to
prepare the way for the Lord in the desert.[19] A slightly different possibility for
understanding the significance of the desert location is suggested by D. R.
Schwartz. The desert may have been seen as an alternative to the Temple,
which was viewed as hopelessly polluted. Sanctity, for these prophetic figures
active in the desert, was now transferred there (at least temporarily), as it was
for the Qumran community. Ultimately, however, they believed, God would
return to Jerusalem.[20]

For these reasons, the leaders of these messianic movements concentrated
on what was to occur in the desert, as that was truly crucial. Once redemption
was underway, perhaps all the rest would follow by itself, in any case. Recognizing the importance of these inaugural stages, the authorities saw to it that
these movements never got past that point in their careers. Perhaps the dreams
spun out by Theudas, the anonymous figures at the time of Felix, the anonymous figure at the time of Festus, Jonathan the Sicarius, or Josephus' John
the Baptist culminated in Jerusalem, but the Romans or Herod Antipas made
certain that these movements were terminated well before they reached that
stage.

Conclusion

Appeal to hypothetical ends of scenarios, such as in the concluding paragraph
of the previous section, is dangerous speculation. Even the temporary transference of holiness to the desert, like so many other temporary actions, has a
way of becoming permanent when repeated for so long that no other way is
ever experienced, thereby acquiring an aura of seeming natural. Thus, even at
Qumran, the archetype model for a transference of holiness to the desert,
speculation was indulged regarding plans for a rebuilt Jerusalem of the end of
days (5Q15). At the same time, however, the community of the end of days,
as well as the banquet in which the messiahs will participate at that time, were
imagined as taking place wherever the יחד happened to be, certainly not necessarily in Jerusalem or at the Temple (1QSa). For example, the work to be
done by the members of this future community is called עבודת העדה (1QSa

i, 12–1., 19–20). This may be military service[21] or some other aspect of participation in the life of the community, but it is explicitly not Temple service, עבודת קדש, in biblical terminology (e.g., Ex. 36:1).

Given the known variety of prophecies for the end of the world, I would rather conclude as I began: the range of hopes of a better world to come, from which there would be no going back to the "bad old days," was broad enough to include movements of despair,[22] as well as of the triumphalist kind.[23] In at least one example, in 4QMMT, the conviction that the end was imminent was based on a combination of success and failure:

> we recognize that some of the *blessings and curses* have come about that are written in the book of Moses. And this is the end of days, when they will return upon Israel forever (C21–23).[24]

Some visions were held by the members of the lower rungs of society and needed to rise from the bottom up, while others were promoted by the elite and trickled from the top down.[25] In some scenarios, there was a specific human figure who played a critical role in the drama of redemption, in others God or the angels did the work, with little or even no human assistance.[26] In some, Jerusalem was the last stop, in others not.

Notes

1. M. Smith, "What is Implied by the Variety of Messianic Figures?," *JBL* 78 (1959), 66–72. Other articles by Smith which I would include in this category are his "The Common Theology of the Ancient Near East," *JBL* 71 (1952), 135–47; "Palestinian Judaism in the First Century," *Israel: Its Role in Civilization*, ed. M. Davis (New York, 1956), 67–81; "The Dead Sea Sect in Relation to Ancient Judaism," *NTS* 7 (1960), 347–60; "A Comparison of Early Christianity and Early Rabbinic Tradition," *JBL* 82 (1963), 169–76; "Goodenough's *Jewish Symbols* in Retrospect," *JBL* 86 (1967), 53–68.

2. For the purposes of this article, messiah will be used in a restricted sense. I will overlook biblical and other evidence for non-eschatological anointed figures called messiah (Smith, "What is Implied" [above, note 1], 67; "just as there are messiahs without ends, so there are ends without messiahs," ibid., 68) and use the term to refer only to figures somehow connected with the redemption at the end of time.
I prefer, however, to put aside the vexed question of whether to use "messianism" and "messianic" for all eschatological movements, whether or not they were based on a redeemer figure. These terms will be employed here in their literal sense only to describe groups whose vision of the end of time included a redeemer, whether human or angelic. See also below, note 26.

3. Smith, "What is Implied" (above, note 1), 71–72.

4. In particular, Smith suggested that attention be turned to disagreements over the law and over legal authority as likelier candidates for filling the role of the source of the sectarian

impulse. This aspect of Smith's proposal has become extremely popular of late, in the aftermath of the discussion and publication of 4QMMT. See, for example, Y. Sussmann, "Research on the History of the Halacha and the Scrolls of the Judean Desert," *Tarbiz* 59 (1990), 11–76 (Hebrew). I have discussed this matter in greater detail in A. I. Baumgarten, "L. Schiffman, *Law, Custom and Messianism* (review)," *Zion* 58 (1993), 509–13 (Hebrew); and in a monograph entitled *The Flourishing of Jewish Sects in the Maccabean Era: An Interpretation* (Leiden, 1997).

5. J. J. Collins, *The Scepter and the Star* (Garden City, 1995), 1–14, esp. p. 4. In Collins' opinion, the variety can be grouped around four basic paradigms: king, priest, prophet, and heavenly messiah. All the figures to be discussed below fall into Collins' category of prophetic messiah.

6. One of the earliest examples appears in Hag. 2:6–9, but see also Tob. 14:5. Herod, according to Josephus, invoked these hopes when speaking to the people, explaining his plans for renovation and expansion of the Temple (*Ant.* 15, 380–87). See also Herod's criticism of the Maccabees for not having rebuilt the Temple (ibid., 17, 161).

7. For a discussion of this aspect of Ben Sira, see B. Mack, *Wisdom and the Hebrew Epic* (Chicago and London, 1985).

8. For an expanded discussion of one such "inelegant landing" in Jewish experience of antiquity, see A. I. Baumgarten, "Josephus on Essene Sacrifice," *JJS* 35 (1994), 169–83. On the one hand, the Temple authorities forbad Essenes to enter because they followed purity rules of their own. We might expect this decision to have caused the Essenes to cut all ties with the Temple. Nevertheless, Essenes were found in the vicinity of the Temple and continued to send money there, perhaps even paying the half-sheqel Temple tax. As Essenes had no money of their own, having transferred their property to the common fund, gifts could only have been sent to the Temple by the group as a whole, making the implicit recognition of the legitimacy of the institution which excluded Essenes even more puzzling.
For the place of the recognition of disorderliness of reality in the work of an outstanding historian of our century, Christopher Hill, see M. Fulbrook, "Christopher Hill and Historical Sociology," *Reviving the English Revolution—Reflections and Elaborations on the Work of Christopher Hill*, eds. G. Eley and W. Hunt (London and New York, 1988), 45; and M. Heinemann, "How the Words Got on to the Page: Christopher Hill and Seventeenth Century Literary Studies," ibid., 85–86.

9. For a comprehensive treatment of these figures, to which my discussion below is much indebted, see R. Gray, *Prophetic Figures in Late Second Temple Judaism—The Evidence of Josephus* (Oxford, 1993), 114–44. See also Collins (above, note 5), 196–210; D. R. Schwartz, *Studies in the Jewish Background of Christianity* (Tübingen, 1992), 29–43.

10. See E. P. Sanders, *Judaism: Practice and Belief, 63 BCE–66 CE* (London, 1992), 368. For an analysis of Josephus' interest in minimizing the political implications of the Jewish religion in his later works in particular, see Schwartz (above, note 9), 32–33.

11. Collins ([above, note 5], 196–99) concludes that the movements of Theudas and the Egyptian, at the very least, had eschatological content. Cf. Gray (above, note 9), 141–43.

12. In modern movements of this sort, the leaders often promise their followers miraculous immunity from the bullets of the opposing army and/or the assistance of divine forces, which will give the believers special weapons with extraordinary powers. See, e.g., P. Worsley, *The Trumpet Shall Sound—A Study of "Cargo" Cults in Melanesia*[2] (New York, 1968), 141. As Worsley notes, in one modern instance the army of the rebels was divided into units, with leaders of various ranks, specialists such as doctors, ministers, and radio operators, and their own flags. The troops were armed with wooden rifles, which would be transformed into real weapons at the Coming. A holy drink guaranteed invulnerability: bullets striking the user's body would turn to water. In that sense, the victory promised is both realistic and miraculous. The

conclusion in these modern examples can be disastrously grim. The results for the followers of the Egyptian were no less catastrophic by the standards of the time than the outcome in modern cases. This encourages me to think that other aspects of the movement led by the Egyptian prophet were analogous to circumstances in equivalent modern movements. If this conclusion were accepted, it would help reconcile the apparent contradiction between the accounts in Josephus' two works. Cf. Gray (above, note 9), 116–18.

13. According to Josephus, as might be expected at such moments of despair, there were numerous prophets assuring the people that help from God was soon to arrive. Josephus felt the need to give these messages an unfavorable interpretation, hence he explained that these prophets were motivated by payment by the tyrants of Jewish Jerusalem who were suborned to delude the people and thus minimize desertions (*War* 6, 286).

14. The willingness to engage in extreme anti-rational behavior, to take possessions, and cross the Jordan shows the high level of commitment that Theudas was able to evoke.

15. See especially J. Meier, "John the Baptist in Josephus: Philology and Exegesis," *JBL* 111 (1992), 225–37. Less successful, and more prone to turning John into a politically correct and socially responsible figure, who appealed to the proper audience in antiquity (those few members of the relatively privileged classes who still had some sensitivity to injustice and were receptive to his apocalyptic-eschatological message), and thus of the sort that every decent liberal modern should admire, is P. Hollenbach ("John the Baptist," *Anchor Bible Dictionary* [Garden City, 1992], III, 887–99).

16. I have discussed the place of interpersonal relations as an explanatory cause in ancient storytelling; A. I. Baumgarten, "Rabbinic Literature as a Source for the History of Jewish Sectarianism in the Second Temple Period," *Dead Sea Discoveries* 2 (1995), 31–34.

17. This is not to claim that Josephus' account was tendency-free. Josephus' interest in playing down the eschatological side of John's career has been noted above. As one expression of that bias, Josephus made a point to stress that John was harmless and that Herod Antipas erred in suspecting him. Herod Antipas, according to the people and Josephus, was appropriately punished for his evil deed. A modern reader may wonder whether John was so politically benign. Indeed, one recent author, J. D. Crossan (*Jesus—A Revolutionary Biography* [San Francisco, 1995], 43) concludes that John was erecting "a giant system of sanctified individuals, a huge web of apocalyptic expectations, a network of ticking time bombs all over the Jewish homeland." While this evaluation draws heavily on John of the gospels, it applies, albeit with diminished force, to Josephus' John as seen in the eyes of Herod Antipas. Is any prophet preaching a message that is received by the multitudes with "an excitement that reached a fevered pitch" (*Ant.* 18, 118), whether in an eschatological context or not, ever free of the suspicion of sedition in the view of the authorities? Whether the historical John was that innocent and/or why Josephus wanted to present John that way are questions we cannot answer with certainty. For a reconstruction of the historical John and a guess at Josephus' motives in his description, see Meier (above, note 15), 234–37. See also H. Lichtenberger, "The Dead Sea Scrolls and John the Baptist: Reflections on Josephus' Account of John the Baptist," *The Dead Sea Scrolls—Forty Years of Research*, eds. D. Dimant and U. Rappaport (Leiden and Jerusalem, 1992), 340–46.

18. See Schwartz (above, note 9), 35.

19. This is quoted in order to explain the fact that its community is at Qumran in 1QS viii, 13–16.

20. Schwartz (above, note 9), 35–43.

21. L. Schiffman, *Law, Custom and Messianism in the Dead Sea Sect* (Jerusalem, 1993), 278 (Hebrew).

22. The classic statement of this position is that of D. Aberle, "A Note on Relative Dep-

rivation Theory as Applied to Millenarian and Other Cult Movements," *Millennial Dreams in Action*, ed. S. Thrupp (The Hague, 1962), 209–14.

23. On this point, see further A. I. Baumgarten, "The Pursuit of the Millennium in Early Judaism," *Tolerance and its Limits in Early Judaism and Early Christianity*, eds. G. Stanton and G. Stroumsa (Cambridge, 1997).

24. This mixture, a bit odd at first sight, can be illuminated by modern Jewish parallels, in which the assessment that now is both the best of times (as proven by Israeli successes, such as that of 1967) and the worst of times (as indicated by specific failures, such as the Holocaust or the blatantly secular nature of the Israeli government) is the most powerful proof that now must be the dawning of the redemption. For the modern evidence, see further A. Ravitzky, *The Revealed End and the Jewish State: Messianism, Zionism and Religious Radicalism in Israel* (Tel-Aviv, 1993), 149 (Hebrew). I owe this idea to a suggestion of Professor Joel Marcus, Glasgow. The dilemma posed by section C of 4QMMT as a whole, and by this passage in particular, is such that even when 4QMMT was finally formally published, after more than a decade of delay, there was no full-scale discussion of section C. As J. Strugnell concludes in his "Afterword," (*Discoveries in the Judean Desert X, Qumran Cave 4, V, Miqsat Maase ha-Torah*, eds. E. Qimron and J. Strugnell [Oxford, 1994], 205): "such an important study remains to be done." My interpretation should be contrasted with that proposed by L. Schiffman, "The New Halakhic Letter (4QMMT) and the Origins of the Dead Sea Sect," *BA* 53 (1990), 66–67, and esp. p. 72, note 7.

25. W. Lamont, *Godly Rule: Politics and Religion 1603–60* (London, 1969). See also the review of this book by B. S. Capp, "*Godly Rule* and English Millenarism," *Past and Present* 52 (1971), 106–17, and Lamont's response, which I find convincing: "Richard Baxter, The Apocalypse and the Mad Major," *Past and Present* 55 (1972), 68–90. I have discussed the implications of Lamont's thesis for the study of Judaism in antiquity in a paper presented at the Second International Taubes Center Colloquium, on "Apocalyptic Time," Bar Ilan University, Ramat Gan, Israel, February, 1996. This paper will be revised and submitted for publication in the proceedings of that conference.

26. In spite of the limitations imposed for the purposes of this paper, some discussion of the accepted range of meaning of the terms "messianism" and "messianic" is necessary. A term means what those who employ it find it useful to mean, and is not limited by its etymology. In discussing the term "messiah" (above, note 2), it was helpful for the purposes of this paper to be bound by one aspect of its literal meaning, but to disregard another. To take another example, scholars have found it enlightening to apply the term "millenarian" to many movements that do not believe in the coming of a thousand-year period of one sort or other, hence its range of meaning has expanded. Should one allow or encourage the same expansion to happen to "messianism" and "messianic"? Would that add confusion, or would it evoke common characteristics among groups which might otherwise be overlooked? My inclination is to expand the permissible range of meaning of "messianic" and to argue that such development is beneficial. In the contemporary Jewish world at the time of writing this study, there are two active movements regularly called messianic—one of Habad hasidism and the other of the religious-political right in Israel, to be roughly categorized as Gush Emunim. The former has a specific human candidate for the role of messiah and remains convinced of his appropriateness for the role in spite of the apparent disconfirmation dealt their beliefs by his death, while the latter does not have a specific candidate for the role, but is nevertheless widely (and I would argue, correctly) viewed as a messianic movement. There is much that unites these groups, from the circumstances which encouraged their flourishing, to their responses to events in Israel, to the risks they would encourage the larger society to take as a result of their convictions, and to their possible fates if irrevocably disconfirmed. These similarities emerge more clearly when both

movements are designated as "messianic." The same is true, I propose, for ancient Judaism. Cf. Y. Talmon, "Millenarian Movements," *Archives Européennes de Sociologie* 7 (1966), 169; Collins (above, note 5), 11–14, 33–37. For a position closer to mine, see G. Nickelsburg, "Salvation Without and With a Messiah: Developing Beliefs in Writings Ascribed to Enoch," *Judaisms and Their Messiahs at the Turn of the Christian Era*, eds. J. Neusner et al. (Cambridge, 1987), 49–68, esp. the summary, p. 65.

7

Jerusalem and its Temple in
Early Christian Thought and Practice

E. P. SANDERS

This paper will be divided into four parts: Jesus, Paul, Luke, and "everybody else." There is quite a lot to say about Jesus, Paul and Luke, and so everybody else will receive very little attention.

Jesus

I assume that Jesus was born into an average Jewish Galilean family and that he inherited views typical of his time and place. New Testament scholars are presently suffering through one of the periodic attempts to reevaluate Jesus, and this has resulted in new views about Jesus and his society: Galilee was as hellenized as any part of the Roman empire, Jesus spoke Greek, he attended the theater at Sepphoris where the Greek classics were performed (difficult to do, since the theater was built at least fifty years after his death[1]), his teaching relates more closely to Greek cynicism than to Jewish prophecy or wisdom instruction, and he was more likely to travel to Tyre or Sidon than to Jerusalem.[2] I think that the explanation of these views is simple. Some New Testament scholars are disturbed by the fact that Jesus was thoroughly Jewish, and they are responding to this problem by claiming that the Galilee was thoroughly hellenized, and Jesus along with it.

I shall not discuss this view any further, but merely offer my understanding of the form of Judaism that Jesus inherited. I think that Jews in the Galilee spoke Aramaic as their principal language, that they attended the synagogue on Shabbat, that they were immersed in the Bible and its depiction of Jewish history and God's will, that the farmers were fairly reliable to tithe and offer first fruits, that most people regularly purified themselves by immersion in *miqva'ot*, and that they made pilgrimage to Jerusalem to attend one of the festivals as often as they reasonably could, offering the appropriate sacrifices there.[3] In the words of S. Freyne, "insofar as any urban center dominated the cultural life of the Galilee, it would seem that it was Jerusalem, not the Hellenistic cities, that had the controlling influence over the majority of the population."[4]

If this is true, Jesus inherited the view that Jerusalem and the Temple were of prime importance. Accordingly, I assume that before he began his public career as healer, prophet, and teacher, Jesus had traveled to Jerusalem several times, that on each trip he spent a week being purified of corpse-impurity, and that he then worshipped in the Temple by offering birds or quadrupeds to be sacrificed.

Despite this, Jerusalem and its Temple are not major themes of Jesus' teaching as we now have it. The surviving material in the gospels, of course, was collected in Greek, and the gospels were written after the destruction of the Temple. Moreover, they were transmitted and used by an increasingly gentile Christian movement, for which Jerusalem was not very important. Some material dealing with the Temple and its service may have been lost. There are, however, a few passages attributed to Jesus about Jerusalem and the Temple, all of them favorable. I shall mention the most prominent: (1) Jesus told his followers to be reconciled with other people before presenting a gift at the altar (Matt. 5:23–24); (2) after healing a leper, he told the man to show himself to a priest and to offer for his purification what Moses commanded (Mark 1:40–44); (3) he called the Temple the dwelling place of God (Matt. 23:21); (4) he forbade swearing by Jerusalem because "it is the city of the great King" (Matt. 5:35); (5) this passage is a little more complicated. It is a lament over Jerusalem: "Jerusalem, Jerusalem, killing the prophets and stoning those who are sent to you! How often would I have gathered your children together as a hen gathers her brood under her wings, and you would not!" (Matt. 23:37–39; Luke 13:34–35). This lament is obviously a criticism of Jerusalem*ites*, but it implies the importance of the city itself.

In addition to these five passages, we should also note the lack of negative material about the priesthood. The gospels, especially Matthew, contain passages in which Jesus denounces the Pharisees or the scribes (e.g., Matt. 23:1–36; Mark 12:37–40), but not equivalent passages attacking the priesthood or the sacrificial system. There is, however, an implicit criticism that some priests and Levites cared too much about purity in the story called the Parable of the Good Samaritan (Luke 10:29–37).

The material in the gospels that is attributed to Jesus was subject to change, expansion, and reduction before it was written in our gospels, and we cannot know with certainty that Jesus himself uttered all the sayings just listed, nor that he never criticized the priesthood. I think, however, that the gospels are reliable in a general way: they present the main themes of Jesus' words and deeds.[5] In any case, the only information that we have about Jerusalem in the teaching of Jesus is favorable.

If, then, Jesus saw Jerusalem and the Temple in a positive light, why did he, in about the year 30, enter the Temple precincts and overturn some tables used by moneychangers and sellers of doves (Mark 11:15–19 and parallel passages in the other gospels)? There are three theories. One is that he found these transactions to be defiling and that he thought that some of the Temple officials were dishonest. According to this view, he was a moderate reformer: he approved of the Temple but wanted its administration to be more spiritual and more honest. This view has often seemed self-evident because the gospels quote Jesus as saying, after he overturned the tables, "Is it not written, 'My house shall be called a house of prayer for all the nations'? But you have made it a den of robbers" (Mark 11:17, quoting Isa. 56:7; Jer. 7:11). There are, however, reasons to doubt this interpretation. One is simply that the gospel writers often quote passages from the Hebrew Bible to show that Jesus "fulfilled" them. The saying attributed to Jesus, which conflates two prophetic passages, could easily have been supplied later. More telling is the point mentioned above: as far as we know, Jesus did not otherwise attack the priesthood, the Temple, or Jerusalem. His overturning of the tables was probably the immediate cause of his death, and he must have known, before he did it, that it was a dangerous action. It seems probable, then, that there would be some other indication that he was a cultic reformer if that were the explanation of this last, fatal, gesture.[6]

The second interpretation of the overturning of the tables in the Temple area is that Jesus was a radical reformer: he fundamentally disapproved of major aspects of his native religion, especially those having to do with sacrifices and purity. According to one scholar, for example, "House of prayer for all the nations"—that is, the gentiles—indicates the reason for Jesus' action. He wanted Judaism to drop its purity practices, centered on the Temple, and admit gentiles freely.[7] Again, however, the other evidence does not support this view. According to the gospels, Jesus limited his own ministry to Israel (Matt. 15:24; cf. Matt. 10:5–6). He had few contacts with gentiles, and some of these were not overly cordial (Mark 7:24–30; Matt. 15:21–28; the passage includes calling the gentiles "dogs"). Moreover, we should recall once more Jesus' favorable references to Jerusalem and the Temple. These do not reveal that he wanted to open the Temple to gentiles.

The third opinion is that the overturning of the tables should be interpreted in accord with Jesus' sayings about the destruction of the Temple. In this case, the physical action is a symbolic gesture representing destruction. Sayings predicting or threatening the destruction of the Temple are very deeply embedded in the New Testament traditions about Jesus. According to all three synoptic gospels, he predicted that "Not one stone [of the Temple] will be left on another" (Matt. 24:2; Mark 13:2; Luke 21:6). According to the story of Jesus' arrest and trial before the high priest and his council, he was first charged with threatening to destroy the Temple before he was charged with blasphemy (Matt. 26:51; Mark 14:58). While he hung on the cross, some passers-by taunted him: "you who would destroy the Temple, save yourself" (Matt. 27: 40; Mark 15:29–30). The tradition even appears in Acts, according to which the first martyr, Stephen, was accused of saying that Jesus of Nazareth will "destroy this place," obviously the Temple (Acts 6:14).[8]

It is my own view that Jesus' act of overturning the tables of moneychangers should be understood in light of these statements about the destruction of the Temple.[9] Even if someone wishes to maintain the traditional interpretation of the event—that he was cleansing the Temple of dishonesty—it must still be granted that he also threatened or predicted that the Temple would be destroyed. We rephrase our question: Why would a good and loyal Jew, who believed in the Bible, predict the Temple's destruction? It is most doubtful that Jesus had suddenly come to the opinion that the slaughter of animals was inappropriate as a way of worshipping God. Nothing in the gospels points in that direction, and his followers, as we shall see, were not opposed to the Temple as such. The best explanation seems to be that he expected the Temple to be destroyed so that when the kingdom of God arrived a new one would be built, one made without human hands ("without hands": Mark 14:58). I think that Jesus was an eschatological prophet, a prophet who expected God himself to interrupt human history and create a new and better world, one in which Israel was redeemed and restored, and in which the gentiles, too, would come to worship the God of Israel.[10] I shall not elaborate on this general view here, but if it is correct, the prediction of the destruction of the Temple fits perfectly. This eschatological expectation is rare in Jewish literature that is more or less contemporary with Jesus, but it does occur, most notably in the Temple Scroll from Qumran.[11]

To summarize: Jesus held fairly conventional views about Jerusalem and the Temple: he thought that they were central. He was, however, an eschatological prophet, and he expected that the Temple would be replaced in the coming kingdom of God.

Paul

We turn now to Paul, a Jew from Asia Minor, who was first a persecutor of the Christian movement and later a convert to it. He became, in his own words, apostle to the gentiles (Rom. 11:13). He was not the only one, but he clearly considered himself the preeminent one; I am inclined to think that this was, in fact, the case. Paul's letters are the earliest books in the New Testament. Most were written between the years 50 and 60 of the Common Era. The gospels are a few decades later, having been composed in the seventies, eighties, or nineties. The book of Acts, written by the author of Luke, was probably composed in the nineties. Thus, Paul's letters, not Acts, are the best sources for the first years of the Christian movement.

Paul's letters reveal that the disciples of Jesus, all of whom were Galileans, had established Jerusalem, not Galilee, as the center and headquarters of the early movement. Paul had an ambiguous relationship with the Jerusalem apostles, which is revealed in a few sections of his letters. I shall briefly summarize the first two chapters of Galatians, which respond to the charge that he was a second-hand apostle dependent on Jerusalem, and not an authoritative figure who could make important decisions, such as whether or not gentile converts to Christianity had to observe all of the Jewish law. In this conflict, Jerusalem was not the central issue, but nevertheless it reveals the general early Christian assumption that Jerusalem was the natural headquarters of the new movement.

In Galatians, Paul names Peter, James the brother of Jesus, and John as the "pillars" of the church in Jerusalem (Gal. 1:18–19; 2:9). He emphatically insists, however, that his own mission was given to him directly by revelation, and that he was not dependent on the Jerusalem pillars (1:1; 1:11–12; 1:17; 2:6). After the Lord appeared to him, he writes, he went to Arabia, then back to Damascus; he did not even visit Jerusalem until three years later (1:17–18). Fourteen years later he made his second trip to Jerusalem. He insists that he was again guided by revelation (not, therefore, by a summons), and he emphasizes that the Jerusalem apostles "added nothing" to him (2:2; 2:6). But he also confesses that he was worried lest he had run in vain (2:2). The meaning of this phrase is not certain. It is not probable that Paul doubted the truth of his message, but he may have wondered whether or not the church was being split into two factions, one Jewish, the other gentile. In any case, he was eager to prove solidarity between the gentile converts and Jerusalem, and for this purpose he agreed to take up a collection from his gentile churches and give it to the poor in Jerusalem (2:10).

I think that we may assume that in these two chapters of Galatians, Paul overstated his complete independence, but it is also probable that he was basically telling the truth. At one point in the narration of his dealings with the Jerusalem pillars, he takes an oath: "In what I am writing to you, before God, I do not lie" (1:20). Paul believed in God, and I doubt that he would take an oath before God if he were deliberately lying.

We learn from this a lot about Paul's personality and something of his career. We see behind the passions of Galatians, however, not only that Paul considered himself an emissary of God, commissioned directly from heaven, but also that Jerusalem held a central place in the early Christian movement. If Paul's mission resulted in a complete rupture with Jerusalem, he would have run in vain. After shaking hands with the pillar apostles and agreeing to take up a collection, he spent the rest of his life—except when he was imprisoned—collecting and delivering money for Jerusalem.

Jerusalem also figures in one of the more difficult passages in Galatians, an allegory based on the story of Sarah and Hagar. I shall quote it in full.

> Tell me, you who desire to be under law, do you not hear the law? For it is written that Abraham had two sons, one by a slave and one by a free woman. But the son of the slave was born according to the flesh, the son of the free woman through promise. Now this is an allegory: these women are two covenants. One is from Mount Sinai, bearing children for slavery; she is Hagar. Now Hagar is Mount Sinai in Arabia; she corresponds to the present Jerusalem, for she is in slavery with her children. But the Jerusalem above is free, and she is our mother. For it is written, "Rejoice, O barren one who does not bear; break forth and shout, you who are not in travail; for the children of the desolate one are many more than the children of her that is married" (Isa. 54:1). Now we, brethren, like Isaac, are children of promise. But as at that time he who was born according to the flesh persecuted him who was born according to the Spirit, so it is now. But what does the scripture say? "Cast out the slave and her son; for the son of the slave shall not inherit with the son of the free woman" (Gen. 21:10). So, brethren, we are not children of the slave but of the free woman. (Gal. 4:21–31)

This is not a very good allegory, since Hagar has two meanings: both Mount Sinai and Jerusalem. Part of Paul's meaning is nevertheless clear: on one side stand Hagar, her descendants, Mount Sinai, Jerusalem, and slavery; on the other, Sarah, her descendants, and freedom. The descendants of Hagar are *now* ("so it is now") persecuting the descendants of Sarah, and Paul identifies himself and his readers with Sarah's descendants ("we," "us").

What is less clear is the identity of the two sides. For centuries, Christian exegetes have thought that the two covenants of freedom and slavery represent Christianity and Judaism.[12] This interpretation goes along with the view that Galatians is an attack on Judaism. This is a complete misreading. Galatians is an attack on competing Jewish-Christian missionaries who want the gentiles who have faith in Jesus also to be circumcised and accept the entire law of Moses. Paul was of the view that his gentile converts should become monotheists, worshipping the God of Israel, and that they should accept Jewish ethics, especially sexual ethics. They should not, however, be required to accept those parts of Judaism that separated Jew from gentile in the Diaspora— circumcision, food, and "days" (the Sabbath and other holy days).[13] This is the sole topic of the letter. At no point does Paul consider Judaism per se. For that, we must wait until Rom. 9–11.

The allegory of Sarah and Hagar is Paul's third argument from the Abraham story (the first is Gal. 3:6–8, the second 3:15–18). It is very highly probable that it was Paul's Christian opponents who had introduced Abraham into the debate when they tried to persuade Paul's gentile converts to be circumcised. Paul tried to reverse the argument and to prove that the story of Abraham shows that circumcision is not necessary—despite Gen. 17, which he carefully does not mention. The allegory in Gal. 4 should be read in light of the overall argument of Galatians and in particular the arguments from Abraham. That is, it is part of the intra-Christian debate over the requirement of circumcision.

The context in Galatians, almost by itself, determines the meaning of the allegory. I shall, however, briefly indicate some revealing details:

1. Just before the allegory, Paul had written that he was again "in travail"— in the agony of childbirth—"until Christ be formed in you" (4:19). That is, he was afraid that his churches in Galatia had become the offspring of competing Christian apostles and needed to be born again of their true parent—himself. It is no surprise, then, that the allegory deals with childbirth. Paul is, in effect, identifying himself with Sarah and his enemies with Hagar.[14]
2. The contrast of "freedom" and "slavery," and the connection between slavery and Jerusalem, go back to Gal. 2:4, where "false brothers" in Jerusalem tried to force Titus, one of Paul's gentile assistants, to be circumcised.[15] This would have meant slavery not only for Titus, but also for "you," the Galatians (2:5).

These two points suffice to show that the allegory is quite at home in the overall context of the letter, especially the other arguments from Abraham, and in ch. 4 in particular, as part of Paul's argument against the position of "false brothers"—Christians, especially Jewish Christians, who disagreed with him about the conditions that gentiles had to fulfill in order to belong to the people of God in the last days. In Paul's view, the only condition was faith in Jesus Christ, accompanied by monotheism and ethical purity; in theirs, it was faith in Jesus, plus acceptance of circumcision and the rest of the law. Paul viewed his enemies as trying to enslave his gentile converts by requiring circumcision, and their home base was "present Jerusalem."

The reference to persecution in Gal. 4:29 requires an additional word. The allegory applies the story of Sarah and Hagar to Paul's own situation, and the similarity that proves the connection is persecution: "as at that time he who was born according to the flesh persecuted him who was born according to the Spirit, so it is now."[16] In and of itself, persecution in Paul's letters could refer to the persecution of the Christian movement by non-Christian Jews, and that, of course, is the way this verse has usually been read. We know with certainty that at least some non-Christian Jews persecuted some Christian Jews, since Paul attributes this activity to himself prior to his call to be an apostle of Jesus (Gal. 1:13; I Cor. 15:9). This does not, however, establish the conventional view (that the allegory contrasts Christians with non-Christian Jews), since Paul saw all groups other than Pauline Christians as persecuting himself and hindering his mission. He had been:

> in danger from rivers, danger from robbers, danger from *my own people* [non-Christian Jews], *danger from gentiles*, danger in the city, danger in the wilderness, danger at sea, danger from *false brethren* [anti-Pauline Christians]. . . . (II Cor. 11:26)

Every place, every group, was dangerous. Given the overall context of Galatians, we should assume that persecution in Gal. 4:29 refers to persecution of Pauline Christians and especially of Paul himself by "false brothers"—other Christians.

This explanation of the allegory has considerable consequence for understanding the "present Jerusalem" and the "Jerusalem above" in Gal. 4:25–26. Paul is not thinking of the "present Jerusalem," which is in slavery, as the Jewish capital city, but rather as the city that harbors the headquarters of the Christian movement, which is too greatly dominated by the "false brothers" who wish to enslave Paul's gentile converts. "Jerusalem above" is the "mother" of those who maintain that gentiles can belong to the people of God without being circumcised. The contrast of the passage is not Christianity vs. Judaism, but rather Pauline Christianity vs. that of Paul's opponents.

We turn now to a third aspect of Paul's letters, which is, I think, even more interesting and important for the topic of this volume. In Paul's last surviving letter, written to Rome, probably from Corinth, he reflects on his past quarrels and difficulties, his present situation, and his future hopes. Moreover, he describes his vocation. I shall quote a few of the key passages:

- Inasmuch as I am apostle to the gentiles, I magnify my ministry in order to make my fellow Jews jealous, and thus I shall save some of them (Rom. 11:13–14).
- I want you to understand this mystery, brethren: a hardening has come upon part of Israel, until the full number of the gentiles come in, and thus all Israel will be saved (11:25–26).
- I tell you that Christ became a servant to the circumcised to show God's truthfulness, in order to confirm the promises given to the patriarchs, and in order that the gentiles might glorify God for his mercy . . . Isaiah says, "The root of Jesse shall come, he who rises to rule the gentiles; in him shall the gentiles hope" (15:8–9, 12, quoting Isa. 11:10).
- [I am] a minister of Christ Jesus to the gentiles in the priestly service (*hierogounta*) of the gospel of God, so that the offering of the gentiles may be acceptable, sanctified by the Holy Spirit (Rom. 15:16).

These passages and others show that Paul set his career within a framework that is very common in Jewish sources from the exilic period through the first century C.E.; at the end of the ages, or the climax of history, the tribes of Israel will be gathered, and the gentiles will come to Jerusalem bearing gifts and worshipping the God of Israel.[17]

At the time he wrote Romans, Paul had finished taking up his collection for Jerusalem, and he and some gentile delegates were about to take the offering there, before he, Paul, returned to the West. He planned to go to Rome and then on to Spain, so that he would have converted gentiles over a vast area (15:22–29). Then the Lord would return, and all Israel, and in fact all gentiles as well, would be saved (11:25-32). This conception explains why he wrote that he was carrying out a priestly service: he was taking the expected tribute of the gentiles—both money and people—to Mount Zion. This act fulfilled part of the prophecies.

But as he reflected on how close this expectation was to fulfillment, he realized that things were not working out as they should. He had done his job, fulfilled his calling—he had won gentiles. But Peter, James, John, and the others had been less successful in persuading Jews to accept Jesus. This is the implication of much of Rom. 11, where Paul states that he "magnifies" his ministry to the gentiles, "*in order to make [his] fellow Jews jealous, and thus [he would] save some of them*" (11:13–14). Though he was apostle to the gentiles, here he assigns himself some role in winning Jews. It is probable that the need to give himself a part in this endeavor stemmed from his realization that Peter and the others had not, in fact, won enough Jews. The Jewish eschatological scheme that Paul inherited was that first Israel would be gathered, and then the gentiles would bring gifts and join in the worship of God. But, in Paul's view, the gentiles were ready first. Then what about the Jews? To meet this problem, Paul reversed the scheme. The gentiles would come in, and this would make the Jews jealous, so that they would join, and thus he, Paul, apostle to the gentiles, would manage to save some Jews as well. He would do so indirectly, by creating jealousy, but clearly Peter and James needed some help! This conception is surprising, and so I shall repeat one of the passages:

> I want you to understand this mystery, brethren: a hardening has come upon part of Israel, until the full number of the gentiles come in, and *thus* (*houtōs*: in this manner) all Israel will be saved (11:25–26).

The scheme is reversed, Israel will be saved by Paul's gentile mission.

The view that gentiles would be ready for the arrival of the Lord before Jews was, of course, Paul's original contribution to what I have called Jewish restoration theology.[18] But I wish to emphasize once more that the basic scheme was widespread. It appears in the biblical prophets, and in rather a lot of post-biblical literature. Above I proposed that Jesus himself had held at least some aspects of this expectation, and Paul's letters confirm its importance in early Christianity, making it even more likely that the basic hope goes back to Jesus. Jerusalem and the Temple were central to the biblical passages predicting the assembly of the tribes of Israel and the pilgrimage of gentiles, and thus they were also central to early Christian eschatological hope.

There is a fourth and final point to be made about Jerusalem and the Temple in Paul's letters. Already before Paul, early Christians had come to see Jesus' death as an atoning sacrifice. According to Paul's inherited formula, people who believe in Christ are "justified by [God's] grace as a gift, through the redemption which is in Christ Jesus, whom God put forward as an expiation by his blood, to be received by faith" (3:24–25).[19] It would be very easy to draw from this view of Jesus' death the conclusion that the sacrifices of the Temple had become superfluous—and Christians did eventually draw that conclusion. We do not, however, see this in Paul's letters. He thought that the coming of Christ annulled those parts of the Jewish law that separated Jews from gentiles in the Diaspora: circumcision, food, and days. But he did not apply his Christology to the question of Temple worship. He says nothing against it, and in Rom. 9:4 he lists "the service"—the service of the Temple—as one of God's important gifts to Israel.

Romans, written just before Paul took the "offering of the gentiles" to Israel, is his last surviving letter. According to Acts, when he reached Jerusalem with his gentiles and their offering, he was accused of taking Greeks into the Temple (21:28). I do not, of course, know that Paul actually did this, but he could have. He could have had the view that the coming of Christ meant not that the Temple was now useless, but rather that gentiles who believed in him should also have access to it. In any case, there is nothing against the Temple in Paul's letters, and there is the positive point that he saw Jerusalem as the natural end-point of his own mission to the gentiles.

Luke

The same man wrote the gospel according to Luke and the Acts of the Apostles. These works, like most of the other early Christian literature, were written anonymously. The gospels seem first to have been named "according to Luke," etc. in the second half of the second century. For convenience, however, I shall follow the usual custom of calling the author of the third gospel and the book of Acts "Luke." Luke held what New Testament scholars often call a Jerusalemocentric view of the world. This is an ugly word, which simply means that he put Jerusalem in the center of his story as much as he could. One of the concerns of Acts is to show the shift of the Christian community to its next major center, Rome, but the gospel of Luke and most of the book of Acts are indeed Jerusalemocentric; Paul reaches Rome only at the end of Acts.

Luke accepted the fact that Jesus was from Nazareth and that he spent most of his public career in the Galilee, but he still inserted Jerusalem into the story more often than did Matthew and Mark. Luke depicts Mary and Joseph as bringing the infant Jesus from Galilee to the Temple in order to present him to the Lord as the firstborn son (2:22–4). He states that Jesus' family went to Jerusalem for every Passover, and that when Jesus was twelve he entered into a learned discussion with teachers in the Temple (2:41–51).

Most striking in Luke's presentation, after Jesus was crucified, is that the disciples remained in Jerusalem rather than fleeing to the Galilee, as Matthew and Mark have it (Mark 14:28; 16:7; Matt. 26:32; 28:7; 28:16). Consequently the resurrection appearances in Luke and Acts all take place in or near Jerusalem (Luke 24; Acts 1:1–12).

The early chapters of Acts show the disciples as active missionaries in Jerusalem, and Luke also emphasizes that they worshiped in the Temple (3:1).

Finally, according to Acts, Jerusalem was Paul's home base. Paul carried out his first career, persecution of the Christian movement, from Jerusalem. There he obtained letters from the high priest that would allow him to go to Damascus and bring back in bonds those who followed "the way" (as Luke calls the Christian movement). Moreover, after Paul was converted to the Christian cause near Damascus, he made his way as soon as he could to Jerusalem (not three years later, as in Gal. 1:18), where he preached to Jerusalemites and disputed with Hellenists (9:26–30). Paul's own statement contradicts this. He states that he was unknown to the churches in Judaea until his second trip, fourteen years after his first, which was three years after his conversion (1:22). I shall not give the details of the rest of Paul's career according to Acts, but the view of that book is that Paul was under orders from Jerusalem, that the church there sent him on missions to Asia Minor and Greece, and that when each mission was concluded he dutifully reported back to Jerusalem. Paul's own view, as we noted above, was that he was independent of Jerusalem, went there only twice before his final visit, and went in response to revelation. Acts' depiction of Paul's career must be very much like the one that made Paul so angry when he wrote Galatians.

Finally, we should note what is not in Luke-Acts: the eschatological pilgrimage of Jews and gentiles to Jerusalem. Luke was concerned to downplay eschatology. He wanted to depict Christianity as a well-established ongoing movement in the Roman empire, peaceful and non-threatening. Hot eschatology is often a little threatening to society.

How much of Luke-Acts can we believe? The legends of Jesus' infancy and childhood are probably only legends, though in general they are not unlikely: probably Jesus really did go to Jerusalem often. I doubt very much Luke's theory that the disciples stayed in Jerusalem after Jesus' execution. They probably fled to the Galilee, as Mark and Matthew state, though they did not stay there. Their home base was Jerusalem, as Luke says, though Paul's letters are better evidence. There is no reason to doubt that members of the early Christian community in Jerusalem worshipped in the Temple. I do not believe Luke's account of Paul's career. If Acts is strictly correct, Paul was telling lie after lie in Galatians. As I indicated above, I can believe he exaggerated, but not that he swore by God that he was telling the truth, while telling deliberate lies. In short, I find only parts of Luke's Jerusalemocentric theory convincing.

We do, however, see something very important happening in Luke and Acts. By the end of the first century, Jerusalem and the Temple were of historical and symbolic importance, but no longer the focus of Christianity. Luke's biggest concern was the question, Who are the people of God?[20] He, of course, wanted the Christians to be the true people of God. One of his tactics was to show that Christianity grew out of Jewish *Heilsgeschichte* and that the Christians had inherited the right to be the true worshippers of the God of Israel. Luke wanted close continuity with the faith and history of Israel, and he achieved this by tying the Christian movement to Jerusalem even more strongly than it actually was. He no longer, however, thought of the eschatological pilgrimage to the Temple, and so that connection between the Christians and Jerusalem found no place in his account. Jerusalem was rapidly becoming a romantic symbol of the origin of Christianity in the bosom of the biblical faith.

"Everybody Else"

It would be moderately interesting to describe the way in which Ignatius of Antioch used the Temple and the altar as metaphors for the Christian life, or to discuss the typology of Hebrews and the Epistle of Barnabas, or the new Jerusalem described in the book of Revelation.[21] But when we reach Luke, we have come to one of the main ways in which Jerusalem figures in Christian literature after Paul: Jerusalem was of historical importance as the place where Jesus died and as the first center of Christian activity. It was less and less often seen as a center of a living religion. Moreover, although Christian eschatological expectations did not entirely vanish (as R. Wilken has shown),[22] nevertheless Jerusalem was less frequently the object of Christian hope for the future. More often, Christians saw heaven as their future hope, not a new Jerusalem.

I would like to close, however, by returning to the role of Jerusalem in the first Christian generation. Paul's eschatological hope, which was probably shared by all the first Christians, included the expectation of the gentiles' pilgrimage to Jerusalem. When he wrote Romans, he, representative gentiles, and their tribute were about to depart for Jerusalem, in accord with the biblical prophecies, all of which would be fulfilled when the Redeemer came from Zion (Rom. 11:26).

Notes

1. E. Netzer and Z. Weiss, *Zippori* (Jerusalem, 1994), 16–19.

2. Some of the principal works are: F. G. Downing, *The Christ and the Cynics* (Sheffield, 1988); B. Mack, *A Myth of Innocence* (Philadelphia, 1988); T. Longstaff, "Nazareth and Sepphoris: Insights into Christian Origins," *Anglican Theological Review* 11 (1990), 8–15; J. D. Crossan, *The Historical Jesus: the Life of a Mediterranean Jewish Peasant* (San Francisco, 1991); R. Batey, *Jesus and the Forgotten City. New Light on Sepphoris and the Urban World of Jesus* (Grand Rapids, 1991); H. C. Kee, "Early Christianity in the Galilee: Reassessing the Evidence from the Gospels," *The Galilee in Late Antiquity*, ed. L. I. Levine (New York and Jerusalem, 1992), 3–22. There are family resemblances among these scholars, but not all hold all the views in my brief summary. See my "Jesus in Historical Context," *Theology Today* 50 (1993), 429–48.

3. This is the traditional view of Galilean Judaism. For my own treatment of common Judaism, see *Judaism: Practice and Belief* (London and Philadelphia, 1992).

4. S. Freyne, "Urban-Rural Relations in First-Century Galilee: Some Suggestions from the

Literary Sources," *The Galilee in Late Antiquity*, ed. L. I. Levine (above, note 2), 75–91, here p. 81.

5. For an account of the problems involved in studying the gospels, tests for "authenticity," and using the material to reconstruct Jesus' career, see E. P. Sanders and M. Davies, *Studying the Synoptic Gospels* (London and Philadelphia, 1989), esp. chapters 20–22.

6. On "cleansing" the Temple (purging it of dishonesty), which is the majority view, see my *Jesus and Judaism* (London and Philadelphia, 1985), 61–63.

7. M. J. Borg, *Jesus: A New Vision* (New York, 1987), 175. See earlier idem, *Conflict, Holiness and Politics in the Teaching of Jesus* (New York and Toronto, 1984).

8. On the problem of the historicity of this accusation, see C. Hill, *Hellenists and Hebrews* (Minneapolis, 1992), 54–69.

9. Sanders (above, note 6), chapter 1; idem, *The Historical Figure of Jesus* (London and New York, 1993 and 1995), 254–62.

10. Sanders (above, note 6), chapter 3; 237–41; see also the index, s.v. "Jesus: As prophet of restoration." More recently, see my *Historical Figure of Jesus* (above, note 9), 238–39, 259–64.

11. 11QTemple 29.8–10. See further Sanders (above, note 6), 84–86.

12. See the discussion by J. L. Martyn, who opposes this view: "The Covenants of Hagar and Sarah," *Faith and History. Essays in Honor of Paul W. Meyer*, eds. J. T. Carroll, C. H. Cosgrove and E. E. Johnson (Atlanta, 1990), 160–92, here pp. 160–69. The present discussion is deeply indebted to this article. The most insightful treatment prior to Martyn was that of C. K. Barrett, "The Allegory of Abraham, Sarah, and Hagar in the Argument of Galatians," *Essays on Paul* (London, 1982), 154–70 (originally published in 1976).

13. E. P. Sanders, *Paul, the Law, and the Jewish People* (Philadelphia, 1983; London, 1985), 100–104.

14. On the imagery of childbirth, see Martyn (above, note 12), 174–78.

15. Ibid., 181.

16. Paul apparently read Gen. 21:9 as meaning that Ishmael persecuted Isaac, rather than played with him. Scholars often explain this by referring to rabbinic exegetical traditions, such as an interpretation attributed to R. Ishmael in T Sotah 6:6. Paul was also, however, quite capable of reading present events back into the biblical text, as in I Cor. 10:2, where he claimed that "our fathers" "were baptized into Moses in the cloud and the sea," despite the fact that according to Ex. 14:22 they crossed the sea "on dry ground." Paul's "baptized" is necessary in order to make his typological exegesis come out right.

17. On Paul and the eschatological "pilgrimage of the gentiles," see Sanders (above, note 13), 171–73 and notes 3 and 5 there (pp. 199–200). On Jewish eschatological views of gentiles, see idem (above, note 6), 213–18.

18. See the index to my *Jesus and Judaism* (above, note 6), s.v. "Jewish restoration theology."

19. It is generally accepted that Rom. 3:25–26 is based on a pre-Pauline formula. See B. F. Meyer, "The Pre-Pauline Formula in Rom. 3.25–26a," *NTS* 29 (1983), 198–208. The word translated "expiation" is *hilastērion*, which is used in the Septuagint to refer to the lid of the ark of the covenant, on which the blood of the sin-offering was sprinkled on the Day of Atonement (Ex. 25:17; Lev. 16:15).

20. C. C. Hill, *Hellenists and Hebrews* (Minneapolis, 1992), 75, who cites earlier discussions.

21. Both Hebrews and Revelation are discussed by R. Wilken, *The Land Called Holy: Palestine in Christian History and Thought* (New Haven and London, 1992), 52–56.

22. Ibid., esp. chapter 3.

8

Jerusalem as the *Omphalos* of the World: On the History of a Geographical Concept

PHILIP S. ALEXANDER

Jerusalem has evoked many images, but none is perhaps more vivid and abiding than that of the Holy City as the center and navel of the earth. A series of medieval Christian maps, of which the Hereford *mappa mundi* is perhaps the best known, has given this idea graphic expression by depicting the world as a circular landmass surrounded by Ocean, with Jerusalem at its center, the circle of its walls following the line of the earth's rim and hinting at the city's perfection and spiritual supremacy. Often reproduced, the symbolism of these charming artifacts has passed into popular consciousness. But where and when did this concept originate, and what message or messages has it been used to convey?

The first clear reference to Jerusalem as the navel of the earth occurs in the book of Jubilees, a retelling of the book of Genesis composed in Hebrew in Palestine in Second Temple times. The importance of Jerusalem, its favored location, and even its centrality within its region, are certainly mentioned in earlier Jewish texts, but it is only in the second century B.C.E. in Jubilees that we find for the first time a clear cartographic image of the world as a whole, with Jerusalem placed at its center and called "the navel" of the earth. The relevant passage comes from Jubilees' treatment of the division of the world among the sons of Noah after the flood:

> And he (Noah) knew that the Garden of Eden is the holy of holies and the Lord's dwelling place, and Mount Sinai the center of the desert, and Mount Zion the center of the navel of the earth: these three were created as holy places facing each other.[1]

There are problems with this text and unfortunately neither the Greek nor the Hebrew survives to help us solve them. The phrase "the center of the navel of the earth" seems curiously tautologous and we might suspect that "navel" has been added secondarily, perhaps in the Greek or the Geez. Why not simply "center of the earth," matching "center of the desert?" Zion's designation as the "navel" does, I would suggest, have a point and was probably in the original text. It serves to rank Sinai and Zion. Both are "holy," both are "centers," but whereas Sinai is only the center of the desert, Zion is the center of the world and its *omphalos*. The resonant epithet *omphalos* establishes Zion's higher status.[2]

The geographical centrality of Jerusalem is presented by the author of Jubilees in a very concrete way. His treatment of the Table of the Nations in Gen. 10 projects a remarkably vivid *imago mundi*, one so coherent and cartographic that it probably once existed as a drawn map. The world is visualized as a more or less circular landmass surrounded by the waters of ocean, its disc bisected east-west by a median running through the Garden of Eden and the Straits of Gibraltar, and north-south by a median running through Mount Zion and Mount Sinai. The medians intersect at Zion which stands, consequently, at the center of the earth.[3]

What exactly does the author of Jubilees mean by asserting that Zion is the "navel" of the earth? We must be careful not to read too much into his use of the word. The concept of the center of the earth plays an important role in many religious worldviews and is associated with an impressive, and remarkably constant, set of mythological ideas. But it would be wrong to assume that every time the phrase "the navel of the earth" occurs, it invokes automatically this whole nexus of ideas. There may be distant echoes of mythology in Jubilees (note, for example, that the "navel" is a mountain), but fundamentally Jubilees is not expressing mythology. Indeed, its sober geography is remarkable for its *absence* of mythology and stands in striking contrast to the fantastic geography of its contemporary, I Enoch. The Jubilees' reference to Zion as "the navel of the earth" must be considered in the context of the message of the Jubilees world map as a whole, and in that setting it can be seen first and foremost as a political statement. It is part of the anti-Greek political rhetoric of the Jubilees *mappa mundi*.

I would suggest that when the author of Jubilees refers to Zion as the navel of the earth, he does not have earlier Jewish or Semitic ideas primarily in mind,[4] but rather contemporary Greek claims that Delphi is the *omphalos* of the world. There were a number of *omphaloi* in Greece, but Delphi was the *omphalos* par excellence. Its status as such was enshrined in national folklore and literature, and the *omphalos* stone at Delphi was a major tourist attraction which featured on coins.[5] Delphi was a pan-Hellenic shrine and doubtless its claim that it was the navel of the earth was intended to support its national status. Its role within Greek religion can be compared to the role of the Jerusalem sanctuary within Judaism. There is every possibility, then, that the author of Jubilees could have known this Greek tradition.

Early Ionian geographers took up this popular Greek mythology and gave it cartographic form. Although the details of the early Ionian maps are obscure, it is probable that they represented the *oikoumene* as a circular disc (Herodotus derides them for being "compass-drawn"), that Delphi was the midpoint, and that the landmass of the world was divided into three continents—Europe, Asia, and Libya (= Africa). Dicaearchus was later to relocate the midpoint of the world. He envisaged an east-west axis running from the Straits of Gibraltar, through Syracuse, the Peloponnese, along the Cicilian coast and the Taurus mountains (seen as a long spine stretching across northern Syria) to India. His north-south axis was drawn from Lysimachia in Propontis to Alexandria in Egypt and bisected the east-west axis at Rhodes. However, the older maps seem to have had Delphi at the center and it was this image of the world which apparently persisted, largely resistant to advances in geographical knowledge, as the world-map of educated Greeks well into the current era.

The author of Jubilees took this standard Ionian map and recast it unto a biblical frame. He correlated the three sons of Noah with the three Ionian continents—Japhet = Europe, Shem = Asia, and Ham = Libya—using the rivers Nile and Dan (as did certain Ionian cartographers) to demarcate their respective territories. And he relocated the *omphalos* of the world from Delphi to Jerusalem. This view, which I have argued at length elsewhere, has recently encountered some criticism.[6] So let me restate the evidence for it as succinctly as I can. The use of the Don and the Nile to delimit the territories of Noah's three sons is a clear Ionian feature on the Jubilees map, which indicates that the author of Jubilees knew the Ionian geographical tradition. This conclusion is reinforced by the presence of other details on the map which almost certainly did not come from earlier *Jewish* tradition. Note, for example, its visualization of the coastline of the northern Mediterranean, with its "tongues" of land (Italy and Greece) jutting out into the sea.

Where is the Jewish antecedent for this? The image is so vivid that it points to a cartographic precursor. So, too, when Jubilees talks about the "great islands" to the northwest of Europe (the British Isles), where is the Jewish source? This is not just the vague biblical "islands of the sea"; the islands are precisely located. It is true that there are scattered hints in the Bible that the earth is circular, and certain, largely poetic, passages speak of the centrality of Jerusalem to the Land of Israel, or even vaguely to the world, though, as we shall presently see, it is doubtful whether earlier Jewish tradition ever called Jerusalem the "navel" of the earth. It is also true that, according to the Bible, Noah had three sons who parceled out the world between them after the flood.

Jubilees is not saying anything radically new. Its image of the world is consonant with earlier Jewish world geography, such as it was, which is hardly surprising since biblical geography and Ionian geography may have common roots in Babylonian geography. But nowhere before Jubilees do we find these scattered elements drawn together so clearly and convincingly. This synthesis is less easy to achieve than one might suppose. In my view, the crucial stimulus toward achieving it was provided by an encounter with the Ionian world map.

A consideration of the general program of the Jubilees map confirms the impression that its assertion of Jerusalem's centrality is essentially polemical and political. We must recall the historical setting of the book. Jubilees dates to the mid-second century B.C.E. Its appearance coincided with the Hasmonean revolution, which caused a profound intensification of religious life in Palestinian Judaism. The Hasmoneans redefined the concept of Jewish territoriality, the relationship of Israel to the Diaspora, and possibly even the concept of what it meant to be a Jew. They re-drew the political map of the Middle East by first establishing the independence of the Jewish territory from Greek hegemony, and then expanding *Jewish* hegemony over neighboring non-Jewish territory and creating a greater Israel. Jubilees attempts to give de jure justification for both these de facto developments. Note, first, its treatment of the Greeks on its world map. Javan (Greece) is a son of Japhet, and so his patrimony, according to the Jubilees schema, belongs to Europe, which ends at the Bosphorus. The Greeks, therefore, have no right of residence in Asia, and in usurping land there they are breaking the solemn agreement entered into by the sons of Noah after the flood. Positing Jerusalem as the *omphalos* of the world is an integral part of this polemic: it is a political gesture of great symbolic significance.[8]

Jubilees also seems to have tried to underpin the legitimacy of the territorial expansion of the Hasmonean state. In this context, its treatment of Canaan is noteworthy. As a son of Ham, Canaan had to be assigned on the Jubilees schema a patrimony in Africa (the area round Carthage was cleverly chosen for him[9]). However, in migrating from Ararat after the flood, Canaan saw the so-called "Land of Canaan," liked it and seized it, thus violating the covenant between the sons of Noah. The "Land of Canaan" was, in fact, allotted to Arpachshad, the ancestor of Abraham. We have here a polemical reversal of the "Canaanite" "Joshua the brigand" traditions, which claimed that it was the *Jews* who had usurped the Land.[10]

The author of Jubilees used the Medes as a foil to the Canaanites. The Medes, as sons of Japhet, were assigned territory in Europe—the British Isles, in fact—but having migrated to their patrimony they did not like it (the weather may have been a problem), and so they returned to the Middle East

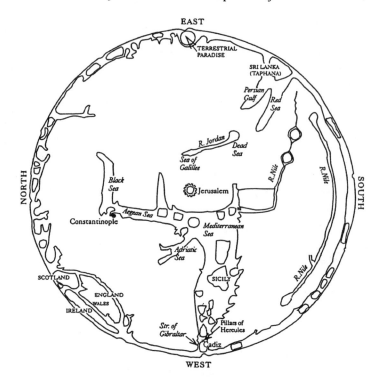

Figure 1: The Hereford *Mappa Mundi*
(after the simplified hand-copy in K. Miller, *Mappae Mundi*, IV [Stuttgart 1896], 2)

and settled in the allotment of Shem. There was, however, a difference. The Medes occupied their new territory amicably, by negotiation and agreement. This story about the Medes is otherwise unknown. The author of Jubilees probably made it up as a telling contrast to the violence of the Canaanites.[11] Maps, even modern scientifically-surveyed ones, are ideological constructs. What features are selected for representation, how they are named, the choice of meridians, the projections used, and the resultant distortions of size and relationship are not value-free, but often involve political statements. The Jubilees map is no exception. It was, arguably, propaganda for the Hasmoneans and embodied their political aspirations in much the same way as Marcus Agrippa's "map" erected in the Forum at Rome embodied Augustus' vision of the Roman world order.[12]

I would like now to consider the question of whether Jerusalem or any other locality is referred to in the Bible as "the navel" of the earth. The expression *tabbur ha-'aretz*, applied to Mount Gerizim in Judg. 9:37 and to

Jerusalem in Ezek. 38:12, has certainly been given this sense, ever since the Septuagint rendered *tabbur* as *omphalos*. But it is very doubtful whether this translation is historically correct. The contexts of both references are vague and it is hard to see why such strong metaphorical language should have been used. It is more likely, as S. Talmon has suggested, that *tabbur* has a neutral geographical sense, perhaps something like "plateau," or "rounded hill."[13] The root טבר is not attested in early Semitic. *Tibbur* occurs in mishnaic Hebrew and in later Jewish Aramaic in the anatomical sense of the umbilicus, and from there it was passed on to modern Hebrew. Particularly noteworthy is B Yoma 85a which states, in accordance with early medical theory, that the formation of the embryo begins from the *tibbur*. But this later usage can hardly be decisive for the early meaning of the word. Old Hebrew had another term for the umbilicus, derived from the root שרר and found in Ezek. 16:4 and Cant. 7:3.[14]

Moreover, mythological motifs normally associated with the navel of the earth—for example, that some physical feature (a rock or a mountain) marks the spot from which the earth grew—are also not prominent in the Bible. These ideas are found in Babylonia and Egypt, but they are not obvious in ancient Hebrew literature. Wensinck tried to prove that belief in a navel of the earth was universal among the western Semites, but his methodology is, to say the least, dubious. He lumps together sources from widely different periods and places to create a highly synthetic picture. When we introduce a diachronic perspective it becomes clear, as Talmon rightly observed, that all Wensinck's clear Jewish evidence comes from post-biblical *aggadot*. Behind Wensinck's account seems to lie the view, fashionable in his day, that there existed in the distant past a universal folk-religion, a sort of perennial philosophy, one element of which was a set of ideas about the navel of the earth. This is speculative and would command little support today.

I know of only two sources that may plausibly be seen as anticipating Jubilees. The first is I Enoch 26:1, where, in his cosmographical account of his world tour, Enoch says: "I was transported to the middle of the earth, and I saw a blessed place, in which were trees and saplings surviving and burgeoning from a felled tree." The "blessed place" here, as in 27:1, is the land of Israel, and the place at the center of the earth is Jerusalem, an unmistakable topography of which follows, though in keeping with the fictional setting of the narrative the name Jerusalem itself is not used. This passage in I Enoch belongs to the Book of the Watchers, which was probably redacted in the second half of the third century B.C.E., that is, earlier than Jubilees. Given that the author of Jubilees unquestionably knew the Enochic literature, we may well conclude that he knew this passage of I Enoch. We are certainly getting close to Jubilees' position, but we are still not quite there. It is one thing to say that Jerusalem is the *middle* of the world and another to say that it is the *navel* of the earth, and to realize this assertion in clear cartographic form. The latter implies the former, but not vice versa.

The other possibly antecedent source is the Septuagint, which, as we have already noted, rendered *tabbur* in Judges and in Ezekiel by the Greek *omphalos*. In the latter text there is a link with Jerusalem. However, we cannot be sure whether the Greek translations of these two books pre-date or post-date Jubilees. The rendering of *tabbur* as *omphalos* is striking and full of potential. It is probable that the Septuagint here, as so often elsewhere, is reflecting Palestinian Jewish exegetical tradition. The word *tabbur*, it should be recalled, occurs only twice in the Hebrew Bible and its sense is very uncertain. This uncertainty may have been exploited already in the late Second Temple period, and Ezek. 38:12 used as a convenient biblical "peg" on which to hang the doctrine of Jerusalem as the navel of the earth. The Septuagint reflects this Palestinian tradition. In other words the equation *tabbur* = *omphalos* in Ezek. 38:12 is not a distinctive Alexandrian invention, but represents Palestinian exegesis—the same Palestinian exegesis as is implied by Jubilees.

To sum up: I would suggest that the doctrine of Jerusalem as the navel of the earth can be traced back no earlier than the Hasmonean revolution of the second century B.C.E. It is first clearly attested in Jubilees, whose author used it for polemical purposes to support aspects of the political propaganda of the Hasmonean state.

Once launched, the idea had a long and vigorous life, in both Christianity and Judaism. First, the Christian tradition. Though explicit statements occur from time to time in Christian writers, asserting the geographical centrality of Jerusalem and calling it the *omphalos* of the earth, it is Christian cartography that expresses this idea most powerfully. This brings us back to the Hereford *mappa mundi*. Even at a glance the similarity of the Hereford map to the reconstructed Jubilees map is striking. Is this accidental? I would argue not: a convincing line of transmission can, in fact, be constructed linking the Hereford map direct to Jubilees.

We know that the author or creator of the Hereford map was one Richard of Holdingham, and that it was drawn, probably at Lincoln, in the late thirteenth century, though it was taken almost immediately to Hereford, where it has remained to the present day.[15] It belongs to a collection of maps which show a strong family likeness. These include both the large, detailed images like the Hereford *mappa mundi*, and the little T-O and T-Y maps, which are probably stylized pictograms or logos created by scribes who were daunted by the challenge of copying the complex, full-scale map. P. D. A. Harvey argues

Figure 2: The Jubilees *Mappa Mundi*
(after P. S. Alexander, *Anchor Bible Dictionary*, II [New York, 1992], 982)

that this whole group of *mappae mundi* belongs to "a single, much ramified tradition which must go back to the Roman period," at least to the fifth century.[16] He suggests that the original was a Roman map "measured" and "reasonably accurate," "showing coastal outlines, mountains, rivers, towns and boundaries of provinces," which has become more and more garbled with successive copying. Parts of this original, more accurate, map have, however, been preserved. In this context he points to the map contained in an eleventh-century Cotton manuscript,[17] which displays a strikingly more correct coast-line for the North Sea and the English Channel. He raises the question of the possible relationship between this original Roman map and the Marcus Agrippa map, set up in Rome on the orders of Augustus and based on a survey of the empire initiated, according to tradition, by Julius Caesar. He notes that Dilke is in favor of such a link, whereas Brodersen is not, on the grounds that the Agrippan map was not an image, but a written text.[18]

Parts of Harvey's tradition-history are plausible, but parts are not. That the ancestor of the Hereford family of maps goes back at least to the fifth century is a conclusion demanded by the basic stemmatics of the manuscripts. But that the ancestor-map was some sort of official Roman world map, based on information derived from the efficient Roman methods of surveying, seems to me to be totally off-target. In fact, I would suggest that Harvey and other historians of cartography are guilty of naively misreading the Hereford map.[19] The Hereford map, and the others like it, were never meant to be "real" geography. Their significance was symbolic and theological right from the start. The Hereford map was so seriously out of joint with the geographical knowledge of its day that it cannot have been intended to be taken literally. Educated people, as Harvey correctly observes, already accepted by the thirteenth century that the world was not a flat disc but a globe, and many would have subscribed to the theory that in the southern hemisphere lay a continent matching our own, the *terra incognita* or *australis,* cut off from northern lands by the burning and impassable tropics.[20] This *terra australis* has actually been added to the Beatus *mappa mundi,* thus destroying its symmetry. There is surprisingly little contemporary information in the Hereford map.[21] Its image was already antiquated when it was produced. It is a survival from an earlier age, cherished more for theological than for strictly geographical reasons. It was not meant to function like a modern school atlas to inform people about the "real" world, but as a stylized visual aid to assist pious meditation and reflection.[22]

The Hereford map belongs primarily to a tradition of Christian symbolic and mythical geography for which the real world was of little moment. Jerusalem was central to this geography, but this "Jerusalem" was not strongly identified with the physical city in the land of Palestine. In certain Christian sources, the physical Jerusalem does indeed stand at the center of the physical world.[23] Thus, a widespread Byzantine tradition puts the *omphalos* in Jerusalem, though significantly—in contrast to Jewish tradition—it is precisely located in the Church of the Holy Sepulchre and not on the Temple Mount. This polemical relocation of the navel of the earth is apparently reflected in the sixth-century Madeba mosaic map, which shows Jerusalem as (more or less) a circle with the Church of the Holy Sepulchre at its center, and which pointedly ignores the Temple area. Christian and Jewish geography thus drew quite different maps of the same small space.

However, for most Christian writers, Jerusalem was a spiritual entity which the Christian could experience anywhere. Other great cities, Rome, Constantinople, Aachen, could become "Jerusalem." "Jerusalem" could even be created in one's local church by the erection of stations of the cross and of "calvaries." Ambivalence towards the Land of Israel goes back to earliest Christianity. The spiritualization of "Jerusalem" is found already in the New Testament: Paul in Gal. 4:25–26 regards the metropolis of the Church as being not the "present Jerusalem" which is "in slavery with her children," but the "Jerusalem above" which is free. It is true that from time to time there have been upsurges of Christian interest in the real Jerusalem. Constantine's beautification of the city with fine buildings in the fourth century raised its importance in Christian consciousness and promoted pilgrimage. At the time of the Crusades, there was a strong feeling that the actual places of Christ's life and passion were important and should be seized back from the Muslims. And in the nineteenth century, European Christianity became obsessed with the realia and archaeology of the Bible. Why these upsurges should have occurred, and what they tell us about the spirituality of the ages which produced them, are intriguing questions which we cannot pursue here. Suffice to note that this interest was the exception rather than the rule. For the most part, Christianity has been indifferent to the actual "Holy Land" and the actual "Holy City." Against this background, to find fault with the cartography of the Hereford map is rather misplaced and involves a misjudgment of its purpose and the nature of its geography.

The ancestor of the Hereford map was probably similar in outline to the Hereford map itself, though occasionally this tradition may have been revised and smartened up, as in the Cotton manuscript, by reference to "real" maps. The roots of this image lie not in Roman "scientific" cartography, but in a symbolic Christian world-map originating in the East, an idiosyncratic version of which is found in the works of the sixth-century writer Cosmas Indicopleustes. This early Christian map was, in turn, more or less identical to the Jubilees map and may well have been descended from it. It should be borne in mind that Jubilees circulated in a Greek version in the Greek East and is quoted by a number of Byzantine scholars.[24] Also relevant is the type of early Christian text known as a "Division (*Diamerismos*) of the World." A classic example of this genre, worked and reworked in Latin and Greek throughout late antiquity, is found in the Chronicle of Hippolytus (§§44ff.). These *Diamerismoi* contain a detailed ethnography based on the Table of the Nations in Gen. 10. They are, in many respects, verbal analogues to the medieval *mappae mundi*, and some of them may show the influence, whether direct or indirect, of Jubilees. I would suggest, then, that a plausible case can be made for the descent of the Hereford map from the Jubilees map. Jubilees represents the *fons et origo* of an *imago mundi* which prevailed in Christian Europe almost down to the time of Columbus.

Finally, some remarks on later Jewish tradition. Jewish-Greek literature yields a few interesting references to the centrality of Jerusalem. Philo, in his *Embassy to Gaius* (§294), claims that Jerusalem is "situated in the center of the world." Josephus, in the *War* (3, 51–52), defines Judaea as stretching from the Jordan River to Jaffa, and writes: "the city of Jerusalem lies at its very center, and for this reason it has sometimes, not inaptly, been called the 'navel' of the country." A similar tradition is echoed earlier in the *Letter of Aristeas* (83), where it says that Jerusalem is "situated in the center of the land of Judah on a high and exalted mountain (cf. Isa. 2:2)."

But the most significant developments of the idea are to be found in rabbinic texts. The *locus classicus* is in the Tanḥuma to Leviticus (Qedoshim 10, ed. Buber, 78):

> As the navel is in the middle of the person, so is Eretz Israel the navel of the world, as it is written, "That dwell in the navel of the earth" (Ezek. 38:12). Eretz Israel is located in the center of the world, Jerusalem in the center of Eretz Israel, the Temple in the center of Jerusalem, the *heikhal* in the center of the Temple, the ark in the center of the *heikhal,* and in front of the *heikhal* is the *'even shetiyyah* from which the world was founded (שממנה הושתת העולם).

What is striking about the rabbinic traditions is how they testify to the remythologization of the concept of the navel of the earth. I argued that in Jubilees there is no sign of mythology; the navel of the earth is a geopolitical concept used to locate Jerusalem on the terrestrial plane and to assert its political importance. In the rabbinic sources, however, the original mythological associations of the idea come flooding back. The mythology is clear in the Tanḥuma passage quoted above. Jerusalem has cosmogonic significance. It is the first created place from which the rest of the world grew outward concentrically. The "navel" is linked with the *'even shetiyyah*, a stone or rock supposedly located within the Temple which marked the exact spot from which the world developed like a foetus from the umbilical cord.[25] Related to this may be the tradition that Adam was created from earth taken from the Temple Mount. The original thought, as found in II Enoch 71:35,[26] was probably that it was appropriate that humanity should arise from the same spot from which the physical world grew; Jerusalem was not only the *tabbur* of the world, but the *tabbur* of humanity as well. In rabbinic tradition, however, the aggadah is given a rather different twist: it was appropriate that Adam should be formed from the place where later atonement should be made for his sins.[27]

In rabbinic literaure, the concept of the navel of the earth belongs to a constellation of mythological motifs which define Jerusalem as an *axis mundi*. In Jubilees, Jerusalem is the focal point only of the horizontal, terrestrial plane. In rabbinic texts, however, it has vertical as well as horizontal centrality: it is the focal point of different, superimposed planes. The Temple in Jerusalem and Jerusalem itself stand over against the heavenly Temple and the heavenly Jerusalem; Jerusalem, the terrestrial midpoint, corresponds to Jerusalem the celestial midpoint.[28] Jerusalem also corresponds, in a downwards direction, to Gehenna, the center of the underworld, an entrance to which is located near the Holy City. And the 'even shetiyyah, on which the Ineffable Name is inscribed, serves as a capstone to seal the waters of the abyss and prevent them welling up and overwhelming the world.[29] Jerusalem is the point where heaven, earth, and the underworld meet—a veritable *axis mundi*.

Here, too, it seems possible to introduce a diachronic perspective. In tannaitic sources, as in the Bible, there are general statements about the centrality of Jerusalem. The map of the concentric circles of holiness surrounding the Temple in M Kelim 1:6–9 is a pertinent example. But this idea undoubtedly gains precision and force in the amoraic period, when it is linked to renewed speculation about the navel of the earth. And although they are occasionally quoted in Babylonian sources, these traditions all appear to be Palestinian in origin. The relationship between M Yoma 5:2 and later texts illustrates this development. There it is stated that the 'even shetiyyah, has been in the Temple "from the days of the first prophets." Even allowing that the time reference of "from the days of the first prophets" is vague and probably means simply "from time immemorial,"[30] the language is odd if the 'even shetiyyah is being thought of as the navel of the earth, since, by definition, the 'even shetiyyah is the oldest thing on earth and has always been there. However, in the corresponding passage of the Tosefta (Yom ha-Kippurim 2:14, ed. Lieberman, 237–38) the cosmogonic function of the 'even shetiyyah is clearly introduced and sets the tone for the comments in the Jerusalem and Babylonian Talmuds, and for later midrashic texts in general. These later ideas were attached to the 'even shetiyyah by the common midrashic device of etymology. The mysterious word shetiyyah is derived either from the root שתת, "to found" (hence "stone of foundation," i.e., foundation stone of the world), or from the root שתה, "to weave" (hence "stone of weaving," involving comparison of the act of creation to the weaving of cloth).[31] Thus the 'even shetiyyah provided a convenient peg on which Palestinian amoraic authorities were able to hang certain speculations about the cosmic and theological centrality of Jerusalem.

Why might these ideas have been stressed in Eretz Israel in amoraic times? Again, we may suspect a political purpose. Rome also regarded itself as the center of the world, the hub of a network of roads leading outward to the edges of its empire. This was symbolized by the *miliarium aureum* in the Forum, the "golden milestone," which "in letters of gilt, indicated the mileage from Rome along the trunk roads to key points in the empire."[32] The amoraic sages seem to have increasingly regarded Rome and Jerusalem as rivals, particularly after the empire became officially Christian and went over to "heresy." J. Neusner has suggested that this rivalry is a major motif of Genesis Rabbah.[33] The rabbinic story which circulated in amoraic times, that Rome was founded when an angel stuck a reed into the sea and a mud-bank grew round it on which the city was built,[34] reads like a parody of the story of the creation of the world from the *'even shetiyyah* in Jerusalem. The new emphasis on Jerusalem as the navel of the earth may be part of this anti-Roman rhetoric. Alternatively, it may have been intended for an internal, Jewish audience. I. Gafni has argued that the new stress on the importance and centrality of the Land of Israel which he finds in Palestinian amoraic sources reflects an emerging political struggle between the rabbinic schools of Eretz Israel and Babylonia.[35] The religious authorities in Palestine, alarmed by the growing reputation of the Babylonian academies, began to highlight ideas which asserted or implied the primacy of Eretz Israel. Perhaps the *tibbur ha-'olam* and the *'even shetiyyah* traditions were employed as part of this propaganda. If either of these suggestions is correct—and they are not mutually exclusive—then, once again, for all its mythological color, the assertion that Jerusalem is the navel of the earth is intended, as in Jubilees, primarily to serve political ends.

Notes

1. Trans. R. H. Charles, revised Ch. Rabin in H. D. F. Sparks (ed.), *The Apocryphal Old Testament* (Oxford, 1984), 38.

2. It is also possible that the *omphalos* here is the city of Jerusalem, which could not, in keeping with the fictional standpoint of the narrative, be named, and that Zion is the center of Jerusalem. The author of Jubilees may also have intended a contrast between "the desert" (= the uninhabited world) and "the earth" (= the inhabited earth, the *oikoumene*). The implication that the place of the giving of the Law was in the center of unoccupied territory to which no people had laid claim could have aggadic overtones. Neither of these readings of the text would materially affect my argument.

3. This I take to be the meaning of the statement, "these three were created as holy places *facing each other.*"

4. On these, see A. J. Wensinck's classic study, *Ideas of the Western Semites concerning the Navel of the Earth* (Amsterdam, 1916). It should be noted, however, that the vast majority of Wensinck's sources date from well after the time of Jubilees.

5. W. H. Roscher, *Omphalos* (Leipzig, 1913; repr. Hildesheim, 1974).

6. See my essay "Notes on the 'Imago Mundi' of the Book of Jubilees," *JJS* 33 (1982), 197–213, and my article "Early Jewish Geography" in the *Anchor Bible Dictionary,* II (New York, 1992), 980–82. J. M. Scott (*Paul and the Nations* [Tübingen, 1995], 16–24) thoroughly reviews my position and makes some constructive criticisms. Less satisfactory is J. Maier, "Zu

ethnographisch-geographischen Überlieferungen über Japhetiten (Gen 10, 2–4) im frühen Judentum," *Henoch* 13 (1991), 157–94.

7. A point well argued by F. Schmidt in his "Naissance d'une géographie juive," *Moïse géographe*, ed. A. Desremaux and F. Schmidt (Paris, 1988), 13–30.

8. It would also have served as a useful reminder to the Jewish Diaspora of the centrality of Jerusalem. Propaganda is usually aimed as much at "insiders" as "outsiders."

9. The choice is clever because it exploits the fact that Carthage was a Punic (i.e., Canaanite) settlement. This lends an aura of historical credibility to the claim. The implication may be that at least *some* Canaanites did finally reach their patrimony, perhaps having been sent on their way by Joshua and the Israelites.

10. Procopius, *De bello vandalico* X, 13–22.

11. However, as with the Canaanites, there may be an element of historical realism in the Jubilees account of the Medes. The author of Jubilees knew full well that the Medes historically lived in Asia. That caused problems for his neat schematization, which the story of relocation helped to solve. He probably arrived at the British Isles as their original patrimony by a process of elimination. Having assigned the other parts of Europe to the sons of Japhet, only the northwest was left for the Medes.

12. On the Agrippan map, see below, note 18. The suggestion that Jubilees intends to support the Hasmoneans may be greeted with some scepticism. Jubilees is normally regarded as anti-Hasmonean. It was certainly popular with the Dead Sea sect, who were bitter opponents of the Hasmoneans. Moreover, Jubilees advocated a solar calendar and not the luni-solar calendar which prevailed in the Hasmonean-controlled Jerusalem Temple. However, it is not implausible to suggest that Jubilees and the Dead Sea sect may have supported the concept of a greater Israel, while denying the Hasmonean claim to the high priesthood and the legitimacy of the Temple cult. Significantly, the doctrine of a greater Israel is found not only in Jubilees but in the Genesis Apocryphon as well (1QGenAp. XXI).

13. See his excellent article *har* in *TDOT*, eds. G. J. Botterweck and H. Ringgren (Grand Rapids, 1978), III, 437–38; and further: H. Eshel and Z. Erlich, "The First Battle in the War of Abimelech with the Lords of Shechem and the Question of the *Tabbur Ha-'aretz*," *Tarbiz* 58 (1988–89), 111–16 (Hebrew).

14. The absolute form of the word is uncertain. *BDB* and Talmon suggest *shor*, the dictionaries of Alkalay and Even-Shoshan *shórer*. See further below on the possibility that the Septuagint translation of Ezek. 38:12 reflects Palestinian Jewish exegesis.

15. See P. D. A. Harvey, *Mappa Mundi: The Hereford World Map* (London, 1996), where the older bibliography is cited. The map, which is on a single piece of parchment, is 1.58 x 1.33 m.

16. Ibid., p.22.

17. British Library, Cotton ms. Tiberius B.V., f. 56v.

18. Harvey (above, note 15), 24–26. On the Agrippan map, see further C. Nicolet, *Space, Geography and Politics in the Early Roman Empire* (Ann Arbor, 1991), 95–122. Curiously, Julius Caesar's survey of the empire is alluded to in the bottom left corner of the Hereford map, but this, in my view, cannot be used to link the Hereford map to the Agrippan map. It is simply a learned piece of *doctrina* on the part of Richard of Holdingham or some other medieval scholar.

19. The impatient strictures of Beazley, a historian of cartography, on the Hereford map are typical: "The non-scientific maps of the later Middle Ages, contrasted with the portolani, are of such complete futility; they affect the history of earth-knowledge (at least from the thirteenth century) so little; and their chief types have already been so fully discussed, that a bare allusion to the monstrosities of *Hereford* and *Erbstorf* should suffice" (C. R. Beazley, *The Dawn of Modern Geography*, III [Oxford, 1906], 528).

20. See J. K. Wright, *The Geographical Lore of the Time of the Crusades* (New York, 1965), 53–57.

21. On possible contemporary influences on the Hereford map, see Y. Friedman, "The City of the King of Kings: Jerusalem in the Crusader Period," *The Centrality of Jerusalem: Historical Perspectives*, eds. M. Poorthuis and Ch. Safrai (Kampen, 1996), 190–216.

22. The map seems originally to have formed the central element of a triptych (Harvey [above, note 15], 11–15). A location on the wall behind the altar, bringing the image into spatial relationship with the sacrament, would have been highly suggestive. The detail of the map would not, of course, have been visible to the congregation, only the general impression of the outline of the world, though two sites of salvation-history—Jerusalem and the Red Sea, which was colored bright red—would probably have stood out. The map may also have been used for catechetical purposes. In this case, people would have been brought up close to it and had its details pointed out to them.

23. Wright (above, note 20), 259–61.

24. R. H. Charles (*The Book of Jubilees* [London, 1902], xxvi–xxvii) gives a partial list of quotations.

25. See the parallels in T Yom ha-Kippurim 2:14 (ed. Lieberman, 237–38); J Yoma 5, 4, 42c; B Yoma 54b; and further: L. Ginzberg, *The Legends of the Jews*, 7 vols., reprint (Philadelphia, 1968), V, 14–16 (the fundamental discussion of these traditions), and p. 292; Z. Vilnay, *Legends of Jerusalem* (Philadelphia, 1987), 5–36.

26. "He, Melkisedek, will be priest and king in the place Akhuzan, that is to say, in the centre of the earth, where Adam was created, and there will be his final grave" (trans. F. I. Andersen, in *The Old Testament Pseudepigrapha*, I, ed. J. H. Charlesworth [New York, 1983], 208).

27. Genesis Rabbah 14:8; J Nazir 7:2; Pirqei de Rabbi Eliʿezer 12.

28. See Ginzberg (above, note 25), V, 292; Vilnay (above, note 25), 128–32 for references.

29. On the entrance to Gehenna, the center of the underworld, see Ginzberg (above, note 25), V, 14; and Vilnay (above, note 25), 269–70. On the *'even shetiyyah* as the capstone, see Ginzberg, op. cit., V, 15–16, and Vilnay, op. cit., 78–80. Echoes of this latter tradition are found in Muslim sources; see ibid., 19.

30. "The first prophets" are identified in B Sotah 48b as Samuel and David, but this is probably a later attempt to give the vague expression some precision. See further Ginzberg (above, note 25), VI, 69.

31. Ginzberg's proposal (ibid.,V, 15) that *'even shetiyyah* originally meant "fire-stone" and referred to a meteorite that had been placed in the Temple, is ingenious, but hardly consonant with the Mishnah's description of the stone as being only "three fingers high." This suggests a piece of natural rock protruding above the level of the floor. However, Ginzberg's etymology may still be correct. The rock may have been called "the fire-stone" simply because it was the place where the priest rested the fire-pan when he burned the incense in the Holy of Holies on the Day of Atonement. The geography of the Temple area and the relationship of the present-day features, particularly the Rock, to the layout of the ancient Temple is a matter of intense debate among archaeologists.

32. L. Casson, *Travel in the Ancient World* (London, 1979), p. 173. See further Nicolet (above, note 18), passim; and W. Müller, *Die Heilige Stadt: Roma quadrata, himmlisches Jerusalem und die Mythe vom Weltnabel* (Stuttgart, 1961).

33. J. Neusner. *Genesis and Judaism* (Atlanta, 1985). For further evidence of the "rivalry" between Israel and Rome, see P. S. Alexander, "The Family of Caesar and the Family of God: The Image of the Emperor in Heikhalot Literature," *Images of Empire*, ed. L. Alexander (Sheffield, 1991), 276–97.

34. Sifre—Deuteronomy 52; J ʿAvodah Zarah 1:2; B Shabbat 56b. Ginzberg (above, note 25), IV, 128, VI, 280. The story has a moral purpose: Rome was founded to punish Israel for her sins.

35. I. Gafni, *Land, Center and Diaspora: Jewish Constructs in Late Antiquity* (Sheffield, 1997), 71–78.

9

The Many Names of Jerusalem

AVIGDOR SHINAN

While the name "Jerusalem" (which appears in the Bible more than 650 times) can only be found in the books of the Prophets and the Hagiographa, throughout the whole Bible one can find numerous names, epithets, and appellations which allude to this geographical entity, such as "the city of David" (II Sam. 5:7),[1] "Zion" (Isa. 1:27; 33:5), "faithful city" (Isa. 1:26) and many more.

Rabbinic literature—The Mishnah, Tosefta, and the two Talmuds, as well as midrashic compilations and the Aramaic targums—inherited the many names and epithets that the Bible bestowed upon Jerusalem and also added many of its own. These names are scattered throughout the sources, but have also been collected in the form of lists. It is these lists that will be the focus of our discussion.

The rabbinic tendency to call any one entity by many names attests to its multifaceted and complex nature. The rabbis, for example, established that Moses had many names[2]—as did the Angel of Death,[3] the Torah, the people of Israel, and God.[4] Yet, we must admit that the distinction between a name and an epithet is not at all clear, in the same way that in our case the distinction is often blurred between names/epithets given to the entire land of Israel, the holy city, the Temple Mount, or the Temple itself.

In addition to the defined lists, which include ten to seventy items each, names for Jerusalem can also be found scattered throughout rabbinic literature; although a final count is yet to be completed, over 120 different names have already been collected.[5] We shall mention only one example of a name that is not included in the lists to be studied here. It is found in the Aramaic targum to Song of Songs 8:11: כרם היה לשלמה בבעל המון (= "Solomon had a vineyard in Baal-Hamon . . ."). The Aramaic targum on the verse expounds:

אומא חדא סלקת בעדביה דמרי עלמא דשלמא עמיה דהיא מתילא לכרמא
אותיב יתה בירושלם

One nation came up by lot unto the Lord of the universe, the One
that peace is His, a nation that is compared to a vineyard. He settled
her in Jerusalem.

Here, the targum freely interchanges "Baal-Hamon" with Jerusalem, claiming
it as one of her many names, most probably[6] following verses that mention
המון (= *hamon*, crowd) with regard to Jerusalem, such as Ps. 42:5.

Let us move to the focus of our discussion—the rabbinic lists of Jerusalem's
names and epithets. The rabbis particularly favored listmaking as a method
for organizing, remembering and presenting data, and numerous lists can be
found in their literature.[7] Two—or by an alternate count, three—lists of
names for Jerusalem are found in rabbinic literature, two lists of ten names
each, combined to form one list of twenty, and a separate list with seventy
names. Each list will be discussed separately.

The Twenty Names of Jerusalem

The list of twenty names of Jerusalem is found in Avot de-Rabbi Nathan[8] and
finds no parallel in any other rabbinic text. Its placement in Avot de-Rabbi
Nathan comes following the Mishnah in tractate Avot (5:5) that lists ten
miracles that were witnessed in the Temple of Jerusalem, and other lists such
as the ten ways in which Jerusalem is superior to all other lands. The list is
comprised of two parts, the first—Jerusalem's ten names of praise, and the
second—her ten names of disgrace. This is the first part:

עשרה שמות נקראת ירושלים לשם שבח: עיר, קריה, נאמנה, בעולה,
דרושה, חפצי בה, שמה, צדק, שלום, יבוסי

In ten names of praise Jerusalem is called: (1) City (*'ir*), (2) City (*qirya*),
(3) Faithful, (4) Espoused, (5) Sought Out, (6) I delight in her,
(7) The Lord is there, (8) Righteousness, (9) Well being (or: Peace),
(10) Jebusite.

The first three names and the eighth name are drawn from one verse: "After
that you shall be called City (*'ir*) of Righteousness, Faithful City (*qirya*)" (Isa.
1:26). We should note that the word "city" is often part of a pair of words
that form a description or name for Jerusalem, such as "The City of David"
or "The Holy City,"[9] but the use of "city" by itself to specify Jerusalem was
common as well. It explains, for example, the understanding of the phrase

"City of Gold" (עיר של זהב) as referring specifically to a golden ornament in the form of (the walls of) Jerusalem.[10]

The following three laudatory names of Jerusalem are derived from various other verses in Isaiah, all expressing the idea of future-naming. "Espoused" and "I delight in her" relate to the words in Isa. 62:4: "But you shall be called 'I delight in her' and your land (shall be called) 'Espoused' "; "Sought Out" finds its source in Isa. 62:12: "And you shall be called 'Sought Out', a city not forsaken."

The seventh name in the list, "The Lord is there," is based on the last verse in Ezekiel: "and the name of the city from that day on shall be 'The Lord is there' "(48:35),[11] while the ninth name, "Well being" or "Peace," seems to be drawn from Ps. 147:12–14: "O Jerusalem, glorify the Lord; praise your God, O Zion . . . who endows[12] your realm with well-being." To this point, the above names are consistent in their laudatory nature, which only serves to highlight the difficulty of finding the aspect of praise in Jerusalem's final name in that list—Jebusite (from Josh. 15:8: "Along the southern flank of the Jebusites—that is, Jerusalem").

While the main source for the names collected in the list of Avot de-Rabbi Nathan is Second Isaiah, we have yet to determine the nature of the list and the purpose it serves. The same holds true for its time of composition, due to the absence of reliable dating methods for any specific text of Avot de-Rabbi Nathan.[13] The second part of our text—the ten names that denigrate Jerusalem—do not bring us any closer to finding a solution:

ועשרה [שמות נקראת ירושלים] לשם גנאי : אלמנה, זונה, שכולה, גלמודה,
גולה, וסורה, עזובה, ושנואה, ענייה, סוערה

and in ten [names] of disgrace [Jerusalem is called]: (1) Widow, (2) Harlot, (3) Bereaved, (4) Barren, (5) Exiled, (6) Disdained, (7) Forsaken, (8) Rejected, (9) Unhappy, (10) Storm-tossed.

Here, too, the majority of the names find their source in the book of Second Isaiah. The first name, "Widow," is coined according to Lam. 1:1: "The city once great with people . . . is become like a widow," while the slur "harlot" is derived from the words of Isaiah: "Alas, she has become a harlot, the faithful City" (1:21). The next four condemnations are all drawn from a single verse in Isaiah: "Who bore these for me when I was bereaved and barren, exiled and disdained" (49:21). Likewise, the rest of the names find their source in the words of the same prophet. "Forsaken" and "Rejected" appear together in one verse, "And you shall be called 'City of the Lord Zion of the Holy One of Israel' whereas you have been forsaken, rejected" (60:15). "Unhappy" and

"Storm-tossed" are joined in "Unhappy storm-tossed one, uncomforted" (Isa. 54:11). A common thread clearly runs through Second Isaiah's choice of names and epithets for Jerusalem. He draws his metaphors for the city from the semantic field of a woman's relationship with her husband and family, and therefore the great majority of Jerusalem's names are colored with that particular motif.

Is there a correlation between this two lists of names? It seems that there is only a minimal basis for comparison, and even then only for the first few names. The first name of each list—"City" ('*ir*) and "Widow" respectively—stand in contrast to each other in a common source (Lam. 1:1): "the city once great with people . . . is become like a widow," while "City" (*qirya*) and "Harlot" are represented in similar fashion in "Alas, she has become a harlot, the faithful city" (Isa. 1:21). One further correlation between the names that praise Jerusalem and those that shame her is set up in Isa. 62:4: "Nevermore shall you be called 'Forsaken' . . . but you shall be called 'I delight in her' and your land 'Espoused'." Beyond that, however, the names and their meaning vacillate, leaving no means for comparison. It is therefore fair to assume that the two lists before us are independent of each other and that there is no a priori correlation between them.

What compelled an author to compile a list of names that comes to denounce Jerusalem? The equal number of names in the two lists clearly represents the desire of their author(s), or of whomever brought the independent lists together, to highlight the balance between the two faces of the city, a phenomenon that we shall see again later on.

I would like to suggest at least one motive for creating the list that comes in praise of Jerusalem which can be understood by its comparison to a passage from the writing of Marqah the Samaritan,[14] who lived in Palestine in the third–fourth centuries. In his work, *Memar Marqah*, the poet establishes that Mount Gerizim is the chosen place and that "It has thirteen names in the Torah (the Samaritans, as is known, do not accept the prophets and Hagiographa as part of the canon of inspired writings), each declaring its glory."[15] He then lists and explains each name:

> The first: "The Hill Country to the East" (הר הקדם—Gen. 10:30), for the God of the East had chosen it from the days of creation. . . . The second: Bethel (בית אל—Gen. 12:8), for God mighty and awesome is a shield and helper to those who believe in Him. . . . The third: The Abode of God (בית אלוהים—Gen. 28:17), for the holy angels did not cease uttering praise to their Lord, seeking God in it. . . . [Other names are]: Gateway to Heaven (שער השמיים), Luza (לוזה), Sanctuary

(מקדש), Mount Gerizim (הרגריזים), The House of the Lord (בית הי),
Good Hill Country (ההר הטוב), The Chosen Place (המקום המבחר),
The Eternal Hill (גבעת עולם), One of the Heights (אחד ההרים). The
thirteenth name: Abraham's calling the name of that site "The Lord
will see" (הי יראה).

Several of the names that Marqah appropriates for Mount Gerizim are
known through Jewish tradition as names for Jerusalem. This fact fits well
in the framework of the debate between the rabbis and the Samaritans
regarding the identity of the unspecified "Chosen Place" ("המקום אשר
יבחר"—Deut. 12:4 and elsewhere).[16] The term "Sanctuary," for example, is
considered by the rabbis as a name for Jerusalem as well.[17] Three other
names—Bethel, House of God, and Gateway to Heaven—are drawn from
the story of Jacob's dream (Gen. 28). Similarly, we find in rabbinic sources
that the site of Jacob's dream is identified as Jerusalem.[18] The term "Good
Hill Country" that Marqah attributes to Mount Gerizim is based on a verse
in Deuteronomy, "that good hill country and the Lebanon" (3:52), and
here, too, it is necessary to point out that "Lebanon" appears among the
rabbis' names for Jerusalem.[19]

One thing that remains clear is that the idea of listing the many names of
a place in the land of Israel in order to attest to its glory already existed in the
third to fourth centuries. It is possible that at the base of this practice lies a
cultural-religious struggle between different religious sects over who could produce more names to sanctify their holy site. Yet, it is important to note that
Marqah limited his list to names of praise, while the rabbis did not hesitate
to include terms of derision in their list, because for them Jerusalem is not a
paragon of virtue. The city, by nature, contains good and bad, splendor and
wretchedness.

The Seventy Names of Jerusalem

The list of seventy names of Jerusalem is found in a text that was published
by S. Buber (1895) under the name Midrash Shir HaShirim Zuta, and in-
dependently by S. Schechter (1896) under the name Aggadat Shir HaShirim.
Parallel texts are found in two late compositions: Midrash HaGadol to Gen.
46:8 (ed. Margulies, 775) and Yalqut HaMachiri to Isa. 62:4 (ed. Shapira,
253).

The list appears in Shir HaShirim Zuta, in the course of an especially
lengthy exposition whose theme is introduced by "Israel is called by seventy
names (e.g., Orchard, First-born, Palm Tree) and Jerusalem by seventy, and
the Torah by seventy (e.g., Wisdom, Understanding, Renewing Life) in def-

erence to the seventy names of the Lord Blessed Be He (e.g., Most High, Fierce in Wrath, Awesome, Beauty)." The number seventy is well known in rabbinic thought and literature: the elderly of the Sanhedrin, the nations of the world and their languages, the angels in the celestial entourage, the vessels of the Temple, and many more.[20] Seventy is used to convey a high and round number, the number of completeness or wholeness, and the many names for Jerusalem is, at a certain level, a testimony to the special status that she bears the worldover.

The text listing the seventy names is distorted, and at times Buber and Schechter differ in their reading of the text, as each emends it freely. Here, then, is my attempt to translate the complicated text into English:

> Jerusalem was called [or: He called Jerusalem] by seventy names: Jerusalem, Shalem, There is a Vision (יראה), Jebus, Gilead, Lebanon, Zion, Heights (מרומים), Throne of the Lord (כסא הי), City of Israel (עיר ישראל), Fair Crested (יפה נוף), Summit of Zaphon (ירכתי צפון), Joy of all the Earth (משוש כל הארץ), Espoused (בעולה), I delight in her (חפצי בה), A Stone to Lift (אבן מעמסה), Efrata, Region of Yaar (שדה יער), Resting Place (מנוחה), Ariel, Mount of Assembly (הר מועד), Fair (יפה),[21] Maiden (בתולה), Bride (כלה), Wife of Youth (אשת נעורים), Great with People (רבתי עם), Great among Nations (רבתי בגויים), The Princess among States (שרתי במדינות), A City Knit Together (עיר שחוררה לה),[22] House of Prayer (בית ונעולה), Migdal-Eder, Consort (שגל), Stronghold (מצודה), Dearly Beloved (ידידות), Sought Out (דרושה),[23] A city not Forsaken (עיר לא נעזבה), Joy (גילה), Garden of Eden of the Lord (גן עדן הי),[24] Lofty Mount (הר מרום), Sanctuaries (מקדשים),[25] Barren (עקרה), Moriah, High Mountain (הר גבוה), Overbearing City (עיר היונה), Faithful City (קריה נאמנה), City of Righteousness (עיר הצדק), Valley of Vision (גיא חזיון), The Gateways of the Peoples (דלתות העמים), Shrines (במות), Portion (נחלה), Holy Mount (הר הקודש), Desired Mountain (הר חמד), Hill of Frankincense (גבעת הלבונה), City of David (עיר דוד), City of the Negeb (עיר הנגב), Lofty Mount of Israel (הר מרום ישראל), A new Name which the Lord Himself shall bestow (שם חדש אשר פי הי יקבהו).

This list is then followed by scriptural proofs that verify twenty different names, e.g.:

> She (= Jerusalem) is called Shalem as it says "And king Melchizedek of Shalem" (Gen. 14:18). She is called "There is a Vision" (יראה) as it says "(on the mountain of the) Lord there is a vision (בהר הי יראה)"

(Gen. 22:13). . . . [She is called] Lebanon as it says "that good hill country, and the Lebanon" (Deut. 3:25).

Yet, only fifteen of the names from the abovementioned list of "seventy names" are presented here alongside scriptural proofs (followed occasionally by some discussion in which the name is explained or otherwise dealt with[26]). On the other hand, six new names were added in the course of gathering textual evidence for Jerusalem's names:

> [She is called Waters (ים)] as it says "and all nations shall assemble (ונקוו) there in the name of the Lord, at Jerusalem" (Jer. 3:17) [and it says] "Let the water below the sky be gathered (יקוו) into one area" (Gen. 1:9) and just as the waters accepted all the water from creation, so, too, is she destined to accept all of her children. . . . She is called City of the Great King (קרית מלך רב—Ps. 48:3), for she is the city of the King of all Kings the Holy One Blessed be He. She is called Perfect in Beauty (כלילת יופי), as it says "Perfect in Beauty, Joy of all the Earth" (Lam. 2:15). . . . She is called Bashan, as it says "O jagged mountain, Mount Bashan" (Ps. 68:16). She is called Hadrach, as it says "in the land of Hadrach" (Zech. 9:1) that she trembles[27] before the King on High. She is called Rammah (or: On a Height), as it says "A cry is heard on a height (קול ברמה)" (Jer. 31:15).

In total, sixty-five (according to Schechter's reading: sixty-three) names can be gleaned from the list itself and from the scriptural proofs that follow it. Additional names, though without textual backup, are listed in the parallel texts of Midrash HaGadol and Yalqut HaMachiri—such as "Palace" (ארמון), Rachel, Cattle (צאן), or "Center of the Earth" (טבור הארץ)—but in these texts as well the count of names does not reach seventy (HaMachiri—fifty-seven, Midrash HaGadol—sixty-nine).

As yet, I have been unable to determine why some of the names warrant textual backing while others appear alone, just as I have been unable to discern any particular order to the list. The names are not listed alphabetically, they do not follow the order in which they appear in the biblical text, nor are they organized by themes. It would seem that there was no a priori order at all, and that if there was, the texts we have in our hands do not allow for its retrieval.

How were the seventy names chosen? The text seems to present a few viable ways. According to the first, the most obvious one, the compiler uses verses that directly address Jerusalem, as for example, in Isa. 62:4: "You shall be called 'I delight in her'." According to a second way, the names for Jerusalem were drawn from verses that contained the root קרא (= to call by name) in connection with the city, as we find for example in Jer. 3:17: "At that time, they shall call Jerusalem 'Throne of the Lord'." Amazingly, however, several of the names are derived from a play on the root שים (to put), while reading שׁ (*sin*) as שׁ (*shin*), understanding it as somehow derived from the word שֵׁם (= name). This play on words is employed, for example, in creating the names "Eden" and "Stone to lift" (אבן מעמסה), based on Zech. 12:3: "I will make (אשים) Jerusalem a stone for all the peoples to lift," and on Isa. 51:3: "Truly the Lord has comforted Zion . . . He has made (וישם) her wilderness like Eden." Apparently all measures were considered acceptable in establishing names for Jerusalem.

Jerusalem's names portray her as a city complex by nature. Unlike the list of twenty names of both praise and condemnation in Avot de-Rabbi Nathan, most of the names in the list of seventy come to praise Jerusalem and only few of them describe her negatively. At times, however, through the recycling of versions or copies, even the few negative epithets for Jerusalem were distorted and evolved into names of praise. "A Bowl of Reeling" (סף רעל), for example ("Behold, I will make [שָׂם!] Jerusalem a bowl of reeling for the peoples all around" [Zech. 12:2]), appears in different versions of our list as יפה (Fair) or ספה על (= Couch + on). The name "Exiled" (גולה), from "who bore these for me when I was . . . exiled and disdained" (Isa. 49:21), becomes גילה (Joy, as in Isa. 65:18: "For I shall create Jerusalem as a joy and her people as a delight"), and the epithet מוראה (Sullied, as in Zeph. 3:1: "Ah, sullied, polluted, overbearing city") evolves as Moriah (מוריה). It seems that at the heart of the copyist's treatment of Jerusalem's names lies the assumption that the text before us is actually one of praise, and therefore it is necessary to distort any indications to the contrary despite the fact that our text in its original form most probably included negative attributes side by side with positive ones.

The list of ten names of denigration in Avot de-Rabbi Nathan and the few remaining negative epithets from the list of the seventy names testify to the rabbis' realistic outlook on Jerusalem. As in many areas—such as their attitude toward the people of Israel, the fathers of the nation, and the rabbis themselves—they subject any entity to intense scrutiny and criticize it for what it is without any partiality. Rabbinic literature is filled with passages about Jerusalem and its people, built on the rebuke of Jerusalem found in the biblical prophecies and in the stories of the destruction of the Temple,[28] and there is an abundance of tales about the hatred that reigned amongst the city's residents and the religious, moral, and social transgressions that overtook her.

The rabbis' preoccupation with Jerusalem does not merely represent an effort to glorify past history or lament the splendid city of yore. Nor do they only seek to portray a brilliant image of the future on which to hang the nation's hopes. The prominence of Jerusalem in rabbinic literature also serves as a signpost of caution engraved with the woes of a city whose many transgressions led to her destruction, forcing the readers to pay heed that such sin and punishment should never be repeated. Jerusalem of the rabbis—as reflected inter alia in her names—differs greatly from Mount Gerizim as perceived by the Samaritans. She is complex in nature, and is not exclusively virtue and glory.

During the rabbinic period, when Jews did not inhabit Jerusalem, the city was upheld as a remembrance from time past and as a foundation for hope in the future. The coexistence of praise and condemnation embodied in Jerusalem's many names demonstrates that the remembrance that by nature was inclined toward nostalgia and hyperbole, and that the hope that offered a promise of a bright future and an escape from the grim reality of life, did not in any measure diminish the criticism that the rabbis conferred upon Jerusalem.[29]

Notes

1. All biblical texts are translated according to The Jewish Publication Society's *A New Translation of the Holy Scriptures* (Philadelphia, 1982).

2. Leviticus Rabbah 1:3 (ed. Margulies, 7–12) and many parallels. See also: Ch. Beer, "The Names of Moses," *Maḥanaim* 155 (1967), 140–47 (Hebrew).

3. B Bava Batra 16a.

4. See our discussion below.

5. See S. D. Goitein, "On the Arabic Names of Jerusalem," *Mincha Le-Yehudah* (Jerusalem, 1950), 62–66 (Hebrew); Z. Vilnay, *Jerusalem—the Capital of Israel*, I (Jerusalem, 1970), 152–75 (Hebrew). See also the vast material collected recently by I. Katzenelbogen, "Seventy Names of Jerusalem," *Sinai* 116 (1995), 141–59 (Hebrew). For earlier attempts in Hebrew scholarship at gathering the various names of Jerusalem, see ibid., 141–42, note 8.

6. See Rashi, ad loc.

7. W. S. Towner, *The Rabbinic "Enumeration of Scriptural Examples"* (Leiden, 1973).

8. Avot de-Rabbi Nathan, B, 39 (ed. Schechter, 106–107). For an English translation, see A. J. Saldarini, *The Fathers According to Rabbi Nathan—Version B* (Leiden, 1975).

9. In one of the manuscripts of our text (ibid.) we indeed find "Holy city" (Isa. 52:1) replacing "City."

10. M Shabbat 6:1 (and B Shabbat 59a). See also T Maʿaser Sheni 5:3 (cf. S. Lieberman, *Tosefta ki-Fshutah*, II [New York, 1955], 778 and note 8).

11. According to B Bava Batra 75b, the Hebrew יי שָׁמָּה (i.e., "The Lord is there") could also be read as יי שְׁמָהּ (= Her name is "The Lord").

12. It seems that the Hebrew הַשָּׁם (= who endows) is understood as related to the word שֵׁם (= name)—a phenomenon not uncommon in forming new names for Jerusalem, as demonstrated below.

13. See M. Kister, "Avot de-Rabbi Nathan—Studies in Text, Redaction and Interpretation" (doctoral dissertation, Hebrew University of Jerusalem, 1993), 6–7 (Hebrew).

14. See Z. Ben-Hayyim, תיבת מרקה—*A Collection of Samaritan Midrashim* (Jerusalem, 1988), 150—51 (Hebrew). For an English translation of the passage, see J. MacDonald, *Memar Marqah—The Teaching of Marqah*, BAZW 84 (Berlin, 1963).

15. It is interesting to note that the Moslem writer A-Suyuti (who wrote his book in 1470–1475) mentions seventeen names of Jerusalem, claiming that "the multitude of names proves the excellence of their bearer" (cited by Goitein, [above, note 5], 65 and note 11). The Arabic names of Jerusalem and their relationship with the (late) rabbinic lists deserve special treatment. See, in the meanwhile, *The Encyclopedia of Islam*, V (Leiden, 1986), s.v. al-Kuds, 322–23.

16. See J. Heinemann, "Anti-Samaritan Polemics in the Aggadah," *Proceedings of the Sixth World Congress of Jewish Studies*, III (Jerusalem, 1977), 23–35.

17. The name מקדשים appears in the list of seventy names of Jerusalem which is studied below. Its biblical origin seems to be Ezek. 21:7: "Set your face toward Jerusalem/and proclaim against Miqdashim (מקדשים)."

18. For example, B Pesaḥim 88a and Pirke de-Rabbi Eliezer 35 (as opposed to Genesis Rabbah 69:7 [ed. Theodor-Albeck, 796]).

19. Sifre—Deuteronomy 28 (ed. Finkelstein, 44–45); Leviticus Rabbah 1:2 (ed. Margulies, 7), and parallels. See Katzenelbogen (above, note 5), 152–53.

20. See L. Ginzberg, *The Legends of the Jews* (Philadelphia, 1967), Index, 429.

21. On this name, see our discussion of the name סף רעל (= Bowl of Reeling), below.

22. This name is discussed in my article " 'A House of Prayer for All Peoples' in Rabbinic Literature," to be published in the proceedings of a symposium held by the Studium Biblicum Franciscanum (Jerusalem) in February, 1997.

23. I follow here Buber's reading, The text reads ירושה (= Inheritance), but I could not find a clear biblical origin for this name (but cf. Deut. 2:12), while "Sought Out" (דרושה) is found already in the list of Avot de-Rabbi Nathan.

24. Buber emends the text and divides this term into two names: עדן and גן ה'. Both names find a biblical origin in Isa. 51:3.

25. See above, note 17.

26. For example: "She is called Summit of Zaphon because all of the possessions of Zaphon (i.e., the wealth of the northern kingdoms) are destined to come to her."

27. A play on words on the name חדרך which is explained as: "היא מחרדת למלך שבמרום".

28. As demonstrated, for example, in B Gittin 55b–56a, Yoma 9b, Shabbat 119b, and in Midrash Lamentations Rabbah. See the recent study of G. Hasan-Rokem, *The Web of Life—Folklore in Rabbinic Literature: The Palestinian Aggadic Midrash Eikha Rabba* (Tel-Aviv, 1996) (Hebrew).

29. I wish to express my thanks to Ms. Esti Baron for her valuable help in writing this article and to Ms. Pearl Kaplan for translating it from the Hebrew.

· III ·

BYZANTINE
JERUSALEM

10

Byzantine Jerusalem:
The Configuration of a Christian City

S ome sixty years elapsed between the destruction of Jerusalem by Titus and the decision of Hadrian, the neoclassicist Roman emperor, to rebuild the city. Many historians believe that the imperial initiative was a major factor in the outbreak of the Bar-Kokhba revolt.[1] Hadrian's plan materialized only after the suppression of the revolt in 135 C.E. The new Roman city, now named Aelia Capitolina, was built upon the ruins of Jewish Jerusalem, whose rubble was reused for building their new colony.[2]

Aelia Capitolina

The change of Jerusalem's name to Aelia Capitolina is indicative of the loss of Jewish dominance in the city. Hadrian also changed the name of the province from Judaea to Syria-Palaestina. A third decision in Hadrian's rule was a bitter act of suppression: Jews who had survived the massacre and exile were not permitted to settle in Aelia Capitolina or its vicinity. In fact, our sources inform us that one small Jewish congregation did indeed manage to survive in Jerusalem,[3] even though the city had become predominantly pagan. Later Christian sources (mostly from the early fourth century on) express enormous theological interest in describing the Jewish loss in the Bar-Kokhba revolt, emphasizing the fact that the bishops of the See of Jerusalem were chosen not from among the members of the Judaeo-Christian community (*ecclesia ex circumcisione*), as they were expelled from the city together with the Jews, but from among the ordinary Christians (*ecclesia ex gentibus*).

The pagan city of Aelia Capitolina enjoyed no more sanctity or centrality than any other colony in the eastern provinces. Caesarea, the official capital of the province of *Palaestina*, later *Palaestina Prima*, preserved its title and function throughout the Byzantine period, and even after the foundation of *Palaestina Secunda* and *Palaestina Tertia* in the late fourth or early fifth century it remained the metropolis of the senior province in the region. In terms of town-planning and architecture, Aelia Capitolina had the same character as any other city in Palestine or Arabia, the best-preserved of which is Gerasa (modern Jerash).[4]

The various modern maps of Roman Jerusalem illustrate the scholarly consensus for reconstructing the two main streets of the city, the *cardines*, along the major north-south arteries of the present-day Old City. These maps also agree in their reconstruction of the *decumanus*, an east-west street which was divided into two main sections, the eastern end north of the Temple Mount (along the present-day Via Dolorosa) and its continuation along the course of the central Cross Valley (today's David and Chain Streets). Moreover, scholars locate the camp of the Roman Tenth Legion in the southwestern part of the city (in the present-day Armenian Quarter) and suggest that the forum of the city was close to the city-center, south of the Church of the Holy Sepulchre (in the area of today's Muristan). Various archaeological discoveries corroborate some of the abovementioned assumptions, particularly the course of the streets, while others—such as the reconstruction of the forum and the Roman camp—remain hypothetical, although very likely. Other Roman monuments that have survived in the Old City, or that have been discovered in archaeological excavations, are the monumental arch in the Russian Hospice (the monumental gate of the forum?), the arch of the Ecce Homo on the Via Dolorosa, the ancient remains of the northern Porta Neapolitana (Damascus Gate), the remains of the monumental *quadriporticus* decorating the Siloam pool, the public bathhouse west of the Temple Mount, and others. The early seventh-century *Chronicon Paschale*, in its rather obscure description of Roman Aelia, mentions other monuments as well.[5] The location of the center and perhaps residential area of the small Jewish and Christian minorities is not clear but, as we shall see below, the sources indicate that they existed on Mount Zion, outside the southern wall of Aelia,[6] near the traditional tomb of David and the chapel of the *caenaculum*.

Byzantine Jerusalem

The Jews who lamented their ruined Temple and prayed for Jerusalem, and the Christians who perceived themselves theologically, ideologically, and historically as *verus Israel* and reveled in the destruction of the Jewish city, were referring to the formerly Jewish city of David, Solomon, and the prophets, the city of the Hasmoneans and the First and Second Temples. For example, the Christians perceived of Mount Zion as both the Citadel of David—the historical founder of Zion—and the Seat of Jacob the Less—Jesus' brother and founder of the first church of Jerusalem, the Mother of all Churches.[7]

In reality, however, the architecture and topography of Christian Jerusalem since the fourth century followed the city-plan and architectural configuration of Aelia Capitolina. Indeed, some monuments of Second Temple Jerusalem survived the sack, such as the *temenos* of the Temple Mount or the wall and towers to the west and southwest that were saved by Titus.

The Bordeaux Pilgrim, who visited Jerusalem around 333 C.E., describes Aelia in its very first stages as a Christian city.[8] Among the city's monuments he lists the Temple Mount and several sites in its vicinity: the spring of Siloam, the *praetorium* of Pontius Pilate, and the Bethesda pools. Of particular interest is the description of the Temple Mount, where two statues of Hadrian stood, and not far from them, still on the site of the ruined Temple, a stone with holes which the mourning Jews would come to anoint every year. The Bordeaux Pilgrim also mentions that during his visit to the site of the newly-discovered Holy Sepulchre and the hill of Golgotha he saw a basilica of remarkable beauty being built by the Emperor Constantine.[9] He distinguishes this basilica from other multipurpose civic basilicas, so common in Roman cities, by calling it the "basilica of the Lord" (*basilica . . . id est Dominicium*).[10]

The Constantinian basilica was incorporated into the already existent city-plan of Aelia.[11] The entrance to its front courtyard or atrium was from the main colonnaded north-south street of Jerusalem (*cardo*). The complex of the Holy Sepulchre included: the congregational basilical church (referred to by the pilgrim Egeria as the Martyrium); the site of Jesus' tomb, above which an enormous rotunda, known as the Anastasis, was built; the Hill of the Crucifixion (Golgotha or Calvary); and an inner atrium in front of the rotunda which connected the various parts of the complex. A large baptistery, composed of an antechamber and the room of the baptismal font, was built as an annex, probably south of the main building. Cyril of Jerusalem informs us that in the mid-fourth century the baptistery was the main site for the conversion of pagans and Jews to Christianity.[12] Beneath the basilica was the Cave of the Finding of the Cross. The center of Christianity in Jerusalem now shifted to this place from its first center on Mount Zion. The focal position of the Holy Sepulchre in the hierarchy of ecclesiastical institutions in Jerusalem and throughout Palestine was established with the dedication of the church in 335 C.E.[13] The festival of the *encaenia*, i.e., the dedication of the church of the Holy Sepulchre in mid-September, developed into a large fair of commercial and social significance and continued to function as such during the early Islamic period as well.[14]

✦ ✦ ✦

The orientation of the basilica and entire complex of the Holy Sepulchre to the west, and not as was commonly the case in Palestine—to the east,[15] was dictated by Jerusalem's topography and city-plan. If the architects would have followed the canonical orientation, then their alternative would have been to build the main complex west of the Holy Sepulchre. By doing so, they would have had to insert the *propylaeum*, atrium, and basilica between the western wall of the city and the hill of Golgotha, far from the city-center, the main street, and the forum. Such a location would have considerably harmed the centrality of New Jerusalem. As we shall discuss below, the church is located on the Madaba map, where—in contrast with its actual geographical location—its entrance appears in the very center of the city.

✦ ✦ ✦

The church of the Holy Sepulchre was founded by Constantine following his mother Helena's pilgrimage to the holy places around 326 C.E.[16] The act of building the first churches in Jerusalem, Bethlehem, and Mamre had an enormous impact on the Christianization of Palestine and the development of ecclesiastical architecture in general.[17] Eusebius quotes a letter to Macarius, Bishop of Jerusalem, in which Constantine himself speaks about his enthusiasm to embellish the tomb of Christ: ". . . I have no greater care than how I may best adorn with a splendid structure that sacred spot which, under Divine direction, I have disencumbered. . . ."[18] The destruction of the temple of Aphrodite and the building of the church marked Christianity's major initial triumph over paganism. The act of building a church directly on top of the temple's ruins calls for a special study. Suffice it to say for the present that such an act apparently needs no explanation, as it demonstrates the victory of the church over the temple. In practice, however, such an act was very rare. Worshippers were aware of the demonic powers or curse of the impure site where the shrine of the demon had once stood.[19] In most cases Christians refrained from building churches directly on top of a pagan shrine (i.e., on its *cella* and *adytum*, but not in its courtyard or *pronaos*) unless a solemn purification ceremony was carried out. Only at a later date, at the end of the fifth or early sixth century, did Christians acquire enough self-confidence to build on top of temple ruins (or, primarily in the West, even integrate a church into the desecrated temple's structure, as, for example, at the Parthenon in Athens or the temple of Concordia in Agrigento).

The building of the church of the Holy Sepulchre on the very spot of the temple of Aphrodite was inevitable, since the temple covered the site of the holy tomb. At the turn of the fourth century and into the fifth, we learn from Mark the Deacon that the main temple of Gaza—the Marneion—was de-

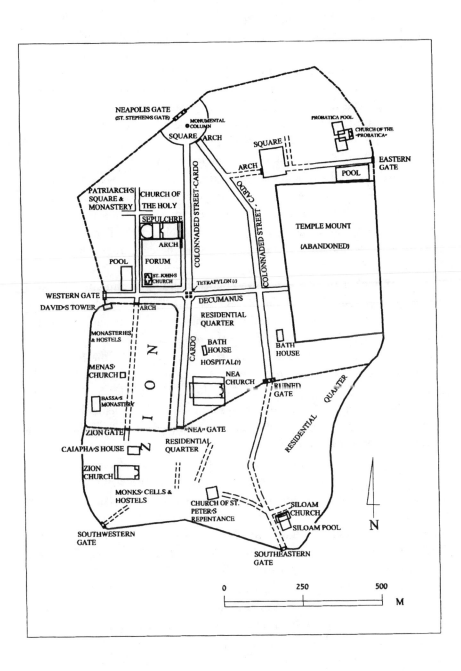

NEAPOLIS GATE
(ST. STEPHEN'S GATE)

MONUMENTAL
COLUMN

SQUARE ARCH

PROBATICA POOL

CHURCH OF THE
"PROBATICA"

SQUARE

ARCH

EASTERN
GATE

POOL

PATRIARCH'S
SQUARE &
MONASTERY

CHURCH OF
THE HOLY

SEPULCHRE

ARCH

FORUM

ST. JOHN'S
CHURCH

POOL

COLONNADED STREET-CARDO

TETRAPYLON (?)

CARDO

COLONNADED STREET

TEMPLE MOUNT

(ABANDONED)

WESTERN GATE

DAVID'S TOWER

ARCH

DECUMANUS

RESIDENTIAL
QUARTER

MONASTERIES
& HOSTELS

Z I O N

BATH
HOUSE

BATH
HOUSE

MENAS'
CHURCH

HOSPITAL(?)

CARDO

BASSA'S
MONASTERY

NEA
CHURCH

RUINED
GATE

ZION GATE

"NEA" GATE

RESIDENTIAL QUARTER

CAIAPHA'S HOUSE

RESIDENTIAL
QUARTER

ZION
CHURCH

MONKS' CELLS &
HOSTELS

CHURCH OF ST.
PETER'S
REPENTANCE

SILOAM
CHURCH

SILOAM POOL

N

SOUTHWESTERN
GATE

SOUTHEASTERN
GATE

0   250   500

M

stroyed by the Christians who built the church of Eudoxia on exactly the same spot; this was an explicit religious and political demonstration of Christianity's triumph.[20] In both exceptional cases of the church of Gaza and the church of the Holy Sepulchre, a meticulous purification of the polluted site of the temple and the rock beneath it was performed. According to Eusebius, the building of the church in Jerusalem began only after the eradication of the "dreadful grave of souls and the gloomy shrine of lifeless idols to the impure spirit they call Venus." Only at this stage was New Jerusalem built on the site.

The foundation of the church of the Holy Sepulchre (inaugurated in mid-September, 335 C.E.) was followed by intensive building activity of churches and monasteries in Jerusalem and the entire country. This was the main impetus for the emergence of Byzantine Jerusalem.[21] Constantine himself founded, probably at the same time as the Holy Sepulchre, the church of Eleona on the Mount of Olives,[22] the Church of Nativity in Bethlehem,[23] and the church of Mamre near Hebron, on the site where the angels visited Abraham.[24]

Constantine's activity was followed by the building of churches and monasteries throughout Palestine in places mentioned in the Hebrew Bible or connected with the life of Jesus and his disciples. On the one hand, the Christians had limited success at converting the region of Tiberias, Nazareth, and the Sea of Galilee, which was densely settled by Jews. On the other hand, neither Jerusalem nor Bethlehem presented a serious obstacle in building *loca sancta* and in converting the region, since the suppression of the Bar-Kokhba revolt left this region bereft of any significant Jewish settlement. The new settlers, the pagans, seemed to have embraced conversion. Classical paganism, which had lost its attractive powers already before the fourth century, was easily defeated by Christianity after the Christianization of the state and the imperial court. Christian eagerness to possess the holy sites was translated into the intensive building of churches. Among the most important foundations of the later fourth or fifth century in Jerusalem are the Church of the Ascension, located on the summit of the Mount of Olives,[25] and the church of Gethsemane in the Qidron Valley (or the Valley of Jehoshaphat).[26] The entire area of the Mount of Olives (from Bethpage and Bethany in the east to the Valley of Jehoshaphat in the west, between the Mount of Olives and Jerusalem) became occupied by many churches and monasteries.[27] The most famous monasteries on the Mount of Olives, those of Melania the Younger and Gerontius, became a center for Latins who came to visit or settle in Jerusalem.[28] The excavations at the site of Dominus Flevit, on the western slopes of the Mount of Olives, reflect a typical example of a small-sized Byzantine monastery.[29] Located on a Jewish cemetery of the Second Temple period, the edifice was a

combination of both rock-cutting and building, and the entire complex consisted of an inner courtyard surrounded by cells, a chapel, and an oratory
decorated with a handsome mosaic pavement.

The Mount of Olives and its slopes were recognized as part of Jerusalem,
and its *loca sancta* became an integral element of the cultic and religious life
of the city. Nevertheless, from an urban point of view the Mount of Olives
always remained outside of Jerusalem, connected with the main city by long
and steep paths sloping down toward the Valley of Jehoshaphat and then rising
to the summit of the Mount of Olives. One of these paths was a flight of
several hundred steps mentioned in several sources.[30]

The summit of Mount Zion, which is geographically the higher part of the
southwestern hill, was left outside the walls of Aelia Capitolina[31] and was only
later incorporated into the city. In the eighth century B.C.E., Mount Zion
was included in the city by the building of the walls later mentioned in Neh.
3:8 ("the Broad Wall"). With the building of the Hasmonean "First Wall,"
it was again included within the built area of Jerusalem as the "Upper City."[32]
After the destruction of the Second Temple, the area probably hosted the
Christian congregation of Jerusalem. Traditions have located the House of
Caiaphas and the Church of the Apostles there, the latter being the site where
the Holy Spirit descended from Heaven.[33] A small Jewish congregation may
have also been located in this area. Thus, both Jews and Christians were situated in the same area, near the present-day Church of the Dormition. The
identification of the Jewish synagogue on Mount Zion or its vicinity is derived
from the writings of three fourth-century authors: the Bordeaux Pilgrim, Epiphanius, and Optatus of Milevis.[34] J. Pinkerfeld discovered that the original
building of the present-day Tomb of David was originally a Roman building,
perhaps a synagogue; M. Avi-Yonah connected Pinkerfeld's discovery with the
above-mentioned sources.[35] The original Roman building was a broadhouse
made of smoothly-cut stones and containing a niche facing (though not accurately) the Temple Mount. The ground plan and the interior arrangement
resemble the synagogues of Eshtemoa and Susiya in southern Judaea. It seems
that the synagogue on Mount Zion (whether identified with the Tomb of
David or not) went out of use in the first half of the fourth century,[36] when
the Christians took over Mount Zion and began the long process of building
a vast Christian complex on the site.

No remains have been found of the early Church of the Apostles, which
might have been housed in a private dwelling (*domus ecclesiae*). Cyril of Jerusalem mentions the existence of the Upper Church (ἀνωτέρα ἐκκλεσία)
on Mount Zion and the church which stood there in the mid-fourth century,[37]
however there is no indication whether he was referring to the early church

(i.e., *domus ecclesiae* of the second–third centuries) or to another medium-sized church built on the site in the first half of the fourth century. A large church was built there in the time of Bishop John II (386 or 387–417 C.E.).[38] Fragments of walls and trenches of this later church were detected, enabling the reconstruction of a large basilica.[39] The Zion Church gained its fame from its association with the early Christian congregation of Jerusalem, or Mother of All Churches (*mater omnium ecclesiarum*). This noble origin became the main argument of Juvenal, archbishop of Jerusalem in the Council of Chalcedon, for gaining the nomination of Jerusalem as the fifth patriarchate of the Christian world.[40]

The area of Zion was encircled by a city-wall in the mid-fifth century, when the Empress Eudocia built the southern wall of Jerusalem along the line of the "First Wall" of the Second Temple period.[41] The area of Mount Zion was rich with Christian buildings and holy sites. Some, like the House of Caiaphas and the Church of Siloam, were known already in the early fourth century; others, such as the Church of St. Peter's Repentance and various monasteries, were added during the fifth–sixth centuries. Egeria and the Armenian Calendar emphasize the role of the churches on Mount Zion in the city's liturgy.[42] These sites, together with those on the Mount of Olives, formed the nucleus of liturgical processions to and from the Holy Sepulchre. These processions enabled the participants to imitate Jesus' movements in Jerusalem and read the appropriate phrases and prayers at the right time and the right place.[43] The monk Strategius, who describes the route taken by the captured Patriarch Zacharias (with the Life-Giving Cross) from Golgotha to Zion, and then to exile in Ctesiphon in 614 C.E., mentions that Jesus himself carried the cross through the gate of Zion on his way to Golgotha. This account leaves room for the suggestion that processions from the Church of Zion through the gate of Zion to Golgotha reenacted Jesus' last walk to his crucifixion.[44] This was most probably the original "Via Dolorosa," which changed its course in a later period, eventually reaching the present-day Via Dolorosa in the eastern part of the city.

A major effort to deepen the Christianization process in the northern suburbs of Jerusalem took place in the mid-fifth century, when the Empress Eudocia built the new martyrium of St. Stephen, where the remains of the saint were deposited[45] and which was inaugurated in 460 C.E. The identification of its remains, which were found in the compound of the present-day church (the French St. Étienne, or the École Biblique) north of Damascus Gate, with the ancient St. Stephen is plausible but not beyond doubt.[46] Recent archaeological excavations have shown that the entire northern suburb (or at least its western part) abounded with monasteries. Excavations in the area west of the

Church of St. Stephen, north of the Damascus Gate, have revealed remains of other monasteries, at least some of which were held by Armenians.[47] The compound of the Church of St. Stephen was, however, the only place in the city in which multitudes of monks and other supporters of Orthodoxy, lead by the holy monks Sabas and Theodosius and the Patriarch John, could find room to gather together during the Origenist dispute in 516 C.E.[48]

Christian building activity on the outskirts of Jerusalem widened the city's boundaries, but not necessarily on account of earlier Roman buildings. In many places, especially in the north, we learn that ecclesiastical as well as residential buildings were situated amidst earlier cemeteries without clearing away the older tombs.[49] More explicit in this regard was the incorporation of newly-built churches into the existing network of streets, monuments, and residential quarters of Roman Aelia. In addition to the complex of the Holy Sepulchre, some other major Christian foundations were found within the city as well.

The transition from paganism to Christianity is very clear in the case of the Church of St. Mary of the Probatica (the Sheep Pool), located in the modern-day compound of the Church of Santa Anna, in the northeastern quarter of Jerusalem's Old City,[50] near the large pools of Bethesda which were famous for their healing powers (John 5). Several votive gifts of pagan character, and a votive foot made of marble dating most probably to the second–third centuries, support the suggestion that this area was a pagan healing precinct (Asclepeion) also in the time of Aelia Capitolina. The building of the Church of St. Mary of the Probatica indicates the conversion of this pagan center into a Christian site. If the analysis of the archaeological remains from the Byzantine church is correct, we may well have here one of the boldest architectural projects ever undertaken in Byzantine Jerusalem. The accepted reconstruction is that of a large church partially supported by huge piers and vaults above the twin Bethesda pools.

The largest and most grandiose structure in Jerusalem was the Nea church, or the New Church of Mary, built in the southern part of former Aelia Capitolina with funds donated by the Emperor Justinian and inaugurated in 543. Procopius' enthusiastic description of this prestigious building project and its adjacent buildings is confirmed by the archaeological finds. Some of its remains, such as two apses, the threshold, and several marble pavers, were discovered in the excavations of the Jewish Quarter.[51] Enormous vaults were built in order to raise the level of the building and provide more space for the Nea; they were also used as water cisterns, and on the wall of one of them a dedicatory inscription was found moulded in plaster. The inscription praises the munificence of the Emperor Justinian and the care of the Abbot Constantine, under whose supervision the work was executed. The financial outlay was great, especially for a site that was not considered a major *locus sanctus.*

The central position, size, and beauty of the church, with its annexed hospital, demanded repaving the southern end of the *cardo.* This section of the street, which was originally Roman, was removed, leveled, and then rebuilt at great expense,[52] as it was adorned with porticoes and shops. The Madaba map clearly depicts this new stage of the street.

The depiction of Jerusalem on the Madaba map helps immensely in appreciating the full extent of Jerusalem's Christianization. Many buildings identified (by their red gabled roofs) as churches or ecclesiastical buildings are shown on the map. However, only five or six of them can be identified with certainty: the complex of the Holy Sepulchre, the Church of Zion, the Nea Church, the Church of St. Mary of the Probatica, and probably also the Church of Siloam and the Church of St. Sophia (the Holy Wisdom) on the site of the *praetorium.*

The northern part of the city, including its network of streets, follows the original plan of Roman Aelia Capitolina. The Byzantine churches were incorporated into the existing urban setting. Archaeology shows that some features evident in the rigid planning of the Roman city were forfeited in favor of a more practical and utilitarian approach in the Byzantine period. This change in priorities should not by any means be construed as a deterioration of the city as an urban center. In fact, the southern part of Jerusalem exhibits a clear Byzantine character[53] and is also reflected in the Madaba map. As noted, the southern area was encircled by a wall only in the time of the Empress Eudocia. A rather loose plan dictated by the topography is evident in this area, as is the strong touch of "comfortable disorder" so typical of Byzantine architecture and city-planning.

✦ ✦ ✦

The Church not only governed Jerusalem's religious life, but also founded social and welfare institutions—hostels for pilgrims, hospitals, and shelters for the elderly—which were established and maintained by the Patriarchate or by individual monasteries. These include, for example, the hospital (νοσουκομεῖον) annexed to the Nea church, the shelter for the poor (πτωχεῖον) built by the monk Passarion near the eastern gate of the city, and hostels (ξενοδοχεῖα) for pilgrims and the elderly (γεροκωμεῖα) built by monks. Literary sources write amply on ecclesiastical and religious matters, yet they reveal very little information concerning the municipal and provincial administration. This unbalanced state of information is partially due to the nature of the sources, which are in large part theological, hagiographical, and pilgrims' reports. Nevertheless, there is no doubt that it also reflects the fact that the real hegemony of life in Jerusalem remained as much in the hands of clerics of the Patriarchate as in those of municipal leaders or the provincial governor.

Paradoxically, Jerusalem became the fifth patriarchate following the council of Chalcedon (451 C.E.), while Caesarea remained the metropolis of *Palaestina Prima*. Officially, not only the civil governor, the dux, or military governor resided in Caesarea, but the metropolitan bishop of the province as well. Moreover, the pro-Chalcedonian desert monks, Sabas and Theodosius, together with the Patriarch John in 516 C.E., were the real spiritual leaders of the Jerusalem community.[54] Before ten thousand monks and other supporters (this figure may be exaggerated) of the Chalcedonian decree in the St. Stephen church, they anathematized Severus, Patriarch of Antioch, as well as other anti-Chalcedonian leaders. By this act they secured the Orthodox hegemony in Palestine, unlike other countries of the East, including Syria and Egypt.

Sabas was a great spiritual and practical leader.[55] By purchasing properties and building a hostel in Jerusalem for his monastery, the Great Laura, he followed the example of earlier prominent monks of the Jerusalem (or Judaean Desert) community. Building monasteries within the city-walls was mostly common in Jerusalem's southwestern quarter, between the gate of David's Tower (in the area of today's Jaffa Gate) and Mount Zion. This area was most probably occupied by the Roman Tenth Legion until the end of the third century; after it was removed from the city, it gradually became settled, enabling monasteries to acquire the land and deserted buildings there. The most explicit example is the story of Peter the Iberian, who built his monastery between David's Tower and Mount Zion, in an area which, according to his biographer, was by municipal regulations open for settlement since the days of Constantine.[56]

The Madaba map reveals how its artist (and his patrons) perceived the image of Jerusalem. Two features are most prominent. The first, as noted, is the location of the gates to the church of the Holy Sepulchre in the exact center of the oval-shaped city. Jerusalem itself is located in the center of the map, demonstrating that the Holy City was perceived as being in the very center of the Holy Land, which itself is the center of the earth. The *omphalos*, which now stands in the Greek Catholicon of the Church of the Holy Sepulchre, reflects the tradition (which still exists today) that the church is the navel of the earth—in contrast with the former Jewish tradition which placed the navel on the Temple Mount. In order to depict such a central position for the entrance to the church (which is located north of the actual city-center), the artist had to distort the geographical reality and shrink the southern part of the city. The real question is whether the artist was conscious of his change and deliberately did so in order to give priority to this notion of the *omphalos,* or did he, in fact, have no sense of the actual topography and believe that the church was in the very center? It is not impossible that he might have perceived Jerusalem as an oval-shaped city, as depicted in the map, and that the Holy Sepulchre was indeed located in its center.[57]

The second striking feature of the Madaba map is the absence of the Temple Mount from the depiction of Jerusalem.[58] The Temple Mount, even in its ruined state, was the largest area in Jerusalem and yet is not shown on the map. The omission of the Temple Mount from the city's topography probably occurred in the later fourth century. The Bordeaux Pilgrim in 333 visited the area and described the monuments on it, some of which seem to have been venerated by Christians. Later sources, however, beginning with Egeria in the 380s, did not mention the Temple Mount at all; only the walls and pinnacle that bordered it were noted on several occasions.[59] Jerome is the only writer who described the Temple Mount when relating how the Jews had to purchase the right to lament at the site of their ruined temple.[60] It is very likely that the Christian change of attitude towards the Temple Mount occurred after the death of the Emperor Julian in 363. The Christians, alarmed by the Jewish attempt to rebuild the Temple under imperial initiative and support, preferred to abandon the area and leave it empty and unvisited or, as later traditions call it, a place of refuse. The elimination of the Temple Mount from the Madaba map thus reflects its elimination from Christian memory.

The process of Christianization was most probably quicker and more intensive in Jerusalem than in other cities of Palestine. Still, we find echoes of the struggle between Christianity on the one hand, and the memories and sympathy for the classical tradition on the other. This is evidenced by the Orpheus mosaic which was found in a house or chapel north of the Damascus Gate.[61] This mosaic, depicting Orpheus, Pan, and the Centaur, reflects the vividness of the classical, even pagan, cultural heritage. Indeed, Orpheus (but not Pan or the Centaur) was converted rather easily into a Christian hero who brings peace and harmony to nature's wild.[62] The mosaic remains unique and its presence in Jerusalem calls for further investigation.

One cannot understand Byzantine Jerusalem without considering the multitude of pilgrims who flooded the city. We assume that many thousands of visitors from the various parts of the Christian world came to Jerusalem and stayed there for long periods, sometimes even two or three years, and that many remained for the rest of their lives.[63] Jerusalem became the basis for their travels throughout the Holy Land, including Arabia and Sinai. Many pilgrims were poor and did not contribute much to the city's economy, but others paid for food and lodging, made use of local guides, and bought relics and souvenirs. Some of these souvenirs are better known, such as the metal *ampullae* depicting the Holy Sepulchre, the crucifixion, and other scenes,[64] or the hexagonal glass bottles that were sold to pilgrims in the markets of Jerusalem.[65] The majority of these bottles were moulded with Christian symbols, but many were also decorated with seven-branched *menorot* and may be indicative of the fact that during the late Byzantine period a remarkable number of Jewish pilgrims visited the Holy City and bought its souvenirs. Most of the pilgrims, however, were undoubtedly Christians who hailed from all corners of the world. As mentioned above, many lived in hostels for pilgrims or in shelters for the poor and elderly, and the infirm were cared for in the local hospitals; most of these welfare institutions were maintained by the church and the monasteries. As a result of the presence of these pilgrims, Jerusalem became one of the most cosmopolitan cities in the ancient world. In addition to the inhabitants of Palestine and Arabia, the sources also mention Greeks, Cappadocians, and Armenians, immigrants from the Latin West and Egypt, and many others who frequented the city.[66]

The Christian character of Jerusalem survived for generations after the Muslim conquest. The great change took place in the days of the Umayyad Caliphs Abd al-Malik and Walid who, in the late seventh and early eighth centuries, built the Dome of the Rock, al-Aksa mosque, and the palaces south of the Temple Mount. Even then, numerous churches and an intensive Christian life flourished in the city.[67] The multifaceted Christian character of the city, which we have tried to describe above, was first and foremost an outcome of the deep religious sentiments and zealous faith of the Christian community and its leaders. On the one hand, they saw themselves as citizens of biblical Zion, the historical city of the Temple which witnessed the crucifixion of the Lord but, on the other, as citizens of New Jerusalem and keepers of the New Temple—the Holy Sepulchre, the place of the Resurrection, the holiest spot of the Christian world. In a letter to his congregation in Jerusalem, the Patriarch Zacharias, who in 614 was exiled to Ctesiphon by the Sassanians together with many thousands of Christians and the Holy Cross,[68] we may find this synthesis of the historical-biblical understanding together with the religious approach of this Christian leader of New Jerusalem. Echoing Ps. 137:1, he writes: "Remember, my brothers, that by the rivers of Babylon, there we sat down, and we wept, when we remembered Zion, and the Golgotha, and the life-giving Tomb, and Bethlehem which is unforgettable forever."

Notes

1. See, for example, E. Schürer, *The History of the Jewish People in the Age of Jesus Christ*, rev. ed., G. Vermes et al. (Edinburgh, 1973), 534–43. On Aelia Capitolina, its foundation, and history, see Y. Tsafrir and S. Safrai (eds.), *The History of Jerusalem*, III (Jerusalem, in press; Hebrew).

2. See the illustrative finds of the Burnt House discovered in the Jewish Quarter of Jerusalem, in N. Avigad, *Discovering Jerusalem* (Jerusalem, 1980), 120–39.

3. S. Safrai, "The Holy Congregation of Jerusalem," *SH* 23 (1972), 62–78; idem, "Jews in Jerusalem in the Roman Period," *History of Jerusalem* (above, note 1).

4. See, for example, the initial reconstruction of Aelia's city-plan by Germer-Durand before the discovery of the mosaic Madaba map; J. Germer-Durand, "Aelia Capitolina," *RB* 1 (1892), 369–87. For the topography and archaeology of Aelia Capitolina, see, inter alia, H. Vincent and F.-M. Abel, *Jérusalem*, II: *Jérusalem nouvelle* (Paris, 1914-26), esp. pp. 1–88; Y. Tsafrir, "The Topography and Archaeology of Aelia Capitolina," *History of Jerusalem* (above, note 1); H. Geva, in *NEAEHL*, II (Jerusalem, 1993), 758–67.

5. *Chronicon Paschale* (Bonn, 1832), 474.

6. On the building of the wall of Aelia, probably under Diocletian, and for its suggested course along or not far from the line of the present Turkish wall, see Tsafrir (above, note 4); as well as idem, "The Gates of Jerusalem in the Description of Mukkadassi—A New Suggestion of Identification Related to Byzantine Sources," *IEJ* 27 (1977), 151–61.

7. See especially idem, "Zion—The South-Western Hill of Jerusalem and Its Place in the Urban Development of the City in the Byzantine Period," Ph.D. dissertation (Hebrew University of Jerusalem, 1975), 91–205 (Hebrew).

8. *Itinerarium Burdigalense* 589-96 (*CCSL* 175, 16–18); R. W. Hamilton, "Jerusalem in the Fourth Century," *PEQ* 84 (1952), 83–90.

9. The Constantinian church of the Holy Sepulchre has been the subject of numerous historical and archaeological studies. See Vincent and Abel (above, note 4), 40–300; Ch. Coüasnon, *The Church of the Holy Sepulchre, Jerusalem* (London, 1974); V. Corbo, *Il Santo Sepolcro di Gerusalemme*, 3 vols., Collectio Maior 29 (Jerusalem, 1981); see recently J. Patrich, "The Early Church of the Holy Sepulchre in the Light of Excavations and Restoration," *Ancient Churches Revealed*, ed. Y. Tsafrir (Jerusalem, 1993), 101–17.

10. R. Krautheimer, "The Constantinian Basilica," *DOP* 21 (1967), 117–40.

11. Following the city's Christianization some time in the late fourth or early fifth century, the second part of its name, "Capitolina," was dropped and the official name remained Aelia until the end of the Byzantine period. The Muslims also referred to the city as Aelia for several centuries, pronouncing it in the Arabic form, Iliya. Its common name in Greek and Latin Christian literature (and, needless to say, in Jewish sources) was Jerusalem, and sometimes Hierosolyma. It is very likely that the name Jerusalem was colloquially and most commonly used throughout the Byzantine period.

12. Cyril of Jerusalem, *Catecheses* XX. According to one opinion, this text was written by Cyril's successor, John II, and thus is to be attributed to the latter part of the fourth century; see, for example, A. Piédagnal, *Cyrille de Jérusalem, Catéchèses mystagogiques*, SC 126 (Paris, 1966), 18–40.

13. This occurred in spite of the rivalry between the leaders of the Jerusalemite See and the metropolitan bishops in Caesarea; see Z. Rubin, "The Church of the Holy Sepulchre and the Conflict between the Sees of Jerusalem and Caesarea," *The Jerusalem Cathedra*, II, ed. L. I. Levine (Jerusalem, 1982), 79–105.

14. Arculf 1, 7–12 (Adamnanus, *De Locis Sanctis* [*CCSL* 175, 185]).

15. This is in contrast to the West, as in Rome for example, where early churches were not oriented in any one direction, but instead were most probably influenced by local topographical and individual considerations. The churches of Palestine and the East generally faced eastward.

16. Eusebius, *Vita Constantini*, III, 25–54. See also E. D. Hunt, *Holy Land Pilgrimage in the Later Roman Empire—AD 312–460* (Oxford, 1982), 6–49.

17. A. Grabar, *Martyrium: Recherches sur le culte des reliques et l'art chrétien antique*, 2 vols. (London, 1972); R. Krautheimer, *Early Christian and Byzantine Architecture³* (Harmondsworth, 1979), 62–67. On the architectural structure and reconstruction of the church, see above, note 9. The aedicula above the tomb is discussed by J. Wilkinson, *Egeria's Travels* (London, 1971), 242–52; and recently by M. Biddle, "The Tomb of Christ—Sources, Methods and a New Approach," *Churches Built in Ancient Times*, ed. K. Painter (London, 1994), 73–147.

18. Eusebius, *Vita Constantini*, III, 30.

19. See especially H. Saradi-Mendelovici, "Christian Attitudes toward Pagan Monuments in Late Antiquity and Their Legacy in Later Byzantine Centuries," *DOP* 44 (1990), 47–61.

20. Marc le Diacre, *Vie de Porphyre, évêque de Gaza*, 20–53, eds. H. Grégoire and M. A. Kugener (Paris, 1930), esp. pp. 17–44; see also G. Downey, *Gaza in the Early Sixth Century* (Norman, 1963), esp. pp. 14–32.

21. On the topography and archaeology of Byzantine Jerusalem, see Vincent and Abel (above, note 4); J. T. Milik, "Notes d'épigraphie et de topographie palestiniennes, IX: sanctuaires de Jérusalem à l'époque arabe (VIIᵉ–Xᵉ s.)," *RB* 67 (1960), 354–67, 550–86; idem, "La topographie de Jérusalem vers la fin de l'époque byzantine," *Mélanges de l'Université Saint Joseph de Beyrouth* 37 (1960–61): 127–89; Geva (above, note 4), 768–81; Tsafrir, "The Topography and Archaeology of Byzantine Jerusalem," *History of Jerusalem* (above, note 1).

22. On the church of Eleona, see Vincent and Abel (above, note 4), 337–60, 374–412; H. Vincent, "L'Eleona, sanctuaire primitif de l'acension," *RB* 64 (1957), 48–71.

23. On the Constantinian Church of the Nativity in Bethlehem, see, inter alia, W. Harvey, *Structural Survey of the Church of the Nativity, Bethlehem* (Oxford, 1935); E. T. Richmond, "Basilica of the Nativity, Discovery of the Remains of an Earlier Church," *QDAP* 5 (1936), 75–81; idem, "The Church of the Nativity, the Plan of the Constantinian Building," *QDAP* 6 (1938), 63–66; H. Vincent, "Bethléem, le sanctuaire de la nativité d'après les fouilles récentes," *RB* 45 (1936): 551–74; B. Bagatti, *Gli antichi edifici sacri di Betlemme* (Jerusalem, 1951); idem, "Recenti scavi a Betlemme," *LA* 18 (1968), 181–236.

24. On the remains, see A. E. Mader, *Mambre*, 2 vols. (Freiburg, 1957).

25. On the remains, see Vincent and Abel (above, note 4), 360–419; V. Corbo, "Scavo archeologico a ridosso della basilica dell'Ascensione," *LA* 10 (1959–60), 240–70.

26. Vincent and Abel (above, note 4), 328–37; P. G. Orfali, *Getsémani* (Paris, 1924).

27. For example, F. G. Bliss and A. C. Dickie, *Excavations at Jerusalem 1894–1897* (London, 1898), 211–24; E. Loukianoff, *"Ὀελαιῶν,"* The Basilica of Eleon in Constantine's Times, *326–333 A.D.*, Mémoires de l'Institut d'Egypte 42 (Cairo, 1939).

28. Y. Tsafrir and L. Di Segni, "The Population and Ethnic Structure of Byzantine Jerusalem," *History of Jerusalem* (above, note 1).

29. B. Bagatti, "Scavo di un monastero al 'Dominus Flevit' (Monte Oliveto-Gerusalemme)," *LA* 6 (1955–56), 240–70; idem, "Nuovi apporti archeologici al Dominus Flevit," *LA* 19 (1969), 194–236.

30. See the discussion by J. Braslavi (Braslavsky), "A Topography of Jerusalem from the Cairo Genizah," *EI*, VII, L. A. Mayer Volume (Jerusalem, 1964), 69–80, esp. p. 75 (Hebrew). The number of steps varies from one source to the next and may reflect various states of preservation of the flight of steps.

31. On the state of Zion in contrast to Jerusalem, see Hamilton (above, note 8), 83–90.

32. Avigad (above, note 2), 64–80; H. Geva, "The 'First Wall' of Jerusalem during the Second Temple Period. An Archaeological-Chronological Note," *EI*, XVIII (Jerusalem, 1985), 21–39 (Hebrew).

33. See references and discussion concerning Zion and the monuments on Mount Zion in Tsafrir (above, note 7), 89–277.

34. *Itinerarium Burdigalense* 592 (*CCSL* 175, 16); Epiphanius, *De Mensuris et Ponderibus* 14 (*PG* 43, col. 261); also in Syrian: J. E. Dean, *(Epiphanius), Treaties on Weights and Measures, The Syrian Version* (Chicago, 1935), 54C (English trans., 30); Optatus Milevitanus, *Liber de Schismate Donatistarum* 3, 2 (*PL* 11, cols. 993–95).

35. J. Pinkerfeld, "David's Tomb, Notes on the History of the Building," *Bulletin of the L. M. Rabinowitz Fund for the Exploration of Ancient Synagogues*, III (Jerusalem, 1960), 41–43; M. Avi-Yonah's editor's note, ibid., 43. See also the discussion by B. Bagatti, *The Church of the Circumcision* (Jerusalem, 1970), 112–22; and Tsafrir (above, note 7), 91–108, 197–205.

36. Epiphanius, in the Greek and Syrian versions (above, note 34) mentions that the synagogue existed until the days of the Emperor Constantine and the Bishop Maximona. The name Maximona was probably the local common Aramaic form of the name Maximus (335–349 CE).

37. This is contingent upon the fact that the text was indeed composed by Cyril, and not John II, as some scholars suggest. Egeria (ca. 381–384 C.E.) mentions the church of Zion as one of the important churches of Jerusalem already before the time of John II; see below, note 42.

38. The fact that the new church was built under John II is derived from the Georgian lectionary of the Church of Jerusalem which mentions the commemoration of the archbishop John, who was the first to build (the church of) Zion, and Modestos, who rebuilt it after the fire; M. Tarchnishvili, *Le grand lectionnaire de l'église de Jérusalem (V–VIII siècles)* (*CSCO* 188–89; *Scriptores Iberici* 9–10) (Louvain, 1959), Latin trans., 565. See also, G. Garitte, *Le calendrier palestino-géorgien du sinaiticus 34 (Xe siècle)*, Subsidia hagiographica 30 (Brussels, 1958), 410–11. See also Tsafrir (above, note 7), 70–71.

39. On the archaeological remains, see M. Renard, "Die Marienkirchen auf dem Berge Sion in ihrem Zusammenhang mit dem Abendmahlsaale," *Das heilige Land* 44 (1900), 3–23; Vincent and Abel (above, note 4), 431–40.

40. E. Honigmann, "Juvenal of Jerusalem," *DOP* 5 (1950), 209–79.

41. The building of Eudocia's wall is mentioned indirectly by Ioannes Malalas, *Chronographia* 14 (*PG* 97, cols. 532-533), by Eucherius (without mentioning Eudocia by name), 3 (*CCSL* 175, 237), and by the (so-called) Antoninus, 25 (*CCSL* 175, 142; recensio altera, 166). The remains of the wall were discovered by Bliss and Dickie (above, note 27, 1–177) and attributed to Eudocia by J. N. Dalton, "Note on the First Wall of Ancient Jerusalem and the Present Excavations," *PEFQSt* (1895), 26–29. See also the discussion by Tsafrir (above, note 7), 132–35, 205–32.

42. Egeria 25, 11; 27, 5, 7; 37, 1; 39, 4–5; 40, 2; 43, 2–3, 8–9; 44, 3. A. Renoux, "Un manuscrit du lectionnaire arménien de Jérusalem (cod. Jer. Arm. 121)," *Le Muséon* 74 (1961), 361–85; 75 (1962), 385–98; idem, *Le codex arménien de Jérusalem 121* (*PO* 35, 1). See also J. Wilkinson, *Egeria's Travels* (London, 1971), 253–77.

43. See in particular J. F. Baldovin, *The Urban Character of Christian Worship*, Orientalia Christiana Analecta 228 (Rome, 1987).

44. Strategius (ch. XIII) mentions that Christ entered the Gate of Zion carrying a cross on his way to Golgotha. See, for example, Arabic manuscript Sinaiticus 428, ed. G. Garitte, *Expugnationis Hierosolymae A.D. 614—Recensiones Arabicae*, CSCO 340; *Scriptores Arabici* 26

(Louvain, 1973), pp. 23–24 (and Latin translation, *CSCO* 341; *Scriptores Arabici* 27, p. 16). See other manuscripts, *CSCO* 340, pp. 76–77 (and Latin translation, ibid., 341, pp. 51–52). See also ibid., 347; *Scriptores Arabici* 28 (Louvain, 1974), pp. 126–27, 165–66 (and Latin translation, *CSCO* 348; *Scriptores Arabici* 29, pp. 85, 113–14); idem, *La prise de Jérusalem par le Perses en 614* (*CSCO* 202–203; *Scriptores Iberici* 11–12) (Louvain, 1960), 22–23 (203 = translation). This course probably began in the *praetorium* or in Pilate's house, which was located in the valley, somewhere in the vicinity of the present-day Dung Gate. See also discussion by Tsafrir (above, note 7), 159–60; on the location of Pilate's house, see idem, "The Maps Used by Theodosius: On the Pilgrim Maps of the Holy Land and Jerusalem in the Sixth Century C.E.," *DOP* 40 (1986), 129–45, esp. pp. 141–45. The ancient Gate of Zion has not yet been discovered and it has no connection with the present Zion Gate of the city's Turkish wall.

45. Cyril of Scythopolis, *Vita Euthymii* 35 (ed. E. Schwartz, *Kyrillos Von Scythopolis* [Leipzig, 1939], 54).

46. On the church and its identification, see M. J. Lagrange, *Saint Étienne et son sanctuaire à Jérusalem* (Paris, 1894); see also Vincent and Abel (above, note 4), 743–804.

47. C. Schick and F. G. Bliss, "Discovery of a Beautiful Mosaic Pavement with Armenian Inscriptions, North of Jerusalem," *PEFQSt* (1894), 257–61; V. Tzaferis et al., "Excavations at the Third wall, North of the Jerusalem Old City," *Ancient Jerusalem Revealed*, ed. H. Geva (Jerusalem, 1994), 287–92; D. Amit and S. R. Wolff, "An Armenian Monastery in the Morasha Neighborhood, Jerusalem," ibid., 293–98; M. E. Stone and D. Amit, "New Armenian Inscription from Jerusalem," *Cathedra* 83 (1997), 27–44 (Hebrew).

48. Cyril of Scythopolis, *Vita Sabae* 56 (ed. Schwartz, 151)

49. G. Avni, "The Necropoleis of Jerusalem and Bet Govrin in the Fourth–Seventh Centuries—An Example of Urban Cemeteries in Palestine in the Roman and Byzantine Periods," Ph.D. dissertation (Hebrew University of Jerusalem, 1997).

50. C. Mauss, *La piscine de Béthesda à Jérusalem,* (Paris, 1888); Vincent and Abel (above, note 4), 669–742.

51. Avigad (above, note 2), 229–46; for an analysis of the sources concerning the church and the adjacent institutions, see also Milik, "La Topographie" (above, note 21), 145–51.

52. On the dating of the street to the sixth century, see Avigad (above, note 2), 213–29; on its supposed Roman origin, see Tsafrir (above, note 4).

53. Compare a similar phenomenon in Bet Shean-Scythopolis; Y. Tsafrir and G. Foerster, "From Scythopolis to Baysan—Changing Concepts of Urbanism," *The Byzantine and Early Islamic Near East*, II: *Land Use and Settlement Patterns*, eds. G. R. D. King and A. Cameron (Princeton, 1994), 95–115. For parallels in various countries, see D. Claude, *Die byzantinische Stadt im 6. Jahrhundert*, Byzantinisches Archiv 13 (Münich, 1969), esp. pp. 15–106.

54. See above, note 48.

55. On Sabas, see recently J. Patrich, *Sabas, Leader of Palestinian Monasticism—A Comparative Study in Eastern Monasticism, Fourth to Seventh Centuries*, Dumbarton Oaks Studies 32 (Washington D.C., 1994).

56. Peter der Iberer (ed. R. Raabe [Leipzig, 1895], 44–45. For monastic buildings in the area of today's Armenian Quarter, between Jaffa Gate and Mount Zion, see Tsafrir (above, note 7), 37–44, 78–88.

57. The perception of Jerusalem as a round city appears in the description of Eucherius 3, wherein "the area of city was encompassed in a circular shape by not a small length of walls" (*situs ipse urbis in orbem circumactus est non paruo murorum ambitu—CCSL* 175, 237). The *Breviarius* completes the description by saying that the basilica of Constantine is in the center of the city: *in medio civitatis est basilica Constantini* (*Breviarius de Hierosolyma* 1 [*CCSL* 175, 109).

58. The attempt of M. Avi-Yonah to trace the esplanade and the Western Wall on the map is rather unconvincing; M. Avi-Yonah, *The Madaba Mosaic Map* (Jerusalem, 1954), 59.

59. See, for example, Bar Ṣauma's account of the monks' struggle with 103(!) thousand Jews near the corner of the Temple Mount; F. Nau, "Résumé de monographies syriaques (Barṣauma)," *Revue de l'orient chrétien* 19 (1914), 122. On the pinnacle of the Temple, where Satan tempted the Lord, see the *Breviarius de Hierosolyma* 6 (*CCSL* 175, 61).

60. Hieronymus, *In Sophoniam* 1, 15–16 (*CCSL* 76A, 1970), 673–74. The author's bitter anti-Jewish description of the Jews is influenced by his theological approach against Judaism; nevertheless, there is no doubt that the description has historical value.

61. H. Vincent, "Une mosaïque byzantine à Jérusalem," *RB* 10 (1901), 436–48; 11 (1902), 100–103.

62. A. Ovadiah and S. Mucznik, "Orpheus from Jerusalem—Pagan or Christian Image?" *The Jerusalem Cathedra*, I, ed. L. I. Levine (Jerusalem, 1981), 152–66.

63. J. Wilkinson, *Jerusalem Pilgrims before the Crusades* (Warminster, 1977); Hunt (above, note 16).

64. A. Grabar, *Ampoules de Terre Sainte (Monza-Bobbio)* (Paris, 1958).

65. D. Barag, "Glass Pilgrim Vessels from Jerusalem," *Journal of Glass Studies* 12 (1970), 35–63; 13 (1971), 45–63.

66. Tsafrir and Di Segni (above, note 28).

67. See for example, Milik, "Sanctuaires" (above, note 21).

68. Zacharia Hierosolymitani Patriarcha, *Epistola* (*PG* 86, 2, col. 3228); see also Garitte (above note 44) (Arabic version), Ch. XXII (*CSCO* 340, pp. 49, 98; 341, pp. 33, 66; 347, pp. 142, 185; 348, pp. 97, 127).

11

The Cult of the Holy Places and Christian Politics in Byzantine Jerusalem

ZEEV RUBIN

O ne of the major problems connected with the acceptance of Christianity as a licit religion and its subsequent endorsement as the only official state religion is the manner in which this process affected time-hallowed norms of hierarchy and provincial administration within the Christian church. The rise of Constantinople as the capital of the new Christian empire, and the consequent elevation of its see to a rank equal to that of Old Rome, is one case in point.[1] Another is how the bishop of Aelia in the Provincia Palaestina would bring all the evangelical associations connected with his see to bear in order to gain official recognition of its status as an apostolic see, although the practice thus far recognized was that such a status was reserved only for metropolitan sees. The See of Caesarea stood to lose from the rise of Jerusalem. The resulting tension is evident in the sixth and seventh canons of Nicaea in 325.[2]

Elsewhere I have argued that Eusebius' account of the discovery of the Holy Sepulchre and the construction of the church there betrays an undercurrent of surging tension between the two sees, not so much in what it says as in what it omits, i.e., that the wood of the Holy Cross was proclaimed to have been discovered near the burial cave, which otherwise would have remained an empty cave without any testimony to authenticate its identity, and that Macarius, bishop of Jerusalem, played an important part in publicizing the discovery. As might be expected, this argument has failed to gain a general consensus.[3] Although this is not the place for a renewed detailed discussion of the problem, I believe it would be useful to point out what I consider to be the main issues involved. It seems to me that there is little doubt today that Eusebius' account of the discovery of the site of the Holy Sepulchre is fraught with silence and evasion, especially about anything that might have any bearing upon the discovery of the Cross in the vicinity of the sepulchral grave.

151

Differences of opinion arise about Eusebius' possible reasons for suppressing the fact that the discovery of the Cross was publicized as evidence for the identification of the cave as the Sepulchre. Fear that this sign which was "the very heart and soul of the faith would be fettered to an imperial standard" has been suggested as one possible motive.[4] This explanation would have gained in likelihood had it not been for Eusebius' own role in promoting the theme of the Cross as a symbol of great power wielded by an emperor who turned out to be a champion of Christianity against its enemies.[5] Other possible explanations have been offered. Eusebius himself, it has been argued, as a man to whom historical truth and authenticity were important, may have had some natural doubts as to the authenticity of the Cross. Yet, assuming that Eusebius really cherished such doubts, would they not inevitably extend to the tomb itself in the absence of any object to authenticate it? It has likewise been proposed that Eusebius may have had some scruples of a theological nature against putting too much emphasis on the Cross because his main purpose was to underscore the Resurrection rather than Christ's death, and for that purpose it would have been much more useful to focus on the tomb. But would not such a procedure be self-defeating when the sole object that might be used as testimony for its authenticity was left unmentioned, or would the mere mention of its discovery indeed run counter to such a purpose? Another explanation of the same character is that Eusebius' tendency to emphasize the spiritual nature of Christianity involved an inclination to shy away from the cult of physical relics. But, then, was the tomb itself—so profusely glorified by Eusebius—any less of a physical relic than the Cross?[6]

Were one to dismiss my thesis as "unlikely," without any serious attempt to show exactly what renders it so,[7] I could only maintain that the conflict between Jerusalem and Caesarea is an undeniable fact of history highlighted by an impressive array of sources, some of which will be referred to in what follows, and especially those that make it amply clear that in this conflict even considerations of doctrinal probity were subordinate to those of mundane ecclesiastical politics. If questions of orthodoxy and heresy might be used as ploys by some of Macarius' successors, would it be too much to assume that Macarius himself made use of the wealth of evangelical associations connected with Jerusalem, associations that were indeed the sole foundation of its claim to ascendancy over Caesarea, and that Eusebius, as the metropolitan of Palestine, had every reason to be concerned about the process of the transformation of Aelia into a holy city? The assumption that Eusebius' account of the discovery of the Holy Sepulchre is colored by his fears therefore cannot be dismissed, at least as a viable hypothesis.

Macarius' personality ought to serve as a starting point for the understanding of the problem. Not much is known about him beyond his involvement in the nascent cult of the holy places in Jerusalem and its environs.[8] The one other sphere of activity where he has left his imprint is the enhancement of the prestige of his see. It is to his presence in the Council of Nicaea that the promulgation of its seventh canon, mentioned above, ought to be ascribed.[9] It is in the context of this activity that Macarius' attempt to nominate Maximus—later himself bishop of Jerusalem—to the vacant See of Lydda (Diospolis) ought to be understood, since it heralded a series of attempts on the part of the bishops of Jerusalem to arrogate themselves a position superior to that of the metropolitan bishops of Caesarea. This idea had already been adumbrated before. It, however, required fuller development and substantiation—and since my own fuller discussion on the subject appears only in Hebrew, it may still require fuller development and substantiation.[10]

Unlike these first phases of the conflict, which may be described by some as too hypothetical and hence doubtful and disputable, there can be hardly any doubt that the conflict between the See of Jerusalem and the See of Caesarea flared up during the episcopates of Eusebius' successor in Caesarea, Acacius, and Maximus' successor in Jerusalem, Cyril. The former is almost uniformly denounced in the sources as a rabid Arian[11] and the latter has been canonized as an orthodox saint, but the picture that emerges from contemporary sources, or from sources written no later than a few decades after his death in 386, is rather different and may be summed up as follows.[12]

Cyril began his ecclesiastical career as a disciple of Maximus, faithful to the Creed of Nicaea. In order to obtain the See of Jerusalem, he joined the camp of Acacius of Caesarea, which at the time was enjoying Constantius' favor. His readiness to compromise on matters of religious doctrine was, however, greater than his willingness to concede in matters of power and hierarchy. Jerome,[13] Epiphanius,[14] Theodoret,[15] Socrates,[16] and Sozomen[17] do not mince words.[18] Cyril's main concern was not doctrinal purity, and his true purpose was to establish the primacy of his see.[19] Acacius of Caesarea was by no means motivated by less mundane considerations.[20] His conduct during the short reign of the Nicene-Orthodox emperor Jovian proves that in his case, too, his insistence on *his* concept of doctrinal purity was no more than a ploy in his struggle to defend the supremacy of his see.[21] A detailed discussion of the different phases of this conflict lies outside the framework set for this paper. Suffice it to say that Acacius of Caesarea enjoyed an initial advantage by virtue of the proximity of his see to the center of secular power. His endorsement of the view prevailing in the imperial court will have had much greater effect than the endorsement of the same view by the bishop of Jerusalem—still a mere suffragan and out of touch with the representatives of imperial government. Cyril seems to have gradually realized that he had much more to gain by joining the leadership of an opposition party. It is thus that his gradual return to the Nicene Creed in the course of a troubled episcopate, that included three periods of exile, is best explained. The rise to power of Theodosius I, a staunch Nicene Orthodox, in 379 found him to be the right man in the right place. In the Council of Constantinople in 381–382, his orthodoxy was vindicated and his church was given the title *mater omnium ecclesiarum*,[22] tantamount to its official recognition as equal in dignity to the apostolic sees of Alexandria and Antioch.

The weakness of Cyril's position at the beginning of his episcopate is reflected in all the sources mentioned above, but perhaps nowhere better than in the *Chronicon* of Jerome, where he imputes to Cyril a renunciation of his ordination as priest by the Nicene-Orthodox Maximus, so that he could accept it again from Eusebius' Arian successor at the See of Caesarea in return for a promise that he would be nominated bishop of Jerusalem rather than Maximus' own candidate, Heraclius.[23] Later sources assert that Acacius and his ally, Patrophilus of Scythopolis, did not even wait for Maximus' demise and evicted him from his throne in order to install Cyril in his stead.[24] Whatever the truth behind these layers of hostile propaganda in our sources, they seem to bear witness to the fact that upon Cyril's accession to his post, the inferiority of the See of Jerusalem to that of Caesarea was more or less universally recognized. Cyril's letter to Constantius, celebrating the appearance of the cross of light in the sky of Jerusalem during the Pentecost of 351, cannot fail to be conceived as an attempt to reassert the unparalleled holiness of Jerusalem. The fact that the cross was described as extending from the Golgotha, the site of Christ's passion, to the Mount of Olives, the site of his ascent to Heaven and his ultimate triumph, demonstrates with the utmost clarity the extent to which the very notion of this holiness came to be dependent on the presence of the holy places in Jerusalem.[25]

It was in the same year that the discovery of the grave of St. James was proclaimed in Jerusalem, according to a tenth-century Latin source, which in all likelihood follows a lost Greek original.[26] The renewed stress on the martyrdom of Christ's brother, the founder of the Church of Jerusalem, may be regarded as accidental only by those who, while forced to admit that doctrinal disputes could be harnessed to political struggles, nevertheless refuse to acknowledge that the encouragement of the cult of the holy places might be used in a similar manner. The document follows a familiar pattern. A recluse named Epiphanius, residing in a cave between the Mount of Olives and the pinnacle of the Temple, has a vision in which St. James reveals to him that this very cave is the place of his burial. A recurrence of the vision helps him to overcome his own doubts, and though he is first dismissed by the bishop, he manages to enlist a notable of Eleutheropolis, Paul, to aid him in exhuming the relics. The bones of St. James, together with those of the priests Zacharias and Simeon, duly turn up. It is only then that Cyril himself endorses the discovery with great enthusiasm and sanctions the construction of a monument next to the burial cave. The close affinity between this story and the one about the bones of the first martyr, St. Stephen, to be discussed later on, has been noted. The skeptics may use the fact to reject the former as modeled on the latter, but is it not equally reasonable to assume that under similar circumstances two different bishops of Jerusalem resorted to similar methods to highlight the unrivaled holiness of their church? After all, it was by virtue of the fact that Christ's brother was regarded as its first bishop that it deserved to be recognized as *mater omnium ecclesiarum* at the Council of Constantinople.

The practical consequences of this recognition are immediately noticeable in the protocols of the council. In the list of participants, Cyril's name appears before that of Gelasius, bishop of Caesarea, also known as an ecclesiastical historian.[27] A more significant fact is that Gelasius was Cyril's relative, his sister's son, who was finally recognized by the ecumenical council after two previously futile attempts by Cyril to install him in that position. Cyril's repeated efforts to involve himself in nominations to the See of Caesarea, which were meticulously and maliciously documented by Epiphanius, had been thwarted by a coalition of semi-Arian Palestinian bishops, apparently headed by Eutychius, bishop of Eleutheropolis. The establishment of Gelasius in the metropolitan see thus marks the apex of the power of its rival, the bishopric of Jerusalem, in the fourth century.[28]

This state of affairs did not endure long after Cyril's death in 386. The resumption of the dispute could hardly have taken place while Cyril was still alive and Gelasius was in the See of Caesarea. Yet Gelasius himself appears to have revived the pristine claims of his see shortly after his patron's death. In a council held in Constantinople in 394 to decide on a schism in Bostra, it was he who represented the bishops of Palestine (he appears fifth in the list of participants, after Nectarius of Constantinople, Theophilus of Alexandria, Flavianus of Antioch, and Palladius of Caesarea in Cappadocia).[29] It is a seductive, though speculative, assumption that the dispute broke out when Gelasius was still alive. Photius' statement, that he translated the *Historia Ecclesiastica* published by Rufinus in 402, has led to some confusion.[30] Together with Winkelmann and others, I believe that the reverse is correct, and that it is a *Historia Ecclesiastica* written by Gelasius which served as Rufinus' main source until the early eighties.[31] In this case, what Rufinus says about Cyril may indicate what he found in his source: *aliquando in fide, saepius in communione variebat,* a statement which strongly implies that his opportunism was by no means irreprehensible.[32] Theodoret and Sozomen will affirm much more frankly (and possibly more clearly reflecting Gelasius' view when he was writing) that his objective in this opportunism was to procure primacy for his see.

In the list of participants in a synod convened in Jerusalem during the Encaenia celebrations of 401, the name of Eulogius, bishop of Caesarea, precedes that of John, bishop of Jerusalem.[33] Thus, the positions of these two prelates in the Council of Constantinople had been reversed already at the very beginning of Eulogius' episcopate, and it was in all likelihood John's disreputable involvement in the Origenist dispute that contributed to the decline of his see's prestige.

The order of participants in the Encaenia Synod of Jerusalem foreshadows that of the council convened in Lydda in 415 to discuss and decide upon the question of Pelagius' doctrinal probity—yet another dispute in which John involved himself in a rather ill-advised manner. Once again, Eulogius' name heads the list of participants and that of John of Jerusalem appears only in second place.[34] The demotion of the See of Jerusalem at that time, in comparison to that of Caesarea, must have been extremely painful to a man who, in the heat of the Origenist dispute several years earlier, had repeatedly insisted on his authority to pass judgment on certain issues by virtue of his position as the holder of an apostolic see (*apostolicam cathedram tenere se jactans*, as Jerome puts it in his *Letter* 82).[35]

Renewed activity in the glorification of the holy places in Jerusalem and its vicinity may mark the counter-reaction of its humiliated bishop. We do not know the exact date of the construction of the basilica on Mount Zion which, according to the Georgian lectionary, took place during the episcopate of John.[36] Any date between the intervention of Theophilus of Alexandria in the Origenist controversy (which marks a turning point in the position of his see) and the Council of Lydda may fit. Let us recall that John's relapse to second place after Gelasius of Caesarea had already become an established fact in 401.

It was while John of Jerusalem was officiating in the Council of Lydda that he heard news about the dream of a priest named Lucianus concerning the location of St. Stephen the Protomartyr's relics. He immediately left the council, accompanied by the bishops of Jericho and Sebaste, and went to supervise the exhumation of the saint's bones at Caphar Gamala. A letter allegedly written by Lucianus himself to commemorate the event (in the Latin translation of Avitus of Braga, who had been staying in the Holy Land together with Augustine's emissary, Orosius) does little to counter the impression that the whole affair was much more than a mere coincidence.[37]

John's policy of propagating the holiness of Jerusalem by every possible means was continued, so it seems, by his successor, Praylius, whose pro-Pelagian position does not seem to have had an adverse effect on the mounting prestige of his see in the long run.[38] Stories about miraculous occurrences in Jerusalem and its environs spread far and wide. One of them, said to have taken place in 419,[39] was in essence a reenactment of a miracle that had occurred in Cyril's time, during the Pentecost of 351, as described in his letter to Constantius.[40] Caesarea ultimately had little to offer in order to stop the flow of prestigious pilgrims to the Holy City. From Theodoret's *Letter* 110,[41] we learn of a fresh reversal in the fortunes of the two sees. Domninus, a successor to Eulogius, was nominated by Praylius in an action whose canonicity was not above dispute. The man had been a *digamus*. The very nomination of a person whose position was inherently weak may have been a ploy, but the very fact that Praylius was again able to act like Cyril, at the highest point of his influence, is significant. In the Council of Chalcedon, Glycon, bishop of Caesarea, appears second in the list of participants, after the notorious Juvenal, bishop of Jerusalem.[42] At that time, the secondary position of the See of Caesarea seems to have become a matter of course. For nearly three decades, the struggle of the bishop of Jerusalem seems to have moved to a more advanced stage. Both in the first and second councils of Ephesus, he had been engaged in an attempt to establish for his see a rank higher than that of the Apostolic See of Antioch. The story of his exploits, plentiful in intrigue and about-faces, is richly documented and has been the subject of at least one brilliant study.[43] At any rate, it concerns the sees of Jerusalem and Antioch.[44] Suffice it to say in the present context that the Council of Chalcedon ultimately recognized the apostolic status of Jerusalem, but preserved that of Antioch.[45]

That the Metropolitan See of Caesarea was no longer in the game is a fact that can be safely attributed to the mounting prestige derived from the cult of holy places in Jerusalem. That this cult was actively promoted by its bishops is much more than a mere hypothesis. Not only Cyril's repeated references to the Cross in his *Catecheseis*, when reflecting, as a priest, upon notions fostered by the reigning bishop (Maximus) and by his predecessor (Macarius), are significant in this context, but also his letter to Constantius, promulgating the theme of the cross of light that illuminated the sky of Jerusalem during the Pentecost of 351. These episodes have been discussed above. Juvenal's report to the emperors Marcian and Pulcheria concerning the Dormition of the Blessed Virgin might have been adduced as further evidence, for it bears upon the sanctity of two sites, both that of Mount Zion and that of Gethsemane. Unfortunately, however, John of Damascus' account concerning this report is highly problematic.[46] A much stronger consideration is the fact that a bishop's doctrinal enemies could cast aspersions on his character on account of an alleged neglect of a holy place. Witness the attack of John Rufus, in his *Plerophoriae*, against that selfsame Juvenal for having allowed the Probatica to become run down with the passage of time.[47]

Notes

1. *Chronicon Paschale*, a. 330 (*CSHB*, 530). Byzantium had been a city in Europa, one of the provinces of the diocese of Thracia, in the Diocletianic division of the empire, when Constantine chose to detach it from its province and turn it into his new imperial capital. The provincial metropolis of Europa was, and remained, Heraclea (Perinthus), proud of traditions that traced the beginning of its Christian community back to the times of the Apostles, of its impressive array of martyrs, and of a few notable bishops, one of them Philip, a martyr himself; see M. Le Quien, *OrChr*, I–III (Paris, 1740), I, cols. 1100–1103. The *Chronicon Paschale* (loc. cit.) makes it plain that the detachment of Byzantium from Europa actually meant its removal from Heraclea's jurisdiction. For further discussion of the anomalous rise of Constantinople in the hierarchy of bishoprics, see Z. Rubin, "The See of Caesarea in Conflict against Jerusalem from Nicaea (325) to Chalcedon (451)," *Caesarea Maritima–Retrospective after Two Millennia* (Leiden, 1996), 559–74.

2. A. H. M. Jones, *The Later Roman Empire 284–602* (Norman, 1964), 882; cf. L. Perrone, "Von Nicaea (325) nach Chalcedon (451)," *Geschichte der Konzilien, vom Nicaeanum zum Vaticanum II*, ed. G. Alberigo (Düsseldorf, 1993), 50–51, although his suggestion that the seventh canon of Nicaea implies a durable and operative compromise concerning the honor of chairmanship in ecclesiastical conferences in Palestine and abroad cannot be accepted (cf. below, notes 22 and 39). I am grateful to L. Perrone for having discussed his view with me and for having provided me with an offprint of his study.

3. Z. Rubin, "The Church of the Holy Sepulchre and the Beginning of the Conflict between the Sees of Caesarea and Jerusalem," *The Jerusalem Cathedra*, II (Jerusalem, 1982), 76–106. For an acceptance of the main argument of this paper, see P. W. L. Walker, *Holy City, Holy Places? Christian Attitudes to Jerusalem and the Holy Land in the Fourth Century* (Oxford, 1990), esp. p. 130; cf. J. W. Drijvers, *Helena Augusta* (Leiden, 1992), 80–92; and more reservedly O. Irshai, "Historical Aspects of the Christian-Jewish Polemic concerning the Church of Jerusalem in the Fourth Century" (doctoral dissertation; Hebrew University of Jerusalem, 1993), I, 49–50 and note 28 ad loc.; II, 60 (Hebrew). For a rejection of the suggestion that the words τὸ γνώριμα τοῦ ἁγιωτάτου ἐκείνου πάθους as quoted by Eusebius (*Vita Constantini* 3.30.1 [ed. F. Winkelmann, *GCS* 1975, 97]), refer to the True Cross; see M. and M. Whitby, *Chronicon Paschale* (Liverpool, 1989), 20, note 62. Their argument, however, seems to be based on a different passage (*Vita Constantini* 28.1 [ed. F. Winkelmann, *GCS* 1975, 96]), where it is Eusebius who speaks, and not the emperor, and what he talks about there is not *the sign of the most holy passion*, which can mean little else than the Cross, but rather *the evidence of the salutary resurrection* (τῆς σωτηρίου ἀναστάσεως μαρτύριον), which alludes indeed to the burial cave, as the words τὸ ἅγιον τῶν ἁγίων ἄντρον clearly indicate. What Constantine himself asserts must be distinguished from what Eusebius says in his own voice. See also H. A. Drake, "Eusebius on the 'True Cross'," *Journal of Ecclesiastical History* 36 (1985), 1–22, esp. pp. 8–9, where much the same interpretation of the phrase τὸ γνώριμα τοῦ ἁγιωτάτου ἐκείνου πάθους is offered (for references to additional literature, see ibid., 8, note 25). This article, which

seems to have been written without awareness of my article, has also reached conclusions similar to mine on the interpretation of the name Martyrion given to Constantine's basilica (ibid., 5–8).

4. Ibid., 15–20.

5. Thus Drake himself, ibid., 18–19.

6. All three explanations are suggested by Walker (above, note 3), 129, who does not, however, reject the more mundane explanation, i.e., the natural concern of the metropolitan of Palestine in view of the growing aspiration of the Jerusalem Church.

7. R. L. Wilken, *The Land Called Holy, Palestine in Christian History and Thought* (New Haven, 1992), 295, note 62; cf. ibid., 27, note 27, where it is admitted, following Walker (above, note 3), that Eusebius was ambivalent toward Jerusalem, and that rivalry between Caesarea and Jerusalem was one of the factors that went into Eusebius' thinking.

8. See E. D. Hunt (*Holy Land Pilgrimage in the Later Roman Empire* [Oxford, 1984], 8, 13, 15, 43, 46, 145) for a digest, more or less, of all the known details about his role in the promotion of this cult, both in history and later legend.

9. See above, note 2, and cf. Hunt (above, note 8), 7.

10. Z. Rubin, "The Episcopate of Maximus, Bishop of Jerusalem, and the conflict between Caesarea and Jerusalem in the Fourth Century," *Cathedra* 31 (1984), 31–42 (Hebrew); cf. Irshai (above, note 3), I, 47–48.

11. See Le Quien ([above, note 1], III, cols. 559–61), whose survey of the source material is still valuable.

12. The following brief survey of the conflict between Caesarea and Jerusalem during the episcopate of Cyril of Jerusalem is based mainly on my *Jerusalem in the Byzantine Era* (Tel-Aviv, 1985), 45–49 (Hebrew), and with fuller annotation in my "The History of Jerusalem from Constantine to the Moslem Conquest," *The Jerusalem* Book, II, eds. M. Stern et al. (Jerusalem, forthcoming) (Hebrew). See also Irshai (above, note 3), I, 82–90. A. Paulin (*Saint Cyrille de Jérusalem Catéchète* [Paris, 1959]) and G. Bardy ("Cyrille de Jérusalem," *Dictionnaire d'histoire et de géographie ecclésiastiques*, 23 vols, eds A. Baudrillart and R. Aubert [Paris, 1912–90], XIII, cols. 1181–83) are clearly biased in favor of Cyril.

13. Jerome, *Chronicon* (ed. R. Helm, *GCS* 47, 237).

14. Epiphanius (*Panarion* 73.27 [ed. K. Holl, *GCS, Epiphanius*, III, 302]) specifically highlights in this context Cyril's personal rivalry against Eutychius of Eleutheropolis.

15. Theodoret, *Historia Ecclesiastica* 2.26.6 (ed. F. Scheidweiler, *GCS*, 157).

16. Socrates, *Historia Ecclesiastica* 5.8 (*PG* 67, col. 570). Both Socrates and Sozomen (see the following note) strongly imply that Cyril's change of heart at the Council of Constantinople was not entirely sincere.

17. Sozomen, *Historia Ecclesiastica* 7.7.3(ed. J. Bidez, *GCS*, 308–309).

18. For Rufinus' assessment of his doctrinal probity, see below.

19. This is admitted explicitly especially by Theodoret (see above, note 15), and Sozomen (*Historia Ecclesiastica* 2.40 [*PG* 67, col. 344]) is especially critical in describing his appeal to the emperor against the verdict of an ecclesiastical council as unprecedented.

20. See above, note 10.

21. Socrates, *Historia Ecclesiastica* 3.25 (*PG* 67, col. 452–53).

22. J. D. Mansi, *Sacrorum Conciliorum nova et amplissima collectio*, III (reprint Graz, 1960), cols. 585–87. The Latin form of this title is that of Sirmond's translation of a letter written by the participants of the Council of Constantinople to Damasus, bishop of Rome, as quoted by Theodoret (*Historia Ecclesiastica* 5.9.17 [ed. F. Scheidweiler, *GCS*, 234]), where the Greek formula is μητὴρ τῶν ἁπασῶν ἐκκλωσιῶν. Yet, possibly the form *mater cunctarum ecclesiarum*, as given by Cassiodorus (*Historia Tripartita* 9.14 [*PL* 69, col. 1134]) ought to be preferred. In

spite of the fact that Cassiodorus is here following the Greek version of Theodoret, he may also have consulted the official Latin version of the letter.

23. See above, note 13.

24. Socrates, *Historia Ecclesiastica* 2.38; Sozomen, *Historia Ecclesiastica* 4.20.

25. Cyril of Jerusalem, *Epistula ad Constantium* (*PG* 33, cols. 1166–77). A detailed analysis of this document is to be found in Irshai (above, note 3), I, 105–30.

26. See F.-M. Abel, "La sépulture de saint Jacques le Mineur," *RB* 16 (1919), 480–99.

27. The list of participants is given by Theodoret, *Historia Ecclesiastica* 8.5 (ed. F. Scheidweiler, *GCS*, 288). In the list of signatories to the Creed of Constantinople as given by Mansi (above, note 22, col. 568),Thalassius is obviously a misreading for Gelasius (cf. ibid., note 2 ad loc.). Perrone's suggestion (above, note 2) that this order may be a reflection of a settlement implied by the seventh canon of Nicaea cannot be sustained. The troubled conditions under which councils were held in the fourth century, when sees were frequently torn by schism and bishops attended councils abroad while banished from their own thrones, do not permit any inference about an arrangement reached in Nicaea if such an arrangement is not explicitly stated. As for the period that followed the Council of Constantinople, there is one piece of circumstantial evidence which points in the opposite direction (see below, note 39).

28. Epiphanius, *Panarion* 73.37 (ed. K. Holl, *GCS, Epiphanius*, III, 312); cf. Le Quien (above, note 1), III, cols. 561–62.

29. See Mansi (above, note 22), 851–52; and cf. L. S. Le Nain De Tillemont, *Mémoires pour servir à l'histoire ecclésiastique de six premiers siècles*, X (Paris, 1705), 705, cf. p. 850; Le Quien (above, note 1), III, cols. 562–63; see also H. Grégoire and M. A. Kugener, *Marc le Diacre, Vie de Porphyre* (Paris, 1930), XXXIX. This council is one of the main considerations against the acceptance of the cautious suggestion made by L. Perrone (above, note 2, 50–51), that the seventh canon of Nicaea actually determined the order of representation of the two leading bishops of Palestine in ecclesiastical councils, so that the bishop of Caesarea should precede the bishop of Jerusalem in councils held within Palestine, whereas the order should be reversed outside Palestine. Perrone argues that this seems to be the practice in the light of the evidence for the fourth and fifth centuries. However, the clearer cases seem to be precisely those of the few decades after the Council of Constantinople, when the tension between Jerusalem's newly-acquired status as *mater omnium ecclesiarum* on the one hand, and that of Caesarea as a metropolitan see on the other, seems to be the best explanation for vicissitudes in the relative positions of these two bishoprics. In our particular case, the bishop of Caesarea represents the church of Palestine outside Palestine as one of the arbitrators in the case of a disputed episcopal nomination. One might have expected the bishop of Jerusalem to have played precisely this role if its position as an apostolic see, or equal to an apostolic see, had been universally recognized.

30. Photius, *Bibliotheca*, cod. 89. For an acceptance of his identification of Gelasius as the translator of Rufinus' *Historia Ecclesiastica*, see, e.g., F. Diekamp, *Analecta Patristica: Texte und Abhandlungen zur griechischen Patristik*, Orientalia Christiana Analecta 127 (Rome, 1938), 16–32; cf. most recently J. Geiger, "Latin in Roman Palestine," *Cathedra* 74 (1974), 17 (Hebrew). Thus also Grégoire (in Grégoire and Kugener [above, note 29], XXXVIII–XXXIX), who identifies the bishop of Caesarea who figures in the *Vita Porphyrii* as Gelasius and refuses to admit the possibility that any John in the See of Caesarea, before the one who took part in the Council of Jerusalem in 518, may be historical, in spite of his basic belief in a sound historical core of this source.

31. F. Winkelmann, *Untersuchungen zur Kirchengeschichte des Gelasios von Kaisarea*, Sitzungsberichte der deutschen Akademie der Wissenschaften zu Berlin 3 (Berlin, 1965), 75–78, cf. p. 105. See also Z. Rubin, "Mavia Queen of the Saracens," *Cathedra* 47 (1988), 34–35 (Hebrew).

32. Rufinus, *Historia Ecclesiastica* 19 (10).26 (ed. Th. Mommsen, *GCS* 9 [2], 989).

33. Jerome, *Letters* 91 and 92; see J. Labourt (ed. and trans.), *Saint Jérôme, Lettres*, IV (Paris, 1954), 148–59, and esp. pp. 148 and 157 for the names of the participants in the Encaenia synod addressed by Theophilus and the response to his letter. That these letters were written before 402 is made clear by Jerome's reference in his *Apologia adversus Libros Rufini* 3.16 (*PL* 23, col. 468), most certainly written in that year; see the introductory note to this work by D. Vallarsi, whose text edition of Jerome's writings is reprinted in *PL* (ibid., 23, cols. 395–96). The reason why these two documents are habitually ignored in the debate about the historicity of John of Caesarea seems to be connected to the fact that negations of his historicity are based mainly on the assumption that Gelasius must not only have still been alive during the year when Rufinus completed his *Historia Ecclesiastica*, but must also have lived on for some time, in order to be able to produce his own translation of it. Such an argument gains little support from the clear evidence that, already in 400 or 401, not Gelasius, but Eulogius, was the bishop of Caesarea. This dating to 400 is suggested by Vallarsi (*PL* 22, cols. LXXVI–LXXVII); cf. F. Cavallera, *Saint Jérôme, sa vie et son oeuvre* (Louvain and Paris, 1922), II, 41; Labourt (op. cit.), 170; and J. N. D. Kelly, *Jerome* (London, 1975), 259. This dating seems to be based on a misinterpretation of Jerome's statements about his translation of a few of Theophilus' letters concerning the Origenist dispute; see Z. Rubin, "Porphyrius of Gaza and the Conflict between Christianity and Paganism in Southern Palestine," *Sharing the Sacred* (Jerusalem, 1998), 31–66, esp. p. 55, note 71, for a discussion of the evidence and the case for 401 as the much more likely date.

34. See above, note 30. The *Vita* ignores Porphyry's participation in this synod, according to Grégoire (in Grégoire and Kugener [above, note 29], LXXIX–LXXX) with good reason. Its favorable attitude toward Pelagius and his teachings will have made it an occasion *dont l'épiscopat palestinien aurait sans doute voulu abolir la mémoire*.

35. For Jerome's involvement in the Origenist dispute, see also above, note 33.

36. See H. Goussen, *Über georgische Drucke und Handschriften, die Forlesung und Heiligen kalender des altchristlischen Jerusalems* (Munich-Gladbach, 1923), 17 (23ʳᵈ March); cf. G. Garitte, *Le calendrier palestino-géorgien du Sinaiticus 34 (Xᵉ siècle)*, Subsidia Hagiographica 30 (Brussels, 1958), 186–87.

37. We possess a number of versions of Lucianus' letter. The two Latin ones (*PL* 41, cols. 805–808) have been known for a long time. A Greek version published by A. Papadopulos Kerameus (Ἀνάλεκτα τῆς Ιεροσολυμιτικῆς σταχυολγίας [Petersburg, 1898], 28–53) is close to the Latin version habitually referred to as Version B, which does not seem to reflect Lucianus' original letter and is a rather late elaboration; see M. J. Lagrange, "Le sanctuaire de la lapidation de saint Étienne à Jérusalem," *ROC* 12 (1907), 412–28, esp. pp. 419–28; and P. Peeters, "Le sanctuaire de la lapidation de saint Étienne, à propos d'une controverse," *AnBoll* 27 (1906), 359–68. This seems to be true also of a Syriac version of the document, in spite of the opinion of F. Nau, "Sur les mots πολιτικός et πολιτευόμενος et sur plusieurs textes grecs rélatifs à saint Étienne," *ROC* 11 (1906), 199–219. On the other hand, the other Latin version, known as Version A, seems to be the verbal translation of Lucianus' letter by Avitus of Braga, whose Greek original has been lost; thus, Lagrange and Peeters in the studies cited above. The detail about the role played by John of Jerusalem in the discovery of the bones during the synod of Diospolis is related in Version A; on its credibility, see Peeters, op. cit., 366–67. It is worth mentioning that Peeters restores here the manuscript reading of the phrase describing the role played by John in the synod (*in synodo agens*), in preference to the arbitrary emendation of the editors in the *PL* (*synodum agens*). The former reading undoubtedly tallies better with Eulogius' precedence over John in the list of participants.

38. See Kelly (above, note 33), 324–26.

39. Marcellinus Comes, a. 419 (*Chronica Minora* 2, 74; cf. B. Croke [trans.], *The Chronicle of Marcellinus*, in *Byzantina Australienia* 7 [Sydney, 1995], 12–13): a cross of light is said to have appeared above the Mount of Olives in the course of an earthquake, and the clothes of those who were baptized under the impact of the miraculous manifestation were stamped with signs of shining crosses; cf. *Consularia Constantinopolitana*, a. 419 (ibid., 246), where the source spreading the rumors concerning these miracles is described in a letter written by a bishop of Jerusalem, mistakenly identified as John (Praylius must be meant, since John had been dead for about two years in 419).

40. See above, note 25.

41. *PG* 83, col. 1305.

42. Le Quien (above, note 1), III, 567.

43. E. Honigmann, "Juvenal of Jerusalem," *DOP* (1950), 211–76.

44. Juvenal's claim to a superior rank of his see over that of Antioch was formulated in the clearest terms already in the Council of Ephesus in 431; see Mansi (above, note 22), IV, col. 1311; *ACO*, 1–3, 18.

45. See Honigmann (above, note 43), 240–47.

46. Johannes Damascenus, *Homilia in Dormitionem Beatae Virginis Mariae* 18 (*PG* 96, cols. 748–52).

47. Johannes Rufus, *Plerophoriae* 18 (*PO* 8, 35–37).

12

"Mapping History's Redemption" Eschatology and Topography in the *Itinerarium Burdigalense*

GLENN BOWMAN

In a recent article, R. Markus queries—with reference to the fourth-century C.E. emergence of a Christian network of holy sites—"why, how was it possible that any place should become holy?" He proceeds to analyze a sacralyzing transformation of places in popular perceptions and practices as the reflection of a shift in Christian devotion "from the eschatological meaning of the historical narratives to their topographical associations."[1] This shift, which prepared the ground for the Constantinian church building program, affecting not only Palestine but the entirety of the Roman empire as well, came about, according to Markus, because early fourth-century Christians felt it necessary to elaborate cult practices around tombs and relics of martyrs in order to assert continuity between their church—increasingly enjoying the support of the Roman state—and the church of early Christians, who discerned the signs of their divine election in the wounds of martyrdom that same state had inflicted on them. Markus writes that "the veneration of martyrs . . . served to assure the Christians of a local church of its continuity with its own heroic, persecuted, past, and the universal Church of its continuity with the age of the martyrs."[2] Martyrs and their relics came to be seen as resting "in place," and the place of the cult became a site for encounter between the sanctifying individuals and events of an increasingly-distant past and contemporary Christians who wished to participate in that sanctity. "Places became sacred as the past became localised in the present,"[3] and the logic of the cult practices that brought fourth-century Christians into contact with their martyred forebears was easily extended from places explicitly connected with martyrdom to sites associated with other elements of Christian and pre-Christian history.

Scripture into Site: Text and Monument in the Fourth-Century Holy Land

In the Holy Land the sites sanctified were less commonly those associated with martyrdoms (notwithstanding the powerful exception of Golgotha) than those linked through biblical narratives with Jesus's prefiguration, his incarnation, and the dissemination of his message through his disciples' activities. Constantine, as is well known, initiated a massive program of church building in Jerusalem in 325 C.E. with the construction of a shrine complex composed of a basilica known as the "Martyrium," a rotunda-shrine over Jesus' tomb named the "Anastasis," and a chapel at Calvary. This was quickly followed by the erection of three other memorial compounds: one near Hebron at Mamre—where Abraham was said to have been visited by God and two mysterious companions (Gen. 18:1–22); another at Bethlehem—where Jesus was reputed to have been born; and a third, the Éléona, on the Mount of Olives from whence, according to Acts 1:6–12, Jesus ascended into the heavens. These and other sites provided local and pilgrim Christians with settings wherein they could engage—in liturgy and the imagination—with signal events drawn from a sanctified past.

We see, for instance, in the enthusiastic narrative of a late fourth-century pilgrim who has come to be known as Egeria,[4] a compulsive siting of biblical referents on the landscape:

> All along the valley [below Mount Sinai] they [local monastics serving as guides] showed us how each Israelite had a house, and they were round stone houses, as you can still see from the foundations. They showed us where holy Moses ordered the children of Israel to run "from gate to gate" (Ex. 32:27) when he had come back from the Mount. They also showed us where holy Moses ordered them to burn the calf which Aaron had made for them; and the bed of the stream from which, as you read in Exodus, holy Moses made the children of Israel drink (ibid., 32:20). And they pointed out the place where a portion of Moses' spirit was given to the seventy men (Num. 11:25), and where the children of Israel had their craving for food (ibid., 11:4). They showed us also the place called "The Fire" (ibid., 11:3), a part of the camp which was burning, where the fire stopped when holy Moses prayed. And they showed us where the manna and the quails descended on the people (Num. 11.6, 31). So we were shown everything which the Books of Moses tell us took place in that valley beneath holy Sinai, the Mount of God.[5]

When Egeria returns from the Sinai to Jerusalem to participate in its extended Holy Week liturgy, she witnesses on Palm Sunday how the Christian liturgy—enacted in the Holy City in the same places the events it celebrates were alleged to have been carried out originally—re-presents and thus reenacts the past:

> the bishop and all the people rise from their places, and start off on foot down from the summit of the Mount of Olives. All the people go before him with psalms and antiphons, all the time repeating "Blessed is he that cometh in the name of the Lord". . . . Everyone is carrying branches, either palm or olive, and they accompany the bishop in the very way the people did when once they went down with the Lord . . . what I found most impressive about all this [the patterns of worship of the Jerusalem community] was that the psalms and antiphons they use are always appropriate, whether at night, in the early morning, at the day prayers at midday or three o'clock, or at Lucernare. Everything is suitable, appropriate and relevant to what is being done.[6]

In Egeria's lauding of the verisimilitude of holy land sites and practices, we see yet another instance of the evolving phenomenon of site sanctification traced by P. Walker through Eusebius of Caesarea's and Cyril of Jerusalem's discourses on the holy places.[7] Egeria *sees* played out before her the forms of Scripture, whether these be read in the details of landscape or reenacted in celebrants' movements across the field of the literal sites. Cyril, addressing catechumens ca. 350 C.E., calls upon them to *read* from the site surrounding them the truth others can only hear: "one should never grow weary of hearing about our crowned Lord, especially on this holy Golgotha. For others merely hear, but we see and touch".[8]

Emerging from these two texts, one may discern the threat Gregory of Nyssa (331–395 C.E.) saw in the growing cult of holy sites—the danger that such sites would come to be seen as inherently sacred and that worship of the sites would come to supplant reverence for the divine events from whence their original significance was metonymically drawn.[9] Cyril, in the lecture cited above, suggests that contact with holy sites adds to the devotion Christians feel when hearing Scripture read; seeing and touching the sites which provide a *mise en scène* for the scriptural events relay a better spiritual charge than merely hearing of the events through a scriptural reading. In Egeria, Scripture begins to dissolve into site; of the holy place which would become St. Catherine's, she writes "nearby you are also shown the place where holy Moses was standing when God said to him (Ex. 3:5), 'Undo the fastening of thy shoes', *and so on.*"[10] More significantly, the sacramental charge put into sites by the past activities of sacred figures begins, in Egeria's rendering of the holy places, to leak out of the places and affect surrounding objects in ways that have little, if anything, to do with the dissemination of the divine truths the Scriptures relay. When Egeria visits Edessa, she sees wonderful fish in the pools of the palace which she discovers are excellent to eat: "I have never seen fish like them, they were so big, so brightly coloured, and tasted so good."[11] This is not, however, a mere intrusion of secular matter into a text marked by its devotion to reading biblical inscriptions off the landscape. The palace visited was that of King Abgar, a monarch who featured in an early Christian legend as having believed in Jesus before seeing him, having written a letter to him attesting to that belief, and having been rewarded by Jesus with a miraculous letter which protected Abgar and his city during an extended Persian siege. During that siege, the people of Edessa had been rescued from death by thirst by a miraculous eruption of sweet water out of dry ground which had occurred after Jesus' letter had been circulated throughout the city. Subsequently, pools were built to hold the waters of the miraculous spring and the fish Egeria enjoyed were spawned in the sanctified waters of those pools.[12] Here the sacred power inherent in Jesus' words is transferred into a text which serves as a miracle-working object and gives rise to a body of water containing the fish which are not only big and beautiful but are also delicious to eat. The word is here in the process of becoming world, and the contagion by which sites in the world borrow sanctity from Scripture only to subsequently appear as holy in themselves does not take long to develop. We read in the *Itinerarium* (ca. 570 C.E.) of the Piacenza Pilgrim that

> We travelled on to the city of Nazareth, where many miracles take place. In the synagogue there is kept the book in which the Lord wrote his ABC, and in this synagogue there is the bench on which he sat with the other children. Christians can lift the bench and move it about, but the Jews are completely unable to move it, and cannot drag it outside. The house of Saint Mary is now a basilica, and her clothes are the cause of frequent miracles. . . . The region is a paradise, with fruit and corn like Egypt. The region is small, but in its wine, oil, and apples it is superior to Egypt. The millet is abnormally tall. . . ."[13]

Here not only has the terrain been transformed by contiguity to biblical events associated with it so that it itself has become miracle working, but elements of the place themselves give rise to "biblical" stories which were not related in the Bible. Place has truly become holy.

Behind this sanctification of site is a shift from the priority of hearing to that of seeing and touching. In some ways this reflects the "coming out" of the church in the period of tolerance which followed the close of the fierce and final persecution Diocletian had launched in 303 C.E. Once it became safe to engage publicly in ritual and in commemoration of Christian ideology, the media of proselytization no longer needed to be the spoken word based on the concealable text, but could become the visual and haptic demonstratives of monument and public liturgy.[14] The "holy land"—like other monumental celebrations of the word made flesh throughout the empire—became, in this sense, a translation of spoken discourse into a discourse of visual and tactile display. The world was in the process of being transformed by the word and it is not, therefore, surprising to see that some domains of the world (the interiors of churches, the surroundings of martyrs' shrines, and the land where the word had walked as a man) could be seen—and read—as the incarnated word.[15]

Locating the Text of the Bordeaux Pilgrim

The *Itinerarium Burdigalense*,[16] which appears to be an account of a pilgrimage from Bordeaux to the Holy Land and back in 333 C.E., is positioned at this transformation's cusp. Despite the significance of its location, modern reception of the text has been dismissive. R. Wilken characterizes the *Itinerarium Burdigalense* as

> a brief, almost stenographic account, noting where he went, what he saw, where he changed his horses, and distances from one place to another. . . . The book exhibits almost no theological interest. It moves indiscriminately from one place to another . . . [and] has no hierarchy of place."[17]

In the work of most commentators, the Bordeaux Pilgrim's narrative is overshadowed by Egeria's "modern" first-person account, which appears to offer a more immediately rewarding access to religiosity of the period. Thus, E. D. Hunt unfavorably compares its "stark narrative" with that of Egeria, which "furnishes a more penetrating glimpse into the devotion of the Christian traveler."[18] Hunt's dismissal resonates with M. Campbell's description of the *Itinerarium Burdigalense* and its source, the "Antonine Itinerary," as "barely more than lists of cities, *mansiones*, places of interest, and the approximate distances (given in *milia*) between them. These works are in effect verbal charts, designed for the convenience of subsequent travelers, not for the reader's spiritual exaltation."[19] I will, however, argue in the following pages that the half century which separates the two texts effected massive transformations in Christians' senses of their world and the place of their religion in it, and these changes deeply effect the narrative economies of the texts. I will contend that the *Itinerarium Burdigalense* is not a mere "verbal chart" for the guidance of travelers, but is instead a carefully structured and deeply theological transposition onto topography of an eschatological history. The text, rather than seeking to direct pilgrims to the holy places of the Roman empire, works to lead catechumens to gateways which open onto a kingdom not of this world.

Egeria's ecstatic response to the conjunction of place, text, and pilgrim was symptomatic of new attitudes toward holy sites developing in the decades following Constantine's conversion. Her narrative celebrates a world in the process of being transformed into a Christian domain, and the tone of her text is redolent with the same holy confidence which inspired Eusebius (ca. 337–339 C.E.) to suggest that the building of the Anastasis was the beginning of an inworldly fulfillment of Revelation's prophecy of a new heaven and new earth:

> on the very spot which witnessed the Saviour's sufferings, a new Jerusalem was constructed, over against the one so celebrated of old which, since the foul stain of guilt brought upon it by the murder of the Lord, had experienced the last extremity of desolation, the effect of divine judgement upon its impious people. It was opposite this city that the emperor now began to rear a monument to the Saviour's victory over death, with rich and lavish magnificence. And it may be that this was that second and new Jerusalem spoken of in the predictions of the prophets.[20]

For Egeria, the newly-Christianized empire is part of the project of world sanctification she and her contemporaries saw prefigured in the texts of Bible; the Christian world, and herself as a Christian in it, are valorized by that continuity, and that engagement renders both self and site worthy. Egeria's narrative is densely charged by enthusiastic first person narration; "we had been looking forward to all this so much that we had been eager to make the climb."[21] It is marked by a confidence in the continuity of biblical past and sanctified present to the extent that Egeria is able to use her contemporary experiences to illuminate and elaborate biblical narrative:

> I kept asking to see the different places mentioned in the Bible, and they were all pointed out to me. . . . Some of the places were to the right and others to the left of our route, some a long way off and others close by. So, as far as I can see, loving sisters, you must take it that the

children of Israel zigzagged their way to the Red Sea, first right, then back left again, now forwards, and now back.[22]

Posteriority—the belatedness of visiting the holy places four centuries after Jesus' death—is not a condition of loss and distance as the world has assimilated the biblical past and built upon it a contemporary structure of Christian community and authority. There is no rupture between the biblical past and the imperial present but only the signs of a community developing its structures and traditions on that past and into its future:

> We were also shown the place where Lot's wife had her memorial, as you read in the Bible. But what we saw, reverend ladies, was not the actual pillar, but only the place where it had once been. The pillar itself, they say, has been submerged in the Dead Sea—at any rate we did not see it and I cannot pretend we did. In fact it was the bishop there, the Bishop of Zoar, who told us that it was now a good many years since the pillar had been visible.[23]

For Egeria, the Holy Land presents a wealth not only of monuments to the founding moments of her faith, but also of testimonies for the expanding power of that faith as it develops the institutions needed for it to grow and spread throughout the known world. It is not surprising that she—having witnessed the monuments to the biblical past and seen the continuity between that past and her present in Jerusalem's fervent transformation into a ritual center manifesting the word made flesh—announces her intention of moving on to visit places beyond the borders of the Holy Land which have been caught up in and render evidence of the expansion of that incarnated and empowered revelation.[24]

Although the Constantinian basilicas were being erected as the *Itinerarium Burdigalense* was being composed, the tone of its discourse differs radically from Egeria's. In it a detached impersonality prevails which tends to efface the subject positions of both narrator and "reader":

> from here to Bethasora 14 miles, where the spring is in which Philip baptized the eunuch. From there it is nine miles to Terebinthus where Abraham lived and dug a well under the terebinth tree and spoke and ate with the angels.[25]

In striking contrast to the passage from Egeria cited above—where the wanderings of the children of Israel are experienced in terms of a network of sites on a contemporary landscape which itself comes to serve as the grounds for biblical exegesis—in the Bordeaux Pilgrim's description of Bethel, the narrator and time of narration at times disappear. In one case the reader is introduced by the text into a landscape which is not coterminous with the contemporary site from whence the narrative is launched, but is present only in the discourse of I Kgs. 13:1–32:

> From here it is a mile to the place where Jacob, on his way to Mesopotamia, fell asleep, and there is the almond tree, and here he saw a vision and the angel wrestled with him. Here was also King Jeroboam, to whom was sent a prophet so that he might be converted to the Most High God; and the prophet was commanded not to eat with the false prophet whom the king had about him, and because he was led astray by the false prophet and ate with him on his way back, a lion met the prophet on the way and killed him.[26]

In the Bordeaux Pilgrim's narrative, the order of events is not organized with reference to the moment of observation, but either in terms of a spatial contiguity which collapses temporality—

> A mile from here is the place called Sechar, from which the Samaritan woman went down to the same place where Jacob had dug a well, to fill her jug with water from it, and our Lord Jesus Christ spoke with her; and where there are plane trees, which Jacob planted, and baths which get their water from this well"[27]—

or, as I will demonstrate below, in terms of an eschatological periodicity which renders the narrator's role extraneous. The Bordeaux Pilgrim's text, rather than portraying the center of an expanding new world order, seems to manifest to its audience a space contiguous to, but not continuous with, the secular world. The pilgrim, who moves out of his or her native land and into that holy space, seems simultaneously to "lose" himself or herself and to "find" a way out of this life and into a world which takes its being from the events and prophecies of the Bible. The *Itinerarium* thus appears to map a passage between two distinct domains—the contemporary and fallen world of the Roman empire and another world where time is eschatological and leads towards the eternity of a promised redemption. The presence on that map of the four Constantinian basilicas would seem, however, to provide a conundrum inasmuch as they would seem to be very much of the time and order of empire. It will be necessary to move through the holy land represented in the *Itinerarium Burdigalense* to understand why, in a text which takes its bearings from a biblical past, the author should emphasize the fact that lately, by the order of the emperor Constantine, was built a basilica, that is a house of the lord, with ponds of remarkable beauty beside it, from which water is taken up, and at the back a font, where children are baptized.[28]

Traversing the *Itinerarium*

The Bordeaux Pilgrim's text poses for the critical reader an immediate set of methodological questions. Is the text—for which we have no contemporaneous history of usage—to be read purely in terms of its internal logic? Insofar as the text is, even with its descriptive addenda, in large part a listing of names, it seems clear that its author expects its audience, in seeking to understand the text, to draw upon extra-textual information pertaining to the sites and events it names. Can we then use the contemporary Holy Land and its topographic peripheries as sources for the information we need to make sense of the Bordeaux Pilgrim's text?

Two things seem to militate against that mode of referencing. The first is that the *Itinerarium* appears to be an unreliable guidebook to a practical trip through Palestine. As Wilken points out, "his route is puzzling; he sometimes turns back to visit places he could have seen when he was in the vicinity, and he makes few observations on the things he has seen."[29] The text's erraticism, as well as its striking ommisions,[30] suggest that it functions not so much as a guide to a literal place than as a discourse using that space as a pretext for another exploration. The second argument against using fourth-century Palestine as a hermeneutic device is that, in the text itself, real places seem to serve as doorways into a literary domain—that of the Bible—as in the passage cited above where the reader is carried into I Kgs. 13 rather than directed along fourth-century roads. One is led to ask, then, whether the text is organized in terms of a logic existing outside of itself, not in the order of sites along fourth-century pilgrim routes but in the biblical texts which early Christians would themselves have used as devices for interpreting events in their own contemporary world? In this case, the literal Holy Land would be presented as a gloss on biblical materials instead of, as it does in Egeria's text, serving itself as a primary text which the Bible serves to explicate. Interpretation would thus have to be based not primarily on the sites visited but—at least in the first instance—on the biblical references to which those sites offer access. In traversing the text of the pilgrim in the following pages, I will reverse the agenda Spitzer discerned in Egeria's gaze (see above, note 5) and direct my eye from "the *locus* (locality) in Palestine" to "the biblical *locus* (i.e., passage)" with which contemporary Christian knowledge would have associated it. In doing so, I hope not so much to show the land as it would have been perceived before place came to be seen as holy as to provide an insight into what the Bordeaux Pilgrim was presenting if it was not a Holy Land.

The presentation of biblical material in the *Itinerarium Burdigalense* is framed, both at the beginning and the close of the narrative, with hundreds of brief entries of which the following, tracing the route between Antioch and Banias, are typical:

City of Antiochia	xvi [miles]
From Tarsus in Cilicia to Antiochia	141 miles, 10 changes, 7 halts
To the palace of Daphne	v
Change at Hysdata	xi
Halt at Platanus	viii
Change at Bacchaiæ	ii
Halt at Catelæ	xvi
City of Ladica	xvi
City of Gabala	xiv
City of Balaneas	xiii
The border of Coele Syria and Phoenicia.[31]	

The massive distances covered between Bordeaux and the borders of the Holy Land (by the text's own calculation the distance between Bordeaux and Sarepta is 3190 miles) are, in large part, rendered as empty spaces by the text. The narrative marks borders (both natural and political) and makes occasional mention of curiosities dealing with water (the ebb and flow of the river Garonne at Bordeaux and "a city in the sea two miles from the shore")[32] but in large part restricts itself to the names of places where the traveler rested or changed horses. Outside of the Holy Land the text proffers little more than the homogenized mapping which characterizes the military itineraries of the period. The only deviations from such models are a number of emendations; on the way out—

Viminatium "where Diocletian killed [Marcus Aurelius] Carinus";

Libyassa where "lies [the body of] King Annibalianus (Hannibal), who was once king of the Africans";

Andavilis where is "the villa of Pampatus, from which came the curule horses"

Tyana where "was born Apollonius the Magician"; and

Tarsus where "the Apostle Paul was born";

and on the return—

> Philippi where the apostles "Paul and Silas were imprisoned";
> Euripides where "is buried the poet Euripides"; and
> Pellas from "whence came Alexander the Great of Macedonia."

It is with the text's advent upon territories which have parts to play in the biblical narratives[33] that the tenor of the *Itinerarium Burdigalense* changes radically. At Sarepta (biblical Zarephath) the narrative begins to sprout novel shoots of discourse: "this is where Elijah went up to the widow and asked for food."[34] A few lines later, another biblical referent emerges from the stem of the itinerary—"this is where Mt. Carmel is; there Elijah made sacrifice,"[35] followed soon after by a third—"There [Caesarea Palaestina] is the bath of Cornelius the Centurion, who gave many alms."[36] A few lines later the city of Isdraela (biblical Jezreel) is described as "where Ahab reigned and Elijah prophesied; there is the field in which David killed Goliath."[37] That is followed by the mention of Aser which—inexplicably according to Wilkinson[38]—the pilgrim claims was the site of Job's house. The text then presents Neapolis (present day Nablus) as:

> the site of Mount Agazaren (Gerizim); the Samaritans say that there Abraham offered sacrifice, and five hundred steps go up to the top of the mountain. From there, at the foot of the mountain, is that place called Sechem. There is the tomb in which Joseph is laid in the villa which his father Jacob gave him. From there Dinah, Jacob's daughter, was abducted by the sons of the Amorites. A mile from here is the place called Sechem. . . . [39]

From that point on, until the confines of the Holy Land are left behind, the form of the itinerary nearly disappears beneath a profusion of commentary binding places to an apparently unstructured glossing of biblical associations and throwing out the occasional contemporary observation. Despite this appearance of unstructured proliferation, which led the above-quoted commentators to characterize the *Itinerarium* as a "verbal chart" which "moves indiscriminately from one place to another . . . [and] has no hierarchy of place," a theme emerges in the opening sections of the pilgrim's presentation of the Holy Land which sets the parameters for the rest of the text, determining what will be included and what excluded in the text's presentation of the territory.

The reader, emerging from a long traverse of the spiritual desert which surrounds the Holy Land, first encounters biblical *manna* at Sarepta where the text's itinerary intersects with that of Elijah who, directed by God, left his desert refuge by the brook Cherith and traveled to Sarepta to dwell in the house of the widow. The next excursus, eight entries later, refers to the site on Mount Carmel where Elijah offered sacrifice. Both incidents are part of a larger narrative (I Kgs. 16:29–18:46) which refers to the apostasy of Ahab and of the larger part of Israel and to Elijah's role in returning Israel from Ba'al worship to its dedication to Yahweh. Central to the story is a fierce drought which Elijah called down upon the land as a consequence of Ahab's following of the Ba'als. While the consequent famine wracked the land, Elijah hid from the wrath of Ahab by the brook Cherith, east of the Jordan, where he was fed by ravens until the brook itself dried up in the drought. He then went to Sarepta where he not only fed the widow and her household with a jar of meal and cruse of oil, which miraculously refilled themselves as long as he took sojourn there, but also resurrected the son of the widow who had fallen sick and died during his stay (ibid., 18:17–24).

Elijah's establishment of a small community sustained by divine power in the midst of a world dominated by famine and disease is followed, in the biblical narrative, by his challenge to the hegemony of the apostate king and the priesthood of Ba'al which propped up Ahab's power. Elijah's sacrifice on Mount Carmel is, of course, the bloody showdown between Elijah and the 450 prophets of Ba'al recounted in I Kgs. 18:20–40. Elijah, setting up the confrontation, challenges the king, the prophets, and all Israel gathered on Carmel: "How long will you go limping with two different opinions? If the Lord is God, follow him; but if Ba'al, then follow him" (ibid., 18:21). The failure of Ba'al's prophets to bring fire down upon their sacrificial offering is countered by Elijah's spectacular success in calling a voracious flame down upon his drenched bull. This is followed by the slaughter of the priesthood of Ba'al and by the torrential closure of the drought which had blasted Israel. Elijah on Carmel not only "repaired the altar of the Lord that had been thrown down" (ibid., 18:30) but also provided a convincing retort to those who, limping with two different opinions, could not decide which god—Yahweh or the deity of the rulers of the state—was the true one.

The richness of detail of these episodes is only alluded to in the text of the *Itinerarium Burdigalense* through the citing of "Sarepta" and "Mount Carmel." The text uses sites as mnemonics to bring strategically signal moments in the history and prehistory of Christianity to the consciousness of a fourth-century audience already knowledgeable about biblical matters. To such an audience, the stories of Elijah would be pertinent on several levels. Elijah's challenge to Israel and his spectacular proof of the power of the only true god would have posed a salient exemplum to early fourth-century neophytes who were poised to commit themselves—or had only just committed themselves—to the worship of monotheistic Christianity and the abandonment of allegiance to the sanctioned divinities of the Roman state. Furthermore, Elijah's experiences at Sarepta would, for them, function typologically; the *Itinerarium*'s reference to Sarepta would—for early Christians to whom "typology, the exposition of the foreshadowings of Christ in the history of Israel, was . . . a subject of elementary catechesis"[40]—have evoked Jesus' feeding of the multitude with loaves and fishes at the Mount of Beatitudes as well as his resurrection of Lazarus at Bethany (Elijah at Sarepta is the first of several Old Testament figures of Jesus which occur in the *Itinerarium Burdigalense*). The progress of Elijah's triumph—his movement from hiding as an isolate bearer of truth in the wilderness through being the mainspring of a small community resident in the world but not subject to its life-destroying regime to becoming the victorious scourge of his enemies and bringer of life-giving rains to Israel—might itself stand as a prefiguration of the Christian community's own sense of past, present, and future. This suggestion is supported by the fact that, throughout the text, an historical motif recurs wherein a dominant old order is mapped, then challenged by a divinely-endowed truth, and then shown to be overcome by that new power. An example, in typical topographical concentration, appears a few lines later: "City of Isdraela [Jezreel]: there Ahab reigned and Elijah prophesied; there is the field where David killed Goliath."[41]

The commentator on the Oxford annotated edition of the Revised Standard Version of the Bible notes, with reference to the opening of the Elijah sequence discussed above, that "the Canaanite (or Phoenician) god Baal (16:31–32) was held by his worshippers to be the one who controlled the *rain*. Elijah intended to show that his God, *the Lord the God of Israel*, was the one who really controlled the *rain*."[42] Elijah's demonstration—graphically rendered in I Kgs. 18:41–46 when the rains pour torrentially over the burnt bull and the hecatomb of the slain Ba'alist prophets—meshes with a less spectacular, similarly pedagogic yet more ambitious, exposition pertaining to water which runs through the whole of the *Itinerarium Burdigalense*. Soon after the pilgrim's siting of Elijah's sacrifice are two excursuses directly associated with water:

> There is the bath of Cornelius the Centurion, who gave many alms.
> At the third milestone from there is Mt. Syna, where there is a spring;
> if a woman washes herself in it, she will become pregnant.[43]

Then, a few lines later, the pilgrim speaks of

Sechar, from which the Samaritan woman went down to the same place where Jacob had dug a well, to fill her jug with water from it, and our Lord Jésus Christ spoke with her; and where there are plane trees, which Jacob planted, and a bath, which gets its water from this well.[44]

If—as the constant mention of water-related sites throughout the text would suggest—water is a significant element in the pilgrim's presentation of the land, then the reader should examine this early congeries of water associations for evidence of the narrator's motivation in including them.

The mention of the spring at Syna develops the theme of the life-giving powers of water earlier raised by the invocation of Elijah at Carmel, where he brought the rains and ended the killing drought. That the spring—even though extra-biblical and contemporary—does not simply maintain already existent life but miraculously engenders pregnancy suggests that water in the Holy Land has a nature-defying power to replace barrenness with life. This link is demonstrated more forcibly later in the text, where the narrator locates, outside of Jericho,

> the spring of Elisha; before if a woman drank from that water she would not bear children. A vessel was brought to Elisha and he put salt in it and came and put it over the spring and said "thus says the Lord: I have healed these waters." Now if a woman drinks from it she will have children.[45]

With the citing of the bath of Cornelius the Centurion, the text again invokes life-giving water and, in so doing, effects not only a movement from the Old to the New Testament, but also the first appearance of another re-current motif of the *Itinerarium*—the overcoming of the old dispensation by the new. Cornelius, whose story is relayed in Acts 10, was one of the first two gentile converts,[46] whose conversion follows on the narrative of Peter being instructed in a vision to reject the dietary restrictions of Leviticus (Acts 10: 10–16). The divine instruction to overturn the Old Testament discriminations between the clean and the unclean is, in the rest of the chapter, extended to the laws separating Jews from gentiles and as a result Cornelius, a gentile believer in the word of Christ, is baptized. Peter, at Cornelius' house, says:

> "Truly I perceive that God shows no partiality, but in every nation any one who fears him and does what is right is acceptable to him". . . . While Peter was still saying this, the Holy Spirit fell on all who heard the word. And the believers from among the circumcised who came with Peter were amazed, because the gift of the Holy Spirit had been poured out even on

the gentiles. For they heard them [Cornelius and his kinsmen and close friends] speaking with tongues and extolling God. Then Peter declared: "Can any one forbid water for baptizing these people who have received the Holy Spirit just as we have?" And he commanded them to be baptized in the name Jesus Christ (Acts 10:44–48).

The bath of Cornelius commemorates the fact that "to the gentiles also God has granted repentance unto life" (Acts 11:18) and thus marks the historical moment at which the promise of divine election, previously restricted to the Jews, becomes universal. It is interesting that the site of this gentile conversion, encountered as the pilgrim's text enters the Holy Land, is balanced later in the text, as the narrative prepares to depart from the Holy Land, by the citing of another water—"the spring . . . in which Philip baptized the eunuch"[47]—where the original gentile baptism occurred. The text transposes onto the spatial boundaries of the Holy Land the temporal borders of the new and old dispensations. The limits of the Old Testament Promised Land are marked simultaneously as the beginnings of the domain opened to redemption by the universal promise of the New Testament. This historical progression seems to be further marked geographically by the pilgrim's noting of Tarsus—where "the Apostle Paul was born," and Philippi—where the apostles "Paul and Silas were imprisoned"—beyond the boundaries of the biblical Holy Land at the front, beyond which pagan holy men and mythographers such as Apollonius of Tyana[48] and Euripides still prevail.

The relation of the Old and New Testament dispensations is further developed in the excursus around the site of Sechem,[49] where the setting of Jacob's well allows the narrator not only to invoke the coming of the Israelites into their inheritance of the land (Gen. 33:18–20 and Josh. 24:32),[50] but also—through the tale of Jesus and the Samaritan woman—to suggest that that literal inheritence is superseded by the spiritual bequest brought by Jesus to Jews and non-Jews alike. In an analogous gesture to Elijah's at Sarepta, Jesus at the well at Sychar asks a woman for water:

The Samaritan woman said to him, "How is it that you, a Jew, ask a drink of me, a woman of Samaria?" For Jews have no dealings with Samaritans. Jesus answered her, "If you knew the gift of God, and who it is that is saying to you, 'Give me a drink,' you would have asked him, and he would have given you living water." The woman said to him, "Sir, you have nothing to draw with, and the well is deep; where do you get that living water? Are you greater than our father Jacob, who gave us the well, and drank from it himself, and his sons, and his cattle?" Jesus said to her, "Everyone who drinks of this water will thirst again, but whoever drinks of the water that I shall give him will never thirst; the water that I shall give him will become in him a spring of water welling up to eternal life" (John 4:9–14).

The woman, acknowledging Jesus as a prophet, queries whether God is to be worshipped—as the Samaritans do—on Mount Gerizim or—as the Jews do—in Jerusalem. Jesus replies:

Woman, believe me, the hour is coming when neither on this mountain nor in Jerusalem will you worship the Father . . . the hour is coming, and now is, when the true worshippers will worship the Father in spirit and truth (John 4:21 and 23).

This desanctification of place, seemingly an example of that early Christian tendency so well described by W. D. Davies,[51] seems to sit oddly in a text which overtly sacralizes a Christian holy land. It is, however, important to recognize that the Bordeaux Pilgrim uses topographical description precisely as a means of transcending the Judaic conception of a physical inheritance and stressing the spiritual, and thus universal, character of the Christian "home-land." This shift is evidenced in the juxtapositioning of Joseph's bones, which lie in a tomb "in the parcel of the ground which his father gave him,"[52] and Jesus' promise of "a spring of water welling up to eternal life" which rests not on a site of land but in the souls of all those who believe. From this point on in the text, the "worldly kingdom" of the Old Testament is increasingly de-valued while the despatialized domain of spiritual salvation is celebrated as the ultimate "holy land."

The pilgrim's presentation of Jerusalem interweaves the abovementioned themes to provide a tapestry densely illustrated with evocations of the collapse of the in-worldly kingdom of the Jews and its supercession by the spiritual empire of their Christian inheritors. The description of the pools of Bethesda, which marks the pilgrim's entry into Jerusalem, is drawn from the chapter in John which directly follows the story of Jesus' encounter with the Samaritan woman at the well below Gerizim. Like that story, the narrative of Jesus' Sabbath healing, without the use of water, of the paralytic (John 5:2–15)—who had lain uncured next to the wonder-working pools for thirty-eight years—serves simultaneously to abrogate Old Testament law and to demon-strate that the "living water" of Jesus' word is more powerful than the life-giving water of the land. The remainder of John 5 distinguishes between the Jews, who sought to kill Jesus for breaking the Sabbath and proclaiming himself equal with God (ibid., 5:16–18), and those who will, in believing the word of Jesus, pass "from death to life" (ibid. 5:24).

The narrative moves from the pools to the Temple Mount itself, where it celebrates the wisdom and power of Solomon, the great kingdom builder of the Israelites, in noting the remains of his palace, his Temple, and the great underground pools and cisterns he had constructed. At the same time, however, by merging elements of the second and third temptations of Jesus relayed in Matt. 4:5–10, the text shows Jesus rejecting the promise of earthly power to which Solomon succumbed.[53] This is followed by the pilgrim's noting of "a great corner-stone, of which it was said, 'the stone which the builders rejected is become the head of the corner'."[54] Matthew sets that psalmic phrase in a chapter in which Jesus demonstrates by a number of parables that the work of God is being taken from those originally assigned it and passed to a new people. In that chapter, mention of the cornerstone is followed by Jesus' statement to the chief priests and the elders at the Temple that "the kingdom of God will be taken away from you and given to a nation producing the fruits of it" (Matt. 22.43).

The *Itinerarium* then demonstrates that Solomon's Temple is ineradicably bloodstained "in front of the altar . . . [by] the blood of Zacharias."[55] The reference invokes Jesus' condemnation of the scribes and Pharisees for killing those God sends to inform them of his will:

> I send you prophets and wise men and scribes, some of whom you will kill and crucify, and some you will scourge in your synagogues and persecute from town to town, that upon you may come all the righteous blood shed on earth, from the blood of innocent Abel to the blood of Zechariah the son of Barachiah, whom you murdered between the sanctuary and the altar (Matt. 24:34–35; see also Luke 11:49–52).

This passage, which the Oxford annotators note refers to "the sweep of time from the first to the last victim of murder mentioned in the Old Testament,"[56] is followed in the New Testament text by Jesus' retraction of the divine dispensation from Israel:

> O Jerusalem, Jerusalem, killing the prophets and stoning those who are sent to you. How often would I have gathered your children together as a hen gathers her brood under her wings, and you would not! Behold, your house is forsaken and desolate (Matt. 23:37–38).

The *Itinerarium* then provides the demonstration offered by the Jesus quote in displaying the statues of the Temple's destroyers built over its ruins and the site of the scattered peoples' lamentations over the loss of their kingdom and their temple: "there are two statues of Hadrian, and not far from the statues a pierced stone to which the Jews come every year to anoint and lament over with sighs, tearing their clothes and then going away again."[57] The contrast displayed by the pilgrim is not only that between the glory of the past and the desolation of the present—a contrast reiterated by the text's mention of Hezekiah who, in II Kgs. 20:16–19, is told by Isaiah that the peace and security of his own days will be traded off against the absolute desolation of his house and his nation in the future—but also between the ruins of the Jewish Temple and the glory of the new Christian temple rising on a facing hill. This demonstration, overt but understated in the *Itinerarium Burdigalense,* is made more triumphantly by St. Jerome later in the century, in *On Zephania* 1, 15–16:

> You can see with your own eyes on the day that Jerusalem was captured and destroyed by the Romans, a piteous crowd that comes together, woebegone women and old men weighed down with rags and years, all of them showing forth in their clothes and their bodies the wrath of God. That mob of wretches congregates, and while the manger of the Lord sparkles, the Church of His Resurrection glows, and the banner of His Cross shines forth from the Mount of Olives, those miserable people groan over the ruins of their Temple. . . .[58]

From the Temple Mount the pilgrim's text moves first to Sion and then across the city to Golgotha. Along this course it catalogues a number of monuments of the Old Dispensation, including Siloam—a pool of water which observes Judaic law by keeping the Sabbath, the remains of David's palace, and the "ploughed and sown" (Isa. 1:8) sites of six of the seven synagogues which had been built around that palace. It also locates the places where a number of salient moments in the trial and execution of Jesus occurred—the ruins of the house of Caiaphas and the praetorium of Pilate, the column where Jesus was scourged, Golgotha, and the "vault, where they laid his body, and he rose again on the third day."[59] The listing of ruined buildings and dead officials is followed by the siting of a death which became a new life. The site of Jesus' resurrection is as well also the site of the "resurrected" Temple which Eusebius, quoted above, referred to as the "new Jerusalem constructed over against the one so celebrated of old which . . . had experienced the last extremity of desolation, the effect of divine judgement upon its impious people." The Bordeaux Pilgrim, having displayed the detritus of Israelite sacred and secular ambitions, here celebrates the fact that God, through the offices of a "new Solomon"—Constantine—has had himself built a new "house of the

Lord" in which He, having abandoned His former "chosen people," will take up residence amongst those to whom His blessing has passed. Here, too, are waters; not only "cisterns of remarkable beauty" which parallel those under Solomon's palace, but also "beside them a bath where children are baptized."[60]

Prior to this attention to the trial, execution and resurrection of Jesus, the sections of the text treating the Holy Land had predominantly focused on Old Testament episodes concerning Israel's establishment and activities. From this point on, the emphasis shifts to the coming of Jesus, the preaching of his message, and the dissemination of his word. Although, as in the earlier sections, there are interjections of material drawn from the other testament, in the latter part of the text (excluding the excursus on Jericho which will be discussed below) Old Testament figures are usually mentioned only to point to the tombs in which they were buried. Thus, after leaving Jerusalem and moving eastward, the pilgrim notes Gethsemane, the palm from which the branches were torn to welcome Jesus on Palm Sunday, the teaching on Éléona (and the basilica Constantine built there), the transfiguration, the raising of Lazarus, as well as "two monuments, built with remarkable beauty by way of a memorial. In one is placed the prophet Isaiah—this one is in fact made from one stone— and in the other Hezekiah, king of the Jews."[61] Similarly, when the itinerary later moves southward, from Jerusalem through Bethlehem to Hebron, it notes the site of Jesus' birth and the aforementioned spring where Philip baptized the eunuch and lists the tombs of Rachel, Ezekiel, Asaph, Job, Jesse, David, Solomon, Abraham, Isaac, Jacob, Sarah, Rebecca, and Leah. The only mention of a living Old Testament figure in this final excursus is that of Abraham at Terebinth (Mamre) who "lived and dug a well under the terebinth tree and spoke and ate with the angels."[62] This episode marks the original choice by God of Abraham as the father of

> a great and mighty nation [by which] all the nations of the world shall bless themselves. . . . I have chosen him, that he may charge his children and his household after him to keep the way of the Lord by doing righteousness and justice; so that the Lord may bring to Abraham what he has promised him (Gen. 18:18–19).

It is followed in the *Itinerarium* by only two more notes before the text departs the Holy Land. The first is that, over the site where the original covenant was forged, the Christian emperor Constantine built "a basilica of remarkable beauty."[63] The second, immediately following, is that in Hebron one may find "a remarkably beautiful tomb"[64] containing the bodies of Abraham, his son, his grandson, and the wives of all three.

The section of the *Itinerarium Burdigalense* pertaining to Jericho and its environs[65] contains a substantial number of Old Testament references—to Elisha's spring (see above), to the house of the prostitute Rahab,[66] to the site of Jericho destroyed by the Israelites,[67] to the twelve stones marking the resting place of the Ark of the Covenant,[68] to the place where Joshua circumcised the children of Israel,[69] and to the hillock from whence Elijah ascended into heaven[70]—of which all but one are enclosed within a framing pair of New Testament sitings: the sycamore that Zacchaeus, the tax collector, climbed to see Jesus[71] and the river in which John baptized Jesus.[72] Also caught within the New Testament frame is a naturalistic description of the Dead Sea: "the waters of this sea are by far the bitterest of any. In them is no fish of any kind nor any ship, and if any man goes in to swim the water turns him upside down."[73]

This juxtaposing of incidents drawn from the Israelites' triumphal entry into the promised land and from Jesus' procession towards the fulfillment of his mission in Jerusalem produces more than a simple parallelism when the reader links up the Old Testament figure of Rahab, the New Testament figure of Zacchaeus, and Jesus' admonition to the chief priests and elders at the Temple in Matt. 21— "the tax collectors and the harlots go into the kingdom of God before you" (21: 31). Rahab the harlot was—alone of all the inhabitants of Canaanite Jericho— saved from death because, having recognized that the spies who approached her were doing God's will, she protected them from her own people. Analogously, Zacchaeus, who had lived a life of sin, was offered salvation by Jesus because he recognized Jesus and answered to his call. This emphasis on seeing and believing is further developed in John. Jesus, seeking to escape the crowds who—having participated in the miracle of loaves and fishes (ibid., 6:5–14)—had taken him for a worldly messiah and "were about to come and take him by force to make him king" (ibid., 6:15), walks across the Sea of Galilee. On the following day, he tells those who sought him out on the other side:

> You seek me, not because you saw signs, but because you ate your fill of the loaves. Do not labor for the food which perishes, but for the food which endures to eternal life . . . you have seen me and yet do not believe" (John 6:26–27 and 36).

Later, in the same chapter, Jesus goes on to develop the distinction between that which sustains life in this world and that spiritual food which gives life unto eternity:

> I am the bread of life. Your fathers ate the manna in the wilderness, and they died. This is the bread which comes down from heaven, that a man may eat of eat and not die. I am the living bread which came down from heaven; if any one eats of this bread, he will live for ever" (ibid., 6:49 and 51).

By imbricating the markers of the Israelites' crossing of the Jordan so as to effect their triumphal entry into the land with references alluding to Jesus' passage through the waters of the Jordan towards his fulfillment in Jerusalem, the *Itinerarium Burdigalense* poses the former as a sign or prefiguration of the latter. The Israelites, who ate *manna* in the wilderness, crossed over into the Promised Land and died, as the proliferation of their tombs in the following section demonstrates. Jesus passed over the waters of Galilee and the Jordan and through death only to be resurrected and to open a pathway for his disciples to follow into an eternal Promised Land.

The exegetical movement from the former to the latter is mirrored in the text's movement from the site where Joshua initiated those Israelites born while the tribes wandered in the desert through the Dead Sea to the site on the Jordan River where Jesus was baptized. The Israelites lived, built a nation, and they and that nation died. The terminus of that process—marked by the tombs in the desert and a water in which nothing can live and which turns those who enter into it "upside down"—is countered by a movement developing out of it and transcending it which is marked by Jesus' baptism in the Jordan:

> when Jesus was baptized, he went up immediately from the water, and behold, the heavens were opened and he saw the Spirit of God descending like a dove, and alighting on him; and lo, a voice from heaven, saying, "This is my beloved Son, with whom I am well pleased" (Matt. 3:16–17).

Interestingly, this vertical passage between heaven and earth, which subsumes and sublimates the earlier lateral passage between desert and promised land, is succeeded by the mention of the site "from whence Elijah was caught up into heaven."[74] The mention of this site—outside the above-cited New Testament "brackets"—not only reminds us that Elijah, alone amongst all of the "dead Jews" mentioned in the *Itinerarium*, was taken up live into heaven but also implies that the mantle of Elijah, which in Old Testament history is caught by Elisha,[75] is in the new dispensation passed to Jesus at the adjacent site of the baptism.

Conclusion

There is no question that, in attempting to recuperate the text of the Bordeaux Pilgrim, I have read into it much that is not overtly there. The fact, however, that the biblical materials associated with the site references made by the *Itinerarium* cohere to make up a systematic and complex discourse on the typological and historical relationships of the Old and New Testaments implies that the text itself would originally have functioned in a setting in which such scriptural supplementation would have been part of its audience's relation to its reading. The consistent attention of the pilgrim to the life-giving qualities of water would suggest that this setting was that in which catechumens were being prepared for baptismal initiation into the Christian church.[76] In the course of such a process the text may have been used as a sort of spiritual itinerary (not unlike today's Stations of the Cross which serve as devotional mnemonics within Latin Christian churches) for pulling together lessons about the new and old dispensations covered throughout the long process of catechetical instruction. The movement of the text's itinerary out of the contemporary secular world and into the space in which biblical history was enacted, and then—through the processes both of Jesus' baptism and of the gentile converts—back into the world of pagans and powers in which, before the hegemonization of the Roman empire by Christianity, the newly baptized Christian would have to live, would offer a prefiguration of the process for which the neophytes were preparing. In that process, of course, both their old lives and the lives of those who lived under the old dispensation would be left behind. As St. Ambrose would later write in describing the rite of baptism in his *De Sacramentos*:

> What was of greater importance than the crossing of the sea by the Jewish people? Yet the Jews who crossed over are all dead in the desert. But, on the contrary, he who passes through this fountain, that is to say, from earthly things to heavenly—which is indeed the *transitus*, that is to say, the Passover, the passing over from sin to life—he who passes through this fountain will not die, but rise again.[77]

Notes

1. R. Markus. "How on Earth Could Places Become Holy? Origins of the Christian Idea of Holy Places," *Journal of Early Christian Studies* 2/3 (1994), 268.

2. Ibid., 270.

3. Ibid., 271; cf. his *The End of Ancient Christianity* (Cambridge, 1990), 92

4. Egeria, *Itinerarium* (*CCSL* 175, 27–90). I will use John Wilkinson's translation from *Egeria's Travels* (London, 1971), 91-147.

5. Egeria, *Itinerarium* 5:5–8, in ibid., 107. L. Spitzer ("The Epic Style of the Pilgrim Aetheria," *Comparative Literature* 1/3 [1949], 239) points out that "the eye of the pilgrim wanders incessantly from the Biblical *locus* (i.e., passage) to the *locus* (locality) in Palestine."

6. Egeria, *Itinerarium* 31:2–3 and 25:5, in Wilkinson (above, note 4), 133 and 126, respectively.

7. P. Walker. *Holy City, Holy Places? Christian Attitudes to Jerusalem and the Holy Land in the Fourth Century* (Oxford, 1990).

8. Cyril of Jerusalem, "Catecheses XIII:22," *The Works of Saint Cyril of Jerusalem*, II, ed. L. McCauley (Washington, D.C, 1968), 19.

9. See "On Pilgrimage," *Selected Writings and Letters of Gregory, Bishop of Nyassa*, V, eds. W. Moore and H.Wilson (Oxford, 1892), 382–83.

10. Egeria, *Itinerarium* 4:8, in Wilkinson (above, note 4), 96; the emphasis is mine.

11. Ibid., 19:7, in Wilkinson (above, note 4), 116.

12. Ibid., 19:6–19, in Wilkinson (above, note 4), 115–17.

13. Antoninus of Piacenza, *Itinerarium* (*CCSL* 175), 79–89, translated by J. Wilkinson, *Jerusalem Pilgrims before the Crusades* (Warminster, 1977), 79 and 81.

14. The term "haptic" is drawn from A. Wharton's stimulating study of transformations of space and sensoria with the "victory" of Christianity, in *Refiguring the Post-Classical City: Dura Europos, Jerash, Jerusalem and Ravenna* (Cambridge, 1995).

15. G. Dix's theories of the transformations effected in Christian liturgy by the correspondent move from private to public worship suggests, interestingly, that as monuments and ceremonials proliferated, so the access of the lay public to Scripture grew increasingly more attenuated; see his *The Shape of the Liturgy* (Westminster, 1945), 303-96.

16. I will provide my own translation drawn from the text in *CCSL*, 1–26, and will follow its editors (and Wilkinson) in citing P. Wesseling's pagination from his *Verera Romanorum Itinera* (Amsterdam, 1735). A complete English language translation is available in the *Itinerary from Bordeaux to Jerusalem: "The Bordeaux Pilgrim" (333 A.D.)*, trans. A. Stewart, PPTS 1 (London, 1896), 1–35. Wilkinson includes a substantial and well-annotated selection in his *Egeria's Travels*, 153–63. The itinerary is dated by the pilgrim's reference by name to the consuls who were in power as he passed through Constantinople and by his references to the days of the months during which he passed through that city on going out and returning; Wesseling, op. cit., 571.

17. R. Wilken, *The Land Called Holy: Palestine in Christian History and Thought* (New Haven, 1992), 109 and 110.

18. E. D. Hunt, *Holy Land Pilgrimage in the Later Roman Empire AD 312-460* (Oxford, 1982), 86.

19. M. Campbell, *The Witness and the Other World: Exotic European Travel Writing, 400-1600* (Ithaca, 1988), 27.

20. Eusebius, "The Life of Constantine," *Eusebius: Church History, Life of Constantine the Great, Oration in Praise of Constantine*, ed. E. C. Richardson (Oxford, 1890), 529.

21. Egeria 4:1, *Itinerarium*, in Wilkinson (above, note 4), 95.

22. Ibid., 7:2–3, in Wilkinson (above, note 4), 101.

23. Ibid., 12:6–7, in Wilkinson (above, note 4), 107.

24. Ibid., 23:10, in Wilkinson (above, note 4), 122.

25. Wesseling (above, note 16), 591: 3–5. Wilkinson (above, note 4) renders the text as though the pilgrim addresses the reader directly in the second person ("you"), Stewart's translation (above, note 16) retains the coolness of the original Latin in its occasional use of the pronoun "one."

26. Wesseling (above, note 16), 588:9–589:3 (*CCSL* [above, note 16], 95). An interesting analogy to the Bordeaux Pilgrim's use of the site of the village of Bethel as a means of entering the narrative space of the Bible is the way in which Greek Orthodox pilgrims ignore the specificities of events commemorated at holy places and use the places as "doors" providing access

to a generalized communion with the saints in the "paradise" manifest to believers in the icon-dense interiors of all Orthodox churches; see G. Bowman, "Contemporary Christian Pilgrimage to the Holy Land," *The Christian Heritage in the Holy Land*, ed. A. O'Mahony (London, 1995), 298–99.

27. Wesseling (above, note 16), 588:2–6.

28. Ibid., 594:2–4.

29. Wilken (above, note 17), 110.

30. The pilgrim, for instance, makes no mention of Nazareth or the Sea of Galilee, despite apparently passing within a day's journey of those salient sites in the life of Christ; see C. W. Wilson, "Introduction," *Itinerary from Bordeaux to Jerusalem* (London, 1896), viii–ix.

31. Wesseling (above, note 16), 581:11–582:8.

32. Ibid., 582:11.

33. Tarsus and Philippi are, of course, biblical sites insofar as they are mentioned in Acts and Philippians with reference to the events the pilgrim cites. As I will demonstrate below, they can—according to the logic of the text—be mapped as being within the "Holy Land."

34. Wesseling (above, note 16), 583:12; see also I Kgs. 17:10–16 and Luke 4:25–26.

35. Wesseling (above, note 16), 585:1; see I Kgs. 18:19–21.

36. Wesseling (above, note 16), 585:7–8; see Acts 10:19–48.

37. Wesseling (above, note 16), 586:4–6.

38. Wilkinson (above, note 4), 154.

39. Wesseling (above, note 16), 587:3–588:3.

40. J. Daniélou, *A History of Early Christian Doctrine Before the Council of Nicea*, I (London, 1964), 406.

41. Wesseling (above, note 16), 586:4–6.

42. H. May and B. Metzger (eds.), *The New Oxford Annotated Bible (Revised Standard Version)* (New York, 1973), 442 (note on I Kgs. 17:1).

43. Wesseling (above, note 16), 585:7–586:2.

44. Ibid., 588:3–6.

45. Ibid., 596:7–10. See II Kgs. 2:19–22, of which this is a close rendering. Elisha's making the water sweet and wholesome by salting it parallels Elijah's counterinductive preparation of the sacrifical bull for immolation by pouring over it twelve jars of water (I Kgs. 18:33–35). In each case, what is treated is not simply water, but water which, when brought into association with divinity, operates supra-naturally.

46. The Oxford annotations (May and Metzger [above, note 42], 1332–33—note on Acts 10:1–48) refer to Cornelius as the first gentile convert, but Acts 8:26–39 describes Philip's baptism of the Ethiopian eunuch, who W. H. C. Frend calls "the first non-Jewish convert recorded" (*The Rise of Christianity* [London, 1984], 89). That the *Itinerarium Burdigalense* treats both conversions indicates that it is concerned to mark the breaking out of the salvatory work from the confines of the Jewish people.

47. Wesseling (above, note 16), 599:1–2; see Acts 8:26–40.

48. Apollonius of Tyana was an itinerant Neopythagorean teacher born early in the Christian era who was alleged to have had magical powers and to have traveled widely, including to India. Flavius Philostratus (ca. 170 C.E.) wrote a *Life of Apollonius of Tyana*, in which the philosopher was attributed with a miraculous birth and the ability to work miracles. More significant, however, was the virulent anti-Christian polemic Sossius Hierocles presented as a biography in 302 C.E.. Hierocles here contended that Apollonius was an excellent philosopher and exorcist and was in all ways far superior to Christ; see Frend (above, note 46), 497–98. John Elsner has examined the role of Apollonius of Tyana in pagan hagiography in "Hagiographic Geography: Travel and Allegory in the *Life of Apollonius of Tyana*," *Journal of Hellenic Studies* 117 (1997), 22–37.

49. Wesseling (above, note 16), 587:5–588:6.

50. Interestingly, in the following section on Bethel, the pilgrim confounds Bethel with Peniel as the site where Jacob wrestled with the angel (Gen. 32:24–30). Wilkinson ([above, note 4], 155, note 6) sees this confusion arising from the fact that Peniel may have been commemorated at Bethel in the fourth century, but it is also salient that at Bethel, as at Peniel, Jacob's name became "Israel" (Gen. 35:10).

51. W. D. Davies, *The Gospel and the Land: Early Christianity and Jewish Territorial Doctrine* (Berkeley, 1974).

52. Wesseling (above, note 16), 588:1; see Josh. 24:32.

53. The second temptation—in which the devil calls upon Jesus to throw himself from the pinnacle of the Temple so that the angels will prove his divinity by bearing him up—takes place where the *Itinerarium Burdigalense* cites the story, but the pilgrim appends to Christ's refusal a phrase—"and him only shall you serve" (Matt. 4:10)—which associates the pilgrim's rendering of Jesus' temptation with Satan's offer—from the peak of a very high mountain—to give Jesus power over all the kingdoms of the world.

54. Wesseling (above, note 16), 590:3–4; see Ps. 118:22–23 and Matt. 22:42.

55. Wesseling (above, note 16), 591:1–4.

56. May and Metzger (above, note 42), 1203, note 35.

57. Wesseling (above, note 16), 591:4–6.

58. Quoted by F. E. Peters, *Jerusalem: the Holy City in the Eyes of Chroniclers, Visitors, Pilgrims and Prophets from the Days of Abraham to the Beginnings of Modern Times* (Princeton, 1985), 144.

59. Wesseling (above, note 16), 594:1–2.

60. Ibid., 594:4. On the Constantinian baptistry, see S. Gibson and J. Taylor, *Beneath the Church of the Holy Sepulchre Jerusalem: The Archaeology and Early History of Traditional Golgotha* (London, 1994), 77–78.

61. Wesseling (above, note 16), 595:2–4.

62. Ibid., 599:3–5; see Gen. 18:1–19.

63. Wesseling (above, note 16), 599:5–6.

64. Ibid., 599:7–9.

65. Ibid., 596:4–598:3.

66. Ibid., 597:1; see Josh. 2:1–21.

67. Wesseling (above, note 16), 597:2–3; see Josh. 6.

68. Wesseling (above, note 16), 597:4–5; see Josh. 4.

69. Wesseling (above, note 16), 597:5–6; see Josh. 5:2–9.

70. Wesseling (above, note 16), 598:3; see II Kgs. 2.

71. Wesseling (above, note 16), 596:5–6; see Luke 19:1–10.

72. Wesseling (above, note 16), 598:1–2; see Matt. 3:13–17.

73. Wessling (above, note 16), 597:7–10.

74. Ibid., 598:3.

75. Who, in the the same section of the text, turns killing water sweet and life-giving.

76. For a thorough description of the process of catechesis leading up to early Christian baptism, see Wharton (above, note 14), esp. pp. 75–85. W. Meeks (*The First Urban Christians: the Social World of the Apostle Paul* [New Haven, 1983], 150–57) provides a nuanced description of early Christianity's transformation of periodic Judaic ritual purification processes into what is, effectively, a permanent transubstantiation of the initiate's being.

77. Ambrose, *De Sacramentos* I:12, quoted in J. Daniélou. *The Bible and the Liturgy* (Notre Dame, 1956).

13

The Attitudes of Church Fathers
toward Pilgrimage to Jerusalem
in the Fourth and Fifth Centuries

BROURIA BITTON-ASHKELONY

The sporadic testimonies about pilgrims to Palestine before the rise of Constantine, and the few traditions regarding holy places which are related to the life of Jesus are well known to students and scholars of this period.[1] Evidence of pilgrimage to Palestine was on the rise from the mid-fourth century on, and by the eighties of that century Egeria and Jerome defined this activity as a mass phenomenon.[2] John Chrysostom has described it as follows: "The whole world runs to see the tomb which has no body."[3] This new reality has led a number of scholars to attribute this dramatic change to the policy of the emperor Constantine. Recently, this thesis was clearly formulated by Joan Taylor: "Suddenly, with Constantine, the church began to focus on earth: the divine substance intermixed with certain material sites and resided in things which could be carried about."[4] Nevertheless, it seems to me that the penetration of the idea of earthly "holy space" into the Christian consciousness, which was contrary to the Pauline conception in the New Testament, as well as the development and localization of myths connected with the life of Jesus, could not be the result of one man's actions, even the emperor himself!

Besides Taylor's theory, and that of J. Smith, stating that "Constantine created, for the first time, a Christian 'Holy Land',"[5] there are several other competing theories. The first one is that of the sociologist M. Halbwachs, in a study published over fifty years ago, *La topographie légendaire des evangiles en terre sainte.*[6] Halbwachs discusses the importance of collective memory in the process of formulating Christian traditions regarding holy places. This theory views holy places as an outcome of Christian collective memory, which was nurtured by the roots of Jewish collective memory regarding biblical sites.

The localization of biblical and New Testament myths is the last stop on the winding and dynamic road of collective memory. This theory enables us to give greater weight to local pilgrimages and to the visits of some personages to third-century Palestine, even though their statements are devoid of details regarding the holy places. These examples reflect a curiosity about the holy places and throw light on the process described by Halbwachs. Another theory for the religious development of pilgrimage was the cult of the martyrs, which existed in the Christian world since the third century and has recently been discussed at length by R. Markus: "to give the first importance to the 'local', the cult of the martyrs, in bringing about the transformation we are concerned with."[7]

This paper will focus upon the tension between local places of pilgrimage and one central place of pilgrimage—Jerusalem. My basic assumption is that pilgrimages to holy men, tombs of martyrs and saints, and holy places in Palestine are various expressions of a single religious phenomenon called "pilgrimage." Close examination of the different components of this phenomenon will enable us to understand the attitudes of Christian thinkers toward pilgrimage to Jerusalem. I do not intend to deal with the entire range of factors that shaped these attitudes;[8] rather, I have confined myself to examining the views of two figures: Augustine, who is enigmatic and generally not discussed in this context; and Gregory of Nyssa and his well-known opposition to pilgrimage in *Letter* II.[9] How did these two figures cope with this new religious reality, which diametrically contradicts the New Testament or, if you will, the traditional Pauline view?

Augustine

In Augustine's day, pilgrimages to the tombs of martyrs and holy places were quite a common pattern of religious behavior among Christian intellectuals and in Roman aristocratic circles. When examining the attitudes of Christian thinkers to pilgrimage in late antiquity, it seems that Augustine, more than any other Church Father, presents the greatest difficulty in solving this issue, since he does not deal with this phenomenon directly in his broad range of works. In contrast to other thinkers in his day from the Latin-speaking West, Augustine never visited the holy places in Palestine; nor do his writings reveal any hint or expression of such a desire. Unlike him, his contemporary, Paulinus of Nola,[10] considered the idea—although he, too, never set foot in the holy places.[11] Jerusalem—the Christian city of the late fourth and early fifth centuries—with its growing number of churches, monasteries, and holy relics, did not especially attract Augustine's attention. On the other hand,

Paulinus of Nola enthusiastically describes the churches of Jerusalem, the discovery of the cross,[12] and the settlement on the Mount of Olives by sisters from the West headed by Melania the Elder.[13] This reality, various elements of which contributed, directly or indirectly, to the establishment of Jerusalem as a Christian city and to its penetration into the general Christian awareness, did not arouse any sort of reaction from Augustine. There is no doubt that the differences in approach between these two prominent figures of the Latin West's intellectual elite are marked and perhaps hint at the problematics involved in Augustine's perception of the existence and establishment of earthly Jerusalem as a Christian city.

Augustine is silent about this religious phenomenon that, already in his day, had existed for several generations. For him, Palestine was not a remote and forgotten province, as is evidenced by his correspondence with Jerome.[14] One may assume that this exchange of letters made Augustine more aware of the attraction of the holy places to Christians, even though this issue was not raised in their correspondence. In this context, we should also mention among the many visitors and pilgrims to Palestine in Augustine's day one Orosius, a young presbyter apparently of northwestern Spanish origin, who arrived in Bethlehem in 414/415 in Augustine's service to Jerome.[15] Upon his return to the West, he brought relics of Stephen the Protomartyr that were discovered near Jerusalem in 415. We do not have specific information as to whether Orosius himself brought these relics to Hippo, home of Augustine, but they nevertheless found their way to that community.[16] The transference of Stephen's relics was a signal event for the proliferation of the cult of the martyrs in North Africa. Augustine was well aware of these discoveries, and was even involved in the building of memorial churches to Stephen. The miracles performed by this martyr via his relics in Augustine's community and nearby occupy a large part of the last book of *The City of God.* This is not the only instance when Augustine was a first-hand witness to the arrival of relics from the Holy Land, as we can see from the story about Hesperius, who received a box containing a holy relic from a friend who had made pilgrimage to Jerusalem. The holy relic was soil taken from Jesus' tomb or, as reported by Augustine himself, *terra sancta.*[17] The manifold dimensions of this story will not be discussed in this framework; nevertheless, it demonstrates beyond all doubt that Augustine was familiar with the various traditions associated with holy places and holy relics.

As a Christian thinker, Augustine saw no need to devote a special discussion to this religious reality, and especially to the question of the role of the holy places in Jerusalem and its environs to which many Christians streamed. Unlike Augustine, other theologians at the end of the fourth and beginning of the fifth centuries discussed the issue, either supporting or negating the phenomenon.

One would assume that for the author of *The City of God*, earthly holy space and the religious emotions of believers toward this space were insignificant. However, his deep involvement in encouraging and shaping the cult of the martyrs within his bishopric in North Africa, as reflected in many sermons he delivered at the martyr celebrations and in his other writings, does not permit us to make such an assumption.[18]

In light of the above, how is one to perceive Augustine's silence? Was this incidental, or did he intentionally choose silence as his way of dealing with this religious reality in Palestine? Does his position reflect early Christianity's a-territorial trend?[19] Is Augustine's attitude rooted in his theological doctrine and adherence to the Pauline position regarding earthly holy space only?

"The generation of Paul"—this is how P. Brown characterized the circle of Christian intellectuals in the West at the end of the fourth century, including Augustine.[20] Such a definition seems to correspond, directly or indirectly, to Augustine's positions regarding pilgrimage and holy places in Palestine. Augustine's loyalty to the Pauline conception of Divine Presence in the world and to the spiritual conception of the temple of God is apparent throughout his many writings.

In his commentary on John, Augustine writes that one hears the prayer that dwells within, in a secret place called "bosom" in the Scriptures (Ps. 35:13: "and my prayer returned into mine own bosom"). For this reason, a Christian does not need to travel far or to raise himself up as if he could reach God with his hands. There is no need to raise one's eyes to the mountains, stars, or sun; rather, one should purify one's heart, and everywhere man wishes to pray, that is where God dwells, as he writes: "He who hears you is within you."[21] According to this pattern of thought, which is based on Paul's words in II Cor. 6:16 ("for you are the temple of the living God"), the true cult has no temple and no place.

In his commentary on the Sermon on the Mount, Augustine develops at length a spiritual conception of Divine Presence.[22] In it, he repeatedly declares that God does not dwell in any space, but rather he dwells within the saints and the righteous.[23] Contrary to those who claim that God physically resides in the heavens, Augustine demonstrates the absurdity of this belief: if God was physically in the heavens, then no one in the world would be happier than the birds, who were closer to him than any other creature. Referring to the popular practice of praying toward the east, he emphasizes that we should not err in thinking that God dwells only there, since He dwells everywhere.[24] Augustine further stresses that while claiming God's omnipresence, one should not mistakenly think that he is referring to an earthly place; one should dismiss any concrete—*carnali*—thought.[25]

A similar a-territorial view is indicated in Augustine's commentary on Ps. 76:2: "In Judah is God known: His name is great in Israel." Augustine explains that one should not erroneously conclude from this verse that God is found in any one place more than in another.[26]

Thus, Augustine's writings clearly reflect his spiritual conception of the temple of God and Divine Presence. The idea of a network of holy places connected with God's name was therefore alien to him.

Augustine's detachment from the idea of Christian holy topography in Palestine is demonstrated in his commentary on Psalms 132:2–7 (LXX: 131:2–7), and especially the last verse: "Let us go to his dwelling place; let us worship at his footstool" or, as other Christians have translated, "where his feet stood." Whereas Eusebius, Jerome, and Paulinus of Nola interpreted the verse in relation to holy places and pilgrimage to Palestine,[27] Augustine, in a long and complex commentary on this Scripture, stripped these verses of their simple meaning and dressed them in the pure Pauline conception.[28] Verse 6, "Lo we heard of it at Ephratah, we found it in the fields of the wood," moves Augustine to relate the *essence* of what they heard, unlike other commentators who dealt with the *place* in which it was heard. To this he responds that these things refer to the place of the Lord, but first he chooses to explain the meaning of the name "Ephratah." He does not regard Ephratah as a geographical location in Palestine; this is in contrast to its identification as Bethlehem, which was accepted by Christian writers based upon the biblical identification in Gen. 35:19 and Mic. 5:1.[29] According to Augustine, "Ephratah" is derived from the Latin *speculum*, symbolizing the future prophecy and the house found in the "fields of the wood." He expounds upon this enigmatic explanation at length: the future house of the Lord has been pronounced in the form of a prophecy. Therefore, "Ephratah" symbolizes the prophecy of the future and explains the second half of the verse, "we found it in the fields of the wood." Even here Augustine rejects any possibility of understanding this verse by its simple meaning. "Field of the wood," *saltus*, generally means "an unworked and forested place," symbolizing, according to Augustine, the nations of the world, idol worshippers who have yet to receive the Word of the Lord. In the next verse, "We will go into His tabernacles," commentators generally interpret "His tabernacles" as the holy places in Jerusalem.[30] Augustine, on the other hand, asks "Whose Tabernacles?"—to which he replies, "Those of the God of Jacob." Therefore, the tabernacles are the soul of the believer, and it is here, in the soul, that God should be worshipped. The verse continues: "We will worship on the spot where His feet stood." Unlike other commentators,

Augustine does not question the geographical place where this takes place. Rather, he states that the feet stand in Christ, and this is the way of the truth. Thus, we have seen consistently that in this interpretation he makes no reference to holy places in Palestine.

The cult of the martyrs, which essentially defined the boundaries of Christian holy space in the Christian communities, flourished in Augustine's day. Here the question arises, how did Augustine deal with the reality of many memoria to martyrs, to which masses of pilgrims streamed? Does not this reality, in fact, conflict with his Pauline view regarding holy space? Or, alternatively, did Augustine try to bridge between his theological positions and the religious reality he witnessed around him?

We should emphasize here that Augustine regarded the tombs of the martyrs as holy places par excellence. Thus, he viewed the tomb of Felix of Nola as a place where a possible theophany or intervention by God could occur (*Letter* 78).

The process of creating holy places, essentially converting a neutral space into a holy one via holy relics, which was a growing trend toward the end of the fourth century, did not engender any reservations on Augustine's part; in fact, he even gave it his support.[31] Augustine's view regarding the process of creating holy places and their role is largely explained by the Hesperius incident.[32] As noted, Hesperius kept a box in his room containing soil (*terram sanctam*) from Jesus' tomb. From the day the box was brought into his home, evil spirits attacked the members of his household. Thereupon, Hesperius wished to remove the soil from his house, bury it, and build there a place of prayer, where Christians would gather to worship God. When approached for their advice, neither Augustine nor Maximinus, a bishop of the neighboring region, objected, and Hesperius' wish was thus fulfilled. The continuation of the story, as told by Augustine, indicates that this place became holy for Augustine, both by the terminology he used in describing it and in its function as a holy site for believers.

The Hesperius incident concludes with yet another story about a paralyzed young man who heard the news and asked his parents to let him visit the *locum sanctum*, whereupon a miracle occurred and the boy stood on his feet. The story of the miracle is cited by Augustine for one purpose: to confirm the status of the new place and to validate it as holy by virtue of the soil from Jesus' tomb. In this incident, the soil from Jesus' grave was considered a holy relic, and it is this that converted neutral earthly space into holy space. The origin of this relic or its inherent significance is of no concern to Augustine; the heart of the story is the miracle and the process by which a local holy place came into being, in this case with Augustine's blessing. R. Wilken has remarked that "here, as elsewhere, Augustine's piety collides with his theology."[33]

However, the literary context in which Augustine chose to mention the Hesperius story is crucial for understanding his perception of this account. Here, Augustine rejects the pagan doubt in past Christian miracles, which he claims came about in order to negate the miracle of Jesus' resurrection and ascent to Heaven.[34] For Augustine, the miracles that occurred in the tombs of the martyrs in his day are living proof that Christian miracles indeed occurred in the past. Therefore, the cult of the martyrs and the miracles there were a means of reinforcing and proving the truth of the Christian faith.

Augustine did not confine himself to preaching the virtue of the martyrs and their role; he even tried to influence the shaping of cultic practice— primarily by rejecting ancient pagan customs and by preventing unethical behavior in cultic places. This position is predominant in two letters, XXII and XXIX, which he wrote from 392–395, at the beginning of his career as a bishop, and which express his explicit reservations against the customs of the pilgrims and local participants in the celebrations of the martyrs.

Gregory of Nyssa

Gregory of Nyssa and his brother Basil of Caesarea both visited Palestine. Basil journeyed to the East around 357, but never mentioned visiting the holy places.[35] On the other hand, Gregory's visit—and especially the letter he wrote following his visit—continued to make waves for hundreds of years in debates regarding the religious value of the pilgrimage act.[36] This letter, from the eighties of the fourth century, may be considered one of the most explicit reservations regarding pilgrimage to Jerusalem ever expressed by a Christian theologian.

Three historical sources attest to Gregory's visit to Jerusalem: *Letters* II and III, and his hagiographical *Vita Macrinae*. These sources contradict one another, both with regard to his reason for coming to Jerusalem and vis-à-vis his views on pilgrimage to Jerusalem and his relationship toward the city and its inhabitants. The varying weight scholars accorded each of these sources or, at times, their disregard for any one of them, is what determined their diverse assessments of Gregory's visit and his attitude to the phenomenon. I do not intend to discuss here all of Gregory's arguments. Rather, I would like to consider one basic question: to what extent did Gregory express theological positions about pilgrimage in *Letter* II, and to what degree did his words echo his debate with the Jerusalem Church? Let us first consider the reasons which brought Gregory to Jerusalem in 381. In *Letter* II (11–13), Gregory writes that there is no contradiction between his criticism of pilgrimage and his visit to Jerusalem. In this way, he wished to remove all doubt that it was religious motivation that brought him to the city. He presents himself as a mediator in the service of the church. Therefore, by presenting his visit solely as a diplomatic mission, devoid of any pilgrim dust, he contradicts his statement in *Vita Macrinae*.

In *Vita Macrinae*, which he wrote after his visit to Jerusalem, ca. 382–383, Gregory reminds the recipient of this treatise that he did not forget their meeting after his return from Jerusalem "for the sake of the prayer (κατ᾽ εὐχήν), in order to see in these places the signs (σημεῖα) of the Lord's coming in the flesh."[37] Scholars have had difficulty in interpreting the expression κατ᾽ εὐχήν in this context. The term ἡ εὐχή usually means prayer, wish, or vow.[38] Maraval, in his translation of *Vita Macrinae*, preferred at first to interpret "à la suite d'un vœu."[39] Recently, however, he has retracted this translation, preferring "en vue de la prière."[40] Maraval bases this change of mind on similar expressions in pilgrimage literature, in which prayer in a specific place marks the act of pilgrimage. If we adopt Maraval's interpretation, then Gregory's words in his introduction to *Vita Macrinae* attest that religious motivation was at the root of his journey to Jerusalem.

It should be noted that this source is an innocent statement, which had no bearing at all on the question of the holy places. Gregory relates here to the journey as a chronological landmark; the journey itself is not a subject of discussion, but merely an interjection. There is not necessarily a contradiction between these two purposes for Gregory's journey to Jerusalem. Nevertheless, there is certainly no reason to repress or downplay his religious motivation. I believe that both motivations, religious and diplomatic, existed side by side, but we are unable to determine the order of events. It appears that the apologetic character of *Letter* II is what led Gregory to deny the religious motivation for his journey to Jerusalem. If this is correct, then there is a great dichotomy between Gregory's religious behavior as a pilgrim in Jerusalem and Cappadocia, and his theological positons regarding pilgrimage as expressed in *Letter* II. This is not the only difficulty that arises when comparing the sources dealing with his visit; a different tone is heard in each of his letters.

In *Letter* III, which he wrote immediately upon his return home from Jerusalem, we detect a positive tone with regard to the places he called "holy" and the people he met there: he tells us that when he saw and felt the holy places, he was filled with an indescribable joy (*Letter* III, 3). Gregory tells about his meeting good people in these places (Jerusalem) and the signs of the Lord's great philanthropy that people bestowed upon him in these places and which gave him an enormous sense of joy. It is in Jerusalem that he met souls in which one spiritually sees signs of the Lord's kindness, to the extent that one could think that Bethlehem, the Golgotha, the Mount of Olives, and the Anastasis dwell in their hearts (*Letter* III, 1). Immediately following this enthusiastic description, Gregory goes on to paint an ambivalent picture of his visit, for, he says, the sense of joy is accompanied by a feeling of bitterness, and thus he returned sadly to his homeland (*Letter* III, 4). After these introductory words, Gregory proceeds to expose before his readers the christological issues that caused opposition to him by certain figures (in Jerusalem), who turned out to be a source of disappointment for him.[41] Gregory does not divulge the names of his adversaries, nor does he mention the names of his supporters. One may assume, as Maraval has suggested, that Cyril of Jerusalem, who was then bishop of the city, was among his adversaries.[42]

Contrary to the contents of Gregory's *Letter* III, his *Letter* II leaves no traces of his joy upon seeing the holy places in Jerusalem. The term ἅγιοι τόποι was absent from this letter, although he used it when referring to the tombs of the martyrs.[43] This small difference joins his general negative description of the city. Not only did the holy places not bring him joy, as stated in *Letter* III, but he even asks in a harsh and mocking manner what the sense there was in seeing these places and what advantage was to be gained by visiting them? One would think that the Holy Spirit dwells within the inhabitants of Jerusalem and could not reach Cappadocia (*Letter* II, 8)! Gregory presents a grim description of Jerusalem, city of sin and evil-doing which has not been spared of even one type of sin (prostitution, theft, murder, idolatry, incest). Let us not forget that this is the same city in which the people and places aroused joy in Gregory according to his *Letter* III!

There is no doubt that the opposition he had met in Jerusalem explains his harsh criticism of the city and its inhabitants, and this essentially explains his contradictory positions regarding the holy places in *Letters* II and III. But to what degree *Letter* II indeed reflects his basic opinions about pilgrimage and what are the special features behind his claims?

At the beginning of *Letter* II, Gregory raises doubts whether seeing Jerusalem, where one may witness the signs of the Lord's physical realization, is part of religious piety (εὐσέβεια). While Gregory raises this question with regard to visiting the holy places in Jerusalem, this does not apply to the cult of the martyrs. His position on this issue is clear; those who recognize the fruits of piety must participate in the cult of the martyr.[44] In other words, unlike pilgrimage to Jerusalem, the cult of the martyrs was perceived by him as belonging to the realm of religious piety.[45]

One of Gregory's main reasons for opposing pilgrimage to Jerusalem is that this act does not belong to the canon (κανόνα). Basing himself on Matt. 25: 34, he writes: "When the Lord called the chosen to inherit the Heavenly Kingdom he did not include the journey to Jerusalem among the good deeds" (*Letter* II, 2–3). This act is not included in Jesus' instructions to his disciples in Matt. 5:3–11. Gregory goes on to declare that if there were any merit in this act, then one would not chose to fulfill it in this way, since the act causes "spiritual harm" to those who chose a monastic way of life. Of course, this is a fundamental claim which is difficult to reject out of hand. Moreover, it should be noted that the use of this claim was rare in the fourth and fifth centuries and Gregory's decision to use it is original. However, despite the absence of any instruction in the New Testament making pilgrimage obligatory, the phenomenon gained momentum and developed, and was indeed witnessed by Gregory when he was in Jerusalem.

Gregory deliberately asserts that there is no contemplative value in seeing these places. If one indeed can argue Divine Presence through visible objects, one may conclude that God dwells in Cappadocia more than in any other place since it has an abundance of cultic places (θυσιαστήριον).[46] Gregory announces his conclusion unequivocally; everywhere the believer is found, he may glorify and praise God. A change of place does not necessarily bring about closeness to God. Paraphrasing II Cor. 6:16, Gregory states that he whose soul will be worthy of God dwelling and walking in him, God will reach him. However, he who has evil thoughts dwelling within him, "whether you are on the Golgoltha or the Mount of Olives, or at the Anastasis tomb, you are far from receiving Christ within you" (*Letter* II, 17). Jerusalem has no advantage over any other region in the world, and because of its sins it is not even worthy of the Divine Presence dwelling within it. Basing himself on Paul in II Cor. 5:8, Gregory proposes to his reader to advise the brothers to leave their body in order to go before the Lord, and not to leave Cappadocia in order to visit Palestine (*Letter* II, 18).

However Gregory still fears that someone will make the claim, according to Acts 1:4, that the Lord commanded his disciples "not to depart from Jerusalem, but to wait there for the promise of the Father" (*Letter* II, 18). Against this possible claim he responds that these words were said before the Holy Spirit was divided among the disciples (Acts 2:1–4), and thus the Lord commanded them to remain in the same place "until you are clothed with the power on high" (Luke 24:49). Jerusalem, the place in which the Holy Spirit descended, thus had a role in history, however from the moment the Holy Sprit was divided among the disciples its role ended. Thus, there is no importance to the place with regard to the presence of the Holy Spirit, since the Holy Spirit blows wherever it pleases (John 3:8). The believers in Cappadocia, according to Gregory, also "share the grace . . . according to the proportion of faith" (Rom. 12:6), and not because of their journey to Jerusalem (*Letter* II,19). With these decisive words, Gregory hopes to abolish the special status accorded to Jerusalem that may be deduced from the New Testament.

Until now, we have shown that Gregory judiciously used traditional theological views anchored in the New Testament that essentially reject the role and significance of earthly holy space. It should be noted that the "substitute" proposed by Gregory to the Christian believer is not traditional, at least in part. I am implying that in *Letter* II Gregory does not discuss the value of heavenly Jerusalem instead of the earthly city, as do other Christian thinkers. One could easily anticipate that Gregory would do this and would pronounce these conceptions which are anchored in the New Testament (Heb. 12:22, Gal. 4:26) and in the Christian tradition of scriptural interpretation of early Christian thinkers, such as Origen and Eusebius. However, instead of the traditional conception that glorifies the importance of heavenly Jerusalem, Gregory places the newly created network of holy places on a par with the cult of the martyrs in Cappadocia, which he and his brother Basil were among its founders.[47] Emphasis upon the local network of holy places, as opposed to the holy places in Jerusalem, robs the city of its historical uniqueness and reveals the author's preference for local pilgrimage to the tombs of martyrs in Cappadocia over pilgrimage to Jerusalem. This standpoint sets Gregory of Nyssa apart from other late fourth-century thinkers in the debate about the holy places and pilgrimage.

Gregory raises yet another claim in *Letter* II in order to prove the insignificance of the holy places for Christians. He rejects their value as evidence for the truth of Christianity and of Jesus' divinity (*Letter* II, 15). Gregory denies the contemplative value of pilgrimage to Palestine; seeing the holy places— which is the essence of the religious experience of pilgrimage—is completely unimportant for Christian faith.

Our sources clearly testify that other perceptions about the pedagogical role of Jerusalem existed in Gregory's day. The most prominent personality in his time, who had placed great religious and pedagogical weight on the holy places so as to reinforce Christian faith, was Cyril, bishop of Jerusalem.[48] It would not be unimaginable to assume that Gregory's words here basically echo a direct or indirect debate between these two figures.

In his *Catechetical Lectures*, Cyril has interpreted the main events in the life of Jesus by relying upon references from the Bible and from geography which emphasize the importance of earthly Jerusalem for Christian faith in his time. Cyril tried to persuade his congregants not with profound theological arguments, but with concrete evidence that could be seen and touched in

Jerusalem and around it. Cyril repeatedly emphasizes to his audience that the testimony for the truth of Christianity and the divinity of Jesus, as learned in the Holy Scriptures, is found "among us" (παρ' ἡμῖν), and that the main events of holy history occurred here (ενταυθα) in Jerusalem.[49]

This motif reflects not only Cyril's desire to teach the importance of historical Jerusalem in order to strengthen the Christian faith, but also his aim to confirm the special status of Jerusalem of the here-and-now and to emphasize the privilege afforded those living in it in the present. In his *Catechetical Lecture* X, 19, Cyril states and enumerates the abundant evidence relating to the life of Jesus. One chain of testimony is borrowed from the miracle acts performed by Jesus and another is borrowed from the geographical realm, from the places where Jesus and his disciples performed their acts, such as the Jordan River and the Sea of Galilee. After reviewing this geographical evidence before his congregants, he brings the concrete evidence found in their geographical proximity. Firstly, he mentions the holiest relic of them all, "the holy tree of the cross bears witness, it is found among us to this day." From this place it now fills almost the entire world who takes part in its faith. Gethsemane, the Golgotha, "the holy hill standing above us here"; the holy tomb bears witness and so does the stone placed there until this very day, and also the Mount of Olives bears witness.[50] According to him, the many and varied pieces of evidence are valid to both convince the non-believers and bolster the faith of those who were already adherents of Christianity.[51]

In *Catechetical Lecture* XIII, Cyril searches for proof of Jesus' crucifixion. And, indeed, he finds a boundless reservoir of evidence for the crucifixion in the books of the Prophets. However, he finds concrete evidence at the place "you see, at the Golgotha." He does not hesitate at all in asserting that this place, which serves as evidence for the crucifixion of Jesus, is the center of the earth (τῆς γὰρ γῆς τὸ μεσώτατον ὁ Γολγοθᾶς). Cyril is apparently aware of the importance as well as the difficulty in this assertion, and he hastens to say that these are not his words, but rather those of the prophet.[52]

By this same method, Cyril seeks to prove Jesus' resurrection. He first brings the evidence from the Bible and then attempts to confirm the faith of his congregants through the places in which these events occurred. Thus, proof of the resurrection of the Lord is "the place itself."[53] Gregory of Nyssa categorically rejects this concept: his faith neither increased nor decreased by seeing the places connected with Jesus' activities.

> For us, we believed that Christ who appeared on earth is the true God before we came to these places, as we did afterwards; our faith in light of this has neither increased nor decreased. We knew about incarnation

through the Virgin before we saw Bethlehem; we believed in resurrection before we saw the tomb; we believed in the truth of the ascent to heaven without seeing the Mount of Olives.[54]

Cyril also seeks proof for Jerusalem's supremacy over other places. For example, he attempts to derive some purpose from the descent of the Holy Spirit upon the city (Luke 24:49). As already mentioned, Gregory of Nyssa draws clear boundaries between events of the past and present-day life, between the role of historical Jerusalem and that of the present.

We have only glimpsed at Cyril's views which attribute to the holy places a religious-pedagogical role of the first order, and which demonstrate the supremacy of Jerusalem over other places. This position reflects the deep division between the conceptions of Gregory of Nyssa and Cyril of Jerusalem regarding this issue. We have no solid proof for a direct debate between these two figures. Cyril indeed wrote about thirty years before Gregory arrived in Jerusalem (ca. 381), but it is possible that Gregory became aware of Cyril's perceptions regarding the value and role of the holy places during his stay in the city.

The fact that Gregory did not suffice only with theological claims in order to reject the religious significance of the pilgrimage act, but rather added to it a vehement attack against the city and its inhabitants, is indicative of the personal dimension which influenced his reaction in *Letter* II; *Letter* II is not a theoretical theological treatise against the significance of the pilgrimage act. It should be remembered that Gregory was spurred to react to the phenomenon of pilgrimage following his visit to Jerusalem; for this reason, I believe that we should not divorce the contents of *Letter* II either from the historical context or the hostile attitude which he encountered in Jerusalem. It is possible that Gregory indeed held these views regarding the role of the holy places. However, it is precisely Gregory's originality and divergence from the classic set of claims expressed when heightening the value of the local holy places in Cappadocia, and not the value of heavenly Jerusalem, that succeeds in expressing the author's position. Gregory used the traditional conceptions of Christian holy space for his apologetic purposes against Jerusalem and its inhabitants. The reasons mentioned here lead us to conclude that *Letter* II is not only a systematic theological document against the phenomenon of pilgrimage, but also an apologetic document against religious conceptions claiming the supremacy of Jerusalem by virtue of the pedagogical role of its holy places. This conclusion slightly weakens the extreme dichotomy between Gregory's attitude toward local pilgrimage and pilgrimage to Jerusalem. Gregory's theological claims in this context undermined and injured the standing and prestige of the bishop of Jerusalem, who had invested much effort to establish the special status of the Jerusalem Church on the basis of its geographical proximity to the holy places.

Conclusion

From the writings of Gregory of Nyssa and Augustine, it may be said that neither of these figures rejected pilgrimage as a pattern of religious behavior; rather, they rejected Jerusalem or disregarded the city as a center for pilgrimage. More precisely, they preferred the local cult and local pilgrimages over pilgrimage to Jerusalem for both theological and political reasons. At the end of the fourth century, and throughout the entire Byzantine period and beyond, we are witness to competition between the local cult and the holy places in Jerusalem. Gregory of Nyssa was among the first promulgators of this debate and among the most radical speakers against the holy places in Jerusalem.

Notes

1. H. Windisch, "Die ältesten christlichen Palästinapilger", *ZDPV* 48 (1925), 145–58; B. Kötting, *Peregrinatio Religiosa: Wallfahrten in der Antike und das Pilgerwesen in der alten Kirche* (Münster, 1950), 85–89; E. D. Hunt, *Holy Land Pilgrimage in the Later Roman Empire, AD 312–460* (Oxford, 1982), 3–4; P. Maraval, *Lieux saints et pèlerinages d'Orient. Histoire et géographie des origines à la conquête arabe* (Paris, 1985), 26–27; K. G. Holum, "Hadrian and St. Helena: Imperial Travel and the Origins of Christian Holy Land Pilgrimage," *The Blessing of Pilgrimage*, Illionis Byzantine Studies, 1, ed. R. Ousterhout (Urbana, 1990), 66–81.

2. Egeria, *Travels* (ed. & trans. P. Maraval, *SC* 296), 25, 12; 45, 1–2 (*SC* 255, 318–319); Jerome, *Letter* LXVI, 14 (ed. & trans. J. Labourt), III, 180.

3. John Chrysostom, *Hom. in Ps.* 109, 5 (110, 5) (*PG* 55, 274a).

4. J. E. Taylor, *Christians and the Holy Places. The Myth of Jewish-Christian Origins* (Oxford, 1993), 314. See also J. Z. Smith, *To Take Place. Toward Theory in Ritual* (Chicago & London, 1987), 76–77.

5. Smith (above, note 4), 79. For reviews of Taylor's book from several points of view, see O. Irshai, *JRS* 84 (1994), 264–65; J. D. Wilkinson, *JTS* 45/1 (1994), 304–306; J. W. Drijvers, *VC* 48 (1994), 84–86.

6. M. Halbwachs, *La topographie légendaire des évangiles en terre sainte: Etude de mémoire collective* (Paris, 1971).

7. R. A. Markus, "How on Earth Could Places Become Holy? Origins of the Christian Idea of Holy Places," *Journal of Early Christian Studies* 2/3 (1994), 268.

8. On this issue, see B. Bitton-Ashkelony, "Pilgrimage: Perceptions and Reactions in the Patristic and Monastic Literature of the Fourth–Sixth Centuries," Ph.D. dissertation (Hebrew University of Jerusalem, 1995) (Hebrew).

9. Gregory of Nyssa, *Lettres* (ed. & trans. P. Maraval, *SC* 363), II, 106–23; on Augustine, see Bitton-Ashkelony (above, note 8), 136–64.

10. On the relations between Augustine and Paulinus of Nola, see P. Courcelle, "Les lacunes dans la correspondance entre saint Augustin et Paulin de Nole," *REAN* 53 (1951), 253–300. On Paulinus of Nola and his ties with the intellectual elite of the Latin West at that time, see W. H. C. Frend, "Paulinus of Nola and the Last Century of the Western Empire," *JRS* 59 (1969), 1–11.

11. Jerome, *Letter* LVIII; Paulinus of Nola, *Ep.* XXXI, 4 (*CSEL* 29, 272); *Ep.* XLIX, 14 (*CSEL* 29, 402).

12. *Ep.* XXXI, 4–6 (*CSEL* 29, 271–75). On Paulinus of Nola's version of the discovery of the cross, see Hunt (above, note 1), 39–49; H. J. W. Drijvers, *Helena Augusta—The Mother of Constantine the Great and the Legend of Her Finding of the True Cross* (Leiden, 1992), 113–17, 120–23.

13. *Ep.* XXXI,1 (*CSEL* 29, 267–68); *Ep.* XXXII, 7, 11 (*CSEL* 29, 282–83, 286–87).

14. On the contents of the correspondence between these two figures, see F. Cavallera, *Saint Jérôme: sa vie et son oeuvre*, Spicilegium sacrum Lovaniense I-II (Louvain, 1922), I, 297–306. Chronological questions regarding their correspondence are discussed in ibid., II, 47–50, 60–61; J. N. D. Kelly, *Jerome: His Life, Writings, and Controversies* (London, 1975), 263–72.

15. Orosius' visit to Palestine and his participation in the Lydda synod are discussed by Hunt (above, note 1), 208–20.

16. On the discovery of Stephanus' remains and their distribution among various communities, see H. Delehaye, *Les origines du culte des martyrs* (Bruxelles, 1912), 96–98, 105–106; P. Peeters, *Le tréfonds oriental de l'hagiographie byzantin* (Bruxelles, 1950), 53–58; Hunt (above, note 1), 211–20; Maraval (above, note 1), 266–67.

17. *The City of God* XXII, 8. The Hesperius incident is mentioned by R. Wilken (*The Land Called Holy. Palestine in Christian History and Thought* [New Haven, 1992], 125).

18. A comprehensive study of Augustine's sermons for the martyrs celebrations and their contribution to our understanding of this cult in North Africa was undertaken by G. Lapointe, "Le culte des martyrs en Afrique d'après les sermons de saint Augustin," Ph.D. dissertation (Inst. Cath., Paris, 1968); C. Lambot, "Les sermons de saint Augustin pour les fêtes de martyrs," *AnBoll* 67 (1949), 249–66.

19. On this trend in ancient Christianity, see W. D. Davies, *The Gospel and the Land. Early Christianity and Jewish Territorial Doctrine* (Berkeley, 1974); Wilken (above, note 17), 52–81.

20. P. Brown, *Augustine of Hippo, a Biography* (London, 1967), 151.

21. *Tract.* X, 1, *In Ioh.* II, 12 (*CCL* 36, 100–101). See comment by R. Markus, *The End of Ancient Christianity* (Cambridge, 1990), 139–40 and notes.

22. *De sermone Domini* II, 5, 17–18 (*CCL* 35, 107–108).

23. Ibid. II, 5, 17.

24. Ibid., 5, 18.

25. *Ep.* 187, 11.

26. *De sermone Domini* II, 5, 19 (*CCL* 35, 109).

27. On the interpretation of Eusebius see, *Life of Constantine* III, 42 (*GCS* 7, 95). See also P.W. L. Walker, *Holy City, Holy Places? Christian Attitudes to Jerusalem and the Holy Land in the Fourth Century* (Oxford, 1990), 183–84; Wilken (above, note 17), 97–99; Jerome, *Letter* CVIII,10; V, 170; *Letter* XLVII, 2; II, 115; Paulinus of Nola, *Letter* XXX, 4 (*CSEL*, 29, 272); *Letter* XLIX, 14 (*CSEL* 29, 402).

28. *Enarr. in Psal.* CXXXI, 2–7 (*CCL* 40, 1911-15).

29. Eusebius, *Onomasticon*, Εφραθα (ed. E. Klostermann, *GCS* III¹), 82, 10; Theodoret of Cyrrhus, *In Psal.* CXXXI, 6 (*PG* 80, 1905); Jerome, *Tract. de Psal.* CXXXI (*CCL* 78, 275); John Chrysostom, *In Psal.* CXXXI (*PG* 55, 382).

30. See above, note 29.

31. This is attested, for example, when he approaches Heraklius the Diakon with a request to build a memoria in which to place the remains of the protomartyr Stephen as well as a hostel for pilgrims who would visit it; *Sermone* 356, 7 (*PL* 39, 1577); *Sermone* 390, 8 (*PL* 38, 1442).

32. See above, note 17.

33. Wilken (above, note 17), 125.

34. *The City of God* XXII, 5, 1.

35. Basil of Caesarea, *Letter* 223 (*LCL* 3, 286–312); *Letter* 1 (*LCL* 1, 2–6).

36. *Vita Macrinae* 1, 7–9. The polemical history of *Letter* II is discussed at length by P. Maraval, "Une querelle sur les pèlerinages autour d'un texte patristique (Grégoire de Nysse, Lettre 2)," *RHPhR* 66 (1986), 131–46; Wilken (above, note 17), 118.

37. P. Maraval (ed. & trans.), *Grégoire de Nysse: vie de sainte Macrine* (*SC* 178, 138).

38. G. W. H. Lampe, *A Patristic Greek Lexicon* (Oxford, 1982), s.v. "ἡ εὐχή," 580; Maraval (above, note 37), 139; Wilken (above, note 17), 117.

39. Maraval (above, note 37), 139.

40. P. Maraval (ed. & tr.), *Grégoire de Nysse: Lettres* (*SC* 363, 37 and note 2); idem, "Egérie et Grégoire de Nysse, pèlerins aux lieux saints de Palestine," *Atti del Convegno Internazionale sulla Peregrinatio Egeriae* (Arezzo, 1990), 328.

41. The most comprehensive and thorough study of this issue was conducted by P. Maraval, "La lettre 3 de Grégoire de Nysse dans le débat christologique," *RSR* 61 (1987), 74–89; Maraval (above, note 40), 36–37.

42. Maraval (above, note 41), 88; Maraval (above, note 40), 37.

43. *In S. Theodorum* (*PG* 46, 736; 737b–c).

44. Ibid. (*PG* 46, 737b).

45. On Gregory of Nyssa's support of the local cult of the martyrs in Cappadocia and his participation in the martyr celebrations, see Ashkelony (above, note 8), 39–42.

46. Lampe (above, note 38), 660, IIIb.

47. On Basil of Caesarea's attitude on the cult of the martyrs and his propaganda in support of this cult, see: M. Girardi, *Basilio di Cesarea e il culto dei martiri nel IV secolo, Scrittura e tradizione* (Bari, 1990); Bitton-Ashkelony (above, note 8), 39–42.

48. Walker (above, note 27), 311–45.

49. *Cat. Lect.* XVII, 13, 22; XIV, 23. See also Walker (above, note 27), 331–33.

50. *Cat. Lect.* X, 19.

51. Ibid., X, 20.

52. Ibid., XIII, 28.

53. Ibid., XIV, 22–23.

54. *Letter* II, 15.

14

The Jerusalem Bishopric and the Jews in the Fourth Century: History and Eschatology

ODED IRSHAI

I n a well-known passage in his *Martyrs of Palestine*, Eusebius of Caesarea, father of church history and the metropolitan bishop of Provincia Palaestina, recorded the following dialogue which took place on the 16th February, 310 between the local Roman governor Firmilianus and a Christian prisoner named Pamphilus:

> Firmilianus . . . next asked him what his city was. But the martyr let fall a second expression in harmony with the former one, saying that Jerusalem was his city—meaning, to be sure, that one of which it was said by Paul: "But the Jerusalem that is above is free, which is our mother". . . . This was the one he meant. But the other (the governor) had his thoughts fixed on this world here below, and enquired closely and carefully as to what city it was, and in what part of the world it was situated; and then applied tortures as well. . . . But our martyr . . . stoutly affirmed that he spoke the truth. The judge next asked him again and again as to what and where situated that city was of which he spoke, and he replied that it was the country of the godly. . . . The judge, on the other hand, was puzzled and shook with impatience, thinking that the Christians had certainly established a city somewhere at enmity and hostile to the Romans; and he was much occupied in discovering it and enquiring into the said country in the East.[1]

This dialogue took place in the midst of the most extensive and ruthless persecutions of the Christians by the pagan Roman state. What we have here, as clearly stated by D. Hunt, is a vivid illustration of two worlds apart. At one extreme was the practical Roman governor who, so it seems, had not heard of a city called Jerusalem and, on the other, was the Christian martyr, obsessed with a Christian dream about a heavenly Jerusalem, a dwelling place for the godly alone which is bound to descend in the "end of days." Both of them did, however, agree on one thing, namely, there was no place on earth named Jerusalem.[2] Even if we ignore the somewhat legendary features of this story, we are still faced with an emphatic conclusion that Hadrian's pagan city Aelia Capitolina managed to obliterate the memory of the older and more famous Hierosolyma. With only a small trickle of pilgrims from outside Palestine,[3] how many of the Christians living outside the region were still aware of the fact that the Church of Aelia was actually the oldest apostolic see?[4] From a modern perspective, one is inclined to endorse J. Wilkinson's remark that "Christianity in Jerusalem makes depressing reading."[5]

The enigma of early Christian Jerusalem becomes even more apparent if we pause to observe the fundamental ecclesiastical-political transformation this church underwent in a relatively short time: in the course of just over a century (ca. 330–430), the Jerusalem Church ascended from the position of a somewhat peripheral church to one of the five leading centers (patriarchates) of the Christian world.[6]

Z. Rubin's colorful description of the accomplishments of the local church's political wizards at the time is most informative,[7] but neither the miraculous discovery of the holy cross (fifteen years after the abovementioned dialogue took place) nor the building of the Church of the Holy Sepulchre later on—both carried out by members of the imperial family[8]—were enough to facilitate the remarkable transformation in the history of that community. Nor could it be attributed entirely to the sudden concerted surge in devotional pilgrimage to the holy city to see "the places where it all happened," to touch the holy relics of the past, and to participate in the newly-formulated liturgical ceremonies and processions *apta diei apta loco* (befitting in time and place) described by Egeria.[9] The ever-growing sacerdotal and imperial interest in reviving the notion of "navel of the earth" had deep roots in the past and was connected with the tradition of the Apostolic Church, going back to the period of the Mother Church of the first century. The image of the first-century Jerusalem Church, with its local founders Stephen and, later on, James, and its concept of the brotherhood (ἀδελφότης) of love and spiritual alliance and sharing (κοινός), still fascinated church fathers such as Basil of Caesarea.[10] This deep sense of enduring respect for that cradle of Christianity was the outcome of what I believe H. Chadwick meant years ago by his reference to that church's "living mystique," which manifested itself in its authority and which "a network of communities linked themselves to by their common origin and events occurring there." However, he described this early mystique and its later manifestations as unrealistic, "in one sense poetry rather than truth, literature rather than dogma, symbol rather than cold reality."[11]

Chadwick explored the tension between two different concepts of authority within the church, the one emerging from Rome the other from Jerusalem, and their imprint on the church at large ("the circle and the ellipse"). However, he paid less attention to the presence and function of these models within the constraints of the abovementioned centers themselves, in our case the formation of the Jerusalem Church's self identity.[12] Contrary to Chadwick's moderation or even dismissal of the essence of the local history as something denoting "symbol rather than cold reality," it is my contention that the history of that see during the first three centuries of the Common Era might serve as an important tool for understanding later developments in Jerusalem, most of all the great transformation of the fourth century.

Close examination of the handful of historical traditions concerning the Jerusalem Christian community, preserved mainly in Eusebius' *Historia Ecclesiastica*, reveals a somewhat overbearing presence of a local "Jewish element" in them. I am not referring here to late Second Temple Jerusalem, the last generation of which coincided with the formation of the local Christian community, but rather to the continued presence of a Jewish element in the history of that Christian community in the post-70 era. This Jewish element determined and shaped the self-perception of the Jerusalem Christian community, whose entire history may be seen in terms of a long and enduring confrontation with its Jewish past.

The rise of the new Christian Jerusalem in the early decades of the fourth century in a way eased this struggle with the past. However, extraordinary events in the second half of the century, perceived locally as signifying the "End of Days," a scenario in which the Jews were allotted a key role in their unfolding, added both a new dimension to these ongoing polemics with the Jews and a new sense of the local Christian mission. In what follows, I shall try and demonstrate the existence of these two dimensions in the evolving history of the Christian community of Jerusalem.

✦   ✦   ✦

The Apostolic Church in Jerusalem, led by James, Jesus' brother, between the early forties and early sixties of the first century, was, according to J. D. G. Dunn, "in no sense part of a new religion, distinct from Judaism."[13] The famous apostolic decree (Acts 15) from ca. 48 C.E., whereby James required all gentile converts to adhere to some basic requirements of the Law, is a clear indication of the spirit in which this community was run.[14]

Moreover, James was martyred in the year 62 by the Sadducees, headed at the time by the High Priest Hanan son of Hanan. This event, according to Josephus,[15] caused some uneasiness among the Pharisees, who most probably viewed his execution as a strictly political act with no foundation in the Law. In early Christian circles, James became a symbol of exemplary fidelity to the Law, and his martyrdom was utilized for local anti-Jewish polemics. It was claimed to be the last straw that brought about the destruction of the city and its Temple. Eusebius records the following tradition, learned from one of his second-century sources, Hegesippus: "and they buried him (James, following his martyrdom) on the spot by the Temple . . . and at once Vespasian began to besiege them."[16] Anyone with only a rudimentary knowledge of the chronology of that period would have noticed the flaw in this assertion. While the former event occurred in 62 C.E., the latter happened a number of years later. However, when faced with a clear case of divine retribution, who would have paid attention to such chronological inaccuracies, especially when the Jerusalem community could assert through such a tradition its own special role in the divine punishment that was visited upon the city and attributed by the church at large to the crucifixion of Jesus?[17]

The following era in the history of the church (70–135 C.E.) was designated the age of the Church of the Circumcision, which was characterized by its Jewish leadership. At its head stood a series of fifteen bishops whose names we first learn from the abovementioned Hegesippus, who availed himself of the local archives.[18] These leaders no doubt continued to govern the community in accordance with James' teachings. In fact, according to some later sources, this Jerusalem community was comprised of the Nazarene sect of Jewish-Christianity. Although by then it was adopting some form of Christology, accepting the virgin birth and referring to Jesus as divine, at the same time this community adhered strictly to the law and emphasized its deep bond with Jerusalem.[19] It seems that it was at this time that the ascetic high priest-like image of James, celebrated leader of the early church, began to evolve.[20] However, by the standards of the Pauline gentile church, this community was probably considered in many respects heretical. The formative periods in the evolution of the Jerusalem community's heritage were thus Jewish-Christian in character, a fact which may have caused some embarrassment to later generations of the local gentile church. The early history of the latter community is thus the cause of a major change in its character.

This change occurred immediately after, and as a result of, the Bar-Kochba revolt. Tradition has it that the Romans issued a decree banning all Jews from entering Jerusalem or its vicinity, and according to Eusebius this action brought about the cessation of the Jewish-Christian community as well:

> Thus, when the city came to be bereft of the nation of the Jews, and its ancient inhabitants had completely perished, it was colonized by foreigners, and the Roman city which afterwards arose changed its name, and in honor of the reigning emperor Aelius Hadrian was called Aelia. The church, too, in it was composed of Gentiles, and after the Jewish bishops the first who was appointed to minister to those there was Marcus.[21]

If we combine Eusebius' description with his unmistakably polemical statement found in his *Chronicon*, namely, that this ban was first and foremost in accordance with a heavenly command and in fulfillment of ancient prophecy, we may also detect in the above description an anachronistic sigh of relief.[22] However, eradicating the past from the local tradition was out of the question, as doing so meant creating a vacuum in the line of the local succession of leadership. This, in turn, meant creating a breach in what was called the ἀληθής λόγος, i.e., the authentic tradition.[23] The essential thing, therefore, was to downplay the importance of that period or create a dignified apostolic-like image for the new gentile leadership. Thus, close examination of Eusebius' account of the second century in his *Historia Ecclesiastica* reveals not only the complexity of the situation, but also the way in which the newly-established gentile leadership tackled it.[24]

By the third century, the Church of Aelia became a regional center, taking an active part in combating heresies with strong monotheistic leanings, such as those which sprung up in the Roman provinces of Arabia and Syria. The cases in question concerned Beryllus of Bostra and Paul of Samosata.[25] These were the early signs of a new assertive church resuming its role of apostolic authority, guidance, and leadership. By the turn of the fourth century, Jerusalem had its share of martyrs, and from the outset of the most bitter dogmatic strife of the fourth century, i.e., the Arian controversy, this church was recognized as a bastion of orthodoxy and its bishop Macarius was acknowledged as one of the most avowed enemies of the heretic Arius of Alexandria. It appears that the Church of Aelia did, after all, manage to build for itself some sort of reputation as being an active anti-heretical center.[26]

The third decade of the fourth century brought about a radical change in the lives of Jerusalem Christians, as they prepared to take part in the active formation of a Christian Holy Land. With the final demise of the pagan Roman state, Constantine devised his "Holy Land" plan, in the center of which was the uprooting of pagan shrines, particularly in and around Jerusalem. According to recent studies, a pagan presence was very much in evidence in Palestine, and especially in Aelia,[27] and is attested in an abundant number of contemporary sources. Hadrian established a pagan center in Aelia which both Jews and Christians assumed was established in order to subvert their own past.[28] I am referring, on the one hand, to the pagan temple built on the site where, according to local tradition, Jesus was crucified and buried, and, on the other hand, to the ploughing of the Temple Mount, a tradition appearing in rabbinical sources.[29] This initial phase in the re-creation of earthly Christian Jerusalem is of little concern to us here. However, it was the second phase in the appropriation of Jerusalem, this time from its ancestral inhabitants, the Jews, that demanded a much more subtle approach. As we shall see below, events occurring in Jerusalem presented a far greater challenge to the local church fathers. A few illustrations should suffice to demonstrate my argument.

The dedication ceremony of the Constantinian Church of the Holy Sepulchre on 14th September, 335 marked a new era in Jerusalem, in which new imagery was appropriated, contrasting the New Jerusalem with the Old.[30] This annual ceremony at first carried with it a strong anti-pagan sentiment; gradually, over time, it assumed a profound anti-Jewish symbolism. The ceremony was described in terms of the consecration of the Temple in the days of King Solomon.[31] Christian pilgrims flocking to Jerusalem from all over the world were constantly reminded that the new church on Golgotha faced the old Temple ruins of the Jews.[32]

Moreover, it seems that the local bishopric contrived to convey the same message to the Jews as well. It brought about the relaxation of the old Hadrianic decree for just one day in the year, on the 9th of the Jewish month of Av, so that the Jews could come and mourn on the site of the Temple ruins and no doubt see with their own eyes the new and prosperous Christian city.[33] Both the desolate Temple Mount and the thriving Church served as testimonies to Jewish crimes against Jesus or, perhaps in accordance with local tradition, against James, the founder of the Jerusalem Church. By the middle of the century, the local church felt very secure and even its Jewish-Christian roots were utilized in catechetical lectures in an anti-Jewish polemical context.[34] It is therefore not surprising that in those years, according to a later tradition, James' remains were found buried near the Temple[35] and the only remaining (Jewish-Christian) synagogue which stood on Mount Zion was demolished by Maximus, the local bishop.[36]

The most profound development in the Jerusalem Church's evolving self-identity was yet to come—in the course of Cyril's service as bishop between

348 and 386 C.E. This church father, whose checkered career is of less importance to us here,[37] was the true founder of the "new" church of Jerusalem and an ardent local patriot. Although his literary output was meager, consisting of one sermon and one known epistle to Emperor Constantius II, he became most famous for his eighteen Catechetical Lectures, a preparatory course on the Christian creed delivered during Lent to candidates for baptism.[38] His patriotic spirit is openly expressed in his sixteenth lecture: "for in all things the choicest privileges are with us";[39] nevertheless, he was well aware of the Jewish history of Jerusalem and indeed of the Jewish-Christian roots of his community. These facts played a major role in his theology of holy places which formed the basis for the local liturgical rite he created and which is preserved until today through Egeria's unique diary from 383/384, and the fifth-century Armenian Lectionary.[40]

The Jews and their traditions were singled out in his lectures as the archenemies of the Church, second only to heretics, whom he despised even more for holding Jewish views. His lectures were to constitute a set of arguments buttressed by prooftexts from the Bible and the New Testament, to serve his listeners, the new converts "as armor"[41] in their future battles with the enemies of the Church. He therefore tried to remove all allegorical interpretation from his exegesis and tended to use only the literal and historical sense.[42] Thus, it is not surprising that Cyril's theology centered around the first advent of Jesus by emphasizing his incarnation and crucifixion in Jerusalem, i.e., the historical and earthly existence of Jesus as opposed to his Divine existence.

Did Cyril express any interest in the expected Second Coming of Jesus in the End of Days? The answer to this lies in the way Cyril addressed two significant events, each twelve years apart, that occurred in Jerusalem. The first, in 351, had local significance; the other, in 363, was to shake the entire Christian world:

> On the morning of May the 7th of the year 351, at the third hour of the morning, there appeared in the skies of Jerusalem a great luminous cross which extended from the hill of Golgotha to the Mount of Olives, and was seen by all the inhabitants of the city. The whole population of the city made a sudden concerted rush into the Martyry, seized by a fear that mingled with joy . . . they poured in, young and old, men and women of every age, even to the maiden hitherto kept in seclusion of their homes, local folk and strangers, not only Christians but pagans from elsewhere sojourning in Jerusalem all of them as with one mouth raised a hymn of praise to Christ our Lord.

This description is taken from the earliest testimony of the apparition in Jerusalem—Cyril's letter to Emperor Constantius II, which was written shortly after the event.[43] As the letter is most probably authentic, it constitutes a firsthand account of this incredible event, the impression it left, and—above all—the interpretation it engendered. The historicity of the actual event is secondary. At the time of the miraculous event, the emperor to whom Cyril sent this description was in great distress, facing a decisive battle with Magnentius, usurper to the throne in the West and, at the same time, a period of unrest in the East. He was in great need of a heavenly omen in his favor. There was already a precedent for this in his father's days, the famous Milvian Bridge apparition of the year 312 which also occurred on the eve of a decisive battle. Following Constantius' victory, contemporary sources did, in fact, interpret the miraculous event in this manner. The anonymous Arian historian transferred its location to Mursa, where the actual battle took place.[44]

However, Cyril saw something entirely different. After emphasizing to the emperor the unique location of the apparition, Jerusalem (mentioned seven times in the course of the epistle), he contrasted it with the finding of the Cross on Golgotha while, at the same time, totally ignoring the apparition seen by Constantius' father.[45] Cyril went on to state that the wonder was the present fulfillment of biblical and New Testament prophecies at the time, though their ultimate fulfillment would only come to pass in the future. Cyril was probably referring to the eschatological scheme at the "end of days" described in detail in Matt. 24, where the first sign of that new age leading to Jesus' Second Advent was "the appearance of the sign of the Son of Man (בן האדם) in heaven (verse 30)." Subsequently, Cyril encouraged the emperor to study the gospels on this matter with diligence and patience as a necessary precaution against "the opposing force" (ἀντικείμηνη ἐνεργείας).[46] By Cyril's time, there was already an established tradition that the "sign" referred to in the gospel was the sign of the Cross[47]—but who was the "opposing force?"

The general meaning of this term in the New Testament was adversary or enemy; in Cyril's vocabulary, however, it had a special connotation. In his fifteenth lecture, dedicated to Christ's Second Coming, Cyril defined this opposing force as the Antichrist—the evil/satanic king who would fight the final battle against Christ in the end of days—who, at the same time, would be the King of Jerusalem and, above all, the benefactor of the Jews. According to Cyril, the "sign," a luminous cross appearing in the sky, declares the coming of Christ so that the Jews who pierced him and plotted against him would "mourn tribe by tribe"[48] (a phrase taken from the prophecy of Zechariah on the "end of days"). If the Jews would contemplate flight from Christ's wrath, the angel hosts accompanying him would surround the Jews so as to prevent them from fleeing. Cyril ended this chilling description by stating that the "sign of the Cross shall be a terror to his foes but joy to his friends who have believed in him." I doubt whether this interpretation of the significance of the apparition was fully grasped by the emperor, but this seems to be the lesson Cyril wished to convey to his flock, and to others as well, specifically the bishop of the Metropolitan See of Caesarea, an avowed rival of the political aspirations of the Jerusalem Church. It is not surprising, therefore, that a few years later Cyril was banished from office with trumped-up charges.[49] Cyril was very cautious in his representation of the whole event, and did not cultivate false hopes, yet he nevertheless managed to rescue this incredible occurrence from potential political exploitation and adorn it with a far more lofty meaning. By so doing, he clearly indicated the centrality of Jerusalem and the Jews in his eschatological scheme. It is not surprising, therefore, that the 7th of May became a date to commemorate on the local Christian calendar.[50]

Twelve years following the abovementioned event, again in the month of May, Jerusalem was placed once more in the center of anxiety of a troubled Christian world. This was the age of the famous pagan emperor and usurper of the Christian empire, Julian the Apostate. He is often portrayed as contriving to change the course of history by halting the process of Christianization thoughout the empire;[51] he was now out to create new horizons for his preferred religion, i.e., polytheism with its universalism,[52] basing it on Neoplatonic concepts together with an active sacrificial system. This principle, coupled with Julian's Christian upbringing, drew his attention to the religion of the Jews. In his famous polemical manifesto "Against the Galileans," written in Antioch late in 362, Julian stated clearly that in his religious system there was a place for the Most High God, the God of the Jewish nation, and indeed for its ancient sacrificial cult. Thus, during his sojourn in Antioch in the cold winter of 362–363, Julian planned to rebuild the Temple in Jerusalem, and proceeded to inform the Jews of his projected plan, to be executed following his return from his campaign against the Persians.[53]

However, there was a hidden agenda in this scheme which undoubtedly caused much apprehension among the Christians. Julian proposed to strike Christianity at the heart of the newly-founded Constantinian Jerusalem. By erecting the Jewish Temple, Christian symbol of Jewish desolation, Julian aspired to nullify Jesus' famous words concerning that very same Temple: "There shall be left no stone upon another in this house."[54] The work on the site, supervised by imperial officials, began in May, 363, but soon came to a halt. According to an apocryphal tradition in Syriac, this happened on the night of the 18th of May, and the entire plan was abandoned.[55]

Much has been written on the circumstances of this sudden development, most probably caused by an earthquake. It provided contemporary Christian writers not only with all they required for the portrayal of this episode, but also yet another sign of divine retribution on their behalf. It gave them the opportunity to embellish their traditions with many miracles and marvels.[56] Julian's subsequent death at the end of June, 363, on the Persian front, added to their elation. The atmosphere of anxiety followed by relief among Christians was expressed in the hymns of the Syrian church father, Ephrem. Writing less than a year after the event, Ephrem described it in apocalyptic terms, using imagery culled from prophecies in the book of Daniel and the New Testament.

However, in all the tremendous upheaval caused by Julian, one voice was missing—the voice of the Jerusalem community. Was this really the case? Knowing that Cyril was in Jerusalem at the time,[57] and knowing his ability and eagerness to promote the cause of his see, such silence is striking. It seems to have prompted a later writer with considerable knowledge of the Jerusalem scene to forge in Cyril's name an epistle describing the whole affair.[58] It is possible, of course, that such a source once existed, but the fact that none of Cyril's contemporaries knows about it makes its existence quite unlikely. However, I believe that a plausible solution to this age-old enigma is to be found in Cyril's existing lectures and lies with Ephrem's elucidation of the affair as an event of apocalyptic dimensions. It is widely assumed that Cyril's lectures were delivered *ex tempore* ca. 350/351 and came down to us without subsequent editing. I am suggesting that this is the case with all of his lectures, save the one in which he expounded the eschatological scheme of the Church— the signs of the end of days, the acts of the Antichrist, and the Second Coming of Jesus—i.e., the fifteenth catechetical lecture.

W. Telfer, an authority on Cyril's work, once remarked: "In this lecture we see how a mid-fourth century churchman looked round him and looked forward."[59] Whereas there are signs of editing in the opening section of the lecture, the real surprise lies in its second section dealing with the Antichrist and his actions. As I have tried to show elsewhere, this section was based on Julian's image and actions. A careful study of the imagery and other hints Cyril dropped in the course of the lecture leaves no doubt as to whom he was referring. Yet, as we have stated before, Cyril was extremely cautious in his presentation so as not to arouse false hopes among his listeners in an imminent Second Coming. As always, he based his message on Scripture and structured it according to the outlines he found in the writings of earlier unnamed church fathers. This whole section can thus be regarded as a *Vaticinium ex eventu*. Cyril's Antichrist is a Roman king (and not a Jew, as can be found in some of the earlier traditions) who usurped the throne. He is a Homo Magicus, a person initiated into magic practices, thus echoing Julian's active participation in magical activities, which was part of the *cultus deorum*[60] in his brand of the Neoplatonic cult. He abhorred idols, a notion somewhat surprising when attributed to Julian but, nevertheless, it is not far off the mark, for Julian wanted to reform paganism and integrate it into a centralized system revolving round the cult of one God, Helios.[61] The Antichrist will beguile the Jews and build their Temple for them, he will come to them as a Messiah. Although the latter three characteristics appeared in one form or another in earlier traditions, they nevertheless are reminiscent of genuine images and actions of Julian, notably his image as the Messiah of the Jews in Ephrem's hymns and Gregory of Nazienzus' invectives.

I believe that one of the most revealing attributes of the Antichrist's beguiling reign was the way it was to change in the course of the days, "at first making a pretense of benevolence, but afterwards displaying his relentless temper chiefly against the saints of God (the Christians)."[62] This two-phased reign entirely resembles what happened in Julian's time.[63] All told, it seems quite plausible to assume that Cyril's Antichrist was based on Julian's figure. Cyril might have delivered this updated and adapted lecture the following year. If my reconstruction is correct, Cyril's eschatological proof shifted the polemics with Judaism from the past to the future, from history to eschatology, and gave the Christians of Jerusalem a new and deeper sense to their mission.

Notes

1. Eusebius, *Martyrs of Palestine*, XI, 9–12 (short recension; trans. H. J. Lawlor and E. L. Oulton (London, 1927), 385–86. On the background as well as the outcome of this massive wave of persecution, see R. L. Fox, *Pagans and Christians* (London, 1986), 585–608.

2. E. D. Hunt, *Holy Land Pilgrimage in the Later Roman Empire AD 312–460* (Oxford, 1982), 4–5.

3. It is difficult to assess how many did actually make their way to Palestine during the centuries preceding Constantine's reign. It is also difficult to assess whether the few that came (according to Eusebius' accounts) were motivated by devotional reasons or were mere tourists on a "study tour" of biblical sites. This matter has received ample attention lately and seems to have created diametrically opposing views. On the one hand, there is the view that Christian devotional pilgrimage originated in the prototypical visits to Palestine of the famous pious female members of the imperial family Helena and Eutropia; see J. E. Taylor, *Christians and the Holy Places: The Myth of Jewish-Christian Origins* (Oxford, 1993), 306–18. The older and more widespread view, on the other hand, takes into account the impression emanating from Eusebius' statements, that the early pilgrims were students of the Bible (an impression which could be endorsed by Eusebius' own contribution to this phenomenon by producing the very tool for the study of the biblical sites, namely his *Onomasticon*; D. E. Groh ("The Onomastikon of Eusebius and the Rise of Christian Palestine," *Ninth Patristic Studies Conference* [Oxford, 1983], 23–32) does not attribute the origins of devotional pilgrimage to the age of Constantine.

4. It was Origen (third century) who did much to "dispel the mistaken notion that the sayings about a good land promised by God . . . have reference to the land of Judaea" (*Contra Celsum* 7, 28). With it, the much-cherished memory of events and places in Christ's life and the ensuing history of the local community, enhanced by second-century church fathers, were toned down. On Origen's influence, see, inter alia, P. W. L. Walker, *Holy City Holy Places? Christian Attitudes to Jerusalem and the Holy Land in the Fourth Century* (Oxford, 1990), 25 (passim).

5. J. Wilkinson, *Jerusalem as Jesus Knew It: Archaeology as Evidence* (London, 1978), 176.

6. This has been attributed entirely to the efforts of one of the assertive leaders of the Jerusalem Church during the greater part of the first half of the fifth century, Juvenal. See E. Honigmann's classic work, "Juvenal of Jerusalem," *DOP* 5 (1950), 209–79, and below, note 7. It is my contention however, that Juvenal's great political achievement was based on the growing spiritual and liturgical reputation of Christian Jerusalem, the foundations of which were laid by Cyril of Jerusalem more than half a century earlier; see below, note 40. The influence of the local liturgical rite on the formation of liturgical rites in other Christian centers is now a well-established fact. See, for example, E. C. Ratcliff, *Liturgical Studies* (London, 1976), 135–54 (esp. p. 146); R. S. J. Taft, "The Liturgy of the Great Church: An Initial Synthesis of Structure and Interpretation on the Eve of Iconoclasm," *DOP* 34–35 (1980–81), 65–66. See, however, the remarks of P. Bradshaw in this volume.

7. See Z. Rubin's contribution to this volume.

8. The discovery of the Cross and the legends surrounding it, as well as their diffusion, were recently the subject of exhaustive studies; see J. W. Drijvers, *Helena Augusta: The Mother of Constantine the Great and the Legend of Her Finding of the True Cross* (Leiden, 1992; S. Heid, "Der Ursprung der Helena legende im Pilgerbetrieb Jerusalems," *JbAC* 32 (1989), 41–71; S. Borgehammer, *How the Holy Cross was Found: From Event to Medieval Legend* (Stockholm, 1991).

9. *Itinerarium Egeriae* XLII (eds. Aet. Franceschini and R. Weber, *CCSL* 175 [Turnhout, 1965], 84, passim).

10. Basil of Caesarea, *Regulae fusius tractatae*, VII, 4 (*PG* 31, col. 933). On this, see P. J. Fedwick, *The Church and the Charisma of Leadership in Basil of Caesarea* (Toronto, 1979), 1ff. (esp. pp. 20–21).

11. H. Chadwick, "The Circle and the Ellipse: Rival Concepts of Authority in the Early Church," Inaugural Lecture, Oxford 1959, (= idem, *History and Thought of the Early Church* [London, 1982],Variorum reprints).

12. Chadwick's reconstruction was recently endorsed in a convincing manner by R. Williams, "Does it Makes Sense to Speak of Pre-Nicene Orthodoxy?" *The Making of Orthodoxy: Essays in Honor of Henry Chadwick*, ed. R. Williams (Cambridge, 1989), 1–23. Though Chadwick stressed the fact that Jerusalem's fame was based on its historical mystique, I have tried elsewhere to portray in detail the reality behind this concept; see my study "The Jerusalem Christian Community: From the Church of the Circumcision to the Church of the Gentiles," *The History of Jerusalem: Roman and Byzantine (70-638)*, eds. Y. Tsafrir et al. (Jerusalem, in press) (Hebrew).

13. J. D. G. Dunn, *Unity and Diversity in the New Testament: an inquiry into the character of earliest Christianity*[2] (London, 1990), 239.

14. A different view of the Jerusalem leadership's requirements of gentiles who wished to join the Christian movement and of the eschatological context in which the Apostolic Decree was formed has been offered recently by R. Bauckham, "James and the Jerusalem Church," *The Book of Acts in its Palestinian Setting*, ed. R. Bauckham (Grand Rapids, 1995), 416–80.

15. *Ant.* 20, 200. On the importance of the reference here to Jesus and its bearing on the

understanding of the celebrated *Testimonium Flavianum* (*Ant.* 18, 63–64), see the recent remarks of J. P. Meier, "Jesus in Josephus: A Modest Proposal," *CBQ* 52 (1990), 77–81.

16. *Historia Ecclesiastica* 2, 23, 18. Very little is known about Hegesippus. W. Telfer's suggestions ("Was Hegesippus a Jew," *HTR* 53 [1960], 143–53) are untenable; see also T. Halton, "Hegesipp," *TRE* 14 (Berlin, 1985), 560–62 (and the extensive bibliography there). On the fragments of Hegesippus' *Hypomnemata* (*Mémoires*) preserved in Eusebius' *Historia Ecclesiastica*, see N. Hyldal's comprehensive study, "Hegesippus Hypomnemata," *StTh* 14 (1960), 70–113.

17. On this, see Irshai (above, note 12), 19–20.

18. H. Y. Gamble, *Books and Readers in the Early Church: A History of Early Christian Texts* (New Haven, 1995), 154.

19. The Nazarenes preserved a special relationship toward Jerusalem; see Epiphanius, *Panarion* XXIX, 8 (ed. K. Holl, *GCS* 25 [Leipzig, 1915], 330–31). It seems that this special attitude was what prompted them to return to the Jerusalem ruins and reestablish their community. Recently it has been proposed that they settled on Mt. Zion; see S. C. Mimouni, "La synagogue judéo-chrétienne de Jérusalem au Mont Sion," *POC* 40 (1990), 215–34. Against this view, see Taylor (above, note 3), 207–20. On the Nazarene sect in general, see R. A. Pritz, *Nazarene Jewish Christianity From the End of the New Testament Period Until its Disappearance in the Fourth Century* (Jerusalem and Leiden, 1988). Even scholars who dismiss the historicity of a Jewish-Christian milieu tend to see some kernel of truth in the traditions concerning the Nazarenes; see J. E. Taylor, "The Phenomenon of Early Jewish-Christianity: Reality or Scholarly Invention," *VC* 44 (1990), 313–34.

20. Hegesippus apud Eusebius, *Historia Ecclesiastica*, II, 23, 4–18 (ed. E. Schwartz, *GCS* 9/1 [Leipzig, 1903], 166, 168). James' priestly and Nazarite-like image, and his supplication on behalf of the Temple and Jerusalem, described in detail by Hegesippus, carry with them a great resemblance to the traditions about the Rechabites (Jer. 35) found in the enigmatic text *Narratio Zosimi* (edited from two Greek mss. and published by M. R. James, *Apocrypha Anecdota*, Texts and Studies II, 3 [Cambridge, 1893], 86–108), which still awaits a thorough treatment. Such a study on the traditions concerning James the Just and their relationship to the *Narratio Zosimi* traditions is currently being prepared.

21. Eusebius, *Historia Ecclesiastica* IV, 6, 4 (above, note 20), 308, quoting Aristo of Pella on the imperial decree banning the Jews from entering Jerusalem.

22. Cf. Jerome, *The Chronicon of Eusebius*, Olympiad 228 (ed. R. Helm, *GCS* 47 [Berlin 1956], 201). The decree banning the Jews, though alluded to by other church fathers (Justin Martyr; Tertullian) as well, has been called into question; see my recent remarks, "Constantine and the Jews: The Prohibition Against Entering Jerusalem—History and Hagiography," *Zion* 60 (1995), 129–78 and esp. pp. 129–35 (Hebrew).

23. According to Eusebius (*Historia Ecclesiastica* IV, 8, 1 [above, note 20], p. 314), this was Hegesippus' main aim in assembling the episcopal lists from the leading centers of Christendom. The chronological data and the symbolic nature of these lists have yet to be determined. On this matter, see H. von Campenhausen, *Ecclesiastical Authority and Spiritual Power* (Berkeley, 1969), 164–65; L. Abramowski, "Alethes logos und Diadoche bei Hegesipp," *ZKG* 87 (1976), 321–27; V. Twomey, *Apostolikos Thronos: The Primacy of Rome as Reflected in the Church History of Eusebius and the Historico Apologetic Writings of Saint Athanasius the Great*, Münsterische Beiträge zur Theologie 49 (Münster, 1982), 41–90.

24. O. Irshai, "Narcissus of Jerusalem and His Role in the Enhancement of the Apostolic Image of the Church of Jerusalem," *Aux origines juives du christianisme*, Cahiers du centre de recherche français de Jerusalem, eds. F. Blanchetière and M. D. Herr (Jerusalem, 1993), 111–31.

25. Irshai (above, note 12), 51–53.

26. The chronology of the unfolding Arian controversy, from its inception until the Council of Nicaea, is not entirely clear. H. G. Opitz's reconstruction of events (ed., *Athanasius Werke*, III/1: *Urkunden zur geschichte der arianischen Streites* [Berlin and Leipzig, 1935] was endorsed by R. P. C. Hanson (*The Search for the Christian Doctrine of God* [Edinburgh, 1988], 134–35). However, a revised chronology of events and the role of the Palestinian bishops in the evolving controversy based on documents amassed by Opitz was presented by R. D. Williams (*Arius: Heresy and Tradition* [London, 1987], 48–59).

27. See recently Taylor (above, note 3), 88–142 (Mamre, Bethlehem, Golgotha).

28. *Itinerarium Burdigalense* (eds. P. Geyer and O. Cuntz, *CCSL* 175 [Turnhout ,1965], 16); Eusebius, *Vita Constantini*, III, 26 (ed. F. Winkelmann, *GCS* 7 [Berlin, 1975²], 95); Jerome, *Epistulae* 58, 3 (ed. I. Hilberg, *CSEL* 54 [Leipzig, 1910], 531–32); Sulpicius Severus, *Chronicon* II, 31, 5–6 (ed. C. Halm, *CSEL* 1 [Vienna, 1866], 85–86); Socrates, *Historia Ecclesiastica*, I, 16 (ed. G. C. Hansen, *GCSNF* 1 [Berlin, 1995], 55)—with no mention of Hadrian; cf. Sozomenos, *Historia Ecclesiastica* II, 1, 3 (eds. J. Bidez and G. Hansen, *GCS* 50 [Berlin, 1960], 47).

29. The tradition appears to have little foundation. See Deuteronomy Rabbah, Eqev, 13; B Ta'anit 29a. The Hadrianic attempt to construct a pagan temple dedicated to Jupiter on the Temple Mount appears in the account of Dio Cassius (*Historia Romana* LXIX, 12, 1) with no apparent parallel in Christian sources. Some prominent scholars doubt its historicity; see G. W. Bowersock, "A Roman Perspective of the Bar-Kokhba War," *Approaches to Ancient Judaism* II, ed. W. S. Green (Chico, 1980), 135, 137. A seventh-century Byzantine tradition might preserve a faint allusion to the pagan tradition; see B. Flussin, "L'esplanade du Temple à l'arrivée des Arabes d'après deux récits byzantins," *Bayt Al-Makdis: Abd al-Malik's Jerusalem*, eds. J. Raby and J. Johns (Oxford, 1992), 17–31, esp. pp. 27–28.

30. Whether Jewish Jerusalem (Eusebius, *de Laudibus Constantini* IX, 16 [ed. I. A. Heikel, *GCS* 7 [Leipzig, 1902], 221); idem, *Vita Constantini* III, 33 (ed. F. Winkelmann, *GCS* 1 [Berlin, 1975²], 99) or pagan Jerusalem (ibid., III, 26, pp. 95–96). On Constantine's attitude toward the city, see A. Linder, "Ecclesia and Synagoga in the Medieval Myth of Constantine the Great," *Revue Belge de Philologie et d'Histoire* 54 (1976), 1016ff.

31. See J. Schwartz, "The Encaenia of the Church of the Holy Sepulcher, the Temple of Solomon and the Jews," *TZ* 43 (1987), 265–81. For a different view, see my study (above, note 22), 170–73.

32. See Eusebius, *Demonstratio Evangelica*, VI, 18 (composed ca. 315) and, later on, idem, *On Christ's Sepulchre* XVII, 8 (ostensibly the second part of what is known as the *Tricennial Oration* (*In Praise of Constantine*) (ed. I. A. Heikel [above, note 31], 256).

33. For a long time, scholars believed that this relaxation originated in imperial circles; according to this view it was Constantine himself who reenacted Hadrian's decree banning the Jews from entering Jerusalem. However, there is no solid evidence to support this, and it is more reasonable to assume that the entire issue was a local one and part of the local bishopric's polemical campaign against the Jews and their heritage. See Irshai (above, note 22). On Jews flocking to Jerusalem on the 9th of Av, see the descriptions in the *Itinerarium Burdigalense* (above, note 28), 16; and especially Jerome, *Commentarius in Soph.* I, 15–16 (ed. M. Adriaen, *CCSL* 76A [Turnhout, 1970], 673).

34. Thus, Cyril of Jerusalem's interpretation of the famous Apostolic Decree initiated by James the Just tends to describe it in terms entirely divorced from its Jewish context. See his *Catechetical Lectures* IV, 28 (*PG* 33, col. 492).

35. See F.-M. Abel, "La sépulture de saint Jacques le Mineur," *RB* 16 (1919), 480–99, based on the Latin text published in *AnBoll* 8 (1889), 123–24.

36. Epiphanius, *De Mensuribus et Ponderibus* 14 (Syriac ed. & trans. J. E. Dean [Chicago,

1935], 30). Epiphanius' testimony is dubious, to say the least. The presence of a Jewish-Christian community on Mount Zion as late as the fourth century has not been established beyond a doubt; see G. G. Stroumsa, " 'Vetus Israel': les juifs dans la littérature hiérosolymitaine d'époque byzantine," *RHR* 205 (1988), 115ff, esp. pp. 125–31; S. C. Mimouni, "Pour une définition nouvelle du Judéa-Christianisme ancien," *NTS* 38 (1992), 171–75. An opposing view was proposed by P. Maraval, "La lettre 3 de Grégoire de Nysse dans la débat christologique," *RSR* 61 (1987), 85–86.

37. Cyril's biography has yet to be written. For the present, see E. J. Yornold, "Cyrillus von Jerusalem," *TRE* 8 (1981), 261–66.

38. On Cyril's literary output, see J. Quasten, *Patrology*, III (Utrecht and Antwerp, 1975), 362–75. Recently it has been suggested that Cyril most probably delivered his *Catechetical Lectures* during the Lent of 351; see A. Doval, "The Date of Cyril of Jerusalem's Catecheses," *JTS* 48 (1997), 129–32. If Doval's suggestion is correct, it would indeed enhance my interpretation of Cyril's epistle to Constantius II (see below).

39. *Catechetical Lectures* XVI, 4 (*PG* 33, col. 924); cf. ibid., XIII, 22 (col. 800).

40. For an analysis of this rite in its Jerusalem setting and historical context, see J. Z. Smith, *To Take Place—Toward Theory in Ritual* (Chicago, 1987), 74–95. On Cyril's theological approach to Jerusalem and its holy sites, see Walker (above, note 4), 311–46. However, Walker's most inspiring and groundbreaking study is lacking in one major area, namely Cyril's *Contra Judaeos* stance; see my remarks, "The Christianization of Palestine" (a review of Walker's book), *Cathedra* 74 (1994), 39–47 (Hebrew).

41. *Procatechesis* 10 (*PG* 33, col. 349).

42. Cyril was closer to what has been termed the Antiochene school of scriptural exegesis, displaying a preference for literal and typological methods of interpretation (as against the allegorical method of exegesis propounded by the Alexandrian school. Cyril was, in fact, a product of a middle-of-the-road trend which developed in Palestine that sought to moderate the extreme allegorical methods emanating from Alexandria. Cyril deviated only once from this local brand of exegesis, opting for a more allegorical interpretation in his sermon on the Paralytic (John 5) delivered ca. 346 when serving as a presbyter. For a short survey on the Antiochene school, see M. Simonetti, *Biblical Interpretation in the Early Church: An Historical Introduction to Patristic Exegesis* (Edinburgh, 1994), 59–77. Cyril's exegetical method still awaits a thorough investigation. See, however, some important suggestions by P. Jackson, "Cyril of Jerusalem's Treatment of Scriptural Texts Concerning the Holy Spirit," *Traditio* 46 (1991), 1–31.

43. See my "Cyril of Jerusalem: The Apparition of the Cross and the Jews," *Contra Iudaeos: Ancient and Medieval Polemics between Christians and Jews*, eds. O. Limor and G. G. Stroumsa (Tübingen, 1996), 85–104. A critical edition of the epistle was published by E. Bihain, *Byzantion* 43 (1973), 286–91. A Syriac version of the letter was published by F. J. Coakley, *AnBoll* 102 (1984), 70–84.

44. Apud Philostorgius, *Ecclesiastical History*, III, 26 (ed. J. Bidez and F. Winkelmann, *GCS* 21 [Berlin, 1972²], 51–52). On the anonymous fourth-century source of this tradition, see P. Batiffol, "Un historiographe anonyme arien du IVᵉ siècle," *RQ* 9 (1895), 60, 78 (frag. 5).

45. *Epistle*, sec. III (ed. Bihain [above, note 43], 288).

46. Ibid., sec. VI (p. 290).

47. G. Q. Reijners, *The Terminology of the Holy Cross in Early Christian Literature Based Upon Old Testament Typology* (Nijmegen, 1965).

48. *Catechetical Lectures* XV, 22 (col. 899). The description is based on a fusion of the prophetical utterance of Zech. 12 and the text of John 19:37.

49. Socrates, *Historia Ecclesiastica*, II, 40 (ed. Hansen, *GCSNF* 1 [above, note 28], 175–

76). Socrates did not disclose the reason for Cyril's banishment. However, Sozomenos (*Historia Ecclesiastica* IV, 25, eds. Bidez and Hansen [above, note 28], 181) held that Cyril was charged with selling a veil and some sacred ornaments of the church to support the poor in a period of famine. The ornaments, as it happened, turned up in the possession of an actress. Cf. Theodoret's insinuation on the matter (*Historia Ecclesiastica* II, 27, ed. L. Parmentier, GCS 19 [Leipzig, 1911], 159). A similar, if not more complicated, affair with an altogether different outcome occurred in the sixth-century church of Gaul. See W. Klingshirn, "Charity and Power: Caesarius of Arles and the Ransomming of Captives in Sub-Roman Gaul," *JRS* 75 (1985), 183–203..

50. A. Renoux, *Le Codex Arménien Jérusalem 121*, PO 36 (Turnhout, 1971), 332 (fasc. 2, no. 168; 417-439 C.E.). Cf. the Georgian Lectionary (ed. M. Tarchonischvili, *Le Grand Lectioner de l'Eglise de Jérusalem*, CSCO 205, Scriptores Iberici 14 (Louvain, 1960), 9; 117–21. See G. Kretchmar's discussion, "Festkalender und Memorialstatten Jerusalems im altkirchlischer Zeit," *ZDPV* 87 (1971), 189–93. The great importance of the 7th of May was not lost on the founders and leaders of the Judaean Desert monastic movement, for they chose that very date to celebrate the consecration of a church (428 C.E.) on the one hand, and the deposition of martyr's bones (475 C.E.) on the other. See Cyril of Scythopolis, *Life of Euthymius* 16 and 42 (ed. E. Schwartz, *TU* 49/2 [Leipzig, 1939], 26 and 61–62, respectively).

51. See P. Brown, *Society and the Holy* (Berkeley, 1982), 94–98.

52. A. Momigliano, "The Disadvantages of Monotheism for a Universal State," *CP* 81 (1986), 295–97 (= idem, *On Pagans, Jews and Christians* [Middletown, CT, 1987], 153–55); G. Fowden, *Empire to Commonwealth: Consequences of Monotheism in Late Antiquity* (Princeton, NJ, 1993), 52.

53. The authenticity of Julian's epistle to the Jews has been contested in the past. However, any reservations have been dispelled by M. Stern, *Greek and Latin Authors on Jews and Judaism*, II (Jerusalem, 1980), 559–68 (no. 486a) and extensive bibliography there.

54. Matt. 24:2, 15. Socrates, *Historia Ecclesiastica*, III, 20 (ed. Hansen [above, note 28], 215).

55. S. P. Brock, "A Letter Attributed to Cyril of Jerusalem on the Rebuilding of the Temple," *BSOAS* 40 (1977), 267–86. Since its publication, the historical value of this tradition has been debated. D. Levenson ("A Source and Tradition Critical Study of the Stories of Julian's Attempt to Rebuild the Jerusalem Temple," doctoral dissertation [Harvard University, 1979], 82–97) claims that it is a sixth-century forgery. Opposing this view, P. Wainwright ("The Authenticity of the Recently Discovered Letter Attributed to Cyril of Jerusalem," *VC* 40 [1986], 286–93) claims that it is a genuine letter composed by Cyril.

56. The main invectives against Julian were composed by Ephrem the Syrian and Gregorius Nazienzus within months after the disastrous outcome of Julian's plan and his own demise. On Ephrem's *Hymns against Julian*, see the translation and useful commentary by S. N. C. Lieu, *The Emperor Julian: Panegyric and Polemic*, Translated Texts for Historians—Greek Texts 1 (Liverpool, 1986), 91–134. On Gregory's *Oration IV—Against Julian*, see J. Bernardi, *Grégoire de Nazienze. Discours 4–5 contre Julien (Introduction, Texte critique, Traduction et notes)*, SC 309 (Paris, 1983). Later traditions concerning Julian's plan and failure, which are found in historiographical sources, are discussed by R. B. E. Smith, *Julian's Gods: Religion and Philosophy in the Thought and Action of Julian the Apostate* (London, 1996).

57. Theodoret, *Historia Ecclesiastica* III, 14 (ed. Parmentier [above, note 49], 190–92).

58. Brock (above, note 55), 283.

59. W. Telfer, *Cyril of Jerusalem and Nemesius of Emessa*, LCC 4 (London, 1955), 147, note 1.

60. It is Ammianus Marcellinus' criticism of Julian's *cultus deorum*, with its excessive num-

ber of sacrifices, which reveals the dimensions of the emperor's obsessive behavior. See R. L. Rike, *Apex Omnium: Religion in the Res Gestae of Ammianus* (Berkeley, 1987), 52–56.

61. P. Athanassiadi-Fowden, *Julian and Hellenism: An Intellectual Biography* (Oxford, 1981), 173–80 (passim).

62. *Catechetical Lectures*, XV, 15 (col. 892). Cyril (ibid., 16, col. 892) goes on to use this two-phased scheme to interpret Daniel's famous prophecy (9:27). The question whether Julian was at first tolerant toward the Christians and during the course of his reign turned against them, or whether he was utterly intolerant towards them from the start, has been revisited recently by R. B. E. Smith, who argues that Julian's hatred of the Christians did not undergo any transformation; see Smith (above, note 56), 208ff. Though Smith does allow some "change of tack" on Julian's behalf, in the case presented here images and appearances are the key factors.

63. Julian actually reigned from the time of his usurpation (February, 360) until his death on the Persian front (June, 363), three-and-a-half years, unlike what we still find in many studies devoted to Julian's career. This period is divided by contemporary historians into two phases. In the first, he gradually unveiled his intentions; see G. Bowersock, *Julian the Apostate* (London, 1978), 55. Julian is described by Ephrem the Syrian as: "A wolf (who) had borrowed for itself the clothing of the lamb . . . and the simple sheep smelt him and did not recognize him" (*Hymns against Julian* II, 1 (ed. Lieu [above, note 56], p. 112). Later on, Julian revealed his full anti-Christian venom; see R. Browning, *The Emperor Julian* (Berkeley, 1976), 159–86. This two-phased reign of the Antichrist, so it seems, was to become a central component in later Byzantine eschatological schemes; see E. Sackur, *Sibilynische Texte und Forschungen* (Halle, 1898), 185–86. A fuller discussion of the *Demonstratio Eschatologica*, the Antichrist, Julian, and the Jews in Cyril's fifteenth *Catechetical Lecture* is currently in preparation.

15

"The Mystery of Judaea" (Jerome, *Ep.* 46) The Holy City of Jerusalem between History and Symbol in Early Christian Thought

LORENZO PERRONE

A Historical Faith Without a Sacred Space?

If we look at the symbol of Nicaea (325) and Constantinople (381), that basic summary of Christian beliefs elaborated by the early Church and still used today by most Christian communities, we may at first be rather surprised by a fact which has to do with our theme. The second section of the Creed, devoted to the "Lord Jesus Christ, the only-begotten son of God," while presenting his incarnation, life, death, and resurrection, makes no mention at all of places. The only allusion to space appears in the rather symbolic, if not altogether mythological, indication of his coming "from the heavens" to the earth, but no concrete land is recorded. What a contrast with the historical precision of the sentence pointing to the circumstances of Jesus' passion: "He was crucified for us under Pontius Pilate!" It seems, then, that early Christians were concerned only with knowing "when" the events of Jesus' life had taken place, while no attention was apparently paid to "where" they had occurred.

It would indeed be misleading to overemphasize this contrast between history and geography, especially when we recall that the Niceno-Constantinopolitan creed probably adopted a form originally employed within the Palestinian church, if not in Jerusalem itself. At the least, we find this same model as the object of explanation in the pre-baptismal homilies of Cyril of Jerusalem, which exploit the local setting for the audience of the Holy City. But, even if this were not the case, the same explanation could still be given for the absence of any geographical details in the Creed: the early church had no need to be reminded of the places which had represented the scenes of

Jesus' life. The ancient "rule of faith" (*regula fidei*)—which finally led to the synods of the fourth century—was always related to Scripture as a sort of key to the understanding of its contents and, at the same time, a way of summing them up authoritatively. The Old and New Testaments continually speak of the Land of Israel and Jerusalem as the essential scene of the history of salvation. Even later on, in patristic times, when pilgrimage to the Holy Land had already become fashionable, the first connection with it was through the Bible. We can see it very clearly in a man like Augustine, who was never eager to travel to Jerusalem or to stay in the Holy Land; in this way, he differentiated himself from many contemporaries who, like Rufinus and Jerome, had taken the road to the East. Nevertheless, Augustine, as a priest of Hippo, when discussing the correct interpretation of the Bible with his Manichaean friend, Honoratus, and reminiscing over the errors made by both of them in their youth, suggests a visit to the land of the Bible as the ultimate recourse to a final understanding concerning its true meaning.[1]

On the other hand, it would be mistaken to consider the absence of references within the Creed to the land and the city of Jesus' life as totally irrelevant. As we shall see, this silence is not in the least accidental, but can be taken as a sign of a problem for the early Christian mind. The difficulty with such a geographical and topographical context could be overcome not only with time but, more specifically, only in a new historical constellation. It is not necessary to insist here on the reasons for this uneasiness towards the places of the gospel on the part of the early Church, inasmuch as the story has recently been told again in a most satisfactory way.[2] It is true that the first Christian community had its origins in Jerusalem and maintained its center there during the initial period. But even before the fatal consequences of the first Jewish revolt, with the ensuing destruction of the Temple, began to be felt, and the parting of the ways between Christians and Jews became effective, Paul had already articulated his reservations about the religious and political core of the Israelite people and its tradition, opposing earthly Jerusalem in favor of the heavenly one, which is the only true mother of Christians (Gal. 4:25–26). The powerful impulse to detach oneself from the concrete, historical, city and to opt for a symbolic and spiritual one was thus accomplished, even if Paul's relation to Jerusalem retained a certain ambivalence due to the respect paid by him both to the first Christian community (Rom. 15:19, 26–31) and to the forms of traditional Jewish devotion to the Temple (Acts 24:11).

This tendency to abandon any connection with land and places in favor of a spiritualization is the main thrust of the New Testament, though the memory of Jesus weeping over the fate of his beloved city (Luke 19:41) was never forgotten in the Church, whose preaching based itself upon the narration of the gospels. Furthermore, it should be remembered that it was also the city that the evangelist Matthew continued to call "holy," even after it had seen the crucified Jesus (Matt. 4:5; 27:53). In contrast, the climax of detachment from Jerusalem was attained in the famous sentence pronounced by Jesus in his dialogue with the Samaritan woman (John 4:21–24): "Believe me, O woman; the time is coming when you will adore the Father neither on this mountain nor in Jerusalem. . . ." Here, the relativization of Jerusalem as the place chosen by God for his presence within and adoration by the chosen people is clearly transcended in the name of a spiritual cult, without giving special status to any particular site. This position, although implying a very idealistic and ultimately problematic attitude with regard to sacred space, would consequently offer the mightiest support to all spiritualistic critics of the idea of a Christian Holy Land.

I deliberately speak of a main trend, since the wealth of references to Jerusalem contained in the New Testament reveals, on close examination, the same sort of ambivalence and mixed feelings that we met above for the Creed. It may be possible to anchor Jesus' conduct toward Jerusalem more deeply inside the religious tradition of Israel as a continuation and fulfillment rather than as a real break, as suggested by Jesus' words to the Samaritan woman.[3] Nevertheless, the image of Jerusalem in the first Christian centuries was either nourished retrospectively through the records of the past (albeit not in a way which could confer any actual religious value to the place itself) or substantiated by the expectations concerning the future. Such expectations had been expressed in the New Testament by the author of Revelation, who adapted materials deriving from both the Old Testament and from the apocalyptic literature through the image of a new Jerusalem, a splendid city coming down from above (Rev. 21–22). If the symbolic meaning of this "new Jerusalem" could be partially juxtaposed to "Jerusalem above" of Gal. 4:26 and to "heavenly Jerusalem" of Heb. 12:22, then a further stage of this eschatological thrust was introduced by the same author through the idea of a millenary kingdom (Rev. 20:1–7). Such a prospect was to accompany early Christian eschatology for a long time, mostly in connection with Jerusalem, thereby opposing or moderating the spiritual transformation of the Holy City.[4]

Earthly and Heavenly Jerusalem
in the First Three Centuries

As we have seen, the principal issue brought to light by the New Testament image of Jerusalem is that of the shift from the "historical" to the "symbolic."[5]

Such movement was to be further developed during the first three centuries C.E. Apart from marginal Jewish-Christian groups like the Ebionites (who are said to have continued to venerate Jerusalem "in the Jewish manner," as the "House of God"),[6] what is important now is no longer the city itself in its present state but what it represents: on the one hand, it was the center of biblical history and the cradle of the new religion; on the other, it was the illustration of the coming Kingdom of God. To sum up the terms of this problem, the coupling "earthly Jerusalem-heavenly Jerusalem" may be acceptable, provided that we recognize also the symbolic implications of the former. This will be better understood if we provisionally avoid going over the well-known route of the investigations regarding "heavenly Jerusalem"[7] by first taking into account the research into the "earthly" one. Since my purpose is only to delineate a general background for a more detailed examination of a later patristic source (Jerome, *Ep.* 46), it will suffice here to summarize the results of N. Brox's enquiry into this subject.[8]

Brox describes a wide range of themes, combining both historical and symbolic aspects. Jerusalem is of permanent value as the starting point of the Christian mission throughout the world as, for instance, Justin had asserted in the first Jewish-Christian debate and in his defense of Christianity vis-à-vis the pagans.[9] This lasting salvific significance of the old Jerusalem (even if just as a provisional stage in preparation for the New Alliance) explains why Irenaeus opposes the negative view of the gnostics toward the Holy City, which only left room for a totally different heavenly Jerusalem. Bearing in mind the picture of the desolated city after the destruction brought about by the two Jewish revolts, they refused to recognize in it the "city of the great king" (Ps. 48:3) as it had been described by the first evangelist (Matt. 5:35): the God of this Jerusalem could not be the God of Jesus Christ.[10] Although the gnostics' refusal is quite radical, the anti-Judaic exploitation of the present unhappy condition of the city was a well-known apologetic argument for ecclesiastical writers. Yet, the early church's main difficulty with respect to Jerusalem was that the city had been the site where Jesus died on the cross.[11] As we shall see later, such uneasiness was not completely eliminated even in the days of Christian Jerusalem.

At the beginning of the third century, Tertullian, too, opposed the spiritualistic criticism of the gnostics, and praised Jerusalem as the embodiment of the biblical mind and ethos in contrast to Athens and its classical values: historical Jerusalem represented the symbol of faith and of the believer's disposition as distinguished from reason and Hellenic philosophy.[12] Though the major trend in early Christian literature led to the reconciliation of Jerusalem with Athens (mainly via Alexandria), this polemical contrast remained alive and well in later patristic authors, as we shall partially verify from Jerome's writings. At the same time, one should not forget that a similar antithesis was also evoked by Revelation (14:8; 17:5; 18:2; elsewhere) between Jerusalem and Babylon (the former being the city of God and his heavenly reign, and the latter being a symbol of Rome or, more generally, of an earthly reign, dominated by the devil) and was to play an important part in the theology of martyrdom and subsequently in the writings of Augustine.[13] If we move briefly to the fourth century, the peculiar role of Jerusalem within the history of salvation was stressed by Ephraem of Edessa, who seems to have taken advantage of motifs circulating in his semitic context and therefore probably deriving from older Jewish traditions concerning the Holy City as the center of God's plan for mankind.[14]

The ecclesiological relevance of Jerusalem was exploited by Cyprian who, in the middle of the third century, had stressed the authoritative model of the early community as portrayed by Acts. With regard to this biblical reference, we should notice how the symbolic development was already anticipated within the original narration, with its ideal picture of the community life in early Christian Jerusalem, as the manifestation of "one heart and one soul" (Acts 4:32).[15] If such a model further nourishes the historical memory of the Holy City, then the movement toward a spiritualization of the earthly, historical, Jerusalem reaches a decisive phase with Origen.

The great Alexandrian theologian (who came to live in Caesarea and knew the church of the Holy City intimately, since he had been invited to preach there by his friend, the bishop Alexander) preferred to think of Jerusalem as an allegory of the church, or of the soul and its spiritual life, ignoring the historical significance of earthly Jerusalem, which had been darkened by its responsibility for the death of Jesus.[16] Such identifications were accompanied by the explicit claim of the church as the "new Israel," that the promise of the land once addressed by God to Abraham and to the chosen people, reinterpreting it in a spiritual sense which rejected any attachment to a place.[17] Moreover, if the whole earth had been condemned because of Adam's sin (Gen. 3:17), then there could be no exception to that, not even for Judaea and Jerusalem.[18] In conformity with such spiritualization, Christians are regarded by Origen as the children of "Jerusalem above" (Gal. 4: 26), the mother being a city in heaven and not on earth.[19]

The equation of Jerusalem with the soul, in turn entering into a process of greater symbolic appropriation, would be universalized by monastic spirituality in the following period. The monastic way of life drew its inspiration, on the one hand, from the model of the first community and, on the other, from the ascetic existence understood as a spiritual journey toward Jerusalem, thought of symbolically as a synonym for perfection.[20] With this latter phenomenon we have already reached the age of pilgrimage and of the new Christian Jerusalem, which is my main concern. In fact, the witness upon whom I intend to rely as evidence for a different awareness of the Holy City (i.e., Jerome) unites both dimensions of the early Christian image of Jerusalem (the historical—both past and present—and the symbolic). But there were other aspects as well in the interplay between history and symbol, especially as regards Jerusalem and the eschatological perspectives within early Christianity.

For much of the first three centuries C.E., and probably for a very large number of the churches at that time, eschatological hopes focused on Jerusalem. The expectations of the "millenarists," appealing to Old Testament prophetic passages, sayings of Jesus, and the book of Revelation, were in many cases closely linked to the Holy City as the future horizon of the final Kingdom of Christ on earth. The complexity of sources and attitudes which inspired the chiliastic position has been illuminated by recent research, especially in the thorough investigation of S. Heid.[21] His conclusions provide us with a more balanced assessment of the shift toward the symbolic or spiritual Jerusalem that we described earlier. According to Heid, the widespread presence of chiliastic ideas from the second to the fourth centuries shows that early Christianity had, in fact, much more interest in Jerusalem and the Holy Land than the *communis opinio* would allow us to think.

Early chiliasm was originally influenced by the prophet Isaiah (primarily chapters 53–54) rather than by the seer of Revelation (chapters 20–21), thus assuming a Christian version of the prophetic "Jerusalem ideology." As the prophecy of the suffering Servant (Isa. 53) had been fulfilled through Jesus' passion and death, so, too, was the following promise of a reconstructed Jerusalem (ibid., 54) to be accomplished. Meanwhile, this latter hope had been further reinforced by the destruction of Jerusalem during the first Jewish war (66–74 C.E.) and had become a point of discussion between Christians and Jews, as we see in Justin's *Dialogue with Trypho.* Answering his Jewish partner, who wanted to know whether the Christians truly believed that Jerusalem would be rebuilt, Justin assured him that this was indeed the opinion of orthodox Christians, based on the promises of Ezekiel, Isaiah, and other prophets.[22] If such a generalization is not without problems for Justin himself (since he does not ignore gnostic criticisms or other spiritualistic concepts), his position reflects a specifically apologetic concern with regard to the Jews. A concern of this kind regarding a Christian annexation of the biblical promise of the land, once made by God to the people of Israel, was motivated so as to avoid a break in the history of salvation and to lead it to its fulfillment in Christ.

This line was to be pursued by Irenaeus, who saw the millenary kingdom of Christ and his saints located in Jerusalem as the last act in the plan of salvation. Once again, it is a realistic eschatology: to be complete, the economy of redemption requires that an earthly reign be established, so that the saints may exert their rule over the adverse powers who tyrannize them. Otherwise, salvation—being purely spiritual—would be only partial.[23] Irenaeus' view is based upon the Pauline notion of "recapitulation" (Eph. 1:10) and is connected to the promise of the land to Abraham (Gen. 13:14–17; 15), in this way exploiting anew the biblical "restorationist" motif. While doing so, Irenaeus differs from Justin, inasmuch as he does not claim Jerusalem and the land of Israel in direct competition with the Jews.[24] Since Abraham could not see this promise realized, but lived in the land as "a stranger and a pilgrim," its fulfillment was assured by Christ in a church composed of both Jews and Gentiles. Nevertheless, this realization would be perfect only in the final kingdom, after the Antichrist has been defeated. Irenaeus strenuously opposes every effort to allegorize: instead of being a symbol, Jerusalem is a city on earth, a definite historical reality; however, this earthly Jerusalem, in its final form, has to be transformed according to the model of the heavenly one. Irenaeus, therefore, succeeds in integrating into his eschatological vision the perspective of Gal. 4 on "Jerusalem above."[25]

We have already discussed how the realistic interpretation of Jerusalem and the Holy Land promoted by chiliastic eschatology was resisted by a spiritual exegesis developed first and foremost by Origen. In a similar fashion, such a radical redefinition was followed by later chiliasts as well. The Montanists, for example, had relativized the geographical fixation on a historical Jerusalem, having substituted for themselves a new one, which would soon descend from heaven to two little towns in Phrygia.[26] Tertullian, the most important theologian who shared Montanist convictions, at least for a while provides evidence of this trend towards a spiritualization of the millenaristic perspective. His Jerusalem is no longer the reconstructed city of Justin and Irenaeus, but rather one that descends from heaven.[27] Jerusalem is thus a spiritual reality and its connection with the city in Palestine is purely nominal. In the final analysis, even that very current which had made the most significant efforts to maintain the link with the biblical tradition of the Holy City and the Land of the patriarchs, thus assuring the continuity of God's salvific plan centered on the earthly Jerusalem, was recast into a symbolic mode.[28]

With the slow but steady disappearance of chiliasm as an important current of patristic theology, one might have thought that the religious significance of historic Jerusalem would actually be confined only to its past, but this was not the case. After the discovery of the tomb of Christ under Constantine, the building of basilicas in the holy places of Palestine and the development of pilgrimage to them on an unprecedented scale—the dominant spiritualizing approach expounded at that time by as important exponent of the Origenian tradition as Eusebius of Caesarea—were no longer tenable. It had to be tempered, or even transformed, in face of the new reality of a Christian "Holy City" in a "Holy Land." The time had come for a new Christian Jerusalem, which would be religiously relevant in its present condition, both as the historic and geographical scene of Jesus' death and resurrection and as the permanent memory of those salvific events.

The New Christian Jerusalem of the Fourth Century: A New Image for Theologians and Pilgrims

The emergence of this new Christian Jerusalem can be reconstructed especially through two authors, who were also the principal protagonists of ecclesiastical life in fourth-century Palestine: Eusebius of Caesarea, an eyewitness to the momentous changes under Constantine, and Cyril of Jerusalem, bishop of the city in the second half of the century, when this transformation had already been consolidated.[29] Together with them, an important source for appreciating the novel awareness which emerges with respect to the religious importance of the present Holy City can be found in the *Itinerary* of Egeria. Again, it is my intention only to note the main features of the historical background against which to read Jerome, our key source for reviewing early Christian thought on Jerusalem at the end of that same century.

There is a debate among scholars as to what extent Eusebius really changed his mind when he saw the effects of Constantine's innovative policy towards Jerusalem. This affects not only his long-established theological views, but also relates to the rivalry which would inevitably ensue between Jerusalem and his own metropolitan see of Caesarea.[30] Nevertheless, it is impossible not to perceive Eusebius' different tone in his depiction of Constantine's Christian Jerusalem in the encomiastic *Life* he dedicated to the emperor just after the latter's death, or perhaps even in the official discourse he delivered in Jerusalem on the occasion of the dedication of the Constantinian martyrium (335).[31] Instead of clinging to his earlier contrast between earthly and heavenly Jerusalem (following his Origenian approach, whereby the Old Testament promises of the land should be interpreted spiritually), the bishop of Caesarea now tends to present the actual Jerusalem in a pronounced eschatological aura in fulfillment of the prophetic expectations.[32] In this way, history and symbol are for the first time reconciled—albeit tentatively—within a Christian framework. Eusebius contrasts the new Christian Jerusalem with the ancient one, which was destroyed because of its responsibility for Jesus' death. The place where Jesus had been buried is the beginning of a new epoch of salvation grounded on the resurrection of Christ, whose perennial memory and triumphant demonstration are attested by this sacred cave.[33]

However, Eusebius' new understanding of the local and physical aspects of the Christian faith is not without certain reservations, as may also be inferred from his somehow disconcerting silence on the most precious relic of the Cross, whose veneration presumably emerged already during his lifetime.[34] Two decades later, Cyril of Jerusalem went a step further in recognizing the special importance of the Holy City. Jerusalem—and in it, more specifically, Golgotha, the place where Christ, the head of the Church's body (Col. 1:18) and of every power (ibid., 2:18), came to suffer his death—is explicitly claimed to be the center of the earth. Thus Cyril coopts, in a very pregnant Christian form, claims found in Jewish tradition with regard to the Temple Mount.[35] Moreover, the centrality of Jerusalem is supported and amplified in the consciousness of the Church by fragments of the Cross which, according to Cyril's testimony, had been dispersed "throughout all the inhabited world."[36]

We thus find in Cyril a new awareness of the special privilege attached to the Holy City within the Christian world. This is why—although still confronted by the ruins of the Temple—he can say that everything good originates in Jerusalem.[37] What is even more striking is a frequent motif in Cyril's catechetical homilies regarding the holy places. These places are taken as a document, or better, as proof of the contents of the Creed that he is explaining to his catechumens.[38] In this way, the historical elements of the Christian faith are authenticated by local and visual aspects which, in Cyril's eyes, themselves assume the role of very eloquent witnesses. There are several instances where it may not be out of place to speak of the holy places of Jerusalem as a kind of "fifth gospel"; at least we see that their testimony is inserted (apparently on the same level and with a corresponding value) in long passages of biblical references to historical events: sacred geography is now fully integrated into the salvific history.[39] We would probably be mistaken to claim a quasi-sacramental power of places in Cyril's words, yet we cannot deny that they lay the foundation for premises in this direction. In expressing the Christian faith, the experience of seeing the places had also become important: as a matter of fact, Cyril already knows well that to look at them helps in some way to reenact the facts of the past.[40]

These perceptions fully corresponded to the primary expectations and feelings of the pilgrims when they visited the Holy Land.[41] From Egeria's travelogue, we can sense the importance of sacred space in connection with the historical narratives of the Bible; for her, past and present, history and symbol go hand in hand. During her travels, this Spanish lady thus performs a double instruction: a biblical catechesis—since the Bible is her chief source and guidebook; and a historical-geographical account, which depends not only on Scriptures, but in some cases indicates that some information derives from oral traditions connected in some way to those holy places.[42] The synthesis of both aspects, besides Egeria's personal prayer and forms of devotion at the different stations of her pilgrimage, occurs especially in Jerusalem thanks to the carefully planned liturgical framework which the local church provides for its own community and which exerts a particular attraction on the monks and pilgrims. Once more, its underlying conception consists largely of the combination of history and geography: as Cyril had stressed earlier, pilgrims now reenact the events of Jesus' life, death, and resurrection "at the very spot."[43]

Until now, I have tried to describe the principal consequences regarding the patristic image of Jerusalem created by the new historical constellation of the fourth century. If we could continue to listen to other voices from the following centuries, we would discover further evidence for this new reality. For example, in pronouncements of Palestinian monks at the beginning of the sixth century, they exploit the motif of Jerusalem and the Holy Land as a *locus theologicus* on behalf of their own doctrinal pro-Chalcedonian stance.[44] Nevertheless, I shall restrict myself to a very interesting document from the end of the fourth century, *Ep.* 46 in Jerome's epistolary. Its interest lies in the fact that it not only gives evidence of the new Christian attitude toward the Holy City in a rather impressive form but, at the same time, does not conceal the traditional difficulties with regard to Jerusalem on the part of Christian authors. Through this source, we may therefore be able to ascertain the degree to which the changed perception of Jerusalem succeeded in shaping the Church consciousness, inasmuch as further statements on Jerusalem and the Holy Land contained in other letters of Jerome point in a different direction.

Jerome and the "Sacrament of Judaea": New Insights and Old Reservations

Ep. 46, addressed in the name of Paula and Eustochium to their Roman friend Marcella, but probably written by Jerome himself, has been transmitted by several manuscripts under the title of "Exhortatory letter regarding the Holy Places," which correctly sums up its content and aim.[45] The letter was written soon after Jerome and Paula had settled in Bethlehem (386) and is therefore full of the happy atmosphere of a new beginning in a long-desired setting. We are thus able to discern therein the typical spiritual condition of pilgrims coming to the Holy Land, but what concerns us here is, first of all, the image of Jerusalem emerging from the text. From the outset, the city is closely associated with the Holy Land as its center and heart, to the point that its name is practically interchangeable with that of Judaea.[46] It is not by chance that such connection with the land is expressed through the revealing quotation of Gen. 12:1—i.e., the passage first containing the promise of the land to Abraham: Paula and Eustochium, having established themselves in the Holy Land, have so far accomplished the divine command addressed to Abraham. Their exodus from Rome—which Marcella is invited to imitate and to perform herself—is in this sense the ascetic-monastic equivalent of the patriarch's journey to the Promised Land.[47]

The picture of this land in Jerome's text mixes inextricably concrete and symbolic aspects: it is a hilly, uncomfortable landscape but, at the same time, is characterized allegorically as spiritual ascent, even at the cost of somehow forcing the geographical evidence.[48] Jerome explains this ascent with the example of Mary, leaving the "fields" of Nazareth and coming to the "mountains" of Judaea after she had received the announcement of Jesus' birth and knew that her womb would become the house of the Son of God. This last image invites, in turn, an association with the Temple, built on the site of the previous Jebusite city, and therefore interpreted by Jerome as a figure of the future Church that would be assembled among the gentiles. But the relationship of Jerusalem with the "Christian mystery" is already prefigured in the Bible through the person of Melchizedek.

It then becomes clear that in a few condensed sentences the letter has assembled some of the main Old Testament traditions regarding the Holy City,[49] giving, as we might expect, the symbolic interpretation characteristic of the patristic authors. But what is new here is that instead of moving as usual into a spiritual allegory, such interpretation serves to raise the status of the present Christian Holy City. Moreover, though there might be several other obvious passages from Scripture to support this, Jerome also cites extrabiblical traditions, like the connection between Adam's burial place and Golgotha. The drama of mankind, from its sinful progenitor to its redeemer, the "second Adam," was in this way bound to the place of Jesus' death, as per Cyril, though the bishop of Jerusalem had not appealed to such legend in order to develop his idea of the universal centrality of the Cross.[50]

For Jerome, biblical and extrabiblical motifs emphasize the unique status of the Holy City, which alone, through its three scriptural names (Jebus, Salem, and Jerusalem), is to be regarded as a summary of the "Christian mystery" when interpreted etymologically. Such a categorization seems at first to point to the Trinitarian faith but, in fact, is applied to the essential stages of the monastic experience as the Christian way of life par excellence: from the fight against the passions (Jebus as *calcata*), through the impassibility gained from it (Salem as *pax*), up to the beatitude of perfection (Jerusalem as *uisio pacis*).[51]

This initial praise of Jerusalem as the most celebrated city, with its attempted reconciliation of history and symbol, must nevertheless face a serious question concerning the possibility of actually preserving such a privilege within Christianity. It is an objection which echoes the old criticisms of the Christian claims advanced for Jerusalem as a "city of God." Such criticisms were widespread, as we already know, especially among the gnostics, but had not been ignored by Origen and other exponents of spiritualistic hermeneutics. We cannot exclude the possibility that they had again been brought to light, especially in the Roman ecclesiastical milieu, in opposition to the increasing attraction of pilgrimage to the holy places among the western aristocracy.[52] According to these reservations, the old economy of salvation, whose center was Jerusalem, had come to an end with the death of Christ. Therefore, it was legitimate to ask whether the "mystery of Judaea" and the tradition of "familiarity with God" centered on Jerusalem had by now been completely transferred to the gentiles by means of the mission undertaken by the apostles.[53] This had indeed been the line of thought followed by early Christian authors up to the fourth century. No wonder, then, that the question had not yet disappeared, even in the face of the new reality represented at the time by Christian Jerusalem.

Nevertheless, replying without any apparent embarrassment to that traditional objection, Jerome reasserts the unique value of Christian Jerusalem. On the one hand, he says, it was not the place itself that was guilty of the death of Christ, but rather the people living in the city at that time. On the other hand, the present reality of the city is much greater than it had been in its Jewish past. Jerome here makes a comparison between the sanctuary of the Temple and the Holy Sepulchre, stressing the superiority of the latter. At the same time, he betrays the persisting complex of envy as well as the Christian need for compensation with regard to the ancient religious institution of Israel.[54] Furthermore, to what extent this position is weakly supported by Jerome from a theological point of view can be seen in the main argument he puts forth for the superiority of the tomb of Jesus. Jerome simply exploits the basic experience of pilgrims in the holy places, which is propitiated by their evocative power. To enter the cave of the sepulchre helps one to imagine the body of Christ lying there dead, and the angel announcing the resurrection. In this way, the reenactment of the past is enhanced by the recollection of the visitor at the very spot.[55]

We have to admit that Jerome—whether or not he is original (the question may for the moment be left open)—is not at his best with theological elaborations, but rather when he deals with the text of Scripture, for instance, when he rejects the application to Jerusalem of Rev. 11:8. This passage cannot mean an identification of Jerusalem with Sodom and Egypt because of Jesus' crucifixion, since these places have to be interpreted spiritually as equivalent of "this world." Besides that, their supposed identification with Jerusalem is even more problematic, if we realize that, on the one hand, Rev. 11:2 speaks of the "Holy City" and, on the other, Matt. 27:51–53 still presents Jerusalem in such terms after the death of Christ on the Cross.[56] The conclusion of this biblical *quaestio de Jerusalem* is offered by the assertion of a complete continuity between the new Christian Jerusalem and the old one, inasmuch as Jerusalem through all the Scriptures is declared "holy" and also in Jesus' words appears to be the "city of the great King" (ibid., 5:35).[57] Jerome's Christian Jerusalem is, then, no longer the cursed land of previous Christian authors, but must be regarded as the most precious soil inasmuch as the blood of Christ had been poured onto it.

Interestingly enough, this last claim about Christian Jerusalem takes advantage of the new historical situation created in the Constantinian church by the steady development of the cult of martyrs—a feature which, together with monasticism and pilgrimage, distinguishes the spiritual landscape of this period and leaves room for a different appreciation of Jerusalem and the holy places. How could the tomb of Christ be neglected when the burial places of the martyrs were the object of such wide, universal veneration? Moreover, proof of the special sacred quality inherent in Christ's sepulchre could be shown by its connection to a popular religious phenomenon, i.e., miracles performed on the possessed before the tomb.[58] This thaumaturgical argument rounds off the picture of contemporary Jerusalem in the presentation made by Jerome, who shows himself as capable of integrating into his argument even the most concrete and popular expectations of pilgrims coming to venerate the holy places.[59]

Nevertheless, this is not yet the end of this remarkably dense apology for Jerusalem. To compensate for the concession made to popular religion, and to restate the spiritual utility of pilgrimage to the Holy Land on a more demanding level, Jerome recalls how many protagonists of the religious and intellectual life of the church—bishops, martyrs, and theologians—had visited it, making their journey to Jerusalem a formative experience, both for their knowledge and virtue. With regard to the first aspect, we find once again the motif alluded to at the beginning of this paper in Augustine's words, from *De utilitate credendi*, and reinforced by our information on the few famous pilgrims of the pre-Constantinian period who, from Melito to Origen, had sought Jerusalem and other places in Palestine for the sake of deepening their knowledge of Scripture. The unique opportunity provided by Jerusalem to become acquainted with the Hebrew Bible makes this city the "Christian Athens," as Jerome says, thus recalling and, at the same time, overcoming the previously-mentioned antithesis of Tertullian.[60] As for virtue, Jerusalem and the Holy Land are the ideal setting for a monastic existence, as is demonstrated by the fact that the best representatives of monasticism come here from all over the world. We clearly perceive at this point a strong element of ascetic aristocracy emerging in Jerome's group but, at the same time, this elitist consciousness is moderated by the cosmopolitanism of the monastic milieu, which impresses on it the characteristic atmosphere of a new Pentecost.

To sum up, Jerome's vindication of the peculiar status of the new Christian Jerusalem, though essentially influenced by a presumed critical attitude toward the Holy City, succeeds in uniting in an organic manner theological, exegetical, pastoral, and devotional motifs. These reasons, mixing questions of principle and situations of fact, largely reflect the developments which had taken place during the fourth century. They finally lead Jerome to draw an ideal picture of the city and its surrounding land as the most suitable context for a monastic way of life.[61] We can even guess how this rediscovered preeminence of Jerusalem in Christian eyes could have been exploited in order to enhance the ecclesiastical importance of the city outside Palestine, when we observe how Jerome places Jerusalem in opposition to Rome. This contrast is emphasized by means of a forced comparison between the rich church buildings of Rome and the poor simplicity of the manger in Bethlehem, seen moreover against the background of the idyllic rural atmosphere of Jesus' little village. Despite the emphasis placed on Jerusalem, this epilogue shows the attachment to and the preference for Bethlehem on the part of Jerome and his community.[62]

The last point may perhaps help to explain, at least in part, why in later letters Jerome disconcertingly formulates a quite reserved, if not a completely contradictory, point of view with regard to Jerusalem as the "Holy City" of Christians. Nevertheless, personal and theological reasons played a more important part, especially after 393, when Jerome found himself involved in a deep controversy with John, bishop of Jerusalem, over the heritage of Origen's thought. This is the context of his *Ep.* 58 to Paulinus of Nola (395), wherein Jerome, trying to dissuade his correspondent from traveling to the Holy Land, describes Jerusalem as a city similar to all others, devoid of any special sanctity, which is exclusively dependent on the moral conduct of the individual.[63] We find here, once again, the same constellation of biblical passages (as, for instance, Gal. 4:24–26 and John 4:21–24) which traditionally supported the spiritualistic detachment from historical Jerusalem in the name of the heavenly one.[64] Finally—as Jerome says, resuming in this sentence the manifesto of the spiritualistic attitude—"the kingdom of God is within our soul," and thus to see the holy places is not necessary to the faith of Paulinus.[65]

With such statements, Jerome approximates the view of Gregory of Nyssa in his famous *Ep.* 2, written a few years before Jerome's letter to Marcella (between 383 and 385). This document expresses a violent critique of the practice of pilgrimage to Jerusalem on the part of the monks, given the fact that, on the one hand, the grace of God does not abound there more than in Cappadocia and, on the other, the city appears to be full of vicious behavior. In principle, then, Christian faith had no need of seeing the places in order to manifest itself; it was neither less before the pilgrimage nor greater after it.[66] However, even in Gregory's case, it is possible to note a certain contradiction, since his preceding *Ep.* 3 (dated around 379) spoke not without some emotion of his visit to the "salvific symbols" of Jerusalem and Bethlehem, nor did it emphasize the contrast between the way of life in the Holy City and the exigencies of the gospel.[67]

Finally, even more drastic and fundamentally negative than the attitude toward the Holy City exhibited in *Ep.* 58 was Jerome's rejection of Palestine as the "promised land" in *Ep.* 129 to Dardanus (414). Though this polemic was directed against the messianic hopes of the Jews, its basic point of view was again the traditional spiritualistic approach to the city and the land as figures and symbols of spiritual entities, and not as concrete historical realities of the present Christian world.[68]

An examination of these last sources is out of place here. I would like just to point out how Gregory's, and partly also Jerome's, arguments renewed the old spiritualistic reservations which had been typical of the early Christian tradition and still continued to find adherents in their own time.[69] In these and other positions expressed by contemporary and later patristic authors, there are certain limitations (as is the case of Augustine) due to the necessity of taking into account the flourishing of Christian holy places and pilgrimage during the fourth century onwards. But their basic orientation was not so well disposed as to promote the veneration of the holy places and to encourage the journey to them. One might think at first that the new reality of Christian Jerusalem had not yet penetrated the consciousness of theologians, despite the efforts made by some of them to give it greater value. In this sense, it would be reasonable to presume that, as is normally the case, a gap remained between realities and ideas, the former having this time gone a step further than the latter. But at least both Gregory of Nyssa and Jerome knew very well what they were speaking about, so that their reservations have to be understood rather as timely reactions to a contemporary devotional phenomenon, which was becoming not only more and more fashionable but also controversial.[70]

It is altogether questionable whether the above-mentioned gap between reality and ideas was ever bridged in later patristic times. There were indeed important individual voices (not only those of pilgrims and monks) defending the theological status of Jerusalem and the Holy Land, like the noteworthy pronouncements made by Pope Leo the Great in the mid-fifth century.[71] Nevertheless, most ancient Christian theologians were inclined to maintain the tension between history and symbol: Jerusalem continued to be the symbol of a different reality pertaining to a spiritual realm, an order superior to the historical one; the latter could only claim for itself a secondary and relative value.

Notes

1. This thought is formulated in *De utilitate credendi*, chapter 17; see *Augustinus, De utilitate credendi. Über den Nutzen des Glaubens*, ed. A. Hoffmann (Freiburg, 1992), 126, 13–19.

2. Thanks especially to R. Wilken, to whom I refer for a general outline: *The Land Called Holy. Palestine in Christian History and Thought* (New Haven, 1992).

3. See, for example, R. Wilken's interpretation of Jesus' triumphal entrance into Jerusalem (Mark 11:1–10) and the cleansing of the Temple (Mark 11:15–17): both stories are evidence of the eschatological hopes shared by the first Christian community, expecting in the first case a restoration of the kingdom of Israel, and in the second a new temple "not made by the hand of man," as stated by Mark 14:57–58; Wilken (above, note 1), 46 52; B. Kühnel (*From the Earthly to the Heavenly Jerusalem. Representations of the Holy City in Christian Art of the First Millennium* [Rom, Freiburg and Vienna, 1987], 50) supposes instead Jesus' desire for reform of the Temple worship.

4. For the wider context of the patristic interpretation of Revelation, see esp. G. Kretschmar, *Die Offenbarung des Johannes. Die Geschichte ihrer Auslegung im 1. Jahrtausend* (Stuttgart, 1985).

5. See K. Thraede, "Jerusalem II (Sinnbild)," *RAC* 17 (Stuttgart, 1995), 725.

6. Irenaeus, *Adv. haer.* 1, 26, 2.

7. Besides Kühnel (above, note 3), see E. Lamirande, "Jérusalem celeste," *Dictionnaire de Spiritualité*, VIII (Paris, 1974), 947–50; and esp. C. Mazzucco, "La Gerusalemme celeste dell'Apocalisse nei Padri," *La dimora di Dio con gli uomini (Ap 21, 3). Immagini della Gerusalemme celeste dal III al XIV secolo*, ed. M. L. Gatti Perer (Milan, 1983), 49–75.

8. N. Brox, "Das 'irdische Jerusalem' in der altchristlichen Theologie," *Kairos* NF 28 (1986), 152–73.

9. See *Dial.* 110, 2–4, but also *I Apol.* 39, 3; 45, 5–6; 49, 5. Regarding the desolation of Jerusalem and the land of the Jews, see ibid., 47.

10. *Adv. haer.* 4, 4, 1–2. Irenaeus, on the contrary, considers the actual state of Jerusalem vis-à-vis the progress of the times, i.e., the accomplishment of the Law and of the coming of the new alliance (4, 4, 2).

11. See, for instance, Origen, *Hom. in Ier.* 13, 1: Christians do not become sad in their face (Jer. 15:5) because of the fate of Jerusalem, since "it has killed my Jesus."

12. *De praescr. haer.* 7, 9.

13. See W. M. Frend, *Martyrdom and Persecution in the Early Church* (Oxford, 1965), 89;

J. van Oort, *Jerusalem and Babylon: A study into Augustine's City of God and the sources of his Doctrine of the Two Cities* (Leiden, 1991).

14. *Sermo de fide* 5, 61–65.

15. See P. C. Bori, *Chiesa primitiva. L'immagine della comunità delle origini—Atti 2, 42–47; 4, 32–37—nella storia della chiesa antica* (Brescia, 1974), 64–83.

16. The equation Jerusalem = church can be found, for instance, in *Hom. in Ier.* 9, 2 (the church is the "city of God" and the "vision of peace," according to an etymology of Jerusalem already present in Philo and then in Clement of Alexandria; for its identification with the soul, see ibid., 13, 2 (the soul, previously "trampled" by the adverse powers—i.e., in a historical sense, still "Jebus"—becomes through Christ "Jerusalem," i.e., a vision of peace).

17. *Hom. in Ier.* 9, 3.

18. *C. Cels.* 7, 28–30. Cf. also *De princ.* 4, 3, 8.

19. *Hom. in Ier.* 5, 13.

20. With respect to the first aspect, see again Bori (above, note 15), 145; as for the second aspect, cf. for example Evagrius, *Ep.* 39; and Dorotheus of Gaza, *Instruct.* 10, 107.

21. S. Heid, *Chiliasmus und Antichrist-Mythos. Eine frühchristliche Kontroverse um das Heilige Land* (Bonn, 1993).

22. *Dial.* 80, 1–5.

23. *Adv. haer.* 5, 32, 1.

24. See Heid (above, note 21), 234.

25. *Adv. haer.* 5, 35, 2.

26. Eusebius, *Hist. Eccles.* 5, 18, 2.

27. *Adv. Marc.* 3, 24, 3–5.

28. Heid (above, note 21), 235–36.

29. On both figures, see P. W. L. Walker, *Holy City, Holy Places? Christian Attitudes to Jerusalem and the Holy Land in the Fourth Century* (Oxford, 1990).

30. While Walker recognizes the role of Cyril in developing a new theological consciousness of the Holy City, Wilken ([above, note 2], 81) presents Eusebius as the true initiator. As for his political reservations, see Z. Rubin, "The Church of the Holy Sepulchre and the Conflict between the Sees of Caesarea and Jerusalem," *The Jerusalem Cathedra*, II, ed. L. I. Levine (Jerusalem, 1982), 79–105; as well as Rubin's article in this volume.

31. This oration, known as the *De sepulchro Christi*, has become part of the *De laudibus Constantini* (chapters 11–18). On both texts, see the study of H. A. Drake, *In Praise of Constantine. A Historical Study and New Translation of Eusebius' Tricennial Orations* (Berkeley, 1976).

32. *V. Const.* 3, 33, 2.

33. Ibid., 3, 33, 3.

34. Z. Rubin ("Holy Sepulchre" [above, note 30], 82–85) has reasonably argued that Constantine's letter to Macarius of Jerusalem (325), reported by Eusebius, alludes to the supposed discovery of the cross; see *V. Const.* 3, 30, 1. In contrast, E. D. Hunt (*Holy Land Pilgrimage in the Later Roman Empire A.D. 312–460* [Oxford, 1982]) stresses the silence both of Eusebius and the *Itinerarium Burdigalense*.

35. *Cat.* 13, 28. The Christological foundation is given in 13, 23.

36. See esp. *Cat.* 4, 10 and 10, 19.

37. For his anti-Judaic polemics, see, for instance, *Cat.* 10, 11; with regard to the preeminence of Jerusalem, see *Cat.* 3, 7; see also the contribution of Irshai to this volume. The same emphasis on the salvific role of the city characterizes Cyril's letter to Emperor Constantius II on the apparition of the Cross (*PG* 33, 1165–76; see esp. 1173A).

38. See *Cat.* 4, 10 and esp. 10, 19.

39. Ibid., 10, 19, while presenting a whole series of testimonies on behalf of Jesus Christ the Lord, records the evidence provided by places in Jerusalem and the Holy Land together with passages from the New Testament; see also 12, 32; 13, 38–39; 14, 22–23.

40. See *Cat.* 10, 19 and 14, 23.

41. For the continuity between Eusebius, Cyril, and the experience of pilgrims, see Wilken (above, note 2), 90–91. The importance of seeing and touching, besides the scope of prayer, is properly stated by P. Maraval, *Lieux saints et pèlerinages d'Orient. Histoire et géographie des origines à la conquête arabe* (Paris, 1985), 137–38.

42. The opening sentence of the preserved manuscript begins characteristically so: "... *ostendebantur iuxta Scripturas*" (*Itin. Egeria* 1, 1). For a good example of private "stational" office, see ibid., 10, 7.

43. G. Kretschmar ("Festkalender und Memorialstätten Jerusalems in altkirchlicher Zeit," *ZDPV* 87 [1971], 178) considers the stational liturgy of Jerusalem influenced by the practice of pilgrims. Its growing "historicism" has been noted by A. Renoux, *Le codex arménien Jérusalem 121*, PO 35/1 (Turnhout, 1969), 184.

44. See Cyril of Scythopolis, *V. Sab.* 57.

45. For the text, see the edition of I. Hilberg (*CSEL* 54, 329–44). The attribution to Jerome was asserted by P. Nautin, "La lettre de Paule et Eustochium à Marcelle (Jérôme, *Ep.* 46)," *Augustinianum* 24 (1984), 441–449, and has been accepted by P. Maraval, "Saint Jérôme et le pèlerinage aux lieux saints de Palestine," *Jérôme entre l'Occident et l'Orient*, ed. Y.-M. Duval (Paris, 1988), 323–42.

46. See esp. *Ep.* 46, 3, 4.

47. Ibid., 46, 2, 2. The same biblical reference, which both illustrates and justifies the monastic choice, can be found in *Ep.* 108, 31, 2 and, more synthetically, in *Ep.* 58, 3, 1.

48. Ibid., 46, 2, 3: *Haec terra montuosa et in sublimi sita, quantum a deliciis saeculi uacat, tantum maiores habet delicias spiritales* (p. 331).

49. See, for instance, the part played both by II Sam. 24:16, 18, 25 and Gen. 14, 18–20 in forming the Jewish image of Jerusalem as the city of God; see Kühnel (above, note 3), 22–26.

50. *Ep.* 46, 3, 2. As to the origins of this tradition, see Walker (above, note 29), 255, note 58.

51. *Ep.* 46, 3, 3. *Ep.* 108, 9, 1 and 129, 5, 3 bring the three names of Jerusalem without an etymological explanation, significantly adding that of Aelia and thus preferring history to allegory. Meanwhile, Jerome had abandoned the connection between Salem and Jerusalem, as can be seen in his treatment of the *quaestio* of Melchizedek in *Ep.* 73, 7, 1 to Evangelus (390). The explanation furnished in *Ep.* 46, 3, 3 is not devoid of Origenian echoes (see above, note 16).

52. Maraval (above, note 45), 347–48.

53. *Ep.* 46, 4, 3: *tunc omne sacramentum Iudaeae et antiquam dei familiaritatem per apostolos in nationes fuisse translatum* (p. 334).

54. Ibid., 46, 5, 2. For the concurrence between Holy Sepulchre and Temple, see J. Wilkinson, "Constantinian Churches in Palestine," *Ancient Churches Revealed*, ed. Y. Tsafrir (Jerusalem, 1993), 23–27. Kühnel ([above, note 3], 83–84) mentions also the ring of King Solomon and the anointment horn of the kings of Judaea which Egeria declares to have seen in the Holy Sepulchre as objects of veneration together with the Cross (*Itin.* 37, 3).

55. *Ep.* 46, 5, 2.

56. This point is the object of a broader and very accurate treatment (ibid., 46, 6–7). It gives Jerome the opportunity to make some hermeneutical statements, starting with the impossibility that Scripture contradicts itself (6, 2). He then proceeds to lose the *quaestio*, first by

denying that Rev. 11:1–2 refers to the heavenly Jerusalem of Rev. 21:16–21. To support the idea that Sodom and Egypt are synonymous with the fallen "world," Jerome observes, among other things, that Scripture never uses the name "Egypt" in a metaphorical sense for Jerusalem (7, 3).

57. *Ep.* 46, 7, 6.

58. Ibid., 46, 8, 2.

59. For the expectation of miracles among the aims of pilgrimages, see Maraval (above, note 41), 150–51. Jerome's understanding of this aspect is also demonstrated by his polemic against Vigilantius (406), wherein he rejects his critique of the miracles at the tombs of the martyrs; *Contra Vigilantium* (*PL* 23, 353–68, esp. 363B–364C).

60. *Ep.* 46, 9, 2.

61. Ibid., 46, 12.

62. Jerome's complex attitude toward Rome and his relationship with Jerusalem and Bethlehem are examined by P. Antin, *Recueil sur saint Jérome* (Brussels, 1968), 375–89.

63. See esp. *Ep.* 58, 3–4.

64. See, for instance, ibid., 58, 2, 3. The appeal to John 4:21–24 appears in *Ep.* 58, 3, 1.

65. Ibid., 58, 3, 3.

66. Gregory of Nyssa, *Ep.* 2, 15.

67. See esp. ibid., 3, 3–5.

68. Among other things, Jerome stresses the exiguity of the land and restates the traditional argument concerning the end of the Jewish economy: *Omnia illius populi in imagine et umbra et typo praecessisse, scripta autem esse pro nobis,* "in quos fines saeculorum decucurrerunt (*Ep.* 129, 6, 3 [ed. Hilberg, *CSEL* 56, p. 173]). See the comments of Wilken (above, note 2), 128–32.

69. See, for instance, Hilary of Poitiers, *Tract. in Ps.* 124, 2; or Ambrose of Milan, *De Cain et Abel* I, 3, 9, both ignoring the reality of Christian Jerusalem.

70. I agree in this sense with Maraval (above, note 45), 353.

71. See *Acta Concil. Oec.* (ed. E. Schwartz, II, IV, 92); and above, note 44.

16

Loving the Jerusalem Below:
The Monks of Palestine

ROBERT L. WILKEN

Christian Jerusalem is at once a fact of history and a work of the imagination. The actual city, the place where King David ruled and Jesus of Nazareth was crucified, is irrevocably part of Christian memory. What happened there—whether one thinks of the siege of Nebuchadnezzar in 586 B.C.E., the destruction of the Temple by the Romans in 70 C.E., or the advent of Muslim rule in the seventh century—is no less constitutive of the Christian past than of Jewish history. When the Persians occupied Jerusalem in 614 C.E., it was a Christian monk from Mar Saba who wrote a lament mourning the destruction of the city. What he lamented was not a heavenly city, the new Jerusalem, but the actual city of stone and wood, its marble columns and mosaic floors, its magnificent portals, and, of course, the temple of God, the holy Anastasis. John the Almsgiver, patriarch of Alexandria, lamented the Persian conquest of Jerusalem not for one day, not for a week, not for a month, but for a full year. "Wailing and groaning bitterly, he strove by his lamentations to outdo Jeremiah, who of old lamented the capture of *this same city*, Jerusalem."[1]

But for Christians, Jerusalem is also the city of Ps. 87, "Glorious things are spoken of you O city of God," and Isa. 60, "And nations shall come to your light," a spiritual and theological reality that came into being with the coming of Christ. When Christians pray the words of Ps. 46, "There is a river whose streams make glad the city of God, the holy habitation of the Most High," they think of the Church, not the city located on the edge of the Judaean Desert. The sublime words and soaring images of the psalms and prophets, though anchored in the singular hopes of the ancient Israelites, brought into existence something that was not there previously. Isaiah's Jerusalem (and the Jerusalem of the Apocalypse) is unlike any city that ever existed. It will be a city in which "the Lord will be [the] everlasting light" (Isa. 60:19).

The spiritual Jerusalem of Christian prayer would, however, never have come into being had things not taken place in the historical city. Just as it is not possible to tell the Christian story without reference to time, "crucified under Pontius Pilate," in the words of the creed, so one cannot speak of the Christian mysteries without reference to place. When Cleopas and another disciple met Jesus on the road to Emmaus, Cleopas said to him, "Are you the only visitor to Jerusalem who does not know the things that have happened *there* in these days?" (Luke 24:18) From the very beginning Christian belief was oriented to events that had taken place in Jerusalem. Early on this topographical fact embedded itself deep within the Christian memory, so much so that in the second century a Christian bishop could say that Jesus was crucified "in the middle of Jerusalem."[2] Where Jesus suffered and died and was buried helped impose order on the memory of his life and sowed seeds for the sanctification of space.

✦ ✦ ✦

The Christian Church had its beginnings in the city of Jerusalem. In the book of Acts it is reported that Jesus' disciples, as well as his followers—Mary and other women—gathered in a room in Jerusalem after his death. As they were offering prayer to God, the Holy Spirit descended on them like a rushing wind. Filled with the Spirit, Peter went out into the streets and preached to the "inhabitants of Judaea and all who dwell in Jerusalem" (Acts 2:14). The first Christian martyr, Stephen, met his death in Jerusalem, and in the fifth century a great church was built in Jerusalem to house his relics and honor his memory. In a sermon preached in Jerusalem to venerate Stephen, Hesychius, a presbyter in Jerusalem, declaimed: "Among us Stephen fixed his courtyards and his tents, among us he received the lot of his ministry and the part of his martyrdom."[3] Only Christians whose home was Jerusalem could say that these things have been accomplished "among us."[4]

It is this identification with the actual city of Jerusalem, its saints and martyrs, its holy places and history, that gives Palestinian monasticism a singular place in the history of Christian Jerusalem. The monks of Palestine did not come to Jerusalem as pilgrims, to worship at the holy places and carry home tales of the wonders they had seen; they came to live in the desert near Jerusalem, to make this land their home, to build communities of faith and piety contiguous to that place where God was shown forth.

The first monks in Palestine had little interest in the desert surrounding Jerusalem. Hilarion, whom Jerome calls the "founder and teacher of this way of life [monasticism]" in this "province," i.e., Palestine, came from a tiny village, Thabatha, five miles south of Gaza.[5] Geographically Gaza was closer to Egypt than to Jerusalem, and spiritually the most compelling ideal of the solitary life had been set by Antony. Hence Hilarion modeled his way of life on Egyptian practice, i.e., by Antony's example. On one occasion (but only on one, according to Jerome), Hilarion went up to Jerusalem to venerate the "holy places," but he chose *not* to live in the desert of Jerusalem. "The blessed Hilarion, a Palestinian who lived in Palestine, set eyes on Jerusalem for only a single day, lest one who lived so close to the holy places appear to despise them, yet . . . he did not wish to appear to confine God within prescribed limits."[6] Hilarion believed he would be as close to God in the desert near his home as he would be in Judaea.

The first monk to settle in the Judaean Desert was Chariton, a native of Iconium in Asia Minor (present-day Konya) who came to Jerusalem as a pilgrim in the fourth century.[7] In contrast to Hilarion, he seems to have made his home in the Judaean Desert *because* it was close to Jerusalem. By the end of the fourth century, during the reign of Emperor Theodosius (379–395), the presence of the "holy places" in Jerusalem and vicinity had begun to beckon wealthy and well-connected men and women from the West. The most famous of these women was Melania, who renounced her husband and children to pursue an ascetic way of life in the East. She first traveled to Egypt to visit the monastic communities, but eventually settled in Jerusalem where she and her friend and companion, Rufinus, founded monasteries on the Mount of Olives. Not to be outdone by Melania and Rufinus, Jerome and Paula founded a monastery in Bethlehem near the Church of the Nativity. Jerome's letter to Marcella, written in the name of Paula and Eustochium, is one of the first documents urging someone to leave her home and take up residence in the Holy Land.

But the future of monasticism in Palestine did not lie with monks from the west. At the beginning of the fifth century, Euthymius, a monk from Armenia, made the long journey from his native land to settle permanently in the Judaean Desert. Unlike the intellectual Jerome, who came to the Holy Land to investigate biblical geography and to impress friends in Rome by transmitting Eastern learning in Latin dress, Euthymius' only desire was to live and pray in the desert that touched the Holy City. His sentiment was like that of T. S. Eliot on his visit to Little Gidding. "You are not here to verify/Instruct yourself, or inform curiosity/Or carry report. You are here to kneel/Where prayer has been valid."[8]

Euthymius' life, and that of his industrious disciple, Sabas, were written by Cyril, a native of Palestine from the city of Scythopolis, south of the sea of Galilee in the Jordan Valley, and the first self-consciously Palestinian writer in Christian history.[9] Cyril's book takes its shape from *place*, the desert that was contiguous with Jerusalem the Holy City. There were deserts aplenty in Egypt, Syria, Cappadocia, and Armenia, but only this desert was called "the desert of Jerusalem" or "the desert east of the holy city," "the desert of the holy city" or simply the "dear desert."[10]

Cyril begins his account of the monks of the Judaean Desert with the arrival of Euthymius in Palestine in 405 C.E. "Our great father Euthymius led by the Holy Spirit came to Jerusalem in the twenty-ninth year of his life and adored the Holy Cross and the Holy Anastasis and the other holy places. He visited the God-fearing fathers who lived in the desert, and as he learned the virtue and way of life of each one, he stamped this on his own soul. Then he *came to live* at the laura at Pharan, six miles from the Holy City."[11]

Euthymius sowed the seed in the "desert of Jerusalem," but his disciple, Sabas, would nurture the young plants, uproot the weeds, hoe and cut and prune, and bring the garden to full bloom. Euthymius was a "lover of solitude" who desired only "to commune with God in silence through prayer." Sabas, however, was a "jolly builder," as the Byzantinist H. G. Beck called him. Unlike Euthymius he was no recluse. He loved the sound of the hammer and saw, the scrape of a trowel on stone.

Of him Cyril writes: "Eager to advance from glory to glory, conceiving in his heart the ascent to God, and completing ten years in his monastery, he had the god-pleasing desire to go to the Holy city and to live the solitary life in the desert surrounding it. For it was necessary through him by *colonizing* it to fulfill the prophecies about it of the sublime Isaiah."[12] The term *polisai*, translated "colonize," means "build" or "found" a city (*polis*) and is seldom used in early Christian literature. It does, however, occur in Athanasius's *Life of Antony*, a work that Cyril knew. In Cyril, however, it has a much more particular reference. It refers to the desert of Elijah, John the Baptizer, and Jesus, and the work of colonization is seen as the fulfillment of biblical prophecy. "The Lord will comfort you, O Zion, and give courage to all its deserted, and will make her wilderness like the garden of the Lord; joy and gladness will be found in her, thanksgiving and the voice of song" (Isa. 51:3).

Though the monks lived in the desert, Jerusalem was only a short walk from their monasteries, and the city itself, its churches, holy places, and history, were never far from their minds. The key text for understanding the attitudes of the Palestinian monks to Jerusalem is found in a petition sent by the monks to Emperor Anastasius at the height of the controversy over the dogmatic definition of the person of Christ. Elias, the patriarch of Jerusalem, refused to support the emperor when he deposed Macedonius, the Chalcedonian patriarch of Constantinople. To mollify the emperor he sent his famous monk, holy Sabas, on an embassy to Constantinople to plead the Chalcedonian cause and, according to Cyril, to insure that the "*mother of the churches* be protected from all disturbance."[13] It was an uncommon assignment for this man of the desert.

Leaving his responsibilities in Judaea, Sabas traveled to Constantinople, where he stayed the winter to press his case before the emperor. Anastasius was unmoved. He removed Elias from office and, over the protest of the monks, exiled him to Aila (Elath) on the Gulf of Aqaba, a garden of delight for twentieth-century sun-worshippers, but to a bishop in the sixth century a miserable and inhospitable town on the edge of civilization.

On their return to Jerusalem, Sabas and Theodosius, the leaders of the cenobitic communities in Palestine, took it upon themselves to address a petition directly to the emperor:

> Theodosius and Sabas, Archimandries, and all the other abbots and monks who dwell in the Holy City of God and all the desert around it and the vicinity of the Jordan send this petition to the God beloved and very pious emperor, Augustus and Pantokrator by God's grace, Flavius Anastasius, friend of Christ. The king of all, God and ruler of all things, Jesus Christ, only Son of God, has entrusted to your authority the scepter of rule over all things after him, to arrange, through your piety, the bond of peace for all the holy churches, but especially for the mother of the churches, Zion, where was revealed and accomplished for the salvation of the world, the great mystery of piety. . . . From that precious and supernatural mystery of Christ, through the victorious and precious cross and life-giving Anastasis, indeed all the holy and adored places, receiving by tradition from above and from the beginning through the blessed and holy apostles, the true confession, a confession without illusion, and faith, we, the *dwellers of this Holy Land,* have kept it invulnerable and inviolable in Christ, and by the grace of God, we maintain it always without being intimidated in any way by our adversaries. . . . [14]

They express their astonishment that the emperor, who had been nourished in the true faith, has allowed "such turmoil and trouble to be poured over the Holy City of Jerusalem, to such an extent that the *mother of all the churches,* Zion, and the Holy Anastasis of our God and Savior . . . has become a common place. . . ." Jerusalem is the "eye and light of all the world" and "we, the inhabitants of Jerusalem, as it were, *touch with our own hands* each day the truth through these holy places in which the mystery of the incarnation of our great God and savior took place. How then, after more than five hundred years after the savior's presence among us, can we Jerusalemites learn the faith anew?"

The language of this petition is without precedent in Christian history. Many of its central ideas had been germinating for generations, but here, for the first time, they are united in a series of theological conceptions that bring together history, practice, and belief. Already in the middle of the fifth century, at the time of the Council of Chalcedon, no less a figure than Leo the Great, Bishop of Rome (d. 461), had appealed to the testimony of those places "by which the whole world is taught" as evidence of the truth of the doctrine of the "two natures" formulated at the Council of Chalcedon.[15]

There is, however, a notable difference between Leo and the monks of the Judaean Desert. Leo was interested only in the theological significance of the "holy places" and showed no interest in the Christian community that lived in Jerusalem. For Leo, the holy places do not imply "Holy Land," and certainly not the authority of the bishop of Jerusalem. He would not have suffered himself to be instructed in matters of faith by the bishop of Jerusalem or the monks of the Judaean Desert. But it is precisely this link between place and people that was central to the petition to Emperor Anastasius.

In the petition, the earlier pilgrimage piety centered on "holy places" gave way to a theology that includes the Christian community living in Jerusalem and vicinity, the bishop, priests, monks, and the faithful. Only the "inhabitants of Jerusalem" had a tangible relation to the places, for they were able to "touch" with their own hands the truth through these holy places. The city conferred on its inhabitants a unique status. The point of the petition is not that the emperor should venerate the "places," but that he should show deference to the Christians living in Jerusalem. Contrast the words of Jerome little more than a century earlier: "It is not being in Jerusalem, but living a good life there that is praiseworthy"[16] The monk Hilarion, it will be recalled, chose *not* to live in the vicinity of Jerusalem.

The purpose of the petition to Emperor Anastasius was, of course, political; it had to do with a struggle over the theological definition of the person of Christ that had gone back to the early fourth century. Its language, however, is sacramental. The arresting term is "touch." Its appearance here recalls the opening lines of the epistle of I John, where the same term is used: "That which was from the beginning, which we have heard, which we have seen with our eyes, which we have looked upon and touched with our hands, concerning the word of life. . . ."

Though the term "touch" is the same in both texts, what is being touched is, of course, not the same. John, a disciple of Jesus, was speaking about the person of Jesus who could be embraced by the disciples during his earthly life and touched after his resurrection. According to the gospel of Luke, Jesus addressed his disciples: "Why are you troubled and why do questionings rise in your hearts? See my hands and my feet, that it is I myself; touch me and see" (Luke 24:39). But the monks of Palestinian were not speaking of touching Jesus; what they could touch were the places and things which Christ's body had touched during his days in Jerusalem, the cross on which Jesus had died, the stone of the tomb in which he had been buried, the walls of the room in which he had celebrated the Last Supper, the street on which he had carried the cross to his death. In the words of Paulinus of Nola: "No other sentiment draws people to Jerusalem than the desire to *see* (*videant*) and *touch* (*continguant*) the places where Christ was physically present, and to be able to say from their own experience, 'We have gone into his tabernacle, and have worshipped in the places where his feet stood'."[17] Through seeing and touching the places one sees and touches the "truth," that is Christ.

Another Palestinian monk, John of Damascus who lived at Mar Saba in the eighth century, was to give these ideas philosophical and theological coherence. In his treatise *On the Images,* written at the height of the iconoclastic controversy, he treats the "holy places" in Jerusalem and "holy things" associated with Christ in the same terms he uses for icons, i.e., holy pictures. Just as one bows before "images of Christ, the incarnate God, our Lady, the *theotokos* and mother of the son of God and the saints," so one venerates these holy places. Among the places "by which God has accomplished our salvation" John mentions the cave in Bethlehem, the wood of the cross, the nails, the lance, the seamless tunic, the holy tomb, the stone of the sepulchre, Mount Zion and the Mount of Olives, the pool of Bethesda, the garden at Gethsemane. All these are to be "honored and venerated" as "God's holy temples." His term for such places is "receptacles of divine power."[18] Through things that can be seen and touched, God is known and made present to human beings. This sacramental principle, founded on the Incarnation, is not confined to the bread and wine of the Eucharist, but is here extended to other material objects, to icons, and to things and places found in Jerusalem.

The heavenly Jerusalem now had an image on earth. In earlier Christian tradition, the Jerusalem above was the "mother of believers," but for the Judaean monks the church of the earthly Jerusalem is the "mother of the churches." By the sixth century, the Christian monks of Jerusalem and the Judaean Desert had created a new spiritual and political fact within the Christian world. These monks had a cool indifference to the stratagems and blandishments of the emperor in Constantinople. For them, Jerusalem—not Rome—was the apostolic see par excellence. Since the time of the "savior's presence among us," they insisted, the inhabitants of the Holy Land have handed on the faith pure and undefiled.

The petition to Anastasius is the most luminous text on Jerusalem from the monks of Palestine, but I would be remiss were I not to call attention to two other monastic writers who offer a different, but no less significant, perspective on the attitude of Palestinian monks to Jerusalem.[19] I refer to the monk from Mar Saba, Strategos, whose *Capture of Jerusalem* is an account of the Persian conquest, and a poem by the monk Sophronius, who was later patriarch of Jerusalem when the Muslims took the city in 638.[20]

Strategos wrote a lament over the city following its Persian occupation, when churches were pillaged and Christians were killed. What impresses the reader of this work is the intensity of feelings reflected in his account of the occupation. The text reaches its emotional zenith as the patriarch of Jerusalem, Zachariah, bound, is led with a band of captives down into the Qidron Valley and up to the Mount of Olives, where the fearful band halted briefly. Strategos writes, "They raised their eyes and beheld Jerusalem ablaze with flames and began to lament with tears. Some struck their faces, and others threw ashes over their heads, and some threw dirt in their faces, and some pulled hair from their scalps. Some struck their breasts, and others lifted their hands to heaven crying out and saying, 'Have mercy on us, O Lord; have mercy on your city, O Lord, have mercy on your altars. . . . O Lord, look how your enemies are rejoicing in the destruction of your city and of your altars . . . .'."[21]

When Zachariah saw the people throwing ashes over their heads and beating their breasts, he raised his hand to calm them. Before being led away

> he turned to Zion, and as a husband consoles his wife, so Zacharias, comforting Zion as he wept, extended his hands, crying out and saying, "O Zion, with a sorrowful word that makes one weep I speak peace to you; peace be with you, O Jerusalem, peace be with you, O *Holy Land*, peace on the whole land; Christ who chose you will deliver you. . . . O Zion, what hope do I have, how many years before I will see you again." "What use is there for me, an old man, to hope? How will I see you again? I will not see your face again. I beseech you, O Zion, to remember me when Christ comes to you. O Zion, do not forget me your servant, and may your creator not forget you. For if I forget you, O Jerusalem, let my right hand wither. Let my tongue cleave to the roof of my mouth if I do not remember you. Peace on you, O Zion, you who were my city, and now I am made a stranger to you."[22]

This extraordinary scene is reminiscent of David's departure from Jerusalem after the revolt of Absalom. As David left the city, crossed the Qidron brook, and ascended the Mount of Olives he was followed by the people of the city. The ancient Israelite historian describes the scene in these words, "But David went up the ascent of the Mount of Olives, weeping as he went, barefoot and with his head covered; and all the people who were with him covered their heads, and they went up, weeping as they went." (II Sam. 15).

The other lament over Jerusalem was also written during the time of the Persian conquest. Composed by Sophronius, who became patriarch of Jerusalem after the Byzantine emperor Heraclius had recaptured the city, it belongs to a quite different literary tradition, the Greek *anacreonticon*, a showy and pretentious genre of poetry favored by rhetors in this period. Even though Sophronius' language is ostentatious and affected, the poem has an immediacy to it. One scholar observed, somewhat myopically, that the poem is a "tearful lamentation" that is "more credit to Sophronius' feelings than his talents as a historian." But that is precisely the point; what is most interesting about the poem is not the bits of information it provides about the occupation, but what it tells us about Sophronius' love for Jerusalem. He sings:

> Holy City of God
> Home of the most valiant saints
> Great Jerusalem
> What kind of lament should I offer you?

> Children of the blessed Christians
> Come to mourn high crested Jerusalem

> In the face of such tragedy
> The flow of my tears is too brief
> The dirge of my heart
> Too measured before such suffering.

> Nevertheless, I shall sound forth a lament
> Weaving my garment of groans for you
> Because you have suffered such brigandage
> Concealing the rushing forth of my tears.[23]

Like Strategos, Sophronius views Jerusalem as a political as well as religious center. In Strategos' threnody it was the "great city of the Christians," and in Sophronius' poem it was the "great Jerusalem" and the city of the "children of the blessed Christians." In the war between the Roman and Sassanid empires, Jerusalem was the emblem of the Christian empire. The capital of the empire may have been located in Constantinople but its spiritual shield and buckler was Jerusalem. Sophronius presents the occupation of Jerusalem as an attack on Rome, using the ancient term "Edom":

Deceitfully the Mede
Came from terrible Persia
Pillaging cities and villages
Waging war against the ruler of Edom [Rome]

Advancing on the Holy Land
The malevolent one came
To destroy the city of God, Jerusalem.

All together
They raised on high their holy hands
Beseeching the Lord Christ
To fight on behalf of their city.[24]

The profound transformation in Christian attitudes toward Jerusalem is summed up in one sentence from Strategos' *Capture of Jerusalem*: "And the Jerusalem above wept over the Jerusalem below." For Christians, these terms, "the Jerusalem above" and "the Jerusalem below," derive from St. Paul: "Now Hagar . . . corresponds to the present Jerusalem, for she is in slavery with her children. But the Jerusalem above is free and she is our mother"(Gal. 4:25–26). Paul's allegory was taken over by Melito of Sardis in the second century. In his paschal homily he wrote: "The Jerusalem below was precious, but it is worthless now because of the Jerusalem above."[25] Five hundred years later, after the building of Christian Jerusalem, and generations of Christian life in the city, a monk from Mar Saba wrote: "The Jerusalem above wept over the Jerusalem below."[26] So great was the sorrow in heaven that "on that day a great darkness came over the city" and people were reminded of the darkness at Christ's crucifixion.

It is now recognized that the monks of Palestine are a significant chapter in the history of Jerusalem and of the Holy Land. What I have suggested is that they are a precious repository not only of historical information and theological ideas, but of profound human emotions. It is not a little paradoxical, and at the same time alluring, that it was monks who wrote with such passion and fervor about the actual city of Jerusalem. After all, these were men who had left home and family and goods, all the natural bonds that kindle human affections and bind us to place, to seek God in a place they had never seen. Yet it is these same men, solitaries given to lives of prayer and fasting, who in antiquity conveyed the deepest feelings of Christians about the earthly Jerusalem. That is why they remain for us not simply witnesses to a distant past; their voices find a place deep within our own hearing. They remind us that to love God alone does not mean turning away from other loves; it deepens and intensifies them. Only in loving the heavenly Jerusalem can we truly love the earthly Jerusalem.

Notes

1. *Life of John the Almsgiver* by Leontius, bishop of Neapolis, chapter 9, ed. H. Delehaye, "Une Vie inédite de Saint Jean l'Aumonier," *AnBoll* 45 (1927), 23.

2. Melito of Sardis, *Paschal Homily* 94.

3. M. Aubineau, *Les Homélies Festale d'Hésychius de Jérusalem*, Sussidia Hagiographica 59 (Brussels, 1978), I, 244.

4. On Christian Jerusalem, see R. L. Wilken, *The Land Called Holy. Palestine in Christian History and Thought* (New Haven, 1992). See also N. Rosovsky (ed.), *City of the Great King. Jerusalem from David to the Present* (Cambridge, 1996).

5. Jerome, *Vita S. Hiliaronis eremitae* 14.

6. Jerome, *Ep.* 58.3.

7. *La Vie prémétaphrastique de S. Chariton*, ed. G. Garitte, *Bulletin de l'institut historique belge de Rome* (Rome, 1941), 5–50.

8. The passage is from "Little Gidding" in "Four Quarters" in T. S. Eliot, *The Complete Poems and Plays 1909–1950* (New York, 1930), 139.

9. On Cyril of Scythopolis and his presentation of Euthymius and Sabas, see Wilken (above, note 4), 149–73, with bibliography. For a recent study of Sabas, see J. Patrich, *Sabas. Leader of Palestinian Monasticism* (Washington, D.C., 1995).

10. The text of Cyril's *Lives* has been edited by E. Schwartz, *Kyrillos von Skythopolis*, Texte und Untersuchungen 49.2 (Leipzig, 1936); English trans.: R. M. Price, *Cyril of Scythopolis: The Lives of the Monks of Palestine* (Kalamazoo, 1991).

11. On the monks of the Judaean Desert, see Y. Hirschfeld, *The Judean Desert Monasteries in the Byzantine Period* (New Haven, 1992).

12. Schwartz (above, note 10), 90.

13. Ibid., 139.

14. Ibid., 152–57.

15. Leo, *Ep.* 113, 109, 123.

16. Jerome, *Ep.* 58.2.

17. Paulinus of Nola, *Ep.* 49.14.

18. *Contra imaginum calumniatores* 3.34.

19. See Wilken (above, note 4), 216ff.

20. Arabic version (with Latin translation) of the Greek original; G. Garitte (ed.), *Expugnatio Hierosolymae A.D. 614*, CSCO 340 (Louvain, 1973).

21. *Expugnatio* (above, note 20), 13. 14–20.

22. Ibid., 14.12–16.

23. *Anacreonticon* 14.1–4; *Sophronii Anacreontica*, ed. M. Gigante, *Opuscula*, Testi per esercitzaione academiche 10/12 (Rome, 1957).

24. Ibid., 19 and 20.

25. Melito of Sardis, *Paschal Homily* 45.

26. *Expugnatio* (above, note 20), 8.9.

17

The Influence of Jerusalem on Christian Liturgy

PAUL F. BRADSHAW

A search of Christian liturgical texts from all time periods and in all ecclesiastical traditions reveals the regular occurrence of references to Jerusalem, but the word is almost invariably employed as a symbol of the
eschatological age to come,[1] picking up the language of the book of Revelation,
which speaks of "new Jerusalem, coming down out of heaven from God" (21:
2; see also 3:12; 21:10); of St. Paul, who refers to "the Jerusalem above" (Gal.
4:26); and of the Letter to the Hebrews, which talks of "the heavenly Jerusalem" (12:22). For the influence that the earthly city itself might have had
on Christian worship, we must turn our attention instead to Christian pilgrimages to Palestine from the fourth century onwards.

Even if the phenomenon of pilgrimage was not initiated by the emperor
Constantine's attention to the holy places,[2] what had previously been no more
than a trickle of pilgrims had certainly turned into a flood after the identification and building of shrines at the sacred sites associated with Old and New
Testament events. Nor were the monastic guardians of these places slow to
respond to the devotional needs of those who visited them. A pilgrimage-diary
of the late fourth century, usually attributed to a nun from France or Spain
named Egeria, tells how at various biblical sites at which her party stopped
there was a short act of worship, which normally included an appropriate psalm
and reading as well as prayer.[3] While it is possible that these liturgies were
composed and conducted by those leading the particular pilgrimage group—
some sort of early ecclesiastical tour guides—it seems more likely that they
were "staged" by the resident religious community in each place in order to
provide a suitable means for the visitors to express their piety.

If this was true of such sites as Mount Sinai and Jacob's Well, how much
more would it have been of Jerusalem itself? Once again, Egeria's description
suggests that the core liturgical practices of the Holy City had been expanded

to include appropriate devotional stations at the sacred places within it, some on a daily or weekly basis, others on annual occasions particularly associated with them. So, for example, every day in the year, after the celebration of evening prayer in the Anastasis, the worshipping community went in procession to the site of the crucifixion, where a further short act of worship was led by the bishop.[4]

In the light of both the popularity of pilgrimages to the Holy Land and the prestige which Jerusalem enjoyed as the cradle of Christianity among the other churches in the ancient world, it is not at all surprising to find that many of its liturgical practices were imitated by Christian communities elsewhere. This is particularly well exemplified by the liturgy of the city of Constantinople, a liturgy which eventually became the basis of the standard practice of eastern Orthodox Christians. It is important to remember that this city only became an important center in the ancient world after Constantine expanded it in the fourth century. It therefore had no significant Christian community resident there prior to that time, and so possessed no ancient indigenous liturgical traditions. Hence, it was forced to borrow from elsewhere, and two of the principal sources of its later practices are the churches of Antioch and Jerusalem. Often practices derived from both these traditions were absorbed into a single rite, rather than just one or the other being selected, a process which resulted in much duplication.[5]

Whilst borrowing from Jerusalem may not have been quite as extensive elsewhere, various elements from the liturgy of the Holy City nevertheless found their way into the practices of Christians throughout the ancient world. One example would be the widespread adoption of the Sunday "cathedral"[6] vigil. This was a gathering which took place very early every Sunday morning throughout the year, and consisted of a series of psalms and prayers followed by a reading of the account of the death and resurrection of Jesus from one of the four canonical gospels. Although there is evidence for the existence of this ritual in the late fourth century in Antioch as well as Jerusalem, there can be little doubt that its true place of origin was Jerusalem, where the celebration took place at the very hour and in the very spot—the Anastasis—where the resurrection of Jesus was believed to have happened. This office forms a part of the regular Sunday services of all later eastern rites, and although it was not preserved in full in the West, traces of it can be seen in some traditions, suggesting that there, too, it once had a more prominent place.[7]

The imitation of Hagiopolite customs by other churches is particularly evident with regard to practices connected with different occasions in the liturgical year. A very good example is the midnight mass of Christmas, copied throughout the Christian world. Although it is true that this was originally celebrated in Bethlehem rather than Jerusalem, representatives of the Jerusalem church always went down to Bethlehem for the occasion. Here the nativity of Jesus was commemorated on the 6th January, rather than the 25th December as at Rome, and it began with a service in the late afternoon of the 5th January at the site where the angels were believed to have appeared to the shepherds in the fields to announce the birth of the Savior. The worshippers then moved on to the cave of the nativity to keep a vigil until midnight, when the Eucharist was celebrated. After this was over, the bishop and monks left for Jerusalem to lead the celebration of the feast there at dawn.[8] Although the full details of this liturgical sequence were not adopted elsewhere, we do find most other churches adding a similar midnight celebration of the Eucharist to their older liturgy of the day for the feast of the nativity. In Rome, of course, and in the other churches which eventually copied its practice, this celebration was on the night of the 24th–25th December rather than of the 5th–6th January.

But above all, the emergence of what western Christians later came to call "Holy Week" and eastern Christians "Great Week"—the attempt to commemorate liturgically the detailed events of the last week of Jesus' life on the particular days on which they were thought to have occurred—has traditionally been thought to have been a fourth-century creation which began in Jerusalem, and has been often attributed to "its liturgically-minded bishop," Cyril.[9] It is certainly true that by the late fourth century, Jerusalem possessed a well-developed series of liturgical practices for this particular time of the year, and that similar practices were found in the later traditions of other churches throughout the ancient world. It is also natural that we should expect them to have originated in Jerusalem itself, where the events of those crucially significant days for Christians could be commemorated at the very sites where they were believed to have taken place, just as the Sunday cathedral vigil and the midnight mass of Christmas appear to have done. However, we need to exercise some caution before assuming that everything we find in the Jerusalem Holy Week liturgy of the fourth century necessarily originated there, or that all later Holy Week practices of other churches were copied from the customs of Jerusalem. The true story appears to be rather more complex than that.

While it is highly likely that some elements of what later became standard Holy Week liturgy in many parts of the world owe their origin to the desire of pilgrims to commemorate the gospel events in the very places and on the very days that they were said to have happened, the leading liturgical scholar R. Taft has demonstrated that such so-called "historicizing" tendencies already existed among Christians long before the fourth century, and that the degree of "historicism" in the fourth-century Jerusalem liturgy can be overstated. No attempt was made, for example, to locate the Holy Thursday liturgy at the supposed site of the Last Supper, nor did the procession through the city early on Good Friday seek to replicate exactly the route taken by Jesus, with detours to the house of Caiaphas or Pilate, but instead went directly to Golgotha.[10] Thus, whatever motivated these liturgical developments, it was obviously not a desire to follow in every single footstep of Jesus in the last days of his life. For that reason, "historicism" may not be the most appropriate expression to use; what the Christians were doing was attaching importance first to time, and then to place, as a means of entering into communion with the Christian mysteries.[11] For this they already had the precedent of the cult of the martyrs, celebrated on the anniversary of the death at the place of burial.

Much more significantly still, the research done by the American scholar T. Talley points to the conclusion that Jerusalem may have been as much an importer of liturgical practices as an exporter at this period, with different groups of pilgrims bringing their own local customs and traditions with them and introducing them into the liturgical cycle of the city, as well as carrying back with them ideas for innovations in the worship of their home churches.

Talley has claimed that some elements of the Jerusalem Holy Week liturgy in this period appear to have been imported from elsewhere rather than being local creations.[12] His case rests on the supposition that the indigenous Jerusalem tradition followed the chronology of the passion and death of Christ recorded in the gospel according to Matthew. And certainly, when one looks at the various gospel readings prescribed in later Jerusalem lectionaries for the different liturgical occasions during this particular season, and to some extent at other times of the year as well, the gospel according to Matthew is the most common choice and seems to form the core of the system of readings.[13]

According to Egeria's description, Holy Week began with the celebration of Lazarus Saturday and Palm Sunday. The first of these commemorates Jesus' raising of Lazarus from the dead just outside the city, in Bethany, an event recorded only in the gospel according to John. Palm Sunday commemorates Jesus' triumphal entry into the city, when the crowds shouted praises and strewed his way with branches pulled from trees, and the Jerusalem church imitated this liturgically by a procession to the city from the Mount of Olives in which the participants carried branches of palm. While this latter event is described in all four canonical gospels, it is assigned to a particular day only in the gospel of John, where it is said to take place five days before the Passover. Thus, Matthew's gospel alone would not have led the Jerusalem church to celebrate the event on this particular day, even though the reading used at the celebration was apparently from that gospel, and hence the selection of the day would have had to come from a Christian community that was following a Johannine chronology of the Passion.

From this evidence Talley concludes that the celebration of Lazarus Saturday and Palm Sunday did not belong to indigenous Jerusalem practice but were brought there from Constantinople which, in turn, derived the observances from Alexandria, where they had originally formed the festal conclusion of the forty-day fast, as they continued to do in Constantinople. While accepting the general outline of Talley's thesis, another American scholar, J. Baldovin, has suggested that it is more likely that Jerusalem inherited the Lazarus Saturday/Palm Sunday tradition directly from Alexandria rather than via Constantinople and that Constantinople itself may have received it from Jerusalem.[14]

Talley also offers another apparent example of liturgical importation during the celebrations of this particular week. Egeria's description of Holy Thursday indicates that there were two celebrations of the Eucharist in Jerusalem on that day. The first took place in the afternoon between 2 p.m. and 4 p.m. in the Martyrium basilica, and the later Jerusalem lectionaries indicate that the theme of the readings was the Last Supper eaten by Jesus with his disciples on the day of the Passover, according to the chronology of Matthew's gospel. The second eucharistic celebration occurred immediately afterwards in the place Egeria describes as "behind the Cross" (*post crucem*). She comments that "on this one day the Offering is made behind the Cross, but on no other day in the whole year" (35, 2).

The existence of this double liturgy has puzzled scholars, since more than one celebration of the Eucharist in a single day would be very unusual in ancient times, although more common in later centuries in the West. Talley, however, has put forward the hypothesis that the second celebration may have been a concession to pilgrims who came from a liturgical tradition that followed the Johannine chronology of the Passion and who wanted a separate eucharistic celebration at the site of the crucifixion on the day and at the hour of Jesus' death according to that chronology.[15] For, while in the other canonical gospels Jesus is said to have celebrated the Passover with his disciples on the night before he died, in John's gospel his death is said to have taken place one day earlier, on the day and at the hour that the Passover lambs were being sacrificed in the Temple.

In support of Talley's general proposition that the Jerusalem Holy Week did not develop as a single integrated whole, but by the piecemeal addition to the local core of elements from other places and differing traditions, we may point to some signs of similar importation in other areas of that city's liturgical practices. For example, the rites of initiation of new converts to the faith as celebrated in late fourth-century Jerusalem included both a threefold credal interrogation of the candidates and also a post-baptismal anointing with oil.[16] Such practices were previously unknown anywhere else in the East, but belonged exclusively to the liturgical traditions of Rome and North Africa. It is true that the details of the anointing as practiced in Jerusalem were not identical with those of these western traditions; as well as the head, as in the West, the Jerusalem anointing also included the ears, nose, and chest. Yet, it is hard to avoid the conclusion that the idea of adding a post-baptismal unction to the rites had been brought there from the West along with the credal interrogation. Similarly, a number of years ago, the British liturgical scholar G. Cuming argued that several features of the Jerusalem eucharistic rite were not those found in Antioch and the rest of the surrounding region, but more closely resembled the practices of Alexandria.[17]

Even the celebration of the paschal triduum (the three-day observance of Good Friday, Holy Saturday, and Easter Day) appears to have roots outside Jerusalem. The earliest Christians kept a single annual festival which commemorated the whole paschal event—the death and resurrection of Jesus—as a unity. At first this took place on the night of the Jewish Passover itself, but later generations of Christians tended to favor the Saturday night following the Passover instead. It was preceded by a day of fasting, but since all Fridays in the year were regular fast days for Christians, the Saturday night–Sunday celebration soon gained a continuous two-day period of preparatory fasting on the preceding Friday and Saturday. However, at first these days were not understood as commemorating particular events connected to the death of Jesus; the whole paschal event was still celebrated in the one unitive feast.[18]

By the middle of the third century, on the other hand, the days had begun to acquire a new significance. A Syrian document known as the *Didascalia Apostolorum*, although cognizant of six days of fasting before the annual feast, stresses the particular importance of the fast on the last two days as recalling, respectively, the crucifixion of Jesus and his sleep in death.[19] A similar development can also be seen in the writings of Origen in Egypt at the same period. He viewed the paschal events as extending over three days, in fulfillment of Hos. 6:2: "Now listen to what the prophet says: 'God will revive us after two days, and on the third day we shall rise and live in his sight'. For us the first day is the passion of the Savior; the second on which he descended into hell; and the third, the day of resurrection."[20]

Although it is unlikely that in either case the days were marked liturgically in any special way, it can be seen that what happened in Jerusalem in the fourth century was not a complete novelty, but merely the natural outcome of this line of thinking. All that Jerusalem was doing by developing special ritual practices on Good Friday was giving concrete liturgical expression to the events that the day was already understood to commemorate at the very sites where they had happened.

It is also questionable how far we should speak of these Jerusalem liturgical practices as really being "imitated" elsewhere. Although some form of liturgical celebration of Good Friday begins to be found in other places before the end of the fourth century, two important facts should be noted. First, this development did not spread rapidly everywhere, as there were some signs of reluctance to make the transition from the single unitive feast. So, for example, while in some cities of northern Italy Easter was focused upon the resurrection of Jesus before the end of the fourth century, with his death being commemorated on Good Friday, in others there was a continuing emphasis on the passion in the celebration of the paschal feast. What made some local churches here adopt Good Friday appears to have been not so much the pressure of returning pilgrims as the assistance that it gave to attempts at the formulation of Christological doctrine; the separation of the commemoration of the death of Jesus from his resurrection helped efforts to distinguish the human and divine aspects of Christ's person.[21]

Second, what actually went on in other parts of the world, and especially in the West, does not closely resemble the particular customs of the Holy City. The Jerusalem liturgy of Good Friday began with the veneration of the supposed cross on which Jesus had been crucified and of other relics. This lasted from 9 a.m. to noon. From noon until 3 p.m. there was a service of biblical readings interspersed with prayers in the courtyard between Golgotha and the Anastasis. Then followed another lengthy service of readings and prayer in the Martyrium basilica—this last having been a feature of every day in Holy Week—and the day's liturgy ended with a commemoration of the burial of Jesus inside the Anastasis, although individuals who were able also kept up a vigil throughout the following night.[22]

While the veneration of the cross captured popular imagination and spread to other churches of the East, no attempt was made to copy every one of the other practices in exact detail throughout the world. Even the dissemination of this particular devotion was impeded at first by the need to obtain a fragment of the true cross from the Jerusalem church. Thus, we hear of public veneration of a remnant of the cross in Antioch on Good Friday, and in Constantinople on the last three days of Holy Week. In Rome, on the other hand, while the Good Friday liturgy from quite early times certainly included readings appropriate to the day, it was otherwise indistinguishable from any Friday in the year, and it is not until the end of the seventh century that there is evidence of the adoption of the veneration of the cross on that day, a development apparently influenced by the practice in Constantinople. The papal liturgy involved an elaborate procession with the relic to the Church of the Holy Cross, its veneration, and then the traditional service of the word followed. It is interesting to note that the ritual directions speak of the arrival at the church as being "in Jerusalem," suggesting that the procession was seen as a symbolic pilgrimage to the Holy City. In other churches in Rome there was no procession, and the veneration followed rather than preceded the service of the word. Later, the ceremony spread throughout the West, with ordinary wooden crosses being used where relics were lacking.[23]

A similar slowness to imitate the Jerusalem traditions in the West can be seen in relation to Palm Sunday. Once again, in Rome the focus of the day was not on Jesus' triumphal entry into Jerusalem, but the principal reading was the account of his passion and death from Matthew's gospel. While the gospel reading in Spain and Gaul included the record of the entry from John's gospel, the primary reason for its selection seems to have been the passage which preceded it, the account of Jesus' anointing by Mary. It was not until the seventh century that the Sunday was called *in palmis* in Rome, and not until the ninth century in France that we encounter a procession with palms like that in Jerusalem; in Rome, which was even more conservative, it does not seem to have been the practice until, perhaps, the eleventh century.[24]

We may conclude this survey, therefore, by agreeing that the city of Jerusalem was certainly an important influence on Christian liturgy throughout the world, but not always through either a simple or rapid imitation of its practices carried home by early pilgrims, as has sometimes been asserted. In part those pilgrims themselves brought practices to Jerusalem, and imitation elsewhere was generally highly selective and often very slow in happening. In reality, the imitation owed as much to the particular doctrinal and pastoral needs of the various local churches as to the prestige enjoyed by the Holy City in the Christian world.

Notes

1. One of the rare exceptions is the eucharistic prayer of the ancient eastern Liturgy of St. James, which intercedes "for your holy places . . . principally for Zion" and for "your holy and royal city," reflecting its origin in the Jerusalem church itself. For an English translation, see R. C. D. Jasper and G. J. Cuming (eds.), *Prayers of the Eucharist: Early and Reformed*[3] (New York, 1987), 94.

2. On this, see J. E. Taylor, *Christians and the Holy Places: The Myth of Jewish-Christian Origins* (Oxford, 1993).

3. For an edition of the text, see P. Maraval (ed.), *Egéria. Journal de voyage*, SC 296 (Paris, 1982); for an English translation, see J. Wilkinson (ed.), *Egeria's Travels* (London, 1971).

4. Egeria, *Itinerarium* 24,7. See P. F. Bradshaw, *Daily Prayer in the Early Church* (London,

1981; New York, 1982), 77–81; J. Mateos, "Quelques anciens documents sur l'office du soir," *OCP* 35 (1969), 347–74.

5. See R. F. Taft, *The Byzantine Rite: A Short History* (Collegeville, 1992); idem, "The Liturgy of the Great Church: An Initial Synthesis of Structure and Interpretation on the Eve of Iconoclasm," *DOP* 34/35 (1980–81), 45–75.

6. "Cathedral" is the standard technical term used to distinguish liturgical gatherings which involved the whole church—bishop, clergy, and people—from those that were primarily monastic in character; it does not mean that they always took place in a cathedral as such.

7. See Bradshaw (above, note 4), 84–87; J. Mateos, "La vigile cathédrale chez Egérie," *OCP* 27 (1961), 281–312; R. Zerfass, *Die Schriftlesung im Kathedraloffizium Jerusalems* (Münster, 1968), 121–27.

8. See J. N. Alexander, *Waiting for the Coming: The Liturgical Meaning of Advent, Christmas, Epiphany* (Washington, D.C., 1993), 80–90.

9. See esp. G. Dix, *The Shape of the Liturgy* (Westminster [London], 1945), 334, 348–53; and also Wilkinson (above, note 3), 54–55; K. Dedden, "Cyrille de Jerusalem et l'année liturgique," *Questions Liturgiques* 56 (1975), 41–46.

10. R. F. Taft, "Historicism Revisited," *Studia Liturgica* 14 (1982), 97–109; reprinted in idem, *Beyond East and West* (Washington, D.C., 1984), 15–30.

11. On the Christian use of space, see further J. F. Baldovin, *The Urban Character of Christian Worship*, Orientalia Christiana Analecta 228 (Rome, 1987).

12. T. J. Talley, *The Origins of the Liturgical Year* (New York, 1986), 176–89, 203–14.

13. For the later Armenian and Georgian lectionaries in use in Jerusalem, see A. Renoux (ed.), *Le Codex Arménien Jérusalem 121*, PO 35/1 and 36/2 (Paris, 1969 and 1971); M. Tarchnischvili (ed.), *Le grand lectionnaire de l'Église de Jérusalem*, CSCO 189 and 205 (Louvain, 1959 and 1960).

14. J. F. Baldovin, "A Lenten Sunday Lectionary in Fourth Century Jerusalem," *Time and Community: Studies in Liturgical History and Theology*, ed. J. N. Alexander (Washington, D.C., 1990), 115–22.

15. Talley (above, note 12), 44–45.

16. Cyril of Jerusalem, *Mystagogical Catecheses* 2 and 3; English translations by E. Yarnold, *The Awe-Inspiring Rites of Initiation* (Slough, 1971), 76 and 79–83.

17. G. J. Cuming, "Egyptian Elements in the Jerusalem Liturgy," *JTS* 25 (1974), 117–24. For an alternative point of view, cf. B. D. Spinks, "The Jerusalem Liturgy of the *Catecheses Mystagogicae*: Syrian or Egyptian?," *Studia Patristica* 18/2 (1989), 391–95.

18. See Talley (above, note 12), 1–27.

19. *Didascalia Apostolorum* 5, 19, 9–10; English translation in S. Brock and M. Vasey, *The Liturgical Portions of the Didascalia*, Grove Liturgical Study 29 (Nottingham, 1982), 28.

20. Origen, *Hom. in Exod.* 5, 2; English translation by R. Cantalamessa, *Easter in the Early Church* (Collegeville, 1993), 55.

21. See M. Connell, "The Liturgical Year in Northern Italy (365–450)," Ph.D. dissertation (University of Notre Dame, 1995), 54–127.

22. Egeria, *Itinerarium* 37.

23. See further P. Regan, "The Veneration of the Cross," *Worship* 52 (1978), 2–13.

24. See P. Jounel, "The Easter Cycle," *The Church at Prayer*, IV, ed. A.-G. Martimort (Collegeville, 1986), 70–71.

18

Jerusalem in the Early Seventh Century: Hopes and Aspirations of Christians and Jews

GÜNTER STEMBERGER

The early seventh century was a period of tumultuous upheaval and revolutionary change for most of the Byzantine empire, but especially for
its East and, above all, for the Holy Land with Jerusalem at its center. The
city changed hands several times within a few decades: in 614, Jerusalem fell
to the Persians and was for some time entrusted by them to Jews;[1] about 617,
the Persian occupants reinstated a Christian administration, and in 628 they
had to surrender their conquests to Heraclius who had besieged Ctesiphon
when the Persian king Chosroes suddenly died. In 630/31, Heraclius brought
the relic of the Holy Cross triumphantly back to Jerusalem, but a few years
later, in 637 or 638, the Christian patriarch of Jerusalem had to hand over
the keys of the city to Arab conquerors who were to rule the country for
centuries to come.

These events gave most participants the impression of living at the end of
times and provoked a wave of apocalyptic writings in which Jerusalem played
a central role. Christians could, at first, hope that these events were only
temporary setbacks; only a few decades later they realized the real impact of
the events. Palestinian Jews, on the other hand, recognized immediately how
extraordinary the events were to which they were witnesses. Fortunately, we
have quite a number of literary sources, some of them contemporary, others
much later or at least less easily dated, which offer us enough information for
an analysis of Jewish and Christian reactions to these events.

On the Jewish side, the outstanding documents are Sefer Zerubbabel, several *piyyutim* by Eleazar ha-Qallir (most important among them is a *silluq*,
published by E. Fleischer) or attributed to him, and some midrashic texts
which, although not easily dated (chapters 28 and 30 of Pirqe de Rabbi Eliezer,[2] perhaps also Pesiqta Rabbati 34–37,[3] etc.), have been used in the history

of research. On the Christian side, we have the writings of Strategius and Sophronius, some hints in the Doctrina Jacobi[4] with its quite extraordinary apocalyptic mood, and, above all, a number of Syriac apocalyptic texts, the most important of which is the apocalypse of Pseudo-Methodius. In order to capture the spirit of the period, some of these texts will be analyzed separately and then briefly compared with each other in search of common elements of interpretation of this revolutionary period.

CHRISTIAN SOURCES

The Capture of Jerusalem by Strategius

(Antiochus) Strategius, also known as Eustratius,[5] a monk of Mar Saba, was an eyewitness of the Persian conquest of Jerusalem and the events which followed it. The Greek original of his description, the *Expugnatio* (or: *Devastatio*) *Hierosolymae*, is almost completely lost, but a Georgian and four Arab versions survive.[6] In this context, the main point of interest is not so much the historical facts he describes (or the legendary material his account includes) as their interpretation.

Strategius laments the fate of "Jerusalem, the city of Jesus Christ, the son of David, the son of Abraham, the city of God, Jerusalem." This introduction seems to emphasize the biblical heritage of Christianity and, above all, of the Christian city of Jerusalem. But the author continues and explicitly rejects weeping over the Jewish Temple, over the priests who killed the prophets, over those who crucified Jesus: "they only received what they deserved" (1, 12–16; the passage is missing in Version D). He thus contrasts the Persian conquest of the Christian city of Jerusalem with the destruction of Jewish Jerusalem, not only the fall of Jerusalem to the Babylonians in 586 B.C.E.,[7] but even more so with the conquest of the city by Titus in 70.

As in 70, so also in 614 did a number of *omina* announce God's withdrawal from the city: monks saw angels standing on the walls of Jerusalem with fiery spears in their hands. At first they rejoiced, believing that the angels were there to protect the city (5, 28f.); but then they saw another angel descending from heaven, telling the angels to depart because God himself would throw fire on the city and hand it over to the enemies (5, 31f.). Another monk saw Christ on the Cross who did not accept his supplications, but rather turned his head away (6; the versions differ regarding the details of this vision).

Time and again, the author insists that the sins of the inhabitants of the city are responsible for the great catastrophe. Jerusalem is condemned because of the crimes of the circus parties: they are the main reason that Jerusalem's condemnation as pronounced in Ezek. 16 is now to be fulfilled (2, 2–8); the depravation of the priests and the people in general produce a stench which only fire and sword can purify (7, 9–11).

The Persians forced their way into the city, killing all the Christians they found while destroying and razing churches. Then heavenly Jerusalem wept over earthly Jerusalem (8, 9), but to no avail. The sun was covered with darkness as at Jesus' crucifixion (8, 10).

Only now Jews enter the story as told by Strategius; where they come from—whether they had already lived in Jerusalem, entered the city together with the Persians, or had come after them, he does not say. "Cursed Jews" tell the Persians that many Christians are still hidden in cisterns and caves. Deceived by a proclamation of peace, they come out of their hiding places and are made prisoners, guarded by Jews in the pool of Mamilla (9). Only Version C mentions Jews at this stage, whereas the Georgian and the other Arab versions have the Jews come on the scene only when the Christians were already confined in the pool. Strategius says that the Jews had an excellent standing with the Persian king and came to the pool to tell the Christians that everybody who would convert to Judaism would be redeemed from the Persians (10, 2); but the Christians preferred martyrdom to the prospect of being thrown into the fire of hell together with the Jews (this last part appears only in Version D). The furious Jews then bought many of the captives from the Persians and slaughtered them like sacrificial lambs (10, 6). Version C gives the precise number of Christian martyrs: 4518 Christians were killed by the Jews on May 20th, the day of the destruction of Jerusalem. All texts agree that while the Persians led the remaining Christian captives, together with the patriarch Zachariah, out of the city, the Jews began destroying and setting fire to the Christian churches (10, 9).

We shall not deal here with the historical question of Jewish participation in the conquest and devastation of Jerusalem, and the massacre of its population, nor with the question of the real measure of destruction;[8] to say the least, the accounts are highly exaggerated and dictated by typological rather than historical interests. The author—or those who later revised his text— evidently intended to underline that it was not so much the Persians, but rather the Jews who were responsible for the destruction of the Christian city and the killing of Christians, as they had been responsible for Christ's death.

This typological interest is again evident in the scene where the patriarch Zachariah bids farewell to Jerusalem. Having crossed the Qidron Valley and gone up to the Mount of Olives, the patriarch who is to be deported into Persian captivity with most of the Christian community of Jerusalem stops to get a last glimpse of the burning city. He wishes peace for "Jerusalem, Golgotha, Sion (Bethlehem: not in Version D), Gethsemane, and all the holy places" (15, 4–5), and recites Ps. 137:5: "If I forget you, Jerusalem, let my right hand wither. . . ." R. Wilken has pointed out the parallel with David's farewell to Jerusalem which he had to leave in Absalom's revolt (II Sam. 15).[9] Another parallel which comes to one's mind is Christ weeping on the Mount of Olives over the fate of Jerusalem (Luke 19:41–44; see also 21:20–24).

Having arrived at "the river of Babylon" (18, 8), Zachariah is reminded of the first Babylonian captivity and explicitly compares what had happened in the time of Moses (!) to what was happening now, in the time of Christ's disciples (18, 9). He again recites Ps. 137, recalling the fate of Jerusalem's holy places, the Holy Sepulchre, and the Anastasis. And again, in the letter which he writes from Persia to the renewed Christian community in Jerusalem,[10] the patriarch recalls Sion, the Anastasis, Gethsemane, Mary's Tomb, Bethlehem, the holy places, all the monasteries and their inhabitants—exclusively Christian points of interest (22, 30–32); in spite of understanding his fate in line with Israel's Babylonian captivity, no memories of the biblical tradition connected with the holy city come to his mind.

A few years later, when the emperor Heraclius returned the relic of the Holy Cross to Jerusalem and provided for the funding of the repair of the Holy Sepulchre in Jerusalem (some reconstruction had taken place when Jerusalem was still under Persian occupation), it seemed to Strategius that Jerusalem was to be reinstated to her former glory once the divinely ordained punishment of her inhabitants was over.

Sophronius of Jerusalem

The reaction to the catastrophe is not very different in Sophronius' poems. This monk had left his monastery, St. Theodosius on the outskirts of Jerusalem, together with his mentor John Moschus, already at the first signs of the impending catastrophe: in 603 they departed for Egypt, and later for Rome, where John Moschus died. Sophronius brought his friend's body for burial to St.Theodosius in 619, but left Jerusalem again in 628 for Africa; when he returned in 633, he was elected patriarch of Jerusalem, a position he still held when negotiating surrender to the Arabs.[11]

In poem 14, Sophronius describes how Jerusalem was conquered by the Persians. Not having been an eyewitness, he does not give any details. Contrary to Strategius, he does not blame the inhabitants of Jerusalem. He does not interpret the fall of the city as a punishment for the sins of the Christians; he even emphasizes the holiness of so many people who gave up their homes, left their cities and families (lines 33–36), and came to the city of Jerusalem as if it were the celestial pole, living like angels on earth (53–54). The Persian king is thus not sent by God—he is a demon, driven by his furious folly, to destroy cities holy to God (25–27) and to burn down the holy places of Christ, together with his friends, the Jews (62). Sophronius, therefore, feels entitled to ask God for vengeance: "O Christ, let us soon see Persia burning in exchange for the conflagration of the holy places" (73–74).

A few years later, while Sophronius was still out of the country, he wrote a poem (no. 18) in honor of the return of the Holy Cross to Jerusalem: "The time of the lawless people is past . . . the cloud of the godless people has gone" (1–3). Astonishingly, Sophronius now contradicts his former interpretation: the Persian conqueror took Jerusalem because of God's wrath (25) and because Christ led him to despoil his own city (31f.).[12] Driven by God, he drowned the whole city in a torrent of fire (35f.). But he then overstepped his command; taking the wood of the Cross to Persia (37), the conqueror caused his own downfall: "When the Parthian country saw the divine wood (of the Cross), it killed Chosroes, the Persian king" (53–55). Sophronius was convinced that now, since the Holy Cross had returned to Jerusalem, "the insult of the lawless Jews has been turned on their own heads" (85f.) and a lasting peace had come (11f.). Written a little later, when Sophronius was temporarily away from Jerusalem, poem 20 expresses his longing for Jerusalem with her earthly monuments, above all the rock, the navel of the world (29f.), on which the Cross stood. It is as if nothing had happened.

Pseudo-Methodius

There are only a few passages in Sophronius that might be interpreted as expressions of a feeling to live at the end of history. The hymn of the return of the Cross to Jerusalem comes closest to it. We have to look to a slightly later text, Pseudo-Methodius, to find a completely eschatological reading of these and the following events. The advent of Arab rule led an eastern Christian writer, living in formerly Persian, now Arab, territory, to compose an apocalypse in Syriac (differently dated to the period between ca. 644 and 692, now most commonly to the end of this period) which soon became highly influential and was subsequently translated into Greek and Latin.[13]

In this text, the stage for the final war at the end of history is set in the last—the seventh—millennium: since the Greeks "devastated the kingdom of the Hebrews and of the Persians, they too will be devastated at Gab'ot by Ishmael, 'the wild ass of the desert', who will be sent in the fury of wrath against mankind" (XI, 3). Many Christians will then give up their faith (XII, 3), "the Divine Office and the Living Sacrifice will come to an end in the Church" (XIII, 1). But when the crisis has reached its climax, "the king of the Greeks shall go out against them in great wrath. . . . And the sons of the kings of the Greeks will descend upon them . . . and finish off with the sword the remnant left over from them in the Promised Land" (XIII, 11). A period of peace is to follow in which "the king of the Greeks will come down and reside in Jerusalem for one week and a half of a week, ten and a half years in number [cf. Dan. 7:25; 9:27]. Then the Son of Perdition shall appear, the False Messiah. He will be conceived and born in Chorazin, brought up in Bethsaida, and he will reign in Capernaum" (XIII, 21–XIV, 1). The places are those cursed by Jesus because of the unwillingness of their inhabitants to believe in him (cf. Luke 10:13–15). Being close to the rabbinic center, Tiberias, they of course also point to contemporary Judaism; is it only a coincidence that, according to Sefer Zerubbabel, the Messiah Son of Ephraim shall be born in Rakkath, i.e., Tiberias?

This is the decisive turning point in history: at the appearance of the Son of Perdition, "the king of the Greeks shall go up and stand on Golgotha and the Holy Cross shall be placed on that spot where it had been fixed when it bore Christ. The king of the Greeks shall place his crown on the top of the Holy Cross . . . and hand over the kingdom to God the Father. And the Holy Cross . . . will be raised up to heaven, together with the royal crown" (XIV, 2–4). The restoration of the Holy Cross to Jerusalem by Heraclius is not explicitly mentioned, but it is to be understood as central to the scene when all earthly rule comes to its end. Then the Son of Perdition will be revealed: He "will enter Jerusalem and take his seat in God's Temple, acting as if he were God [cf. II Thess. 2:4]. . . . But at the Advent of our Lord from heaven he will be delivered to the 'Gehenna of Fire' and to 'outer darkness' " (XIV, 10–13).

There are many problems in the interpretation of Pseudo-Methodius which have to be left to specialists of Christian-Syriac apocalypticism. The important element in our context, however, is clear: the consummation of history is to take place in Jerusalem. Jerusalem is the city where the last Christian emperor hands over his dominion to God; Jerusalem's Temple is the place where Satan's representative on earth challenges God's rule, but is thrown out by God or the returning Christ. It is the city of David, and not the new Rome, where all earthly kingship ends and God will be king over the whole earth.

There is some debate whether Pseudo-Methodius is to be interpreted within the tradition of Jewish apocalypticism or not. P. J. Alexander has most forcefully argued

> that the expectation of a Last Roman Emperor derived from the Jewish (post-canonical) national hope for a Messiah, an anointed king of the Jews who would free the Jewish people from the oppression by foreign

powers. Indeed, as one compares the details of the Byzantine expectation with the corresponding Jewish material, one finds that so far as the basic features are concerned, the agreements in content, and sometimes also in literary and linguistic form, are so striking that they cannot possibly be accidental.[14]

Others have emphasized, however, that these seemingly Jewish features derive from the Syriac Christian tradition (above all, the Cave of Treasures) and that the emphasis on Jerusalem is to be understood as a "reaction to ʿAbd al-Malik's foundation of the Dome of the Rock on the site of the Jewish Temple" interpreted in light of what Julian the Apostate had done.[15] Wherever the direct inspiration of the author may have come from, it seems clear that Jewish tradition—at whatsoever point it entered the stream of Christian apocalypticism—was of great importance in the further development of the apocalyptic tradition. Even if there was no direct Jewish influence on Pseudo-Methodius, it is intriguing to read his work, at least to some extent, as a Christian answer (or, to remain more neutral, a Christian parallel) to Jewish apocalyptic interpretations of the events of this century.

JEWISH TEXTS

Jewish texts are, as is to be expected, even more focused on Jerusalem and very eager to interpret the turmoil of these decades as signs of the imminent end. Sefer Zerubbabel, Sefer Eliyahu, and three *piyyutim* are closely related to each other and follow the same eschatological scheme, although they seem to reflect different stages of the historical events.

Sefer Zerubbabel

This apocalypse, ascribed to Zerubbabel, one of the Jewish leaders at the return from the Babylonian exile, is known in several different versions; there is no critical edition (given the state of the textual tradition, one may even doubt how such an edition could be realized).[16] I. Lévi was able to prove that this apocalypse, dated by earlier authors to the time of the crusades, was written in the context of the Persian rule over Jerusalem and the years afterwards. The main clue to solving the riddle of the apocalypse was the list of the last ten kings who rule the nations: the ninth king is Shiroi, king of Persia, the tenth Armilus, the son of Satan, born of a statue of stone (p. 80). The only Persian king of this name is Shīrūya who, after the death of his father Chosroes, ascended to the throne as Kavad II. He negotiated the peace treaty with Heraclius, who is to be identified with the Armilus (Romulus) of the apocalypse. The text (agreeing with rabbinic tradition) says that the Second Temple will be destroyed after 420 years; 990 years later the redemption will come (p. 76). Contrary to the manuscripts, when we count the 990 years from the building of the Second Temple, and not from its destruction, we arrive at 638 which fits well the general scheme of the apocalypse.

The details given in the apocalypse for the events in the years before the expected coming of the redemption lack any precision and are too confusing to be used in an historical reconstruction. Only with difficulty can its allusions be pieced together with information we have from other sources. Nehemiah ben Ḥushiel, the warrior messiah from the house of Joseph, is to bring all Israel to Jerusalem where they will offer sacrifices to the Lord. But then the Persian king will come to wage war against Jerusalem (p. 78) and Nehemiah will be killed, his body left without burial before the gates of Jerusalem (p. 81). Armilus will extend his rule over the whole earth; he will build seven altars of stone in the form of a woman from which he was borne, and everybody will venerate it (p. 82; evidently an allusion to the veneration of Jesus' mother, Mary).

In this final affliction, the Davidic messiah, Menaḥem ben Ammiel will appear, Nehemiah will rise from the dead and, together with the prophet Elijah, they shall lead the whole people of Israel to Jerusalem, rebuild the city, renew the sacrifices, and then go out to the Mount of Olives where God is to reveal himself (p. 84).

In a kind of appendix, the apocalypse sums up the signs of the end in their temporal sequence in the last week of years (which seems to begin, not to end, with the year 990 after the destruction of Jerusalem). In the last year of this week, Menaḥem ben Ammiel will kill Armilus with the breath of his mouth (cf. Isa. 11:4), but the final battle against the forces of Gog and Magog will be led by God himself (pp. 85–88).

This is not the place to go into details of the text (as, for example, the role of Ḥeftzibah, the mother of the Davidic messiah, as opposed to Armilus' mother, or the origins of the Messiah and the Antichrist in comparison with what Pseudo-Methodius has to say). Sefer Zerubbabel does not even mention the Persian conquest of Jerusalem at the beginning of the series of events; the Jewish leader is said to have taken Jerusalem (without a war) on his own. The renewal of some form of sacrifices after 614 is frequently taken as an historical fact;[17] this is not impossible, but the text may quite as well just take up what is said about Zerubbabel in Ezra 3:2–6. What the apocalypse depicts as the Persian war against Jerusalem probably corresponds to the reversal of Jewish fortunes in Jerusalem about 617, when the Jewish leader—here symbolically named Nehemiah—was deposed and, so it seems, executed. The atmosphere in the short period of renewed Christian rule is well described, and one may easily understand the heightened messianic expectations of many Jews when the attacks of the Arab troops were to bring to an end centuries of Christian rule over Palestine. But, once again, one must know the history of these years (details of which have been reconstructed on the basis of this apocalypse!) in order to make full sense of this text. One has to remain conscious of this vicious circle. In any case, if this apocalypse (at least in an early version) was written in these decades, it certainly captures well the general atmosphere of these years and the excitement of the Jewish population.

Eleazar ha-Qallir

L. Zunz had already pointed to parallels between a poem by ha-Qallir and Sefer Zerubbabel.[18] What they really meant, however, was discovered only much later. A *piyyut* found among the texts of the Genizah, published and interpreted by E. Fleischer,[19] clearly presupposes Sefer Zerubbabel. Fleischer dates the *piyyut* because of the events described in it (the Arabs are not yet seen as the new power) to the years between 629 and 634. Whereas the apocalypse seems to have been frequently altered and adapted to new circumstances, the *piyyut*—because of its form and the mode of transmission of poetical texts—is not likely to have been tampered with and adapted to later conditions.

In this *piyyut*, ha-Qallir expresses his conviction that the time has come to rebuke the "beast of the forest," Rome, at the hands of the Messiah (the "red one") and Elijah, the "hairy one" (1–5). "[And Ass]ur will come over her [the beast], and will plant its tabernacle in her territory [cf. Dan. 11:45] . . . All her judges will be put to shame and all her idols exposed to contempt" (8–12). These words sound very general; that the Persian conquest of Jerusalem is alluded to becomes clear from what follows:

> And the holy people will have some repose because Assur allows them to found the holy Temple; and they will build there a holy altar and offer sacrifices on it. But they will not be able to erect the sanctuary because the 'staff from the holy stump' has not yet come (16–21).

This is the first really clear testimony we have that the Persians allowed the Jews to renew the Temple, and that an altar was built and sacrifices were offered on it. But this restoration of the cult was not completed because the Davidic Messiah had not yet appeared. At first, the "the strength of the head"

(22; cf. Ps. 60:9: "Efraim is the strength of my head"), i.e., the Messiah ben Joseph, had to come, as did the Jewish leader of Jerusalem during the Persian occupation: "He will be set up as officer and head—within three months he will reach the top" (24–25). Not much later, however, the Persian chief officer[20] killed him in the small sanctuary and the Jewish people mourned him as the "Anointed One for the War" who had perished (26–30).

Then arises the enemy, the "headstone," the small horn which arose among the ten horns (Dan. 7:7) and brings destruction on the holy people; his name is [Armal]ios (32–39). He erects an idol in his name, and whoever does not bow to him will be destroyed (41–44). But then, so the poet hopes, comes the Messiah ben David (92–96). He will awaken the slain Messiah ben Joseph (97) and the three Fathers of Israel (101) from the dead; both messiahs will cooperate in complete harmony under God's rule.

The second part of the *piyyut* (113ff.), published by Fleischer from another manuscript, returns to an earlier stage of the eschatological events. Here, the poet dreams of the punishment meted out to Israel's enemies, corresponding exactly to what the had done to Israel: "they ploughed Zion as a field; therefore they will be destroyed by a fire, ploughing their backs" (190f.); they will receive their punishment because they made Jerusalem a ruin (192), destroyed the Temple and caused the end of the morning sacrifice (196), burnt down the Holy of Holies, etc.: the main emphasis is on what they had done to Jerusalem and its Temple.

In the following lines, the poet describes the ingathering of all the Israelites to the Holy Land and the Temple Mount (228), the rebuilding of the Holy City, surrounded by a wall of fire and that of God's glory (234f.). Then, Jerusalem will greatly expand: the three holy mountains (Carmel, Tabor, Sinai) will come and form the base of the Temple; the City's territory will be expanded and reach until Damascus, in order to fulfill Cant. 7:5: "your nose is like a tower of Lebanon, overlooking Damascus," and Zech. 9:1: "Damascus is his resting place."

This tradition, which in Sefer Zerubbabel is mentioned only briefly (p. 85; but here five mountains are named: Lebanon, Moriah, Tabor, Carmel and Hermon), is first attested in Sifre–Deuteronomy 1 and taken up in Pesiqta de-Rav Kahana 20, Pesiqta Rabbati 21, 6, Song of Songs Rabbah 7, 11, and Tanḥuma, Tzav, 12 (ed. S. Buber, §16, p. 20). This tradition is based on a material reading of biblical poetry. Most of the texts regarding the eschatological expansion of Jerusalem are to be found in later midrashim (Sifre–Deuteronomy is the only early text of any importance) and in the Bavli, but never in the Yerushalmi. These traditions are drawn together in a systematic way in the eschatological midrashim and related *piyyutim*.

In its final part (246ff.), the *piyyut* describes how the holy people of Israel, with the Messiah at their head, enter the city. God himself comes (251) and the gates of the Temple are opened (Zech. 14) to receive the holy ark (253f.). God will rule in Jerusalem forever (268), David will be *Nasi* and his throne will stand forever in the Temple which was prepared before the world existed (272–275). Sacrifices are mentioned only in the first stage of the restoration, in the beginning of the Persian rule, but once the full redemption has come, there will be no more sacrifices since the Temple is to be a spiritual center.

The *piyyut* is generally very close to what we know from Sefer Zerubbabel; it does not give the names of the two messianic figures, nor does it mention the mother of the Messiah. The symbolic names of the two messiahs are, however, to be found in another *piyyut* attributed to Qallir, the one which Zunz already compared with Sefer Zerubbabel. Here, the poet enumerates the events of the months of the year which brings the final redemption, beginning with the appearance of Menahem ben Ammiel in Nisan and ending with Adar, when (Elijah) the Tishbite, Menahem, and Nehemiah will be together in the rebuilt Jerusalem and everybody praises God. A number of motifs known from Sefer Zerubbabel and other texts reappear in this *piyyut* which, however, does not contribute anything new and, above all, is completely timeless, giving no hint to the historical context in which it might have been composed.

More important is another *piyyut*— *Oto ha-yom*—which is also attributed to Qallir. Parts of it have been known for long; the full text has been found in the Genizah and published by J. Yahalom.[21] This text clearly situates the messianic hope in history: the king of the West (Byzantium) makes war against the king of the East (Persia) and remains victorious; but then a king from Arabia (Yoqtan) comes forth, puts up his camps in the country, and fights against the Romans in the plain of Akko. The Jews leave Jerusalem (Qiryah) and fast for forty days; then their messiah will be revealed. As Yahalom points out, the historical setting of this first part of the poem is in the early years of the Arab invasion, just before the capitulation of Jerusalem. Now, so the poet hopes, the visions of Sefer Zerubbabel will be realized. He quotes explicitly (32–33: "And there will come the vision of the son of Shealtiel which God had let him see"), as well as paraphrases and elaborates upon in the second part of his poem, which focuses on Jerusalem. In this part, he names Heftzibah and Menahem ben Ammiel, but not Nehemiah: Menahem is identified with the Messiah ben Joseph who will be killed by Heramlios,[22] but brought to life again by the Davidic messiah (46–55). The poem ends with the description of the eschatological expansion of Jerusalem and a string of biblical verses praising the holy city.

SUMMARY

No Christian text dealing with the Persian conquest of Jerusalem interprets it in a clearly eschatological key. Sophronius' hymn to the Holy Cross, written when the imminent danger was over, comes closest to such a reading. Jewish texts, on the other hand, immediately interpret the Persian victory as a decisive sign of the imminent end, following the maxim attributed to Simeon ben Yohai: "If you see a Persian horse tethered in Eretz Israel look out for the feet of the Messiah" (Lamentations Rabbah 1, 41; Song of Songs Rabbah 8, 9). The subsequent setbacks were not seen as indicating the incorrectness of this interpretation, but rather as facts which had to be built into the scenario which proved to be more complicated than at first foreseen. This may be the main reason for the seemingly irrational structure of several of these texts. But the earliest Christian text which unequivocally gives an apocalyptic interpretation of the events of this century, Pseudo-Methodius, is no less embarrassing in its structure and may point to a longer prehistory of this interpretation than we can document today.

Notes

1. A. Cameron ("The Jews in Seventh-Century Palestine," *SCI* 13 [1994], 75–93, 79–80) hesitates to accept this tradition because of the bias of the Christian sources, but Jewish sources also seem to corroborate this.

2. A. H. Silver, *A History of Messianic Speculation in Israel* (Boston, 1959), 37–42.

3. B. J. Bamberger, "A Messianic Document of the Seventh Century," *HUCA* 15 (1940), 425–31.

4. New edition and discussion of the text: G. Dagron and V. Déroche, "Juifs et Chrétiens dans l'Orient du VIIe siècle," *Travaux et Mémoires* 11 (1991), 17–274; see also D. M. Olster, *Roman Defeat, Christian Response, and the Literary Construction of the Jew* (Philadelphia, 1994), 158–79.

5. Some distinguish Antiochus, the author of the *Epistula ad Eustathium* and a number of homilies (*PG* 89) from the author of the *Capture of Jerusalem*, called Strategius in the Georgian version and Eustratius in the Arab versions.

6. They have been edited by G. Garitte, CSCO 202–203 (Georgian version and Latin translation), 340–41, 347–48 (four Arab versions and a Latin translation; Louvain, 1960, 1973–74. The versions differ in their presentation of the Jews and other details, and deserve a special analysis. We generally follow the Arab Version C (Sinaiticus), and point only to significant differences in the other versions.

7. This parallel is shown in detail by R. L. Wilken, *The Land Called Holy* (New Haven and London, 1992), 220, 325–26.

8. Archaeological evidence is not as clear as one might wish. The measure of destruction seems to have been much smaller than suggested by the literary sources. See J. Magness, "A

Reexamination of the Archaeological Evidence for the Sasanian Persian Destruction of the Tyropoeon Valley," *BASOR* 287 (1992), 67–74; K. Bieberstein, "Der Gesandtenaustausch zwischen Karł dem Großen und Harun ar-Rašid und seine Bedeutung für die Kirchen Jerusalems," *ZDPV* 109 (1993), 152–73, 157: the devastation of only three churches—Anastasis, Hagia Sion and Ascension—is certain, that of St. Mary's at Bethesda at least credible. In excavations carried out in 1989–93 on Mamilla Street, a mass grave was discovered which is to be dated to the Persian conquest; a Greek mosaic inscription commemorates "those whose names are known to the Lord,", i.e., unidentified people who have been buried there; see R. Reich, E. Shukrun and Y. Bilig, "Jerusalem, Mamilla Area," *ESI* 10 (1992), 24–25; R. Reich and E. Shukrun, "Jerusalem, Mamilla," ibid., 14 (1995), 92–96; R. Reich, "The Cemetery in the Mamilla Area of Jerusalem," *Qadmoniot* 26 (1993), 103–109 (Hebrew).

9. Wilken (above, note 7), 223.

10. A Greek version of the letter has survived: *PG* 86, 2, 3227–34.

11. Ch. von Schönborn, *Sophrone de Jérusalem*, Théologie Historique 20 (Paris, 1972). Edition of his poems: *Sophronii anacreontica*, ed. M. Gigante, Coll. Opuscula (Rome, 1957).

12. Contrary to his view of the Persian conquest, Sophronius interprets the invasion of the Saracens from the very beginning as a punishment for the sins of the Christians, see D. M. Olster (above, note 4), 101–108.

13. *Die Syrische Apokalypse des Pseudo-Methodius*, ed. G. J. Reinink, CSCO 540–541 (Louvain, 1993). English trans.: P. J. Alexander, *The Byzantine Apocalyptic Tradition* (Berkeley, 1985), 36–51. I follow S. Brock's translation (only the second half) in A. Palmer, S. Brock and R. Hoyland, *The Seventh Century in the West-Syrian Chronicles* (Liverpool, 1993), 230–42.

14. P. J. Alexander (above, note 13), 151–84, quotations 175–76.

15. G. J. Reinink, "Ps.-Methodius: A Concept of History in Response to the Rise of Islam," *The Byzantine and Early Islamic Near East.*, I: *Problems in the Literary Source Material*, eds. A. Cameron and L. I. Conrad (Princeton, 1992), 149–187, quotation 185.

16. The text most frequently quoted is Y. Even-Shmuel, *Midreshei Ge'ulah²* (Jerusalem, 1954), 71–88; but it freely rearranges the order of the text and emends it. The page numbers given refer to his text. Other editions: A. Jellinek, *Bet ha-Midrasch²* (Jerusalem, 1938) II, 54–57; S. A. Wertheimer, *Batei Midrashot²* (Jerusalem, 1968), 497–505; I. Lévi, *Le Ravissement du Messie à sa naissance et autres essais*, ed. E. Patlagean (Paris, 1994), 175-88 (reprint from *REJ* 68 [1918]).

17. M. Avi-Yonah, *The Jews under Roman and Byzantine Rule* (Jerusalem, 1984), 266: "Apparently Temple services were resumed for the third time after the destruction of the Temple, following previous efforts under Bar Kokhba and Julian."

18. L. Zunz, *Literaturgeschichte der synagogalen Poesie* (Berlin, 1865; reprint Hildesheim, 1966), 31.605–606. The *piyyut* for the Ninth of Av is to be found in the Roman Maḥzor, as well as in Even-Shmuel (above, note 16), 113–16.

19. E. Fleischer, "Solving the Qilliri Riddle," *Tarbiz* 54 (1984-85), 383–42.

20. Another manuscript introduces a little change in the text which makes the "headstone" (Zech. 4:7), i.e., Armilus, the one who kills the Jewish leader; ibid., 401–402.

21. J. Yahalom, "On the Validity of Literary Works as Historical Sources," *Cathedra* 11 (1979), 125–33 (Hebrew).

22. Yahalom (ibid., 129) points out that this form of the name Armilus is a play on the name of Heraclius, who is designated as a *herma*, a statue of stone, thus alluding to the story of his birth from a statue in the form of a woman.

· IV ·

JERUSALEM
IN THE EARLY
MIDDLE AGES

19

Space and Holiness
in Medieval Jerusalem[1]

OLEG GRABAR

The usual way in which medieval Jerusalem is reconstructed and explained is both simple and logical. Leaving aside for the moment the imperial Roman paganism which ruled the city between 70 C.E. and the fourth century, three systems of religious beliefs and practices—Jewish, Christian, and Muslim, each with ethnic, social, economic, political, ideological, and linguistic variables—were present and active in the city during the medieval millennium. One of them always dominated, the Christian one from Constantine to the early seventh century and in most of the twelfth, the Muslim one the rest of the time. It is easy to demonstrate that the monumental infrastructure of the city—the Holy Sepulchre and the Nea during the so-called Byzantine Christian rule; the Holy Sepulchre and a host of other churches, few of which have remained, during Latin Christian times; and the Haram al-Sharif and its immediate surroundings in Umayyad, Fatimid, or Mamluk guises under Muslim rule—expressed religious and ideological values and ambitions characteristic of whatever system predominated. Significant Jewish monumental presence appears only in the nineteenth century, partly because Jews were not directly connected to political power since the second century and partly because post-Temple Judaism did not need or require monumental expression until the modern era.

Domination was rarely total in medieval times, except perhaps in the Late Antique Christian town; as a result, it is reasonable and proper to posit, underneath the large constructions and shiny effects sponsored by princes, patriarchs, abbots, and civil or military governors, a daily life of multiple pieties and ethnicities. How these different communities lived and operated is often difficult to imagine for the first half of the Middle Ages, roughly before the Crusades, for the very interesting reason (which is still partly true of the Jerusalem of today) that the communities were (and are) closely connected to their coreligionists or compatriots elsewhere, but not to each other in Jerusalem itself. In most of the sources dealing with Jerusalem, groups other than one's own are hardly ever mentioned, except for occasional complaints about some humiliation or levy imposed by whoever dominated.

Studies on Jerusalem in the Middle Ages have tended to concentrate on five neatly-separated chronological segments—Late Antique or Byzantine, early Islamic, Latin, Ayyubid, Mamluk—or on the three ethno-religious communities and their subdivisions. This is so largely because of the linguistic competencies required to handle these fifteen academic boxes. Original sources on Jerusalem are in eight or nine languages, and secondary literature in at least six additional ones. When one further adds the literary genres of written sources, matters become even more complicated. Inscriptions in Greek, Arabic, Syriac, or Armenian, Genizah fragments in Hebrew or Arabic written with Hebrew characters, travelbooks from many lands endowed with varying degrees of imagination, court documents in Arabic, endless diplomas in Latin, grand chronicles from remote capitals like Cairo, Baghdad, Constantinople, Moscow, or Aachen, locally-sponsored guidebooks, and pious eschatological meditations and proclamations all require awareness of specialized issues and vocabularies and of many other cultural milieux than strictly Palestinian ones. A similarly vast comparative baggage, together with considerable linguistic skills, are required to learn and understand the archaeological and visual data available for Jerusalem in unusually large and varied quantities.

It is indeed nearly impossible to handle all this information and, as a result, the vision we tend to have of medieval Jerusalem (when we actually do try to have one, for the period is remarkably telescoped in most surveys or guidebooks) is that of a relatively small number of discrete periods following each other. In each one, Jews, Christians, and Muslims organized their lives and structured their behavior according to whatever constraints or opportunities affected each one of them. There were unusual moments involving all of the city's inhabitants, as when the emperor Julian returned to paganism in the middle of the fourth century; when out of nowhere Persian invaders arrived around 614 and allegedly sacked the city; when the caliph al-Hakim initiated measures against Christians and Jews which culminated in the looting and destruction of the Holy Sepulchre in 1009, or when Frederic II set up his own peculiar arrangement in a presumably Ayyubid city. Nevertheless, however interesting and important these episodes may be, the overwhelming picture offered of medieval Jerusalem is that of separate religious communities, and the academic result is the ecumenical juxtaposition of the lives and activities of these communities in whatever sequence editors and organizers of symposia have chosen. Compelled in part by the nature and accessibility of sources, this juxtaposition also corresponds to a very peculiar paradox of our own time to cultivate differences without realizing incompatibilities and to feel satisfied with an acknowledgment of variety while maintaining the indivisible unique-ness of one's own faith and nation. This paradox, I shall try to suggest, is deeply embedded in the very fabric of Jerusalem, medieval and probably con-temporary.

Regardless of one's views about the ethics of a scholarship of juxtaposition, even when apparently compelled by the sources and by the limitations of any one scholar, this is not the only way to look at the history of medieval Jeru-salem. In fact, the physical space of the city and the components of its holiness are constant features which are partly independent of the faiths with which they are associated. They defined the city far more consistently than the chang-ing mosaic of men and women, of authority and religion. These factors may, in fact, have shaped the ways of the faiths that came to them. Therein lies what seems to me to be the true originality of Jerusalem: alone among all the cities of God (whoever or whatever the divinity may be) known to be, it is a holy city for three religions, rather than for a single one, that can accommodate an unusual variety of subsets of these three religions. There are a few examples elsewhere of this sort of internal ecumenism.

I will first identify the key components of the space and holiness of Jeru-salem and then give three examples of what could be called the "petrification" or "inlocation" of the holiness, that is to say, the transformation of a priori neutral spaces and stones into holy ones. I will suggest something of the dia-lectic whereby hallowed spaces generate their own holiness which, if evicted, must find a place elsewhere. My examples are medieval, but some of the remarks which follow may have implications for earlier times in the city. I suspect, although I have not studied the matter, that the very nature of Israeli and Palestinian nationalism has been modified by being associated with Je-rusalem, as contemporary emotional allegiances are no less affected by the character of the city than were the old traditional religions.

The key event that created medieval Jerusalem was the destruction of the Herodian city after the two Jewish revolts of the first and second centuries and its transformation into Aelia Capitolina. The following two results en-sued:

1. the Roman military establishment took over and transformed an enclo-sure hugging the ridges of sharply-rising hills into a more or less square walled city with fixed gates, a backbone of regular main streets, parts of which were excavated in the seventies and successfully incorporated into

the contemporary restoration of the Jewish Quarter, and a number of water reservoirs. These walls, gates, reservoirs, and streets have remained the main axes of the city's composition until today. The city included what is known as the "western" hill, a ridge with a succession of high points from Golgotha in the north to Mount Zion in the south; the upper and middle parts of the Tyropoeon Valley; and the eastern hill, strikingly modified by Herod the Great, where the Temple stood at the northern edge of the earliest city. A deep ravine on the eastern side, the Qidron Valley, was used for centuries as a cemetery. Beyond it rose the steep slope of the Mount of Olives, dominating the city and extending one's vision to the Mediterranean or to the Dead Sea. In ways for which there are parallels elsewhere (Montmartre and Montparnasse in Paris, seven hills in Rome, Istanbul, and San Francisco), here, in a strikingly small area, an east-to-west sequence of high ridges and narrow gullies created a daunting setting for any sort of urban design. The genius of the Roman military establishment was to know how to form a coherent quadrilinear space with strong axes wherever it had to show its presence, and it is fascinating to see how that presence has remained in the present configuration of the Old City as well as in a Late Antique representation like the Madeba map, where an irrationally ovoid city totally focused on Christian buildings still identifies Roman imperial walls, gates, and main streets.

The Roman order highlighted for all times (or at least until the city became affected by the modernism of our own times) the physical shape of Jerusalem—both the key natural elements of the landscape, like the high ridges and deep gullies, and the artificial limbs forced on that land-scape, like the flattened Mount Moriah transformed into a huge plat-form. Since there are other imperial examples, Jerash for instance, of adapting standard plans to terrains ill-suited for quadrilinear orders, there is perhaps no need to attribute a profound ideological significance to the design of Roman Jerusalem and to consider it merely as a standard operational procedure. However, a deeper purpose cannot be entirely excluded because of the second unique effect of the failed Jewish revolts of the first and second centuries. Before turning to it, it is worthwhile to point out that, in our own times and under the effect of modernism in general and of tall buildings in particular, a new artificial and arbitrary pattern of planning and construction is being imposed on a much en-larged city. Romantic antiquarians and believers in history regret it, worshippers of the future and devotees of change love it. But, even if modern Jerusalem is not my concern here, the medieval city can either be incorporated into the language of modernism (or whatever follows post-modernism) or else be swallowed and trivialized by it. For better or for worse, the Roman system of destroying and rebuilding is no longer morally viable.

2. The second major result of the fateful events of the first and second centuries may be called the liberation of memory from space. The Roman city was provided with a number of monuments commemorating or expressing standard pagan and imperial themes—temples to Venus and Jupiter, a statue of Hadrian, an ensemble which became known in later sources as a "capitol"—although the exact quality and character of these constructions may well have been exaggerated by later Christian writers. We tend to assume that Roman official art did not look like Caesar's Palace in Las Vegas, but I have often wondered about the true scale of architectural and artistic investment made by the empire for a troublesome provincial city. Whatever may have been the case, the important point is that none of these buildings was in honor of anything that heretofore had been holy in Jerusalem and, thus, memories were released from the spaces they had occupied. These memories were colored in Jewish and Christian terms, but I prefer, at this stage, to divide them into historical, sacred, pious, and eschatological categories, although the boundaries between them are not always clear and a considerable amount of overlap does occur.

Historical memories are those of clearly-delineated events which are not necessarily transformed into places of holiness or worship; in Jerusalem, the most obvious examples are the memories of David and Solomon, the real as well as the mythical creators of the city's importance. Sacred memories also include events, but these are associated with sacred figures. On the basis of evidence from later times, which can reasonably be used for earlier ones, Moses, Abraham, Adam, and, of course, Jesus were the principal agents of memory; over the centuries, many others will be added.

Pious memories are memories requiring or inviting behavior, specific actions, or contact with hallowed places. The main expression of pious behavior in Jerusalem was pilgrimage, and one of my arguments is that pilgrimage eventually became an activity independent of religious affiliation but demanding a religious allegiance. Thus, Islam in the seventh and later centuries developed pilgrimage to Jerusalem not because it was required by the faith itself, but because Islam became part of the city. A sociologist could well point out that tourism in Jerusalem has a pilgrimage-like aspect which is absent from tourism in Cairo or in Paris, but is partly present in Rome.

Finally, there are eschatological "memories." It is, of course, not very logical to talk about a memory of something that has not yet happened, but at some point in history Jerusalem became infused with the expectation of the end of time in the space of the city. Whether it is reasonable to assume this expectation as early as the second century of the Common Era is unclear to me, just as I am not certain about the ways in which, and the times when, the cemeteries and mausoleums or caves, eventually the garden of Gethsemane to the east of the city, affected the emotions which became part of Jerusalem. Nevertheless, the presence of the dead, mighty, or humble, in the hope of resurrection and eternal life, became an essential psychological component of the city.

However one is to interpret the eschatological component need not affect the general point that we can reconstruct and imagine for, let us say, around 200 C.E., a walled Roman garrison and administrative town containing services associated with such functions artificially imposed on a rugged and waterless terrain, as well as a host of displaced memories—some involving concrete events, others determining modes of behavior. The vast majority of these memories was Jewish, but a Christian differentiation had appeared, and the southeastern corner of the Roman city with its presumed "capitol" was going to be the place where Jews sought (or were going to seek) traces of the ruined Temple, while Christians looked for the place of Jesus' preaching or of St. Stephen's martyrdom. What is curious about the few accounts we have of these early times (the point even applies, I believe, to the "invention" of the Holy Sepulchre) is that there were searches because of memories without a clear sense of where the searches would end.

The Middle Ages were the time when the space of Jerusalem and the memories associated with the city were transformed by Christians, and then Muslims, into monuments, stones—what I call the "petrification" (or *eislithosis*) of the memories. Christians and Muslims could do that because they exercised political and financial power, but it is also possible to construe the relationship between the successive monotheistic versions of divine revelation in another way, which may become clearer after I sketch out reconstructions of the medieval city in three early medieval instances.

The Christian transformation was simple. The western hill was sanctified through the building of the Holy Sepulchre complex, the Zion complex, and, somewhat later, the Nea or New Church of the Theotokos as major monuments in the midst of many other, lesser, constructions. The eastern hill was left in ruins as a sign of God's wrath upon the Jews and as the fulfillment of the prediction in the gospels that no stone shall remain upon another stone. Beyond the ruinous Jewish space, the Mount of Olives—scene of the Ascension and location of the forthcoming Resurrection—rises beyond the valley of pain and death. The whole city could become monumentally organized around foci of architectural or liturgical attention because enough memories existed which could embody the space of the city. As one walked out of the Holy Sepulchre, one could see the destroyed Temple area with its pagan remains and the Nea's mighty substructures facing Herod's tremendous western wall, which at that time was probably already associated with Solomon—although I have not yet found a clear source to prove or disprove this assumption. Procopius' account of the building of the Nea emphasizes primarily the engineering feats needed to carry stones into the building site and "forty oxen were specially selected by the emperor for their strength" to pull the carts that brought the stones. It is not easy, in this text, to separate the hyperbole of a Constantinpolitan publicist from what actually happened (for instance, carts were never used in Syria and Palestine at this time), but it is reasonable to assume that someone had persuaded Justinian to outdo Solomon's or Herod's work. This is not the only time that Justinian compared himself to Solomon.

There was also a second level of "petrification" of memories. The Piacenza Pilgrim in 570, and other pilgrims around that time, actually *see* the fig tree on which Judas hanged himself, the altar on which Abraham was meant to sacrifice Isaac, which is also Melchizedek's altar, the wood of the Cross, the sponge and the reed of the Passion, the onyx cup of the Last Supper, the Virgin's girdle and headband, the stones with which St. Stephen was killed, the ring of Solomon, the silver bowls with which Solomon ruled the demons, the horn with which David was anointed, and so on. In addition to an architecture that organized the space of the city, there was also a reification of the memory of things, at times with movements from one place to the other, so that the same object could be seen in two different sanctuaries or in the treasury of two different churches.

The first Muslim transformation was that of the seventh century. Its key act was the resacralization of the area of the Herodian Temple. There are many reasons for this transformation, and many different interpretations of it now exist, as they have since the ninth century. From the perspective of this paper, the causes of the event are less important than its results.

Instead of the willfully ruinous area of the Temple, the faithful Christians coming out of the Holy Sepulchre see now the shining and colorful Dome of the Rock. In stages which will probably never be known, Abraham, Moses, several Zacharias, Jesus, Jacob, and Joseph acquire their Muslim embodiment in the stones of what becomes the Haram al-Sharif. David and Solomon are also present, but in a different way, due to their double quality in Islam of kings *and* prophets and because of a historical as well as mythical kernel associating them with Jerusalem.

The details of these changes are almost impossible to disentangle either chronologically or typologically, but two points are essential. One is that a space inherited by a very young Islam required specifically Islamic meanings; within a century, beyond the early connection with the "miḥrab of David" mentioned in the Koran (38:21), or with a place seen by the Prophet (there is much scholarly debate on both of these issues), the combined themes of the Prophet's *isra* and *mi'raj*, Night Journey and Ascension became the dominant theme of the Haram. The other point was the Muslim adoption of the general themes of resurrection, judgment, and eternal life. Typologically, the themes of mystical visits and ascension were already present in Jerusalem; only now, however, did they acquire a Muslim connotation.

The impact of this early Islamic transformation on the character of the physical city was, first of all, that the whole city became, so to speak, religiously charged rather than contrasted through an active western Christian pole and a negative, ruined, eastern one. It is, as far as I have been able to see, impossible to imagine the actual physical presence of Jews in the city; this is unfortunate, as these must have been extraordinary decades—from ca. 640–690—when very different and hardly homogeneous members of all three faiths were seeking or holding on to *their* place in Jerusalem and where there must have been a whole crowd of intermediaries ready to suggest where memories could find a place and which places needed memories. Let us just try to imagine *in their actual places* what Arculfus described around 670, after he identified the footprints of Christ before his Ascension:

> . . . on the west of the round building [of the Ascension] described above there are eight upper windows paned with glass. Inside the windows, and in corresponding positions, are eight lamps, positioned so that each one of them seems to hang neither above nor below the window, but just inside it. These lights shine out from their windows on the summit of the Mount of Olives with such brilliance that they light up not only the part of the Mount to the west . . . but also the steps leading all the way up from the Valley of Jehosaphat to the city of Jerusalem, which are lighted, however dark the night. Most of the nearer part of the city is lighted as well. The remarkable brilliance of these eight lamps shining out by night from the holy Mount and the place of the Lord's Ascension brings to believing hearts a readiness for the love of God.[2]

Arculfus' emotions were affected by a spectacle of *lumière* whose *son* may have been provided by liturgical singing, yet it affected the whole part of the city which by then was supposed to be Muslim and to contain a Jewish Quarter.

The second important aspect of the early Islamic transformation of the city is, once again, difficult to explain but easy to see—the building of the Dome of the Rock. Much has been, is, and will be written about the construction, iconography, history, patronage, and holiness of this most extraordinary and unique monument. But, for an understanding of the visual history of the city, it does not really matter why it was built by and for Muslim purposes. The important point is that it was a truly unique work of art in its shape and in its decoration of shiny gold and mosaic on the outside, and with an extraordinary interior spatial order and marble as well as mosaic decoration. It was and still is a work of art because its aesthetic magnetism and power kept it from destruction, because the abstract values by which it was (and is) perceived and judged could be adapted to the memories of Abraham or Solomon, to changing moods of Muslim piety, to a church, to a mosque, to Palestinian nationalism, or to Israeli tourist posters—to anything that required physical beauty and attraction. Urban planners see such buildings as challenges, if not even real problems, because they dominate space and constrict invention and innovation. They are also a problem for strict religious leaders because they overwhelm the perception of space and lead one's emotions in directions other than strictly pious ones. It is possible that the edifice was built in this fashion because it is only by abstracting them into geometry and color that the Mediterranean, and possibly even local, builders and decorators could express the complex religious and ideological motivations of the building's patrons into terms understandable to all the inhabitants of Jerusalem.

My last vision of urban medieval Jerusalem is roughly that of the mid-eleventh century, when we have an important eyewitness account by the Persian traveler Nasir-e-Khosrow who, like a contemporary trained anthropologist, used fieldnotes, measurements, and drawings in remote northeastern Iran to relate what he saw and did in Jerusalem. It is also the time of thousands of Genizah fragments with considerable information about Jews in the city, of Latin Christian pilgrims, and of the first *fada'il* or "praises" of the city for Muslims.[3]

The main spatial changes were: shortening of the walls of the city to the south; reconstruction of the complex of the Holy Sepulchre after its destruction by order of al-Hakim; reconstruction of the Aqsa mosque and a new dome on the Dome of the Rock after an earthquake; abandonment and eventually closing of the southern gates of the Haram (the ones under the Aqsa mosque); a number of additions to the Haram itself, including a fancy new gate on the spot of the present Gate of the Chain, facing westward and dominating the city across the Tyropoeon Valley, which was still very much a valley at that time. Most of these changes were the result of perfectly normal maintenance requirements. Some also reflected political decisions. The Holy Sepulchre was looted probably because it was alleged to be filled with expensive objects. Moreover, Fatimid ideology was expressed through the dynasty's control of Jerusalem in particular and of Muslim piety in general, as is clear from the inscriptions found near the Holy Sepulchre, in the Dome of the Rock, and, most spectacularly, on the triumphal arch of the new Aqsa mosque. In the latter, the Koranic mention of the *masjid al-aqsa* (17:1) is the earliest remaining use of that important reference associated with Jerusalem and it is followed by the full titulature of the ruling caliph al-Zahir and the names of his local representatives.

These spatial changes both reflected and affected holiness. They reflected it primarily in the Muslim sanctuary, with the full establishment through buildings and inscriptions of the two dominant themes of Muslim piety: the Prophet's Journey and the Resurrection and Judgment. But this is also the time when the *fada'il*, those wonderful accounts of pious memories in Jerusalem, enshrined the prophet-kings David and Solomon in the Muslim stones of the city. These changes also reflected a new trend toward the withdrawal of religious systems into themselves. The new gate to the Haram dominates the city, but the Holy Sepulchre is closed unto itself; the probable completion of the colonnade on the north, west, and south of the Haram, as well as the building of parapets and formal gateways to its upper platform, are all features which emphasize the boundaries between spaces and, therefore, between groups. Two aspects of these changes remain unclear to me. One is why Mount Zion, the highest point in the city, with a church built or rebuilt in the late tenth century, was kept outside the walled city. The other one is why there is no evidence for Jewish holy spaces, as opposed to religious or otherwise restricted institutions which existed, among other places, on the Mount of Olives.

Both Mount Zion and the Mount of Olives deserve a monographic history as spaces with considerable modifications in the nature of the holiness and piety which surrounded them. But, in a general sense, and if one excludes relatively minor modifications like the shifting of the names of gates from the south of the Haram to the north, the image suggested by this second definable moment in the history of Islamic Jerusalem is that of confessional communities acting out their lives and beliefs separately from each other in their minds, if not necessarily in the streets they shared. They rarely talk about each other, except at carefully-staged moments when a Nasir e-Khosrow is shown in the Holy Sepulchre paintings depicting the "Last Judgment" or the "Entry into Jerusalem," that is to say, images which reflect shared beliefs or innocuous events in the life of Christ—not the "Crucifixion" or the "Resurrection," which must have existed in that sanctuary. A small group of tenth-century inscriptions do suggest something a bit different. They are epitaphs of Muslims and Christians which contain unusual curses on those who would deface the tombs or jump over them. They provide a curious glimpse of a time when relative peace in the living streets was possible because one could play one's antagonisms out in the cemeteries.

The time of the crusades will see an explosion of Christian buildings and a partial eradication of Muslim memories; the latter will be revived in Ayyubid and Mamluk times. Under the less tolerant and more arbitrary late medieval domination of the latter, separate lives in separate quarters becomes the lot of Jews, Christians, and Muslims. Their stories are better known, as they have been studied more frequently than the early medieval period, which has been my primary concern.

What I have tried to show here can be summed up in the following manner. An artificial Roman imperial space over ragged hills and valleys contained a rich trove of holy memories associated with the real and the mythical history of the Jews and the first Christians, as well as with pious practices like pilgrimage or the deeper expectation of existence beyond time. Between 350 and 700, these memories (or most of them) found spaces, and these spaces acquired holiness—first a Christian holiness and then a Muslim one. Over the centuries, memories changed location as well as confessional allegiance—Abraham in particular, but also Jesus, Adam, and David—and spaces changed their holy names. But sooner or later, sometimes as late as the nineteenth century, holy memories were still seeking a space in Jerusalem and its surroundings, and at times insignificant stones were suddenly given a meaning from the rich source of the Scriptures in order to please a wealthy visitor. At the same time, large- and small-scale pilgrimage continued regardless of religious affiliation, and the expectation of the end of time and the beginning of eternity drew people, living and deceased, to the city. They still do so today.

The further uniqueness of Jerusalem is that most of its memories were Jewish, but that these Jewish memories became Christian, and Christian and Jewish memories became Muslim. Alone, of all the holy cities of the world, the space of Jerusalem could accommodate all these pious expressions in every one of their confessional garbs. This was so in part because it is the same God who appeared differently to Jews, Christians, and Muslims. It was also so because Islam, which dominated the city during most of the Middle Ages, acknowledged and formalized the rights and beliefs of those who remained within the fold of older traditions. Finally, it was so because the Roman empire had freed the memories of the city from the places they had occupied and also freed the city from being a political capital. During 1800 years or so, Jerusalem was an administrative and political *sous-préfecture* for all but one unsuccessful century. This, I submit, allowed for another set of values than those of power—values of belief and piety—to define the purpose of the city. Yet, in a striking paradox, it is political and ideological power that, under Constantine, Justinian, ʿAbd al-Malik, al-Walid, al-Maʾmun, al-Hakim, and al-Zahir, created the monuments of the city which shaped the way we perceive it. And, as a further paradox, it is the Dome of the Rock, the one building whose exact original function is still something of a mystery, that dominated the city in the past. In it the brilliant manipulation of space and decoration restricted the certainty of holiness, but the aesthetic quality given to the holiness made the space sacred.

Today, this old Roman city is a small part of a large metropolis teeming with different expectations and varied agendas. Whether the holiness of its spaces is still meaningful in terms other than those of contemporary ethnic and political passions, or whether it is destined to be transformed into the post-modernist spaces of contemporary architecture needed for international tourism and worldly taste, will not be known for a while.

Notes

1. This paper is substantially the one delivered at the conference, with only a few rhetorical devices removed. The bibliography on Jerusalem, even for its medieval centuries, is immense, and most of it, as well as the justifications for some of the arguments in this paper, will be found in O. Grabar, *The Shape of the Holy, Jerusalem 600–1100* (Princeton, 1996). Maps, references, and drawings can be found on the three sheets (1992) of the Tübinger Atlas der Vorderen Orient, in K. Bieberstein and H. Bloedhorn, *Jerusalem: Grundzüge der Baugeschichte,* III (Wiesbaden, 1994), and in D. Kroyanker, *Jerusalem Architecture* (New York, 1994), which summarizes his multi-volume series in Hebrew.

2. J. Wilkinson, *Jerusalem Pilgrims before the Crusades* (Warminster, 1977), 107.

3. See also M. Rosen-Ayalon's article in this volume.

20

Jerusalem and Mecca

HAVA LAZARUS-YAFEH

Jerusalem and Mecca are two of the most famous holy cities in the world. Although a vast amount of literature and scholarly treatises has been written about each, very little has been done by way of comparative study. Most comparisons treat the relationship between the sanctity of Jerusalem and Mecca in Islam, or the sanctity of Jerusalem in Judaism, Christianity, and Islam. I propose to compare the sanctity of Jerusalem and Mecca in their original, "natural" original surroundings in order to gain a broader picture of Judaism and Islam. In other words, if the basis for the sanctity of Jerusalem in Judaism differs from the basis for the sanctity of Mecca in Islam, then what does this say about Judaism and Islam ? Perhaps it is no more than different historical contexts that shaped their sanctities. Or perhaps the most essential characteristics of each religion shaped the sanctity in its own particular way. If, on the other hand, their sanctity is basically the same—taking into consideration, of course, their different histories and religious sources—we may then draw some more universal conclusions with regard to the religious character of holy cities in general.

Three Similarities

Let us begin by mentioning only three of the many basic similarities between the two holy cities—the ancient pre-monotheistic source of their sanctity, the expansion of this sanctity to the respective cities, and the strict regulations for pilgrims and inhabitants of these cities.

The ancient pre-monotheistic source of sanctity. Scholars have stressed the fact that the sanctity of both cities stems from pre-monotheistic times and from a specific locale in the city. In Mecca, the Ka'ba shrine and the small Black Stone in its eastern wall, and perhaps also other stones in and near the Ka'ba and

287

Mecca, were all ancient sites of pre-Islamic pagan worship. In Jerusalem, Araunah's threshing floor (II Sam. 23:18ff.) was the site which King David bought (apparently from the Jebusite king) and where he erected an altar and gave burnt offerings to God, and where King Solomon built the Temple. Because of the huge rock on the site, this may well have been an early pre-monotheistic place of worship.

The expansion of the sanctity. Both the Temple Mount and the Ka'ba imparted their sanctity to their respective cities. Although these are two very different shrines (for instance, no offerings are burnt at the Ka'ba and there is no priesthood in Islam), the same process of sanctification of the city took place in both. The cities became holy because God was said to dwell in each— even though this notion was discarded long ago by all three monotheistic religions. After building the Temple in Jerusalem, King Solomon asked: "But will God indeed dwell on the earth? The heaven and heaven of heavens cannot contain Thee, how much less this house that I have built?" (I Kgs. 8:27). Isaiah (66:1) repeats almost the same question, and Paul is quoted in the Acts of the Apostles (17:24) as saying: "God that made the world and all things therein . . . dwelleth not in Temples made with hands." In the same way, Al-Ghazzālī (d. 1111), one of the greatest Muslim writers, states clearly that people make pilgrimage to God's house in Mecca, "although everyone knows that no house can contain the transcendent God, nor can any city harbor Him."[1] Nevertheless this ancient pre-monotheistic notion survived as a metaphor and the cities became holy because they encompassed the site in which God—as the ancient kings—chose to dwell. Slowly, but surely, the distinction between temple or shrine on the one hand, and city on the other, was blurred, and the city itself became the holy site. Thus, Jerusalem was termed "the city of God, the holiest dwelling place of God Most High" (Ps. 46:5), and the entire country was considered sacred for the same reason. In Al-Ḥidjāz as well, a huge area of sacred territory—*Haram*—surrounds Mecca. A long process of discovering other holy sites in and around the cities then began, sites which pilgrims added to the primary goal of their pilgrimage, i.e., the Temple in Jerusalem or the Ka'ba in Mecca. The pilgrims to these cities and shrines came to be considered visitors of God Himself and were urged to behave accordingly throughout the entire city, and not only at the Temple or the Ka'ba mosque.

Strict regulations for pilgrims and inhabitants. The pilgrim's behavior in both cities is scrupulously regulated, especially in Islam, where no one may enter Mecca and the holy territory without undergoing special purification. At specific points along the periphery of the holy territory (*Mawāqīt*), the Muslim male pilgrim has to wash his whole body, remove his everyday clothes, and dress in the white garb of holiness (*Iḥrām*), which consists of two unsewn sheets thrown around the body in such a way so as to cover the left shoulder, back, and breast, but leaving the right shoulder and arm bare. Dressed in this garb, the Muslim pilgrim to Mecca is considered to be in a state of holiness and many prohibitions are imposed upon him, such as washing, shaving, cutting his hair and nails, or having sexual relations. Arriving in Mecca in this state, he has to perform certain rituals at the Kaʿba (*Ṭawāf*—circumambulation) and near the mosque surrounding it (*Saʿy*—running between two hills) before he can remove his *Iḥrām* garb. This holds true for the pilgrim who arrives in Mecca before the general Ḥajj-pilgrimage begins (for which he will then once more put on the *Iḥrām* dress) and for the ordinary visitor to Mecca who cannot enter the city merely as a casual visitor. The city and its surroundings thus became as holy as the Kaʿba itself which first sanctioned them.

It is a small step from here to the discussion whether the pilgrim to Mecca should stay longer in the holy city. This practice was very common and considered to be a pious and recommendable act. However, the holier the city became in the eyes of the believers, the more some Doctors of Law and mystics hesitated to recommend such an act of piety. Below are some of the great Al-Ghazzālī's thoughts on this matter:

> The very cautious among the *ʿUlamā* did not like people to stay on in Mecca because of three reasons: first, because people may became bored and too familiar with the House [e.g., the Kaʿba] and this will extinguish the flame of reverence in their heart. Therefore, ʿUmar [the second caliph, 634-644] used to strike the pilgrims after they had performed the rituals and say: "O People of Yemen, go home to your Yemen; O people of Syria, go home to your Syria; O People of Iraq, go home to your Iraq". . . . The second reason is that in order to raise the yearning to return, one has to leave. . . . Therefore someone said: "To be in another place while your heart yearns for Mecca and is connected with this House is better for you than to be in it, while you are bored and your heart is in another place." And someone else said: "How many are those who are in Khorasan and are closer [to the Kaʿba] than those who circumambulate it". . . . The third reason is the fear to commit sins in Mecca, which is a very dangerous thing to do, as it may bring the wrath of God [upon you] because of the honored place. . . . People say that sins are multiplied in Mecca as are the good deeds [done there] . . . Ibn ʿAbbās said: "I prefer to commit seventy sins in Rakiyya than one in Mecca"[2] . . . and some people who stayed in Mecca [for longer] never relieved themselves there but used to go everytime outside

the holy territory to do so; others, who stayed for months, never lay down there [to sleep]. . . . Do not think that opposing staying [in the holy city] stands in contrast to the city's excellence, because its real cause [has nothing to do with the city itself but] with the weakness of man and his inability to live in the way demanded [that is] worthy of the city. Therefore, we mean that leaving the place is better than living there in boredom and disrespect, but [it certainly is not better] than living there while living up to the city's demands.[3]

Some of these considerations bear a strong resemblance to views expressed about a thousand years earlier by the so-called Qumran sect in the Temple Scroll, for example. It should be borne in mind, however, that the Temple Scroll refers primarily, though not exclusively, to future Utopian descriptions of the city rather than to actual practice. These regulations mean that the sanctity of the Temple or the Ka'ba spilled over to the city itself, placing—in theory at least—unbelievable hardships on its inhabitants or at least on those who aspired to live by the holy law. In the Temple Scroll, these regulations were much stricter and included various sources of defilement and impure relations that were forbidden in the city. Some of these rules were known from the Bible and rabbinic literature, but were much more strictly applied here, others were totally unknown to the sages or were clearly at odds with their views.

In the chapter "Bans on entering the Temple and Temple city,"[4] God decrees: "and the city which I will hallow by settling my name and my Temple within it shall be holy and clean." Therefore, no impure person should enter it before special purification as, for example, he who had sexual relations (outside the city) or contact with the dead, or even nocturnal emissions.[5] In the same way, "no blind man shall enter the Temple city so that they will not defile the city in which I dwell," nor should a leper or diseased person, to whom separate places are allotted in other cities.[6] Not only were sexual relations forbidden in the city, so, too, was relieving oneself within the city: "And you shall make them a place for a hand outside the city, to which they shall go out to the northwest of the city-roofed houses, with pits within them to which the excrement will descend."[7] It was stipulated that this place was to be 3000 cubits outside the city—about 1500 meters according to some—and therefore Yadin supposed that those Essenes who actually made the attempt to live in the city according to such rules tried not to relieve themselves on Shabbat (perhaps they ate accordingly) because they could not travel this far on Shabbat without transgressing the Sabbath limits. They may also have lived near the Essene Gate (which was named after them) which led to the "hand" outside and was perhaps closer to it than the other gates.

In the same way, Mecca is considered the city in which God built His house and the pilgrims are His visitors. According to some, a pilgrim even shakes hands with Him by kissing the Black Stone which is considered to be His right hand, as it were.[8] Being rooted in a social reality, however, the Ḥajj regulations regarding Mecca are more tempered than those of the Temple Scroll referring to Jerusalem, although they may not seem so evident. As noted, after entering the city in the special *Iḥrām* garb—which has no counterpart in Judaism—and after performing several rituals at the Ka'ba, the Muslim pilgrim may remove his *Iḥrām* dress and is thus relieved of its concomitant personal prohibitions. He may now wash, cut his hair, or have sexual relations—even inside the holy city. Only the general prohibitions not to hunt, cut trees, or shed blood in Mecca remain in force at all times.

Three Differences

Having mentioned—if only briefly—three basic similarities between the two holy cities and their sanctity, we shall now focus on three important points of differences between them: the destruction of the Temple and the hopes for its rebuilding and the redemption of Israel; the competition of Al-Madina with Mecca; and the spiritual symbolism of Jerusalem as compared to the earthly image of Mecca.

The destruction of the Temple in Jerusalem. The destruction of the First and Second Temples of Jerusalem and the dispersion into exile had far-reaching ramifications, and not only in the political sphere. The political and religious trauma was great. Life had ceased, as it were, and there was a general feeling that all comforts and pleasures should be discarded until the rebuilding of the Temple and the ingathering of the exiles could once again reinstate the proper equilibrium in history. People even thought that the cosmic order was interrupted:

> Rabbi Joshua testified that from the day the Temple was destroyed there is no day without a curse, the dew has not descended for a blessing and the flavor has left the fruits. Rabbi Jose says the fatness [nourishing quality] was also removed from the fruits.[9]
> So long as the Temple service is maintained, the world is a blessing to its inhabitants and the rains come down in season.[10]

Without the Temple offerings, however, there appears to have been no venue for the atonement of sins; even the gates of prayer seemed to be sealed.[11] The sages, of course, reorganized the spiritual life of Israel without the Temple, but mourning upon its destruction and the destruction of Jerusalem remained an integral part of Jewish life ever since, and for some it became the central idea of their entire life. Every Jew cited the words of the Psalmist: "If I forget thee, O Jerusalem, let my right hand forget its cunning, let my tongue cleave to the roof of my mouth if I remember thee not, if I prefer not Jerusalem above my chief joy" (137:5–6). For centuries, Jews the worldover remembered Jerusalem—more so than the Temple itself—on various occasions:

- when a man built his house he was to leave a small part of the wall unfinished in memory of Jerusalem;
- no festive banquet could be complete, but some things were to be omitted in memory of Jerusalem;
- to this very day, a glass is broken at a wedding in remembrance of Jerusalem and a special blessing is recited: "May she who was barren [Zion] be exceedingly glad and exult when her children are gathered within her in joy";
- in the prayers to be recited several times daily, mention of Jerusalem has a permanent place connected with both one's misery and as well as hopes for redemption: "Let our eyes behold thy return in mercy to Zion" (from the daily *Amidah*);
- after the reading of the haftarah on Shabbat, one recites: "Have mercy upon Zion, for it is the home of our life, and save her that is grieved in spirit—speedily, even in our days. Blessed are thou, O Lord, who makest Zion joyful through her children";
- finally, in the Grace after Meals one recites: "And rebuild Jerusalem thy holy city speedily in our days. Blessed are thou, O Lord, who in thy compassion rebuildest Jerusalem."[12]

This historical difference brought about deep religious changes in Judaism which had no counterpart in Islam; some of these developments were even frowned upon by Islam and ridiculed by its Doctors of Law.[13] In Judaism, the hopes for rebuilding the Temple and Jerusalem and the restoration of the Davidic dynasty became associated with the more general eschatological hopes for a golden messianic age, the redemption of Israel and all mankind, and the eternal prophetic search for justice, righteousness, piety, charity, and peace. Although Jerusalem had been an important part of the eschatological prophetic visions before its destruction (see, for example, Isa. 2:2–4), its role became central to them after the destruction.

Jewish literature abounds with descriptions linking the rebuilding of Jerusalem and the ingathering of exiles with a dramatic eschatological change of heart in man and the inauguration of a new golden age for man, city, land, and even the world. Jerusalem in ruins became the symbol of Israel's misery[14] and future rebuilding—the redemption of Israel, all mankind, and the beginning of the messianic era. In certain kabbalistic circles, the longing for Jerusalem took the form of erotic yearning; the synonymous terms Jerusalem and Zion were explained, under gnostic influence, as symbols of the majestic male and earthly female (Jerusalem the city), elements in God Himself which would reunite at the end of days, as it is written: "Awake, awake, put on thy strength, O Zion; put on thy beautiful garments, O Jerusalem, the holy city" (Isa. 52:1).[15]

These are, of course, only a few hints of what is elaborated upon in the various corpora of Jewish literature over the centuries; it has no parallel in Muslim medieval literature with regard to Mecca and the Ka'ba, neither of which has ever suffered a traumatic history or destruction. Mecca is never mentioned in Islam's daily prayer which, in any case, is not very verbal although the direction of prayer is always toward Mecca, nor is the city mentioned during festivals although it is present in the mind of every Muslim who wishes to perform the Ḥajj pilgrimage at least once in his lifetime. Moreover, Mecca plays no central role in the eschatology of Islam (according to some, this will be the first place of resurrection; according to others, Jerusalem—like in the Judaeo-Christian tradition—will be the place where the great Judgment will commence and take place). Eschatology in Islam has remained marginal in Muslim theology,[16] probably because there was no destruction or exile which demanded spiritual compensation in the form of a theory of redemption.

Muslim mystics, the Ṣūfis, were also very reserved about their feelings and yearnings for Mecca and the Ka'ba; many of them even advised their disciples against making pilgrimage, as "the knowledge of God is more urgent than the visit to His house"; they explained the Qur'ānic verses about pilgrimage as referring to "the pilgrimage of the profession [in your heart] of the essence of the one true God," and the verses about sacrifice as referring to "the sacrifice of the desires of the heart in the courtyard of the Ka'ba of the heart."[17] Some even spoke out explicitly against pilgrimage to the Black Stone at the Ka'ba:

> Muhammad b. Al-Faḍl says: "I wonder at those who seek His temple in this world: why do they not seek contemplation of Him in their hearts? The temple they sometimes attain and sometimes miss, but contemplation they might enjoy always. If they are bound to visit a stone, which is looked at only a year—surely they are more more bound to visit the temple of the heart, where He may be seen three hundred and sixty times in a day and night. But the mystic's every step is a

symbol of the journey to Mecca, and when he reaches the sanctuary he wins a robe of honour for every step."[18]

It may well be that such sayings, together with the general reserved or even ambivalent Muslim attitude to the holy Black Stone,[19] contributed their share to the astonishing fact that when the Black Stone was robbed by the Ismaʿīlī Qarmatians, who considered its worship as idolatrous, and held by them for twenty years (930–950),[20] no great religious outcry was heard in the Islamic world. It is also interesting to note that, due to Jewish-Christian influence, early Muslim mystics became more attached to Jerusalem and the Land of Israel[21] than to Mecca and Al-Ḥidjāz. It might have been easier to accept the given sanctity of the Holy Land and Jerusalem than to risk the over-cultivation of the sanctity of Mecca, the Kaʿba, and the Black Stone. This may be true in other spheres as well, and not only with regard to the Ṣūfi mystics, and is certainly deserving of a separate study.

The rivalry between Mecca and Al-Madina. Al-Madina, and Jerusalem to a lesser extent, were and still are great rivals to the primacy of Mecca in Islam. In early Judaism, Jerusalem was also rivaled by other sacred places and holy cities, such as Beth-el (Gen. 28:16) and Dan (I Kgs. 12:28). Later on, the Samaritans made Shechem their holy city instead of Jerusalem. Nevertheless, there can be no doubt that Jerusalem prevails as *the* holy city of Judaism which has no rivals and shares its holiness with no other city in the world.

Mecca, however, is a different story. From the outset, Mecca and Al-Madina competed for primacy in Islam. Muhammad was born in Mecca, the city of the holy Kaʿba, but had to leave it in 622 because of the inhabitants' hostile attitude to his religious message. He found a place of refuge for himself and his company in Yathrib-Al-Madina, and from there established his leadership throughout Arabia. He dreamt of returning to Mecca and reinstating monotheistic worship at the Kaʿba. Muhammad's dream came true eight years later, in 630, when he returned to Mecca as victor. However, he did not stay for long in his birthplace, now the holy city of nascent Islam, but returned to Al-Madina, where he died and was buried two years later.

The rivalry between Mecca and Al-Madina was very serious and the literature in praise of each is great, constituting part of the popular genre in Arabic literature in praise (*Faḍāʾil*) of different cities, objects, or people. But the competition between these two cities encompasses more than just local or tribal rivalry. Mecca is the place of the Kaʿba and the great holy mosque (*Al-Masdjid Al-Ḥarām*) surrounding it. Every Muslim has to make pilgrimage to it and to the other sacred places in its vicinity at least once in his lifetime: to the neighboring hills of Safa and Marwa, where the ritual of *Saʿy* (running back and forth in memory of Hagar's searching water for her son Ishmael) is performed; to the plain of ʿArafāt, where the dramatic "Standing" (*Wuqūf*) and hearing of the sermon takes place; and to the small places of Muzdalifa and Minā nearby. None of these sites competes with the Kaʿba and Mecca, but early on they became part of the Muslim Ḥajj-pilgrimage.[22] Al-Madina, however, is an independent holy city some 400 kms. north of Mecca. It harbors the Prophet's mosque (*Al-Masdjid al-Nabawī*) and his burial nearby, which is considered one of the gates to heaven. No pilgrim to Mecca returns home without visiting the holy tomb although this is not considered part of the pilgrimage, and everyone prays there although it is explicitly forbidden to pray *to* the Prophet. According to classical Islamic theory, there is no holiness but that of God and no tomb should be worshipped, and even prophets are considered to be ordinary humans only.[23] Al-Madina is not part of the holy territory of Al-Ḥidjāz, and the pilgrim may enter this city in his everyday clothes (it is only forbidden to shed blood, hunt, or cut trees there). Even non-Muslims who may never enter Mecca are allowed to enter Al-Madina, but only for a couple of days. Nevertheless, Al-Madina aspired for centuries to surpass Mecca's primacy and become the first holy city of Islam.

We shall not dwell here on this fascinating competition. Mecca is the city wherein every prayer and good deed is multiplied, as are the sins committed there. Every prayer there is worth a hundred thousand prayers in any other mosque; to live there is as if one lives in constant prayer, or as if one is stationed on a dangerous frontier (*Ribāṭ*); if one dies there, it is as if one has died in lower heaven; to be resurrected there almost assures one of God's forgiveness. The people of Mecca are God's people (*Ahl Allāh*), and even the simpletons among them are deserving of paradise. The Prophet said: "By God, you, Mecca, are the best on God's earth and the most beloved earth to God, and had I not been evicted from you I would never have left you. . . ."[24] Other cities (Jerusalem, for example) also tried to compete with Mecca, but to no avail. Only the rivalry of Al-Madina was never to be trifled with and often overshadowed the unique place of Mecca in Islamic religious thought and history.

It seems that because of this rivalry the amount of literature in praise of Al-Madina is legion, perhaps even more than that in praise of Mecca! Al-Samhūdī (d. 1505), a native of Al-Madina, is a late author who collected in the two volumes of his *A Complete Account of the History of the Abode-City of the Chosen Prophet*[25] all the praises of Al-Madina. This book comprises Ḥadīth and other sayings, as well as stories extolling Al-Madina, some of which clearly attempt to undermine the special status of Mecca: to visit the Prophet's tomb and to stay in Al-Madina is the best of all good deeds; when God created the Prophet, He commanded Gabriel to bring to him dry dust from the future burial place of the Prophet in Al-Madina which He kneaded with the nectar of paradise and immersed in the rivers of paradise; every prophet is buried in the place he loves most; before the excellence of Al-Madina became clear to everyone, the Prophet said in a Ḥadīth that Mecca is the best of all cities of God and the one He loves most—but when the Prophet stayed in Al-Madina for many years and proclaimed his religion from there, the blessings of Al-Madina became greater than those of Mecca. Mecca was then reconquered by the Prophet in the same way as all the other lands were conquered later (e.g., without any special distinction), but the Prophet never returned to settle there. Al-Madina thus became the most beloved city of God where all prayers are answered and in which it is best to die and be buried because the Prophet will intercede for all its people on the day of Judgment. A visit to Al-Madina is equivalent to a private pilgrimage to Mecca ('Umra), and a prayer in the Prophet's mosque in Al-Madina is equal to the Ḥajj-pilgrimage, and so forth. Even the holy places outside Mecca are recruited into this competition, as it is stated that on certain days of the pilgrimage prayer on Mount 'Arafāt and in Minā is better than in Mecca—thus demonstrating that God's grace is boundless and not restricted to Mecca alone.

There can be little doubt that such rivalry did, in fact, undermine the primacy of Mecca, which could not develop as the holy city of Islam par excellence. Mecca is usually considered the first of the three holy cities of Islam, as is expressed in the famous Ḥadīth: "You shall only set out (lit., fasten your saddles) for three mosques: the Sacred Mosque (in Mecca), my (i.e., the Prophet's) mosque (in Al-Madina), and the Aqṣā mosque (in Jerusalem),"[26] or in many Ḥadīth traditions such as the following: "One prayer in my mosque (in Al-Madina) is worth ten thousand prayers, and one prayer in the Aqṣā mosque is worth a thousand prayers, and one prayer in the Sacred Mosque (of Mecca) is worth one hundred thousand prayers." Sometimes only two of the three cities are mentioned: "A prayer in my mosque is worth more than one thousand prayers elsewhere, except (for a prayer)in the Sacred Mosque (of Mecca)." Sometimes a fourth city is mentioned (for example, Al-Kūfa) or a different, third, one, but more often than not Mecca is the first of three— a phenomenon with which Jewish Jerusalem never had to wrestle.

Symbolic Jerusalem and the shunning of symbols in Islam. We now turn to the most basic point of difference between the status of Jerusalem in Judaism and that of Mecca in Islam. At the end of the entry "Jerusalem" in the *Encyclopaedia of Religion*, F. E. Peters writes:

> Jerusalem is more than a city or even a capital. It is a [biblical] idea. People, city, and temple became one . . . linked in destiny and in God's

plan, then transformed and apotheosized into Heavenly Jerusalem . . .
[even after its destruction Jerusalem remained] not as a vaguely remembered nostalgia, but as a symbol built solidly into the thought and
liturgy of Jerusalem.

We know that this idea and symbol of Jerusalem, and especially heavenly
Jerusalem, became very important in Christian thought,[27] and it may well be
that the unique position of Jerusalem in Islam was a continuation of this
Judaeo-Christian heritage. Mecca, on the other hand, never became a symbol
of Islam or in Islam. It was neither a capital nor even a spiritual capital, and
despite the myth of the heavenly Kaʿbas—seven above the earth and seven
below of exactly the same measurements as the earthly Kaʿba in Mecca—there
is no real Islamic counterpart to the Judaeo-Christian heavenly Jerusalem.[28]
Why is this so? I believe the answer has less to do with Mecca itself than
with the more general characteristics of mainstream Islam as a puritan, almost
spartan, religion which aspires to understand and express the unity and tran-
scendence of God (*Tawḥīd*) in the most abstract way possible. Islam knows
of no visual symbols, just as it shuns icons, liturgy, music, drama and processions, festivals, myths, and even—to some extent—allegory. Of course, no
religion is devoid of symbolic language, and in Islam there were mystics and
Shīʿites as well as others who cultivated this language. Nevertheless, of the
three monotheistic religions, mainstream Islam avoided symbols and symbolism more than the other two, apparently because it was always devoted to
attaining the highest level of perfect, pure, and abstract monotheism without
succumbing, as it were, to any human need for symbolism and allegory.
Therefore, Islam has, for example, no visual symbol[29] like the cross and no
parallel to the lulav or the symbolic parts of the Passover seder, or to the
incense bowl or shofar of Jewish mosaic art. We shall not examine here either
the details of this claim or whether the Qurʾān, the Arabic script, the *Miḥrāb*-
prayer niche, or even the Kaʿba and other items could be considered symbols
of Islam. Suffice it to say that if we define symbol as something "presented to
the senses or the imagination which stands for something else,"[30] Islam may
perhaps have "marks or signs of identification," but no visual symbols. With
regard to Mecca, it is certainly true that Muslim authors explicitly and pur-
posefully denied any symbolic status to the holy city, or to any other place,
just as they denied any religious symbolism to special weekly or yearly times.
Friday, for example, is not a day of rest because God never needed any rest
after the six days of creation![31]
Thus, this deep difference between the two holy cities has its roots not only
in the different historical circumstances that shaped their destinies, but also

resulted from the very basic differences in their character. While Judaism accepted, to a certain extent at least, the pagan legacy of holy places and holy times, as well as symbolic signs, thereby catering to the needs of the people who cannot live with a totally abstract religion, mainstream Islam tried to avoid symbolism even of holy times and places, leaving holiness and symbolism to God alone. (This—at least on the theoretical level; in practice, however, this attitude failed completely and popular religion offered copious answers to the demands of the people in terms of festivals, holy places, and holy times.) In this regard, we should examine the unique quotation which Al-Samhūdī quotes from one Ibn ʿAbd Al-Salām (a Damascene Shafiʿite Doctor of Law who died in Cairo in 1262) and which he, like most of his sources, cannot accept as he strives to prove that Al-Madina and the Prophet's tomb therein are the most holy places in the world:

> All times[32] and all places are equal and they differ in merit only because of what happens in them, not because of any inherent quality in them. In the same way also the merit of Mecca and Al-Madina is connected only with what a person performs in them and with the fact that God Almighty is most generous to his servants and multiplies the rewards of deeds done in those cities.[33]

This is the religious ideal of Islam which only few have dared to formulate in such an explicit manner and which was seldom achieved in reality. Regarding Mecca, however, it seems to have succeeded in putting limits on the city's sanctity, denying it the symbolic status which Jerusalem has attained in Judaism.

Notes

1. Abū Ḥāmid Al-Ghazzālī, *Iḥyā ʿUlūm Al-Dīn* (Cairo, 1356 Hg.), I/7, 485 (Arabic).

2. Some Jewish halakhic decisions which deal with the commandment to live in the Land of Israel also state that sins will be punished there more severely than anywhere else. See, for example, I. Schepansky, *Eretz Israel in the Responsa Literature*, I (Jerusalem, 1996), 121 (Hebrew). I thank David Golinkin for this reference.

3. Al-Ghazzālī (above, note 1), 444–45. See also W. Ende, "Mudjāwir," *Encyclopedia of Islam*², VII (Leiden, 1993), 293–95.

4. Y. Yadin (ed.), *The Temple Scroll* (Jerusalem, 1983), 285–94.

5. Because of these difficulties, some scholars erroneously thought that these prohibitions relate only to the Temple and Temple Mount, and not to the entire city. See J. Milgrom, "The City of The Temple: A Response to L. H. Schiffman," *JQR* 85 (1994), 125–28.

6. Yadin (above, note 4), 289.

7. Ibid., 294. Cf. Deut. 23:13–15.

8. Al-Ghazzālī (above, note 1), 490.

9. B Sotah 48a.

10. *ARN*, A, Chapter 4 (ed. S. Schechter [Vienna, 1887], 19). See also Version B, Chapter 5, there.

11. B Berakhot 32b.

12. There are, of course, many more examples of this kind. The English translation of the blessings is taken from the J. H. Hertz, *The Jewish Prayer Book* (New York, 1965).

13. For example, they ridicule the idea that God Himself—the Shekhina—went into exile. The Spaniard Ibn Ḥazm (d. 1064) vehemently attacked the talmudic anthropomorphic myth (Berakhot 3a and 7a) about God plucking His hair, moaning like a dove, or meeting with Rabbi Ishmael among the ruins of the Temple while mourning its destruction. Cf. H. Lazarus-Yafeh, *Intertwined Worlds, Medieval Islam and Bible Criticism* (Princeton, 1992), 31–32.

14. Y. Yahalom, "The Temple and the City in Hebrew Liturgical Poetry," *The History of Jerusalem*, I, ed. J. Prawer (Jerusalem, 1987), 215–35 (Hebrew).

15. M. Idel, "Jerusalem in Jewish Thought in the Thirteenth Century," *The History of Jerusalem*, II, ed. J. Prawer (Jerusalem, 1991), 267–69 (Hebrew); see also J. Dan, "Jerusalem in Jewish Spirituality," *City of the Great King: Jerusalem from David to the Present*, ed. N. Rosowsky (Cambridge, MA, 1996), 60–73.

16. See my "Is There a Concept of Redemption in Islam?" *Some Religious Aspects of Islam* (London, 1981), 48–57.

17. See *Al-Risāla Al-Qushayriyya* (Cairo, 1940), 201 (Arabic); Pseudo-Ibn ʿArabī, *Commentary to the Qurʾan*, I, (no place, no date), 66, 68–70 (Arabic). Cf. my "The Religious Dialectics of the Ḥadjdj," *Some Religious Aspects of Islam* (above, note 16), 33–34.

18. R. A. Nicholson (trans. from the Persian), *The Kashf Al-Maḥjūb* by ʿAlī Al-Hujwīrī (London, 1959), 327. See also p. 328 there.

19. See my "Religious Dialectics" (above, note 17), 28–29.

20. See M. G. Hodgson, *The Venture of Islam*, I (Chicago, 1961), 491.

21. See S. D. Goitein, "The Sanctity of Jerusalem and Palestine in Early Islam" in his *Studies in Islamic History and Institutions* (Leiden, 1966), 135–48.

22. Only during the personal ʿUmra pilgrimage is one not to leave Mecca for these places outside Mecca.

23. Therefore, one may pray *over* the Prophet, but not *to* him. The Wahhabis tried unsuccessfully to demolish the Prophet's tomb in order to stop its veneration and worship.

24. See Taqī Al-Dīn Muḥammad Al-Fāsī Al-Makkī, *Shifā Al-Ghurām fī Akhbār Al-Balad Al-Ḥarām*, I (Cairo, 1956), 74–83 (in Arabic).

25. Nūr Al-Dīn Al-Samhūdī, *Wafā Al-Wafā bi-Akhbār Dār Al-Muṣṭafā* (Cairo, 1326 Hg.) (Arabic).

26. M. J. Kister, "You shall only set out for three mosques: a Study of an Early Tradition," *Le Muséon* 82 (1969), 173–96.

27. See, for example, R. J. Z. Werblowsky, "The Meaning of Jerusalem to Jews, Christians and Muslims," *The Charles Strong Memorial Lecture* (Australia, 1972; reprint Jerusalem, 1978); J. Prawer, "Jerusalem in the Christian Perspective of the Early Middle Ages," *History of Jerusalem* (above, note 15), 249–82; as well as the articles by L. Perrone and R. Wilken in this volume.

28. Nor are there any medieval religious representations of Mecca the city (although there are paintings of the Kaʿba) or any other cities called after her. See G. Stroumsa's article in this volume; and cf. O. Grabar, "Jerusalem Elsewhere," *City of the Great King* (above, note 15), 333–43.

29. See O. Grabar, *The Formation of Islamic Art* (New Haven, 1973), 138.

30. This definition is based on E. Bevan, *Symbolism and Belief* (Boston, 1957), 11.

31. See Lazarus-Yafeh, *Some Religious Aspects of Islam* (above, note 16), 41.

32. Ibid., 38–47 (Muslim festivals).

33. Al-Samhūdī (above, note 25), 21.

21

Pilgrims and Pilgrimage to Jerusalem during the Early Muslim Period[1]

AMIKAM ELAD

The Historical Framework

The politico-religious status of Jerusalem in the Muslim world was established at the beginning of the second/eighth century, during the Umayyad period (661–750). However, from the mid-eighth century, and even prior to it, Jerusalem lost its central political, though not religious, status, and throughout most of the Middle Ages it was an outlying city of diminished importance.

The effort made by the Umayyads to exalt and glorify the religious and political status of Jerusalem was enormous. The evidence for this is to be found in the scope of the Umayyad building program in Jerusalem, in the sanctification of the Ḥaram, and in the rituals instituted there. The building program included not only Qubbat al-Ṣakhra and al-Masjid al-Aqṣā, but also the smaller-domed buildings on the Ḥaram (Qubbat al-Silsila, Qubbat al-Nabī, Qubbat al-Miʿrāj; the Ḥaram wall with its holy gates, which have combined Jewish and Islamic resonances (Bāb al-Nabī, Bāb al-Sakīna, Bab Ḥiṭṭa); the six large structures outside the Ḥaram, including the large two-storied palace, from the second floor of which a bridge led apparently to al-Aqṣā Mosque; and, finally, the roads to and from Jerusalem built and repaired by ʿAbd al-Malik.[2]

This intense building activity must be seen in the context of the sanctification of the Ḥaram and the rituals performed there. Although there is no explicit written testimony that the Umayyads considered Jerusalem to be their capital, their extraordinary investment of material and human resources in the city leaves no doubt that this was so. Certainly, at the local level, it would seem that the city was for some time the political and administrative center of the district (*jund*) of Filasṭīn. The abundance of "Traditions in Praise of Jerusalem," including the exegeses of passages of the Qur'ān which are devoted to the city, and the "historical" traditions concerning the conquest of the city and the peace treaty granted it, all belong to this concerted effort on the part of the first Umayyads to give exceptional status to Jerusalem.

It therefore seems evident that the Umayyads intended to develop Jerusalem into both a political and religious center which, if not intended to surpass Mecca, would at least be its equal. This effort began with the reign of Mu'āwiya b. Abī Sufyān (661–680) and ended during the reign of Sulaymān b. 'Abd al-Malik (715–717), when he began to build the city of Ramla. Sulaymān, apparently, did not share the adoration of Jerusalem which his father and brother had demonstrated before him.[3]

Muslim Worship on the Ḥaram during the Umayyad Period

Ritual ceremonies in Jerusalem in the Umayyad period (and later as well) were mainly concentrated on the Ḥaram. There are a number of early testimonies of these services, and they certainly confirm the trend developed and encouraged by the first Umayyad caliphs. Many of these rituals were performed in and around the Dome of the Rock (Qubbat al-Ṣakhra).

During the time of 'Abd al-Malik, the Dome of the Rock was opened to the public on Mondays and Thursdays only (!); on the other days only the attendants entered. These attendants cleansed and purified themselves, changed their clothing, burned incense, and anointed the Rock with all kinds of perfume. Prayers were held after incense was burnt. Ten gatekeepers were responsible for each gate.[4] During 'Abd al-Malik's reign, the Dome was coated with gold and the Rock was surrounded with an ebony balustrade, behind which—between the pillars—hung curtains woven with gold. Jews and Christians were employed in different services on the Ḥaram: they cleaned the dirt there, made glass for the lamps and goblets, and prepared wicks for the lamps. They were exempt from the poll tax and passed these tasks on as an inheritance.[5] Apparently, the gatekeepers mentioned above do not refer to these same Jews or Christians.

Another early tradition says that there were forty guards, one of whom belonged to the *Anṣār*. Also serving on the Ḥaram were *al-Akhmās*, slaves of the caliph who belonged to the State Treasury as the fifth part (*khums*) of the booty or who were acquired by the Treasury on account of this *khums*.[6]

A chain hung from the middle of the Dome of the Rock. An interesting tradition relates that at the time of 'Abd al-Malik a precious stone was suspended from this chain together with two horns of the ram sacrificed by

Abraham, and the crown of *Kisrā*, king of Persia. According to another tradition, prior to the siege of Mecca by ʿAbdallāh b. al-Zubayr in 683–684, the two horns of the ram sacrificed by Abraham in redemption of his son were hung in the Kaʿba. According to one version of the latter tradition, they were placed on the fence of the Kaʿba at the time it was built and renovated by Ibn al-Zubayr, and were shattered there.[7] Less than ten years later, horns of the ram were allegedly found at the Dome of the Rock in Jerusalem.

Evidently, already in the Umayyad period there were a number of places venerated within the Dome of the Rock where the Muslims performed ritual ceremonies. Two of these, the Black Paving Stone (*al-Balāṭa al-Sawdāʾ*) and the Gate of Isrāfil, were of special significance.[8]

During the season of the *ḥajj*, the same ritual ceremonies were held on the Ḥaram as were held in Mecca. One interesting tradition, parts of which are unparalleled in the known sources, describes in great length the ritual ceremonies customary on the Ḥaram during the time of ʿAbd al-Malik. The text is found in the book of Sibṭ b. al-Jawzī (1186–1256), *Mirʾāt al-Zamān*, which is still mainly in manuscript form.[9]

Analysis of Sibṭ b. al-Jawzī's Description

Generally, the text can be divided into two parts. From the first part it is learned that the politico-religious situation, i.e., the struggle with ʿAbdallāh b. al-Zubayr, drove ʿAbd al-Malik to prevent *Ahl-al-Shām* from going to Mecca to perform the *ḥajj* and then build the Dome of the Rock as a replacement for the Kaʿba. The second part (much longer than the first) deals mainly with the actual building of the Dome of the Rock, its special attendants, the rituals held within, some physical characteristics of the Ḥaram, and in this connection the description of the building and renovations on the Ḥaram during the reign of the ʿAbbāsid caliphs, al-Manṣūr (754–775) and al-Mahdī (775–786).

Many passages in the second part have almost identical parallels in the "Literature in Praise of Jerusalem" (*Faḍāʾil Bayt al-Maqdis*). The first part, which deals with the motives for the building of the Dome of the Rock, has almost no parallels in this genre. This description reported by Sibṭ b. al-Jawzī is much longer and detailed than the well-known tradition of al-Yaʿqūbī (d. 897), which was one of the main sources for scholars debating the reasons and circumstances for the erection of the Dome of the Rock.[10]

Notably, while many identical parallels are found in Sibṭ b. al-Jawzī's book and in the *Faḍāʾil* literature, the sources of *Mirʾāt al-Zamān* are al-Wāqidī (d. 823), Hishām b. al-Sāʾib al-Kalbī (d. 764), and his son Muḥammad (d. 819), whereas the sources for this tradition in the *Faḍāʾil* books are a Jerusalem family.[11]

The account of Ibn al-Jawzī has bearing upon some historical as well as historiographical problems. It has significant implications for the importance of Jerusalem during the Umayyad period. The importance of the Dome of the Rock and the reasons for its erection are also part of this vast problem.[12] There is good reason to discount the objections of Goitein and adhere to the earlier contention of Goldziher that it was the struggle with Ibn al-Zubayr which caused ʿAbd al-Malik to build the Dome of the Rock and to attempt to divert the *hajj* from Mecca to Jerusalem. This in no way conflicts with what appears to have been two other important considerations in ʿAbd al-Malik's development of the Ḥaram: the association of the spot with the Last Days and with the Temple of Solomon.

Although the immediate cause for the construction of the Dome of the Rock and the attempt to divert the *hajj* from Mecca to Jerusalem may have been his struggle with Ibn al-Zubayr, ʿAbd al-Malik was also concerned with emphasizing the central place of Jerusalem, of the Ḥaram and the *Ṣakhra*, within the religious landscape of early Islam. There is no contradiction in arguing that he built the Dome of the Rock on the site of the Temple of Solomon as a symbol of the Last Days and also as a rival to Mecca, which was then in the hands of his opponent Ibn al-Zubayr.

Worship on the Ḥaram after the Umayyad Period: The Wuqūf

Additional testimonies on the performance of the *wuqūf* ceremonies in Jerusalem on the Ḥaram come from later periods. Nāṣir-i Khusraw, who visited Jerusalem in the year 1047, describes the performance of *al-taʿrīf* opposite the Rock on the Ḥaram, the offering of the ʿĪd al-Adḥā sacrifice on the Ḥaram by those Muslims who were unable to make the pilgrimage to Mecca. Al-Ṭurṭūshī, who was in Jerusalem in the last decade of the eleventh century, notes that on the day of ʿArafāt, in the mosque in Jerusalem, the people from that city and the neighboring villages stood in prayer with their faces turned to Mecca, raising their voices in *duʿāʾ* (prayers of request, invocations) as though they were standing before Mount ʿArafāt in Mecca.

In the year 1189 Ṣalāḥ al-Dīn traveled from Ṣafad to Jerusalem for the explicit purpose of celebrating the holiday of the sacrifice there. Ibn Taymiyya (d. 1329) also tells of the existence of the *wuqūf* custom in Jerusalem. Toward the middle of the fourteenth century, ʿAlāʾ al-Dīn, Abū al-Ḥasan composed a poem (*qaṣīda*), whose verses blatantly condemn a number of the rituals held in Jerusalem which related to the Holy Rock and other places on the Ḥaram.[13] Muslims from Jerusalem and the adjacent areas, as well as pilgrims from all over the Muslim world, most certainly took part in the rituals held on the Ḥaram in the course of their visit to the holy places in the city.

The Visit and Pilgrimage to Jerusalem and Its Holy Sites

Christian and Jewish Pilgrims to the Holy Land

There was a long and developed tradition of Christian worshippers visiting the Holy Land already before the early Muslim period (634–1099).[14] Its roots were still deeply embedded in the early period of the Christian church, but the real impetus was in the days of Constantine, following the pilgrimage of his mother, Helena, to the Holy Land.[15]

The pilgrims set out for the Holy Land with guidebooks which were widely circulated in the Christian world. One of the first guides, already heard of at the beginning of the fourth century, was Eusebius' *Onomasticon*, "The Guide to the Land of the Bible."[16] There were short guides written for the Christian pilgrim at the beginning of the sixth century which were prepared for the pilgrim to carry about during his travels to the holy places and were already distributed to him at his place of origin in the West.[17] A number of descriptions of Christian pilgrims' routes in the Holy Land in the early Muslim period seem to follow such itineraries.[18]

Many testimonies exist of pilgrimages by Jews to the Holy Land, especially from Syria but also from places farther away in the Muslim world. We have almost no information about Jewish pilgrimages from European countries during this period, which were ongoing whenever external circumstances made it possible.[19] It is noteworthy that the first guidebook for the Jewish pilgrim to Jerusalem (and Palestine?) was most probably the one published by J. Braslavi[20] from the eleventh century. Guidebooks for Jewish pilgrims to the Holy Land existed from the twelfth century on.[21]

Muslim Pilgrimage to the Holy Land

We have no testimony during the early Muslim period for the existence of a guide for Muslim pilgrims to the Holy Land. The earliest-known book concerning the visits to the known Muslim holy sites (in the Islamic caliphate) dates to the ninth century. Three more treatises on this subject, dating to the end of the tenth century, are known, however none of them has survived. Their authors were Shī'ites (apparently not by coincidence), and it is clear that they discussed, first and foremost, visiting the sites holy to the Shī'ites.[22]

The Umayyad and Early ʿAbbāsid Periods[23]

From the beginning of the Umayyad period, Muslim visitors and pilgrims came to Jerusalem to pray in its holy places. A few very early testimonies of this have been collected and are cited here. However, even partial conclusions regarding the scope of the phenomenon cannot be drawn from them, nor are specific pilgrim itineraries or a complete list of the holy sites that pilgrims visited and prayed at given. What is known is that the places visited were concentrated mainly on the Ḥaram, and that the itinerary also included the Place of Prayer of David (Miḥrāb Dāwūd), the Spring of Silwān, the Valley of Gehenna (mainly the Church of Mary), and the Mount of Olives.

Many traditions were circulated in the Umayyad period in an attempt to encourage pilgrimage to Jerusalem and prayer there. These constitute a part of the "Traditions in Praise of Syria" (Faḍā'il al-Shām).[24] In addition, special traditions in praise of places in Jerusalem itself were circulated at the beginning of the Umayyad period as part of the Faḍā'il literature, and this certainly encouraged pilgrimages and visits there. Thus, we have a rather early tradition that was circulated no later than the first quarter of the eighth century that "he who comes to Jerusalem and prays to the right of the Rock [on the Ḥaram] and to its north, and prays in the (holy) place (al-mawḍi') of the Chain, and gives a little or much charity, his prayers will be answered and God will remove his sorrows, and he will be freed of his sins as on the day his mother gave birth to him."[25]

Tradition has it that the Prophet "prayed" to the right of the Rock on the night of the isrā', and it was there that the Qubbat al-Nabī was later built.[26] It should also be remembered that he who prays to the north of the Rock unites the two qiblas.[27] As for the place of the Chain, this may mean Qubbat al-Silsila (or perhaps the chain that was suspended from the center of the Dome of the Rock).[28]

Another early tradition (the isnād concludes with Khālid b. Ma'dān, d. 103 or 104/721–722) encourages visits to the holy places in Jerusalem: "Whosoever comes to Jerusalem must come to the eastern Miḥrāb Dāwūd and pray there and bathe in the spring, the Spring of Silwān, for it is one of the springs of Paradise, and he is not allowed to enter the churches and buy anything from there."[29]

The pilgrims came to Jerusalem from nearby locales (from Syria[30] and from more distant regions. Some came in fulfillment of personal vows.[31] Anyone who could not make the pilgrimage and pray in Jerusalem could send olive oil instead to illuminate the Mosque of Jerusalem.[32] Goitein thinks that Jews and Christians also donated oil for illumination of the mosque.[33]

Some pilgrims came to Jerusalem before the season of the ḥajj in order to sanctify themselves and prepare themselves for the ḥajj or the 'umra. This santification ceremony was called iḥrām or ihlāl (meaning that the person sanctifying himself, the muḥrim, announced out loud his intention and readiness to enter into a state of iḥrām).

Early traditions, which can be dated back to at least the first quarter of the second/eighth century, extol the sanctification of the *ḥajj* or the *ʿumra* from Jerusalem.[34] There is information on a number of important Muslim scholars who went up to Jerusalem to perform the *iḥrām* there before the *ḥajj*, namely ʿAbdallāh b. ʿUmar (d. 74/669), ʿAbdallāh b. al-ʿAbbās (d. 58/678), Maḥmūd b. al-Rabīʿ, Abū Nuʿaym (d. 99/717), and a little later Wakīʿ b. al-Jarrāḥ (d. 812), who performed an *iḥrām* in Jerusalem.[35] All these were famous people; some of them did not live either in Syria or Palestine. Obviously scholars and other residents of Palestine were also present on the Ḥaram during the *iḥrām* ceremony before the *ḥajj*, and it may be assumed that they constituted the majority of those sanctifying themselves. It is related, for example, that Ṣāliḥ b. Yūsuf, Abū Shuʿayb, a resident of Palestine who died in Ramla in 282/890, performed the *ḥajj* ninety (or seventy) times, and each time he would perform the *iḥrām* from the Rock of Jerusalem [or the Ḥaram: *min Ṣakhrat Bayt al-Maqdis*].[36]

There is great virtue in combining the visit to Jerusalem with one to Hebron. All those who visit Jerusalem and afterwards go to the tomb of Abraham in Hebron will there recite five prayers; their requests from God will be granted and all their sins will be forgiven.[37] Another tradition combined the pilgrimage to Mecca and the visit to al-Madīna with that to Jerusalem, praising and recommending prayer in the three mosques of these cities during the same year.[38] Perhaps in this light one can understand the words of al-Muqaddasī (second half of the tenth century) who, when describing the Berbers in North Africa, says that there are very few of them who do not visit Jerusalem (*wa-aqallu man lā yazūru Bayt al-Maqdis minhum*).[39]

A rare testimony combining the pilgrimage to Mecca with the *ziyāra* to Jerusalem is found in a poem by al-Muʿallā b. Ṭarīf, the *mawlā* of Caliph al-Mahdī (775–786).

Kāmil Muraffal:
Yā ṣāḥi innī qad ḥajaj / tu wa-zurtu Bayta ʾl-Maqdisi
Wa-dakhaltu Luddan ʿāmidan / fī-ʿidi Māryā Jirjisi
Fa-raʾaytu fīhi niswatan / mithla ʾẓ-ẓibāʾi ʾl-kunnasi.[40]

Translation:
Oh, my friend:
I have already performed the pilgrimage / and visited Jerusalem
And I entered [the city of] Lod intending to visit / the St. Georgius Festival
And I saw there women / who looked like gazelles gathering to their shelter.[41]

Al-Muʿallā b. Ṭarīf visited Lod for the St. Georgius festival, one of the Christian festivals recognized by the Muslims in Palestine according to which they calculated the seasons of the year. The festival of Lod (*ʿĪd Ludd*) is the festival of the sowing season.[42] Exactly when al-Muʿallā visited Jerusalem and Lod is not known, however it may have been at the time of al-Mahdī's visit to Jerusalem in 163/780.[43]

Jerusalem also constituted a unique center for the early ascetics and Muslim mystics, the *zuhhād*, who developed and circulated the "Traditions in Praise of Jerusalem." Some resided in the city and others made pilgrimages to it from all corners of the Muslim world. They often combined their visit to Jerusalem with visits to other border towns (*ribāṭāt*) in Palestine and other parts of the Muslim world.[44]

The testimonies for visits to Jerusalem and its holy places are very early, but what the pilgrim's itinerary was is not known, nor is there a full list of the holy sites which they visited or where they prayed. It was said of the well-known scholar al-Awzāʿī (d. 157/774)[45] that he prayed on the Ḥaram with his back to the Rock, saying: "Thus did ʿUmar b. ʿAbd al-ʿAzīz" (717–720). The transmitter of the tradition continues: "And al-Awzāʿī did not come to any of the holy places which are generally visited."[46] It was also said of the scholar Wakīʿ b. al-Jarrāḥ (d. 812) "that he did not visit a single one of the holy places [which it was customary to visit]."[47] The latter two traditions are evidence of the controversy between the scholars in the second century of the *hijra* (eighth century of the Christian era) regarding the holiness of Jerusalem and the holy places there, especially of the Rock.[48]

A tradition which emphasizes the controversy between the Muslim scholars on this question and, at the same time, offers evidence of the itinerary of the Muslim pilgrim at the end of the eighth century was reported by Jaʿfar b. Musāfir (d. Muḥarram 254/January, 868),[49] who states:

> I saw Muʾammal b. Ismāʿīl (d. 206/821–822)[50] in Jerusalem give [a small] amount of money to people (*aʿṭā qawman shayʾan*) and they went round with him to those [holy] places (*fī tilka 'l-mawāḍiʿ*). His son said to him: "Oh my father, Wakīʿ b. al-Jarrāḥ has already entered [Jerusalem?] and he did not make a course [of the holy places]." [Muʾammal] said: "Each person does as he pleases."[51]

Although specific places were not mentioned in the sources, from the evidence compiled of visits to the holy places in Jerusalem from the Umayyad period to the early ʿAbbāsid period, approximately to the year 800, it can safely be assumed that, first and foremost, they included sites on the Ḥaram, e.g., the Dome of the Rock, the Aqṣā Mosque, the Dome of the Prophet, the Dome of Ascension, and the Dome of the Chain. A number of gates on the Ḥaram were surely included: the gates of Mercy, Ḥiṭṭa, the Divine Presence (Sakīna), the Tribes (al-Asbāṭ), and the Prophet. And, finally, there were additional places outside the Ḥaram, such as Miḥrāb Dāwūd, the Spring of Silwān, and the Mount of Olives.[52]

The description by Ibn Kathīr, who outlines the existing situation in the Umayyad period, informs us that visitors to Jerusalem saw pictures of *al-Sirāt*, Paradise, and other scenes connected with the Latter Days on the Ḥaram. Ninth- and tenth-century geographers, Ibn al-Faqīh, Ibn ʿAbd Rabbihi, al-Muqaddasī, and also the Muslim traveler Nāṣir-i Khusraw, describe or mention numerous structures on the Ḥaram, many of which were no doubt erected in the Umayyad period. It is difficult to determine exactly where they were located, since their names and locations changed over the years.[53]

The First Guide for the Muslim Pilgrim from the Beginning of the Eleventh Century

It has been clearly shown that from the earlier periods (seventh–ninth centuries) there is much evidence of pilgrimage and visits to the holy places in Jerusalem, especially on the Ḥaram. The "Literature in Praise of Jerusalem" supplies much information concerning religious and learned men who dwelt in Jerusalem or who came to visit its holy sites, however at this stage of research it is very difficult to assess the nature and especially extent of these pilgrimages in the early Muslim period. It has already been stressed that a complete description of the pilgrim's stops during this period is lacking and we know of no guidebook for the Muslim traveler from this early period.

It was only in the early eleventh century that a complete and detailed itinerary of visits to the Muslim holy places in Jerusalem was recorded by Ibn al-Murajjā. It is the first of its kind known,[54] and its influence is well attested in the late compilations of the "Literature in Praise of Jerusalem." Some of these late authors copy the itinerary almost verbatim, while others present only parts of it. A few scholars mentioned this guidebook and briefly stressed its importance.[55] A separate discussion was dedicated to it by Livne.[56]

Ibn al-Murajjā describes more than twenty recommended sites in Jerusalem. In some of them the Muslim must pray and in other places he need only perform the invocation or combine prayers with invocations. Livne came to the conclusion that the majority of these prayers have no direct link to the specific places in which they are said. Prayers and invocations are already found in the early compilations of *ḥadīth* and in the early *adab* literature; some of the prayers "give the impression that they paraphrase some verses from the

Bible, especially from Psalms." The prayers which have a special link to places in Jerusalem are those said in Miḥrāb Dāwūd (*sūrat ṣād*) and Miḥrāb Maryam (*sūrat Maryam*). Summarizing this topic, Livne concludes that the prayers were probably compiled artificially by Ibn al-Murajjā himself.[57]

Dating the Guide of Ibn al-Murajjā

Unlike most of the traditions in Ibn al-Murajjā's book, which can be dated to a much earlier period with the help of the *isnād*, the traditions in the "Muslim Guide" (except for the prayers) are not preceded by an *isnād*. Therefore, it appears that Ibn al-Murajjā composed the guide himself during the first half of the eleventh century. It is highly probable, however, that this itinerary, or a similar one, was known to visitors to the holy places in Jerusalem already at the beginning or middle of the tenth century. This can be deduced from an interesting tradition, recorded by Ibn al-Murajjā with an *isnād* which concluded with Abū Muḥammad, ʿAbdallāh b. Muḥammad al-Khūlī [?], relating that on the tenth of Muḥarram, in the year 335 [= 12th August, 946], he had a dream wherein he visited the holy places on the Ḥaram in Jerusalem. In this dream he visited:

1. The Dome of the Rock. Within the Dome.
2. The Black Paving Stone (al-Balāṭa al-Sawdāʾ). Then to:
3. The Dome of the Ascension (of the Prophet) to Heaven (Qubbat al-Miʿrāj).
4. The Dome of the Prophet (Qubbat al-Nabī).
5. The Gate (Bāb) of Ḥiṭṭa.
6. The Cradle of Jesus (Mahd ʿĪsā) and Miḥrāb Maryam.
7. Miḥrāb Zakariyyāʾ.
8. The Gate of Mercy (Bāb al-Raḥma).
9. Al-Masjid al-Aqṣā.[58]

All these sites, and several others, are mentioned (though not in this order) by Ibn al-Murajjā.[59] This tradition most probably testifies to the existence of an itinerary to the holy places on the Ḥaram. Its purpose is most probably to reinforce and praise their sanctity.[60]

Stops in the Visitors' Itinerary to the Holy Places in Jerusalem, according to Ibn al-Murajjā

1. The Dome of the Rock (Qubbat al-Ṣakhra). Within the Dome of the Rock the Muslim should pray in the following holy places:

1a. The Black Paving Stone (al-Balāṭa al-Sawdā').

1b. The Cave under the Rock.

1c. Maqām al-Nabī. Then the Muslim must turn toward the east, stand and pray at the eastern gate of the Dome of the Rock, which is:

1d. The Gate of [the Angel] Isrāfil (Bāb Isrāfil). Then he goes out of the Dome towards:

2. The Dome of the Chain (Qubbat al-Silsila). Then to:

3. The Dome of Ascension [of the Prophet] to Heaven (Qubbat al-Miʿrāj). Then to:

4. The Dome of the Prophet (Qubbat al-Nabī). Then to:

5. The Gate of Mercy (Bāb al-Raḥma). Then to:

6. Miḥrāb Zecharia (Zakariyyā'). Then to:

7. Solomon's Chair (Kursī Sulaymān), which is located on a rock at the backside [= the southwest] of the mosque [i.e., the Ḥaram]. Then he goes on toward:

8. The Gate of the Shekhina (Bāb al-Sakīna). Then to:

9. The Gate of Ḥiṭṭa. Then to:

10. Al-Masjid al-Aqṣā. Within the Mosque the Muslim should pray in:

10a. Miḥrāb ʿUmar.

10b. Miḥrāb Muʿāwiya.

10c. All the *miḥrāb*s within the Mosque. Then he ought to descend to:

11. The Gate of the Prophet (Bāb al-Nabī). Then he continues toward:

12. Miḥrāb Maryam, also known as the Cradle of Jesus (Mahd ʿĪsā). From there he goes down to:

13. The place which the Angel Gabriel drilled with his finger and tied up al-Burāq. From this place the Muslim can ascend to:

14. Al-Sāhira, which is the Mount of Olives (Ṭur Sīnā [= Ṭur Zaytā],[61] or enter:

15. Miḥrāb Dāwūd, which is [located] at the western gate of the city.

Notes

1. This article is based largely on Chapter II of my book, *Medieval Jerusalem and Islamic Worship: Holy Places, Ceremonies, Pilgrimage* (Leiden, 1995).

2. For a comprehensive discussion, see ibid., Chapters I and III.

3. A full discussion appears in ibid., Chapter IV.

4. Abū Bakr, Muḥammad b. Aḥmad al-Wāsiṭī, *Faḍā'il al-Bayt al-Muqaddas*, ed. I. Hasson

(Jerusalem, 1979), 81–83, no. 136—the tradition of the Jerusalem family of ʿAbd al-Raḥmān, from Rajāʾ b. Ḥaywa and Yazīd; Mondays and Thursdays were the days the Jews read the Torah; see also O. Livne, "The Sanctity of Jerusalem in Islam," Ph.D. dissertation (Hebrew University of Jerusalem, 1985), 327, note 154, about Mondays and Thursdays, the days the Dome of the Rock was opened to the public; cf. the interesting tradition in the Ṣaḥīfa of Ibn Lahīʿa: Khoury, Raif Georges. ʿAbdallāh Ibn Lahīʿa (97–174/715–790), juge et grand maître de l'école égyptienne (avec édition critique de l'unique rouleau de papyrus arabe conservé à Heidelberg) (Wiesbaden, 1986), 288, ll. 298–301.

5. Al-Wāsiṭī (above, note 4), 43–44, no. 60 and the parallel sources; Abū 'l-Maʿālī, al-Musharraf b. al-Murajjā, Faḍāʾil Bayt al-Maqdis wa-'l-Shām wa-'l-Khalīl (ms. Tübingen VI 27), ed. by O. Livne (Shfaram, 1995), 58–62 (no. 47); both sources and others are mentioned by M. Gil, Palestine during the First Muslim Period (634–1099), 3 vols. (Tel-Aviv, 1983), 72, no. 86 (Hebrew) (= A History of Palestine, 634–1099, vol. I trans. from Hebrew by E. Broido [Cambridge, 1992], p. 60); see also Mujīr al-Dīn, Abū 'l-Yumn, ʿAbd al-Raḥmān b. Muḥammad, al-Ḥanbalī, al-ʿUlaymī. Al-Uns al-Jalīl bi-Taʾrīkh al-Quds wa-'l-Khalīl, I (Beirut-Amman, 1973), 281; Livne (above, note 4), 295.

6. Elad (above, note 1), 51–52.

7. Ibid., 52 (and the discussion therein).

8. On al-Balāṭa al-Sawdāʾ, see ibid., 78–81; on the Gate of Isrāfīl, see ibid., 81–82.

9. B. M. Add, 23, 288, fols. 2b-3a; and Bodleian Library, Marsh 289, fols. 153b-155b; A. Elad, "Why Did ʿAbd al-Malik Build the Dome of the Rock? A Re-examination of the Muslim Sources," Al-Ḥaram al-Sharīf: ʿAbd al-Malik's Jerusalem, eds. J. Raby and J. Johns, Oxford Studies in Islamic Art IX (Oxford, 1992), 33–58.

10. Aḥmad b. Abī Wāḍiḥ (known as al-Yaʿqūbī), Taʾrīkh, II (Leiden, 1882), 311.

11. Elad (above, note 9), 39–40.

12. For a detailed discussion of this text, the reader may consult Elad (above, note 9); idem (above, note 1), Chapter II.

13. For a full discussion and documentation, see ibid., 61–62.

14. But cf. J. A. Taylor, Christians and the Holy Places: The Myth of Jewish-Christian Origins (Oxford, 1993), esp. the last chapter (Conclusion).

15. A selected bibliography on the itineraries of Christian pilgrims to the Holy Land may be found in M. Ish-Shalom, Christian Travels in the Holy Land, Descriptions and Sources on the History of the Jews in Palestine (Tel-Aviv, 1965), 3 (Hebrew).

See also J. Prawer, Histoire du Royaume Latin du Jérusalem, I (Paris, 1969), 127–34; A. Grabois, "The Christian Pilgrimage in the Mediterranean during the Middle Ages and its Consciousness Projection," The Mediterranean: Its Place in the History and Culture of the Jews and Other Nations, ed. The Historical Society of Israel (Jerusalem, 1970), 68–85 (Hebrew); J. Wilkinson, Jerusalem Pilgrims Before the Crusades (Jerusalem, 1977); Gil (above, note 5), Eng. trans., I, 482–86, nos. 719–23; E. D. Hunt, Holy Land Pilgrimage in the Later Roman Empire AD 312–460 (Oxford, 1982); Taylor (above, note 14).

16. Hunt (above, note 15), 97f.

17. Wilkinson (above, note 15), 1, 4–5.

18. English translation in the Palestine Pilgrims Text Society, II (London, 1896); III, (London, 1895); IV (London, 1893), which should be compared and often corrected against Wilkinson's translation.

19. Gil (above, note 15), Eng. trans., I, 624–31, nos. 829–34; see also idem (with the participation of S. Safrai, A. Grossman, H. Ben-Shammai), "Immigration and Pilgrimage in the Arab Period (634–1099)," Cathedra 8 (1978), 123–35; and the discussion, ibid., 136–46 (Hebrew).

20. J. Braslavi, "A Topography of Jerusalem from the Cairo Genizah," *EI*, VIII, *L. A. Mayer Memorial Volume* (Jerusalem, 1964), 69–80; mention also should be made of the Genizah document from the eleventh or twelfth century, dealing with the special prayer of the Jewish pilgrims at the gates of Jerusalem (*Ṣalawāt al-Abwāb fī 'l-Quds*). The document was first published by J. Mann, *Texts and Studies in Jewish History*, II (Cincinnati, 1931), 458, and was republished by L. N. Goldfeld, "A Version of Prayer at the Gates of Jerusalem," *Ha'aretz (Literary Supplement)* from 18th May, 1972.

21. A. Ya'ari, *Jewish Pilgrims' Travels to Eretz Israel from the Middle Ages until the Beginning of the Return of Zion* (Ramat Gan, 1976).

22. Y. Raghib, "Essai d'inventaire chronologique des guides a l'usage des pèlerins du Caire," *Revue des Études Islamiques* 41 (1971), 259–60. Raghib maintains that these early works did indeed deal with pilgrimage to the important Muslim holy sites, such as the Mosque of al-Madīna, Jerusalem, the tombs of the Prophet, 'Alī in najaf, al-Ḥusayn in Karbalā', etc.; see also J. Sourdel-Thomine's introduction to the French trans. of 'Alī b. Abī Bakr, al-Harawī, *Guide des Lieux de Pèlerinage* (Damascus, 1957), XXX–XXXV; I. Goldziher, "Veneration of Saints in Islam," *Muslim Studies*, II, ed. S. M. Stern (London, 1971), 290, esp. note 2.

23. Elad (above, note 1), 62–68.

24. See, for example, S. D. Goitein, "The Sanctity of Jerusalem and Palestine in Early Islam," *Studies in Islamic History and Institutions*, ed. S. D. Goitein (Leiden, 1968), 28–30; Livne (above, note 4), 278–79.

25. Al-Wāsiṭī (above, note 4), 23, no. 29; Livne (above, note 4), 296.

26. Al-Wāsiṭī (above, note 4), 73–74, no. 119.

27. See Elad (above, note 1), 30–31.

28. Ibid., Chapter II, note 5.

29. Al-Wāsiṭī (above, note 4), 13, no. 13; 44, no. 61, and the comprehensive bibliography of the editor therein; Livne (above, note 4), 301.

30. For example, 'Abdāllah b. Abī Zakariyyā' al-Khuzā'ī, a well-known scholar from Damascus (d. 117/735–736) who, whenever he came to Jerusalem, would ascend the Mount of Olives; see Ibn 'Asākir, *Ta'rīkh*, XX (biographies of 'Ubāda b. Awfā-'Abdallāh b. Thawb) (Damascus, 1402/1982), 413 (his biography, ibid., 403–15); for more on him, see Abū Nu'aym, Aḥmad b. 'Abdallāh, al-Iṣfahānī, *Ḥilyat al-Awliyā' wa-Ṭabaqāt al-Aṣfiyā'*, V (Cairo, 1351 H.), p149–53; al-Dhahabī, Shams al-Dīn, Muḥammad b. Aḥmad, *Ta'rīkh (ḥawādith wa-wafayāt 101–120)* (Beirut, 1990), 396–97; idem, *Siyar A'lām al-Nubalā'*, V (Beirut, 1982–85), 149–53.

31. See, for example, al-Wāsiṭī (above, note 4), 30, no. 42 (the end of the Umayyad period), and the editor's note therein; Livne (above, note 4), 280–81.

32. Al-Wāsiṭī (above, note 4), 24–25, no. 32, and the exhaustive bibliography therein; see also S. D. Goitein, "Jerusalem during the Arab Period," *Palestinian Jewry in Early Islamic and Crusader Times in the Light of the Geniza Documents* (Jerusalem, 1980), 13 (first published in *Jerusalem Researches of Eretz Israel* [Jerusalem, 1953], 82-103) (Hebrew); Livne (above, note 4), 281.

33. Goitein (above, note 32); Goitein quotes the Muslim jurist, al-Khaṣṣāf (d. 874/875 A.D.; *Aḥkām al-Awqāf*[Cairo, 1904–1905], 341), who permits Christians and Jews to send oil to illuminate the mosque in Jerusalem. Goitein comments: "And it is possible that the words of the *Ahima'az Scroll* hint at this custom: 'Rabbi Shmuel . . . donated . . . and oil to the Temple at the Western Wall and to the altar within'." And see also idem, "Did 'Umar Prohibit the Stay of Jews in Jerusalem," *Palestinian Jewry* (above, note 32), 41 (supplement) (first published in *Melilah* 3–4 (1950), 156–65, Hebrew); this is contrary to B.-Z. Dinaburg, " 'House of Prayer and Study' for the Jews on the Temple Mount in Arab Times," *Zion* (Anthology) 3 (1929), 62 (Hebrew).

34. Elad (above, note 1), 64 and the bibliography therein.

35. Ibid., 64–65.

36. Abū Muḥammad, Aḥmad b. Muḥammad b. Ibrāhīm b. Tamīm b. Surūr, al-Maqdisī, *Kitāb Muthīr al-Gharām ilā Ziyārat al-Quds wa-'l-Shām*, ed. al-Khaṭimi (Beirut, 1994), 359; in the printed edition of the last part of the book, ed. Aḥmad Ṣāliḥ al-Khālidī (Jaffa, 1365 H.), 56: seventy (*sab'īn*) instead of ninety (*tis'īn*).

37. A. Elad, "Pilgrims and Pilgrimage to Hebron (al-Khalil) during the Early Muslim Period (638?–1099)," *Pilgrims and Travelers to the Holy Land, Proceedings of the Seventh Annual Symposium of the Philip M. and Ethel Klutznick Chair in Jewish Civilization, October 2 and 3, 1994*, eds. B. F. Le Beau and M. Mor, Studies in Jewish Civilization 7 (Omaha, 1996), 28.

38. Elad (above, note 1), 65.

39. Muḥammad b. Aḥmad, al-Muqaddasī, *Aḥsan al-Taqāsīm fī Ma'rifat al-Aqālīm*, BGA III (Leiden, 1866), 243. In the preceding sentence, al-Muqaddasī mentions the pilgrimage customs of the Berbers. It may have been this that prompted Goitein to explain the sentence on their visit to Jerusalem as if the Berbers used to go up to Jerusalem to perform the *iḥrām* from the Rock before their journey to Mecca for the *ḥajj*. However, the text is not so unequivocal, and could be understood otherwise—as if the Berbers came to Jerusalem after the pilgrimage, or perhaps even without any connection with Mecca and the *ḥajj*. Thus, the sentence just affirms generally the visit of the Berbers from North Africa to Jerusalem in the tenth century.

40. Elad (above, note 1), 65–66.

41. Cf. *Qur'ān* 81, v. 16; the visit to Mecca is the *ḥajj* or pilgrimage, whilst to Jerusalem it is simply a visit, *ziyāra*. In the second century, the primacy of Mecca is unchallenged.

42. Al-Muqaddasī (above, note 39), 183; G. Le Strange, *Palestine under the Moslems* (London, 1890), 21.

43. Elad (above, note 1), 17.

44. Ibid., 66, note 76.

45. On al-Awzā'ī, see F. Sezgin, *Geschichte des Arabischen Schrifttums* I (Leiden, 1967), 516–17; J. Schacht, *Encyclopaedia of Islam*[2], V (Leiden, 1986), s.v. "al-Awzā'ī."

46. *Muthīr al-Gharām* (above, note 36), 354, (*wa-lam ya'ti shay'an min al-mazārāt*); Livne (above, note 4), 300–301.

47. *Muthīr al-Gharām* (above, note 36), 356 (*wa-lam yazur shay'an min tilka al-amākin*).

48. For this controversy, see M. J. Kister, "You Shall Only Set Out for Three Mosques," *Le Muséon* 82 (1969), 193. (= *Studies in Jāhiliyya and Early Islam*, Variorum reprints XIV [London, 1988]).

49. On Ja'far b. Musāfir, see Elad (above, note 1), 67.

50. On Mu'ammal b. Ismā'īl, see ibid.

51. Ibid.

52. It was related about 'Abdallāh b. Abī Zakariyyā' (on this figure, see ibid., 63, note 60), that whenever he came to Jerusalem he used to ascend the Mount of Olives (Abū Zur'a < Abū Mushir < Ibrāhīm b. Abī Shaybān < *qāla lī Ziyād b. Abī 'l-Aswad: kāna ṣāḥibukum, ya'nī Ibn Abī Zakariyyā', idhā qadima hāhunā ya'nī, Bayt al-Maqdis, ṣa'ida hādhā 'l-Jabal, ya'nī Ṭūr Zaytā*).

53. Ibid., p. 68, note 85 and the references therein.

54. Ibn al-Murajjā (above, note 5), 66–81, nos. 54–69.

55. H. Busse, "The Sanctity of Jerusalem in Islam," *Judaism* 17 (1968), 466; I. Hasson, "Jerusalem in the Muslim Perspective: The *Qur'ān* and Tradition Literature," *The History of Jerusalem: The Early Islamic Period (638-1099)*, ed. J. Prawer (Jerusalem, 1987), 301 (Hebrew); Livne (above, note 4), 302; Elad (above, note 1), 69.

56. Livne (above, note 4); see also E. Sivan ("The Beginnings of Faḍā'il al-Quds Litera-

ture," *Israel Oriental Studies* 1 [1971], 271), who stressed the importance of the description of the itinerary by Ibn al-Murajjā.

57. Livne (above, note 4), 302–303.

58. Ibn al-Murajjā (above, note 5), 268, no. 407; Livne (above, note 4), 302; Abū ʿAbdallāh, Muḥammad b. Shihāb al-Dīn, Aḥmad b. ʿAlī b. ʿAbd al-Khāliq al-Minhājī, Shams al-Dīn, al-Suyūṭī. *Itḥāf al-Akhiṣṣāʾ bi-Faḍāʾil al-Masjid al-Aqṣā*, I, ed. Aḥmad Ramaḍān Aḥmad (Cairo, 1982), 110–11: a corrupt tradition. The name of the dreamer: Abū ʿAbdallāh b. Muḥammad al-Ḥarīzī. The entire section dealing with the holy places visited is omitted.

59. All of these sites are discussed at length, in Elad (above, note 1), Chapters II and III.

60. Livne (above, note 4) also reached this conclusion.

61. Ibn al-Murajjā (above, note 5), fol. 31a: Ṭūr Sīnā; Ibn al-Firkah (C. Matthews, "The K. Baʿith al-Nufus of Ibnu-l-Firkāḥ," *JPOS* 15 [1953], 68) copies Ibn al-Murajjā: Ṭūr Zaytā.

22

Jerusalem and the Genesis
of Islamic Scripture

ANGELIKA NEUWIRTH

Jerusalem's Honorary Names in Islam[1]

Looking for an Islamic expression of the spiritual meaning of Jerusalem through history, one inevitably comes across a triple honorary name that the city has borne for at least ten centuries[2] and which is still in use among believers as a mnemotechnical device to remind them of the complex significance of the sanctuary:

Ūlā al-ḳiblatayn	(First of the two directions of prayer)
Thānī al-masjidayn	(Second of the two sanctuaries)
Thālith al-ḥaramayn	(Third after the two places of pilgrimage)

At first glance, the three attributes appear surprising: instead of presenting panegyric expressions of the particular "merits of Jerusalem," they rather seem to mirror the inconsistent historical process of attraction and repulsion which this city, as a complex religious symbol, underwent a process which, superficially viewed, may be taken as a steady decrease in recognition during the formative period of Islamic religious development. To do justice to the titles, we should, however, attempt to re-read them within a broader semantic and religious context. Obviously, two of the three titles immediately touch on the process concerning us here, i.e., the genesis of Islamic Scripture. Thus, the epithet "first of the two directions of prayer" relates to the earliest phase of scriptural genesis, recalling a ritual custom—the physical orientation of the worshipper toward Jerusalem—which was practiced by the emerging Muslim community during the Meccan phase of the prophet's activities. The middle epithet, "second of the two sanctuaries," also recalls a development still from the time of the prophet. It refers to the tension emerging between the two foundation places of monotheist worship which were becoming rivals: on the one hand, the Ka'ba of Mecca, soon after the Hijra, had become celebrated as the place from where the Abrahamic worship, i.e., primarily the *rites* of pilgrimage (the ḥajj), had originated; on the other hand, Jerusalem, the "further sanctuary" (*al-masjid al-aqṣā*), presented itself as the center of the "Blessed Land" (*al-arḍ allatī bāraknā fīhā*), the homeland of those Qur'anic prophets whose message had survived in *verbal*, not ritual, forms, i.e., Moses and Jesus. Since the Abrahamic sanctuary should be, of course, more ancient than the sanctuary of the people of Moses (the Banū Isrā'īl) built by Solomon, Jerusalem falls into second place, after Mecca. The last honorary name, "third after the two sanctuaries,"[3] reflects a later compromise. It expresses the ultimate concession that some religious scholars, a few generations after the prophet, would grant those growing circles within Islam who, to the orthodox, exaggerated their esteem for Jerusalem. The epithet, therefore, expresses restriction rather than approval. Jerusalem is conceded third rank only, after Mecca, and now that the prophet's tomb had become a place of pilgrimage—after Medina as well.

Of course, the titles would hardly have survived into modern times as honorary names had they been meant to describe a successive loss of significance. They should, therefore, allow for a different reading. To approximate their intended meaning, we have to ask what particular experiences relating to Jerusalem might be hidden behind these titles, experiences deemed worth preserving by the Muslim community. For our present purposes, we will limit ourselves to an inquiry into the history of the first and the second of these titles.

Ūlā al-ḳiblatayn

The first epithet draws our attention to the peculiar *body* language[4] implied in the Islamic ritual, more precisely its introductory gesture which, however modified, characterizes the prayer worship until today. As is well known, the ritual custom of facing the Ka'ba was preceded historically by the worshippers' orientation toward Jerusalem; this practice was upheld for a few years until it was changed by a revelation dating from the year 2 Hijra.[5] Thus, the ḳibla is to be considered as part and parcel of the emerging Islamic worship from its formative, i.e., middle/late Meccan, period onward. In order to understand the particular consciousness that might have found its expression in the earliest worshippers' adoption of a ḳibla, their orientation toward a distant sanctuary, we have to consider the particular communication process that is implied in Islamic worship. Our source—the Qur'an—the only contemporary one we possess, must be viewed in a novel way: not in its paraenetical function, i.e., as a canonized corpus of narrative, edificational, or legal texts, but rather in its liturgical function, i.e., as the document of, and a kind of "libretto" for, a very complex *communication* process.

When we turn to the kibla, three contextual associations closely connected with it come to mind, associations that seem to point to particular experiences of the early community as underlying the adoption of the gesture: firstly, taking up the kibla is always performed at a cosmically-determined *time* of the day; secondly, it is closely connected to the evocation of a *topographia sacra* as the place of remembrance of divine self-manifestation; and thirdly, it attests to the ever-renewed staging of divine communication to man through the *recitation* of Scripture.

The Emergence of Muslim Worship as Mirrored in the Early Surahs

Since the Islamic practice of facing a kibla in worship appears to have been adopted at a particular historical stage, we should undertake a short survey of the Qur'anic texts that yield some information about the body language in the Meccan pagan and ever-increasing Islam-imprinted worship. A number of early surahs present similar scenarios: the prophet recites verses in front of two groups of listeners: one, the God-fearing, responds to the Qur'an recitation through prostration, thereby acknowledging the spiritual presence of the divine sovereign and displaying strong emotions; the members of the other group "turn their backs," thereby rejecting, or even mocking, participation in the worship as they witness it. What kind of service is to be presupposed here as the framework of this interaction? We may assume that it was composed of two basic elements: the first should have been the ritual which, already in pre-Islamic times, bore the name *salāh*, an Aramaic loanword used in the Qur'an for both the ancient Arabian and the emerging Islamic community's worship. This suggests that the ritual had already been in use in a relatively fixed form, presumably consisting of a sequence of gestures of self-humiliation in front of the divine King, similar to those of the later canonized Muslim *salāh*. Some Qur'anic passages explicitly state that Muhammad himself was exhorted to partake in this ritual at the Ka'ba. The second element may be considered Muhammad's own innovation, i.e., the recitation of the speech conveyed to him. Since, in some metatextual passages, his listeners are reprimanded because of the negligence displayed in their performing the traditional *salāh*, and in others because of their rejection of Muhammad's recitation, we learn that both types of worship were celebrated together and that the whole scenario was supposed to be staged at the Ka'ba.

The Community's Dissociation from the Kaʿba and Their "Exodus" into the Imaginary Space of the Banū Isrāʾīl

Striking signs of change in the surahs of the later Meccan periods. The collision between the adherents to the ancient Arabian worship and the followers of its monotheist reform, which is already heralded in the metatextual parts of the early surahs which comment upon the poor reception given Muḥammad's recitation, leads to the final emigration of the early community from Mecca to Medina. Not only the biography of the prophet, the *sīra*, but, indirectly, the Qurʾan as well, reflect at least one intermediate stage which has been termed in western scholarship the "Second Meccan period."[6] At this stage, we find a new framework for the recitation of the surahs. The earlier metatextual references to hostile behavior are missing, and the surah is addressed exclusively to believers, and only indirectly to nonbelievers, by noting their positions in the frequent polemical passages which often contain stereotypical simulations of arguments.

There are, however, further hints of progress in the development of worship. One Qurʾanic verse affirms that now, in addition to the Qurʾanic recitation, there is a communal prayer transmitted in the Qurʾanic text as the "Opening Chapter" (*al-fātiḥa*),[7] in which the believers express themselves as "We," thus responding to the speech of God transmitted by the recitation. Finally, this recitation itself has gone through changes: the new surahs have become longer and more composite. Indeed, they seem to reflect the shape of worship familiar to neighboring religions, featuring in their central parts a narration of salvation history, a kind of recasting of the Torah- or gospel-reading, which is absolutely novel in the Qurʾanic development. This narrative nucleus of the surah is framed by other typical features of monotheistic worship, such as hymns, litanies, exhortations, and, finally, polemical sermon-like elements. The emphatic introductory section, instead of alluding to the rites of the Kaʿba, now refers to writing or to instruments of writing such as the pen, parchment, etc.[8] What has happened? What was it that replaced the Kaʿba's significance?

◆   ◆   ◆

The "Exodus". The only Qurʾanic verse of this period of development that still refers to Mecca, surah 17.1, appears to be of key importance to our problem. It alludes to a nocturnal exodus:

> Glory be to Him, who carried his servant by night
> from the Holy mosque (*al-masjid al-ḥarām*) to the Further Mosque
> (*al-masjid al-aqṣā*)

the precincts of which We have blessed,
That We might show him some of Our signs.
He is the All-hearing, the All-seeing.

This somewhat cryptic verse mentions a nocturnal journey, more precisely a flight, conceived as an experience of liberation and viewed even in analogy to the exodus of Moses,[9] leading the prophet out of Mecca toward "the other sanctuary" par excellence, which in the context of the religio-geographical horizons of the early community can hardly be located elsewhere than on the Temple Mount of Jerusalem, the "*masjid* of the Banū Isrāʾīl".[10] The simplest explanation of the event alluded to in this verse would be to assume the experience of a dream.[11] In Islam, this explanation has been upheld by only a minority of the exegetes, yet it has been incorporated into the most renowned tenth-century commentary on the Qurʾan by al-Ṭabarī, wherein a cousin of the prophet, ʾUmm Hāniʾ, is quoted to have related the following:

> As to the nocturnal journey (*isrā*) of the Messenger of God the follow-ing took place. He had been staying in my house over night. After performing the last evening prayer he retired to sleep and so did all of us. At dawn the Messenger of God woke us up for morning prayer, and when we had performed it together, he said to me: ʾUmm Hāniʾ, you remember that I performed with you in this very place the evening prayer. Thereupon, however, I was in Bayt al-Maqdis and have prayed there. And now I have been praying again with you the morning prayer in this place.[12]

It should not detract from the convincing force of this simple and sober account that a short time later the same Qurʾanic verse, 17.1, was to become the *locus probans* for the elevation of the prophet to the rank of an ecstatic with the ability to perform a miraculous ascent to heaven. In later exegetic traditions, verse 17.1 is usually understood as an allusion to a unique nocturnal voyage (*isrā*), miraculous not only insofar as time and space are reduced to *quantités négligéables*, but in other respects as well; the prophet is imagined to be riding a fairy tale-inspired, pegasus-shaped beast, the Burāq, on whose back he travels from Mecca to Jerusalem, passing by diverse stations of significance for salvation history. At a further stage of the exegetic development, the journey is even imagined as going beyond Jerusalem and ascending through the seven celestial spheres to heaven itself. This ascent (*miʿrāj*)—according to the tradi-tion reported from the prophet's scribe, Ibn Masʿūd—reaches its climax when God himself gives Muḥammad the institution of the five Islamic prayers.[13]

The images of the prophet underlying these two interpretations of verse

17.1 stand in sharp contrast. Still, the sober descriptive version and the fantastic mythifying interpretation have one trait in common, namely, the realization that the aim of this journey, the revelation of the "signs," is nothing other than an expression of the unique closeness to God granted to the prophet through *prayer*. In both accounts, the voyage out of Mecca is associated with prayer, the prophet himself performing or even leading the prayer (*ṣalāh*) in the midst of the other prophets in the Jerusalem sanctuary in one version, and the prophet being granted the very institution of prayer by his divine Lord in the other. Thus, in view of the identical nucleus of both accounts, namely the concept of prayer as connected to a particular site, it is suggestive to interpret the nocturnal journey, the exodus to the sanctuary of the Israelites, the *masjid Banī Isrāʾīl*, as a spiritual movement continuing the journey already started in the imagination of the prophet by his facing the ḳibla, unto the "further sanctuary" which, newly introduced as the orientation for prayer, may be assumed to have been still forcefully present in the worshippers' minds.

✦   ✦   ✦

The spiritual dimension of the "exodus". How is it to be explained that adopting the ḳibla could appear as so significant a departure as to be conceived as an exodus into the space of the memory of the Banū Isrāʾīl? It appears that the Jerusalem sanctuary, in its function as the object of ritual orientation, as the focus of an imaginary space becoming accessible in prayer, did not reach the consciousness of the community as an isolated discovery or at a haphazard time.

As has been mentioned, the process of segregation from the traditional Meccan rites is clearly reflected in the evolution of new Islamic forms of worship, less dependent now on the presence at holy places and concentrating more strongly on elaborated verbal compositions than on the earlier ritual gestures. The new surahs show clear compositional patterns, extending over numerous complexly-built verses[14] and reflecting in their central parts important episodes of biblical history. This process of development is, however, not to be understood simply as a change in forms, but its full dimensions run much deeper. What is mirrored here is the radical break with the inherited tradition which is caused by the intrusion of writing into the space of memory. It should be stressed that, according to the most widely-accepted hypothesis, it was still during Muḥammad's Meccan career that the medium of writing was, for the first time in Arabic literature, consistently integrated into the composition of texts and the techniques of their preservation. Nevertheless, the wording may not yet have been fixed for an envisaged individual reader, but rather still for a secondary mediator, that is, a reciter of texts. Thus, there were two essential novelties: (1) the newly-attained state of convergence of the Qur'anic revelation with the previous Scriptures, represented primarily by the Torah, the scripture of the Banū Isrāʾīl; and (2) the simultaneous adoption of the *topographia sacra* of that very group, by fixing the direction of prayer toward their central sanctuary. Together, these developments created a new self-consciousness of the young community, which was no longer based only on the rites as practiced at the Kaʿba, but much more on the new awareness among the receivers and bearers of a Scripture, thus giving them a share in the memory of salvation history transmitted by the medium of writing.

The particular type of change in orientation, described by J. Assmann[15] as the transition of a society from ritual coherence to textual coherence, seems to have been at work here. The ḳibla toward Jerusalem points to a close connection between the emerging Islamic community and the older religions, and thus to a newly-attained "textual coherence." Thus, it is not surprising that the Qur'anic allusions to the Meccan sanctuary and its rites as the previous guarantors of societal coherence, allusions which used to be so numerous until then in the introductory sections of the Meccan surahs, were soon replaced by a stereotypical introductory evocation of the Book (*kitāb*), now realized as the most significant common spiritual possession, and even more as the token of God's presence.

The images now appearing in the beginning sections of the surahs, the book and its requisites, point unequivocally to the awareness that a stream of tradition has come to a standstill and now has become accessible through the means of writing. It is a new form of remembrance that finds expression here and which would soon penetrate daily ritual practice. The strong attachment to the local Meccan place which was characteristic of the worship at the Kaʿba gives way to a new situation for the Muslim worshipper in a spiritual space reaching far beyond the horizons of the inherited rites into the world and the history of the others, of the Banū Isrāʾīl. Accordingly, there is a substantial change in orientation—in terms of time as well. Instead of the numerous allusions to ritually-relevant times of the day appearing at the beginnings of the early surahs, the surahs in the new phase of development display a substantially new time-setting; they culminate in an oft-repeated appeal, formally introduced with a simple referential "at the time when" (*idh*) or "remember when" (*udhkur idh*), to the examples of former prophets reaching far back into the history of their spiritual forebears, the Banū Isrāʾīl.[16] Jerusalem is the central sanctuary of the space marked by this Scripture and thus by history and, on the medial level, by writing. All prayers gravitate in the direction of Jerusalem as their natural destination and the worshipper turns his *face* to Jerusalem, seeking his Lord via the remembrance of salvation history.

Thānī al-ḥaramayn:
The Image of Mecca from the Perspective of Exile

The Muslim community at Medina, as is well known, dissociates itself from Jerusalem in the process of the growing precariousness of its relations with the Medinan Jews. At the same time, this dissociation is nothing other than the reverse recollection, the rediscovery of Mecca as the essential destination for the longing of the exiles at Medina. Hardly two years after the Hijra, there is a change of orientation, this time attested by a Qur'anic passage (surah 2.143–45):

> The fools among the people will say,
> "What has turned them from the direction
> they were facing in their prayers aforetime?"
> Say: "To God belong the East and the West.
> He guides whomever He will to a straight path."
> We have seen you turning your *face* about
> in the heaven, now we will surely turn you
> to a direction that shall satisfy you.
> Turn your *face* toward the Holy Mosque (*al-masjid al-ḥarām*);
> and wherever you are, turn your *faces* toward it.

The spiritual return of the worshippers to the Ka'ba at Mecca heralded in these verses dislocates Jerusalem from the center. However, as a prototype of a center to be visited in the believer's imagination and headed for from afar, it survives, becoming reembodied in the ḳibla toward Mecca. The replacing of the actual Jerusalem ḳibla, therefore, should not, as has been done until now, be viewed merely from a negative point of view, i.e., as a solely pragmatic politico-religious step. A ritual reorientation in space, expressed by so dominant a gesture in worship, reflects the reality of a genuine change of spiritual longing. Mecca was able to replace Jerusalem since the memory shared with the Banū Isrā'īl by the Medinan community had, in the meanwhile, been blotted out to some degree by a novel experience of real exile, within which the symbolic value of the Meccan central sanctuary had increased substantially. One should also bear in mind that, although there had been a decisive leap in spiritual development, a total break with *ritual practices* with regard to their timing and gestic performance, had not taken place. Once the evocation of a central sanctuary through ritual gesture had been realized as a precondition of prayer, it would be difficult, if not impossible, to conceive of any orientation other than toward the Meccan Ka'ba, after the symbols shared with the Banū Isrā'īl had become problematic.

What is even more important, however, is that the "ideal Mecca" as conceived in exile had itself gone through a substantial change; it had become integrated into that particular form of memory borne by the medium of writing that bestowed on it the rank of a place honored by a significant episode of salvation history. Mecca had become center stage in the career of a great biblical protagonist, Abraham, and thus entered biblical space.

Mecca—Part of Biblical History

Abraham's inauguration prayer of the Ka'ba (surah 2.126f.) is reminiscent of Solomon's inaugurational prayer of the Temple (I Kgs. 8:41–43) in its essential verses:

> My Lord, make this a secure *temenos*
> and make us submissive to You,
> and of our seed a nation submissive
> and show us our holy *rites* and
> turn Your Face toward us, surely You turn
> and are the All-compassionate.
> And our Lord do You send among them a Messenger, one of them,
> who shall recite to them thy signs and teach them the *Book*
> and the Wisdom and purify them, You are
> the Almighty, the All-wise.

What is elsewhere expounded in detail is only alluded to in this passage, namely, that Abraham institutionalized the rites, the most essential being the ṣalāh and the ḥajj (the pilgrimage). However, Abraham's inaugurational prayer culminates with his plea that there shall take place not only rites, but verbal worship and reading of Scriptures as well, and that a prophet should arise, to read out of the Book to the worshippers at the Ka'ba. Abraham's prayer was fulfilled with the appearance of the prophet Muḥammad, who was sent to complete the complex structure of Islam as a religion whose cult is based equally on ritual and verbal worship.

Through this new development in meaning, Mecca has for the second time taken over part of the aura of Jerusalem. After the change of the ḳibla moved the focus of prayer from Jerusalem to Mecca, with these Qur'anic verses Mecca was now honored with what had been a prerogative of Jerusalem, as attested by the words of the prophet Isaiah (2:3): "Torah will go out from Zion and the word of the Lord from Jerusalem." In fulfillment of the prayer of the first propagator of monotheism, Mecca had again become a place of theophany which, through the mediation of a prophet reciting scriptural verses, proves capable of satisfying the new expectations which, aroused by examples of salvation history, demand that a genuine theophany—a divine revelation—should take the shape of a book, a Scripture.

Conclusion: The Ḳibla Conceived as a Vector Pointing toward Scriptural Memory

If one were to spell out the main characteristics of Islam, then a visual and an auditive dimension certainly would have to figure prominently: the worshipper facing Mecca on the one hand, and the announcement of prayer through liturgical words and followed by Qur'anic recitation at certain times of the day on the other. Prayer's demand for an orientation in space—to the center of the world, which is paramount to the place of divine self-manifestation—is valid for Judaism as well; yet regarding its realization, there is no apparent comparable practice in Jewish worship. The particular pathos of the practice in Islam seems to be due to its dramatic history, where the introduction of the ḳibla or, more precisely, the two successive ḳiblas, marked important steps in the community's progress on its way toward a new collective identity. The ḳibla was first oriented toward Jerusalem, the sanctuary of the People of the Scripture, the center of the space of the memory of the Banū Isrāʾīl. By associating themselves with them, the new community entered the space of the earlier adherents of the scriptural religions. By reverting the ḳibla to Mecca, they reentered a space of their own memory. But this could no longer be a mere return to an earlier stage of development, since relevant space had now been coupled with the command to seek God's face. This was to be accomplished not simply in the given place of ritual worship inherited from the forefathers, but essentially in an imaginary space charged with the memory of more universal salvation history, that is, with scriptural memory. For once and for all, holy space entered into a close relationship with Scripture and thus with the Qur'an and its recitation. The community's realization of Jerusalem as the center of the imaginary space of salvation history may duly be considered a crucial stage in the development of the Islamic concept of Scripture, which itself combines memory of scriptural history and ongoing divine-human communication to form an inseparable unity.

Notes

1. For a more detailed survey of the significance of Jerusalem for Islam, see A. Neuwirth, "The Spiritual Meaning of Jerusalem in Islam," *City of the Great King. Jerusalem from David to the Present*, ed. N. Rosovsky (Cambridge, MA., 1996), 93–116, 483–95.

2. The triple epithet can be traced back to the Ayyubid era. It is cited by the preacher Zakiyyaddīn in his sermon in praise of the reconquest of Jerusalem by Saladin. See Ibn Khallikān, *Obituaries of Prominent Men*, ed. I. Abbas, 8 vols. (Beirut, n.d.), IV, 232 (Arabic).

3. The classical rendering of the concept of three Islamic sanctuaries is a tradition ascribed to the prophet (*ḥadīth*): "You shall only set out for three mosques, the Sacred Mosque (in Mecca), my Mosque (in Medina) and al-Aqṣa mosque (in Jerusalem)." On its socio-religious context, see M. J. Kister, "Studies in Jahiliyya and Early Islam" (London, 1980), 173–96.

4. For a first attempt to interpret the body language implied in facing a ḳibla, see A. Neuwirth, "Face of God—Face of Man: Some Observations about the Significance of the Direction of Prayer in Islam," *Soul, Body and Self*, ed. A. Baumgarten (Leiden, forthcoming).

5. There is no consensus about the duration of the first ḳibla; see A. Duri, "Jerusalem in the Early Islamic Period: 7th–11th Centuries A.D.," *Jerusalem in History*, ed. K. J. Asali (Essex, 1989), 105–28.

6. For a more comprehensive survey on the formal development of the surah during the Meccan periods, see A. Neuwirth, "Vom Rezitationstext über die Liturgie zum Kanon—Zu Entstehung und Wiederauflösung der Surenkomposition im Verlauf der Entwicklung eines islamischen Kultus," *The Qur'an as Text*, ed. S. Wild (Leiden, 1996), 69–106.

7. For the place of the *fātiḥa* as against Qur'an recitation in the performance of the Islamic prayer service, see A. and K. Neuwirth, "Sūrat al-Fātiḥa—'Eröffnung' des Text-Corpus Koran oder 'Introitus' der Gebetsliturgie?" *Text, Methode und Grammatik. Festschrift für Wolfgang Richter*, eds. W. Gross, H. Irsigler and Th. Seidl (St. Ottilien, 1992), 332–57.

8. See A. Neuwirth, "Der Horizont der Offenbarung—Zur Relevanz der einleitenden Schwurserien für die Suren der frühmekkanischen Zeit," *Gottes ist der Orient, Gottes ist der Okzident: Festschrift für Abdoldjavad Falaturi*, ed. U. Tworuschka (Köln, 1991), 3–39. See the abridged English version of the German: "Images and Metaphors in the Introductory Sections of the Makkan Suras," *Approaches to the Qur'an*, eds. G. R. Hawting and A.-K. A. Shareef (London, 1994), 3–36.

9. The equation of *isrā'* with "exodus" is based on J. Wansbrough's observation, that the verb *asrā* mentioned in the context of "servant(s)" more than once points to Moses' exodus; see J. Wansbrough, *Quranic Studies. Sources and Methods of Scriptural Interpretation* (Oxford, 1977), 66–69.

10. The interpretation of *al-Masjid al-Aqṣā* in surah 17.1 is still subject to controversy in research. The opinions held here are ultimately dependent upon the researcher's position in the debate over the historicity of the basic traditions about the prophet Muḥammad; on the problematics of this issue, see A. Neuwirth, "Erste Qibla—Fernstes Masǧid?: Jerusalem im Horizont des historischen Muhammad," *Zion—Ort der Begegnung. Festschrift für Laurentius Klein*, eds. F. Hahn, F.-L. Hossfeld, H. Jorissen and A. Neuwirth, Bonner Biblische Beiträge 90 (Hanstein, 1993), 227–70.

11. On this interpretation, see ibid.

12. Al-Ṭabarī, *Ingathering of Eloquence—On the Exegesis of the Qur'an*, 30 vols. (Cairo, n.d.), 15.3 (Arabic).

13. See Ibn Hishām, *The Biography of the Prophet*, ed. A. M. Shakir, 2 vols. (Cairo, 1373H/ 1954), II, 36–50 (Arabic); for an analysis in typological terms, see Neuwirth (above, note 10).

14. For the particular composition of verses of both textual and metatextual elements, see A. Neuwirth, "Zur Struktur der Yūsuf-Sure," *Studien aus Arabistik und Semitistik: Anton Spitaler zum siebzigsten Geburtstag*, eds. W. Diem and S. Wild (Wiesbaden, 1980), 123–52.

15. J. Assmann, *Das Kulturelle Gedächtnis. Schrift, Erinnerung und politische Identität in frühen Hochkulturen* (Munich, 1992).

16. For details, see Neuwirth (above, note 6).

23

Three Perspectives on Jerusalem: Jewish, Christian, and Muslim Pilgrims in the Twelfth Century

MYRIAM ROSEN-AYALON

The Crusader period has been described as the "Golden Age" of medieval pilgrimage to the Holy Land. In his study of medieval pilgrims, the Holy Land, and its image in European culture, A. Grabois refers, of course, to the Christian pilgrims.[1] However, it appears that non-Christian pilgrims also benefited from the conditions at the time. The flow of Muslim and Jewish pilgrimage was far from attaining the dimensions of the deluge of Christian pilgrims, but must have been more extensive than the surviving evidence attests. We shall refer to some of these pilgrims in this study.

The first, al-Harawi, was a Muslim who compiled an elaborate compendium of Muslim pilgrimage sites, including Jerusalem.[2] The second was Rabbi Benjamin of Tudela of Spain, whose stay in Jerusalem was rather brief.[3] The third pilgrim, apparently of German origin, was a Christian monk named Theoderic.[4]

Al-Harawi states clearly that he visited Jerusalem in the year 569/1173; since his visit is dated, he has been chosen as the first of the three to be discussed. As for the other two, studies have shown that their visits took place around the same date.

I. THE ITINERARIES AND THE MONUMENTS

Al-Harawi (Plate I)

We do not know where al-Harawi entered the city. However, his report clearly establishes three different areas that he visited. The first group of sites revolves

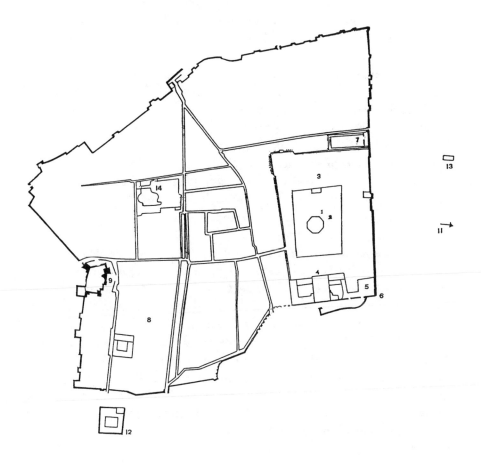

Plate I: The Itinerary of 'Ali al-Hawari

1. Dome of the Rock
2. Dome of the Chain
3. Dwellings of the Canons
4. Al-Aqṣa Mosque
5. Solomon's Stables
6. Cradle of Jesus
7. Pool of the Sons of Israel

8. Church of the Jacobites
9. Tower of David
10. Pool of Siloam
11. Church of Ascension
12. Church of Zion
13. Tomb of Mary
14. Holy Sepulchre

primarily around the Temple Mount. He begins with the Dome of the Rock and the monument immediately next to it, which he clearly states lies to its east—the Dome of the Chain. From there he moves to the north of the Temple Mount, to the Dwellings of the Canons (a crusader addition), and then to the extreme south of the Temple Mount, to al-Aqṣa mosque. In the vicinity of this monument he mentions Solomon's Stables and the Cradle of Jesus. He then returns to the north of the Temple Mount, this time outside its limits, referring to the Pool of the Sons of Israel (*Birkat Banū Israil*). From there he could have walked along any of the streets running east-west until he reaches the Church of the Jacobites (*Kanisat al-Yaʿakiba*). He subsequently reached the Tower of David (*Burg Dawud*) at the entrance to the city and opposite the point from where he had started, the Temple Mount. This group contains all of the monuments inside the city, with one exception (and to which we shall return).

The second group consists of sites visited by al-Harawi outside the city. In fact, his itinerary is rather confused. He sets out in the south, at the Pool of Siloam (*Ayn Silwan*), then refers to the Church of the Ascension (*Kanisat al-Saliq*) on the Mount of Olives in the east, and again returns to the south, to the Church of Zion (*Kanisat Suhyun*). From there he goes on to speak of the Tomb of Mary in the Valley of Jehoshaphat, and finally returns to the Mount of Olives, where he mentions some tombs and a memorial. In his description of the Mount of Olives, he merely notes that *bi-ljabal* ("on the mountain") there is a saint's place and his tomb (*Maqam Rabiʿa al-Adawiya*). There were apparently more tombs of saints and disciples on the Mount of Olives, but al-Harawi was unable to identify them (*Salahines wa-ltabaʿin*). Al-Harawi mentions the existence of two tombs to the east, that of Saddad b. Aws al-Hazragi and that of Du-l Asabiʾ at-Tamimī.

In the third and last group, al-Harawi introduces the Christian pilgrimage sites. However, after announcing this new category, he basically describes only the Holy Sepulchre;[5] he has already described several other Christian sites in the previous two groups.

Rabbi Benjamin of Tudela (Plate II)

Rabbi Benjamin begins his itinerary by mentioning the existence of three (!) walls. The first building he encounters is the Tower of David, and he then apparently walks along what is known today as David Street to the Muristan (Hospital), although at the same time he refers to the existence of *Templum Solomonis*, which in all probability he has not yet visited; we shall return to this later. He then mentions the large altar (*bamah*), called *shiporki* (sepulchre),

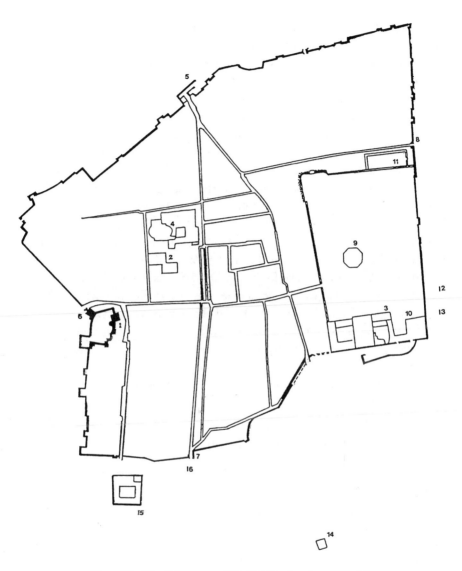

Plate II: The Itinerary of Rabbi Benjamin of Tudela

1. Tower of David
2. Muristan
3. *Templum Solomonis* (al-Aqṣa mosque)
4. Holy Sepulchre
5. Abraham's Gate (Damascus Gate)
6. David's Gate (Jaffa Gate)
7. Zion Gate
8. Gate of Jehoshaphat (Lions' Gate)

9. Temple (Dome of the Rock)
10. Solomon's Stables
11. Pool of the Sheep
12. Tomb of Absalom
13. Tomb of King Uzziah
14. Pool of Siloam
15. Church of Mount Zion
16. Jewish cemetery

taking the trouble to specify that this is where "that man is buried." From here he has easy access to the northern gate, with which he begins his enumeration of the city's gates: the Gate of Abraham (Damascus Gate) in the north, David's Gate (Jaffa Gate) in the west, Zion Gate in the south, and the Gate of Jehoshaphat (Lions' Gate) in the east. This last gate brings him to the Temple, which he refers to as *Bet Hamiqdash*, adding the words *biy'mei qedem* ("in the past"). He also calls it "Tinpoli Domini" (*Templum Domini*). He then mentions the Western Wall and Solomon's house (*bayt asher haya l'Shlomo*) and the stables that he (i.e., Solomon) built. Next on his itinerary is the pool where the priests slaughtered their sacrifices. This is probably the Pool of the Sheep, since immediately afterwards he refers to the Gate of Jehoshaphat, walking through it to the Valley of Jehoshaphat.

Once outside the city, he lists the Tomb of Absalom, the Tomb of King Uzziah, and the Pool of Siloam. From the Valley of Jehoshaphat, he ascends the Mount of Olives and overlooks the Dead Sea as far as Mount Nebo. To the southwest, he refers to Mount Zion and its *bamah* (in reference to a church, as he does with the Holy Sepulchre), and the Jewish cemetery.

Like al-Harawi, Rabbi Benjamin organizes his itinerary in three coherent categories: first the city itself, with the Tower of David, the Hospital, and the Holy Sepulchre; then the Temple Mount and its vicinity; and, finally, the sites outside the city-walls. Nevertheless, Bejamin's itinerary is quite different from that of al-Harawi.

Theoderic (Plate III)

In Theoderic's account, it is difficult to discern a rational itinerary, as he seems to describe his visit to Jerusalem in several spheres. He begins with an introduction containing a general overview of the topography, and then relates more specifically to the sites and monuments, but, as we shall see, with varying emphases and degrees of interest.

Thus, he notes Mount Moriah with the Temple of the Lord and the Mount of Olives, which is higher. Between the two he mentions the Brook of Qidron and the Valley of Jehoshaphat, as well as the Church of the Blessed Mary by the Tomb of Jehoshaphat. He then notes, below the Pool of Siloam, a new cistern between Mount Zion and Akeldama. He follows the two walls enclosing the city and returns to the Tomb of Jehoshaphat, noting that its masonry resembles that of a pyramid. He states that the city is "united" by towers, walls, and bulwarks; in all probability, this should be understood as an "enclosure" or "encirclement." Outside the wall is a valley or ditch, protected by yet another wall, bulwarks, and a fosse. Note that he speaks of two walls while

Rabbi Benjamin mentions three. Theoderic goes on to list Jerusalem's seven gates. Six of them are locked every night until dawn; the seventh is blocked and opened only on Palm Sunday and the Exaltation of the Holy Cross.

Thus far the general description. Theoderic now proceeds to describe the monuments. The first is the Tower of David, with Mount Zion to its south and the Mount of Olives to its east (as indeed they are). Also south of the Tower of David, outside the walls, is the Church of the Blessed Mary. He then mentions the Palace of Solomon and the Beautiful Gate, as well as the Field of Akeldama for the burial of strangers. The next group of sites he mentions begins with the House of Pilate, which is next to the House of St. Anne and the Pool of the Sheep. He mentions one side of Herod's palace, the Antonia, and the gate outside the court.

Everything up to this point has been introductory, since Theoderic proceeds, in his own words, "now to describe the Holy Places." He begins, of course, with the Holy of Holies, i.e., the Holy Sepulchre, and follows with a detailed description of the monuments and all their trappings—decorations, chapels, icons, and the like. His itinerary goes on to list the Church and the Hospital of St. John the Baptist, and near it another Church of Mary. From there, in the south, one proceeds to the Beautiful Gate (of the Temple) and to the Temple of the Lord. Descending twenty-two steps, one reaches the Great Pool with its underground passages leading to the Church of the Holy Sepulchre (rather strange),[6] where the sacrifices were washed. (Theoderic later also mentions an "abandoned pool" where sacrifices were washed.)

Having already mentioned the Cloisters and the Dwellings of the Canons at least twice, he once again gives a detailed description, reporting their position as lying to the north (of the upper platform). He also infers that a slab (or altar) to the southeast may be either the mouth of a pool or the site of the killing of Zachariah son of Berachia. Afterwards, he points out "above the steps . . . in front of the pool" to the east, four columns with arches (what we would call a *mawazin* today) as well as the tomb of a wealthy man made of beautifully carved alabaster and surrounded by iron lattice work. Above the southern steps are two more arched columns on the right and three on the left. On the east, and toward the platform, are fifteen double steps (which indeed are very large) by which one goes up from the Golden Gate to the Temple. South of the platform are two small houses; at the western angle is the School of the Blessed Mary. Theoderic then turns to the southern end of the Temple Mount, mentioning the Palace of Solomon (al-Aqṣa mosque), describing it as an "oblong church." Next to the palace lie the Stables of Solomon.

After discussing the city and its surroundings, albeit summarily, Theoderic

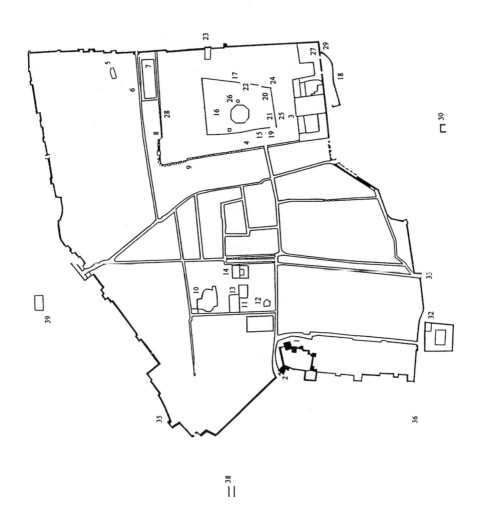

332

Plate III: The Itinerary of Theoderic (the most salient sites)

1. Tower of David
2. South Gate (Jaffa Gate)
3. Palace of Solomon (al-Aqsa mosque)
4. Beautiful Gate
5. House of St. Anne
6. House of Pilate
7. Pool of the Sheep
8. Antonia
9. Gate outside the Court
10. Holy Sepulchre
11. St. John's Church
12. St. John's Hospital
13. St. Mary
14. St. Mary
15. Gate
16. Cloisters
17. Steps from the Golden Gate
18. Wall built by the Templars
19. School of the Blessed Mary
20. Small house
21. Small house
22. Arches
23. Golden Gate
24. Arches
25. Arches
26. Temple (Dome of the Rock)
27. Solomon's Stables
28. Wall of Herod
29. Cradle of Jesus
30. Pool of Siloam
31. Chapel
32. Church of St. Mary
33. Lithostratos
34. Tomb of Mary
35. Church and house for lepers
36. New Cistern
37. Gethsemane
38. Toward the Monastery of the Cross
39. Armenian church

now turns to a new "cycle"—in his words, "that of the order of Christ's suffering"—which constitutes an itinerary in itself.

The cycle begins in Bethany, in the valley to the east of the Mount of Olives, at the House of Simon the Leper and of Lazarus and his sisters Mary and Martha where Jesus used to visit. On Palm Sunday, Jesus went from Bethany to Bethphage, half-way from the Mount of Olives to the Beautiful Chapel. The route runs across the Valley of Jehoshaphat and the Qidron Brook to the Golden Gate. Theoderic now refers to the Church of St. Mary on Mount Zion, but immediately returns to the Valley of Jehoshaphat, to the Tomb of Mary. He returns to the Golden Gate, mentioning the existence of a chapel commemorating the passage of Christ through the gate (this is perhaps the chapel seen on some of the late medieval prints). He also notes at this point the passage of Heraclius through the Golden Gate, an event we know to be debatable. After passing the Cradle of Jesus, at the southern corner of the city, near the Temple Mount, the route descends the steep slope through the advance wall, which the Templars may have built to defend their homes and palace. From there it leads to the ancient City of David and the Pool of Siloam. He then mentions the Beautiful Chapel containing the Prison of St. Peter on the road from the Temple to Mount Zion. From there he proceeds to the Valley of Jehoshaphat and the Tomb of Mary, and then to the Church of Gethsemane. Theoderic next speaks of a "New Church" very close by. From the Lithostratos, one moves eastward to St. Peter of Galicante (also known as Galilee). Turning to a different part of the city, he returns to St. Anne's and the nearby Pool of the Sheep.

From here on, it seems that our pilgrim leaves the city, passing through the Tower of David (probably corresponding to the Jaffa Gate), the Church and House for the Lepers, continuing on to the Church of Blessed Stephen and the Cistern of the Hospitalers. He mentions an Armenian church dedicated to a saint called Cariton, the Church of the Ascension on the Mount of Olives, and then a "dark chapel" with the body of the Blessed Pelagia.

To the west, on the road to Bethany and on the slopes of the Mount of Olives, Theoderic mentions a church where the Savior used to sit, as well as an underground cave. Has he now come full circle?

Finally, outside the city and beyond the Tower of David, he refers to two monuments: one to the south, the New Cistern, and one to the west, the Monastery of the Cross, in a fertile valley.

II. COMMENTARY

Al-Harawi

On the whole, al-Harawi's account does not appear to be very systematic. Toward the end of his account, he says: "and the Christians have their own sites of pilgrimage" and then proceeds to describe the Holy Sepulchre. He also lists some of its adjacent monumental elements but, in fact, lists no other churches, although he has already mentioned several of them in passing. He is completely silent about many other sites whose existence is well known.[7] While three of the churches he has mentioned (the Tomb of Mary, the Church of the Ascension, and the Church of Zion) are, in fact, extramural, it is nonetheless strange that he neglects to list them with the Christian monuments. Moreover, he mentions the Church of the Jacobites only casually during his walk through the city.

We have seen the way in which al-Harawi relates to monuments outside the walls of the city; he has nothing to say about the walls or the gates. As a matter of fact, he does not enter the city at all, but rather begins his account with the words *Bihi Qubbat al-Sahra* ("in it is the Dome of the Rock"). Clearly, in his view this is the most important monument of all and the one that must be mentioned first, though we have no idea of how he reached it, which route he took, or what he saw on the way. At the same time, he emphasizes the fact that he himself has visited it, and gives a detailed description of it on several occasions.

On the first, he deals with it on the theological level, and this is the tone that prevails. This is where the Prophet ascended to Heaven and where al-Harawi saw the footprint of the Prophet in the rock. He gives the rock's measurements and even describes the iron grille, which is indeed an extraordinary piece of craftsmanship.[8] He adds that in his day (i.e., 1173), only the southern part of the grille remains; this may well account for the wooden screen erected by the Ayyubids which can still be seen all around the rock.[9] The next element he discusses is the grotto beneath the rock, Magarat al-Arwāh, with its attached legend, as well as the possibility that Zachariah's tomb is located there.

Al-Harawi now gives us very important information, as he describes and furnishes us with the full text of an inscription in the Dome of the Rock that no longer exists (Qur'ān 2, 255–56). He goes on to state that the inscription was executed in gold mosaic, which was the medium of all mosaic inscriptions in the Dome of the Rock up to the Mamluk period[10] (only in the Ottoman period were other techniques used, such as inscriptions in stucco).

Another interesting item of information is al-Harawi's account of the paintings of Suleiman b. Daoud and the Messiah. He refers to them as *Ṣūrat*, and these may very well have been icons. In her commentary to the text, J. Sourdel-Thomine draws attention to the fact that this information is repeated in some of the accounts of western pilgrims.[11] However, as we shall see below, Rabbi Benjamin of Tudela completely contradicts these accounts, leaving us with an enigma.

When describing the monument with its four doors, Al-Harawi states, once again, that he entered it in the year 569/1173, under the Franks. Surprisingly, it seems that there was no objection to the building being entered by non-Christians; as we shall see, Rabbi Benjamin visited it, too.

Approaching the Dome of the Rock's eastern door, al-Harawi mentions another inscription located above it, while providing additional information that this door faces the Dome of the Chain. He quotes from the inscription (which has been discussed extensively by van Berchem), giving the name and another *ṣurat*. Interestingly, al-Harawi does not say here that the inscription was made of gold mosaic—a piece of circumstantial evidence, for the eastern wall has no mosaic decoration and thus the inscription above the eastern door was not made of mosaics. The inscription mentioned above, however, fits the monument's scheme of decoration perfectly and undoubtedly was executed in mosaic. Al-Harawi remarks that he noticed Qur'ānic inscriptions above all four doors. It is evident that the inscriptions were not covered up, since al-Harawi was able to read them and identify their contents. To dispel any doubt, he clearly states that "the Franks have not altered anything here."

He next refers to the Dome of the Chain, noting the tradition linking this monument with the Judgment of Solomon, and then discusses the Dwellings of the Canons north of the Temple Mount's upper platform. He is apparently unable to refrain from mentioning the columns and other artistic marvels, "which he intends to discuss separately." Comments of this kind recur frequently in al-Harawi's text; unfortunately, however, this promised work on architecture and decoration has not come down to us. When describing the Pool of the Sons of Israel, al-Harawi adds an account of the slaughter of the children of Israel. However, Rabbi Benjamin does not mention this tradition—yet another discrepancy between the two visitors to Jerusalem.

Al-Harawi now goes on to describe al-Aqṣa mosque. He speaks of the *miḥrab* of 'Umar b. al-Ḥattab, which provides him with an opportunity to stress the fact that the Franks had changed nothing. Once again, he quotes an Arabic inscription, *Ṣurat al-Mi'radj* (Qur'ān 17, 1). This inscription might be one that has recently been cleaned. He then cites the name of a Fatimid caliph, al-Zahir, followed by the name of the person who was in charge of the building and gilding of the dome (the vizir) and the date (426/1035). These details are followed by the names of the craftsman and mosaicist, al-Misri. Once again, al-Harawi expresses his amazement that the Franks have retained all these Arabic inscriptions. Subsequently, the inscription apparently disappeared, but, as has already been pointed out by Sourdel-Thomine, was extensively documented by van Berchem. It seems likely that the rediscovered inscription in al-Aqsa mosque referred to by R. W. Hamilton[12] may be connected with al-Harawi's account.

After mentioning the famous stone that gives the measurements of the Temple area, al-Hawari returns to the Dome of the Rock and gives a detailed description of the building—the number of its columns and pillars (he differentiates between them by the use of the words *ustawāt* and *arkān*) and, once again, the measurements of various parts, including the dome, and the number of windows. He again notes the four doors, this time giving their names. G. Le Strange, in the nineteenth century, published some passages from al-Harawi, whom he called ʿAli of Heart; he noted that al-Harawi's measurements correspond perfectly to the state of the monument today.[13]

Al-Harawi now lists other monuments and their measurements, including the Dome of the Chain and the Grotto. These are followed by very detailed measurements of al-Aqsa mosque. In fact, this order may correspond to a deliberate scheme, in which al-Harawi first introduces the monuments and then returns to each of them to describe them in greater detail. Having spoken of al-Aqsa mosque, he mentions Solomon's Stables and the Cradle of Jesus, and, as noted above, he proceeds northward, to the Pool of the Sons of Israel, telling the story of the children of Israel slaughtered by Nebuchadnezzar whose heads filled the pool. He then mentions the Church of the Jacobites, linking it to a well where Christ washed and was revered by the Samaritan; strangely, this tradition is otherwise unknown.[14] He concludes this section with the Tower of David, mentioning that it contained a *mihrab* and apparently even a Qurʾānic inscription (37, 20/21–21/22).

Turning to monuments outside the city, he points out the Pool of Siloam, comparing it to the Zamzam well in Mecca and noting the belief that the water derived from beneath the rock in the Dome of the Rock. He then mentions the Church of the Ascension and the Church of Zion, the site of the Last Supper. Al-Harawi describes the Tomb of Mary in great detail, even noting the different colors (green and red) of marble used for the columns. Curiously, he does not note this feature for the Dome of the Rock, though it is an equally magnificent building and one which al-Harawi knew had been built by Muslims. Nevertheless, he does relate some Muslim traditions connected with the Tomb of Mary. There is no doubt that al-Harawi was sensitive to architecture. Just as he commented earlier on the Dwellings of the

Canons north of the Temple Mount's upper platform, he now states that the Tomb of Mary has many columns that, together with the various antiquities, form a wonderful work of art. It is noteworthy that when speaking of the numerous tombs of saints and disciples, al-Harawi makes his first complaint that since the Frankish occupation of the country the tombs cannot be identified.

He now proceeds to describe the Christian pilgrimage sites. He begins with the Church of the Holy Sepulchre, which he mockingly describes as *Qumama* (a dung heap) rather than *Qiyama* (a resurrection). Nevertheless, he is duly impressed by its architecture, which he promises to describe in detail in his projected volume on that subject. He goes on to explain that the place was actually called *Qumama*, since this was where all the city's refuse was discarded. The area is thus correctly identified as having been located outside the city in the time of Christ. This, he relates, was the place where the hands of criminals were amputated and where thieves were crucified. At this point, one may wonder whether an interesting transposition has taken place on the Temple Mount, which was also on the fringe of the city and where heaps of refuse had piled up until the Islamic conquest.[15]

When al-Harawi mentions the descent of the Holy Fire, he says: "I have lived long enough in Jerusalem to know how it works." Unfortunately, he does not describe it or give the length of his stay in the city. These words, however, do imply that Muslims were permitted to reside in Jerusalem at the time, and this is confirmed by Rabbi Benjamin, who enumerates the various communities living in the city, including the "Ishmaelites" (Muslims). Curiously, al-Harawi says nothing of the Muslim community; in fact, apart from the various monuments of the Temple area, he mentions no Muslim monument within the city. However, there must have been a mosque for the Muslim community, which was not permitted to pray on the Temple Mount during the crusader occupation.

Al-Harawi's account of his pilgrimage to Jerusalem is only a small part of his entire work. This may well reflect an interesting aspect of Muslim pilgrimage to the Holy Cities. In an article published a few years ago, Sourdel-Thomine studies some documents that are, in fact, certificates attesting to pilgrims' visits to the Holy Cities.[16] Several of these certificates are accompanied by sketches confirming the authenticity of the pilgrimage.[17] On close examination, it is obvious that the space allotted to Jerusalem is far smaller than that devoted to Mecca and Medina. Sourdel-Thomine argues that this reflects the importance traditionally given to the cities and compares it with the importance of prayer in the various cities as related by Nasir-i Khosro, for whom prayer performed in Jerusalem had a lesser weight than prayer performed in Mecca or Medina. The relatively short narrative of al-Harawi may thus reflect these traditional proportions.

Rabbi Benjamin of Tudela

Rabbi Benjamin's primary concern when describing his visit to the Holy Land is for the Jews and the Jewish community, as well as Jewish traditions. However, even on these subjects relatively little can be learned from his account. Each place he visits is described principally in terms of the presence or absence of Jews; if no Jews are present, he has nothing further to say.

Arriving in Jerusalem, his first comment is that it is a small city. We would naturally like to know to which cities he is comparing it. We should note that earlier he referred to "the great city of Gibeon"; can he mean that Gibeon was larger than Jerusalem? At the same time, however, he is struck by Jerusalem's great demographic diversity, mentioning that it is densely populated by all kinds of communities. Interestingly enough, the first one he mentions is the "Ishmaelites" (Muslims), a group not mentioned by Theoderic or even al-Harawi. Rabbi Benjamin then lists the Jacobites, Aramaeans (or Armenians), Greeks, Georgians, and Franks, again emphasizing the large variety of communities. In view of this list, and the monuments that Rabbi Benjamin identifies, this Jerusalem was undoubtedly a Christian city.

He goes on to state that Jerusalem was fortified by three walls, This is a rather puzzling comment: there was, indeed, a fortification wall around the city, but what of the other two? It is possible that one of these surrounded the citadel, to which he refers separately. The third may have been the wall built by the Templars in the south, close to the Temple wall, which is referred to by Theoderic as well.

Although Rabbi Benjamin is primarily concerned with the Jewish theme, and the fact that his information is rather scanty, one of his most important contributions, nevertheless, concerns a concession for "dyeing" granted to the Jews, a fact that probably would have escaped us were it not for Rabbi Benjamin's eagerness to record every scrap of information related to the Jews. The Jews paid the king annually for this concession, which was an exclusive one in Jerusalem. This may imply that the Jews were engaged in a complete textile industry, which probably included the production of souvenirs and relics. Rabbi Benjamin states that the Jews numbered 200[18] and that they lived under the Tower of David; another edition mentions "walls" in the plural, giving rise to the abovementioned suggestion regarding the identity of one of the two extra walls.

Our Jewish traveler, like his Muslim counterpart, seems to have had a penchant for architectural detail. The power construction of the Tower of David impressed Benjamin of Tudela, and he clearly states that there is no building in the entire city as strong as this one. This was the dominant military element of the city under the crusaders, despite the fortification walls they constructed. Rabbi Benjamin's understanding of the Tower of David is almost that of an archeologist, distinguishing between the different periods of its construction. Describing the lower part, he says that it is huge, measuring 10 ells (*amot*), and adds "that was the doing of our ancestors." The implication is that the upper part, built by the Muslims, is both of a later period and is less impressive than the lower part, which, of course, is the Herodian Tower of Phasael and may have received special attention because of its connection with the Jewish past and due to its massive proportions.

Rabbi Benjamin begins his itinerary from the Tower of David, undoubtedly because this was the entrance to the city, and lingers there for a while, in all probability because of the concentration of Jews in this part of the city. He then enters the city and mentions two buildings, which are rather far apart: the Hospital and the *Templum Solomonis*. He clearly has not yet reached the *Templum Solomonis*, but merely mentions it, perhaps because he assigns a similar function to both buildings, stating that the Hospital housed 400 people and the *Templum Solomonis* 300 people, not including horsemen. We know that St. John's Hospital was under the control of the Hospitalers and that the Temple Mount (including Solomon's Stables which Rabbi Benjamin attributed to King Solomon) was under the control of the Templars.

Next to St. John's Hospital is the Holy Sepulchre, of which, as noted earlier, Rabbi Benjamin mentions only a *bamah* ("altar" or "platform") called *shiporki* (sepulchre) which, he adds, is the tomb of "that man." It is surprising that the church itself is not mentioned, since Rabbi Benjamin does refer to other churches of lesser importance.

In fact, this is practically all he has to say about the inner city. He enumerates the gates, naming them in a counter-clockwise fashion, starting with the Gate of Abraham (Damascus Gate). He thus encircles the city in order to reach the Temple Mount directly, without crossing the city or paying attention to its buildings or inhabitants. He knows that in former times the Temple stood there and that today, precisely where the Temple stood, is a monument called "Tinpoli Domini." He does not attribute its construction to the Muslims, but names 'Umar b. al-Ḥattab as its builder, reflecting the crusader tradition connecting the Dome of the Rock with the Mosque of 'Umar. Rabbi Benjamin's only reference to aesthetic criteria surfaces when he describes the Dome of the Rock as a large and most beautiful building. However, he does not comment on its exterior or interior decoration. On the contrary, he makes a most unexpected remark: that the gentiles do not permit sculptures or figurative depictions, and only come there to pray. Though he apparently entered the building, this detail indeed contradicts al-Harawi's account. Another omission is equally difficult to understand: Rabbi Benjamin of Tudela, a resident of medieval Spain, undoubtedly knew Arabic, but he has nothing to say about all the inscriptions read by al-Harawi.

He then mentions the Western Wall, though this passage is somewhat confused; the Western Wall is identified as one of the walls remaining from the Holy of Holies, but at the same time is called the Gate of Mercy.

Now reaching "Solomon's House" (al-Aqṣa mosque), Rabbi Benjamin mentions the stables built by Solomon. Once again, as with the Tower of David, he feels the need to emphasize the remarkable nature of the architecture, reporting that the building stones are such as cannot be seen anywhere else in the country. The so-called "Solomon's Stables" are another Herodian building, combining massive construction with an historical connection in the Jewish past.

He proceeds to describe the pool where the priests slaughtered their sacrifices. For Rabbi Benjamin this is another opportunity to link a monument with memories of the Jewish Temple, giving an account of the priests and the ritual of that period; as already mentioned, al-Harawi offers a different account of the pool. The nearby Gate of Jehoshaphat is mentioned immediately afterwards as leading to the Valley of Jehoshaphat. The monuments in this vicinity are, once again, essentially Jewish in nature: the tombs of Absalom and King Uzziah, the Pool of Siloam, and "a large building from the time of our ancestors." He notes that there is little water there and that the people of Jerusalem store rainwater, an observation made by Theoderic as well. Between Jerusalem and the Mount of Olives, only the Valley of Jehoshaphat is mentioned, an additional point of similarity with Theoderic's account. To the east, Rabbi Benjamin notes the view of the Dead Sea, Lot's Wife, and Mount Nebo.

He then turns to Mount Zion, where he states clearly that there is no building other than a *bamah* at the site, though we know that there was a Church of St. Mary. The term *bamah* is the same as that used for the Church of the Holy Sepulchre. His emphatic denial that there is any other building on Mount Zion is puzzling. Presumably, he means that there is no building apart from the church, or perhaps he is referring to the absence of any Jewish buildings.

The last site mentioned by Rabbi Benjamin is the Jewish cemetery, which apparently lies not far away since, on the whole, there is a logical order in his account. The description of the cemetery, with its references to royal tombs, including that of David, tends to associate it with the Cenaculum (the Church of St. Mary). Two stories are related in connection with the cemetery. The first is factual in nature, telling of the robbery of tombstones for the building of houses either by *Benei Adam* (people) or, in another version, *Benei Edom* (Edomites, as distinct from the Christians mentioned earlier).[19] The second story belongs more to the realm of legend, telling of two people who enter a grotto and visit the tombs of Judaean kings, finding there extraordinary treasures and gold and marble objects.

Theoderic

At the beginning of his account, Theoderic mentions the existence of seven gates, though he notes that the Golden Gate is blocked while the others are locked at night and reopened in the morning. He does not list the gates in any order, nor does he name them as does Rabbi Benjamin.

Several comments may be made on his account of the Temple Mount. He informs us that both the courtyard and the upper platform are paved with wide stones—undoubtedly the paving that still survives today. He adds that two sides of the Mount are unchanged (without specifying which sides), and then refers to the Canons and the Templars who built houses and gardens at its southeastern end.

When referring to Solomon's Stables, he describes them as a structure "that is remarkably complex," with vaults, arches, and roofing of different kinds that can house 10,000 horses and their grooms. The area is so great that a single crossbow shot could not encompass its length or breadth.

From the courtyard, he looks up to the *mawazin* on the upper platform and notes two arched columns on the right and three on the left, while on the east he counts fifteen steps from the Golden Gate to the Temple. He goes on to mention the existence of "large pools" around the Temple and beneath the pavement.

Returning to the Temple (the Dome of the Rock), Theoderic gives a detailed description of its doors, columns, piers, marble panels, and mosaics (outside), as well as its inscriptions, starting from the west, though he cites them in Latin rather than in Arabic. He relates the traditions connected with Christ as well as those of the Old Testament, such as Jacob's Ladder, and then describes in detail the Dome of the Chain, which he calls the Chapel of the Blessed James and says it is well decorated with pictures. He appears to imply that at the time the monument was walled, a phenomenon known elsewhere even today.

Curiously, he refers to the Dome of the Rock as a church consecrated to Our Lady Mary, describing it as a monument in honor of Jesus Christ and his revered mother. He proceeds to trace the history of the monument, which he says was first built by Queen Helena and her son, the Emperor Constantine. He now attempts to describe the earlier history of the Temple founded by Solomon. Interestingly, he specifies that the building was rectangular, and not round as it was in his day, until Zedekiah was captured by Nebuchadnezzar and taken to exile. He mentions the destruction of the First Temple by Nebuzoradan and accurately describes the return of the Jews to Jerusalem after seventy years of exile, led by Zerubabel and Ezra and under the patronage of Cyrus, and the rebuilding of the Temple, which he correctly numbers "the second." He quotes Neh. 4:17, which describes the rebuilders as "everyone with one of his hands wrought in the work, and with the other hand held a weapon."

He further recounts the destruction of the Temple by King Antiochus of Syria and the rebuilding of the Temple, which he terms "the third," by Judah Maccabee. This brings him to the time of King Herod, of whose role Theoderic is well aware in the history of the Temple: he relates that Herod razed the building and built a new and larger one, which he calls "the fourth," which stood until the days of Vespasian and Titus, who brought about the fourth destruction.

As for the "Palace of Solomon" (al-Aqṣa mosque), Theoderic goes into great detail, describing its pillars and recording that at the end of the sanctuary the building rises to a circular roof, round and large; this is apparently the dome, though this is not stated specifically. He notes that this and neighboring buildings are in the possession of the Templars, who store arms, food, and clothing there and have their stables there as well. Above the stables, the area is full of houses, dwellings, and outbuildings for every kind of purpose. He also says that the area contains walking places, lawns, council chambers, porches, consistories, and reservoirs of water in splendid cisterns, and below—washrooms, stores, and granaries.

On the other, western, side of the palace, the Templars built a new house, of which the height, length, and breadth are given; its cellars and refectories, staircases and roof are most unusual.

It is evident that the city walls surround the dwellings of the Templars on the south and east. To the north and west, the wall built by Solomon surrounds the buildings, together with the outer court and the Temple; the northern wall of the Temple and the gate of the Antonia are mentioned at the very beginning of his account. It is striking how much of Theoderic's account is borne out by the archaeological evidence.

From there, passing through a narrow passage that runs between the city-wall and the garden of the Templars, he refers to the Cradle of the Lord. When speaking of the Golden Gate, he correctly identifies it as a double gate.

Important evidence for the topography of Jerusalem is contained in Theoderic's statement that "most of Mount Zion is situated outside the walls of the Holy City on its south." He goes on to add, however, that there is a church (that of St. Mary) that is well defended by walls, towers, and bulwarks. This may account for one of the three walls mentioned by Rabbi Benjamin which are not well identified (see above). He gives a very detailed description of the Church of St. Mary (the Cenaculum) and its decoration, including "a round ciborium" (apparently a dome).

His description of the Tomb of Mary in the Valley of Jehoshaphat is very different from that of the Via Dolorosa or the sites connected with the life of Christ. Like al-Harawi, Theoderic is overwhelmed by the beauty of the monument; he, too, praises the marbles and mosaics. Once more, he states that "this church and all its neighbouring buildings are strongly defended by big walls, strong towers, and bulwarks," and notes that there are many cisterns in the vicinity.

Theoderic makes a rather puzzling comment about the Church of the Ascension on the Mount of Olives: ". . . for it is not the custom in these parts to use any consecration for the places glorified by Our Lord's presence, except for this particular mountain height."[20] It is not clear how this applies to the other churches mentioned earlier, particularly the Holy Sepulchre. He gives a detailed description of the decoration of the church, adding that it, too, is well defended against the infidels by towers, great and small walls, and bulwarks, as well as by sentries at night. Also when speaking of the Monastery of the Cross, Theoderic remarks that its fortifications are "strongly defended against the attacks of infidels by towers, walls, and bulwarks."

Theoderic also makes some general comments about the city. He notes that it is in the shape of a polygon, with five angles, one of which projects inward. He apparently noticed the paving of the streets, for he says that underfoot "nearly all streets are made with closely-lodged stones." He notes that many of the houses have stone roofs as well as windows to let in light. The houses have carefully-made walls reaching a considerable height, but the roofs are not raised in "our manner with beams," but are flat. The rainwater drains into cisterns and there is no other water supply; this observation is similar to one made by Rabbi Benjamin. Theoderic also adds a fact well known to us, that there is no wood in the area.

Theoderic, as Rabbi Benjamin, was greatly impressed by the Tower of David. He gives an accurate description of this monument, stressing the fact that it is an incomparably strong construction made of enormous square blocks. He adds that the tower is adjacent to the newly-built palace, which is also heavily defended by ditches and a barbican. He observes that from here the road to Bethlehem runs to the south.

III. CONCLUSIONS

All three accounts share similar basic interests, as they are all primarily concerned with the monuments and very little with the people living around them.

Al-Harawi is not very curious about the city or its inhabitants; the existence of a Muslim community is not even mentioned, though it is implied, and, of course, it is mentioned by Rabbi Benjamin. Al-Harawi relates to the city in a very limited way; interestingly, he is rarely impressed or excited. Only in two or three instances does he express admiration, always in relation to the architecture. Unfortunately, the book in which he promised to discuss the marvels he saw and admired either was never written or has not survived.

Although Rabbi Benjamin speaks about the Jews and the Jewish tradition in Jerusalem, an emotional chord is hardly every struck. Two minor exceptions are when he describes those who come to mourn at the Western Wall, and when he relates that they write their names; nevertheless, these remarks are never accompanied by any feelings of personal involvement. On the other hand, he cannot help but be impressed by the institution of the Hospitalers, as well as by the diversity of the city's population. On the whole, he tells us little.

For Theoderic, everything is both real and mythical. He retraces the itinerary of a real pilgrimage, but each detail relates to the biblical legacy. Neither of the other two pilgrims observes a heavenly Jerusalem, nor does Theoderic, but his earthly Jerusalem has an important substratum of ancient Jerusalem. The historical details mentioned by both al-Harawi and Rabbi Benjamin do not seem to have this dimension.

There are, of course, many questions that remain unanswered. However, on the purely factual level, some interesting comments may be made. For example, while Theoderic gives a very detailed description of the Holy Sepulchre and its marbles, mosaics, and columns, he says nothing of the sort about the Dome of the Rock. After describing the Holy Sepulchre in great detail, he devotes a few words to the forum in front of the church, where commercial activity took place, as well as the "roofed street" (the covered market) full of items for sale. He speaks with amazement of the wealth of the Hospital of St. John and of the help provided to the poor and destitute: ". . . no king or tyrant would be powerful enough to feed daily the great number fed in this house and it is not surprising, for besides the properties they have abroad . . . they possess almost all the cities and villages which once belonged to Judaea and were destroyed by Vespasian and Titus . . . all the fields and vineyards." This is a rather strange interpretation of the past; Theoderic mentions the Jews and the Romans, but not the Muslims from whom the crusaders conquered the country.

None of our three pilgrims refers to the city's administration,[21] institutions, or buildings. They seem to resemble the later travelers and explorers who may have been a continuation of the pilgrim tradition.

Each of the three narratives may be viewed as a microcosm, illustrating the sanctity and centrality of Jerusalem to Judaism, Christianity, and Islam at one and the same time.

Notes

1. A. Grabois, "Medieval Pilgrims, the Holy Land and Its Image in European Civilization," *Pillars of Smoke and Fire*, ed. M. Sharon (Johannesburg, 1988), 69.

2. ʿAli al-Harawi, *Guides des Lieux de Pèlerinage*, ed. J. Sourdel-Thomine (Damascus, 1953), 24–28; trans. J. Sourdel-Thomine (Damascus, 1957), 62–69.

3. *The Itinerary of Rabbi Benjamin of Tudela*, ed. and trans. A. Asher (new York, 1840), 68–75; *The Itinerary of Rabbi Benjamin of Tudela*, ed. M. N. Adler (London, 1907), 23–26.

4. *Theoderich's Description of the Holy Places*, trans. A. Stewart, PPTS (London, 1891); *Theodericus, Libellus de locis sanctis*, ed. M. L. and W. Bulst (Heidelberg, 1976), xxvii–cciii, 10–34; see also J. Wilkinson, *Jerusalem Pilgrimage 1099–1185* (London, 1988), 276–308.

5. Sourdel-Thomine, trans. (above, note 2), 68–69.

6. For a study of underground passages in Jerusalem in medieval times, see A. Shalem, "Biʾr al-waraqa: legend and truth. A note on medieval sacred geography," *PEQ* 127 (1995), 50–61.

7. See the map of crusader monuments in Jerusalem in J. Prawer and H. Ben-Shammai, *The History of Jerusalem—Crusaders and Ayyubids (1099–1250)* (Jerusalem, 1991).

8. M. S. Briggs, *Muhammedan Architecture in Egypt and Palestine* (New York, 1974), Fig. 8.

9. M. van Berchem, *Matérieux pour un Corpus Inscriptionum Arabicarum, Jérusalem, "Haram"* (Cairo, 1927), 301–303.

10. M. Rosen-Ayalon, "Jewish Substratum, Christian History and Muslim Symbolism: An Archaeological Episode in Jerusalem" (in press).

11. Sourdel-Thomine, trans. (above, note 2), 23, note 3.

12. R. W. Hamilton, *The Structural History of the Aqsa Mosque* (Jerusalem, 1949), 9, Pl. III.

13. G. Le Strange, *Palestine; Under the Moslems* (London, 1890; reprint Beirut, 1965), 132.

14. Sourdel-Thomine, trans. (above, note 2), 66, note 4.

15. H. Busse, "The Sanctity of Jerusalem in Islam," *Judaism* 17 (1968), 451.

16. J. Sourdel-Thomine, "Une image musulmane de Jérusalem au début du XIIIème siècle," *Jérusalem, Rome, Constantinople: L'image et le mythe de la ville*, ed. D. Poirion (Paris, ;1986), 217–33.

17. Ibid., 231–32.

18. For an alternative reading of this number, see Adler (above, note 3), 23, note 26.

19. Ibid., 25, note 8.

20. Wilkinson (above, note 4), 302.

21. It is worth noting that Christian pilgrims in the later medieval period were required to pay considerable fees to the Muslim rulers in order to visit Christian sites such as the Holy Sepulchre, though no such fees are noted in the accounts of Theoderic and Rabbi Benjamin. On entrance fees to churches, see G. Weiss, "The Pilgrim as Tourist: Travels to the Holy Land as Reflected in the Published Accounts of German Pilgrims between 1450 and 1550," *The Medieval Mediterranean: Cross-Cultural Contacts*, eds. M. J. Chiat and K. L. Reyerson (Minnesota, 1988), 124–25.

· V ·

JERUSALEM
IN MEDIEVAL
JEWISH
AND CHRISTIAN
TRADITIONS

24

Mystical Jerusalems

GUY G. STROUMSA

Vincet pax et finietur bellum. Quando autem vincet pax, vincet illa civitas quae dicitur visio pacis (Augustine, *Enarr. in Psal.* 64, 4).

In his book *The Martyrs of Palestine*, Eusebius reports the following conversation between the Roman governor of Palestine and the Christian Pamphilus in late third-century Caesarea:

—"Where do you come from?" asks the Governor.

—"From Jerusalem," answers Pamphilus.

—"Where is that?"

—"It lies toward the Far East and the rising sun."[1]

This exchange is revealing on two counts. Not only does it show that the Roman governor in Caesarea was ignorant of the former name of Aelia Capitolina, but it also reflects Pamphilus' intention to describe heavenly Jerusalem, rather than the earthly one, as his true homeland—a characteristic Christian attitude in the pre-Constantinian period.[2] Incidentally, the governor was not the last person to be ignorant of the geographical location of Jerusalem. Some twenty years ago, when my wife and I told a major American poet that we came from Jerusalem, she asked, "Is it far from Israel?"

The idea of a heavenly Jerusalem as a model of the earthly city was, of course, originally a Jewish idea, which owes its centrality in Christian literature to the fact that it was picked up and developed in the book of Revelation. This text, as well as the Letter to the Hebrews, propounded a conception of heavenly Jerusalem as the perfect model of which earthly Jerusalem was, at best, a pale reflection.[3] In Christian thought patterns, heavenly or new Jerusalem soon achieved autonomous status, as it were, from earthly Jerusalem, a phenomenon which has no parallel in Jewish thought.

The noble status of Jerusalem did not stem only from its having been the home of the first Christian community, the "Mother Church." It soon achieved mythic status. In various strata of early Christian literature, for instance in some New Testament apocryphal texts, the Mount of Olives in particular became the mythicized place of dialogues between the resurrected Christ and his disciples. Since its appearance in Zech. 14:4 (a radically eschatological passage and the only time it is mentioned in the Hebrew Bible), the Mount of Olives had achieved eschatological importance; in Christian consciousness it was not affected by the curse on Jerusalem.[4] So, too, Golgotha was not simply the place where Jesus had been crucified, but it soon became identified with the burial place of Adam in an adaptation of Jewish traditions regarding Mount Moriah. Like its Jewish antecedent, the early Christian conception of Jerusalem as the *omphalos* did not only imply that it was the center of the inhabited earth, the *oikoumenè* (as represented in medieval maps), but also the locus of a direct connection between heaven and earth. Fifth-century Christian Jerusalem, for instance, was a place where letters could fall from heaven, offering the possibility of new divine revelations.[5]

The singing of the praises of *urbs beata Hierusalem* in medieval hymns and religious poetry refers to the heavenly city, not to its earthly *figura*. This dual nature of Jerusalem and, more specifically, the dialectical relationship between earthly and heavenly Jerusalem, is crucial for any understanding of medieval attitudes to the holy city.[6]

In contradistinction to heavenly Jerusalem, the earthly city was charged with a deep ambivalence in early Christian literature.[7] Indeed, Jerusalem in the writings of the New Testament had left a powerful yet ambivalent impact upon the early Christian mind. In the gospels, Jesus had predicted the destruction of the Temple. Paul's career, moreover, symbolized the passage of the new religion from Jerusalem to Rome, from a marginal provincial city to the empire's capital, in a movement which has been described as "elliptical" by Henry Chadwick.[8] In the first centuries, we can detect in the main a trend of de-territorialization, which denied any central importance—at least implicitly—to earthly Jerusalem. The City of David retained in Christian consciousness a deeply ambiguous position: its inhabitants had been guilty of Deicide. The destruction of the Temple predicted by Jesus was soon perceived as divine punishment inflicted on the city for this crime.

An indication of the permanence of this ambivalence of Jerusalem in Christian consciousness perhaps is reflected by the fact that although there are at least five Bethlehems in the U.S.A., the only other Jerusalem I could find in the atlas is located in Olutanga, a small, remote island in the southern Philippines.

The Constantinian revolution brought with it the reconstruction of Jerusalem as a sacred city, its *renovatio*, mainly through the building of the basilica of the Anastasis. During three centuries, until the Islamic conquest, Byzantine Jerusalem would be invested with earthly as well as heavenly glories, adorned with churches and sanctuaries; the city had become the recipient of much respect and the source of some spiritual influence. Holy places were discovered not only in Jerusalem, but also throughout Palestine, soon transforming the latter into a *terra sancta*, a "Holy Land," during the fifth and sixth centuries—a process well described by Robert Wilken.[9]

And yet, the Temple Mount remained barren until the end of the seventh century, when the Kubbet a-Sahra, the Dome of the Rock, was built. This building is the first extant architectural monument of Islamic civilization, and remains to this day the most majestic structure in Jerusalem. According to the theology first propounded in the Letter to the Hebrews, Jesus was both the High Priest and the Sacrifice. His body was the new Temple. Hence, the theologically central position of Constantine's Church of the Anastasis, which was meant to replace the Temple.[10]

As is well known, the birth of Christian pilgrimages to the Holy Land and the Holy City in the fourth century took place despite reticence or objection by some of the leading teachers of the Church.[11] In a dialectical way, it is this movement back to Jerusalem which led the way to the reproductions of Jerusalem—more precisely, of its heart for Christians, the Holy Sepulchre—in various cities of western Europe throughout the Middle Ages. Often built by personalities, such as bishops back from Holy Land pilgrimage, these reproductions permitted those who could not go on pilgrimage themselves to experience it without leaving home, as it were, "abroad at home"—to use the motto of a *New York Times* columnist. The Holy Sepulchre, then, can be said to represent the core of the emerging "cultural memory" of the Christian people. Its symbolic reproduction throughout Europe reflects the organization and institutionalization of this memory.

In a sense, both the reproductions of Jerusalem and the idea of a heavenly Jerusalem represent two different metamorphoses of Jerusalem which run parallel to the Church's understanding of itself as *verus Israel*: if the name "Israel" refers to believers in Christ, this entails the expropriation of its earlier owners from their identity. If the true Jerusalem is located in heaven or elsewhere upon earth, the Old City upon the hills of Judaea has lost its unique significance. The desacralization of the Judaean space, however, can also be seen as the reverse side of the sacralization of the European soil; Jerusalem is not only elsewhere, to use Oleg Grabar's term, but everywhere. There is, then, another side to the radical metamorphosis of Jerusalem: the multiple senses and references of the name also reflect the spiritual conquest of a whole continent by the faith born in Judaea.

In the following pages, I shall focus upon the connections between two strikingly different phenomena, the reproductions of the Holy Sepulchre and the metaphor of heavenly Jerusalem. Both reflect central aspects of the metamorphosis of Jerusalem in medieval consciousness, or what the French call "l'imaginaire médiéval." To be sure, both phenomena have been studied often and well. Oddly enough, however, they never seem to have been approached simultaneously in their possible relationships. This is precisely what will be attempted here. I shall first refer to the intriguing phenomenon of the duplication of sacred places—the medieval *translatio* of Jerusalem to various European cities. I shall then discuss the idea of a new or heavenly Jerusalem and the spiritual metaphors of Jerusalem which have been prominent in Christian spiritual and mystical literature since the patristic period. Prima facie, these two ways of "uprooting" Jerusalem do not seem to be connected to one another; one reflects an "overdose," as it were, of the spatial, earthly dimension of Jerusalem, while the other represents its very negation. I shall argue that both phenomena dialectically complement one another, functioning like a pendulum of sorts in medieval thought patterns. In other words, the way to heavenly Jerusalem does not pass as much through earthly Jerusalem as it does through the multiple Jerusalems disseminated throughout western Europe. It should be noted here that these phenomena have no real counterpart in Byzantium, for complex reasons which reflect the vast difference between eastern and western Christendom. In particular, the status of Constantinople as the new Jerusalem has no equivalent in the West. In the fourth century, Rome in a sense came to be considered a *nova Hierusalem*. Santa Croce in Gerusalemme was built as early as the second half of the fifth century.[12] The Hierosolymitan influence was not only architectural, but also liturgical, especially during the paschal period. However, when Rome was sacked by Alaric in 410, Augustine could explain the collapse of the empire's capital precisely by recalling its pagan past and by contrasting it in a radical fashion to the *Civitas Dei*—another name for heavenly Jerusalem. Indeed, the Crusaders' *Iter Hierosolymae* did not have a Byzantine equivalent either. In a sense, then, this will be an investigation into the mythopoieic power of Jerusalem in European religious imagination.

◆　◆　◆

The idea of a Christian *translatio Hierosolymae* seems to occur for the first time with Montanus who, according to the testimony of Eusebius, "gave the name of Jerusalem to Pepuza and Tymion, little towns in Phrygia."[13] As confirmed by Tertullian, who knew Montanist beliefs as an insider, this probably means that heavenly Jerusalem was thought to have descended upon Pepuza and Tymion. The heretic status of the Montanists in the third century, and the Christian invention of the idea of Holy Land in the fourth century, probably prevented the *translatio Hierosolymae* from becoming implanted in patristic literature. Nevertheless, this conception never quite disappeared, remaining an endemic expression of sectarian eschatology throughout Christian history, from the Hussite reconstitution of the Holy Land in Bohemia, and the Taborites' Tabor, up to nineteenth-century Russia, for instance, where the sectarians of New Zion were expecting the descent of heavenly Jerusalem.[14]

If the new Jerusalem can descend from heaven on Pepuza, a small town in Asia Minor, who needs the City of David anymore?[15] To be sure, new Zions exist in various cultural surroundings. A famous case is that of the churches carved in the rock in Lâlibalâ, Ethiopia. This new Jerusalem became a major goal of pilgrimages at times when Axum was inaccessible.[16] In the modern world, we think mainly of Baptist churches in the southern United States or in sub-Saharan Africa or the Swedenborgian churches "of the New Jerusalem."[17] It should be pointed out that the idea of *translatio* from the Holy Land to Europe was not limited to the Holy Sepulchre and Jerusalem. In the last decade of the thirteenth century, for instance, the house of the Blessed Virgin Mary was transposed from Nazareth to Tersatz in Dalmatia, and from there to Loreto, near Ancona.[18]

Since Carolingian times, the symbolic transference of shrines from the Holy Land could bring considerable prestige and charisma to spiritual and political centers in the West.[19] The clearest and earliest example, perhaps, is Aachen (Aix-la-Chapelle), where the political stakes were particularly high. Charlemagne wished Aachen to be perceived in the sequence of Jerusalem, Rome, and Constantinople. The *Libri Carolini* call the city *sedes davidica* and New Jerusalem. The *translatio* here directly reflects the political claim of Charlemagne to be Constantine's, and ultimately Solomon's, successor.[20] Moreover, in his competition with the Byzantine emperor, he had succeeded in being granted by Harun al-Rashid a kind of protectorate over the Christian holy places in Jerusalem, with the right, for instance, to build *xenodocheia* for western pilgrims. Eusebius had specified that the dome of the Anastasis should "make conspicuous an object of veneration to all," the Holy Sepulchre. So the Rotunda Church of Aachen, Charlemagne's Capella Palatina, was perceived in typological association with the Church of the Holy Sepulchre.[21] Let us also mention, among others, the case of Orléans, where a crucifix was seen weeping on the eve of the year 1000. Within the context of the changing religiosity at the turn of the millennium, such a prodigy was thought by some to foretell "far greater matters, some kind of *translatio Hierosolymae*, in which Orléans would play the role of the New Jerusalem."[22]

The most sustained effort to concretize such a *translatio* was the actual building of a city according to the ideal plan of Jerusalem. Heavenly Jerusalem was often represented as *urbs quadrata*—but also as a circle[23]—and the sacral topography of the city could be perceived as a mental map, a mandala of sorts, reminding one of Christianity's central belief and offering an immediate object for meditation.[24] A clear example is that of Constance, mentioned by Christoph Auffarth in his study of the significance of Jerusalem in the realized eschatology in the wake of the Crusades. Auffarth points out that such mental maps also became mental timetables as pilgrimage loci.[25]

From the early ninth to the early twelfth centuries, at least nineteen churches were built in western Europe which were meant to be copies of the Holy Sepulchre, imitating its main characteristics.[26] The first such edifices were built on a smaller scale than the original. So, for instance, Saint Maurice of Constance, was built between 934 and 976, following that of Saint Michael of Fulda, which was built already in 820 as a copy of the Anastasis. Konrad, bishop of Constance, had gone on pilgrimage to the holy city. In his *Vita* (dating from 1123), mention is made of the reconstruction of the Holy Sepulchre with wonderful goldwork, *mirabili aurificis opere*.[27] The church in Paderborn, built between 1033 and 1036, was the first one to be built *ad mensuras ejusdem ecclesiae et sancti Sepulchri*. The oldest such church, however, seems to be the Narbonne Holy Sepulchre, built in white Pyrenean marble in the fifth century. The first real reproduction of the tomb in Jerusalem, complete with antechamber, was built in Eichstätt, Walbrun around 1160. Examples of similar churches from the twelfh century are numerous, from Northampton and Cambridge to Augsburg. Moreover, there exist ten round churches built by the Templars and the Hospitaliers, as well as the Pisan baptistery.[28] These churches, which evoke the image of the Holy Sepulchre, express a devotion to the first shrine of Christendom.

One striking example of a new Zion in Europe is the Chiesa di Santo Stefano in Bologna, also called Sancta Jerusalem Bononiensis, one of the earliest and certainly the most famous of the many similar churches in western Europe. The Santo Stefano rotunda was conceived as a reproduction of the church of the Anastasis but, at the same time, was also meant to refer to the Hierusalem coelestis and the Santa Maria rotunda in Rome, i.e., the Pantheon. According to some traditions, Petronius, bishop of Bologna ca. 431–450, upon returning from a Holy Land pilgrimage, had a replica of the Holy Sepulchre built in his city and consecrated to the protomartyr Saint Stephen. This reproduction is, in a sense, an *eidolon* of Jerusalem, a portable Jerusalem, as it were, whose function was to remind one of the great and original shrine, the *omphalos.*[29] A representation of Petronius, Bologna's patron saint, depicts him holding the city in his hands. Bologna itself is thus represented as a *forma orbis*, similar, in a way, to Jerusalem.[30] The first testimony for the name of Jerusalem granted to the Petronian Church in Bologna, it would seem, is found in a document by Charlemagne, dated to 887; it confirms to Wibodus, bishop of Parma, the acquisition of various churches in Bologna, including that of *Sanctum Stefanum qui dicitur sancta Hierusalem.*[31] The earliest mention of a *Hierusalem* in Europe seems to go back to a document dating from 716 where mention is made of the church *Sancti Andrae, ubi est baptisterium, una cum ecclesia Sancte Hierusalem.*[32]

The numerous scholars who have studied the impressive compound, its architecture, and history agree that it is quite distinct from the many other round churches, imitations, or copies of the rotunda of the Holy Sepulchre (or, rather, copies of an idealized Holy Sepulchre). The church as it exists today seems to have been erected upon the ruins of an earlier, Roman building, which may date to Saint Petronius' time. As is well known, in 1048 Constantine X Monomachos had rebuilt the church of the Anastasis, which in 1009 had been destroyed by the Caliph Al-Hakim. The Crusaders, in turn, launched extensive rebuilding activities at the Holy Sepulchre from 1099 to 1161. The plan of S. Stefano relies on the arrangement that existed in Jerusalem prior to the Crusaders' extensive rebuilding of the Holy Sepulchre. The Bologna church thus remains, to this day, the only concrete testimony to the original form of the Anastasis, after the radical changes made in the Jerusalem sanctuary itself in the eleventh century. This original form was known accurately, since plans of the Holy Sepulchre, similar to those drawn by the seventh-century pilgrim Arculf, had been brought back to Europe by the Crusaders.

But the church did not stand alone. It seems that, originally, Sancta Hierusalem consisted of a reproduction of the various holy places in Jerusalem that was created at the eastern end of Bologna. Already in the tenth century, mention is made of San Giovanni in Monte Oliveti, and also of a church of S. Tecla, built as a *similitudo* of the Valley of Jehoshaphat, whose identification with the Qidron Valley is attested already in Eusebius' *Onomasticon*. This Valle di Giosafat is located between the Oliveti and Sancta Hierusalem, in other words, corresponding to the topography of Jerusalem. Indeed, the claim that the distances between the different loci reproduce precisely those between their models in Jerusalem is not quite accurate. The distance between S. Giovanni in Monte Oliveti and S. Stefano varies by almost one kilometer from the distance between the Anastasis and the Mount of Olives. The field of Akeldama and the pool of Siloam are also mentioned in the sources, although their location remains undetermined. The whole complex, then, was created as a "theme park" of sorts, the first Eurodisney, offering a reproduction of Jerusalem, its hills and valleys, and permitting a short escapade into the mythical Holy Land without the vagaries of the voyage. This was a new Jerusalem, neither a faithful reproduction of the earthly city nor a completely mythical one. Actually, neither "reproduction" nor "myth" quite fits the nature of this reconstructed Jerusalem, no more than either fits the maps of Jerusalem drawn by pilgrims and travelers throughout the centuries. Rather, its most obvious character lies in what can be called the *actualization* of the Holy City.

The Church of St. Stephen itself did not originally possess a precise symbolism as did the Holy Sepulchre. This was added later by the Benedictine monks who rebuilt the original church in the Middle Ages. It is reasonable to postulate the First Crusade offered the impulse for the reconstruction of Sancta Hierusalem. We know of the great enthusiasm generated by the First Crusade among the Bolognese.[33] With the first Crusaders returning from the liberated holy city, the time was ripe for a new symbolism, more powerful and more complex than the earlier tradition, itself inherited from the late antique pilgrimages to the Holy Land.

The Nuova Gerusalemme, however, was meant to be more than just a souvenir reproduction of the holy city. It had obvious liturgical dimensions that are referred to in our sources. In the twelfth century, we know of processions from S. Stefano to S. Giovanni in Monte that were organized by the returning Crusaders. In the Middle Ages, S. Stefano was also the site of Easter week ceremonies and of an *adoratio crucis* copied from the cult of the Holy Cross in Jerusalem. In its twelfth-century form, S. Stefano offered a clear and specific link to Jerusalem and its holy sites. Through its architectural and liturgical imitations, it gave the citizens of Bologna a visible connection to Jerusalem, both the holy city and the heavenly vision.

The liturgical dimensions of Jerusalem's *memoriae* permitted the performance of the sacred drama of Christ's Passion. Here, too, the developments reflect a deep ambivalence. In the mid-thirteenth century, Urban IV established the *Corpus Christi* feast in order to express his own interest for the Holy Sepulchre.[34] Already in ninth-century Carolingian France, one could observe various liturgical connections with Jerusalem, such as processions of palms. In Santa Croce, Bologna, we can recall the facsimile of the Holy Cross kept at a special locus called Golgotha. This may have been the setting for an *adoratio crucis,* similar to the Exaltation of the Holy Cross described by Egeria on Holy Thursday, when the relic of the True Cross was presented to the faithful to be kissed.[35] In the tenth century, tropes of the *visitatio sepulchri* were chanted in places such as Saint Gallen or Limoges.[36] Altogether, Christian liturgy recognizes a direct relationship between the spatial and temporal dimensions of cultic behavior. It might be worth noting that the liturgy commemorating different events, such as the Annunciation or the Birth of Jesus, which are usually celebrated once a year, can be celebrated *at any time* on the spot itself.[37]

In the same context, one should also understand the development of the Passion mystery plays: Jerusalem is everywhere; the reconstitution of its central shrine performs a role similar to the reenactment of the events which it is intended to recall. Plays about visitation to the Holy Sepulchre were common in western Europe.[38] There is no doubt that the dissemination of such churches reflects the new interest in the earthly Jerusalem inspired by the Crusades. Moreover, the movement for the construction of these churches came to a halt with the conquest of Jerusalem by Saladin. No wonder, then, that there was no similar phenomenon in Byzantium. The question remains, however, of the extent to which the cult in these churches strengthened or weakened the believers' bonds to the holy city. The Holy Sepulchre venerated in western Europe was no longer localized in Jerusalem, and the Passion of Jesus Christ, the Via Crucis, could be reenacted everywhere.[39]

The idea of the Via Dolorosa is a medieval invention of the Franciscans which had been imported to Jerusalem from Europe, as was the rite of the Deposition, which reached Jerusalem only in the sixteenth century. In a sense, therefore, it is the very recovery of Jerusalem in medieval Christendom which brought, in a dialectical way, to its *Aufhebung*, and to the transformation of religious memory. Paradoxically, then, the *memoriae* of Jerusalem played a role in limiting the significance of the actual Holy City in Christian religious consciousness.[40]

In "Calvaries of Convenience," a chapter of his recent *Landscape and Memory*, Simon Schama focuses on mountains transformed into symbolic Golgothas in the Middle Ages.[41] Schama begins his analysis with Monte Verna, the Piedmontese mountain chosen in 1224 by St. Francis as an alternative calvary and where he received the stigmata; "And this, God willed, should manifestly appear on Mount Verna because there the Passion of our Lord Jesus Christ was to be renewed through love and pity in the soul of Saint Francis." In the following centuries, the Franciscans would continue converting mountains into inspirational theaters. Schama mentions the case of the Franciscan Friar Bernardino Caimi who, having seen the real Mount Zion while acting as patriarch of the Holy Land, determined in 1486 to create on Monte Verna a more readily-available version. On the mountain, various chapels were built, called by names such as "Nazareth" or "Bethlehem" and adorned with paintings from the "parallel lives" of Jesus and Francis. At these chapels, the pilgrim would pause for prayer and contemplation during his (or her) ascent. Monte Verna, therefore, was not only transformed into a new Golgotha, but into a new, symbolic Holy Land—a fact which emphasizes the abstract nature (or spiritualization) of the idea of the Holy Land in the Middle Ages.[42]

The piety which encouraged the development of the Via Dolorosa went against the grain of the *Iter Sancti Sepulchri* and Crusader piety.[43] Inspired by their love of the heavenly city, pilgrims and Crusaders came to earthly Jerusalem: *Terrestram celestis amore Jerusalem cum aliis currens.*[44] As pointed out by Bernard McGinn, we cannot recapture the power evoked by the name "Jerusalem" at the time of the First Crusade if we ignore the full scope of the name's meaning. In the piety of the Crusaders, engaged in a mixture of holy war and pilgrimage, there was also room for *concordia*, the peace of the hearts, which was necessary for a pilgrimage of penance.

This kind of piety, however, did not go unchallenged. The growth of a new, local religiosity in western Europe tended to belittle or even ignore the significance of, or the need for, Holy Land pilgrimages. One can also follow a trend of opposition to the Crusades in the Middle Ages.[45] After their final failure, the reconquest of earthly Jerusalem had paved the way, as we have seen, for a radical spiritualization of the *Iter Sancti Sepulchri*.

◆　◆　◆

The failure of early Christian apocalyptical movements, illustrated by the perception of the Montanists as heretics and the postponement *sine die* of the *parousia*, had direct implications for the representations of Jerusalem. Rather than alternative earthly locations, or the idea of an eschatological *renovatio*, it is the metaphor of a *spiritual* Jerusalem which became prevalent in the early Christian mind. This Jerusalem was the Christian's true fatherland, and it was in heaven. Indeed, early Christian writers were here following in the footsteps of Jewish apocalypticism; in the book of Revelation, the new Jerusalem was to descend from heaven (Apoc. 21:1–5). For IV Esdras, a Jewish text redacted at the end of the first century C.E., the eschatological element is still prominent: Jerusalem would be established by God in messianic times. The Syriac Apocalypse of Baruch weakens this element by pointing out the direct relationship between *Urzeit* and *Endzeit*: heavenly Jerusalem had been prepared by God since the origin of the world.

The transformation of the ideal city was completed in the late second century with Clement of Alexandria, who recalls that the Stoics referred to the heavens as the true city.[46] For him, as a Christian, the obvious parallel to the heavenly city of the Stoics was heavenly Jerusalem, which he calls "my Jerusalem."[47] We reach here the roots of the mystical meaning of Jerusalem.

For Origen, who follows and develops Clement's views on the *polis*, Jerusalem (whose Hebrew name means "vision of peace") could mean the Church, but also, in the tropological sense, it could mean the soul.[48] A similar allegorical interpretation is found in the writings of the fourth-century Origenist, Didymus the Blind. For him, too, Jerusalem could be understood in a threefold way: it is at once the virtuous soul, the Church, and the heavenly city of the living God. We shall return to the *visio pacis* metaphor of Jerusalem, which runs like a thread throughout the centuries.[49] One should at least mention here another formative metaphor, stemming directly from Paul: the Jerusalem above, the Christians' mother, is also called free, *eleuthera* (Gal. 4:26). *Caelestis Hierusalem, quae est mater libertatis, chorus libertatis*: this is a Leitmotif of medieval Latin Christian literature.[50]

As is well known, the Augustinian typology of the two cities finds its roots in Tyconius, whose *Commentary on the Apocalypse* referred to two *civitates*, Babylon *versus* Jerusalem.[51] It is impossible here to offer even a brief overview of Augustine's perception of spiritual Jerusalem, whose praise he sings: *Quando de illa loquor, finire nolo.* For him, heavenly Jerusalem represents the Church, the wife of Christ, while Babylon represents power and politics. In his *de Civitate Dei*, the *civitas dei* is also called "Jerusalem." It is needless to dwell upon the major formative influence of this typology on medieval perceptions.[52] Augustine's most interesting developments regarding Jerusalem, perhaps, occur in his *Enarrationes in Psalmos*. Jerusalem is placed in opposition to Babylon, as in Revelation (and also to Sinai, as in Galatians). While Babylon refers to present life, in this world, Jerusalem alludes to future life. Then the boundaries of time will be overcome and God will be praised forever, *in saecula saeculorum*. In his commentary on Psalm 64.2, for instance, Augustine begins by referring to the etymologies of Babylon and Jerusalem.[53] One means *confusio*, (Heb. *bilbul*) and the other *visio pacis* (Heb. *yr'e shalom*). The major problem facing the relationships between these two opposite entities is the fact that they are inextricably intertwined throughout history: *Permixtae sunt . . . usque in finem saeculi*. Jerusalem represents the love of God, while Babylon signifies the love of the world: *Duas istas civitates faciunt duo amores: Ierusalem facit amor Dei; Babyloniam facit amor saeculi*. Hence, the criterion for anyone to recognize his own identity: ask yourself what you love, and you'll know where you belong. Such an understanding of Jerusalem, then, denies any localization of the city: Jerusalem is everywhere or, more precisely, in the hearts of those who love God.

The full-fledged spiritual interpretation of Jerusalem, with its multiple levels of meaning, is first found in the writings of John Cassian (fifth century). For him, Jerusalem could be understood as referring to the human soul:

Si Hierusalem aut Sion animam hominis uelimus accipere secundum illud: lauda Hierusalem dominum: lauda deum tuum Sion. Jerusalem, he goes on, can be understood in four ways, according to the four senses of Scriptures. According to history (*secundum historiam*), it is the city of the Jews, the earthly Jerusalem. According to allegory (*secundum allegoriam*), it represents the Church and Christ. According to anagogy (*secundum anagogem*), it is "that city of God which is the mother of us all." Finally, Jerusalem is identical to the human soul when understood according to tropology (*secundum tropologiam*).[54] Jerusalem thus becomes the most privileged symbol. *In nuce*, this name includes the entire Old Testament, the city of God, the mystery of the *Virgo singularis*, the total presentation of Christian mystery.[55]

Throughout the Middle Ages, these various senses of Jerusalem appear among different writers, from the Venerable Bede and Hrabanus Maurus to Nicolas of Lyra, for whom Jerusalem is the best example illustrating the fourfold sense of Scriptures. Such conceptions of the spiritual meaning of Jerusalem should be understood in the tradition of its fourfold meaning stemming from Cassian, as, for instance, in Nicolas of Lyra, or in Hugh of Fouilloy's *De claustro animae*, a treatise in forty-three chapters on the four senses of Jerusalem: historical, ethical, anagogical, and mystical.[56]

Cassian's *Collationes* was one of the most influential books in the formative period of monastic spirituality. No wonder, then, that Jerusalem is one of the preferred symbols of contemplative life in medieval literature. More precisely, it would seem that the use of Jerusalem in medieval Christian spiritual and mystical literature stood at the intersection between two traditions, that of Cassian and that of Augustine. It is the combination of these two which permits the emergence and development of Jerusalem as the natural symbol of the contemplation of the divine glory shared by angels and those leading the monastic *vita angelica*.

The most obvious author for the medieval spiritual meaning of Jerusalem, however, is Bernard of Clairvaux. The following quotation is representative of his understanding of Jerusalem:

> You have two from heaven, both Jesus the Bridegroom and the Bride Jerusalem. . . . When the holy Emmanuel brought to earth the teaching of heavenly discipline, when the visible image and beautiful appearance of that heavenly Jerusalem which is our mother became known as revealed to us in and through Christ.[57]

For Bernard, the monastery was a training camp for heavenly Jerusalem.[58] He intended to model the church after heavenly Jerusalem.[59] In a famous letter from about 1129 to Alexander, bishop of Lincoln, which has become the *locus classicus* of the new religious sensitivity, Bernard identifies Clairvaux in so many words with heavenly Jerusalem: *Et, si vultis scire, Clara Vallis est. Ipsa est Ierusalem, ea quae in coelis est, tota mentis devotione, et conversationis imitatione, et cognatione quadam spiritus sociata.* Bernard was referring to Philip, a monk from England who, on his way to Jerusalem, had made a stop in Clairvaux. Bernard convinced him that his monastery was the new and true Jerusalem and that there was no need for him to continue his exhausting voyage.[60] His conception of spiritual pilgrimage is developed in his writing "on conversion."[61] The monastery was not only conceived as a *paradeisos*, but also as a new Jerusalem, the heavenly city of peace, already in the patristic tradition.

For Bernard, then, the cloister of Clairvaux is a Jerusalem in anticipation. The monk dwells in Jerusalem: this name refers to those who in this world lead a religious life; by a virtuous and orderly life, they seek to imitate the way of life of the Jerusalem above:

> *Puto enim hoc loco prophetam Ierusalem nomine designasse illos, qui in hoc saeculo vitam ducunt religiosam, mores supernae illius Ierusalem conversatione honesta et ordinata pro viribus imitantes; et non veluti hi, qui de Babylone sunt. . . . Mea autem, qui videor monachus et Ierosolymita, peccata certe occulta sunt. . . .*[62]

In the second half of the twelfth century, the school of St. Victor provides other instances of a similar conception of Jerusalem. Explaining the parable of the Good Samaritan, for instance, Richard of St. Victor sees not only Christ in the Samaritan, and the fallen man in the traveler attacked by the thieves (both interpretations revert to patristic literature), but also argues that the city of Jerusalem, which the traveler left, represents contemplation, while Jericho symbolizes fallen man's misery; the descent from Jerusalem to Jericho represents sin.[63]

Dom Jean Leclercq, the great scholar of medieval monastic spirituality, has edited an anonymous sermon, probably written in the eleventh century by a disciple of Jean of Fécamp.[64] This text, written with profound enthusiasm, makes generous use of quotations from the Psalms and appears to reflect widely-shared images. It begins by praising the frequent recollection of Jerusalem as a spiritual exercise of great value: *Ciuitatis et regis Hierusalem frequens recordatio dulcis est nobis consolatio, religiosae exercitationis grata occasio, onerosae sarcinae nostrae necessaria subleuatio.* I wish to call attention here to the direct link between the representation of a place (even if only a metaphorical, ideal one) and religious meditation, or, as the text has it, an exercise.

This would be recognized by Ignatius of Loyola who, in his *Spiritual Exercises*, emphasized the need to identify a place with oneself in order to meditate on the mysteries of Christ's earthly life. This trend in Ignatian spirituality clearly reflects medieval patterns of thought, especially since the Crusades.

◆   ◆   ◆

The coupling of opposite entities, Jerusalem/Babylon, is not limited to Latin and ecclesiastical literature. Its important influence upon European culture is reflected by its presence in the earliest strata of Italian vernacular literature of the *duecento*. Such texts may reflect Joachite influence. Giacomino of Verona, for instance, writes, in Veronese:

> Ierusalem celeste   questa terra s'apella
> citˆ de l'alto Deu   nova, preclara e bella
> dond e Cristo segno. . . .
> . . . contraria de quella   ke per nomo se clama,
> citˆ de gran pressura   Babilonia la magna
> un la qual Lucifer. . . .[65]

Similar perceptions of Jerusalem are found in the *Libro delle tre Scritture* of the poet Bonsevin de la Riva, one of Dante's precursors:

> . . . quella città soprana   si è pur d'or lucente
> Le plaze delectevre   le mure resplendante
> . . . Oi De, splendor purissimo   in la città celesta . . .
> . . . Oi De, com pò godher   lo just in paradisò. . . .[66]

In what can be described as a pendulum movement in the *longue durée*, the image of a golden Jerusalem was to cross centuries (and religious boundaries) as well as continents. From the song *Urbs beata Ierusalem, dicta pacis visio*, known to have been written for Vespers in the eighth century, a straight line goes up to the Victorian hymns on "Jerusalem the Golden," and from these to the Hebrew song of Naomi Shemer which was to become one of the main symbolic and cultural expressions of Israeli triumphalism in 1967.

Bernard of Clairvaux, Richard of St. Victor, Joachim of Fiore, and Giacomino of Verona have been brought here as examples of the understanding of Jerusalem as a symbol of spiritual life. Throughout the Middle Ages, and up to the early modern period, heavenly Jerusalem has represented for this trend of thought the ultimate goal of the pilgrim on his way to spiritual vision. The total transformation of the symbol, with the complete disappearance of any reference to earthly Jerusalem, will be accomplished in spiritual writings such as those of Bonaventure in the thirteenth century. He speaks of St. Francis, in his insatiable thirst for peace, as a citizen of heavenly Jerusalem, which the soul reaches when it enters into itself.[67] At the dawn of modern times, the Spanish mystics continued this trend. Bernardino of Laredo, for instance, published in 1535 his *Ascent to Mount Sion.* The work's historical importance stems from Teresa of Avila's predilection for it. The ascent to Mount Sion has now become totally metaphorical:

> So that the ascent of Mount Sion is the same as the ascent to Jerusalem. . . . And this temporal Jerusalem denotes for us the eternal and sovereign city for which God created us and to which we shall not go unless we ascend from the knowledge of ourselves to the following of Christ.[68]

The message has undergone a radical spiritualization, earthly Jerusalem has disappeared from sight, and the whole pilgrimage to the holy city is a journey of the soul:

> The fire of the Lord is in Zion, since contemplative souls possess it in this life, and finally are perfected in Jerusalem, since such souls as these, who here begin to love, and persevere in love, grow in love continually as they proceed along the road of this exile, then are led . . . into the Jerusalem which is above, where in that fire which had its beginning in this exile of ours burns without intermission. . . .[69]

In the late Middle Ages, we can follow the development of new, radical beliefs in a kind of pilgrimage. This can be described as internal and quite atopical, a pilgrimage accomplished not in space, with no need of dangerous and expensive travel to a foreign land, not even in a conveniently miniaturized space at home, but within the soul itself. The traditional images of Holy Land pilgrimage are reinterpreted metaphorically, and the earthly pilgrims are a figure of the march toward spiritual Jerusalem. Such an idea is found, for instance, in the sermons of Bernardino of Siena, probably the most influential spiritual force in Italy in the first half of the fifteenth century. Toward the end of Chaucer's *Canterbury Tales,* it is also reflected in the words of the country priest, who views Canterbury as the Holy Land for everybody, since earthly pilgrimages are but the image of the spiritual march toward Jerusalem.[70]

✦ ✦ ✦

I have dealt briefly above with two different phenomena: the imaginary visit to Holy Land shrines at their local replicas, and the tradition of a heavenly Jerusalem, up to the development of spiritual pilgrimages to Jerusalem in the later Middle Ages. I have argued that these two phenomena are related. Various "spiritual pilgrimages," which began to be printed as early as the first half of the fifteenth century, were meant as spiritual guides for those who could not afford the expense of the pilgrimage itself or who were unwilling to suffer its vagaries. In a sense, Christian spirituality was thus rediscovering themes already found in late antique patristic spiritual and monastic literature. The Christian was defined anew as *homo viator*.

Such patterns of thought reflect, in a sense, a return to some fundamental Augustinian attitudes. No wonder, then, that in the fifteenth century Nicolas of Cusa was able "to transpose these themes of spiritual experience to the level of philosophical and theological reflection, and to elaborate a mystical synthesis."[71] For him, it is not only man who could be defined as *viator*. Rather, it is the whole life of the Church on earth which should be understood as a pilgrimage in the footsteps of Jesus Christ.

We can perhaps describe schematically the dialectical evolution of pilgrimage ideas in the following way: the holy places gave birth to the development of pilgrimage in early Christianity. At a later stage, translations of these holy places brought them to European cities. Finally, the pilgrimage to the local replica of the Holy Place was transformed into a spiritual pilgrimage.

Apocalyptic spirituality permits the actualization and vivification of perceptions often muted or neutralized in mainstream Christian tradition. The great Calabrian visionary from the twelfth century, Joachim de Fiore, is said to have experienced a conversion to internal life precisely during a pilgrimage to the Holy Land which he undertook as a young man. He was to make great use of the name of Jerusalem in his *Liber Figurarum*. The most puzzling pair of figures in this book is perhaps the antithesis of Jerusalem/*Ecclesia* and Babylon/Rome. Note that the Roman church, for Joachim, is always Jerusalem, never Rome. While Babylon is the realm of the devil, the heavenly kingdom of God is symbolized by Jerusalem. The theme of the figures is the pilgrimage of the faithful people of God. "The sons of Jerusalem are pilgrims sojourning in the midst of Babylon. . . . The *Liber Concordiae* . . . starts from the concept of the earthly pilgrimage and throughout makes much use of the figures of pilgrimage and journeying.[72] At the end of history, there will be a third apotheosis of Jerusalem, after the reign of David in earthly Jerusalem and the pontificate of Pope Silvester in Rome.

In his *Eternal Gospel*, Joachim goes into a detailed description of heavenly Jerusalem as described in Rev. 21, seeing a precise symbolism in its various components, such as the different precious stones from which it is built. He insists on the fact that in heavenly Jerusalem there is no Temple built by men, since the Father and the Son are themselves the only Temple of the Spirit.

In the fourth century, Eusebius and Jerome pointed out the traditional etymology of Jerusalem, *Yerushalaim*, as referring to a vision of peace, *visio pacis* in Jerome's words. This interpretation was picked up by Augustine and Isidore of Sevilla.[73] Through their mediation, this traditional etymology had become prominent in medieval texts.[74] The last avatar of the perception of earthly Jerusalem in the later Middle Ages and at the time of the Renaissance reflects a new dimension given to the mystical *visio pacis*. From a purely spiritual vision, it also becomes the best metaphor of an eschatological dream of peace upon earth among religions and civilizations.

In his *De pace fidei*, Nicolas of Cusa dreams of a religious concordate agreed upon in heaven, i.e., in the only rational region, by wise Christians, Jews, and Moslems. Given full powers, they then meet in Jerusalem, the common religious center, in order to receive in the name of all the single faith, and they establish upon it perpetual peace, "in order that in this peace, the Creator of all things be glorified in all *saecula*. Amen."[75]

The development of ethnological curiosity, also vis-à-vis "Turks" (i.e., Muslims) and Jews, together with the sorrow generated by religious strife throughout Europe, encouraged a renewal of utopian thought. Jerusalem provided here a ready-made symbol, understood by all. Tomaso Campanella, another visionary from Calabria (this time a Dominican), dreamed at the beginning of the seventeeenth century of a new kind of *recuperatio Terrae Sanctae*, which would be the utmost expression of the *renovatio saeculi*: "The Church was born in Jerusalem, and it is to Jerusalem that it will return, after having conquered the whole world." The former presence of the Crusaders in Jerusalem is perceived by Campanella as a step toward the instauration of the messianic kingdom in that kingdom: Jerusalem, indeed, is the Holy City, where Jews, Christians, and Muslims can become united in communion.[76]

A similar mixture of mysticism and politics linked to Jerusalem is found also in the thought of the sixteenth-century Jesuit, Guillaume Postel, an Orientalist who became the first holder of the Chair of Hebrew at the Collège de France and one of the great "illuminés" of the Renaissance. For Postel, Jerusalem, true mother of the universe, is the *figura* of the building of the third Temple, a Temple to serve the whole earth and to permit the spiritual rebirth of humankind in the final kingdom of Jesus Christ and the restitution of all things, the *apokatastasis pantôn* dear to the Stoics and to Origen:

> Ceste unité unique, et du tout differente de toutes celles qui ont esté, ou sont, ou jamais seront au monde inferieur, est la personele Jerusalem, de laquelle David escript: Yerusalaim sehubeerah lah yiheddow, Jerusalem cujus associatio aut participatio pro ipsa fit una cum eo. Nos

pieds sont establis en tes portes, o Jerusalem. Jerusalem qui es edifiée comme une cité, mais non pas une cité, ains une personne, de laquelle l'accompaignement est pour elle avec un luy, qui en est le chef. Or est il du tout certein et necessaire qu'entre toutes et sur toutes les congregations, polices, estats ou eglises du monde, il y en aye une tele qu'elle soit du tout excellente et differente de tout aultre . . . car oultre l'estre un corps mystique ou civil et politique, elle est personele et vive union come chascune aultre mere ou vierge ou femme du monde. . . . C'est donc la finale victoire d'une seule et unike colombe et espouse. . . .[77]

One could go on quoting Postel's lucubrations on messianic Jerusalem, for him both a political and spiritual entity. His naiveté and messianic patterns of thought reflect a recurrent trend in modern religious attitudes, with which we are unfortunately all too familiar. We are here far away from another early modern reinterpretation of Jerusalem, Pico della Mirandola's *De dignitate hominis*, where heavenly Jerusalem is the goal of a spiritual flight kindled by the Socratic delirium described in Plato's *Phaedrus*, a flight which takes the mystical philosopher far from this world ruled by Satan.[78]

◆ ◆ ◆

In these pages, I have sought to focus on medieval mental representations of Jerusalem and to suggest some main lines of their development and transformation processes. As we have seen, these processes are dialectical in the sense that they fuel one another. The heavenly or spiritual Jerusalem lies at the base of Holy Land pilgrimages and crusades, while pilgrimages to the earthly city, in turn, permit the development of "new Jerusalems" throughout Europe. Ultimately, it is such *memoriae* of Jerusalem which permit a constant passage between earthly and heavenly Jerusalem in the "imaginaire médiéval." The spiritualization of Jerusalem and its "multiplications" are two sides of the Christian "uprooting" of Jerusalem, reflecting a fundamental ambivalence in Christian attitudes to the Holy City. In the religious history of Europe, Jerusalem is no longer located "toward the Far East," as it had been for the Palestinian martyr Pamphilus. Jerusalem is both in heaven and at home.

Notes

1. Eusebius, *Martyrs of Palestine* 11, 9–12.
2. P. Walker, "Jerusalem and the Holy Land in the Fourth Century," *The Christian Her-*

itage in the Holy Land, eds. A. O'Mahony et al. (London, 1995), 23–24. Cf. E. D. Hunt, *Holy Land Pilgrimage in the Later Roman Empire, A.D. 312–460* (Oxford, 1984), 4–5.

3. On heavenly Jerusalem, see E. Lamirande, "Jérusalem céleste," *Dictionnaire de Spiritualité*, VIII (Paris, 1974), 944–58, and bibliography there. See further W. D. Davies, "Jerusalem and the Land in the Christian Tradition," *The Jerusalem Colloquium on Religion, Peoplehood, Nation and Land*, eds. M. A. Tanenbaum and R. J. Z. Werblowsky (Jerusalem, 1972), 115–57; idem, *The Gospel and the Land: Early Christianity and Jewish Territorial Doctrine* (Sheffield, 1994).

4. See O. Limor, "The Place of the End: Eschatological Geography in Jerusalem," *The Real and Ideal Jerusalem*, ed. B. Kühnel (forthcoming).

5. See M. van Esbroek, "La lettre sur le dimanche, descendue du ciel," in his *Aux origines de la dormition de la Vierge* (London, 1995), XIII.

6. See K. L. Schmidt, "Jerusalem als Urbild und Abbild," *Eranos Jahrbuch* 18 (1950), 207–48. See further the important work of B. Kühnel, *From the Earthly to the Heavenly Jerusalem: Representations of the Holy City in Christian Art of the First Millennium*, Römische Quartalschrift für christlische Altertumskunde und Kirchengeschichte 42, Supplementheft (Rome, Freiburg & Vienna, 1987).

7. On Jerusalem in earliest Christian thought, see especially N. Brox, "Das 'irdische Jerusalem' in der altchristliche Theologie," *Kairos* 28 (1986), 152–73. Brox rightly emphasizes the theme of the Mother Church in Jerusalem as a regulating model in patristic literature and its importance also for the construction of the monastic ideal. See also P. C. Bori, "La référence à la communauté de Jérusalem dans les sources chrétiennes orientales et occidentales jusqu'au cinquième siècle," *Istina* 19 (1974), 31–48. See further P. Fredriksen, "The Holy City in Christian Thought," *City of the Great King: Jerusalem from David to the Present*, ed. N. Rosovsky (Cambridge, MA, 1996), 74–92. On the ambivalent status of Jerusalem in early Christian thought, see G. Stroumsa, "Which Jerusalem?" *Cathedra* 11 (1979), 119-24 (Hebrew).

8. H. Chadwick, "The Circle and the Ellipse: Rival Concepts of Authority in the Early Church,", in his *History and Thought of the Early Church* (London, 1982).

9. See R. Wilken, *The Land Called Holy: Palestine in Christian History and Thought* (New Haven, 1992), 149–72.

10. See J. Z. Smith, *To Take Place* (Chicago, 1986).

11. See Hunt (above, note 2). See also Bitton-Ashkelony's chapter in this volume.

12. On Rome and Jerusalem, see C. Auffarth, "Himmlisches und irdisches Jerusalem: ein religionswissenschaftlicher Versuch zur 'Kreuzzugseschatologie'," *Zeitschrift für Religionswissenschaft* 2 (1993), 101–104.

13. *Historia Ecclesiastica* 5, 18, 2; LCL, II, 486–87. On Pepuza and Tymion, see now C. Trevett, *Montanism: Gender, Authority and the New Prophecy* (Cambridge, 1996), 15–26.

14. See P. Kovalesky, "Messianisme et millénarisme russes?," *Archives de sociologie des religions* 5 (1958), 47–70.

15. On Montanist conceptions of heavenly Jerusalem, see P. de Labriolle, *La crise montaniste* (Paris, 1913), 86–95, 330–32.

16. See, for instance, M. Heldman, "Legends of Lâlibalâ: the Development of an Ethiopian Pilgrimage Site," *Res* 27 (1995), 25–38.

17. For the meaning of "heavenly Jerusalem" in the thought of Emanuel Swedenborg, see, for instance, his *The True Christian Story* (London, 1936), §782. *The Book of Mormon* offers another self-understanding of a modern religious movement issuing from Protestant Christianity as "the new Jerusalem."

18. For a similar puzzling contemporary phenomenon, see the recent exact replica in Kefar Habad, Israel of the late Lubavitscher Rebbe Menahem Schneersohn's house in Brooklyn.

19. S. Nichols (*Romanesque Signs: Early Medieval Narrative and Iconography* [New Haven, 1983], 75) points out that renovation and translation are closely associated with artistic creation.

20. On Orléans, see R. Landes, *Relics, Apocalypse and the Deceits of History* (Cambridge, MA, 1995), 304, and Nichols (above, note 19), 75.

21. Ibid., 70.

22. Landes (above, note 20), 304.

23. See B. Narkiss, "Round is Perfect: Ideal Jerusalem as a Circle," *Real and Ideal Jerusalem* (above, note 4).

24. Auffarth (above, note 12), 25–49 and 91–118; see also pp. 98–100. The main thrust of Auffarth's learned study is to insist on the importance of the medieval "realized eschatology" and of the image of Jerusalem in the genesis of the Crusades.

25. Ibid., 104.

26. For various other copies of the Holy Sepulchre in Italy, see D. Neri, *Il Santo Sepulcro riprodotto in occidente* (Jerusalem, 1971), chaps. 10–12, where references are made to churches in Rome, Tuscany, Florence, and elsewhere, as well as in Granada.

27. See L. Kötzsche, "Das heilige Grab in Jerusalem und seine Nachfolge," *Die Reise nach Jerusalem: eine kulturhistorische Exkursion in die Stadt der Städte—3000 Jahre Davidsstadt*, eds. H. Budde and A. Nechama (Berlin, 1995), 65–66.

28. G. Bresc-Bautier, "Les imitations du Saint-Sépulcre de Jérusalem (9ᵉ–15ᵉ s.): archéologie d'une dévotion," *Revue de l'histoire de la Spiritualité* 50 (1974), 319–42, passim.

29. See R. G. Ousterhout, "The Church of Santo Stefano: a 'Jerusalem' in Bologna," *Gesta* 20 (1981), 311–21, esp. p. 312.

30. See F. Filippini, *S. Petronio, vescovo di Bologna* (Bologna, 1948), 48, on the religious meaning of Petronian Jerusalem.

31. See I. B. Supino, *L'arte nelle chiese di Bologna*, I (Bologna, 1990; first ed. 1932), 45. The name "Jerusalem" may go back as far as the Lombardian kings Liutprand and Ildebrand (736–744), as pointed out by F. Lanzoni, *San Petronio, vescovo di Bologna* (Roma, 1907), 104–18.

32. See A. Sorbelli, "La 'Sancta Jerusalem' Stefaniana," *L'archiginnasio* 35 (1940), 14–28, esp. p. 15. I should like to express my thanks to Saverio Marchignoli, who sent me important material from Bologna.

33. See Ousterhout (above, note 29).

34. On the emergence of the medieval festival of *Corpus Christi*, see M. Rubin, *Corpus Christi* (Cambridge, 1991).

35. Ousterhout (above, note 29), esp. pp. 316–17. The ritual of the Exaltation of the Holy Cross, celebrated on 14ᵗʰ September, was initiated in Constantinople in 614, and the rite was popularized elsewhere in the seventh century. This appears clearly, for instance, in Leontius of Neapolis' *Life of Symeon the Fool*. See D. Krueger, *Symeon the Holy Fool. Leontius' Life and the Late Antique City* (Berkeley, 1996), 17.

36. See Bresc-Bautier (above, note 28), 323.

37. I should like to thank to Laurence Vianès for calling my attention to this fact.

38. Ousterhout (above, note 29), 317.

39. Bresc-Bautier (above, note 28), 321.

40. For a wonderful description of the ways in which memory uses mental images (in a different period), see J. D. Spence, *The Memory Palace of Matteo Ricci* (New York, 1984).

41. S. Schama, *Landscape and Memory* (New York, 1995), 436–42.

42. See G. Constable, "Opposition to Pilgrimage in the Middle Ages," *Mélanges G. Fransen*," Studia Gratiana XIX (Rome, 1976), 125–46 (= G. Constable, *Religious Life and Thought [11th–12ᵗʰ Centuries]* [London, 1979]). For phenomenological parallels, see Rocamadour, which to this day pilgrims climb on their knees, or, further away, the Buddhist temple at

Borobudur. Schama deals at some length with the case of the Mont Valérian near Paris. Referring to its disaffectation in "martyrized Europe" at the end of World War II, he oddly enough
forgets the last transformation of Mont Valérien. The fortress built there in the nineteenth
century had become during the war an execution ground for underground fighters and hostages
caught by the Wehrmacht. It hence received, as it were, a new legitimation as calvary, becoming
after the war a place of annual pilgrimage by the French chief of state (Schama [above, note
41], 444).

43. See B. McGinn, "*Iter Sancti Sepulchri*: the Piety of the First Crusaders," *Essays on
Medieval Civilization*, eds. B. K. Ladner and K. R. Philp (Austin, 1978), 33–71.

44. This text is quoted by Kühnel (above, note 4), 114.

45. Constable (above, note 42), 134–38.

46. *Strom* 172, 2ff. This text is quoted by Schmidt (above, note 6), 239.

47. For a discussion of Clement's attitude, see K. Thraede, "Jerusalem II (Sinnbild)," *RAC*
17 (1995), 718–64, esp. pp. 729–31.

48. *Hom. in Ier.* 9 (on Jer. 11:2); *Com. in Ioh.* 10, 18: "It is Jesus, God's logos, which
enters into the soul, called Jerusalem." See also the triple allegorical interpretation of Jerusalem
by the fourth-century Origenist, Didymos the Blind, in his *Commentary on Zacharias*; this text
is quoted by H. de Lubac, *Exégèse médiévale: les quatre sens de l'Ecriture*, I/2 (Paris, 1959), 645.
See also D. O. Rousseau, "Quelques textes patristiques sur la Jérusalem céleste," *La vie spirituelle*
85 (1952), 378–88.

49. Medieval references in de Lubac (above, note 48), 646.

50. See, for instance, Godefroy of Saint Victor, *Glossa in Ex.*, 20:2, quoted by de Lubac
(above, note 48), 646.

51. See Thraede (above, note 47), 752–54.

52. See J. van Oort, *Jerusalem and Babylon: a Study of Augustine's City of God and the Sources
of his Doctrine of the Two Cities* (Leiden, 1988). For the *Fortleben* of the idea, see E. Gilson,
Métamorphoses de la Cité de Dieu (Louvain and Paris, 1952).

53. I quote according to M. Simonetti (ed. and trans.), *Sant' Agostino, Commento ai Salmi*
(Mondatori, 1988), 182ff. A similar conception of heavenly Jerusalem as delivering us from the
confusion and slavery of the present life is found in Eusebius, *Demonstratio Evangelica*, IV, *in
finem*.

54. See J. Cassian, *Collationes* XIV, 8; (ed. E. Pichery, *SC* 54, 190). Cf. E. A. Matter, *The
Voice of My Beloved: the Song of Songs in Western Medieval Christianity* (Philadelphia, 1990),
54.

55. Similar opposition between free Jerusalem, mother of the Christians and earthly Jerusalem, mother of the Jews, in Marius Victorinus, *Com. Gal.* 19, 22, referred to by Thraede
(above, note 47), 755.

56. Book IV; references in de Lubac (above, note 48), I/2, 646; de Lubac points out that
the second and fourth senses are mixed up in Hugh's text.

57. *SSC* 27, 7. This text is discussed by B. McGinn, *The Growth of Mysticism* (New York,
1994), 178–9. See also Auffarth (above, note 12), 111–12.

58. McGinn (above, note 57), 182.

59. H.-W. Goetz, "Bernard et Norbert [de Xanten]: eschatologie et Réforme," *Bernard de
Clairvaux: histoire, mentalités, spiritualités* (= *Oeuvres complètes*, I; *SC* 380 [Paris, 1992]), 514.

60. Bernard, *Letter* 64 (*PL* 182, 169–70; *Writings*, 281–82). See discussion of this famous
text, inter alia, by Goetz (above, note 59), 505–25, esp. p. 518. Another of his letters, also
discussed by Goetz, reflects his preference for spiritual over earthly Jerusalem. In 1124, he writes
to Geoffroy, bishop of Chartres: "I do not know whether Norbert will go to Jerusalem , as you
ask me. . . ."

61. See Bernard, "On Conversion," Bernard of Clairvaux, *Works*, Classics of Western Spirituality (New York, 1987), 65–97.

62. *Sermon* 55, 2 (*PL* 183, 1045c–d). Cf., for instance, J. Leclercq, *The Love of Learning and the Desire for God: A Study of Monastic Culture* (New York, 1961), 54. To be sure, this was not a new trend; as is well known, opposition to Holy Land pilgrimages began in the fourth century, together with the development of pilgrimages. The *locus classicus* is that of Gregory of Nyssa, who had himself visited the Holy Land on ecclesiastical business, and who argued in one of his letters (*Letter* 2) that Cappadocia was as good a place as Palestine for leading a spiritual life. This text is discussed within the context of a patristic discussion of pilgrimage by B. Bitton-Ashkelony, "Pilgrimage: Perceptions and Reactions in the Patristic and Monastic Literature of the Fourth–Sixth Centuries," Ph.D. dissertation (Hebrew University of Jerusalem, 1996) (Hebrew).

63. *Liber exceptionum* 12, 5, quoted by J Châtillon, *Dictionnaire de Spiritualité*, XIII, 601. See also on Hugh of Saint Victor: P. Dinzelbacher, *Christliche Mystik im Abendland* (Paderborn, 1994), 141.

64. J. Leclercq, "Une élévation sur les gloires de Jérusalem," *RSR* 40 (1951–52), 326–34.

65. G. Contini (ed.), *Poeti del duecento*, I (Milan & Naples, 1960), 625.

66. Idem (ed.), *Le opere volgari di Bonsevin de la Riva* (Rome, 1961), 154.

67. Bonaventure, *The Soul's Journey to God* (transl. E. Cousins), Classics of Western Spirituality (New York, 1978), 51, 90.

68. E. A. Peers, *The Ascent to Mount Sion* (New York, 1951), 66. See the edition of the *Subida* by J. B. Gomis, *Misticos Franciscanos Españoles*, II (Madrid, 1948).

69. Peers (above, note 68), 70, 71.

70. E. Delaruelle, "Le pèlerinage intérieur au XVe siècle," in his *La piété populaire au moyen-âge* (Turin, 1975), 555–61.

71. Ibid., 558.

72. As pointed out by M. Reeves and B. Hirsch-Reich in their magisterial study of the theme, *The Figurae of Joachim of Fiore* (Oxford, 1972), 184–91.

73. See above, note 53. Augustine integrates this etymology of Jerusalem into his thought about war and peace; see for instance *Enarr. in Psalmos*, Ps. 64, 4: *Vincet pax et finietur bellum.*

74. See for instance Haymon from Auxerre: *Jerusalem quae interpretatur visio pacis, significat sanctam Ecclesiam Deum mente videntem. . . .*

75. Nicolas of Cusa, *De pace fidei*, XIX. With the dawn of the modern times, such "interfaith dialogues," as they are now being called, or rather "polylogues," became more common. The most famous example of the genre, perhaps, is Jean Bodin's *Heptahemeres*, written in 1596.

76. A. Dupront, *Du sacré* (Paris, 1987), 301–303.

77. G. Postel, *Le thrésor des prophéties de l'univers*, ed. F. Secret, Archives internationales d'histoire des idées 27 (La Haye, 1969), 157–59. On Venice as the New Jerusalem (and the New Rome) for Postel, see M. Leathers Kuntz, "The Myth of Venice in the Thought of Guillaume Postel," *Supplementum Festivum: Studies in Honor of P. O. Kristeller*, eds. J. Hankins et al. (Binghamton, NY, 1987), 503–23, esp. p. 512: *Esse vero Jerusalem translatam Venetias ab sacrorum inviolabilitatem patet.*

78. I quote according to P. de la Mirandola, *Oeuvres philosophiques* (Paris, 1993), 28–29. I wish to express my thanks to Jean Robert Armogathe for his judicious comments on a draft of this article.

25

Jerusalem and the Sign of the Cross (with particular reference to the cross of pilgrimage and crusading in the twelfth century)*

GILES CONSTABLE

I

It is hard to exaggerate the importance of the cross in the Middle Ages. As the ubiquitous symbol of the power of Jesus, it permeated every aspect of life and thought. The followers of Jesus were told in the New Testament to take up His cross and to follow Him. At baptism they were "signed with the sign of the holy cross" and restored to life "by the imposition of the same cross of the Lord." Leo the Great said that "The cross makes all those who have been regenerated in Christ into kings," and in the tenth-century Romano-Germanic pontifical the cross was called the trophy of Christ's victory and our redemption and "the incomparable sign of Christ, by which the power of the devil is destroyed [and] the freedom of mortals restored." Alan of Lille, in his sermon *On the Cross of the Lord*, which was preached on the occasion of the third crusade, said that

> We bear the glorious figure of the cross on the forehead of the body
> by impression and on the forehead of the mind by faith. . . . The sign
> of the cross is sometimes made for strengthening, sometimes for glo-
> rifying, sometimes for signifying, sometimes for sanctifying. O great

* This lecture is published as it was delivered at the conference. A revised and annotated version will appear at a later date.

mystery of the cross, which drives away the demons, saves men, conquers the world, and weakens sin.

The cross was the *vexillum regis*, the standard or banner of the all-powerful King, which sanctified the rule of Christian monarchs and brought victory in battle. It also brought peace, prosperity, and security. The Council of Clermont in 1095, where Urban II preached the first crusade, decreed that "If anyone flees to a cross on a road when his enemies are in pursuit, let him remain free as if he were in a church." Fields were regularly blessed with the cross in order to assure fertility, and houses as a mark of good fortune. Countless men and women were cured of ailments by the sign of the cross: a blind boy saw after he was "signed" by Bernard of Clairvaux, and a deaf man heard "when the sign of the cross had been imposed."

The development of the cult of the cross in the Latin West has been studied in particular by André Wilmart, who dated "the true advance" of the cult in the eleventh century and studied the works of Peter Damiani and Anselm of Canterbury. Ralph Glaber and John Gualbert were cited by Delaruelle, who also said that "This evolution was completed in the second half of the eleventh century." More recently, Dominique Iogna-Prat stressed the importance of the cult of the cross at Cluny and associated the feasts of the Invention and Exaltation of the Cross with the works of Abbot Odilo in honor of the cross, and Johannes Fried pointed out the significance of the cross in the millennial expectations around the year 1000 and said that the cult of the cross reached a high point in 1060. Jean Leclercq, writing somewhat earlier, distinguished two periods in the history of medieval devotion to the cross: the first from the ninth to eleventh centuries, when the emphasis was on redemption and remission of sins and on the power of the cross, and the second in the twelfth century, when greater attention was paid to patience and suffering, though the older view of the glory of the cross and its redemptive power was still found in the works of many writers.

Every aspect of the cross had a special meaning and was given a symbolic interpretation. For Gregory of Nyssa it was "a visual symbol of the four principal extensions of the universe and its unity in Christ," and for Augustine it represented "four invisible dimensions of man's soul in its capacity to love." The four arms of the cross stood for charity, perseverance, faith, and hope. Christians must extend their arms to the cross in order for Christ's arm to extend to them, wrote Ephraim Syrus: "For he who does not extend his hand to His cross cannot move his hand to His table." The life of monks and nuns was frequently compared to the cross. According to the *Book on Preserving the Unity of the Church*, the monastic habit had "the form of a cross through its four extended parts so that this four-part union through every part restrains and leads to heaven him who is crucified to the world." Later it continues:

> For we call a cross not only that one which was put together out of wood at the time of the passion but also that which is fitted to the virtues of all the disciplines throughout the course of an entire life. Whence not only the whole life and institution of a monk but also every Christian action is described in the sign of a cross.

For Aelred of Rievaulx the order of Cîteaux was the cross of Christ, and Caesarius of Heisterbach described the inner crucifixion of monks by compassion and their outer crucifixion by mortification of the flesh.

It was customary from the earliest times to place a cross in the hand of a new monk and to mark him with the sign of the cross. In the west-Syrian rite the sign was on the shoulder, but the position of the mark may have varied from region to region and even from monastery to monastery. Pseudo-Denis the Areopagite said, in his *Ecclesiastical Hierarchy*, that after the new monk ratified his commitments "the priest marks him with the sign of the cross and cuts his hair, invoking the three persons of the divine beatitude." Arnulf of Lisieux, in a letter written about 1159, said that a monk should express obedience to his superior by voice and in writing "with an oath also physically intervening [and] with the added impression of the saving cross." This suggests that the cross was not seen only as a blessing but also as a sign of confirmation, like a cross put on a document in place of a signature. It marked the monk as the bearer of the cross and also sealed his obligation to renounce the world.

The cross with which a new monk was marked may have been associated with the ancient concept of entry into monastic life as a second baptism, which initiated a new monk into a new life, free of sin. It may also have been an indication of the monk's spiritual orientation toward Jerusalem, with which the cross was associated in medieval devotions and spirituality. In an influential article, "The Cross and Prayer Towards the East," published in 1945, Erik Peterson showed "the close connection," as he put it, "between the East and the cross." The custom of praying in the direction of the cross, the presence of the cross behind (or sometimes in place of) the altar in many ancient churches, and the mystical visions of the cross in the East all reflected, Peterson argued, the belief in the second coming of Christ in the East. Capelle also argued that, "It was in the first place a matter of an 'eschatological cross' since the direction towards the East was eschatological. The cross was evocative and annunciative of Christ." Recent research has confirmed the importance in the works of the church fathers of praying toward the East and of praying with extended arms, which represented the figure of the cross.

The association of the cross with Jerusalem was made clear in the ceremony of carrying the cross in imitation of Christ on Good Friday, in the legends of St. Helen's finding of the cross, in the Roman church known as Santa Croce in Gerusalemme, and in the feasts of the Adoration, Invention, and Exaltation of the cross. Egeria, in the account of her pilgrimage to the East, described vividly the mass of the cross in Jerusalem, and Adamnan, in his book *On the Holy Places*, described the church where the cross was preserved and the sweet odor and oil that emanated from it. One of the most striking statements of the concentration of the cult of the cross on Jerusalem appears in the *Histories* of Ralph Glaber, who attributed the fact that Christianity spread to the north and west of the Holy Land, but not to the south and east, to

> the position of the Lord's cross while the Savior hung there in the place called Calvary. For the rough people of the east were behind the head of the Suspended One, but the west was in the sight of His eyes, ready to be filled with the light of the faith. So too the north, softened by the faith of the sacred word, received His almighty right arm, extended for the work of mercy, while the south, made tumultuous by the peoples of the barbarians, received His left [arm].

This passage is reminiscent of Ephraim Syrus' exhortation to Christians to extend their arms toward the cross, and it underlined the fact that Christ's followers received their faith from the East and faced His cross in Jerusalem, at least in spirit if not in body. Throughout the Middle Ages, Jerusalem was seen as the true homeland of all Christians, and especially of monks. Origen said that "All of us who have learned the holy scriptures, whether we live well or badly, are in Jerusalem," and Augustine, in his commentary on the Lord's choice of Sion in Ps. 131:13, called Sion both the church and "the Jerusalem to whose peace we run, which peregrinates not in the angels but in us." Monasteries were often described as Jerusalem in the twelfth century. "The undertaking of monks," according to Bernard of Clairvaux, "is to seek not the earthly but the heavenly Jerusalem, and this not by proceeding with their feet but by progressing with their spirit," and in a letter about a cleric who became a monk at Clairvaux while on his way to Jerusalem, Bernard wrote that he had quickly reached his destination because Clairvaux was "the Jerusalem that is associated by a total devotion of mind, imitation of way of life, and affinity of spirit with [the Jerusalem] that is in heaven." There is a glowing passage on Jerusalem in Bernard's treatise *In Praise of the New Army*, in which he said, addressing the earthly city, that God had allowed it to be attacked so frequently "in order that you might be an occasion both of virtue and of salvation for brave men."

There is no explicit reference to the cross in these passages, but they date from the first half of the twelfth century, when the cross was firmly associated with crusading and pilgrimage to Jerusalem, and when there was a recognized parallel between going to the heavenly Jerusalem as a monk and to earthly Jerusalem as a pilgrim or crusader. Bernard declared that the pilgrim to Jerusalem who entered Clairvaux had reached his destination, and he wrote to the sister of a man who had become a monk rather than go on a crusade, that by taking the monastic habit he had fulfilled rather than put aside "the intention of the saving sign that he had received," that is, the cross. Geoffrey of Chalard, who died in 1125, was dissuaded by a vision from leaving his monastery to join the first crusade, and Count William of Nevers, who had sworn to take the cross and go to Jerusalem, instead became a lay brother at La Chartreuse, where he bore the cross of Christ daily (according to the *Life* of Hugh of Lincoln) and "as a true pilgrim of the world he did not cease to go from virtue to virtue before he deserved to see the God of Gods in Sion."

Sometimes the distinction between the two Jerusalems is unclear, as in the so-called *Itinerary or Exhortation of a Certain Dermot of Ireland Who was Traveling to Jerusalem*, of which the author, writing about 1117, called himself "an exile for the sake of God" who carried both the cross of Christ and a cross on his clothing and who fled to God "Who is not only in Jerusalem but everywhere." Caesarius of Heisterbach told a story about a canon of Liège who, after hearing Bernard of Clairvaux preach the crusade, took the cross of the Cistercian order rather than of the expedition across the sea because he judged it "more salubrious to impose a continual cross on his mind than to sew a brief sign temporarily on his clothes." Caesarius went on to stress the superiority of the cross of the order to the cross of pilgrimage, saying that whereas "someone signed by the cross or bound by the vow of another pilgrimage" was permitted to join the Cistercians, a monk who took the cross or went on a pilgrimage without permission was an apostate rather than a pilgrim of Christ.

II

Very little is known about the origins of the cross of pilgrimage and crusading, though there is abundant evidence for its use by participants in the first crusade, which Erdmann considered "unquestionably an innovation." It seems to have originated in the initiative taken by Urban II in his preaching of the crusade at Clermont in 1095. The only use of the term *cruce signatus* by Urban himself is in a document now generally considered a forgery, but many contemporary accounts of his preaching show that he ordered the crusaders to wear a cross. Fulcher of Chartres said that "at the order of said pope, after their vow of participation," the pilgrims put "crosses made of silk or woven with gold or adorned with some sort of brocade" onto their mantles, cloaks, or tunics above the shoulder and that "The warriors of God who prepared themselves to fight for His honor were indeed justly marked and strengthened by this sign of victory." According to Baldric of Bourgeuil, Urban cited the exhortation of Jesus to take up His cross, and said "You should apply a cross to your clothes, and from this you will proceed more safely, and you will present both an example and an encouragement to those who see you." Therefore, Baldric continued, "Everyone immediately sewed the standard of the holy cross onto his outer garments. For so the pope ordered, and it pleased those who were about to leave to make this sign."

Almost all the contemporary historians of the first crusade refer to the crosses worn by the crusaders, and their evidence is confirmed by sources from all over Europe. In 1098, a woman named Emerias of Alteias, "who had raised the cross on her right shoulder for the journey to Jerusalem," came for a blessing to Bishop Isarnus of Toulouse, who advised her to found a monastery rather than go on a crusade. Geoffrey of Malaterra, who lived in southern Italy and died before 1101, said that when Bohemund joined the crusade he "put the sign of that expedition, that is, the cross, on his garments." Ekkehard of Aura, writing around 1115, put in his chronicle under the year 1096 that "Many men also showed the sign of the cross on themselves on their foreheads or clothes or divinely impressed on some part of their body, and they believed themselves enrolled by this stigma in the same army of God."

The evidence of charters confirms the connection between taking the cross and going to Jerusalem. When Stephen of Neublens decided in 1100 "to go to Jerusalem where the God-Man was seen and lived with men and to worship in the place where His feet stood," he opened his heart concerning this journey to Abbot Hugh of Cluny, who "placed the sign of salvation, that is, the holy cross on my shoulder and a ring on my finger." When Chalo of Vivonne, whom Pope Calixtus II had excommunicated for failing to settle a dispute with the canons of St. Hilary at Poitiers, subsequently "with rash audacity" took the cross to go to Jerusalem, he was forbidden to leave by apostolic authority. In 1145, a donor visited Saint-Sulpice-en-Bugey "when he was about to begin the journey of pilgrimage to Jerusalem and had received the standard of the holy cross"; Maurice of Glons resigned a fief to St. James at

Liège in 1146, when he was "armed with the sign of the cross and about to travel to Jerusalem"; William of Obey, in 1153/64, proposed to visit the tomb of the Lord after the sign of the cross of the Lord had been taken"; and so on all over Europe.

The dates of these and other charters show that many journeys to Jerusalem were not necessarily connected with one of the great expeditions that later scholars have called crusades. The cross was the mark of a pilgrim whether or not he (or she) was armed and intended to fight the pagans. Later it was adopted by members of the military orders as a mark of their permanent commitment to the defense of Christians and the church, but to consider the cross a sign exclusively of crusading rather than of pilgrimage is an error of hindsight that sees the crusades in the twelfth century as an institution rather than as events. This conclusion is confirmed by the evidence of iconography. The pilgrim whose wallet is marked with a cross on the tympanum of the main portal of the cathedral of Autun, which dates from about 1130, carries no arms, nor does the pilgrim in the sculpture from Belval, now in Nancy, who wears a cross around his neck or perhaps sewn or pinned on his chest. In a canon concerning the defense of Christian people, the First Lateran Council referred to "those who are known to have placed crosses on their clothing for the journey either to Jerusalem or to Spain," but they were not called crusaders as distinct from pilgrims.

In the earliest sources, the crusaders were referred to as *peregrini* or *milites* or simply as *christicolae* or Christians. *Crucesignatus* did not become the established term for crusaders until the end of the twelfth century, and even then may also have been used for simple pilgrims. *Signati* alone was used for Conrad III and his followers on the second crusade in the *First Life* of Bernard of Clairvaux, who cured the blind boy when he was *signatus* and the deaf man *impresso crucis signaculo*. Fulcher of Chartres described the crusaders as *ligno dominicae crucis muniti* and *signo crucis armatus*, and in the anonymous *Deeds of the Franks and Other Jerusalemites* they were called *signo crucis armati*, *signo crucis muniti*, and *signo crucis protecti*.

The precise nature and position of the cross are uncertain. According to both Fulcher of Chartres and Guibert of Nogent, it could be made out of any of several types of cloth and was attached at the shoulder to the tunic, mantle, or cloak. King Louis VII, at the start of the second crusade, received the sign of the cross from the pope, and others were distributed at Vézelay by St. Bernard who, according to Odo of Deuil, "was forced to cut his own clothes into crosses and to sow them after he had sown, rather than distributed, the bundle of them that had been prepared." Some sources specified that they were worn on the right shoulder, but Peter Tudebode said that it could also be between the shoulders, presumably in the middle of the back. The badges of the pilgrims on the Autun tympanum and in the cloister at Silos appear on their pouches, and the Templars wore their cross on the chest, like the pilgrim in the Belval sculpure. Alan of Lille, writing toward the end of the twelfth century, said that crusaders on their way to Jerusalem wore the cross on the shoulder and on the way back on the chest, to show that the burden had become easy. Robert of Rheims said at one point that the sign of the cross was placed on the forehead, chest, or, in the case of returnees, between the shoulders on the back; at another point he said that Bohemund required his followers to wear "the sign of pilgrimage" and to bear "the sign of the cross either on their foreheads or on their right shoulders."

The marks on the forehead or body were apparently made by branding or tattooing. Guibert of Nogent said that Abbot Baldwin of Josaphat, who later became archbishop of Caesarea, "himself carried the sign of the cross, which was customarily placed on the clothing, made out of some cloth, on himself by I know not what means, so that he was inflicted by iron not just with a depicted [cross] but with the image of the military stigma." The westerners who joined the holy army were described in the account of the translation of St. Nicholas, which took place in 1100, as "some imprinting the sign of the cross on their own body with a glowing iron, others marking [it] externally on their clothes." There are also several references to crosses found on the bodies of dead crusaders and pilgrims. "Clear crosses were found . . . above the shoulders" of some crusaders who were shipwrecked at Brindisi, according to Fulcher, for instance, and Raymond of Aguilers said of a group of crusaders who were captured and killed by the Saracens that "All these dead men had crosses on their right shoulders."

It is impossible to say whether the cross was a mark of pilgrimage to Jerusalem, or of pilgrimage generally, or whether it was a specific mark of participants in an armed expedition either in Spain or the East, as the canon of the First Lateran Council suggests. Robert of Rheims and Ordericus Vitalis referred to the cross simply as "the sign of pilgrimage" and "in the manner of a pilgrim," and the Autun and Belval sculptures show that it was used by unarmed as well as armed pilgrims. Very little is known about the early history of pilgrimage badges, but scallop shells have been found in the graves of pilgrims to Compostela in the late eleventh and early twelfth centuries, and there is a reference in the *Pilgrim's Guide* to the sale at Compostela of "the small scallop shells which are the insignia of the blessed James." "Not without reason the prayers returning from Jerusalem carry palms," according to the *Codex Calixtinus*, "and those returning from the abode of St. James carry scallop shells. For the palm signifies triumph and the scallop shell good work."

No clear picture emerges from these sources regarding the history and significance of the cross of pilgrimage and crusading, nor of why Urban chose it as the mark of participants in the first crusade. The cult of the cross was at its height during Urban's lifetime, and it was apparently on his mind at the time of his visit to France in 1095, as Delaruelle pointed out, citing his consecration of a cross at the abbey of the Trinity at Vendôme and the decree of the Council of Clermont concerning roadside crosses. He was also deeply concerned with Jerusalem and may have been inspired by the ancient association of the cross with Jerusalem and the East, but none of the sources says so. Urban chose the cross, according to Baldric of Bourgeuil, to protect and identify the crusaders. For Fulcher it was a sign of victory; for Ekkehard a mark of belonging to the army of God; and for Geoffrey Malatesta and Ordericus Vitalis, the latter writing somewhat later, simply a badge of pilgrimage. Odo of Cheriton said that the cross worn by the Templars and Hospitallers, like the cross of monks, meant that they had the cross in the heart and in the flesh "so that they crucify the flesh from the vices of luxury and greed and the mind from the desires of avarice and pride." Otherwise, he said, they would be donkeys of the devil. Some other ancient themes, which have not perhaps been sufficiently emphasized by crusading scholars, may run through these and other references to the cross as a sign of protection and victory and the ceremonies by which all Christians were *signo sanctae crucis consignati* and restored to life *per eiusdem dominicae crucis impositionem*. There are, too, some striking parallels with the ceremonies for making a new monk who was marked with a cross, sometimes on the shoulder. These parallels suggest that by marking participants with a cross Urban may have had in mind some sort of personal consecration to the holy undertaking rather than a formal sign of pilgrimage. A *benedictio crucis peregrinorum* is found in the pontifical of Magdalen College, which dates from the twelfth century, and later became a standard ceremony, but it has no specific reference to crusading as distinct from pilgrimage.

Alan of Lille mingled the roles of crusaders and pilgrims in the sermon "On the Cross of the Lord" that he addressed to the participants in the third crusade. After giving a brief history of the cross, "the seal of our religion, the banner of the Christian faith," which was at first lost, then found by Helen, taken by Chosroes, and recovered by Heraclius, he said that owing to sin it is now lost without hope of recovery. The loss of the cross showed beyond a doubt God's reproach and Christ's retreat from men.

> Therefore indeed the soldiers of Christ sign themselves with the sign
> of the cross on the body, sign on the heart, sign externally by the image,
> sign internally by penance; they bear the cross of Christ not with Simon

as an obligation but with Christ in patience; with the right-hand robber
in penance, not with the left-hand [robber] in violence. Christians sign
themselves with the cross; crucified they go on pilgrimage in the world;
they reach the place; they seek the tomb with the Magdalen; they run
with Peter; they discover with John. They weep for the taking of the
cross; they labor for its recovery; they avenge Christ's wrongs; they
mourn His insults; they free the land of our inheritance, the inheritance
of Christ, the dowry of the Virgin.

Alan ended this section with the statement, cited above, that pilgrims going
to Jerusalem wore the cross on the shoulder and those returning on the chest.

Writing a few years later, James of Vitry, who was bishop of Acre before
he became a cardinal, said in his second sermon addressed "To Those Signed
or About to Be Signed with the Cross" that

The Lord told us to raise the sign of the cross like the standard of the
highest king in Sion, that is, the church of God, by preaching the power
of the cross and by exalting the praises of the cross by the voice of the
speaker, and by inviting the people to the cross. Just as a house of God
is known by the cross raised above it, so a man is known as a house of
God by the cross affixed to his shoulders; and since we have been signed
with the cross by baptism itself, we should not deny the sign of the
cross.

God could have freed His land by a single word, James continued later in the
same sermon, "but He wished to honor His servants and to have companions
in its liberation, giving you the occasion to save your souls. . . . This holy
pilgrimage has indeed saved many who would have remained in their sins if
the Lord had from the beginning freed that land by Himself." Just as nobles
and great men invest their vassals with precious fiefs by gloves and other tokens
of small value, James said, "So the Lord invests His vassals with the heavenly
kingdom by a cross made out of modest thread and cloth."

These sermons, written by two of the most perceptive churchmen of their
time, bring together many of the themes touched on in this talk, including
the concentration on the cross as a symbol of Christian power and of individual
salvation, the parallel of the crosses of baptism and pilgrimage, and the aim
of freeing the Holy Land and winning the heavenly kingdom, of which the
cross was the symbol. Far more than just an identifying badge or sign, the
cross was granted by God to the crusader to guide his journey both in this
world and to the next. Delaruelle described the crusade as, above all, "an

extraordinary movement of feelings and imaginings evoked by the cross of Christ." The cross thus brought together the earthly and heavenly Jerusalems, toward which respectively (as Bernard of Clairvaux said) monks progress with their spirits and laymen proceed with their feet. Jerusalem has been called "the most authentic reason for the crusade," and pilgrimage "a living witness to the dominant role of Jerusalem in medieval thought." The cross, as the symbol both of Jerusalem and of pilgrimage, thus lay at the heart of the spiritual as well as of the bodily journey of medieval Christians.

26

Jerusalem as Christian Symbol during the First Crusade: Jewish Awareness and Response

ROBERT CHAZAN

W hile scholars have been unable to reconstruct with precision the papal message that set the First Crusade in motion and the complex imagery that animated the Christian warriors who undertook the arduous and dangerous journey eastward, there is no real doubt as to the centrality of Jerusalem in crusader thinking. The three Latin chronicles composed by eyewitness participants feature Jerusalem at the core of the crusading enterprise; even the rather dry letters that have survived, which have added relatively little to modern comprehension of the crusade, project Jerusalem as the centerpiece of the undertaking. To be sure, other emotionally evocative symbols pervaded the crusading campaign. Indeed, the force and success of the endeavor stemmed from the successful interaction of a number of potent images. In this mix of compelling symbols, however, Jerusalem surely dominated.[1]

Crusade historians have by and large paid little attention to the available Jewish materials. More precisely, they have utilized the Hebrew data for reconstructing the Jewish experience during the First Crusade; they have not, however, looked to the Hebrew records for their perspectives on the broad crusading phenomenon. The Jewish evidence consistently reinforces the centrality of Jerusalem in crusader thinking in two ways: first, it overtly depicts the crusaders as focused on the conquest of Jerusalem, a focus that the Jews both admired and denigrated. More subtly, the Jewish materials show the Jews of the 1090s creating their own counter-crusade, Jerusalem-based religious imagery, an imagery that sustained them during a period of tribulation and whipped many of them into a frenzy of martyrological inspiration. Aware of the extent to which their crusader foes were moved by Jerusalem, the Jews asserted the superiority of their own claims to the Holy City, particularly its spiritual dimensions.

Let us begin with the direct testimony of the Jewish sources to the centrality of Jerusalem in crusader thinking. Those sources include three unusual Hebrew narratives and numerous Hebrew elegies written in honor of the European Jewish martyrs to misguided crusading zeal and to the impact of that zeal among burgher circles in the Rhineland. These Jewish sources involve a host of scholarly problems that require extensive treatment, for which the present circumstances are not appropriate. Let me note simply the need to distinguish among these sources, both narrative and poetic, between immediate and later, a distinction with which crusade historians are readily familiar.[2]

Our earliest and, in many ways, richest Jewish source is the so-called Mainz Anonymous, a carefully composed narrative that is particularly sensitive to the early stages of the crusade and to the complex evolution of anti-Jewish sentiment on the fringe of the crusading campaign.[3] Let us note the very beginning of this meticulously constructed Hebrew account:

> It came to pass in the one thousand and twenty-eighth year after the destruction of the [Second] Temple that this disaster befell Israel. Initially, the barons, nobles, and commonfolk in France arose, took counsel, and planned to ascend, to rise up like an eagle, and to clear the way to Jerusalem, the Holy City, and to arrive at the sepulchre of the crucified, a trampled carcass that can neither profit nor save, because it is vanity.[4]

Our Jewish narrator is here, as elsewhere, quite well informed as to the early development of the First Crusade. Note his awareness of the centrality of France and the French in the early preaching of the crusade and of the complex social composition of the campaign, that involved no kings, many barons and nobles, and a significant number of commonfolk. In this perceptive account, we find full Jewish awareness of the role that Jerusalem played in early crusade thinking. For the Jewish author, the Holy City, in particular its Holy Sepulchre, lay at the heart of the agitation that began in France and quickly spread eastward into the writer's own territory, the Rhineland.

Acknowledgment of the elevated goals of the crusade may seem straightforward, with the Jewish narrator simply recognizing the most obvious of realities. In fact, however, the Mainz Anonymous was contravening a rich Jewish historiographic legacy. Prior Jewish tradition included no enemy figures moved by pious goals. The biblical Egyptians, Assyrians, and Babylonians, as well as the more fictionalized and personalized Haman of the book of Esther and Persian courtiers of the book of Daniel, are portrayed in one of two ways—either as figures whose shadowy motives are of no real interest, since they operate as God's agents on the historical scene, or as real human beings moved by the basest of motivations; the Second Commonwealth Seleucids and Romans are generally portrayed along the latter lines. Even for an unusual Jewish observer like Josephus, positive in his orientation to the Roman rulers of Palestinian Jewry, the Romans were moved by concerns of state, tempered by political and ethical largesse; even Josephus did not go so far as to portray the Roman foe as moved by high spiritual objectives. To acknowledge an enemy in pursuit of lofty religious goals required divergence from traditional Jewish patterns of thinking. Committed to accurate portrayal of the late eleventh-century realities, the author of the Mainz Anonymous, as well as other Jewish narrators and even poets, could not disguise the mission of the enemy, even though such acknowledgment meant a break with prior Jewish paradigms and implied grudging respect for the foe. To be sure, this grudging respect ultimately had to be tempered by Jewish denigration, and in fact—as we shall quickly see—it was.

Let us pursue one step further this overt Jewish acknowledgment of the Jerusalem-centered objectives of the First Crusade. The precise language utilized by the anonymous Jewish narrator includes elements with positive resonance to the Jewish ear. He identifies the Jerusalem toward which the crusade was directed as *ʿir ha-qodesh*, the city of sanctity. More interestingly, the Jewish narrator speaks of the crusader effort *le-fanot derekh*, to clear the way, to Jerusalem, an expression taken from Isa. 40 that suggests a genuine redemption of the Holy City.

To be sure, the Jewish author had to temper his acknowledgment of genuine crusader zeal focused on Jerusalem with profound repudiation, and he energetically did so. Most obviously, after identifying the goals of the crusade as clearing the way to Jerusalem the Holy City, he specifies accurately the crusader objective of securing the Holy Sepulchre, which the Jewish writer portrays pejoratively as "the sepulchre of the crucified, a trampled corpse that can neither profit nor save, because it is vanity." The vituperative quality of this depiction is by no means accidental.[5] There were, from the Jewish perspective, noble elements in the crusading endeavor, elements which were, however, thoroughly nullified by the perverted religiosity that lay at the heart of the enterprise. Jerusalem may have constituted the crusade objective, but it was a worthless, indeed shameful, aspect of the Holy City that, from the Jewish perspective, stimulated the mammoth undertaking.

Once again, there are important biblical resonances to the precise language used by the Jewish narrator. The designation of Jesus as a trampled corpse is taken from Isa. 14, one of the prophet's lengthy diatribes against Babylonia.

Isaiah contrasts tellingly the arrogance of the mighty Babylonia, which had visited so much destruction upon the world, with its ignominious end:

> All the kings of nations
> Were laid, every one, in honor,
> Each in his tomb;
> While you were left unburied,
> Like loathesome carrion,
> Like a trampled corpse. . . . (Isa. 14:18-19)

There is much more here than mere vituperation. On one level, the power and the arrogance of the Christian world are, for the Jewish narrator, contrasted with the ignominy of its slain messiah figure. For this Jewish observer, the Isaiah image highlights the essential flaw of the Christian religious vision, its focus on a central figure who represents the opposite of divine majesty. At the same time, the Isaiah citation suggests that the seeming strength and power of the Christian world, so strikingly expressed in the crusading venture, are in fact chimeric: this massive undertaking is destructive in the extreme; it constitutes the embodiment of arrogance; for all the grandeur of the crusade, its eventual fate will be the undoing prophesied by Isaiah, with the peoples of the world rejoicing at the downfall of the haughty.

There is yet a second pointed biblical resonance in the dismissive depiction of the crusader goal. The figure whose sepulchre the crusaders seek is depicted as a power that "can neither profit nor save, because it is vanity." That combination of terms comes directly from the well-known speech in I Sam. 12. There the aged judge upbraids his people for their request for a king, that is to say a human leader to usurp the place of God himself. God sends a miracle to chastise the people, who cry out in remorse over their lack of faith in asking for such a human leader. Samuel, in the face of Israelite contrition, reassures his people:

> Have no fear. You have indeed done all these wicked things. Do not, however, turn away from the Lord your God, but serve the Lord with all your heart. Do not turn away toward vanities which can neither profit nor save, for they are vanity. For the sake of his great Name, the Lord will never abandon his people, seeing that the Lord undertook to make you his people. (I Sam. 12:20–22)

There is a double message here, negative with respect to Christianity and positive with respect to the Jews. Christianity is depicted as yet another sinful search for a human intercessor, along the lines of the Israelites of Samuel's days. At the same time, the Jewish readers are reassured that the God who had remained loyal to them in days of old would continue to hold them dear as his own special people, all seeming Christian power and success notwithstanding.

The depiction of crusader objectives highlights, in a number of ways, the Jewish author's negative assessment of the enterprise. One last manifestation of this negativity should be mentioned, for it constitutes the most regular Jewish denigration of the crusading enterprise. As soon as the Mainz Anonymous begins his description of the movement of the crusaders out of France and into the Rhineland, he introduces a recurring description for these pilgrim-warriors; they are regularly designated as *to'im*, those in movement but in confused, erratic, and pointless movement.[6] The Christian sense of pilgrimage is implicitly acknowledged but in a totally pejorative manner.

Thus, the Jewish author upon whom we have focused recognized the Jerusalem-centered spirituality that lay at the core of the crusade, while rejecting critical elements in that religiosity. Although breaking with prior Jewish perceptions of the enemy, the narrator does link the crusaders with earlier foes of Israel, at least with respect to the outcome of their hostility. Like all historic opponents of the Jewish people, the crusaders are ultimately doomed to failure. In the opening passage of the Mainz Anonymous cited earlier, this sense of eventual outcome is expressed recurrently. We have already noted the use of Isa. 14 to convey the Jewish sense of the ultimate failure of the crusade. Directly related to Jerusalem, the Jewish narrator depicts the crusader intention "to rise up like the eagle" (*le-hagbihah ka-nesher*), thus reminding Jewish readers of the prophecy of Ovadiah. The prophetic warning to Edom, identified in the medieval Jewish lexicon with Rome and Christianity, predicts total destruction, the result of its gleeful participation in the sacking of Jewish Jerusalem. The prophet highlights the haughtiness of Edom: "Your arrogant heart has seduced you, you who dwell in clefts of the rock, in your lofty abode. You think in your heart, 'Who can pull me down to earth?'." The prophet then warns: " 'Should you rise up as high as the eagle, should your eyrie be lodged among the stars, even from there will I pull you down', declares the Lord" (Ovad. 1:3–4). Late eleventh-century Edom, in its campaign to conquer Jerusalem and in its persecution of Jews along the way, is portrayed as recapitulating the arrogance of an earlier Edom; its ultimate fate will be precisely that projected by the prophet.

A bit further in its account, the Mainz Anonymous once more introduces a historic enemy for whom Jerusalem served as the occasion for divinely ordained defeat. The narrator portrays the French crusaders sweeping across into the Rhineland and their impact in the following terms: "When the crusaders came, battalion after battalion, like the army of Sennacherib, some of the barons in this empire said: 'Why do we sit idly by? Let us also go with them. For anyone who goes on this way and clears the way [again *le-fanot derekh*] to ascend to the polluted sepulchre of the crucified will be guaranteed paradise'."[7] While we might note in passing yet another reflection of Jewish acknowledgment of Jerusalem and genuine crusader religious sentiment, I would like to draw attention to the expression "like the army of Sennacherib" and to suggest that the choice of this figure was hardly accidental. The image was intended to conjure up an impression of overwhelming numbers and military power, more than offset by eventual divine undoing of the Assyrian campaign for Jerusalem. This might be taken as a pious pre-1099 Jewish hope. However, even if the Mainz Anonymous was penned subsequent to the remarkable crusader conquest of the Holy City, the expression would still reflect Jewish conviction of ultimate divine reversal of crusader fortunes.

Thus, the Jewish memorializers of the 1096 victims of crusade-related violence were profoundly aware of the Jerusalem-centered crusader imagery. A measure of admiration was more than offset by rejection and vilification. Equally, if not more intriguing, is the extent to which the Jerusalem-centeredness of the crusade conditioned the patterns of 1096 Jewish behaviors and thinking. While the Rhineland Jews who suffered assault and who responded in one of the most unusual outbursts of martyrological enthusiasm in Jewish history were overt in their recognition of Christian zeal, they would, of course, have been quick to reject any suggestion that Christian religiosity conditioned their own heroic postures. Such a suggestion would have been decisively and angrily repudiated, for the eyes of the Christians and Jews of 1096 were firmly fixed on the values and symbols that divided them, rather than the patterns of behavior and thinking that in point of fact united them.

For the Jewish victims of crusader aggression and for those who survived the attacks, the Jewish behaviors of 1096 represented nothing more or less than an unusually high level of age-old Jewish dedication and heroism. As their memorializers regularly proclaimed, they were simply emulating Daniel and his friends, the mother and her seven sons who fell victim to Seleucid persecution, and Rabbi 'Aqiva and his associates who were martyred by the Roman authorities. Yet these memorializers were, in fact, ambivalent on the issue of historic precedent. While regularly reiterating the chain of historical tradition that linked the martyrs of 1096 with their predecessors of the Persian, Seleucid, and Roman periods, they at the same time recurrently felt and emphasized the uniqueness of the behaviors and thinking of 1096. Thus, the Mainz Anonymous, normally restrained in its depiction of tragedy, breaks forth into elegy after describing the battle at the gateway to the archbishop's palace in Mainz, the victory of Count Emicho and his followers over the desperate Jewish defenders, and the beginning of the slaughter that would utterly destroy the Jews who had sought safety in the palace. According to the generally laconic chronicler, the events were unparalleled in the history of the Jewish people, indeed in the history of the world. "Ask and see! Was there ever an *'aqedah* [a human sacrifice, but more on this key term shortly] as numerous as this, from the days of the original Adam."[8] The so-called Solomon bar Simson Chronicle, later and less well-focused than the Mainz Anonymous, embellishes this brief outcry in striking terms: "At such reports, the ears of those who hear must surely tingle. For who has heard the like? Who has ever witnessed such events? Were there ever so many sacrifices like these from the days of Adam? Were there ever a thousand one hundred sacrifices on one day, each one of them like the sacrifice of Isaac the son of Abraham?"[9] The attentive reader knows, of course, that each one of those offerings was in fact a real sacrifice, with no restraining divine hand to hold back the knife at the last moment.

We would do well to follow the late eleventh- or twelfth-century Jewish narrators in seeing the Jewish behaviors of 1096 as simultaneously a continuation of prior Jewish martyrological patterns and an innovative and precedent-setting departure. Our focus will, for this occasion, be on the new and different and the impact of crusading fervor on that innovation. The altered Jewish patterns of behavior and the thinking that underlay this unprecedented martyrdom show unmistakably the influence of the religious zeal evident in a general way in the First Crusade and, more specifically, of its focus upon Jerusalem and the epic of self-sacrifice played out in a number of ways in its sacred precincts.

On the behavioral level, what is striking about the Jewish actions of 1096 is the movement from traditional patterns of passive martyrdom, that is to say willingness to accept death at the hands of the oppressor, to the preponderance of activist martyrdoms, that is to say acts of suicide or homicide in which beleaguered Jews took matters into their own hands and dispatched themselves or their loved ones in advance of slaughter by the enemy. Prior Jewish religious injunction prescribes only passive martyrdom, and that under limited circumstances; the normative precedents advanced in the 1096 narratives and poetry, those of the Seleucid and Roman periods, all involved passive martyrdom. The only early model that shows real activism is that of Masada, nowhere alluded to in the 1096 Jewish sources because of rabbinic distaste for the radical groups who had made Masada their last refuge.[10]

Our focus, however, is less upon the Jewish behaviors than upon the symbolism that sustained such acts. A variety of present-day observers agree to the centrality of Jerusalem and Temple imagery among the 1096 Jewish martyrs, in particular the activist martyrs. One of the earliest poems that has survived from this episode, penned by David ben Meshullam, a well-known leader of the Jewish community of Speyer and a survivor of the assaults, is replete with invocation of the Temple theme. Only two of the many Temple-centered stanzas will be cited:

> Infants and women agreed to the sacrifice
> Of splendid offerings in the sanctuary of the Temple.
> O you who are unique and exalted! For your sake we are tortured and killed,
> Rather than acknowledge an imposter born of lust.
> Year-old lambs appropriate as burnt offerings
> Have been set apart, burnt offerings to serve as peace offerings.
> To their mothers they say: "Do not let your mercies be aroused.
> We have been assigned from on high as a sacrifice to the Lord."[11]

The somewhat later Solomon bar Simson Chronicle preserves, in its Cologne section, a remarkable hortatory address that is similarly rich in Jerusalem and Temple imagery:

> Then the pious and faithful one—the priest who stood above his brethren—said to the congregation seated about him at the table: "Let us recite the grace to living God, to our Father in heaven. For the table is set before us in place of the altar. Now let us rise up and ascend to the house of the Lord and do speedily the will of our Creator. For the enemy has come upon us today. We must slaughter on the Sabbath sons, daughters, and brothers, so that he bestow upon us this day a blessing. Let no one have mercy—neither on himself nor on his companions. The last one remaining shall slaughter himself by the throat with his knife or pierce his belly with his sword, so that the impure and the hand of evil ones not sully us with their abominations. Let us offer ourselves up as a sacrifice to the Lord, like a whole burnt offering to the Most High offered on the altar of the Lord."[12]

In both poetry and prose, imagery of Jerusalem and Temple sacrifice abounds, indeed dominates.

While present-day observers have regularly noted the dominance of Jerusalem and Temple imagery in the depictions of 1096 Jewish martyrdom, they have been slow to set this imagery in a crusading context. The relationship to crusading enthusiasm is patent. On the simplest level, the Jewish martyrs of 1096 saw themselves as the true pilgrims to the sacred places. As noted, the 1096 Jewish martyrs and their memorializers exhibit a grudging respect for the Christian effort to reconquer the Holy City. Yet both the martyrs and their memorializers obviously saw the Jewish ascent to Jerusalem as more spiritual and profounder than that of the crusaders. According to the Solomon bar Simson Chronicle, Rabbi Moses *ha-Cohen*, in his remarkable hortatory address, challenged his listeners to make the excruciating journey to a sublimer Jerusalem. "Let us rise up and ascend to the house of the Lord." Now, the combination of Hebrew verbs—*naqumah ve-naʿaleh*—resonates richly. The combination evokes, first of all, Gen. 35, where God orders Jacob to rise up and ascend to Beth-el—*qum ve-ʿaleh*—and to establish there an altar in honor of the God who had maintained him throughout his wanderings. Jacob delivers the message to his retinue in precisely the terms attributed to Rabbi Moses *ha-Cohen*: "Let us rise up and ascend [*ve-naqumah ve-naʿaleh*] to Beth-el [lit., the house of God], and I shall make there an altar to the God who answered me on the day of my travail and who stood by me on the way on which I have traveled" (ibid., 35:3). The same combination of verbs reappears in Jer. 31, in a messianic passage that speaks of the gleaners on the Mount of Ephraim saying to one another: "Let us rise up and ascend to Zion, to the Lord our God" (ibid., 31:6). The crusaders, misguidedly from the Jewish vantage point, saw themselves as making an exalted pilgrimage to the Holy City; from the Jewish perspective, the genuine pilgrims to the Holy City were the Jewish martyrs who answered the true divine call.

Yet, more significantly, the crusade emphasis on the self-sacrifice of Jesus, with its concomitant call for emulation of this human/divine behavior, clearly called forth a Jewish counter-symbolism that put the notion of sacrifice in a wholly Jewish context. Somewhat ironically, the Christian sense of Jesus as a sacrificial lamb intended to replace the obsolescent Temple ritual of Jerusalem was reworked by the Jews of 1096 in such a way as to project hundreds and even thousands of men, women, and children as superhumanly—although not divinely—prepared to offer themselves up as surrogates for the animal-centered ritual of earlier days. Put differently, the Jewish sacrifice of 1096, in its quantity and quality, surpassed—in Jewish eyes—the human/allegedly divine offering that stood at the very core of the Christian faith. In surpassing the offering of Jesus, the Jewish sacrifice of 1096 reduced purported crusader heroism to puny dimensions indeed.

Related to the Temple imagery was the symbol of Abraham's near-sacrifice of his son Isaac. Again, what happened in 1096 was Jewish rejection of Christian appropriation of the Abraham/Isaac imagery or, perhaps better, Jewish reappropriation of that imagery. In Jewish lore, that critical event in early Israelite history was labeled the ʿaqedah, Abraham's preparatory laying out of his beloved son on the altar. We have already seen both the Mainz Anonymous and the Solomon bar Simson Chronicle speaking collectively of the Jewish martyrdom as an extraordinary ʿaqedah and of hundreds upon hundreds of ʿaqedot. One of the most striking of the individual martyrdoms depicted in the Mainz Anonymous involved a Jew named Meshullam bar Isaac of Worms who invoked in a sustained way the Abraham/Isaac imagery in slaughtering his son, born to him by his wife Zipporah in her old age. The Mainz Anonymous tells this brief tale in language redolent of Gen. 22, reinforcing the overt imagery with recurrent linguistic borrowings from the biblical text.[13] Once again, there is a sharp Jewish challenge to Christian appropriation of the Abraham/Isaac tale and symbol; the real followers of Abraham and his son were the Jews of 1096, ready in fact to move beyond Abraham's readiness for sacrifice to the bloody reality.

The Christian warriors who set forth on the road to Jerusalem saw themselves as undertaking a divinely-ordained pilgrimage and, in so doing, emulating the self-sacrifice of Jesus that took place in the Holy City. This undertaking bore no immediate repercussions for most of the Jews of the late eleventh century. For a small number of major Rhineland Jewish communities, the call to the crusade unleashed potent anti-Jewish sentiment. Many, if not most, of the Jews assaulted in the name of the crusade and confronted with the choice of conversion or death responded with intense rejection of conversion and saw their death as divinely-ordained martyrdom. These Rhineland Jews and those who later celebrated their valor were intensely aware of the place of Jerusalem and its resonances in crusader ranks. At the same time, they denigrated Christian views of Jerusalem and its sanctity and projected the Jewish martyrs as far exceeding their crusading counterparts in depth of religious understanding and zeal. For neither the first nor the last time in its history as reality and symbol, Jerusalem was fiercely contested by its Christian and Jewish devotees.[14]

Notes

1. The three eyewitness Latin narratives are: (1) the anonymous *Gesta Francorum*, ed. and trans. R. Hill (Oxford, 1962); (2) Fulcher of Chartres, *Historia Hierosolymitana*, ed. H. Hagenmeyer (Heidelberg, 1913), trans. F. R. Ryan (Knoxville, 1969); (3) Raymond of Aguilers, *Historia Francorum*, ed. J. H. and L. L. Hill (Paris, 1969), idem (Philadelphia, 1968). The crusader letters are available in H. Hagenmeyer, ed., *Die Kreuzugsbriefe aus den Jahren 1088–*

1100 (Innsbruck, 1902). For the development of crusading ideals and symbols, see the early (1935) and influential study of Carl Erdmann, *The Origin of the Idea of Crusading*, trans. M. W. Baldwin and W. Goffart (Princeton, 1977); P. Rousset, *Les Origines et les caractères de la Première Croisade* (Neuchâtel, 1945); P. Alphandery, *La Chrétienté et l'idée de croisade*, ed. A. Dupront, 2 vols. (Paris, 1954–59); and J. Riley-Smith, *The First Crusade and the Idea of Crusading* (London, 1986). Erdmann disputed the significance of pilgrimage and Jerusalem in the papal call. Erdmann's position on this issue has been challenged by a number of scholars, most tellingly by H. E. J. Cowdrey in "Pope Urban II's Preaching of the First Crusade," *History* 55 (1970), 177–188. Riley-Smith, in the most recent of the comprehensive studies of the crusading idea, stresses the importance of Jerusalem in Pope Urban's call (pp. 20–25). A new perspective on crusading ideals and symbols has been opened by M. Bull, *Knightly Piety and the Lay Response to the First Crusade: The Limousin and Gascony, c. 970–c.1130* (Oxford, 1993). Bull uses narrative and documentary sources to analyze the lay response to the papal call. He finds that pilgrimage and Jerusalem loomed large in that lay response. For a more general discussion of Jerusalem in western-European thinking, see A. H. Bredero, "Jerusalem in the West," A. H. Bredero, *Christendom and Christianity in the Middle Ages*, trans. R. Bruinsma (Grand Rapids, 1994), 79–104. Bredero accepts the possibility that the papal call may not have highlighted Jerusalem, but argues that the popular response surely did (pp. 80–86).

2. These Hebrew narratives were published in a fine scholarly edition by A. Neubauer and M. Stern, *Hebräische Berichte über die Judenverfolgungen während der Kreuzzüge* (Berlin, 1892), and were republished by A. Habermann *Sefer Gezerot Ashkenaz ve-Zarfat* (Jerusalem, 1945). An English translation of all three narratives can be found in S. Eidelberg, *The Jews and the Crusaders* (Madison, 1977). Translations of the Mainz Anonymous and the so-called Solomon bar Simson narrative can be found as an appendix to R. Chazan, *European Jewry and the First Crusade* (Berkeley, 1987).

3. I have studied closely the Mainz Anonymous in an essay to appear in a *festschrift* in honor of Yosef Hayim Yerushalmi.

4. Neubauer and Stern (above, note 2), 47; Habermann (above, note 2), 93; Eidelberg (above, note 2), 99; Chazan (above, note 2), 225.

5. For a study of the use of invective in the Hebrew narratives, see A. S. Abulafia, "Invectives against Christianity in the Hebrew Chronicles of the First Crusade," *Crusade and Settlement*, ed. P. Edbury (Cardiff, 1985), 66–72.

6. Neubauer and Stern (above, note 2), 47; Habermann (above, note 2), 93; Eidelberg (above, note 2), 100; Chazan (above, note 2), 226.

7. Neubauer and Stern (above, note 2), 48; Habermann (above, note 2), 94; Eidelberg (above, note 2), 100; Chazan (above, note 2), 226.

8. Neubauer and Stern (above, note 2), 53; Habermann (above, note 2), 100; Eidelberg (above, note 2), 109; Chazan (above, note 2), 236.

9. Neubauer and Stern (above, note 2), 8; Habermann (above, note 2), 32; Eidelberg (above, note 2), 33; Chazan (above, note 2), 255–56.

10. For a full discussion of the various types of Jewish martyrdoms in 1096, see Chazan (above, note 2), 103–14.

11. Habermann (above, note 2), 70.

12. Neubauer and Stern (above, note 2), 21–22; Habermann (above, note 2), 48; Eidelberg (above, note 2), 57; Chazan (above, note 2), 281.

13. Neubauer and Stern (above, note 2), 50; Habermann (above, note 2), 96; Eidelberg (above, note 2), 103–104; Chazan (above, note 2), 230.

14. As I listened to the papers delivered at the conference, I felt that a central theme was the competition among the three Western monotheisms for domination of the terrestrial Jerusalem and of the spiritual values represented by the Holy City as well.

27

The Loss of Christian Jerusalem
in Late Medieval Liturgy

AMNON LINDER

Almost a century of Christian rule in the Holy Land ended with the defeat of the Latin army in Hattin on 4th July, 1187, and with the capitulation of Jerusalem to Saladin some three months later. Latin Christendom reacted to this new situation in various ways and by various means, but its immediate and most durable response can be observed in the sphere of liturgy.

Adoption of Traditional Liturgical Practices

The liturgy of Christian Europe evolved over more than a thousand years of common practice and was rich and varied enough to meet most new challenges. It offered psalms and prayers traditionally said in times of crisis for individuals and the community at large, as well as Masses for the Dead, which were celebrated more and more frequently as losses accumulated in the Holy Land and in other crusading campaigns. As early as 1190, the Cistercian General Chapter associated the fallen crusaders with the dead commemorated in the daily Mass for the Dead in every Cistercian house.[1] The main burden of commemorating fallen crusaders lay, of course, on their relatives, and though less documented than measures adopted by large organizations like the Cistercian Order, such ceremonies were undoubtedly performed in the usual way and on the appropriate dates in numerous churches throughout Europe for quite a long time.

Traditional liturgy also provided a large number of votive masses, such as the masses *In tribulatione, In tempore belli, Contra paganos, Pro pace,* and *Contra persecutores Ecclesiae.* Each of these could be celebrated—and indeed frequently was—under the specific rubric *Pro Terra Sancta,* and in this way served the specific needs of the crusade. When Oliver Scholasticus from Paderborn preached the crusade in Bethun in June, 1214, he celebrated the Holy Cross

Mass prior to his crusading sermon, as he recorded in his description of the miraculous apparition of the cross in the sky on that occasion.[2] Another example of a traditional votive mass celebrated in this specific context is known from Sicily: toward the end of 1198, the commissioners appointed to preach the crusade on the island informed Innocent III that a weekly mass *Pro tribulatione* was celebrated for the sake of the crusaders in some churches, and asked for his authorization of this practice. The pope confirmed it on 5th January, 1199, and extended it to the whole island.[3]

Besides these general traditional practices, by the end of the twelfth century the corpus of traditional liturgy also comprised several practices specifically bearing on Jerusalem and the Holy Land. There was the old rite of consecrating the *peregrinus* on one's departure on *peregrinatio*, but as that rite was entirely silent with regard to the military character of the *peregrinatio*, it was gradually augmented by new, essentially military, ceremonies. The more the crusader diverged from the prototype of the pilgrim, the more these rites tended to emphasize Jerusalem as his goal and the predominantly military character of his pilgrimage. It was an uneasy combination of ideas, and something of that unease can be detected in the departure ceremony celebrated in honor of Philip Augustus in St. Denis on 24th June, 1191. There the king received the traditional pilgrim's staff and hamper, but also two military standards and two flags,[4] for his *peregrinatio* combined the humble, almost ascetic self-denial of the pilgrim with the military pomp and might of the king of France.

Much more specific—and more poignant after the loss of Jerusalem in 1187—were some traditional triumphal commemorations celebrated on fixed dates. One of these was the Holy Sepulchre Mass celebrated on Holy Saturday in countless churches throughout Europe at least since the eleventh century. It celebrated victory—in the broadest theological sense of Easter and in the limited historical and geographical sense of the Holy Sepulchre of Jerusalem as the chosen venue for that victory. The annual miracle of the Holy Fire embodied these localized aspects in a specific liturgical practice.

Another commemoration of victory was celebrated on 15th July.[5] On that day in 1099, the crusaders "liberated" Jerusalem, and on the very same date fifty years later, in 1149, they also dedicated the new church of the Holy Sepulchre. Both festivities certainly had a grim, hollow sound to them after 1187, but they were maintained, nonetheless, in many European churches right down to the fifteenth century; we can still find them in the Calendars of Alençon, Brouges, Beauvais, the Cluny usage, Laon, Soissons, and elsewhere.

A third commemoration specific to the memory of Jerusalem was the Destruction of Jerusalem Sunday, the ninth Sunday after Trinity Sunday (or

Pentecost), toward the end of July and the beginning of August.[6] This was not by accident, of course: it was meant to be celebrated close to the Ninth of Av, for it commemorated, as it still does today, the destruction of Jerusalem by Vespasian and Titus as a just punishment for the act of Deicide perpetrated by that Jewish city, and the cessation of its Jewish identity from that date on. Clear and straightforward as this message was, it became ambivalent in the crusading context. It could not simply be ignored, for it was held in very close proximity to the Liberation of Jerusalem Day on 15th July and, furthermore, its narrative structure was basically identical to that of the Liberation Day. Both portrayed the destructive siege and occupation of Jerusalem in the context of the cosmic conflict between God and Evil, Salvation and Damnation. The restoration of Christian rule in Jerusalem by the crusaders in 1099 resulted, therefore, in a reappraisal of the traditional commemoration and its contemporary relevance, and led to a reformulation of the old affinity between the ancient signifier and its contemporary signified.

Medieval Christianity in general, and the crusaders in particular, preferred to consider themselves successors to Vespasian and Titus rather than heirs to the high priests of Jerusalem. An impressive body of pious historical works, sermons and legends, poems and plays converged around the memory of the Roman siege and destruction of Jerusalem. We find in it various sub-groups centered on the figures and objects of Veronica, Joseph of Arimathea, the Imago Salvatoris in Rome, the literary cycle of the *Venjeance de Dieu*, and many others. The medieval reputation of Vespasian stood high for several reasons, recreating his image in the form of a proto-Christian emperor, certainly a champion of God; it was but a step to claim (as in *La chanson d'Antioche*[7] and by Matthew of Edessa[8]) that Godfrey of Boulogne conquered Jerusalem with the very same sword that Vespasian wielded in a similar and earlier campaign. Baudry of Dol contested this opinion when he underscored the differences between these two sieges and asserted that the crusaders besieged Jerusalem in 1099, "not in that siege prophesied by the Lord when he said: 'For the days shall come upon thee, that thine enemies shall . . . encompass thee round, and shall confine thee and thy children within thee'; now, on the contrary, she is encompassed by her friends, and her children confine the aliens and the false."[9] It is clear, nevertheless, that the much easier identification with the Romans had a better reception.

The simple equation of the besiegers with the Romans vindicating God's cause and of the besieged with the biblical Jews, God's enemies undergoing their just punishment, runs counter to the crusaders' tendency to see themselves in the light of the Old Testament's history and figures. The royal coronation at Bethlehem more than hinted at the Davidic precursors of the kings of Jerusalem, and the epitaph of Baldwin I—"alter Judas Maccabeus"—referred, once again, to the biblical roots of the kingdom. Ironically, and perhaps tragically, the strong identification of the crusaders with the Old Testament surfaced again after 1187 in attempts to explain and justify their defeat. The crusaders, it was claimed, like the Old Testament inhabitants of Jerusalem before them, paid the price of their iniquity, for the Holy Land, as scriptural history amply proves, does not tolerate sinners on its soil, certainly not for long.

The same commemoration supported two different interpretations with mutually-contradictory messages, from the twelfth century down to the immediate aftermath of the 1187 defeat.

Liturgical Innovations: The *Clamor Pro Terra Sancta*

Our documentation proves that these traditional liturgical practices were not only available in 1187, but also that they were highly relevant to the new situation and were, therefore, applied in that context. It also proves that by themselves they did not suffice. New practices evolved very early on, as early as 1188, and new texts were composed somewhat later, within two decades after the fall of Jerusalem. This burst of creativity suggests that the generation of 1187 felt the need to expand traditional liturgy with new practices and texts, through which it expressed new attitudes toward Jerusalem and the Holy Land, the Moslems, and the crusade. A fairly good insight into this process can be gained by surveying (even in a cursory fashion) the evolution of one of these innovations, the *Clamor pro Terra Sancta* in mass. Introduced immediately after Hattin, it was still practiced in the framework of several liturgical usages by the beginning of the sixteenth century. This is an impressive duration (even when the factor of sheer inertia is taken into account), indicating the long-term vitality of this practice.

Structure, Origin, Diffusion

The *Clamor pro Terra Sancta* probably originated in London in 1188. It consisted of a weekly program of daily masses celebrated in Westminster Abbey (St. Peter) "for peace, and for the liberation of the Land of Jerusalem, and of the Christian captives held in chains by the Saracens." Another account changes the venue to St. Paul's Cathedral, but describes essentially identical proceedings; robbing Peter to give the prayers to Paul is of no consequence in this case.[10] Both accounts describe a sequence of prayers that were introduced into mass immediately after the *Pater noster* and before the *Agnus Dei*, in a seven-day program of daily masses. This sequence consisted of a psalm (a different psalm for every day, seven psalms in all) accompanied by an antiphon, eleven versicles, and a collect.

It was not a complete innovation. Both its appellation (*clamor*) and structure correspond to an earlier liturgical practice, the *Clamor pro malefactoribus* in mass. Evolved toward the end of the tenth century by monastic and capitular communities struggling against lay despoilers, it was maintained in the liturgical heritage of several major monasteries and churches (Farfa, Langres, Tours, Chartres, Corbie, Fleury, etc.) and was practiced at least down to the fourteenth century.[11] By the end of the twelfth century, it served as the model for special *clamor*-type *preces* that were commonly inserted into mass in reference to specific emergencies, either local or general. A *Clamor Pro pace Ecclesiae*, for example, was decreed for the Cistercian Order by its General Chapter ca. 1155.

Recourse to the traditional *clamor* in the post-1187 situation was to be expected, therefore, in the general context of the adoption of traditional liturgical practices, but the *clamor* proved to be particularly relevant to that situation, more so than any of the other traditional practices bearing on crises in general, because its prayer, *In spiritu humilitatis*, presented the desolation wreaked by *invasores* through the figure of the grieving Jerusalem and in terms borrowed from Jeremiah's lamentations over the desolation of the city: *sedet in tristitia, non est qui consoletur et liberet eam.* That prayer alluded to Jerusalem in the traditional allegorical mode via its reference to the actual monastery or church mentioned. In 1188, the London liturgist emphasized the literal aspect of the church *of* Jerusalem rather than its allegorical prefiguration of the church/monastery *as* Jerusalem. It was the same attention to topicality that guided his choice of the daily psalms said during the *clamor*. Tuesday's psalm was Ps. 59, referring to Joab's victories against *Mesopotamiam Syriae et Syriam Sobal*,[12] while its text also mentions "Moab" and "Idumea,"[13] and Friday's psalm (Ps. 82) named God's enemies as *tabernacula Idumeorum et Ismahelitum, Moab et Aggareni, Gebal et Ammon et Amalech.*[14] The topicality of both psalms to Londoners in 1188 was self-evident.

The London observance was not an isolated phenomenon. An almost identical daily program, though limited to one mass and one psalm, was adopted in various other places at about the same time. The psalm chosen for that practice was Ps. 78 [79], *Deus venerunt gentes* (recited in London on Thursday); the entire sequence (psalm, antiphon, versicles, and collect) was said *in prostratione* and was easily inserted into any mass on any day. Monastic congregations could practice this *clamor* daily, whether after a chapter or later, and daily usage is documented in churches serving the public on particular occasions, usually during crusades and in times of crisis; when it was cited on Sunday it had a much larger audience, obviously, with a larger proportion of lay worshippers in the congregation.

A cursory survey of the liturgical manuscripts reveals the wide diffusion of this practice and its duration in time.[15] The earliest manuscript comes from Arles, in the late twelfth century. The *clamor* was enjoined on the universal church by Innocent III in the bull *Quia maior* (1213), included in the Pontifical of Guillaume Durand of Mende and in the Ordinal of the Carmelites. Our latest evidence in print comes from the Marian Sarum Missal of 1555, which restored this practice after it was suppressed in the Book of Common Prayer and, finally, from the printed Braga Missal of 1558. During these centuries, it was included in manuscripts produced or celebrated in the churches of Chartres, Sens, Clermont, Senlis, Fécamp, Valenciennes, Assisi, Avignon, Marseille, Paris (the common Paris usage and the Sainte Chapelle in particular), Seckau, Köln, Reims, Rouen, Sankt Lambrecht, Sarum, York, Durham, Essen, and Monte-Cassino.

This short list illustrates the considerable geographical diffusion of the *clamor* and also raises the question whether some parts of Europe are more prominently represented in the list of extant manuscripts than others and, consequently, whether such a disparity reflects a different attitude toward the *clamor* and its goal—the deliverance of Jerusalem. Our documentation suggests that the *clamor* was mostly practiced in France and England, and to a lesser degree in Germany and Italy, and that it was almost completely unknown in Spain and Scandinavia. These results should be further checked against the relative roles played by members of these cultural-political-national entities in the crusading movement. The complete absence of the Spanish is easily explained; they have had their own infidels to worry about on their very doorsteps. But the relatively minor representation of German and Italian manuscripts calls for further investigation. It may be due, to some extent a least, to the very real threat of the Turks, much nearer to home than the Holy Land, or to the greater accessibility of French liturgical manuscripts (thanks to the monumental survey of Leroquais) than manuscripts "hidden" by catalogues (mostly the old ones) whose editors exercised the utmost self-restraint in their description of liturgical manuscripts, suppressing rather than revealing their detailed contents.

From Temporary to Regular Practice

The London elaborate weekly observance, maintained *sine intermissione*, could not have lasted for a long time, and most probably was not intended to. Like the other *clamor* practices, it was regarded as an exceptional measure devised to respond to an exceptional crisis, and to be applied, consequently, for a short duration only. The 1187 debacle was still regarded at the time as a temporary setback, a transitory crisis that called for a *clamor*-type response. A study of the chronology of this practice highlights its temporary character throughout the thirteenth century in a series of immediate responses to the vicissitudes of the crusade. It appears with an almost constant periodicity, in close association with certain events (crusades, particular dangers and enemies, e.g., the Tartars) and for their duration. Though each of these *clamor* celebrations was essentially temporary, their high frequency and relatively long duration nevertheless coalesced into an almost permanent liturgical activity that responded to frequent alarms and accompanied the organization of crusades, their actual execution, and their usually catastrophic aftermaths. One could always be sure, during most of the thirteenth century, of encountering some crusading venture—with its accompanying liturgical practices—taking place someplace or other in Europe and the Latin East.

The temporary nature of the *Clamor pro Terra Sancta* is reflected in the particular character of its integration into the liturgical manuscripts, mainly missals and sacramentaries. For most of the thirteenth century, it appears in additions written on first and last blank pages and on spaces left blank before the Canon of the Mass, or as marginal additions to written pages. These additions and interpolations answered the need of the moment and served as an update for future use, but the actual process of integration into the standard authoritative missal was rather slow. There is some evidence of integration as early as the beginning of that century, but the process did not accelerate until the last quarter of the century, reflecting the gradual transformation of the *clamor* from a temporary measure wholly dedicated to the Holy Land to a regularly celebrated practice bearing equally on the Holy Land and other issues. The *clamor* became an integral part of the Carmelite conventual daily mass, according to the ordinal composed by Sibert of Beka about 1312, and was declared obligatory by several Chapters General of the Order,[16] but the best example of such a transformation in a use open to the public is that presented by the Sarum Use.

The Sarum Use *Clamor* (documented from the Cathedral of Exeter) was augmented by two additional prayers about the middle of the thirteenth century.[17] These were the *Ecclesie tue quaesumus domine* and the *Deus a quo sancta desideria*, received, respectively, from the votive masses, *Contra persecutores Ecclesiae* and *Pro pace*. The three-tiered structure (three psalms and [probably three] prayers) was adopted by the Archbishop of Canterbury in 1295, when he instructed the English bishops to celebrate special masses as well as a daily *clamor* in Mass for the Holy Land and for the Realm and the King. This was the decisive step towards regular celebration, for the *clamor* became anchored on issues of permanent importance and continued relevance—the well-being of the King and the Realm. The final version was established some time in the fourteenth century.[18] It consisted of three psalms (78 and 66 [identical with the 1295 *Clamor*], and Ps. 20), an antiphon, eight versicles, and three prayers; the first bore on the deliverance of the Holy Land, the second (*Rege qaesumus famulum*) on the diocesan bishop, and the third on the king (*Da qaesumus omnipotens deus famulo tuo regi*). This became the standard form of the *clamor* in England for the next two centuries. It was celebrated daily throughout the year, with the exception of certain portions of the Christmas period and the Paschal time.[19] The new form implied, obviously, a certain dilution of the crusading character of this *clamor* as a purely crusading liturgical practice, but what it had probably lost in this direction it more than certainly gained in enlarged and constant impact thanks to the regularity of its daily celebration in the entire land.

Implementation

If our distinction between temporary and regular practice of the *clamor* is correct, it provides us with a useful tool for evaluating the problematic inquiry regarding the actual performance of the *clamor*. Most of our documentation is prescriptive, consisting of either service-books or documents produced in relation to the implementation of ritual, such as papal or other ecclesiastical directives, while the evidence about actual use and implementation is at best episodic and open to challenges of typicality. Furthermore, by bearing on actual events these documents tend to emphasize commission rather than omission. Let me illustrate this difficulty with three cases of indirect evidence of implementation which are trustworthy in principle because all three sources are manifestly concerned with issues other than the one at hand, i.e., the question of implementation.

The thirteenth-century Customaries of St. Augustine, Canterbury, and St. Peter, Westminster determine that monks *in penitentia* should take the last place among the brethren and prostrate together with the young and the novices whenever *clamor* is said in mass.[20] This casual reference to the *clamor* can be taken as perfectly credible evidence that the *clamor* was indeed practiced in these two Benedictine houses, but it certainly does not prove how often it took place, nor are we in a position to extend this information to any other house or religious community without further evidence.

My second example concerns the crusade led by Frederick II and the treaty he signed with el-Kamil in 1229. Gerold, the Patriarch of Jerusalem, commented on the treaty's clauses point by point in a bitter report he sent to Rome, and this was his angry reaction to the clause that reserved the Temple Mount to Muslim control: *Haec est abusio manifesta que expositione non indiget, hec est conventio Christi ad Belial; per hoc apparet, si frequentatio psalmi illius "Deus venerunt gentes" cessare debeat, cum adhuc templum sanctum polluant infideles.*[21] Here again, we obtain valuable information about the actual implementation of the *clamor*, but we have to delimit its implications very carefully. Crusades in general offer perfect occasions for temporary *clamors*, limited in time and circumscribed to certain territories, and the unique character of this particular crusade, led by an excommunicate emperor, should certainly be considered in any attempt to gauge the measure of support, liturgical and otherwise, that it was able to enlist in Europe. And one might query, finally, how well informed the Patriarch of Jerusalem was in his palace in Acre about what really happened in Europe.

My third and last example concerns the mobilization of the French kingdom during the crusade led by Louis IX in 1248. Salimbene of Adam happened to visit the Franciscans of Provins during the preparations for the crusade and met there two Joachimite friars, who tried to win him over by showing him commentaries and prophecies attributed to Joachim of Fiore:

> *Et cum diceretur per totam Franciam in missa conventuali qualibet die per totum annum psalmus "Deus venerunt gentes in hereditatem tuam" et cet., ipsi similiter deridebant dicentes: "Oportet impleri scripturam que dicit"* [Tren. 3:44]: *"Opposuisti nubem tibi, ne transeat oratio. Nam rex Francie capietur et Gallici debellabuntur et pestilentia multos consumet." Et facti sunt isti duo exosi fratribus de Francia, qui dicebant quod in precedenti passagio fuerant ista completa.*[22]

This evidence is clear and unequivocal, certainly about the Franciscans in France during that specific year, and that year alone; but how much can we deduce from this text concerning other regular communities, clerics, and laymen, at the same time in France, let alone in other countries or at other times? It would be utterly wrong to read into this document more than it really conveys.

The episodic evidence provided by sources like these should be checked against and complemented by evidence of a more serial nature, covering long spans of time and relating to large territories, like the series of relevant decrees issued by the annual General Chapters of the Cistercian Order. They provide us with important information about commission, omission, and repeal in the entire Order year in and year out. After a silence of some forty years—the last time its General Chapter decreed on this matter was in 1197—the Order established special prayers in support of the crusaders and of the Holy Land in 1239,[23] and again in 1245,[24] 1247,[25] 1255[26] and 1258.[27] The *clamor* reappears in the conventual daily mass only in 1245, and the phrasing *prout antiquitus fieri consuevit* suggests that a considerable time passed since past observance. It was reintroduced in 1255, and again in 1261, under the reference *orationes . . . quae . . . antea per nostrum Ordinem dicebantur*[28] and *sicut antiquitus fieri consuevit*,[29] suggesting, once more, a considerable period of non-observance. It was expressly and definitely repealed in the following year.[30] Clearly, the historian will neglect the invaluable information provided by the Cistercian legislation at his own peril, but he should be aware, at the same time, of failing to recognize its character as a prescriptive source always in need of corroborating or invalidating evidence, which not infrequently turn out to be indirect and episodic.

The Prayers of the *Clamor*

The problem we have to address under this heading is topicality. Many of the texts employed in both office and mass were general enough to fit nicely into most particular situations, the sort of *passepartout* texts that can be recycled successfully, texts that transmit ideas and sentiments centered on few pivotal conceptions of the relationship between Man and the Divine. We shall call them the "universal texts."

More limited pivotal concepts like martyrdom, virginity, sacrifice, or priesthood denote relationships general enough to embrace a large number of specific situations, yet delimited, all the same, to the particular clusters of values peculiar to the Christian religion. Let us call them the "Christian common texts."

The last stage in this scale, going down from the universal through the commonly Christian, brings us to the uniquely individual. Liturgy cannot deal with the individual on universal or relatively general grounds alone. Whenever it paints the unique physiognomy of a personality, a specific entity, or a particular historical occurrence, it marks them with particular markers, creating texts or practices which will embody and transmit its recognition of their uniqueness.

We propose to apply this three-level analysis (universal–commonly Christian–individual) to the evolution of the Jerusalem liturgy. The immediate reaction to Hattin was expressed in recycled texts. Some of them were of the first, universal type: a general cry for help when in distress. The Valenciennes antiphon (late twelfth century) cries: *Clementissime deus exaudi preces nostras,*[31] while the London antiphon of 1188, and the Sarum Use right down to the fifteenth century, were more detailed, but no less general: *Tua est potentia tuum regnum domine tu es super omnes gentes da pacem domine in diebus nostris.*[32]

Yet most of the texts chosen immediately after 1187 are of the second type, referring directly and specifically in a typical Christian context to biblical Jerusalem or to the concepts of martyrdom, God's war with Evil, and the Holy War against the heathen.

The prayer said in the first *clamor* in London was a very old one, going back to the Christian Roman empire; this prayer for the Roman empire and the emperor on Good Friday reads as follows:

> *Omnipotens sempiterne deus, in cuius manu sunt omnium potestates et omnium iura regnorum, respice ad Romanum benignus imperium ut gentes, quae in sua feritate confidunt, potentiae tuae dextera comprimantur.*

It was adapted to the more general needs of the Christian society during the eighth–ninth centuries (the Gregorian Sacramentary) by the replacement of *Romanum Imperium* with that of *Christianorum . . . auxilium* (*respice ad Christianorum auxilium*). But it was still too general in terms of the 1188 situation, although the call for God's aid against ferocious (read: barbarous) *gentes* (read: non-Christians) fit the crusading situation quite well. Our 1188 London program in St. Paul's, therefore, went one step further by explicating: *respice ad Christianum benigne exercitum,* and later versions added another explicit reference to *gentes paganorum.* Its concise opposition of God's people with the ferocious pagans was clear enough to express the sentiments of Christians afflicted at the hands of non-Christians, and general enough to fit *any* situation of this type. The best proof of this extraordinary applicability is this prayer's long duration as the main prayer against the heathen. It maintained its role against the non-Christians in the crusading and the anti-Turkish liturgy as long as liturgy was mobilized for these ends, and it is still to be found in the modern Catholic missal as the collect of the *Missa contra Paganos.*

This progression, from the general to the less general, albeit still in need of some explication, did not solve the problem entirely, for it failed to highlight the uniqueness of the Jerusalem crusade, hence of the Jerusalem liturgy. Two new explicit prayers appeared toward the beginning of the thirteenth century.

The first prayer seems to have been created in Germany, as its earliest texts are known from three twelfth-century German manuscripts (copied in Bamberg, Darmstadt, and one of unknown provenance) as well as two twelfth-century manuscripts from Valenciennes and Arles, on the western limits of the empire. It spread to various French (Chartres, Sens, St. Denis) and probably also English centers during the thirteenth and fourteenth centuries. Received by the Carthusians into their breviary, it opened the rather long list of their *clamor* prayers before Prime (mostly five, in one manuscript seven) right down to the fifteenth century. Of a more limited diffusion than that of the competing second prayer, it was still popular enough to survive in some eighteen manuscripts and in seven versions. Its earlier text reads as follows:

> *Deus qui ad nostre redemptionis exhibenda misteria terram repromissionis elegisti, libera eam quesumus ab instantia paganorum, ut gentium incredulitate confusa populus in te confidens de tue virtutis potentia glorietur.*[33]

The second prayer was issued by Innocent III in 1213. It was by far the most popular prayer for the deliverance of Jerusalem, known today in twenty-two versions preserved in a very large number of manuscripts, incunabula, and early prints. This number is further augmented by most of the manuscripts of the Pontifical of Guillaume Durand, which brings this prayer in its *Ordo pro liberatione Terrae Sanctae a fidei inimicis* (III:16). Its text reads as follows:

> *Deus qui admirabili providentia cuncta disponis, te suppliciter exoramus ut terram quam unigenitus Filius tuus proprio sanguine consecravit de manibus inimicorum crucis eripiens, restituas cultui Christiano, vota fidelium ad eius liberationem instantium misericorditer dirigendo in viam salutis aeternae. Per eundem Dominum nostrum. . . .*

Two short prayers present a concise call for action as well as a manifest of the principal ideas subsumed in the general idea of the crusade: that the sanctity of the land derives from the choice, the real presence and the Passion of God; that a fundamental dichotomy divides the Christians from the enemies of the cross and of the Christian cult; that the crusade is an action of restoration and liberation, as well as a way offered to the individual to acquire eternal salvation. Each of these statements is an entire discourse in a nutshell; each of them calls for further elaboration, but in their brevity they can be better perceived and assimilated by the congregation, in the same way that the brief "Symbol" was assimilated through repetition in a liturgical context.

Unlike the first prayer, these two are committed to the liberation of Jerusalem and to this goal alone. They represent the third type of liturgical text in our analysis, the complete mobilization of liturgy in the service of the crusading movement. We have moved all the way down, from the universal to the general Christian concept and, finally, to the uniquely historical and individual in less than one generation, from 1188 to 1213. The last prayer in particular (*Deus qui admirabili*) became identified with the crusading movement to such an extent, that it received numerous additions which echo the concerns and doubts harbored in the minds of the attending believers in an ongoing dialogue conducted between the faithful under the guise of addressing God in prayer. One of the most interesting interpolations of this type can be read in the Reims *Clamor*, documented in manuscripts copied between the thirteenth and fifteenth centuries:

> . . . *de manibus inimicorum crucis eripias, qui eam non tam ex sue virtutis potentia quam ex nostre iniquitatis offensa detinent occupatam, ipsamque restituas cultui Christiano, ad laudem gloriam nominis tui sancti, vota fidelium*. . . .

As late as the end of the seventeenth century, the Franciscans of Jerusalem and Bethlehem used to say this prayer in the following version:

> *Deus qui admirabili providentia cuncta disponis: te suppliciter exoramus: ut hanc terram, quam unigenitus tuus proprio sanguine consecravit: de manibus inimicorum cunctis eripiens, et eam in Christiana religione tuo nomini servire concedas.*[34]

As late as 1670, in Jerusalem and under hostile occupation, this prayer still expressed the same sentiments and ideas that motivated Christian Europe to evolve this special Jerusalem liturgy on the aftermath of Hattin.

Notes

1. J. M. Canivez, *Statuta Capitulorum Generalium Ordinis Cisterciensis* (Louvain, 1933), I, 122, Statut. 16.

2. Oliverus Scholasticus, *Historia regum Terre Sancte*, ed. H. Hoogeweg, Bibliothek des Literarischen Vereins in Stuttgart 202 (Tübingen, 1894), 285.

3. *De Vestra Discretione*, dated 5 January, 1199 (*PL* 214, cols. 470–71, no. 508). The envoys were appointed in July, 1198; see P. Cole, *The Preaching of the Crusade to the Holy Land, 1095–1270* (Cambridge, MA, 1991), 85.

4. Rigordus, *De gestis Philippi Augusti*, Recueil des historiens des Gaules et de la France 17 (Paris, 1878), 29.

5. A. Linder, "The Liturgy of the Liberation of Jerusalem," *Mediaeval Studies* 55 (1990), 110–31.

6. Idem, "The Destruction of Jerusalem Sunday," *Sacris erudiri* 30 (1987–88), 253–92.

7. *La Chanson d'Antioche,* ed. P. Paris (Paris, 1848) V:4, 12–13.

8. *Fragmenta Chronici Matthaei de Edessa,* Recueil des historiens des croisades, Documents armeniens 1 (Paris, 1869), 25.

9. Baldricus Dolensis, *Historia Hierosolimitana,* Recueil des historiens des croisades, Historiens occidentaux 4 (Paris, 1879), IV:9, 97.

10. See [Ps.] Benedict of Peterborough, *The Chronicle of the Reigns of Henry II and Richard I,* ed. W. Stubbs, II, Rolls Series 49b (London, 1867), 53–54; Roger of Howden, *Chronica,* ed. W. Stubbs, II, Rolls Series 51b (London, 1869), 359–60. On the question of the author(s) of these accounts and their authority, consult D. M. Stenton, "Roger of Howden and 'Benedict'," *English Historical Review* 86 (1953), 574–82; J. B. Gillingham, "Roger of Hoveden on Crusade," *Mediaeval Historical Writing in the Christian and Islamic Worlds,* ed. D. O. Morgan (London, 1982), 60–75; D. Corner, "The Earliest Surviving Manuscripts of Roger of Howden's 'Chronica'," *English Historical Review* 98 (1983), 297–310; idem, "The 'Gesta Regis Henrici Secundi' and 'Chronica' of Roger, Parson of Howden," *Bulletin of the Institute of Historical Research* 56 (1983), 126–44; J. Sayers, "English Charters from the Third Crusade," *Tradition and Change, Essays in Honour of Marjorie Chibnall,* eds. D. Greenway et al. (Cambridge, 1985), 195–213.

11. P. J. Geary, "L'humiliation des Saints," *Annales* 34 (1979) 43–60; L. K. Little, "Formules monastiques de malédiction aux IXᵉ–XIᵉ siècles," *Revue Mabillon* 262 (1975), 377–99; idem, "La morphologie des malédictions monastiques," *Annales* 34 (1979), 43–60; idem, *Benedictine Maledictions: Liturgical Cursing in Romanesque France,* (Ithaca, 1993).

12. Ps. 59:2.

13. Ibid., 59:10.

14. Ibid., 82:7–8.

15. A. Linder, " 'Deus venerunt gentes': Psalm 78 (79) in the Liturgical Commemoration of the Destruction of Jerusalem," *Medieval Studies in Honour of Avrom Saltman,* eds. B.-S. Albert et al. (Ramat Gan, 1995), 145–71.

16. B. Zimmerman, *Ordinaire de l'Ordre de Notre-Dame du Mont-Carmel* (Paris, 1910), v, x, xiv. The Ordo (R. XLIII) is published on p. 86. See also M. Rickert, *The Reconstructed Carmelite Missal: An English Manuscript of the Late XIV Century in the British Museum (Additional 29704–5, 44892)* (London, 1952), 37.

17. Manchester, John Rylands Univ. Lib., Latin Ms. 24. J. Wickham Legg identified this version as the earliest form of the Sarum Missal. See his edition, *The Sarum Missal* (Oxford, 1916), 209–10.

18. Documented in the Sarum Usage Missal from St. Mary's, Lapworth (Warwickshire), Oxford, Ms. Corpus Christi College 394, dated to 1398.

19. The prayers were not said in the ferial mass from the Vigil of the Nativity to the second Sunday after Epiphany (*Domine ne in ira*), and from Maundy Thursday to the Sunday following the Corpus Domini Octave (*Deus omnium*).

20. E. M. Thompson (ed.), *Customary of the Benedictine Monasteries of Saint Augustine, Canterbury, and Saint Peter, Westminster,* I (London, 1902), 240, 242; II (London, 1904), 200, 203–204.

21. *Epistolae saec. XIII e regestis pontificum Romanorum, selectae,* I, ed. C. Rodenberg, MGH (Berlin 1883), 297, no. 380.

22. Salimbene de Adam, *Cronica,* I, ed. G. Scalia (Bari, 1966), 339–40.

23. Canivez (above, note 1), II (Louvain, 1934), 201, An. 1239, Statut. 3—special Friday prayers in support of the Duke of Burgundy's crusade *tam pro servitio Terrae sanctae quam pro negotio Constantinipolitano.* A similar disposition was probably decreed in 1238 by the Provincial Council of Bordeaux, convoked at Cognac; see Concilium Copriniacum, ca. 30, in J. D. Mansi, *Sacrorum Conciliorum nova et amplissima collectio* (reprint Graz, 1960), XXIII, col. 873.

24. Canivez (above, note 23), 289, An. 1245 Statut. 2, at the request of the Papal Legate *pro rege Franciae qui signum sanctae crucis assumpsit, et pro terra Sancta.*

25. Ibid., 316, An. 1247 Statut. 4, establishing Friday prayers in support of a long list of persons, beginning with the Pope and closing with . . . *omnibus cruce signatis, maxime qui in comitatu domini regis Franciae erunt.*

26. Ibid., 409, An. 1255 Statut. 2. The prayers are described as *tam pro domino Papa quam pro statu Ecclesiae,* but both their structure and content indicate a typical Jerusalem liturgy.

27. Ibid., 435, An. 1258 Statut. 1, a general confirmation of the *orationes solemenes quae solebant fieri.*

28. Ibid., 409, An. 1255 Statut. 2.

29. Ibid., 475, An. 1261 Statut. 3.

30. Ibid., III (Louvain, 1935), 3, An. 1262 Statut. 13: *Oratio "Deus venerunt gentes," quae ad missam dici consuevit, et responsorium "Aspice Domine," penitus revocantur.*

31. Bar. 2:14, slightly changed.

32. After I Par. 29:11.

33. Hessische Landes- und Hochschulbibliothek Darmstadt Hs. 3183, fol. 188v.

34. Daily Processions carried out by the Franciscans in Jerusalem and Bethlehem, printed in Venice (1623) and Amsterdam (1670).

28

Jerusalem in Jewish Law and Custom:
a Preliminary Typology[1]

DAVID GOLINKIN

J ewish literature written during the past two thousand years has preserved hundreds, if not thousands, of laws and customs related to the city of Jerusalem. This material has been collected in many books and articles, but thus far no attempt has been made to categorize and organize this vast corpus. I shall attempt here to present a preliminary typology of these laws and customs which will enable further study and investigation.

The laws and customs related to Jerusalem can be conveniently divided into three major categories: (1) laws and customs in talmudic literature which are attributed to Second Temple Jerusalem; (2) post-destruction laws and customs observed by Jews throughout the world in order to remember Jerusalem; and (3) post-destruction laws and customs observed by Jewish residents and visitors in Jerusalem itself.

Laws and Customs Attributed to Second Temple Jerusalem

This category contains at least fifty such traditions. We shall only mention them briefly since they have already been listed and investigated by quite a few scholars.[2] About twenty of these laws are contained in a list which has come down to us in four different versions.[3] The most well-known version (B Bava Qama 82b) reads as follows:

> Ten things were said about Jerusalem: that a house sold there can be redeemed even though it is a walled city (Lev. 25:29–30); that it does not bring a heifer whose neck is broken (Deut. 21:1–9); that it can never become a condemned city (ibid., 13:13–18); that its houses cannot be defiled through leprosy (Lev. 14:33–53); that neither beams nor

408

balconies are allowed to project; that no dunghills are made there; that no kilns are made there; that neither gardens nor orchards are cultivated there, except for the rose gardens which existed from the days of the former prophets; that no chickens may be raised there; and that no dead person may be kept there overnight.

Scholarly opinion is divided over the historical veracity of these traditions. Some scholars, such as L. Finkelstein and S. Bialoblocki, accept most of these traditions at face value. A. Guttmann, on the other hand, views most or all of them as apocryphal, pointing out that of the twenty laws found in the four versions of the list, only four occur in all four versions. Furthermore, most of these laws are not cited in the Mishnah. In addition, there are over 300 disagreements in rabbinic literature between Bet Shammai and Bet Hillel, yet none of them concerns the laws of Jerusalem. Lastly, even the four laws found in all four versions are contradicted by other rabbinic sources.[4] He therefore suggests that these laws first appeared in the realm of aggadah: Guttmann states:

> As several of the items concern biblical laws, it stands to reason that the Mishnah disregarded them primarily because it rejected their authenticity. On what grounds? . . . The only satisfying explanation for the disregard of several seemingly important cases is, in our opinion, that the redactors of the Mishnah considered them as belonging to the realm of the *aggadah*. We saw that three of the four lists were given in an aggadic or semi-aggadic context. . . .
>
> The predominant tendency after the fall of the Temple was to emphasize the unique and distinguished status of the city by pointing to its superiority not merely from the viewpoint of beauty, sanctity, historical past, etc., but also from the vantage point of the law. Accordingly, the Tannaim put special effort in finding and creating laws and practices that would set Jerusalem apart from all the other cities of the land. As a consequence, we find that *halakhot* are being used in the same way as *aggadot*.[5]

Finally, a recent study by S. Safrai presents a more balanced view. Regarding the four lists, he admits that "it is not unlikely that some items were not traditions from the time of the Temple, but only imaginary creations . . . that developed after the destruction of the Temple." He then proceeds to examine four specific laws and to show, through careful analysis of rabbinic sources, Apocrypha, Josephus, and the Dead Sea scrolls, that they were "actually practiced in Jerusalem during the time of the Second Temple, or at least . . . reflect the reality of the time."[6] Safrai's approach to these laws and customs is, no doubt, the correct one. We should neither take them at face value nor reject them *in toto* as apocryphal. Rather, we should critically examine each custom using rabbinic and external sources in order to see whether it could be dated to Second Temple Jerusalem.

Post-Destruction Laws and Customs to Commemorate Jerusalem and Its Destruction

The second category consists of at least twenty-five laws and customs observed by many, and sometimes all, Jewish communities throughout the world for hundreds and even thousands of years in order to remember Jerusalem. These customs have yet to be examined in a critical fashion.[7] They can be conveniently divided into five categories: (a) wedding customs; (b) funerary customs; (c) prayer customs; (d) fast days; and (e) general mourning customs observed throughout the year.

a) *Wedding Customs*
   1) Rabbi Yom-Tov Lippman Heller (Moravia and Poland, 1579–1654) was the first to mention breaking a plate at the *tena'im* or *knassmahl* (engagement ceremony) "as a reminder of the destruction of the Temple of Jerusalem."[8] This is no doubt a late explanation for a universal tendency to frighten away demons on happy occasions,[9] but it shows that Jews frequently associated such customs with the destruction of the Temple.
   2) The *ḥassidim* developed a custom of writing in their *tena'im* or engagement contracts as follows:
      The wedding will, God willing, take place in the Holy City of Jerusalem. But if, Heaven forbid, because of our sins, the Messiah will not have come by then, the wedding will take place in Berdichev.[10]
      Today, some Jews write similar phrases in their wedding invitations.
   3) We read in the Babylonian Talmud (Bava Batra 60b):
      What does the verse mean "I shall place Jerusalem *at the head* of my greatest joy" (Ps. 137:5)? Said Rabbi Isaac (third century, Eretz-Israel): "these are the ashes from the hearth which we place *on the head* of the groom."
      This custom was not only codified by the major codes of Jewish law, but we know that it was actually observed by various Jewish communities until the twentieth century.[11]

4) In addition, the verse "If I forget thee Jerusalem" alluded to above is recited at many Jewish weddings today. This custom is first mentioned by Rabbi David Halevi (Poland, 1586–1667) in his commentary to the Shulḥan Arukh.[12]

5) In as early as fourteenth-century Germany, and especially in Italy, brides would wear large, ornate rings in addition to their actual wedding ring. These rings were frequently crowned with an ornate building. I. Abrahams, A. Wolf, and D. Sperber maintain that these buildings represent the Temple in Jerusalem so that the bride, too, should remember the Holy City on her wedding day.[13]

6) Finally, the most well-known wedding custom associated with Jerusalem is that of breaking a glass at weddings. The custom itself is mentioned in the Babylonian Talmud (Berakhot 31a) and is undoubtedly an attempt to ward off demons, as explained above. Nonetheless, by the fourteenth century, it was already explained as a way of remembering the destruction, and this is the explanation that has survived until today.[14]

b) *Funerary Customs*

1) I. Gafni has shown that Diaspora Jews began to be buried in Israel in the third century because they believed that this practice atones for one's sins and that those buried in Israel will be the first to be resurrected.[15] It is clear that Jews held the same beliefs with regard to Jerusalem, and especially about the Mount of Olives where the resurrection was supposed to begin.[16] Thus, it is not surprising that many Diaspora Jews made 'aliyah to Jerusalem in their old age in order to die and be buried there, while many others were brought to Jerusalem for burial after their deaths.[17]

2) Other Jews were not buried *in* Jerusalem, but were buried with their feet *pointing toward* Jerusalem, so that when the resurrection occurs, they will be ready to stand up and walk toward the Holy City. This custom is already mentioned by R. Abraham, the son of Maimonides, who opposes it because it is an imitation of the Muslim custom of being buried toward Mecca.[18] It is also mentioned by R. Moshe Sofer (Hungary, 1763–1839) and other rabbis, and it is still the practice in Israel today.[19]

3) It is a widespread custom to comfort mourners both in the *shurah* (double line) at the cemetery and at the house of mourning with the expression: "May God comfort you among the other mourners for Zion and Jerusalem." It is difficult to trace the exact origin of this phrase, but similar words of comfort were already used by R. Jacob

Moellin in Mainz (d. 1427) and by the Carmi family in Cremona, Italy (ca. 1572).[20]

c) *Prayer Customs*

Aside from the frequent mention of Jerusalem in liturgy,[21] there are a number of prayer customs associated with Jerusalem:

1) The book of Daniel (6:11) indicates that Diaspora Jews used to face Jerusalem in prayer in the second century B.C.E. An oft-repeated *baraita* states that Jews all over the world face Jerusalem, while Jews in Jerusalem face the Holy of Holies.[22] Though the archaeological evidence is mixed, most ancient synagogues also faced Jerusalem.[23] In any case, this was the practice codified in Jewish Law and is the universal practice until today.[24]

2) A corollary of this custom is that the doors or windows in a person's home should face Jerusalem so that he can pray through them. This law is based on a literal reading of the above-mentioned verse from Daniel.[25]

3) R. Meir of Rothenberg (Germany, d. 1293) would bow toward Jerusalem every time he mentioned the word Jerusalem in the Grace after Meals.[26]

d) *Fast Days*

1) Shortly after the destruction of the First Temple in 586 B.C.E., Jews began fasting on the Third of Tishri, the Tenth of Tevet, the Seventeenth of Tammuz, and the Ninth of Av in order to commemorate specific events related to the destruction.[27]

2) The days preceding the Ninth of Av were observed as days of mourning, when haircutting, laundering, betrothals, and marriages were forbidden. In the course of the centuries, the number of prohibitions was gradually expanded to include eating meat and drinking wine, and the period of mourning was extended by many to the three weeks between the Seventeenth of Tammuz and the Ninth of Av.[28]

3) According to rabbinic tradition (M Ta'anit 4:6 and B Ta'anit 29a), both Temples were destroyed on the Ninth of Av. On that day every year, Jews throughout the world abstained not only from food, but also from bathing, anointing oneself, wearing leather shoes, and conjugal relations. They recited the book of Lamentations at night and special *qinot* or elegies during the day while sitting on the ground.[29]

4) Specific Jewish communities added additional mourning customs, such as placing ashes on their foreheads, wrapping the Torah scrolls in black, and announcing the number of years that had passed since the destruction of the Second Temple.[30]

e) *General Mourning Customs*

In addition to the customs described above, which were attached to specific life-cycle events or days of the year, there are a number of general mourning customs which were observed throughout the year.

1) The Mishnah (Sotah 9:11) states:

> When the Sanhedrin ceased [judging capital cases a number of years before the destruction], singing ceased at wedding feasts, as it is written: "They shall not drink wine with a song" (Isa. 24:9).

This prohibition went through many permutations over the centuries, but the general trend was to allow sacred music while prohibiting secular music. Indeed, the latter type of music is prohibited by some Orthodox rabbis until today.[31]

2) A much rarer mourning custom is related by R. Yoel Sirkes (Poland, 1561–1640) in the name of *Sefer Ha'eshkol* (by R. Abraham ben Isaac, Provence, d. 1159):

> If you hear the sound of gentiles dancing and playing flutes and rejoicing, sigh and say: "Master of the universe, Your people whom you took out of Egypt have sinned doubly and been punished doubly . . . You have destroyed their palaces, You have stopped their joy . . . You have cast down their glory from the Heavens to the earth . . . Oh God, do not be angry at us forever . . . May it be Your will that you build Jerusalem Your holy city speedily in our day, Amen."[32]

3) We learn in a *baraita* that after the destruction of the Second Temple, there were many ascetics who refused to eat meat and drink wine, since they were no longer offered in the Temple. Rabbi Joshua scolded them, saying that by that logic we can no longer eat bread, figs, and grapes nor drink water because they, too, were offered in the Temple!

> He said to them: My sons, to mourn too much is impossible and not to mourn is impossible. Rather, thus said the sages: a person plasters his house and leaves a small section unplastered in memory of Jerusalem. A person prepares a feast and leaves a little bit out in memory of Jerusalem. A woman makes jewelry and leaves a small item out in memory of Jerusalem, as it is written (Ps. 137: 5–6): "If I forget thee Jerusalem, may my right hand forget its cunning". . . .[33]

This *baraita* was quoted by the Bavli and standard codes of Jewish law and its customs are still observed by some ultra-Orthodox Jews today.[34]

Post-Destruction Laws and Customs Observed
by Residents and Visitors in Jerusalem

The largest category we shall discuss consists of laws and customs observed by residents of Jerusalem and pilgrims visiting the city since the destruction. These customs, which have never been studied in a critical fashion, can be conveniently divided into five main categories: (a) laws and customs not unique to Jerusalem which reflect the fact that the city was a melting pot for Jews the worldover; (b) unique mourning customs over and above those mentioned above; (c) laws and customs which mimic specific laws and customs of Second Temple Jerusalem; (d) laws and customs which were intended to preserve the chastity of the city's inhabitants; (e) laws and customs which express the Jewish people's love for the city.

A word is in order here regarding the vast number of source used in this category. We rely on five types of sources: (1) bibliographies;[35] (2) Genizah fragments;[36] (3) responsa literature;[37] (4) the *taqqanot* of Jerusalem as well as other collections of local customs;[38] and (5) itineraries and letters from the tenth–twentieth centuries.[39] These latter documents are crucial because they enable us to compare the laws and customs *in theory* with eyewitness accounts of actual *practice*.

a) *Melting Pot Customs*

Rabbi Ḥizkiyah da Silva lived in Jerusalem for most of his adult life (from 1678–95). He stated that "in Jerusalem one must always follow the stricter custom *because all [of her inhabitants] are gathered [= le-kuta'e].*"[40]

This aspect of the laws and customs of Jerusalem is also reflected in a letter sent by Rabbi Yisrael Ashkenazi to his benefactor back home in Italy (ca. 1517–23):

> In the days of Rabbi Ovadiah [of Bertinoro, 1488–ca. 1516], [the prayer customs] were like that of the Jews of Israel . . . but now that the Spanish Jews have been added [due to the Expulsion of 1492] . . . they do as they please. And the cantors: there are three Spanish Jews and one from Israel *and each one of them does as he pleases*. One says the *qedushah* [which begins with] *keter yitnu lekhah*, and one says [*naqdishakh v'na'aritzakh*]. And there are variants in the *qedushah* itself. And there are many examples like this, one [cantor] adds and another detracts. . . ."[41]

Indeed, by far the largest number of laws and customs reflect the fact that Jerusalem was a melting pot for Jews from all over the world. Here is a random sampling of a few such customs:

1) Originally, the *qedushah* was only recited in Israel and Jerusalem on Shabbat or when the *mussaf* was recited. Pirkoi ben Baboi (ca. 800) reports how this custom was changed due to the influence of Babylonian immigrants:

    Until now they do not say [the *qedushah* which includes the *Shema*] in Eretz-Israel except on Shabbat and festivals and only in *Shaharit*, except in Jerusalem and in every city containing Babylonians who caused controversy until [the Palestinian Jews] took upon themselves to recite the *qedushah* every day. But in the other cities and towns of Eretz-Israel which do not contain Babylonians, they do not recite [the *qedushah*] except on Shabbat and festivals.[42]

2) Jumping forward almost a millennium to the *taqqanot* of 1730, we are told that "a betrothed man may not see his fiancée until the night of the wedding," so as to prevent the latter from becoming pregnant before the wedding day. However, upon investigation one discovers that the same *taqqanah* was enacted in Candia in 1228, in the Balkans ca. 1500, in Safed in the sixteenth century, and in Aleppo.[43]

3) When R. Joseph Schwartz arrived in Jerusalem from Germany in 1837, he reported to his brother back home that bridegrooms in Jerusalem read a special portion from the Torah (Gen. 24:1–8) on the Shabbat after their wedding.[44] Yet, in fact, this custom is not indigenous to Jerusalem. It is mentioned in various forms by Rav Sa'adia Gaon (Babylon, tenth century), R. Judah Al-Bargeloni (Spain, eleventh century), R. Nathan ben Yehiel (Rome, eleventh century), Rabbenu Bahya (Saragossa, thirteenth century), R. David Abudraham (Seville, fourteenth century), and the Rashbatz (Algiers, fifteenth century), and is observed by some Oriental Jews until today.[45]

4) Finally, it is stated in the *taqqanot* of Jerusalem of 1883: "It is the custom in the Holy City of Jerusalem, may she be rebuilt, to recite the *tahanun* (a prayer of supplication) even in a place which has no Torah scroll." [46] Yet, investigation reveals that this custom did not originate in Jerusalem, but was, rather, a widespread Sephardic custom following the opinion of R. Joseph Karo.[47]

Thus, a large percentage of the laws and customs of Jerusalem were imported by immigrants from elsewhere and reflect the fact that the city was a melting pot for Jews from all over the world.

b) *Mourning Customs Over and Above Those Practiced Elsewhere*

In addition to the mourning customs described above, pilgrims and natives of Jerusalem observed a number of mourning customs which stemmed from their proximity to the Temple Mount and its ruins:

1) A *baraita* in the Babylonian Talmud (Mo'ed Qatan 26a) rules that one must tear one's garments upon seeing the cities of Judaea, Jerusalem, and the Temple in ruins.[48] R. El'azar adds that one recites a special verse (Isa. 64:9–10) for each type of ruin. This law was not merely codified by the major codes of Jewish law; we know from travelers' itineraries that it was actually practiced by visitors to Jerusalem ca. 100, 1210, ca. 1240, 1481, 1488, 1495, 1879 and 1888.[49] R. Ovadia of Bertinoro, for example, described the ceremony in his famous letter of 1488:

> And at a distance of three quarters of a mile . . . the blessed city was revealed to us . . . and there we rent our clothes as required. And when we continued a bit more, our ruined holy and glorious House was revealed to us and we rent our garments a second time for the Temple. . . . [50]

2) The Itinerary of the Bordeaux Pilgrim, written by an anonymous Christian pilgrim in 333 C.E., contains an oft-quoted description of the observance of the Ninth of Av in Jerusalem at that time:

> These are two statues of Hadrian, and not far from the statues there is a perforated stone to which the Jews come every year and anoint it, bewail themselves with groans, rend their garments, and so depart.[51]

Jerome (ca. 386–420) gives a similar description of Jews mourning in Jerusalem in sackcloth on the Ninth of Av.[52]

3) The *Aveilei Tziyyon* or "Mourners of Zion" lived in Jerusalem and elsewhere from ca. 850–1173. They are variously referred to as "mourners of": "Zion, His glorious height, the Eternal House, the Temple and the Tabernacles, Jerusalem, and Zion and Jerusalem." The sources report that they "desired the Redemption morning, noon and night," "sigh and groan and await the Redemption and mourn for Jerusalem," and that they "do not eat meat or drink wine and they wear black . . . and they fast . . . and they ask for mercy before God." Finally, they composed and recited special poems and elegies for Jerusalem and the Temple.

Since the *Aveilei Tziyyon* are mentioned in both rabbinic and Karaite sources during the same period of time and in very similar language,[53] there is much disagreement as to the makeup of the group. J. Mann and S. Poznanski maintain that they were originally a group of Rabbanites, and when the Karaites came to Jerusalem in the early ninth century they adopted their behavior. M. Zucker, on the other hand, maintains that the rabbinic sources are referring to the Karaite *Aveilei Tziyyon.*[54] This is not the place to settle this disagreement. Suffice it to say that *Aveilei Tziyyon*—Rabbanite and/or Karaite—mourned for the Temple from the ninth to twelfth centuries.[55]

4) Since the 1860s, many of the ultra-Orthodox Jews of Jerusalem prohibit the use of instrumental music even at weddings. This prohibition is attributed to Rabbi Meir Auerbach (1815–78), one of the leading Ashkenazic rabbis in Jerusalem, or to the saintly Rabbi Naḥum Shadik (1813–66). A. M. Luncz says it was enacted because the men and the musicians looked at the women, but today it is explained as a sign of mourning for the destruction. Ultra-Orthodox Jews circumvent this prohibition by holding their weddings at Moshav Orah outside the city limits or by using singers who accompany themselves on drums.[56]

c) *Laws and Customs which Mimic Those of the Second Temple*
   Given the fact that the ruins of the Second Temple are located in Jerusalem, it is not surprising that the Jews of the city developed some laws and customs aimed at imitating laws and customs of the Second Temple.
   1) Rabbi Yaʿakov Hagiz, who lived in Jerusalem between 1648 and 1664, relates:

   > It is a good thing that which is customary here in Jerusalem our holy city, may she be rebuilt, that every Shabbat there is a person who [pays for] lighting the candles in the synagogue . . . . That Shabbat is a holiday for him, and his friends and relatives have ʿaliyot. It seems that they derived this custom from the wood offering.[57]

   The "wood offering" (Neh. 10:35; 13:31 and M Taʿanit 4:4–5) consisted of wood donated to the Temple for use on the altar nine times a year by nine different families, and the day of donation was celebrated by the donors as a holiday. R. Hagiz said that the families in his day who rejoiced on the day on which they donated oil to the synagogue were imitating "the wood offering" of Second Temple days.
   2) M Rosh Hashanah 4:1 relates that when Rosh Hashanah fell on Shabbat, the shofar was blown only in the *miqdash*—meaning the Temple or Jerusalem—and not elsewhere.[58] After the destruction, Rabban Yoḥanan ben Zakkai decreed that the shofar could be blown

on Shabbat wherever there was a *bet din.* Yet, in actuality, this seems to have only occurred in Yavneh, in Eretz-Israel during the geonic period, and in a few specific cities in the Diaspora.[59] In 1881, and again in 1904–1905, Rosh Hashanah fell on Shabbat and Rabbi Akiva Yosef Schlesinger tried to revive the Second Temple custom of blowing the shofar in Jerusalem on Shabbat. Some of his rabbinic colleagues were in favor yet were afraid to say so publicly, but it appears that he did indeed blow the shofar on Shabbat following the practice of Second Temple Jerusalem.[60]

3) The classic list of the laws of Second Temple Jerusalem mentioned above states that "one does not allow a dead body to remain there overnight,"[61] i.e., burial must be performed on the day of death or on that very night. This custom, which mimics Second Temple practice, is explicitly mentioned by five writers between 1837 and 1909[62] and is the accepted custom in Jerusalem until today.

4) The most impressive custom in this category of imitating the Temple is mentioned in eighteen primary sources written between 921-1330 C.E.[63] According to these sources, Jews would gather in large numbers on the Mount of Olives on the three pilgrim festivals, and especially on Hosha'nah Rabbah. They would begin by making a circuit around the gates of Jerusalem reciting special prayers and then ascend the Mount of Olives. There they would perform seven *haqqafot* around a special sacred stone while reciting the traditional *Hosha'nah* poems. The priests would wear special clothing. The Gaon of Eretz-Israel would stand on the special stone and declare the dates of the festivals, bless the Diaspora Jews who had donated money to the Palestinian *yeshivot,* and excommunicate sinners such as the Karaites. It is difficult to reconstruct all of the elements of this fascinating ceremony, but it is clear that during the tenth and eleventh centuries the Mount of Olives became a surrogate Temple Mount on which Jews imitated certain laws and customs of the Second Temple.[64]

d) *Laws and Customs Intended to Preserve the Chastity of the Jews of Jerusalem*
A number of the eighteenth-century *taqqanot* of Jerusalem were aimed at preserving a high level of chastity and sexual purity in the city. Only further study will reveal if such laws were limited to that period of time.

1) A *taqqanah* from 1730 rules that "no woman shall remain in the synagogue for the final *qaddish,* either at *Shaharit, Minhah,* or *Ma'ariv.*"[65] The obvious goal was to prevent men from looking at or mingling with the women after services.

2) A *taqqanah* from 1754 goes one step further and rules that "any woman who has not reached the age of forty may not come to the synagogue for *Minḥah* and *Maʿariv* on the Sabbath and weekdays, except for Rosh Hashanah, Yom Kippur and Simḥat Torah. . . ."[66]

3) As of 1798, we hear of a custom that any girl under the age of twelve may not be married within the city, but rather the wedding is held in a nearby village.[67] It was apparently considered unseemly to marry a girl under the age of twelve in the holy city of Jerusalem.

4) Lest we think that men escaped this trend, a *taqqanah* from 1749 rules that single men between the ages of twenty and sixty had to get married within four months. If not, they had to leave Jerusalem forthwith in order to seek a livelihood and a wife.[68]

e) *Laws and Customs which Express the Jewish People's Love for the City of Jerusalem*

The Jews of Jerusalem and Jewish pilgrims to the city developed various customs which expressed their love for the city in general, and for the Temple Mount and Western Wall in particular:

1) Beginning in the twelfth century, we hear of many customs associated with the Western Wall. Jews visiting the Wall would recite specific passages from the Bible and the Mishnah related to the Temple and the sacrifices,[69] as well as special prayers composed by well-known rabbis.[70]

2) R. Moshe Reisher reports in 1868 that:

it is the custom [in Jerusalem] to circle the city on Hol Hamoʿed— men, women, and children—in order to fulfill the verse (Ps. 48: 13): "Walk around Zion, circle it, count its towers" and this is an ancient custom.[71]

Conclusion

Jewish tradition has always stressed that Torah study and theory must be grounded in practice.[72] The Jewish attitude towards Jerusalem is in keeping with this approach. Love for the city of Jerusalem was not just studied in the Bible and Talmud and mentioned in the liturgy. It was expressed in the concrete form of laws and customs before the destruction, throughout the Diaspora after the destruction, and within the city from 70 C.E. until the present. We have not attempted to list all of these innumerable customs. Rather, we have presented a preliminary typology of the Jewish laws and customs of Jerusalem which will help future scholars deal with this vast corpus of material.

Notes

1. By "Jewish" we mean Pharisaic or rabbinic. On Jerusalem in the Dead Sea scrolls, see L. H. Schiffman, "Jerusalem in the Dead Sea Scrolls," *The Centrality of Jerusalem: Historical Perspectives*, eds. M. Poorthuis and Ch. Safrai (Kampen, 1996), 73–88; E. Qimron, "Chickens in the Temple Scroll (11 QTᶜ)," *Tarbiz* 64 (1995), 473–75 (Hebrew). Due to considerations of space, the references which follow are selective and not exhaustive.

2. For lists of these customs, see J. D. Eisenstein, ed., *Otzar Yisrael*, V (New York, 1907–13), 207–13, s.v. "Yerushalayim" (Hebrew); *EJ*, IX (Jerusalem, 1972), 1553–56, s.v. "Jerusalem"; I. Schepansky, "Taqqanot and Customs of Jerusalem," *Or Hamizrah* 31 (1983), 245–72 (Hebrew). They have been studied critically by S. Krauss, *Qadmoniyot HaTalmud*, I/1 (Berlin and Vienna, 1922), 92–113 (Hebrew); L. Finkelstein, "The Halakhoth Applied to Jerusalem," *Alexander Marx Jubilee Volume*, ed. S. Lieberman (New York, 1950), Hebrew section, 351–69; S. Bialoblocki, "Jerusalem in the Halakhah," *Alei Ayin: Essays Presented to Shlomo Zalmen Schocken* (Jerusalem, 1948–52), 25–46 (Hebrew); A. Guttmann, "Some Aspects of Theoretical Halakhot," *Fifth World Congress of Jewish Studies*, III (Jerusalem, 1972), 67–79 (Hebrew); idem, "Jerusalem in Tannaitic Law," *HUCA* 40–41 (1969–70), 251–75; T. Kahana, "Towards an Understanding of the Baraita about the Laws of Jerusalem," *Bet Mikra* 21 (1976), 182–92 (Hebrew); S. Safrai, "Jerusalem in the Halacha of the Second Temple Period," *The Centrality of Jerusalem* (above, note 1), 94–113.

3. T Negaʿim 6:2 (ed. Zuckermandel [Jerusalem, 1937], 625); ARN, A, Chap. 35 (ed. Schechter [New York, 1945], 104); ibid., B, Chap. 39 (107); B Bava Qama 82b.

4. For example, the regulations regarding gardens, dunghills, and chickens seem to be contradicted by T Bava Qamma 8:10 (ed. Lieberman [New York, 1955–88], 38–39); M Maʿaserot 2:5; and M Bava Qama 7:7.

5. Guttmann, "Jerusalem in Tannaitic Law" (above, note 2), 269 and 274.

6. Safrai (above, note 2), 95. See, for example, his discussion on sounding the shofar and waving the lulav, ibid., 108–113.

7. See, for example, Y. Z. Kahana, *Studies in the Responsa Literature* (Jerusalem, 1973), 436–38 (Hebrew); A. Bloch, *The Biblical and Historical Background of Jewish Customs and Ceremonies* (New York, 1980), 372–75; and Y. Schwartz, *Aveilut Hahurban* (Jerusalem, 1984) 57–105 (Hebrew).

8. J. Z. Lauterbach, "The Ceremony of Breaking a Glass at Weddings," *HUCA* 2 (1925), 375 and note 36.

9. Ibid.

10. R. Charif and S. Raz (eds.), *Jerusalem: the Eternal Bond* (Tel-Aviv, 1977), 70.

11. Maimonides, Taʿaniyot 5:13; Shulhan Arukh, Orah Hayyim 560:2 and Even Haʿezer 65:3; J. Kafih, *Jewish Life in Sanaʾ* (Jerusalem, 1982), 139 (Hebrew); E. Guedj, *Zeh Hashulhan*, II (Algiers, 1889), para. 186 (Hebrew).

12. Magen David to Orah Hayyim 560, subpara. 4.

13. See D. Sperber, "These Candles," *Customs of Israel* (Jerusalem, 1995), IV, 143–49 (Hebrew) for earlier literature as well as illustrations.

14. The first two authorities to connect this custom to the destruction are: *Kol Bo*, Laws of Tisha Bʾav (Lvov, 1860), 25d; *Sefer Minhagim Dʾvei Maharam*, ed. Elfenbein (New York, 1938), 82 (Hebrew).

15. I. Gafni, "Bringing Deceased from Abroad for Burial in Eretz-Israel—On the Origin of the Custom and Its Development," *Cathedra* 4 (1977), 113–20 (Hebrew).

16. For this belief, see, for example, Pesiqta Rabbati 31 (ed. Friedmann [Tel-Aviv, 1963], 147a; Maʿaseh Daniel (Midreshei Geʾulah, ed. Even-Shmuel [Tel Aviv, 1943], 225).

17. See, for example, B. Klar, *Megillat Ahimaaz* (Jerusalem, 1974), 37 (Hebrew); J. Mann,

The Jews in Egypt and Palestine Under the Fatamid Caliphs, I (London, 1920), 165–66; II (London, 1922), 191; M. Gil, *Palestine During the First Muslim Period (634–1099),* I (Tel Aviv, 1983), 517–18 (Hebrew); I. Schepansky, *Eretz Israel in the Responsa Literature,* I (Jerusalem, 1966), 189–92, 433–40 (Hebrew).

18. N. Wieder, *Islamic Influences on Jewish Worship* (Oxford, 1947), 73 (Hebrew).

19. *Responsa Ḥatam Sofer,* Yoreh Deah, no. 332 (Hebrew); Y. Y. Greenwald, *Kol Bo Al Aveilut* (Jerusalem and New York, 1973), 177–78 (Hebrew); Y. M. Tukichinsky, *Gesher ḥayim²,* I (Jerusalem, 1960), 138 (Hebrew).

20. S. Glick, *Light and Consolation: The Development of Jewish Customs of Consolation Following Bereavement* (Efrat, 1993), 35, 149 (Hebrew).

21. See the contribution of S. Reif in this volume.

22. T Berakhot 3:15–16 (ed. Lieberman, 15–16) and parallels.

23. F. Landsberger, "The Sacred Direction in Synagogue and Church," *HUCA* 28 (1957), 181–203; M. Chiat, *Handbook of Synagogue Architecture* (Chico, 1982), 338; J. Wilkinson, "Orientation, Jewish and Christian," *PEQ* 116 (1984), 16–34.

24. Maimonides, Tefillah 5:3; Oraḥ Ḥayyim 94:1.

25. B Berakhot 31a; Maimonides, Tefillah 5:6; Oraḥ Ḥayyim 90:4.

26. I. Z. Kahana (ed.), *Rabbi Meir Ben Barukh (Maharam) of Rottenberg: Responsa, Rulings, and Customs,* I (Jerusalem, 1957), 194, no. 152 (Hebrew).

27. Zech. 7:1–8:19; M. Taʿanit 4:6; D. Golinkin, "Fasting Until after Minḥa on the Ninth of Av," *Responsa of the Vaʾad Halakhah of the Rabbinical Assembly of Israel,* I (Jerusalem, 1986), 29–34 (Hebrew).

28. M Taʿanit 4:7; B Yevamot 43b; Y. Gartner, *The Evolvement of Customs in the World of Halacha* (Jerusalem, 1995), 9–49 (Hebrew).

29. See Oraḥ Ḥayyim 549–59 for the many laws and customs of the Ninth of Av.

30. A. Yaʿari, *Letters from the Land of Israel* (Ramat Gan, 1971), 372 (Hebrew); M. Reisher, *Shaʿarei Yerushalayim* (Lemberg, 1869), 49b (Hebrew); Y. Gellis, *Minhagei Eretz Israel* (Jerusalem, 1968), 159, 161 (Hebrew).

31. See B. Cohen, *Law and Tradition in Judaism²* (New York, 1969), 167–81 for a good historical survey; and M. Feinstein, *Igrot Moshe,* Oraḥ Ḥayyim, I (New York, 1959), no. 166 (Hebrew) for an Orthodox responsum.

32. Bayyit Ḥadash to Tur Oraḥ Ḥayyim 224, s.v. *misefer haʾeshkol.* I have yet to locate the primary source.

33. T Sotah 15:11–12 (ed. Lieberman, 243–44) and cf. the parallels listed there.

34. Maimonides, Taʿaniyot 5:12–15; Oraḥ Ḥayyim 560; and Schwartz (above, note 7), 69–76.

35. M. Rapeld and Y. Tabori, "The Custom—Its Offshoots and Research: A Bibliography," *Customs of Israel* (above, note 13), V, 242–44; *Jerusalem through the Generations: A Bibliographical List* (Jerusalem, 1993), 53 (Hebrew). My thanks to Dr. David Segal for the latter reference.

36. See, for example, A. Harkavy and A. Berliner, in *Magazin für die Wissenschaft des Judenthums* 3 (1876), 217; 4 (1877), 233–34; and in the Hebrew supplement idem, "A Letter from Jerusalem," *Otzar Tov* 1 (1878), 77–81; Mann (above, note 17) and Gil (above, note 17).

37. See Kahana (above, note 7) and Schepansky (above, note 17).

38. For the *taqqanot* of Jerusalem, see I. Badhab, *Kovetz Hayerushalmi,* I (1930); III (1931) (Hebrew); M. Benayahu, "Books of Taqqanot and Customs of Jerusalem," *Kiryat Sefer* 22 (1946), 262–65 (Hebrew); and A. H. Freimann, "Taqqanot of Jerusalem," *Sefer Dinaburg,* eds. Y. Baer, J. Guttmann, and M. Schwabe (Jerusalem, 1949), 206–14 (Hebrew). For the customs of Jerusalem, see, for example, Reisher (above, note 30); Refael Aharon ibn Shimon, *Shaʿar Hamifqad,* 2 vols. (Alexandria, 1908) (Hebrew); Amram Aburbia, *Netivei Am²* (Tel-Aviv, 1969) (Hebrew); and Schepansky (above, note 2), 245–79.

39. J. D. Eisenstein, *Ozar Massaoth* (New York, 1926) (Hebrew); E. N. Adler, *Jewish Travellers in the Middle Ages* (London, 1930); and Yaʿari (above, note 30).

40. Peri Ḥadash to Oraḥ Ḥayyim 496, subpara. 2, no. 22.

41. A. David (ed.), "The Letter of R. Israel Ashkenazi to R. Abraham of Perugia," *Alei Sefer* 16 (1990), 110–11 (Hebrew) along with a correction by J. Borstein, "Comments on 'The Letter of R. Israel Ashkenazi of Jerusalem'," ibid., 18 (1996), 181 (Hebrew).

42. L. Ginzberg, *Geonica*, II (New York, 1909), 52 (Hebrew) = idem, *Geniza Studies*, II (New York, 1929), 555–56 (Hebrew).

43. Freimann (above, note 38), 209, 213.

44. Yaʿari (above, note 30), 372.

45. N. Wieder, "Addenda and Errata to Seder Rav Saadya Gaon," *Sefer Assaf*, eds. U. Cassuto et al. (Jerusalem, 1953), 246–49, 254, 260 (Hebrew); S. Assaf (ed.), *Misifrut Hageʾonim* (Jerusalem, 1933), 141–49 (Hebrew); A. Kohut (ed.), *Sefer Arukh Completum*, 8 vols. (New York, 1955), s.v. *ḥattan* (Hebrew); *Sefer Haʿittim* (Cracow, 1903), 278–79 (Hebrew); Rabbeinu Baḥya to Gen. 24:3; *Abudraham Hashalem* (Jerusalem, 1959), 365 (Hebrew); *Sefer Hatashbatz* (Lemberg, 1858), II, no. 39 (Hebrew); R. Shemtob Gaugine, *Keter Shem Tob* (Kaidan, 1934), 300–302 (Hebrew).

46. Badhab (above, note 38), I, 11, para. 9 (Hebrew).

47. Bet Yosef to Oraḥ Ḥayyim 131; Birkei Yosef, ibid.; Kaf Haḥayyim, ibid.; Gaugine (above, note 45), 78; Gellis (above, note 30), 48–49.

48. For parallel yet different traditions, see Tractate Semaḥot 9:19 (ed. Higger [reprint Jerusalem, 1970], 175–76) and Y Moʿed Qatan 3, 7, 83b–c.

49. The codes of Naḥmanides are quoted by Maggid Mishneh to Maimonides, Taʿaniyot 5:16; Rosh to Moʿed Qatan, Chapter 3, para. 64; Oraḥ Ḥayyim 561; and Yoreh Deʿah 340: 38. For actual testimonies, see: Sifre–Deuteronomy 43 (ed. Finkelstein [New York, 1969], 95) and parallels; Yaʿari (above, note 30), 78, 127, 155, 481–82; Eisenstein (above, note 39), 66–67, 99; and R. Hammer, *The Jerusalem Anthology: A Literary Guide* (Philadelphia and Jerusalem, 1995), 227.

50. Yaʿari (above, note 30), 127.

51. A. Stewart and C. W. Wilson (eds.), *Itinerary from Bordeaux to Jerusalem* (London, 1896), 21–22.

52. In his commentary to Zeph. 1:15ff., translated into Hebrew by Gil (above, note 17), 57.

53. The rabbinic sources are: the special Grace after Meals for the house of mourning which is first found in Halakhot Kezuvot (ed. M. Margaliot [Jerusalem, 1942], 146) and Seder Rav Amram Gaon (ed. D. Goldschmidt [Jerusalem, 1971], 188)—both ca. 850; Derekh Eretz Rabbah 2 (ed. M. Higger, II [reprint Jerusalem, 1970], 287–88)—date unknown; Pesiqta Rabbati 34 (ed. M. Friedmann, 158a–b)—ca. 850; Megillat Aḥimaaz (ed. B. Klar [Jerusalem, 1974], 14, 35, 37)—ca. 850, 970, and 1000; *The Itinerary of Benjamin of Tudela* (ed. M. N. Adler [London, 1907], 26, 47)—ca. 1173. The Karaite sources are: Daniel Alkumisi (late ninth cent.), Salman ben Yeruḥam and al-Kirkisani (early tenth cent.); Sahal ben Mazliaḥ (late tenth cent.), and Yefet ben Ali (d. after 1005)—all of whom are quoted by Gil (above, note 17), 58, 507–508.

54. Mann (above, note 17), 47–49, 61; S. Poznanski, *Yerushalayim* 10 (1914), 90–91 (Hebrew); M. Zucker, "Reactions to the Karaite *Aveilei Zion* Movement in Rabbinic Literature," *Jubilee Volume to Rabbi Hanoch Albeck* (Jerusalem, 1963), 378–401 (Hebrew). For more recent discussions, see Y. Gartner (above, note 28), 15–49; H. Ben-Shammai, "Poetic Works and Lamentations of Qaraite 'Mourners of Zion'—Structure and Contents," *Knesset Ezra: Studies Presented to Ezra Fleischer*, eds. S. Elizur et al. (Jerusalem, 1994), 191–234 (Hebrew).

55. For some late remnants of this type of custom, see Yaʿari (above, note 30), 164–65; Y. Y. Yehudah, "The Western Wall," *Zion* 3 (1929), 142 (Hebrew).

56. Reisher (above, note 30), 49a; A. M. Luncz, *Yerushalayim*, I (Jerusalem, 1882; reprint Tel-Aviv, 1969), 9 and note 21 (Hebrew); E. Cohen-Reiss, *Memories of a Jerusalemite* (Tel Aviv, 1933), 60–61 (Hebrew); B. Yadler, *B'tuv Yerushalayim* (Bnei Brak, 1967), 348 (Hebrew); E. Waldenberg, *Responsa Tzitz Eliezer*, XV, no. 33, para. 3 (Hebrew); P. Kidron, *In Jerusalem* (Dec. 12, 1986), 18; Y. Mazor and M. Taube, "A Hassidic Ritual Dance: The "Mitsve tants" in Jerusalemite Weddings," *Yuval* 6 (1994), 165. My thanks to Yaacov Mazor of the Jewish Music Research Center of the Hebrew University for a few of these references.

57. Responsa Halakhot Ketanot, II, no. 90 (Hebrew) quoted by Schepansky (above, note 2), 275–76.

58. In rabbinic literature, *miqdash* can refer to either the Temple or the city of Jerusalem. See M. Zipser, "The Virtue and the Sanctity of Jerusalem according to the Opinion of the Sages, the Great Commentators and the Halakhic Authorities," *Kevutzat Hakhamim* (1861), 1–5 (Hebrew); H. Albeck, *Six Orders of the Mishnah*, 6 vols. (Jerusalem and Tel Aviv, 1959), II, 489–90 (Hebrew).

59. B Rosh Hashanah 29b; M. D. Herr, "Matters of Palestinian Halakha during the Sixth and Seventh Centuries C.E.," *Tarbiz* 49 (1979-80), 78 (Hebrew); E. Fleischer, "A Piyyut Describing the Blowing of the Shofar on Rosh ha-Shana and Shabbat," *Tarbiz* 54 (1984), 61–66 (Hebrew); L. Moscovitz, "On Sounding the Shofar in the High Court of Palestine on Shabbat Rosh Hashana," *Tarbiz* 55 (1986), 608–12 (Hebrew); Naḥmanides in H. D. Chavel (ed.), *The Writings of Nachmanides*, I (Jerusalem, 1963), 245 (Hebrew); Rabbeinu Manoah to the Rambam, Shofar 2:9; T. Preschel, "Blowing the Shofar in the Palestinian Yeshivah," *Sinai* 58 (1965), 102–103 (Hebrew).

60. S. Hacohen Weingarten, "The Geonim of Jerusalem and the Blowing of the Shofar on Rosh Hashanah Holiday that Falls on Shabbat," *Sinai* 25 (1949), 337–39 (Hebrew); Y. M. Tukichinsky, *The Holy City and the Temple*, III (Jerusalem, 1969), 283–91 (Hebrew).

61. Bava Qama 82b and cf. the parallels cited above, note 3.

62. Ya'ari (above, note 30), 372; E. Cohen-Reiss (above, note 56), 56; Luncz (above, note 56), 12; Tuckichinsky (above, note 19), 88.

63. Lack of space prevents me from listing the primary sources. This custom has been discussed by over forty scholars, beginning with the publication of the first Genizah fragment by Harkavy and Berliner (above, note 36). The most recent discussions are those of E. Reiner: "Concerning the Priest Gate and Its Location," *Tarbiz* 56 (1986), 279–90 (Hebrew); "Pilgrimage to Jerusalem in the Middle Ages," *Moreshet Derekh* 12 (Dec.-Jan. 1986), 7–12 (Hebrew); and in his doctoral dissertation: "Immigration and Pilgrimage to Eretz Israel 1099–1517" (Hebrew University of Jerusalem, 1988), 179–98 (Hebrew), which was reprinted without footnotes in *Ariel* 83–84 (Feb. 1992), 220–35 (Hebrew).

64. For some of the Second Temple parallels, see M Sukkah 4:5; B Sanhedrin 11a; and Barukh 1:10–14. (My thanks to Prof. Martin Goodman for the last reference).

65. Freimann (above, note 38), 208, 210.

66. Badhab (above, note 38), III, 52b.

67. Schepansky (above, note 2), 269, note 136.

68. Badhab (above, note 38), III, 51b–52a.

69. Yehudah (above, note 55), 135, 136, 140, 141.

70. See, for example, R. Ishtori Haparḥi, *Kaftor Vaferaḥ*, ed. A. M. Luncz (Jerusalem, 1897), 114 (Hebrew).

71. Reisher (above, note 30), 47b.

72. See, for example, M Avot 4:5; ARN, A, Chap. 24 (ed. Schechter, 78); Sifre–Deuteronomy 48 (ed. Finkelstein, 113); Leviticus Rabbah 35:7 (ed. Margaliot [Jerusalem, 1953–60], 826) and parallels.

29

Jerusalem in Jewish Liturgy

STEFAN C. REIF

There can be little doubt that Jerusalem occupies an honored place in the
medley of religious ideas formulated and transmitted by Jewish circles
through countless generations. Equally incontrovertible is the notion that liturgy has, during those many centuries, functioned as a central medium for the
expression of Judaism's most cherished principles of faith and practice. In the
words of the late A. M. Habermann, "the mention of Jerusalem was obligatory
in all the statutory prayers."[1] It therefore follows that any characteristic selection of Hebrew literature should include significant examples of the occurrence
of Jerusalem in liturgical texts. The fact is, however, that an examination of
R. Hammer's recently-published volume, *The Jerusalem Anthology: A Literary
Guide*, fails to support such a presupposition. In what is a useful and extensive
volume, all manner of works, of diverse content and from numerous periods,
are cited for their remarks about the City of David, but there is only one
minor reference to the standard rabbinic prayerbook.[2] It seems to me that this
by no means represents an oversight on the part of the learned author but is,
rather, a reflection of a basic problem in the study of Jewish liturgy which is
singularly relevant to any treatment of the subject in hand. As such, it deserves
some attention at the beginning of this paper.

If it is assumed, as the structure and content of the conference in which
this contribution is being offered justify us in assuming, that the liturgical role
of Jerusalem in biblical, apocryphal, qumranic, Christian, and Muslim texts is
being dealt with in different contexts, what remains to be examined here is
the theme as it occurs in rabbinic prayer-texts. If one was of a mind to do so,
one could simply take the traditional *siddur* of any of the major rites, before
the substantial revisions of the modern period, and summarize the cases in
which Jerusalem makes an appearance. One would then have a comprehensive catalogue of texts that had been fairly standard for the best part of a

whole millennium but had also, by virtue of their very canonicity and ritual-ization, lost the link with their original incorporation. Since I regard my in-vitation to contribute to this important scholarly initiative as demanding more of me than the provision of a literary index, I feel obliged to complement what is here being offered by colleagues by tackling the subject of Jerusalem in the first rather than the second millennium of rabbinic liturgical history. It is then that one is likely to find the evidence that will prove so central to any under-standing of what Jews, Christians, and Muslims had in common and how they differed in their approaches to the Holy City. That is the period during which only two major rites appear to have existed, in Babylonia and the Land of Israel, and it predates both the widespread standardization based on the former rite and the subsequent renewal of ritual fractionization in both Europe and the Orient.[3] And here, in the formative era of rabbinic liturgy, one is con-fronted by precisely the problem that apparently faced Hammer; how can one place liturgical texts, which clearly had their origin in that wide span of time, in a particular geographical, chronological, or theological context?

That problem relates to the scientific use of liturgical texts from the talmudic-midrashic literature, from the geonic corpora, and from the earliest sources preserved in the Cairo Genizah. There are, of course, general difficul-ties in dealing with any material of such origins. There are undoubtedly oral and written stages; clear indications of provenance are rare; and traditions often appear isolated. The matter of dating, contextualizing and expounding the texts is consequently a challenging task. As far as liturgy is concerned, that task is made even more complicated by further considerations. To what extent may we assume that the text preserved in one generation precisely matches its format in an earlier one? Is there not a tendency to adjust versions to accom-modate them to current thought? When a scribe cites a prayer, might he not absentmindedly record what is familiar to him rather than what he is supposed to be transmitting? What is more, it is all too facile a solution to subscribe to the general principle that all short, simple Babylonian texts (from the Talmud, for example) represent the pristine form while all longer, more complex Pa-lestinian versions (from the Genizah, for example) may universally be judged to be later accretions. These and other difficulties have led scholars from the period of the *Wissenschaft des Judentums* until our own day to eschew the kind of detailed historical reconstruction of liturgical history that would explain what dictated many textual choices in favor of a less speculative approach that concentrates on an account of what these choices simply were.[4] As D. Rappel has, however, strongly contended, the theological history of rabbinic liturgy deserves no less attention than its text-critical analysis, since every variant carries with it a meaningful religious message of some sort.[5] How, then, shall we best proceed in attempting to meet both these needs in this brief and necessarily modest examination of the place of Jerusalem in the first few centuries of rabbinic liturgy?

I propose to examine a few of the major prayers (but not liturgical poems) that were incontrovertibly central to the rabbinic tradition. Some are documented in the talmudic and geonic sources and are representative of authoritative viewpoints, while others are found in the Genizah fragments and are often more indicative of less conformist trends. Each such examination will include a survey of the role that Jerusalem and closely-associated subjects play in the texts and a report on the nature of significant textual variations that relate directly to that role. I shall deliberately refrain from defining texts as specifically Babylonian or Palestinian in order not to confuse textual evidence with its assumed provenance nor unjustifiably restrict the interpretative possibilities. Some additional information of a similar nature will then be adduced about less prominent prayers. At that point, an effort will be made to summarize the various notions relating to Jerusalem that have been identified and to estimate their individual and overall significance in the realm of religious ideas. In the concluding section of the paper, I propose to offer some options that are available to historians in their analysis of the development and absorption of such ideas among the rabbinic Jews of the period. I am, however, aware that no more than the groundwork will by then have been completed and that the matter of historical reconstruction, speculative as it must remain at this stage of our knowledge, will await attention in another context.

A start may be made with a liturgical tradition that lays strong claim to be one of the earliest to be documented in the talmudic-midrashic literature. It describes a ritual that took place in the Temple on Yom Kippur and, given that it has no real parallels or equivalents in the post-Temple period to contaminate its textual purity, it may be regarded as a reliable testimony to an important list of theological priorities inherited by the rabbis. The beginning of the seventh chapter in the mishnaic tractate Yoma records that after the high priest had recited some relevant pentateuchal passages he pronounced eight benedictions—for the Torah, Temple-service (*'Avodah*), Thanksgiving, Forgiveness of Sin, Temple (*Miqdash*), Israel, Priests, and other (more general) matters.[6] The Tosefta identifies the first benediction as that familiar to us from synagogal (or, perhaps, academic) use; the next three as those included in the *'Amidah*; the fifth, sixth, and seventh as individual (unique perhaps?) benedictions; and the last as a special plea for the security of the Jewish people.[7] Further comment is provided in the talmudic tractates. The Palestinian Talmud cites the doxological conclusions for all the benedictions, and the ones that are of special interest to us in the present context are those for the Temple-service, Temple, and Priesthood. The latter two allude to God's special choice of these two institutions by the use of the phrases *ha-boḥer ba-miqdash* and *ha-boḥer ba-kohanim*, and to the awesome worship of God in the imperfect tense by the use of the phrase *she'otekha nira' ve-na'avod.* What is of special significance here is an alternative phraseology offered for the Temple. Instead of noting its Divine selection, the third-century Palestinian 'amora, Rabbi Idi, opts for a phrase about the Temple that refers to the Divine presence in Zion (*ha-shokhen beṣiyyon*).[8] Little is added to the discussion by the Babylonian Talmud, which merely cites (but not in the Munich manuscript) a tannaitic tradition virtually at one with that of the Tosefta.[9] What, then, of Jerusalem the city? Its only mention in this context is in variant texts of the Mishnah which cite it between Israel and the Priests and therefore create a textual problem by referring to nine, rather than eight items.[10]

Another liturgical phenomenon that is widely recognized as having had its origins in the pre-rabbinic period is the grace after meals. What remain more open questions are the degree to which its four benedictions are a revolutionary innovation of the tannaitic rabbis and whether each was appended to a basic text-form at a different point of development.[11] In this case, however, there is little difficulty in locating the context in which Jerusalem occurs, since the third benediction is devoted to that subject and its doxological conclusion is exclusively concerned with that city. The problem here is that, on approaching the sources emanating from the first Christian millennium, one is confronted with a wide variety of content. The closing benediction itself, if we include both the Sabbath and weekday versions, may refer simply to the building of Jerusalem, to the consolation of Zion through the building of Jerusalem, or to David's God and the building of Jerusalem.

Such complexity appears positively straightforward when compared with the situation regarding the subjects covered in the body of the benediction, according to a variety of textual and literary traditions.[12] It is obviously not possible in the present context to record all the variants, but if the briefest and most extensive lists are set side by side, then the purpose of indicating the range of content will have been well served. The simplest formulation would appear to have included a request for God's mercy to be shown to his people Israel, his city Jerusalem, his Temple (*hekhal, ma'on*), and, perhaps as early additions to such a formulation, to his glorious habitation Zion and to the Davidic dynasty. Some versions place an emphasis on the secure provision of food while others make a link between that subject and the main theme of the benediction by stressing that the worshipper's consumption of food and drink by no means indicates that he has forgotten the plight of Jerusalem and its need for restoration. In a number of texts, the theme of restoration is spelled out, in some cases after the benediction, with pleas for some or all of the developments that are presupposed by references to the consolation of Zion, the building of Jerusalem, and the return there of God's presence and rule, as well as of the Davidic (= messianic) kingdom, the sacrificial system, and the Jewish population.

Given the fact that the fourteenth benediction of the daily *ʿAmidah* shares with the third benediction of the *Birkat ha-Mazon* (Grace after Meals) the central theme of Jerusalem, it is by no means surprising to find that they have in common many of the related topics found in the body of the text.[13] The major difference between them is that in the case of the *ʿAmidah* benediction there are two options, of sound talmudic pedigree, for the treatment of the restored kingdom of David. According to one, it appears as part of the Jerusalem benediction while, according to the other, it is treated in an independent benediction. Inevitably, there are indications of conflated versions and contamination by the text of the Grace after Meals, but three archetypal formulations stand at the center of most textual witnesses, as has recently been pointed out by Y. Luger.[14] The first of these, which is perhaps the closest to the simpler format recorded for the Grace, invokes God's mercy first on Israel his people, Jerusalem his city, and his Temple (*hekhal, miqdash, maʿon*), and then on his glorious habitation Zion; it then pleads for the building of an eternal Jerusalem and concludes with a doxology that refers to God as the builder of Jerusalem. In the second formulation, the messianic kingdom of David is added to the subjects of God's projected mercy which are again Israel, Jerusalem, and Zion, the last-mentioned appearing on its own, without any specific word for the Temple itself. That institution receives attention after the addendum referring to the Davidic kingdom, when a plea is made for the reconstruction of God's house and palace. Since the option to include the Davidic kingdom in the Jerusalem benediction is here being exercised, the doxology understandably describes the recipient of the prayer as the God of David and the builder of Jerusalem. The third archetypal formulation again has the simpler doxology on the one theme, as well as a plea for the building of an eternal Jerusalem, but any similarity with either of the other two formulations ends there. God is in simple terms kindly requested to return to his city of Jerusalem (or, according to a textual variant, make it his habitation), and there is no mention whatsoever of any of its other institutions.

In the context of his study of the talmudic origins of rabbinic liturgy, J. Heinemann helpfully points out that there are three other benedictions which use similar formulations in dealing with the topic of Jerusalem and which occur, respectively, in the service for the fast-day of the Ninth of Av, in the benedictions that follow the *hafṭarah*-reading, and in the benedictions that are

recited at a wedding feast. Although Heinemann's agenda is somewhat different from ours, and his comparative list of readings makes no distinction between the talmudic and geonic evidence on the one hand and the early
medieval sources on the other, a careful and eclectic use of the information he
compiled about these three liturgical items will be of considerable assistance
to us in the present context.[15]

The special prayer formulated in talmudic times for the Ninth of Av, and
inserted at some point in the ʿAmidah during one or all of the services to be
held on that day, is designed to make specific mention of the fate of Jerusalem.
In its simplest form, it first reads very much like the fourteenth benediction,
craving God's mercy (not his compassion)[16] on Israel his people, Jerusalem his
city, and Zion his glorious habitation, while then adding to the list the ruined
city, whose plight and divinely-promised ultimate restoration are duly noted.
As far as the doxology is concerned, God is again cited as the builder of
Jerusalem or, in more complex manner, as either the God of David and the
builder of Jerusalem or the consoler of Zion and the builder of Jerusalem. The
initial word of the second blessing after the prophetic reading is again either
raḥem or naḥem, and the doxological variants once more contain references to
either the consolation of Zion—this time with her children—or to the building of Jerusalem. Since the benediction directly concerns Jerusalem, the remainder of the content is also of importance for our discussion. The titles of
Jerusalem are here given as "Zion your city" and "our house of life,"[17] and
there is also a call for swift vengeance on behalf of those who have been
saddened, presumably by its loss.

If Jerusalem stands as a theme in its own right in both of these benedictions,
its relevance to the wedding feast is somewhat more problematic. One must
assume that the philosophy behind its inclusion is that even at times of self-
indulgence and joy one should remember the tragic loss of the historic and
spiritual center. Be that as it may, there is still ambiguity about whether to
place the emphasis on the joyous occasion or on the loss, and this makes itself
particularly felt in two of the benedictions. In the fourth, the joy of the barren
woman joyfully gathering her children to her clearly serves as a metaphor
alluding to the return of the Jews to Jerusalem, since the doxology praises God
as the one who will gladden Zion through (the return of) her children. The
subject of the fifth benediction is the joy the participants are requesting of
God, such as he produced in Adam by creating a wife for him, but the doxology varies in different traditions. One placed the emphasis exclusively on
God's gift of joy to the bride and groom, another on such a gift to his people
(or Zion) and on the building of Jerusalem, and a third on the creation of his
people's joy in Jerusalem.[18]

Since this analysis has perforce alluded to such Jerusalem institutions (if they may, for want of a better term, be categorized as such), it will not be appropriate to leave the ʿ*Amidah* without devoting some attention to the seventeenth benediction, that entitled ʿ*Avodah* and dealing with the Temple service, at least insofar as the textual data are relevant to the matter of Jerusalem. This benediction is particularly important since it is highly likely that elements of it have their origin in Temple times.[19] Here, the textual options are basically two, even if there is the usual phenomenon of examples that are not wholly consistent with either option but incorporate elements of both. In the first of these, the text remains true to the title given to the benediction in various talmudic passages, namely *Birkat ha-ʿAvodah*, by making use of the root ʿ*avad* twice in the body of the text and once in the doxology. God is asked to express his favor by dwelling in Zion, and a future is described in which his servants will serve him there and the reciters of the prayer will worship him in Jerusalem. In the final phrase of the text God will find favor in them and the doxological conclusion states that the reciters of the benediction will serve him. The second formulation has a somewhat different style, order, and content. It entreats God to favor his people and their prayer, to restore the service to his Temple (*devir betekha*), and to accept favorably their service (ʿ*avodah*), including an ambiguous reference to "fire-offerings" that could allude to either the restoration or the acceptance. There then follows a final appeal to see God's merciful return to Zion, followed by a doxology that describes him as the one who restores his presence to Zion.

It will perhaps be useful to spell out more precisely the differences between the two archetypes. The first formulation has a text that centers on what will happen liturgically in a future Zion followed by a doxology that stresses (and presupposes?) divine service there, while the second has a form of words that centers on God's acceptance of Jewish liturgy, followed by a doxology that stresses (and presupposes?) his return to Zion. The mention of Jerusalem is unique to the first version and that of prayer (as distinct from service) is unique to the second, while the concern with finding God's favor is common to them both. It should be added that in the later midrashic literature there is a conflated reading that simply requests the restoration of the divine presence to Zion and the order of the Temple service to Jerusalem, God's city. It is not clear, however, whether this represents anything more than a late textual variation.[20]

Whether or not the prayer entitled *yaʿaleh ve-yavo* was originally more closely associated with another liturgical context, by the geonic period it had certainly become part of the ʿ*Avodah* benediction and consequently deserves some attention at this point in the discussion.[21] The prayer is inserted on festive occasions and expresses the hope that on this special day God will remember his special Jewish connections. What these connections are is a matter of textual controversy, although it may safely be said that certain circles tended to expand the list into a kind of litany. Perhaps there was a simple form which referred to no more than the divine remembrance of the worshippers, God's people Israel. Be that as it may, one dominant formulation in the post-talmudic period also opted for a number of references associated with Jerusalem, not only mentioning God's city, without specific name, but also using a number of poetic terms for the Temple. The other specified Jerusalem by name, also cited "our fathers," and in some versions included the Davidic messiah—but made no mention of the Temple.

Before an attempt is made to summarize and analyze the textual evidence, attention must be drawn to some additional data relating to Jerusalem's treatment in five other contexts, where it is of less central significance than in the cases noted above. In the *Musaf* prayer for the pilgrim festivals, the basic theme is the future offering, on the respective occasions, of the requisite sacrifices ordained in the Pentateuch. Again there are two basic styles. In the first (thoroughly documented by E. Fleischer), biblical verses play an important part, the formulation is not greatly at odds with those used for the other *'Amidot* of the day, and there are simple references to the return to Zion and Jerusalem, to the joyous view of the Temple, and to the festal offerings. The second version is more complex, differing from the other *'Amidot* and expanding on the theme of the return to Jerusalem and the future offerings in the Temple. It decries the current inability to make the pilgrimage to the Temple site and looks forward not only to the return of the people and the sacrifices but also to the restoration of God's presence and of the specific duties of the priests, levites and Jewish population.[22]

In the second post-*Shema'* benediction of the evening service, God is entreated to protect the worshippers from catastrophes and ensure their peace and security. While one version of the doxology remains with the general theme of God's protection of Israel, the other extends this to include God's "stretching the canopy of peace" over his people Israel, consoling Zion and building Jerusalem.[23] The matter of peace is itself the subject of the final *'Amidah* benediction, and in some versions the blessing is invoked not only on God's people Israel but also on his city or, more specifically, on Jerusalem.[24] As far as the *Qaddish* is concerned, the version that came to be used at the burial service and *Siyyum* ceremony goes beyond the simple praise of God and contains a passage of messianic character. This is regarded by Heinemann as a genuine *bet midrash* element rather than a later addition, as was suggested by I. Elbogen. The theme there is that God will establish his kingdom, revive the dead, build Jerusalem, reconstruct the Temple, and replace heathen ritual with authentic worship.[25] Finally, it is interesting to note that the text of the *ge'ulah* benediction included in the Passover *haggadah* also includes a messianic section, in various formulations, which looks forward to the restoration of the Temple and the sacrifices and to the joy to be engendered by that development and by the "the building of your city." Another version, however, refers more simply to next year's joyous celebration of the Temple service in "Zion your city."[26]

What, then, emerges if we now attempt to capture an image of the thematic wood rather than the textual trees, first bringing into view the overall treatment of the city and its special institutions, and then moving on to the activities of God and of Israel, as they are all described in the sources examined earlier? The city is referred to as Zion, the city of God, and simply Jerusalem. The Temple enjoys a larger number of epithets, the basic forms alluding to it as a holy place (*miqdash*), glorious habitation (*mishkan kavod*) or house of God, while the more lyrical terms include *hekhal, ma'on, devir,* and *bet ḥayyim,* all of which, while clearly conveying the general sense, present problems for the precise translator. The act of liturgy, or divine service, attracts the term *'avodah,* but there are also more specific references to sacrifices, as well as instances in which prostration and prayer are included in the formulations. The Jewish people involved one way or another with Jerusalem were priests, levites, Israel, and Zion's children, and there are also references to the royal Davidic dynasty. Apart from the mention of its worship of God, reports of Israel's activities are fairly limited, with notes about her exile, her renewed sight of the holy place, and her return. As is only to be expected in praises of God and his power, on the other hand, the divine activities vis-à-vis Israel and her institutions receive considerable attention. They include (as well as his divine status) his presence and his potentially favorable treatment of Israel;[27] his mercy, compassion and building program; his vengeance and his blessing of happiness; and his eternal restoration of Israel's lost glories.

The data collected and the themes identified are also capable of being interpreted in the context of the variety of religious ideas to be found in Jewish liturgical material in the period under discussion. There is some ambivalence about whether it is the Temple or the city that is spiritually predominant. While the Temple is sometimes seen as God's place, it also functions in a special way to the benefit of Israel. The service of God may be expressed and his favor obtained not only through the Temple rituals, past and future, but also through other acts of worship. The separate functions of Israel, the priesthood, and the levites are blurred in contexts in which more general reference is made to Zion and her children. The theological and political significance of Davidic rule and the building of Jerusalem are stressed in some prayers, while in others the dominant theme may be the cultic shortcomings of exile and how these will be made good by the restoration, or Israel's tragedy and how its pain may be assuaged by God's mercy, or the exercise of his power as purveyor of joy or recompense. Descriptions of the future may be oriented toward security, the recovery of what was lost, or the messianic eon. It may be presupposed either that it is primarily God's presence that requires to be restored to Zion or that his special favor will be obtained when Jerusalem again becomes the center of his cultic service.[28]

As already indicated earlier in this paper, a chronological approach to the ideas and formulations to be found in early Jewish liturgy is fraught with methodological danger. It is nevertheless an important interpretative option and must be offered as such, albeit with the necessary caution. If it is assumed that the scholar may, with some degree of confidence, identify early tannaitic material, distinguish it from later talmudic and geonic sources, and date the contents of the Genizah texts to the end of the first Christian millennium, a reconstruction of the development of liturgical ideas becomes possible. In the period before 70 C.E., a realistic picture emerges of the Temple and its service, with the priests at their center and the people of Israel at their edge, all of them the beneficiaries of the special favor expressed by God for Zion, a term that alludes to the whole religious arrangement. During the talmudic period, there is the keen anticipation of a recovery from the disasters that befell these institutions and the expectation of an almost imminent restoration of the city of Jerusalem, the Temple and its service, and the special relationship with God that they represent. God's compassion and mercy will bless Israel with security, and the people's prayers, as well as their offerings, will attract divine favor. As the passing of the centuries puts paid to even the vaguest folk memories of actual Jerusalem institutions, so the prayers chosen most commonly to relate to them become less embedded in reality and convey a more futuristic and messianic message.[29] God's infinite power will bring unexpected joy and recompense to those suffering the pain of exile and persecution. A detailed picture is painted of an idealized future, with Jerusalem functioning with more than its former glory. The Temple and the Davidic kingdom are presupposed and each group of Jews is seen to be playing a part in the scene. Economy of expression and simplicity of language, particularly as championed by the Babylonian formulations, give way to the kind of generous augmentation and colorful vocabulary that are more characteristic of Palestinian prayer texts.

What if, however, the dating of tannaitic material is more problematic and the talmudic traditions as they have come down to us are less than reliable witnesses to the precise prayer forms of the talmudic period? Perhaps geonic testimonies are not disinterested records of liturgical developments, but contain more than their share of propaganda on behalf of their own notions and ambitions. Is there always such a clear-cut distinction between what is authoritative and Babylonian on the one hand and what is deviant and Palestinian on the other? Conceivably, Genizah texts of the ninth and tenth centuries are authentic bearers of liturgical traditions that predate the geonic tendency to standardization but became popular only afterwards.[30] It must be allowed that such doubts would call into question some of the chronological reconstruction just attempted. At the same time, however, it would still be possible to maintain that the religious ideas identified in the liturgical texts examined, in all their variety and difference of emphasis, stand testimony to changing conceptions of Jerusalem and its institutions on the part of Jews in the first Christian millennium. The changes may be due as much to the different milieux from which various forms of liturgy emerged as to chronological developments over a period of centuries. A synchronic rather than diachronic analysis would still detect the same rich variety of theological notions pertaining to Jerusalem as that described above. The problem is that any attempt to set their emergence and development in particular historical contexts suffers seriously from a lack of matching historical data. Whatever the methodological preference, there can be no avoiding the conclusion that Jerusalem stood close to the hearts and minds of Jewish worshippers whenever and wherever they formulated prayers that were central to their reflections on the present and their aspirations for the future.

Notes

1. *EJ*, IX (Jerusalem, 1971), 1560–63 also has a useful summary of Jerusalem's appearances in statutory prayer and liturgical poetry.

2. R. Hammer, *The Jerusalem Anthology: A Literary Guide* (Philadelphia and Jerusalem, 1995). The sole reference is to the burial *qaddish* and is included in the "Fourth Gate" of the volume (p. 150), dealing with the geonic period.

3. For an historical overview of liturgical developments in this period, see S. C. Reif, *Judaism and Hebrew Prayer: New Perspectives on Jewish Liturgical History* (Cambridge, 1993), 122–52.

4. For discussion of some of the methodological problems in the scientific study of Jewish liturgy, see Reif (above, note 3), 1–21; and idem, "Jewish Liturgy in the Second Temple Period: Some Methodological Considerations," *Proceedings of the Eleventh World Congress of Jewish Studies*, C/1 (Jerusalem, 1994), 1–8.

5. D. Rappel, "Methodological Problems in the Study of Popular Theology in the Prayerbook" (text of an unpublished lecture in Hebrew delivered in 1993). See now also his "Jerusalem in the Prayerbook," *Ariel* 102–103 (1995), 26–31 (Hebrew), which covers similar ground to this paper but from a different perspective, and also alludes to later developments.

6. M Yoma 7:1; see E. E. Urbach, *The Sages: Their Concepts and Beliefs* (Jerusalem, 1975), 655–67:

ומברך עליה שמונה ברכות על התורה ועל העבודה ועל ההודאה ועל מחילת העון ועל המקדש ועל הכהנים ועל שאר תפלה.

7. T Yoma 3:13 (ed. Zuckermandel, 189); S. Lieberman, *Tosefta Ki–Fshutah*, IV (New York, 1962; Hebrew), 800–803:

שמונה ברכות היה מברך באותו היום על התורה כדרך שמברך בבית הכנסת על העבודה
(ועל ההודאה) ועל מחילת העון כסידרן ועל המקדש ברכה בפני עצמה ועל ישראל ברכה
בפני עצמה ועל הכהנים ברכה בפני עצמה ושאר תפלה בקשה תחינה שעמך ישראל צריכין
להיושע מלפניך וחותם בשומע תפלה כל העם קורין בשלהן כדי להראות חזיתן לציבור.

Although the first benediction is given a synagogal milieu, it seems strange that this should be differentiated from that of the next three, namely, the prayers. Perhaps an earlier version of the text had a reference to the *bet midrash*, where the Torah benediction no doubt originated and was later amended to reflect new realities. See also I. Elbogen, *Jewish Liturgy: A Comprehensive History* (Philadelphia, New York and Jerusalem, 1993), 140–41.

8. J Yoma 7, 1 (ed. Krotoschin, f. 44b):

ומברך עליה שמונה ברכות על התורה הבוחר בתורה על העבודה שאותך נירא ונעבוד על
הודיה הטוב לך להודות על מחילת העון מוחל עונות עמו ישראל ברחמים על המקדש
הבוחר במקדש ואמר רבי אידי השוכן בציון על ישראל הבוחר בישראל על הכהנים הבוחר
בכהנים על שאר תפלה ותחינה ובקשה שעמך ישראל צריכין להיושע לפניך בא״יי שומע
תפילה.

There is some doubt about the precise identification of the Idi cited here since he is entitled "Rabbi" and not "Rav" and is apparently therefore not the Palestinian teacher with the strong Babylonian background.

9. B Yoma 70a; see R. N. Rabbinovicz, *Variae Lectiones (Diqduqey Soferim)*, IV (Munich, 1871), 203–204:

ומברך עליה שמונה ברכות ת״ר על התורה כדרך שמברכים בבית הכנסת על העבודה ועל
ההודאה ועל מחילת העון כתקנה ועל המקדש בפני עצמו ועל הכהנים בפני עצמם ועל ישראל
בפני עצמם ועל שאר תפלה ת״ר ושאר התפלה רנה תחינה בקשה מלפניך על עמך ישראל
שצריכין להיושע וחותם בשומע תפילה ואחר כך כל אחד ואחד מביא ספר תורה מביתו
וקורא בו כדי להראות חזותו לרבים.

10. For the variant texts in the Mishnah, see J. Meinhold (ed.), *Joma (Der Versöhnungstag). Text, Übersetzung und Erklärung* (Giessen, 1913), 79.

11. S. Baer, *Seder ʿAvodat Yisrael* (Rödelheim, 1868), 554–62; B. S. Jacobson, *Netiv Binah*, 5 vols. (Tel-Aviv, 1968–83), III, 33–97; J. Heinemann, *Prayer in the Talmud; Forms and Patterns* (Berlin and New York, 1977), 115–22.

12. J. Mann, "Genizah Fragments of the Palestinian Order of Service," *HUCA* 2 (1925), 332–38; L. Finkelstein, "The Birkat Ha-Mazon," *JQR* 19 (1928–29), 211–62; A. Scheiber, "Qitʿey Birkat Ha-Mazon," *Studies of the Research Institute for Hebrew Poetry*, VII (Jerusalem and Tel Aviv, 1958), 147–53; Y. Ratzaby, "Birkot Mazon Mefuyyaṭot," *Sinai* 113 (1994), 110–33 (Hebrew). Three basic forms are:

a. רחם יי א׳ על ישראל עמך ועל ירושלים עירך ועל היכלך ועל מעונך (ועל ציון
משכן כבודך ועל מלכות בית דוד) בא״יי בונה ירושלים

b. נחמינו יי א׳ בציון עירך ובשכלול בית מקדשך ורחם יי א׳ עלינו ועל
ישראל עמך ועל ירושלים עירך ועל ציון משכן כבודך ועל הבית הגדול שנקרא
שמך עליו ועל מלכות בית דוד משיחך במהרה תחזירנה למקומה כי לך יי
מיחלות עינינו ותבנה ציון עיר קדשך ותמלוך עלינו אתה לבדך ותושיענו למען
שמך ואע״פ שאכלנו ושתינו חרבן ביתך הגדול והקדוש לא שכחנו ואל תשכיחנו
לעד כי חסיד וקדוש וברוך ונאמן אתה ונאמר בונה ירושלים יי נדחי ישראל
יכנס בא״יי הבונה ברחמיו את ירושלים אמן בחיינו אמן במהרה בימינו תבנה
ציון ברנה ותכון עבודה בירושלים וארמון על משפטו ורומי הרשעה תפול

c. רחם יי א׳ . . . רועינו זונו מפרנסנו מכלכלנו הרוח לנו מהרה מצרותינו ועל
תצריכנו לידי מתנת בשר ודם שמתנתם מעוטה וחרפתם מרובה בשם קדשך
הגדול והנורא בטחנו ויבא אליהו ומשיח בן דוד בחיינו . . .

13. Baer (above, note 11), 96–97; Jacobson (above, note 11), 285–86; Elbogen (above, note 7), 47–48; Heinemann (above, note 11), 48–50, 70–76; and 288–91, A. Shinan (ed.), *Studies in Jewish Liturgy,* (Jerusalem, 1981), 3–11 (originally published in *Hayyim [Jefim] Schirmann Jubilee Volume,* eds. S. Abramson and A. Mirsky [Jerusalem, 1970], 93–101 [Hebrew]).

14. Y. Luger, "The Weekday *'Amidah* Based on the Genizah," Ph.D. dissertation, 2 vols. (Bar-Ilan University, 1992), I, 169–79 (Hebrew). The two options are perhaps already presupposed in T Berakhot 3:25 (ed. Zuckermandel, 9). The three archetypal formulations are:

a. רחם יי א׳ עלינו ועל ישראל עמך ועל ירושלים עירך ועל היכלך ועל מקדשך ועל מעונך
ועל ציון משכן כבודך ובנה את ירושלים בנין עולם באי״י בונה ירושלים

b. רחם עלינו יי א׳ ברחמיך הרבים על ישראל עמך על ירושלים עירך על ציון משכן כבודך
ועל מלכות בן דוד משיחך בנה ביתך ושכלל היכלך באי״י אלקי דוד בונה ירושלים

c. לירושלים עירך ברחמים תשוב ותבנה אותה בנין עולם באי״י בונה ירושלים

15. Heinemann (above, note 11), 70–76. See also J Berakhot 4, 3 (ed. Krotoschin, f. 8a); and Tractate Soferim 13:11 (ed. Higger, 247).

16. The Hebrew root *rḥm* is common in the early versions, but the alternative *nḥm* was ultimately preferred for the Ninth of Av, perhaps because it is more closely associated with tragic loss.

17. It is unclear whether the Hebrew *bet ḥayyenu* refers to the Temple's eternal significance, its close association with God as the source of all life, or its function as the guarantor of Israel's survival. This is reflected in the medieval liturgical commentaries.

18. In addition to Heinemann (above, note 15), see B Ketubot 7b–8a; and N. Wieder, "Fourteen New Genizah-Fragments of Saadya's Siddur together with a Reproduction of a Missing Part," *Saadya Studies,* ed. E. I. J. Rosenthal (Manchester, 1943), 270–72.

19. Leviticus Rabbah 7:2 (ed. Margaliot, I, 151); PRK 24:5 (ed. Mandelbaum, II, 353); and Rashi's commentary on B Berakhot 11b, where he interestingly offers a reconstruction of the text in Temple times.

20. Mann (above, note 12), 419–20; Elbogen (above, note 7), 50–51; E. Fleischer, "On the Text of the *'Avodah* Benediction," *Sinai* 60 (1967), 269–75 (Hebrew); Luger (above, note 14), 197–209. Elbogen (op. cit., 212) is correct about variant liturgical texts reflecting changing religious views, but his claims about the theological differences between Babylonia and Palestine in the case of the *'Avodah* benediction are not justified by the additional textual evidence now available. The alternatives are:

a. רצה יי א׳ ושכון לציון [בציון] יעבדוך עבדיך בירושלים נשתחוה לך ואתה ברחמיך
תחפץ בנו ותרצנו באי״י שאותך [ביראה] נעבוד

b. רצה יי א׳ בעמך [ישראל] ובתפלתם והשב [ה]עבודה לדביר ביתך [ואשי] ישראל
ותפלתם תקביל ברצון ותהא לרצון תמיד עבודת ישראל עמך] ותחזינה עינינו בשובך
לציון ברחמיך [ותרצה בנו כמו אז] באי״י המחזיר שכינתו לציון

The later midrashic text is found in Midrash Psalms (ed. S. Buber; Vilna, 1891), §17, p. 64b, and Midrash Samuel (ed. S. Buber, second edition; Vilna, 1925), §31, p. 47b: השב שכינתך לציון וסדר עבודתך לירושלים עירך.

21. Tractate Soferim 19:5 (ed. Higger, 327); L. J. Liebreich, "Aspects of the New Year Liturgy," *HUCA* 34 (1963), 125–31; Luger (above, note 14), 289–91; L. A. Hoffman, *The Canonization of the Synagogue Service* (Notre Dame and London, 1979), 93–100. There is no scholarly consensus about the earliest context(s) of the *ya'aleh ve-yavo* prayer. The alternatives are:

a. וזכרון עמך עירך מקדשך היכלך מעונך נאוך

b. וזכרון אבותינו וזכרון ירושלים עירך וזכרון כל עמך בית ישראל.

22. Mann (above, note 12), 325–32; Elbogen (above, note 7), 111–17; E. Fleischer, *Eretz-Israel Prayer and Prayer Rituals as Portrayed in the Geniza Documents* (Jerusalem, 1988), 93–159 (Hebrew). The alternatives are:

a. ‏והביאנו י׳ א׳ לציון עירך ברנה ולירושלים בית מקדשך בשמחת עולם . . . ועיננו ת. יר.
בבית מאוויינו ושם נראה לפניך . . . ונעשה לפניך את חובתנו . . .

b. ‏אין אנו יכולים לעלות ולראות ולהשתחות לפניך בבית הגדול והקדוש
אשר אתה שמך נקרא עליו . . . שתשוב ותרחם עלי ועלינו . . . ותבניהו . . . והביאנו
לציון ולירושלים עירך בשמחת עולם . . . בנה ביתך כבתחלה כונן מקדשך על
מכונו והראנו בבנינו ושמחנו בתקונו החזיר השכינה לתוכה יעלו כהנים לעבודתם
וליים לשירה ולזמרה השב ישראל אל נוהו ושבטי ישורון אל נחלתם וארמון על
משפטו ישב שם נעלה ונראה לפניך . . .

23. Mann (above, note 12), 302–25, espp. P. 304; Elbogen (above, note 7), 87; Hoffman (above, note 21), 77. See also J Berakhot 4, 5 (ed. Krotoschin, f. 8c):

‏בא״י הפורש סוכת שלום עלינו ועל עמו ישראל מנחם ציון ובונה ירושלים אמן
בא״י שומר עמו ישראל.

24. Mann (above, note 12), 307 and 310–11; Elbogen (above, note 7), 53; Heinemann (above, note 11), 57; Luger (above, note 14), 223–27:

‏שים שלומך על ישראל עמך ועל עירך ועל נחלתך וברכנו כולנו כאחד.

25. D. de Sola Pool, *The Kaddish* (Leipzig, 1909), 79–89; Elbogen (above, note 7), 80–84, esp. p. 83; Heinemann (above, note 11), 266–69. There are also some useful insights and an interesting anthology in D. Telsner, *The Kaddish: Its History and Significance*, completed and edited by G. A. Sivan (Jerusalem, 1995):

‏יתגדל ויתקדש שמה רבא דעתיד לחדתא עלמא ולאחאה מיתיא ולמפרק חייא ולמבני
קרתא דירושלם ולשכללא היכלא קדישא ולמעקר פלחנא נכראה מן ארעא ולאתבא
פלחנא דשמיא לאתרה.

26. M Pesaḥim 10:6 (ed. E. Baneth [Berlin, 1927], 254) and the footnotes there; E. D. Goldschmidt, *The Passover Haggadah: Its Sources and History* (Jerusalem, 1969), 56–57 (Hebrew):

‏הגיענו למועדים ולרגלים אחרים הבאים לקראתנו לשלום שמחים בבנין [נ״א:
בציון] עירך וששים בעבודתך ונאכל שם מן הזבחים ומן הפסחים . . .

On the matter of the phrase *or ḥadash* inserted into the first pre-*Shemaʿ* benediction of the morning prayers, according to some rites, see N. Wieder, "Chapters in the History of Prayer," *Sinai* 77 (1975), 116–18 (Hebrew).

27. Fleischer has indeed identified the central element of the ʿAvodah benediction as the attempt to obtain God's favor (*raṣon*) and suggested that the original doxology was *ha-roṣeh ba-ʿavodah*. It may just as well have been *ha-boḥer baʿavodah* but his basic point remains valid; see Fleischer (above, note 20). See also the relevant text in Ben Sira 51:27 and 33 (ed. M. H. Segal [Jerusalem, 1958]), 355.

28. Many of these notions are, of course, perfectly compatible with each other and even those that appear to stress opposing concepts may be doing so because they are operating in different contexts. One's interpretation of the evidence ultimately depends on the degree to which one expects to find total consistency in a set of prayer texts from a given time or provenance.

29. It is hardly necessary to point out that the predominance of a particular kind of theological message in one historical or religious context does not mean that it was not previously in existence in an earlier or alternative one.

30. What is being touched on here is the wider methodological debate about Jewish liturgical history which is reflected, for instance, in the differences between my views and those of E. Fleischer; see Reif (above, note 3)), 5, 54, 77, 90, 105–106, 119, and 136; Fleischer, "On the Beginnings of Obligatory Jewish Prayer," *Tarbiz* 59 (1990), 397–441 (Hebrew); and his rejoinder to Reif in *Tarbiz* 60 (1991), 683–88 (Hebrew); see also idem, "On the Earliest Development of Jewish Prayer," *Tarbiz* 60 (1991), 677–81 (Hebrew); idem, "Jewish Liturgy" (above, note 4).

30

Jerusalem in Geonic Era Aggadah

BURTON L. VISOTZKY

As we celebrate the three-thousandth anniversary of the founding of Jerusalem, she still faces a somewhat uncertain future. As we look back to the past and forward in our hopes for the future—however it may be that we see Jerusalem—she reflects our deepest hopes, joys, and sorrows. Isaiah teaches us "Rejoice with Jerusalem and be glad for her, all who love her" (66:10), even as the Tosefta[1] teaches of that very verse that "all who mourn Jerusalem will merit seeing her joy."

The same Tosefta text teaches us the piety that "a man makes a banquet but omits one item as a remembrance of Jerusalem"[2] and that "a woman puts on her jewelry yet leaves off an item as a remembrance of Jerusalem." I offer this Tosefta here not only as a recognition of the sanctity and centrality of Jerusalem in rabbinic literature from its earliest times, but also as a caveat that should the following discussion omit any matter, great or small, it should be construed as a pious remembrance of the Holy City and not, Heaven forfend, an error of scholarship.

During the geonic era—particularly from the eighth through tenth centuries—Jerusalem underwent many changes as it came under Muslim rule; she experienced an upsurge of visitation from the Karaite and Rabbanite communities, and perhaps received the attentions of the Samaritan community to her north. I wish to focus here on the traces, if any, that those years of Jerusalem's history have left in the aggadic literature of the rabbis. I have chosen three midrashim as the focus and limits of my study, each from the middle of the era in question, each from somewhere in the Middle East,[3] each exhibiting specific characteristics which distinguish it from the other two.

First, Midrash Mishle is a midrash *cum* commentary to the biblical book of Proverbs. Second, Pirqe Rabbi Eliezer is a Hebrew, targum-like retelling[4] of the pentateuchal narrative from Creation to the death of Miriam. Finally,

Seder Eliahu Rabbah is a meandering narrative of moral sermons, exegeses, law, and lore. In short, I have chosen three disparate genres of midrashic/ aggadic literature for my examination of Jerusalem in geonic era midrashim. In each case I date the relevant midrash to the ninth century.[5]

Before I begin to sketch the evidence or offer analysis and conclusions, a note is in order on date and provenance. I do not intend here to prove definitive date or locale for any of these three midrashim,[6] nor are these facts necessary for the observations which follow.[7] Indeed, one would expect virtually any rabbinic work, authored in virtually any era, to sing the praises of the Holy City, for the psalmist has taught us, "If I forget you, O Jerusalem, let my right hand wither, let my tongue stick to my palate if I cease to think of you, if I do not keep Jerusalem in memory even at my happiest hour" (Ps. 137:5–6).

In order to honor Jerusalem and at the same time respect those of my colleagues who may differ as to date or locality of any of the three texts being examined, I shall survey each separately, offering analyses and conclusions about each individual midrash. Only at the very end of this paper will I attempt to garner what, if any, significance my findings may have about the role of Jerusalem in the literature of the rabbinic community dwelling between the Mediterranean Sea and the Tigris River in the ninth century.

Midrash Mishle

I begin with Midrash Mishle not only because I know it best, but because it presents the simplest body of evidence. I was, I confess, surprised to learn that Midrash Mishle has but two references to Jerusalem in the entire body of the text and these are each borrowed from earlier sources. The first text is to Prov. 1:24:

> "Since you refused me when I called" (ibid., 1:24)—this refers to Jeremiah, who called to Israel in Jerusalem to repent, as it is said, "But they refused to pay heed. They presented a balky back" (Zech. 7:11).

> "And paid no heed when I extended my hand" (Prov. 1:24)—this refers to the angel Gabriel, for his hand was against Jerusalem for three and a half years. He had live coals in his hand to cast upon Jerusalem, yet he cast them not. . . .[8]

What interests me about this text is that there are earlier parallels for the latter half (the part about Gabriel with his hand against Jerusalem). This text has its sources in Leviticus Rabbah, Lamentations Rabbah and/or the Babylonian Talmud.[9] In none of them is Jerusalem mentioned. One wonders if the Muslim conquest of Jerusalem precipitated the city's mention in our midrash.

The second text of Midrash Mishle which mentions Jerusalem is to Prov. 15:30, which invokes the story of Yoḥanan ben Zakkai escaping besieged Jerusalem. This text has sources and parallels galore,[10] all of which, by plot necessity, mention Jerusalem. Here, too, it may be significant that besieged Jerusalem is the subject.

One might briefly note that Jerusalem is *not* mentioned in the first chapter of Midrash Mishle, when the Queen of Sheba makes her famous visit to King Solomon. It might have been appropriate to localize the story in the glories of Solomonic Jerusalem, yet no explicit mention is made. Nor when in chapter twenty-three, Midrash Mishle expands upon on the messianic future and cites the verse, "The city shall be [re]built upon her ruins," is there mention of Jerusalem by name. It is as though Midrash Mishle can only see Jerusalem narrowly, through the lens of conquest or destruction, with no eye to its past glory or future resurrection. Perhaps too much should not be made of this argument *ex silentio*; after all, Midrash Mishle is biblical commentary to the book of Proverbs, which also does not mention Jerusalem by name.

Seder Eliahu Rabbah

Despite famous idiosyncrasies that mark its unique style,[11] Seder Eliahu Rabbah, a.k.a. Tanna DeBei Eliahu Rabbah, shares much in common with Midrash Mishle.[12] Indeed, both texts have a clear anti-Karaite polemic, marked by Midrash Mishle in its famous Rabbanite curriculum in chapter ten and paralleled in Seder Eliahu at the very outset of chapter one. There, it is offered as commentary to Ps. 139:16, where the Day of Judgment[13] and the Sabbath day's study are conflated as the interpretative matrix for the Psalm verse. The Day of Atonement is the next interpretation for that verse of Psalms offered by Seder Eliahu and then the Day of Gog and Magog. It is in this destructive-apocalyptic interpretation that Jerusalem is first mentioned in Seder Eliahu.

> The nations of the world will be found guilty and so be destroyed from the world and descend to Gehenna. Why? For they laid a hand on Israel and *upon Jerusalem* and the Sanctuary. Whence in Scripture do we know this? Know ye, that when Nebuchadnezzar King of Babylonia surrounded *Jerusalem*, the nations of the world, etc.[14]

This is but one of two dozen references to Jerusalem in Seder Eliahu. It represents a class of references to Jerusalem in apocalyptic, end-of-days texts which speak of the destruction of the nations and the retribution which God will bring upon them.[15] Often, these texts are composed of explicit scriptural verses which themselves contain references to Jerusalem, particularly its historic destruction.[16]

Complementary texts speak of messianic hope for Jerusalem, with the general good advice, "each and every sage of Israel . . . should yearn for and desire and look forward to the honor due Jerusalem and the honor of the Sanctuary and the salvation soon to sprout forth, and for the ingathering of the Diaspora. . . ."[17]

There remain yet two more categories (in addition to some random Jerusalem citations[18]) in which Seder Eliahu evokes Jerusalem. The first, which I confess is mystifying, consists of four different references to the "great academy in Jerusalem" (bet hamidrash hagadol beyerushalayim).[19] Since precious little in Seder Eliahu indicates that the author actually knew Jerusalem, I am dubious about the veracity of the reports. One is inclined to consider this "great academy" a fictional device, perhaps on the order of a "heavenly Jerusalem" and any "heavenly academy" that might be found there.

Although the concept of a heavenly Jerusalem is absent in Seder Eliahu, one must admit the possibility that there actually was such an academy in the Holy City. If nothing else, it offers some verisimilitude to the first-person narrator as one who is serious in his studies, ready to dialogue with Karaite and Rabbanite alike, whether on his travels from one locale to the next or in the Holy City itself.

The final category of citations regarding Jerusalem contains five references to the city as part of an extended consideration of Ps. 79.[20] They open with the prayer, "Blessed is the Omnipresent Who remembers Jerusalem at all times," yet include three references to destroyed Jerusalem. Perhaps this juxtaposition of the prayer with the historic fact of destruction can best be understood by the last of the references. There, the heading of Ps. 79 is taken up:

A Psalm of Asaph . . . Thus when Asaph and all the prophets foresaw that the gates of Jerusalem would be rebuilt [in the messianic future] . . . Asaph and all the prophets rejoiced at the matter. Asaph explained, The One Who shall rebuild Jerusalem shall also resurrect my grandfather from the earth.

The messianic hope of bodily resurrection, here tied to the equally messianic hope that the Holy City will be rebuilt, seems to embody the rabbinic prayer for a restored capital. At the same time, it undermines the possibility that the

Great Academy of Jerusalem, just mentioned, existed on any map but that of the rabbinic imagination. Indeed, Seder Eliahu Rabbah closes with a messianic prayer which seems to epitomize the role of Jerusalem:

> All who are resurrected in the days of the Messiah and go to the Land of Israel will never again return to dust, as it is said, "The remnant of Zion and those who remain in Jerusalem, all who are inscribed for life in Jerusalem, shall be called holy" (Isa. 4:3). . . . Thus may it be Your will, O Lord our God, that we may witness the rebuilding of Jerusalem, Amen![21]

For Seder Eliahu Rabbah, then, the restoration of a Jewish Jerusalem is as much a messianic hope as is the prayer for bodily resurrection.

Pirqe Rabbi Eliezer

Pirqe Rabbi Eliezer contains some eighteen references to Jerusalem. They fall in a variety of categories: some serve as incidental prooftexts,[22] others describe, as it were, historic occurrences in the city,[23] including references to the infamous four kingdoms and counting Ishmael or Islam as the final kingdom.[24] Then there are references to messianic Jerusalem, such as in chapter fifty-one, where it is imagined that every variety of fish will gather in the Mediterranean Sea, sweetened by the waters as they travel upstream to Jerusalem, there to be gathered—one supposes for the great messianic fish fry.

Messianic fervor is a leitmotif in the score of Pirqe Rabbi Eliezer, as in chapter thirty-four, wherein God recognizes the misfortunes of the city past and promises succor for the future: "I smote Jerusalem and her people on the Day of My Wrath, so in bountiful mercy shall I heal them." Indeed, Pirqe Rabbi Eliezer's imagination is well exercised on behalf of the Holy City. She is listed among the ten things which God imagined before creation began,[25] and though not named, located in Adam's plans for the Mount Moriah Motel, most probably referring to a monument thought to be his mausoleum.[26] That same Jerusalem mountain serves, quite expectedly, as the object of Abraham and Isaac's famous three-day journey in Pirqe Rabbi Eliezer, chapter thirty-one. There, father and son make a stop on the way, on Mount Scopus, to assure themselves that the journey is going according to divine plan.

Jerusalem also serves as the locus for Jonah's gentile sailors as they journey to Jerusalem to fulfill the vows they took when the ship was in danger.[27] In the same chapter of Pirqe Rabbi Eliezer, Jonah is treated to a tour of the depths of the seas. During the trip, Jonah's fish "showed him the Sanctuary, as it is said, 'To the ends of the mountains I descended,' from which we learn that

Jerusalem stands upon seven hills." One other midrash in Pirqe Rabbi Eliezer, although deemed quite baffling, also refers to the Temple: "Anyone who prays at this place in Jerusalem it is as though he has prayed before the Throne of Glory—for the Gate of Heaven is there with an open door in order to hear prayer, as it is said, 'For this is Heaven's Gate' (Gen. 28:17)."[28] Of course, Genesis itself immediately has Jacob name the site Beth-el and identifies it as Luz of old. Our sages, good Deuteronomists that they were, polemicized against "foreign" altars in their midrashic insistence that this locus, too, was Jerusalem.

This polemic advancing Jerusalem as the only true place of prayer also calls our attention to chapter thirty-eight, where the Samaritans are the object of the preacher's scorn:

> Anyone who eats Samaritan bread is as though he has eaten pork! Nor may one convert a Samaritan and further they have no portion in the bodily resurrection [at the time of messianic redemption] as it is said, "Not for you, but for us" (Ezra 4:3)—Not in this world, neither in the world to come. Nor shall they have any portion or inheritance in Jerusalem, as it is said, "For you shall have neither portion nor justice nor memorial in Jerusalem" (Neh. 2:20).

Here, as above apparently, the very idea of an alternative capital was anathema to the rabbis, whether they dwell in Jerusalem or not. One must wonder if the author did, in fact, dwell in Jerusalem or, perhaps, further north, under the shadow of Mount Gerizim and the Samaritan community. This might account for the sharp, however brief, polemic.

Of course, the very question of whether they merely yearned for Jerusalem or did actually live and study here is most sharply raised by the final midrash of Pirqe Rabbi Eliezer which we will consider here. In chapter thirty we read:

> Rabbi Ishmael said: In the End of Days the Muslims[29] will do fifteen things in the Land [of Israel]. These are: they will survey the land,[30] they will turn the cemetery to a trash heap where sheep graze,[31] . . . the use of paper and quill will diminish,[32] . . . the breaches in the Temple wall will be fenced in, while a building shall be erected in the Temple Court,[33] and two brothers shall rise up as princes over them in the End[34] . . . destructions . . . wars, one in forest to the West[35] . . . one in the Mediterranean . . . and one in the mighty city Rome.[36]

All this suggests a Land of Israel under Muslim rule. Although Jerusalem is not mentioned, she is described as the locus of the Temple Mount. Earlier scholars have placed this text at the time of the Muslim sack of Rome, when the sons of Haroun al-Rashid shared the Caliphate, some two centuries following the land survey of Mu'awiyya.

Did the Rabbanite author of this midrash, then, dwell in Jerusalem, did he study there, pray there, walk her very streets? I limit myself here only to the evidence of the text, for there is outside evidence from Muslim and Karaite sources that does, indeed, indicate the presence in Jerusalem of a Rabbanite community. As far as our text is concerned, however, we might conclude a possible, but not necessary, first-hand knowledge of Jerusalem, for the events referred to would have been known to all Jews under Islam concerned with the sanctity and centrality of the Holy City. These political acts would have been mulled over by Jews in the Land of Israel and throughout the Muslim (and perhaps even Christian) diaspora. Nevertheless, of our three midrashim surveyed, Pirqe Rabbi Eliezer[37] has the best knowledge of the Holy City.

In summary, Midrash Mishle hardly mentions Jerusalem, while Seder Eliahu Rabbah offers a view of the city from afar, a view through the rose-colored glasses of messianic hope for rebuilding and resurrection. Only Pirqe Rabbi Eliezer seems to know of a Jerusalem contemporary with its own redaction. Yet even that midrash is rife with the possibility that the events which overtake Jerusalem may herald the advent of the Messiah. Was the long-awaited redemption finally to come? If Jews could witness the capture of Jerusalem and the sack of Rome from Christianity by Muslim conquerors, was it too much to imagine Jews regaining the Holy City under the rulership of the King Messiah? No more unimaginable, I suppose, than wishing that all three religions share the Holy City with free access to all its holy places for all who revere her. As the prophet Isaiah teaches, "Rejoice with Jerusalem and be glad for her, *all* who love her" (66:10).

Notes

1. T Sotah 15:15 (Erfurt; ed. Lieberman, 244).

2. Ibid., 15:13 and 14.

3. The exact provenance of each of the three midrashim under discussion remains under question; see below.

4. Here, using a technical term coined by G. Vermes in his *Scripture and Tradition in Judaism* (Leiden, 1961).

5. For Midrash Mishle, see my various introductions to my Ph.D. dissertation (Jewish Theological Seminary, 1982), my Hebrew critical edition (New York and Jerusalem, 1990), and my annotated English translation (New Haven, 1992). For Pirqe Rabbi Eliezer, see G. Stemberger (*Introduction to the Talmud and Midrash* [Minneapolis, 1992], 356–57), who cites

G. Friedlander (ed. and trans.), *Pirke de Rabbi Eliezer* (London, 1916; reprint New York, 1981) and adds the material adduced in S. W. Baron, *A Social and Religious History of the Jews*, III (New York and Philadelphia, 1957), 163, with more discussion on Baron's citation below. For Seder Eliahu Rabbah, I follow M. Zucker, *On the Translation of the Torah of Rav Saadiah Gaon* (New York, 1959), 219 (Hebrew), but I am aware that many critics date the work as late as the tenth century and some as early as the Talmud (cf. Stemberger, op. cit., 369–70).

6. Indeed, the only one I would make a case for is Midrash Mishle; on the date of this composition, see the bibliography cited above. As for the others, although I am generally inclined to ninth-century datings, I am open to persuasion that I should date them otherwise. As far as locales, I suspect that the absence of any new versions of the texts or Genizah manuscripts, with autographs from the authors indicating date and place, combined with the traffic in the Levant during the period, make a secure assertion of locale either unsound scholarship or patriotic bias.

7. Except the general assumption of early medieval (i.e., geonic) redaction.

8. For full commentary, see my edition (above, note 5), ad loc.

9. Leviticus Rabbah 26:8; Lamentations Rabbah 1:41; B Yoma 71a. There are parallels in the Tanḥuma literature as well, but I deem this material roughly contemporary to our text and thus not a likely source; indeed, Tanḥuma, Tazria, 12 (ed. Buber) has a vaguely similar story which mentions Jerusalem.

10. See my commentary (above, note 5), ad loc., for the citations.

11. See the introductions in Stemberger (above, note 5), various encyclopedias, the edition of M. Friedmann (Vienna, 1904), and W. Braude's English translation, *Tanna deBei Eliahu* (Philadelphia, 1981).

12. See Zucker (above, note 5) and my introductions to Midrash Mishle (above, note 5).

13. The Day of Judgment is never actually invoked in Seder Eliahu Rabbah, although it might be inferred from the context. It is explicitly invoked in the Midrash Mishle parallel.

14. Seder Eliahu Rabbah (ed. Friedmann, 5).

15. For these texts, see ibid., 5, 96, and 154. More are listed with prooftexts (below, note 16).

16. Ibid., 39, 104, 108.

17. Ibid., 19; cf. p. 63.

18. These include two texts which mention pilgrimage festivals to Jerusalem (ibid., 15 and 81); three more involve various scriptural exegeses (ibid., 83, twice on p. 85).

19. Ibid., 49 (*shebeyerushalayim*); 51, 80, and 122 (omitting *hagadol*).

20. Ibid., 147, 148, 149, 150, 151.

21. Ibid., 164f.

22. I would include here references to Ezek. 33:21 in Chapter 27, and to Judg. 1:21 in Chapter 36. This latter reference contains an identification of Jebusites and Hittites coupled with a depiction of the Jebusites as Roman-like idolators. The text of Pirqe Rabbi Eliezer is taken from the Eshkol edition, with some comparisons to the vulgate Luria edition. I also consulted the variants listed in *Ḥorev* 8–10 (1946–48) (Hebrew).

23. Chapter 9, Hezekiah blocks the water sources of the city, citing II Chron. 32:30; Chapter 17, Jeremiah and the Judahites of Jerusalem offer condolence to Josiah.

24. Chapter 49, with reference to Persia, Media, and Babylonia, twice citing verses of Scripture referring to Jerusalem (Dan. 1:1, Neh. 13:6); and Chapter 28, referring to Greece, Persia and Media, Babylonia, and Ishmael; viz. Islam, with a citation of Isa. 31:9.

25. Chapter 3.

26. Chapter 20. Cf. G. Friedlander's translation (above, note 5), ad loc. This locution (*bet malon*) parallels Karaite tombstones of the period which use similar language (*malon hatov*) also found in Midrash Mishle.

27. Chapter 10.

28. Chapter 35. Cf. the Samaritan Memar Marqa, which equates these loci with Mount Gerizim. See the references to this connection with the Samaritan shrine in A. Shinan's article in this volume.

29. Lit., sons of Ishmael.

30. Lit., measure it with ropes. Baron (above, note 5, III, 163) suggests this took place during the caliphate of Mu'awiyya, ca. 640 C.E.

31. Perhaps referring to the valley before the Golden Gate, between the Mount of Olives and the Temple Mount, where today lies a Muslim cemetery, which is often enough the site of grazing flocks of sheep.

32. Friedlander's translation here is gibberish, but the Hebrew text here (*vyqml hnyr vhqlmos*) is admittedly difficult. The word *qlmos* is undoubtedly reed quill, as *nyr* is paper. The lead verb, *vyqml*, is not found in rabbinic Hebrew, but exists in biblical Hebrew; cf. Isa. 9:6–7, which may have been in the mind of the narrator. My thanks to Prof. O. Grabar for helping me reach this translation.

33. This is understood as a reference to the Dome of the Rock; see S. Krauss apud Friedlander's note, ad loc.

34. Perhaps the sons of the Caliph Haroun al-Rashid; and see Friedlander (above, note 5), who cites H. Graetz (*Geschichte der Juden*, V [Leipzig, 1861], 197f.); as well as Z. Fraenkel (*MGWJ* 8 [1859], 112) who assume the caliphs to be Mohammed Alemin and Abdallah Al-mamun (ca. 809–813 C.E.).

35. Here Friedlander translates Arabia. Our text reads '*arav*, which means West, whereas the rabbis generally refers to Arabia as '*araviah*. Still, the translation is possible, for it would then imply Arabia to the East and the Mediterranean to the West.

36. Which was sacked by the Arabs in 846 C.E., a likely terminus for the redaction of Pirqe Rabbi Eliezer.

37. At least in the version considered. Ed. Luria is lacking the material in Chapter 30 discussed above.

31

Jerusalem in Early Medieval Jewish Bible Exegesis

HAGGAI BEN-SHAMMAI

The earliest systematic Jewish Bible exegesis in the Middle Ages is that of the geonic period (ninth to eleventh centuries) or, to be more precise, the latter part of that period, since the geonic period started after the Savoraim, in the late seventh century. The term "geonic" also indicates the geographical boundaries, namely, the communities that lived under Muslim rule. It has also important linguistic and cultural bearings, as we shall see shortly.

The geonic period opens a whole new chapter in the history of Jewish learning. Emphasis should be put equally on halakhic contributions (to be sure, of different genres), philosophy, and biblical exegesis. It seems that in all these areas the new activity starts suddenly—from nothing, as it were—with very few antecedents on which to rely. The beginning of this new chapter is coupled with a most fundamental cultural change, namely, the adoption of the Arabic language, and indeed Arab culture, by Jews. This important change affected all areas of literary activity, both religious and secular, with the exception of liturgical poetry. Socially, it involved all segments of the Jewish population, including the highest echelons of Jewish spiritual and cultural leadership of the largest communities at the time. The importance of this change cannot be overestimated, as it deeply exposed Jewish spiritual activity to interaction with the cultural environment at large (including Islam, Christianity, and the heritage of classical philosophy and sciences).[1]

The geonic period witnessed also the most important development in the history of Jewish sectarianism during the Middle Ages—the schism between Rabbanites and Karaites. In principle the Karaites rejected the authority of rabbinic tradition in favor of independent interpretation of the Bible. In practice, however, Karaite exegetes often followed exegetical principles and attitudes resembling those of the Rabbanites and also made use of, or reacted to, similar exegetical traditions. Consequently, for the present discussion the Karaite exegesis may be considered part of the same corpus.

The novelty in the genre of biblical exegesis in the geonic period is that, unlike talmudic times, the study of the biblical text now acquired a new status as a legitimate occupation in its own right. This development may have been connected to the Karaite challenge, though it should also be borne in mind that biblical exegesis for ages had enjoyed a similar status in Christianity. This fact could be of significance in the geonic environment, where Christians and Jews participated in one universal civilization, namely, the Arabic-speaking civilization. In addition, Jews and Christians in Arabic-speaking countries had a bilingual channel, since they could communicate in both Aramaic, which for many Christians was still an important vehicle of both secular (written and spoken) and religious expression, and Arabic.

The need, or the wish to rephrase or paraphrase, the Bible in another language was bound to lead to exegesis on two levels: translation and commentary. The rephrasing or paraphrasing of the biblical text was very often greatly affected by the issues that constituted the mental or ideological agenda of the Jewish public, especially the intellectual sector of that public. The fact that this was done in Arabic is not merely a linguistic factor, but clearly indicates the extent to which the Jews felt part of the general culture in which they lived. In the translation, some authors try to incorporate their exegetical views in the most concise way possible. Those whose works combine translation with commentary, perhaps the most common format, try to translate quite precisely the language of the original Hebrew text with respect to both vocabulary (e.g., the use of identical roots) and syntax, even to the degree of awkward or clumsy literalism.[2] They rely on the opportunity to elaborate later, at the level of commentary, on the exact meaning of their translation—and they did so at length, producing numerous lengthy commentaries, as may be discerned from the very caustic remarks made in the twelfth century by the Spaniard Abraham Ibn Ezra, in his introduction to the Pentateuch. Saadya is an especially interesting case; his translations were accompanied by long commentaries, yet even in such recensions one finds numerous deviations from a literal translation. Nevertheless, at least in the case of the Torah, he prepared a separate edition of the translation, which he considered—according to his own testimony in his introduction—a short, concise commentary. Here, of course, Saadya tries his best to include in the translation as many exegetical elements as possible.[3]

Exegesis of the geonic period, in its particular frame of reference, having been written mostly in Arabic, gave ample opportunity not only to paraphrase the biblical text in relation to the issues that occupied the minds of the general public, but also to subject the rabbinic interpretation of the Bible to the same process. This is especially true with regard to Rabbanite exegesis,[4] but Karaite exegesis as well reacted to rabbinic tradition, not always for the purpose of disputing or refuting it, but very often for silently incorporating elements of it into their system.

The harvest of Jewish translations and commentaries on the entire Bible, or on select books from the geonic period, is extensive, one may say even vast. With few exceptions, they were written in Arabic. Most authors originated in the main Jewish centers of the time, Babylonia and Palestine. Of the former, Saadya (to be sure, a native of Egypt who studied for some time in Palestine) and Samuel b. Ḥofni among the Rabbanites figure prominently, as does Qir-qisānī the Karaite. Noteworthy among the Palestinians are the residents of Jerusalem, mostly Karaites, starting with Daniel al-Qūmisī (around 900 C.E.), through Salmon b. Yeruḥim, and Yefet b. ʿEli (tenth century),[5] to Yeshuʿa b. Judah (eleventh century), to name just a few. To these one may add also the Karaite lexicographer David b. Abraham al-Fāsī, of North African origin, who most probably resided in Jerusalem in the second half of the tenth century and composed there the first dictionary of biblical Hebrew in Judaeo-Arabic, which is a treasure trove of exegetical and linguistic materials.

The earlier Karaites of Jerusalem are generally identified with the Mourners of Zion,[6] whose relationship with Jerusalem is strongly colored by messianic expectations. There is another novelty of the geonic commentators, namely, that for all Jews living in the realm of Islam, Jerusalem had again become a concrete, actual reality, and not an abstract concept. It was the seat of a gentile government and also the residence of members of a number of faiths. There was an active, important community there whose influence and jurisdiction were recognized far beyond its immediate environment. People would go on frequent pilgrimage trips to Jerusalem, sometimes more than once a year.

There were, indeed, many more exegetes, less famous or even completely unknown to us. Jewish exegesis of the geonic period has been studied to a rather limited extent, largely due to the fact that most of the primary sources are still unpublished. Even the relatively modest amount preserved in western libraries has not been exhausted to date. The many thousands of additional manuscripts containing such materials that have recently been made accessible in Russian libraries make the exhaustive study of this material seem more distant than ever. This assessment is valid also to very limited topics, such as the one discussed here. Consequently, the following remarks are some im-pressionistic observations, with the very humble aim of putting the subject on the agenda.

The Name of Jerusalem in the Translations and Commentaries

It is well known that the name *al-Quds* became quite common among Muslims already in the beginning of the ninth century.[7] In Judaeo-Arabic documents from the Genizah, Jerusalem is primarily called *al-Quds*, occasionally *Bayt al-Maqdis*. However, initially *al-Quds* (and, of course, *Bayt al-Maqdis*) seems to have indicated the Temple (or the Temple Mount), and the full name of the city as a whole would be *Madīnat Bayt al-Maqdis*, or *Madīnat al-Quds*, i.e., the city of the Temple.[8] Only later, by way of extension, or abbreviation of the long name, would the entire city take on *Bayt al-Maqdis/al-Quds*. The use of *al-Quds* as indicating mainly, but in no way exclusively, the Temple Mount is very common in several early documents. Among them is the famous fragmentary document that contains the story of the return of the Jews to reside in Jerusalem by the permission of Caliph ʿUmar b. al-Khaṭṭāb. One of their requests was to settle near the Temple Mount and its gates.[9] However, in the same document *al-Quds* is also mentioned as indicating the entire city.[10] Judaeo-Arabic translations render mostly Temple or Temple Mount, while *Yerushalayim* and *Ziyyon* in most cases are not rendered at all, but are rather left in their original Hebrew forms. It would seem that the translators felt that even though for everyday purposes also Jews could adjust to the Muslims' use of *al-Quds*, it was not appropriate for rendering the scriptural text. It appears that for them the Hebrew name of Jerusalem was, as it were, not translatable, and even if it were (as will become evident in the exceptions quoted below), the Arabic Muslim equivalents could not be suitable for this purpose. In Judaeo-Arabic commentaries, sporadic use of the Arabic names may be found. So, in his commentary on Isa. 22:1, Saadya[11] remarks that the expression *gey ḥizzāyōn* (Valley of Vision?[12]) indicates *Bayt al-Maqdis*.[13] This comment was later copied by the eleventh-century Spanish exegete, Judah Ibn Balʿamm.[14] Occasionally one may find forms which seem to originate in Syriac translations: *ūrsālim* (אורסאלם). In Saadya's comments on Isa. 62:6, he mentions the watchmen set by God on the walls of *arūsalām* (ארוסלאם).[15] This name may be a corrupt form of the Syriac. It is found also in the commentary on the book of Samuel by the judge Isaac b. Samuel al-Kanzī, a Spaniard who emigrated to the East towards the end of the eleventh century and settled in Egypt.[16] In the course of the commentary, the exegete follows the normal custom of using the Hebrew *Yerushalayim*. He also quotes the famous midrashic etymology that the name *Yerushalayim* is a combination of *yeraʾe* and *shalem*.[17]

When Saadya uses *al-Quds* in his translation of Psalms, he does so in most cases to render terms indicating the Temple, normally the Hebrew *qodesh*. In some comments *balad al-Quds* (which very closely follows biblical *ʿir ha-*

qodesh) refers to Jerusalem,[18] and in a comment on Ps. 45:13,[19] perhaps the reference is to the entire Land of Israel, and elsewhere indeed to the entire land.[20] Hebrew *miqdash* is rendered *maqdis*, e.g., Ps. 68:36, and consequently *balad al-maqdis* (probably a reflection of biblical *miqdash*, rather than rabbinic *bet ha-miqdash* which, in turn, is reflected in the Arabic *Bayt al-Maqdis*) refers to the entire city.[21] In his translation of Daniel,[22] Saadya follows a similar usage and always gives the name of the city in the Hebrew form, and so also in his discussion of the laws of prayer.[23] The appellation *al-Quds* in the course of the comments on Dan. 9:2-3[24] was correctly translated by Qāfiḥ as referring to the Temple.

It is interesting to consider some exceptions to this general trend. Saadya renders the name *Shālēm* (Ps. 76:3 and already Gen. 14:18) by the Arabic *Dār al-Salām* [= the house/abode of peace], and so also the name *Yerushᶜlem* in Dan. 5:3. In the Arabic translation of the Scroll of Antiochos,[25] however, Saadya always renders the name of Jerusalem as *Madīnat al-Salām* (= the city of peace). This last-mentioned rendering is also found in Isa. 40:2; Ps. 48:2 ("the city of our God"), 51:20 ("rebuild the walls of Jerusalem"), 79:1 ("and turned Jerusalem into ruins," but not in v. 3 there), and in a variant reading of the translation of Ps. 122:2 ("Our feet stood on your gates, O Jerusalem"). It is found also in Saadya's (?) translation of Cant. 6:4.[26] This rendering thus appears in a variety of contexts, which may have an eschatological element in common.

The phrase *dār al-salām* (the house/abode of peace) occurs in the Qurʾān twice: 6:127 and 10:26. It may designate Paradise or perhaps some other place which God has allocated to his faithful believers.[27] Concerning the first verse, according to one tradition, quoted on the authority of Qatāda,[28] it indicates Paradise (*al-janna*); according to another, quoted from Jābir b. Zayd, *salām* (= peace) equals God.[29] A harmonizing tradition on the authority of al-Suddī, one of the oldest authorities on Qurʾānic exegesis, says that the abode is Paradise, while peace is God.[30] Fakhr al-Dīn al-Rāzī, the twelfth-century exegete-theologian, in the course of a typical lengthy discussion, also remarks that it is one of God's names.[31] These traditions and exegetical suggestions can be easily traced to other prooftexts in the Qurʾān.[32] It is probably related to the rabbinic statement that *Shalom* is one of God's names.[33] Be that as it may, such traditions or similar ones were possibly in the back of the mind of the ʿAbbāsid Caliph al-Manṣūr, the founder of Baghdad, when he nicknamed his new capital *Dār al-Salām* or *Madīnat al-Salām* (the City of Peace).[34] He may well have had some eschatological motives for doing so, which was very typical of the ʿAbbāsids. While the rendering City/Abode of Peace by Saadya may allude to a plausible etymology for the name *Yerushalayim*, as far as I have been able to trace, there is only one instance in a rabbinic source, Avot de-Rabbi Nathan,[35] where *Shalom* is listed as one of the ten names of Jerusalem. In Saadya's writings, however, no suggestion to that effect has been found as yet.[36] Consequently, I would venture to suggest that Saadya tries through these occasional renderings to offer a Jewish counterweight to some kind of eschatological status conferred upon Baghdad by the ʿAbbāsids. Accordingly, God's gracious assistance to the righteous against Syrian villains was not manifested in the Baghdad of al-Manṣūr, who managed to depose the Syrian Umayyads, but rather a thousand years earlier, in Hasmonean Jerusalem, in the struggle against the Syrian Seleucids. Similarly, the arena for the manifestation of divine justice and salvation in the End of Days will again be in Jerusalem rather than in Baghdad.

Not only in translations, but also in exegetical or other theoretical discussions, does Saadya use *al-Quds* to denote the Temple only. To mention just a few examples: in his introduction to Isaiah;[37] in his commentary on Isa. 26 in the *Commentary on the Ten Songs*;[38] and in his introduction to Psalms;[39] or in his commentary on Isa. 22,[40] where he mentions *ʿīdān al-quds* (= the harps of the Temple). Similarly, Saadya comments on Ps. 24:7 as follows:

> The meaning of "O gates, lift up your heads" is glorification and reverence, meaning to say that His light [= glory] cannot be contained by the heavens and earth, all the less so by the Temple (*al-quds*), as Solomon said: "Even the heavens to their uttermost reaches cannot contain You, how much less this House" [I Kgs. 8:27].[41]

In this comment, *al-Quds* clearly denotes "this House."[42]

The Relationship between City and Temple

A survey of Saadya's renderings of the name of Jerusalem, and of the many quotations from his commentaries, has shown that he preserves the term *al-Quds* mainly to denote the Temple, although among Muslims it had already become the common appellation of Jerusalem as a whole. One may conclude from this fact that the matter is important beyond the limited scope of nomenclature. It touches on the notion of Saadya and his contemporaries, that the Temple is the central focus of the city in general, and in his vision of the Redemption in particular. A relevant illustration appears, for example, in his interpretation of Isa. 62:3, "You shall be a glorious crown (*ʿateret tifʿeret*)," as referring to the Temple (*al-Quds*) and the Nation, although the feminine addressee is explicitly named by the prophet as "Zion and Jerusalem."[43]

If this is the situation with respect to the works of Saadya, who had spent some time as a young man in the Land of Israel, but then preferred the rival center of Baghdad, it is small wonder that similar characteristics may be found, and in a much more emphasized manner, in the exegetical works of the Karaite Mourner of Zion, Salmon b. Yeruḥim (active in Jerusalem in the mid-tenth century). There al-Quds, the Temple, figures prominently. It is not surprising, then, that in Salmon's argument (in his introduction to Psalms) against Saadya concerning the place of the Psalms in the Temple rite, the term al-Quds is in the center of the controversy.[44]

Salmon was a resident of Jerusalem, and yet al-Quds denoted for him mostly the Temple or Temple Mount. In the course of his commentary on Lam. 1: 4, Salmon identifies the term la-parbar (I Chron. 26:18) with the Cattle Gate (bāb al-baqar), which "has remained the gate's name to this [i.e., Salmon's] day." "The gate is known now on the western side of the Temple Mount and was used for bringing sacrifices into the Temple."[45] It is obvious that this can indicate only the Temple.[46] Now, the entire discussion there is about the phrase in Lam. 1:4, "All her gates are deserted"; this is precisely the interesting point, because the verse may, or indeed should, be interpreted as referring to the city, and yet Salmon interprets it as explicitly referring to the Temple, and specifically to "the porters who used to sit at the gates of the House of the Lord" (Hebrew beit YWY is inserted in the Arabic discussion).[47] Yefet ben 'Eli, another Karaite resident of Jerusalem (second half of the tenth century), interprets the verse as referring to Jerusalem.[48]

In a similar instance, Salmon understands Lam. 2:9, "Her gates have sunk into the ground" (again with the feminine pronoun referring to Jerusalem), as indicating the gates of the Temple.[49] Time and again in lengthy exegetical discussions,[50] Salmon distinguishes very clearly between Jerusalem (YRWSLM)[51] and the Temple (al-Quds). Commenting on Lam. 1:17, "Jerusalem has become among them a thing unclean," Salmon interprets Jerusalem as comprehending both entities of the Temple (using the historical Hebrew term bayit sheni, the Second Temple) and the city:

> He means the attitude of Edom [= the Romans and Byzantines]: after they had destroyed the Second Temple, all along [the period of] their control [over the Temple Mount] they used to throw there rags of menstruate [woman], refuse and every [kind of] filth[52]. . . . As for the damned Samaritans, they think that whoever enters Bayt al-Maqdis [= Jerusalem?] is defiled for seven days, and therefore it says "Jerusalem became a menstruate [woman]."[53]

In relation to general references to Jerusalem in the Bible, the commentator may make precise distinctions between the Temple, the Temple Mount, certain sections of Jerusalem, or the entire city. Such distinctions clearly reflect first-hand· acquaintance with the topographical reality and are typical of exegetes who, like Salmon, had such an acquaintance. Commenting on Lam. 1:13, "He left me forlorn," the Karaite commentator expounds a homily with a technique that is typical to geonic exegesis and may be described as systematization of rabbinic homiletics. Around a leading term or root, the exegete assembles several or perhaps all of the available biblical prooftexts in which the root appears. The purpose of the exercise is, of course, the message—historical, moral, ritual, and the like. The leading term in the verse in question is the root *ShMM.* Salmon assembles several occurrences of the root in the Bible which he refers to the relevant parts of Jerusalem or the Holy Land, and then builds a kind of descending hierarchy of deprivations[54] from all honored positions: at the peak is the Temple (Dan. 9:17; "show Your favor to Your desolate sanctuary"); then the Temple gates (Lam. 1:4; "All her gates are deserted"[55]); Mount Zion (Lam. 5:18: "Because of Mount Zion, which lies desolate"); Jerusalem (Isa. 64:9: "Jérusalem a desolation"); other cities [of the land] (Isa. 24:12: "Desolation is left in the town"); [the entire] Land (Zech. 7:14: "and the land was left behind them desolate, without any who came and went"). When Daniel (9:18) used the plural, saying "see our desolations,"[56] he summed up all these pronouncements, in the lowest state of lowliness, after which can come only ascent toward redemption.

It is thus not surprising that Salmon renders "the glory of Israel" in Lam. 2:1 as *al-Quds*, i.e., the Temple is for him the acme of a triangle consisting of kingdom,[57] Temple and glory, and prophecy, while "His footstool" in the same verse refers specifically to the Temple only.[58] Salmon's rendering of the "the glory of Israel" may reflect a widespread tradition with respect to the interpretation of phrases of this kind. Already al-Qūmisī interprets "the Pride of Jacob" in Amos 6:8 as a reference to the Temple; he does it in a complex exegetical maneuver, in which he combines also Ps. 132:14[59] and 47:5 (where the same phrase occurs again).[60] "The Pride of Jacob" in 47:5 was also interpreted by Saadya[61] as a reference to the Temple.[62]

The combination of the Temple with political power in the notion of biblical and eschatological Jerusalem in biblical exegesis of the geonic period has already been noted.[63] The place given to Mount Zion in the hierarchy, adduced in the comments on Lam. 1:13, reflects apparently an element peculiar to the works of Karaite Mourners of Zion mainly in the tenth century, such as Salmon, Yefet ben ʿEli, and Sahl ben Maṣliaḥ. In their works, one finds quite often a distinction between Jerusalem, which symbolizes the Temple (i.e., the religious/spiritual aspect of the city), while Zion figures in such passages as the seat of the kingdom of David and Solomon, and the actual site of their royal magnificent buildings (the secular counterpart of their Temple), which are now occupied and defiled by the idolatry of the uncircumcised (= Christians) but will eventually return to its past glory. This distinction probably reflects these authors' acquaintance with the topographical reality of Jerusalem in their time, when the Western Hill, already identified in this period as the biblical Mount Zion, was the site of a large concentration of major constructions of Christian worship.[64]

Another representative example of the central, focal, place of the Temple in the perception of biblical and actual Jerusalem in Jewish exegesis of the geonic period is found in several of Yefet's commentaries. In his translation to and comments on Ps. 122, the entire psalm concerns pilgrimage (which is evident) and the glory of the City of the Temple (*balad al-quds*[65]). The city itself has no importance other than being the seat of the Temple.[66] The description "Our feet stood inside your gates" in v. 2 of the psalm may refer, according to Yefet, either to the pilgrims who come to mourn the destruction of the Temple (including in his own time) or to those welcoming the pilgrims who will come when the Temple will be rebuilt.[67] The psalmist's call to his addressees "to pray for the well-being of Jerusalem" (*sha'alu shelom Yerushalayim*) is understood by Yefet as referring to enquiries about the condition of the Temple which are posed to the pilgrims who return to their homes by those left behind in their places. The pilgrims who go to the Temple, when it stood or will stand again, go there to offer sacrifices, while those who go there in the period of exile, while the Temple is destroyed, go there to pray and mourn. The psalmist actually prophesied that they will have to inform their fellow-neighbors about the terrible defilement of the Temple by the gentiles, in both theological and ritual aspects, and about the bad conditions in which the Jewish residents of Jerusalem are living.[68] This is the typical linkage of Karaite exegetes, namely, to interpret biblical statements as prognostications of their own time and situation. This is precisely the kind of interpretation which Saadya did his best to avoid. The Karaite views discussed here find an interesting expression in the theology of pilgrimage of the mourners which was aimed at speeding up the restoration of the Temple.

The centrality of the Temple in Yefet's commentaries comes up almost naturally in verses or sections that mention the unnamed "chosen site" and which are so typical to Deuteronomy. On the "rest and the inheritance"[69] in Deut. 12:9, Yefet quotes three interpretations; according to the first, and apparently the one which he preferred, it indicates the Temple (*al-Quds*) and the land which the Tribes would inherit.[70] This is probably why Jerusalem and/or the Temple are often called *beit menuḥah* (cf. I Chron. 28:2).[71] Deut. 16:16 says: "Three times a year all your males shall appear before the Lord your God. They shall not appear before the Lord empty-handed." "Before" is rendered by the Hebrew *et penei*, which Saadya translates by the Arabic *bayna yaday* (= in front, before). Yefet renders it *fī quds rabbika* (= in the Temple/Sanctuary of your Lord), and similarly at the end of verse.[72]

It may be of interest to adduce here some Rabbanite parallels. In a Genizah fragment,[73] probably from a commentary by Samuel b. Ḥofni (the famous Gaon of Sura and father-in-law of Hai Gaon, d. 1013) on Deut. 12:6,[74] the author says that this verse comprises seven things which should be brought to the Temple.[75] He thus takes it for granted that the verse speaks of the Temple, which is a reasonable assumption. Or, he may actually be saying that the "chosen place" denotes the Sanctuary, whatever or wherever this may be. But further on he says:

> If the vows are of the kind which is not offered on the altar, such as wheat, wine, oil, and their likes, these vows should be handled according to the intention of the person who makes them: if he dedicated them to the poor of his locality, he should distribute it to them, but if he intended the vows for those who reside in *al-Quds*, then he has to carry it to *al-Quds*.[76]

"Those who reside in *al-Quds*" could mean the priests in the Temple, but it may equally reflect the language used in the Gaon's time to denote the Jewish inhabitants of Jerusalem who were dependent to a large extent on vows made for them in other communities.

A similar comment on Deut. 12:5[77] is also quite instructive in this regard. It is also found in a Genizah fragment,[78] and is typical of eleventh century exegesis. It may also belong to Samuel b. Ḥofni's commentary, but Karaite authorship, perhaps by Yeshuʿa ben Judah for instance, should not be excluded. It reads as follows:

> He says "unto His habitation" rather than "to His Presence"[79] in order to instruct us that He meant that you should seek the place where the Presence should be, which can be one of two possible situations: either the Glory is actually abiding there, or It is not. There you should set out. This is like the situation in our own time, when the Glory is not present in *al-Quds*, yet we pray in its direction, as it says "To His habitation," which is the place of His dwelling. Therefore it is said, "a glorious high throne from the beginning is the place of our sanctuary [Jer. 17:12]."[80] It does not say "our sanctuary," but "the place of our sanctuary," to teach us that the [designated] location of the Temple is

the chosen one, and that whether the Glory is actually present in the [location of the] Temple or absent from it, there we should aim, as it is said, "the place of our sanctuary."[81]

Clearly, al-Quds here refers to the sanctuary only. The city of Jerusalem at best encompasses the location of the Temple, which is the focus of the Jewish prayers.

Another relevant statement which certainly comes from the pen of Samuel b. Hofni is found in his comments on Deut. 32:11.[82] Having quoted a number of biblical similes that involve eagles, he says:

Similarly the Land of Israel is the highest of lands, and al-Quds is higher than all of it, as it is said: "Then shalt thou arise, and get thee up unto the place which the Lord thy God shall choose" [Deut. 17:8].[83]

On the face of it, al-Quds in this comment may refer to either the Temple or Jerusalem. However, it should be noted that this comment is a faithful reflection of a rabbinic tradition, namely a statement found in the Babylonian Talmud (Sanhedrin 87a), where the geographical and spiritual superiority of the Temple is deduced, as it were, precisely from Deut. 17:8, which is an injunction associated with legal procedure, not with worship or pilgrimage. The unannounced and unascribed integration of such a tradition in Arabic paraphrase is rather typical of Samuel b. Hofni and, in fact, of other exegetes of the geonic period, at least since Saadya. There can be no doubt, therefore, that the Temple is intended here. The Temple functions in this tradition not as a ritual focus, but as the acme of the judicial system.

To this context belongs Daniel al-Qūmisī's interpretation of the enigmatic mention of Beth-el in Zech. 7:1. According to him, it is a reference to the Temple,[84] i.e., the term is not a proper name of a locality, but a description of the Temple, "the House of God"; the persons mentioned there sent their queries to the priests of the Temple. This interpretation is not very common. It is found again in the Judaeo-Arabic commentary of Tanḥum b. Joseph of Jerusalem (late thirteenth century).[85] The old targumic tradition had it that the term referred to the place known by the name Beth-el, and that this was the destination of the query. A quite common approach is that the term is the name of one of the persons who sent the query, i.e., it is not an indirect object in the verse, but one of the subjects.[86]

I would like to mention very briefly just a few examples of exegetical statements found in the Judaeo-Arabic dictionary of biblical Hebrew by the Karaite Abraham b. David al-Fāsī (active in Jerusalem in the second half of the tenth century),[87] which also attest to the centrality of the Temple in the Karaite notion of Jerusalem.

The first case is Cant. 7:3 ("Your navel is like a round goblet"). According to al-Fāsī's allegorical interpretation (in itself not much expected in a dictionary), which he repeats twice, the navel (*shor'rekh*) in this verse alludes to the Temple as it does in the "navel of the earth" in Ezek. 38:12.[88] Now, the exegetical process through which this conclusion is reached seems to be as follows: the rare term in Song of Songs is translated into Arabic by an etymologically-related term and common Arabic word, *surra*.[89] This rendering is then equated with the Hebrew word *ṭabbur* of Ezek. 38:12. The meaning of the latter word itself, navel, was felt to be evident. Its particular meaning in Ezekiel had been associated with the Temple in old midrashic sources,[90] and hence perhaps in very early Islamic sources.[91] On this background of the image of the navel, and the long tradition of allegorical interpretation of Song of Songs, the identification of the navel of the beloved with the Temple is perhaps not so surprising.

Another case is the "nut grove" in Cant. 6:11 which, according to al-Fāsī, also alludes to the Temple.[92] The reason for comparing the Temple to a nut grove is "the commotion, stamping, and crying[93] [heard there] especially in times of hardships, as it is said 'and we shall cry out to You in our distress' [II Chron. 20:9]." The prooftext quoted, which refers explicitly to the Temple, proves that the identification of the nut grove with *al-Quds* is actually with the Temple. According to the Targum on the verse in Song of Songs, the allusion is specifically to the Second Temple.

Jerusalem, as well *Madīnat al-Quds*, is for al-Fāsī the City of the Temple.[94] In his usage, *al-Quds* still refers predominantly to the Temple (I counted over fifty occurrences),[95] while over twenty times the name *al-Quds* refers to the city in general, in both geographical explanations and allegorical interpretations.

The textual evidence of al-Fāsī's dictionary occasionally sheds light on the development of the notion of Jerusalem in Jewish sources of the eleventh century. Mention has been made above of Salmon ben Yeruḥim's interpretation of the term *parbar* (I Chron. 26:18) and his identification of it with the Cattle Gate. Al-Fāsī discusses the term in connection with *parbarim* (II Kgs. 23:11), and says "a place name in *al-Quds*,"[96] which may refer either to the Temple or to the city. In the two abridgments of al-Fāsī's dictionary, composed by the Karaite Levi ben Yefet (son of the famous Yefet ben 'Eli mentioned above; active in Jerusalem in the late tenth century–early eleventh centuries) and the Rabbanite scholar 'Eli ben Israel Alluf (active in Palestine, first half of the eleventh century),[97] the biblical term is identified as "a gate on the western side of *al-Quds.*" This seems to be taken from Salmon, and therefore probably refers to the Temple. In a third abridgment, however, the Karaite scholar ʿAlī b. Sulaymān,[98] says unequivocally: "A place name in the city of *Bayt al-Maqdis* [= Jerusalem]." It may well be that for this prolific epitomizer of old Karaite sources, who spent most of his life in the Diaspora, *al-Quds* came to denote mainly the city; however, in this case, to prevent any possible doubt, he changed the term *al-Quds* to *Madīnat Bayt al-Maqdis.*

✦ ✦ ✦

As mentioned at the beginning of the present study, my intention was merely to suggest a number of observations, which pertain mainly to one aspect of the attitude toward Jerusalem in Jewish exegesis of the late geonic period. We have seen how, in Jerusalem as a real residence and with the Islamic Temple Mount as a concrete presence, the Temple in so many appearances and contexts predominates the concept of biblical Jerusalem in Jewish exegesis down to the mid-eleventh century. This concept may be due to the messianic expectations that were aroused by the advent of Islam and the return of Jewish presence to Jerusalem. It may be that the deterioration of the Jewish presence in the city during the second half of the eleventh century brought with it a change in this concept. Further research into these rich and fascinating materials will certainly bring to light many other interesting aspects.

Notes

1. A very important and new study of the period and the subject of the present observations is D. E. Sklare, *Samuel ben Hofni Gaon and His Cultural World* (Leiden, 1996); see R. Brody, *The Geonim of Babylonia and the Shaping of Medieval Jewish Culture* (New Haven, 1998).

2. An important analysis of early translations of the Bible into Judaeo-Arabic may be found in R. M. Polliack, *The Karaite Tradition of Arabic Bible Translation* (Leiden-New York-Köln, 1997); the author has published some of her findings and discussions in "Medieval Karaite Views on Translating the Hebrew Bible into Arabic," *JJS* 47 (1996), 64–84; idem, "The Medieval Karaite Tradition of Translating the Hebrew Bible into Arabic: Its Sources, Characteristics and Historical Background," *Journal of the Royal Asiatic Society* (July 1996), 189–96.

3. See the detailed discussion by Polliack, *Karaite Tradition* (above, note 2); L. E. Goodman, "Saadiah Gaon's Interpretive Technique in Translating the Book of Job," *Translation of Scripture, JQR* Supplement (1990), 47–76.

4. See my forthcoming observations in "The Rabbinic Literature in Saadya's Exegesis: Between Tradition and Innovation," *Proceedings of the Sixth Conference of the Society for Judaeo-Arabic Studies* (Ramat Gan, 1993) (Hebrew).

5. Especially relevant to the last three is the important study of D. Frank, "The *Shoshanim*

of Tenth-Century Jerusalem: Karaite Exegesis, Prayer and Communal Identity," *The Jews of Medieval Islam*, ed. D. Frank (Leiden, 1995) 199–245. Most extant fragments of al-Qūmisī's commentaries are in Hebrew.

6. Ibid.

7. On the occurrence of the name on ʿAbbasid coins struck in Jerusalem in the early ninth century, see Y. Meshorer, "Coins of Jerusalem under the Umayyads and the ʿAbbāsids," *The History of Jerusalem: The Early Islamic Period (638–1099)*, eds. J. Prawer and H. Ben-Shammai (Jerusalem-New York, 1996), 419; see also M. Gil, "The Political History of Jerusalem during the Early Muslim Period," ibid., 10 (which is based mainly on Goitein's views; see the next note).

8. On the names of Jerusalem in the Muslim period and sources, see S. D. Goitein, "al-Kuds," *Encyclopaedia of Islam²*, V (Leiden, 1986), 322–23. Goitein mentions only literary sources; there seems to be a discrepancy between these sources and the numismatic evidence quoted in the previous note.

9. In the original Arabic: *qurb al-quds wa-abwābihi*; see M. Gil, *Palestine during the First Muslim Period (634–1099)*, II, (Tel Aviv, 1983), no. 1, p. b:13 (Hebrew); p. a:4: ʿUmar "orders to clean the Temple" (*amarahum bi-tanzīf al-quds*); see also idem, "The Jewish Community," *The History of Jerusalem* (above, note 7), 167.

10. Idem, *Palestine* (above, note 9), p., a:15.

11. The names of Jerusalem in Saadya's works have recently been discussed by E. Schlossberg, "The Names of Jerusalem," *Mehqerei Ḥag* 4 (1992), 74–82 (Hebrew). Schlossberg's article contains much valuable information, some of which is used in the present study; at the same time his article needs several corrections, additions and qualifications, both in details and in the general premises and conclusions, which will not be discussed here.

12. As a rule, translations of biblical quotations are given here according to *Tanakh: A New Translation of the Holy Scriptures According to the Traditional Hebrew Text* (Philadelphia, 1985); on some lexicographical and exegetical problems involved in this verse, see also A. A. Macintosh (*Isaiah XXI* [Cambridge, 1980], 138), who interprets the allusion as Jerusalem, but mentions nonetheless Driver's suggested etymology of *ḥizzāyōn* from the (Arabic) root *ḥzy*, and the consequent translation "the valley of calamity."

13. Saadya's translation of Isaiah with the extant fragments of his commentary have been edited twice: first by J. Derenbourg et al., *Oeuvres complètes de Saadia ben Iosef al-Fayyoumi*, 5 vols. (Paris, 1893–99), III, and subsequently (with many more fragments of the commentary) by Y. Ratzaby (ed.), *Saadya's Translation and Commentary on Isaiah* (Kiryat Ono, 1993), with Hebrew translation by the editor. Henceforth quotations will be given from the latter. The commentary on Isa. 22:1 is found on p. 177; see also below, note 60.

14. R. Judah Ibn Balʿamm's *Commentary on Isaiah*, eds. M. Goshen-Gottstein and M. Perez (Ramat Gan, 1992), 112; the editor refers to Saadya and adds that Ibn Balʿamm meant Jerusalem.

15. Saadya on Isa. (Ratzaby [above, note 13], 237). Interestingly, Saadya retains the Hebrew name in the translation of the verse.

16. Translation of II Sam. 5:5, ms. British Library, Or. 2388 (*Catalogue*, no. 167), fol. 22b.

17. Ibid., fol. 24b; the source of this midrashic etymology is Genesis Rabbah 56:14 (eds. Theodor-Albeck, 607–608).

18. J. Qāfiḥ, *Saadya's Translation and Commentary on Psalms* (Jerusalem, 1966), 33 (Saadya's introduction); his comment concerning Ps. 137 (repeated in his comment to the actual verse, p. 272) has been understood as referring even to the entire Land of Israel; see U. Simon, *Four Approaches to the Book of Psalms* (Albany, 1991), 23; this understanding is not compelling.

19. Saadya on Ps. (Qāfiḥ [above, note 18], 129); here, too, the comment may also be understood as a reference to Jerusalem or to the sanctuary only.

20. Ibid., 114 (on Ps. 37:9).

21. In a fragment of *Kitāb al-tamyīz*, published by H. Hirschfeld, "The Arabic Portion of the Cairo Genizah in Cambridge," *JQR* 16 (1904), 104:15–16.

22. Saadya's Judaeo-Arabic translation and commentary on Daniel (with a Hebrew translation) was published by J. Qāfiḥ (Jerusalem, 1981).

23. Ibid., 115:20, 21, 26.

24. Ibid., 160:end (see 9:17).

25. A non-canonical, quite popular work on the wars of the Maccabees, written in Aramaic. It is not possible to date it with certainty, and scholarly views range from the second century C.E. to the early Middle Ages. See *EJ*, XIV (Jerusalem, 1971), 1045–47 (Saadya's Arabic translation is not mentioned there, but only the fact that he mentions the scroll in his *Sefer ha-Galuy*). See H. Malter (*Saadia Gaon: His Life and Works* [Philadelphia, 1921], 173), where Malter remarks that "the translation was intended to counteract the Karaites who had rejected the feast of Ḥanukka as a Rabbanite invention"; see also p. 355, on the history of the ascription of the Arabic text to Saadya. The text was published by J. Qāfiḥ as an appendix to his edition of Saadya's Arabic commentary on Daniel. The edition, notably with Saadya's theoretical introduction to the scroll, has established the Gaon's authorship beyond any doubt.

26. Judaeo-Arabic translations of the five scrolls ascribed to Saadya, with commentaries thereof bearing the same ascription, have been published by J. Qāfiḥ (Jerusalem, 1962). The translation quoted here is found on p. 105. The question of the authenticity of all these works is certainly beyond the scope of the present study. That the translation of Song of Songs was inspired by Saadya seems to be a reasonable proposition.

27. See H. Ringgren, *Islam, 'aslama and muslim* (Uppsala, 1949), 10; "Dār al-Salām," *Encyclopaedia of Islam* (above, note 8), II, 128.

28. An early authority on exegetical traditions (d. 735); *Encyclopaedia of Islam* (above, note 8), IV, 748.

29. al-Suyūṭī, *al-Durr al-Manthūr* (Cairo, 1314 AH), III, 45.

30. al-Ṭabarī, *Jāmiʿ al-bayān ʿan taʾwīl āy al-qurʾān*, 8 (Cairo, 1968), 132.

31. *Mafātiḥ al-ghayb*, 13 (Beirut, 1990), 154.

32. See D. Gimaret, *Les noms divins en Islam* (Paris, 1988), 204–205.

33. E.g., B Shabbat 10b (supported by the prooftext Judg. 6:24).

34. See above, note 27.

35. ARN, B, 39 (ed. Schechter, 107). I am indebted to Prof. A. Shinan for this reference.

36. One could expect an allusion to this topic in a comment on Gen. 22:14; no fragment of Saadya's commentary on that verse has been uncovered until now.

37. See my "Saadya's Introduction to Isaiah as an Introduction to the Books of the Prophets," *Tarbiz* 60 (1991), 401–404 (Hebrew); published again in Ratzaby (above, note 13), 155–56, 250–51; the restoration of the Temple is combined there with the restoration of prophecy (*nubuwwa*) and political power (*mulk*).

38. The commentary is still unpublished; see my survey in "New Findings in a Forgotten Manuscript: Samuel b. Ḥofni's Commentary on Haʾazinu and Saadya's 'Commentary on the Ten Songs'," *Kiryat Sefer* 61 (1986–87), 313–32 (Hebrew). Isa. 26:1–19, according to Saadya, is the tenth song which will be sung on the occasion of the messianic redemption; see ms. Oxford, Bodl. Ms. Heb. d. 57 (*Catalogue* 2745, 23), fol. 87–91; British Library, Or. 8658, fol. 21–22. *Al-Quds* is used there several times to indicate the Temple.

39. Esp. pp. 30–33, in the course of the discussion of the exclusive function of the Psalms in the rites of the Temple; see also Simon (above, note 18).

40. Ratzaby (above, note 13), 178.

41. Saadya on Ps. (Qāfiḥ [above, note 18], 92). "The earth" actually appears in the text in the plural "earths" (Arabic: *al-araḍīn*), which is a typical Arabic usage, specifically in the context of the Creation story. It is found, for instance, in exegetical-aggadic traditions related to Qurʾān 65:12, where the seven heavens that are explicitly mentioned there are said to have seven earthly counterparts; see al-Ṭabarī (above, note 30), 28, 154. The theme seems to be well attested in midrashic sources; the dating, however, is somewhat problematic; see L. Ginzberg, *Legends of the Jews* (Philadelphia, 1947), I, 11; VII, 12, n. 28. On the dating of the tradition about seven heavens, see E. E. Urbach, *The Sages—Their Concepts and Beliefs* (Jerusalem, 1975), 238.

42. The same usage is found in Salmon b. Yeruḥim's introduction to Psalms; see below.

43. Ratzaby (above, note 13), 237.

44. J. Shunary, "Salmon ben Yeruham's Commentary on the Book of Psalms," *JQR* 73 (1982), 172:296–327.

45. S. Feuerstein (ed.), *Der Commentar des Karäers Salmon ben Ierucham zu den Klagelieder* (Cracow, 1898), XVII.

46. That this is so can be also inferred from further references in Salmon's commentaries indicated in the following note; for a different view, see M. Gil, *Palestine during the First Muslim Period* (Cambridge, 1992), 643, note 115, §842; see also H. Ben-Shammai, "The Karaites," *The History of Jerusalem: The Early Islamic Period (638–1099* (above, note 7), 207. Note that in Feuerstein (above, note 45, XVIII:8–10), Salmon refers even to the Tabernacle in the wilderness as *al-Quds.*

47. This leads Salmon to a detailed discussion of the Temple's gates (ibid., XV:25–XVIII: 26); parallel discussions, to the degree of verbal similarity, are found in Salmon's commentary on Song of Songs, preserved in St. Petersburg, ms. Firkovitch II, Evr.-Ar. I, 1406, fol. 125–140; there is not much new or different information there.

48. In his commentary on Ps. 122:2 , ms. Paris 289, fol. 106a.

49. Ms. British Library, Or. 2515 (*Catalogue*, no. 253), fol. 94b.

50. E.g. Feuerstein (above, note 45), XXXVII:26–XXXVIII:11.

51. As a rule, Salmon leaves the Hebrew name of Jerusalem in its original form in his translations and comments. Some exceptions may be found, e.g., Feuerstein (above, note 45), XII:24–25: "Nebuchadnezzar came to *Bayt al-Maqdis* in the year, etc." probably refers to Jerusalem.

52. This is an allusion to the well-known stories about the condition of the Temple Mount during the Byzantine period, when it was used as a depot for refuse.

53. Feuerstein (above, note 45), XLIV:23–30.

54. Arabic *tawḥḥush* renders Hebrew *shomema* in the Lam. 1:13, translated in the *Tanakh* as "forlorn."

55. Actually said of Jerusalem, see above.

56. The *Tanakh* translates desolation in the singular; other translations (e.g., King James) are more faithful to the Hebrew and have the plural here, which corresponds to Salmon's insistence.

57. It should be noted that the exegetes of the geonic period, even those who resided in Jerusalem, felt as if they were living in exile, or at least in an exilic age. The terms used in such contexts are: the age of *dawla* or *mulk*, i.e., government, control, and the age of *jāliya* or *jālūth* (see J. Blau, *The Emergence and Linguistic Background of Judeo-Arabic*² (Jerusalem, 1981), 162.

58. Ms. British Library Or. 2515 (*Catalogue*, no. 253), fol 73a.

59. The term *menuḥati* ("my resting-place") in this verse represents for the exegete the Temple; on this term see below, note 71.

60. Daniel al-Qūmisī, *Pitron Sheneim 'Asar* [Commentary on Minor Prophets], ed. I. D. Markon (Jerusalem, 1957), 36–37.

61. Saadya on Ps. (Qāfiḥ [above, note 18], 131); the prooftext adduced is Ezek. 24:21.

62. Interestingly, Yefet ben 'Eli interprets another occurrence of the "The Pride of Jacob" in Nah. 2:3 as a reference to the messiah; *Jefeth b. Ali's Arabic Commentary on Nāḥūm with Introduction*, Jews' College Publication no. 3, ed. H. Hirschfeld (London, 1911), 22 (Arabic), 36 (English).

63. See above, note 37.

64. I have elaborated on this point at some length in my article "Poetic Works and Lamentations of Qaraite 'Mourners of Zion'—Structure and Contents," *Knesset Ezra: Literature and Life in the Synagogue. Studies Presented to Ezra Fleischer* (Jerusalem, 1994), 220–24 (Hebrew).

65. As already noted, this is a favorite appellation for Jerusalem also with Saadya and other authors.

66. Ms. Paris 289, fol. 105a.

67. Fol. 106a.

68. Complaints of this kind abound in Karaite literature of the period; see for instance my article in *Knesset Ezra* (above, note 64).

69. This is the King James rendering of *ha-menuḥah ve-ha-naḥalah*, which for the purpose of the present study seems much more suitable than the "allotted haven" of the *Tanakh*.

70. Yefet commentary on Deut., Ms. Oriental Institute, St. Petersburg, C41, fol. 10a; according to its colophon the ms. was copied in Jerusalem, 24 Elul, 1825 Sel. = Jumād[!] II 920 AH, by Judah b. Abraham Ibn al-Naqqāsh, for Isaac b. Joseph b. Samuel 'Abd al-Walī. On another ms. copied by the same scribe in the same year, see M. Beit-Arié, "Hebrew Manuscripts Copied in Jerusalem before the Ottoman Conquest," *Jerusalem in the Middle Ages: Selected Papers*, eds. B. Z. Kedar and Z. Baras (Jerusalem, 1979), 275–77 (Hebrew). All the dates in mss. copied by this scribe in that year are somewhat problematic, as Beit-Arié had already pointed out. The reason for this is apparently that 5274 AM was a leap year according to the Rabbanite calendar, but not so in the Karaite calendar. The equivalent Christian dates have therefore to be pushed one month backwards, and the ms. quoted here was completed in the Middle of August, 1514.

71. As has been noted above (note 59), the term *menuḥah* is used already by Daniel al-Qūmisī to denote the Temple, on the basis of Ps. 132:14.

72. Fol. 100a.

73. Cambridge University Library, T-S Ar. 16.50.

74. "And there you are to bring your burnt offerings and other sacrifices, your tithes and contributions, your votive and farewell offerings, and the firstlings of your herds and flocks."

75. ‏וקד גמע פי הדא אלקול ז' אשיא תגאב אלי אלקדס אולהא עלתיכם וכו'.‏

76. ‏פאמא אן כאנת אלנדור מא לא יקרב מתל מן ינדר אלקמח ואלנביד ואלזית וגירה פהו עלי חסב מא יעתקדה צאחב אלנדר אן כאן נדרה עלי ציעפי בלדה פעליהם יקסמה ואן כאן ללמקימין פי אלקדס פאלי אלקדס יחמלה‏

77. It seems that the King James version is here closer to the exegete's interpretation: "But unto the place which the Lord your God shall choose out of all your tribes to put His name there, even unto His habitation shall ye seek, and thither you shalt come."

78. T-S Ar. 46.278.

79. The author discusses the suggestion that Scripture could have used here *sh'khinato* instead of *shikhno*, with complete disregard of the fact that term *shekhina*, which for him seems to be a basic term, is nowhere attested in the Bible. It is obvious that for the author *shekhina* and *kavod* (Presence and Glory) are interchangeable synonyms.

80. Here, too, I found the King James version more suitable to the exegete's purpose.

81. וקולה לשכנו ולם יקל לשכינתו תד' ליערף אנה אלי אלמוצ׳יע אלדי יכון[!] פיה אלשכינה
תדרשו[ן!] והו עלי צ׳ירבין אמא יכון אלכבוד מקים ואמא לא[!] מקים אליה תקצדו מתל הדא
אלזמאן אלדי כבוד יי ליס פי אלקדס ואליה נצלי כ'ק' לשכנו והו מוצ'יע סכנאה. ולהדה[ן!] קאל
כסא כבוד מרום מראי מק' מק' ולם יקל מקדשנו ליערף אן אלמוצ'יע אלדי אלמקדש פיה מכתאר
ואנה אן כאן אלכבוד פי אלמקדש או גאיב ענה אליה קצדנא כ'ק' מקום מקדש'

82. "Like an eagle who rouses his nestlings, Gliding down to his young, So did He spread His wings and taken him, Bear him along on His pinions." On Samuel's commentary, see the reference above, note 38.

83. Ms. British Library, Or. 8658, fol. 46a:11–13: כק' אם על פיך יובא נשר וכי ירים קינו
סלע ישכון ויתלונן על שן סלע ו' מצ'. כדלך ארץ ישי אעלי אלבלדאן ואלקדס אעלי מן גמיעהא כק'
וקמת ועלית אל המקום אש' יבחר ייי אליך בו

84. Markon (above, note 60), 68.

85. *Tanḥum ha-Yerushalmi's Commentary on the Minor Prophets*, ed. with Hebrew translation H. Shy (Jerusalem, 1991), 291:2–3. The same approach seems to have been followed in the King James rendering.

86. Or part of one subject, as is the interpretation of the *Tanakh*.

87. The dictionary was edited and published by S. L. Skoss, *The Hebrew-Arabic Dictionary of the Bible Known as Kitāb Jāmiʿ al-Alfāẓ (Agron)*, I–II, Yale Oriental Series, Researches XX–XXI (New Haven, 1936–45). This edition represents al-Fāsī's short recension of this work. Skoss described the long version in his introductions; I, xcv–cii; II, cl–clx.

88. Ibid., I, 31:34; II, 310:8.

89. This translation is found also in Saadya's commentary on Prov. 3:8 (ed. J. Qāfiḥ [Jerusalem, 1976] 45:7), but not as the main translation of the verse. A dialectal variant, ṣurra, is used by al-Fāsī; see Skoss (above, note 87), II, 6:58–59.

90. See for instance Tanḥuma, Qedoshim 10, in the popular editions.

91. I. Hasson, "The Muslim View of Jerusalem—The Qurʾān and Ḥadīth," *The History of Jerusalem: The Early Islamic Period (638–1099* (above, note 7), 383: "The rock which is in *Bayt al-Maqdis* is the center of the world." Note that in the midrashic sources quoted in the previous note it is the Ark that is in the center of the world, and the rock is situated in front of it.

92. Skoss (above, note 87), I, 31:23.

93. *al-ḥaraka wa-ʾl-ṭaqtaqa wa-ʾl-ṣurākh.*

94. Skoss (above, note 87), II, 58:16.

95. Some of them refer to verses or biblical terms discussed above.

96. Skoss (above, note 87), II, 482:60.

97. In modern publications (such as the ones quoted below in this note), his name is usually given as ʿAli ben Israel. However the biblical name ʿEli seems to have been quite common in the Middle Ages, both among Rabbanites and Karaites, and there is no reason to use the Arabic form for certain people. M. Steinschneider (*Die arabische Literatur der Juden* [Frankfurt am Main, 1902], §68) gives rather little information on him. Much important information is found in J. Mann, *Texts and Studies*, II (New York, 1972) 30–31, 58, and in interesting excerpts from his commentary on Samuel on pp. 95–96. On ʿEli's linguistic work, see Skoss's introduction to al-Fāsī (above, note 87), I, cvi–cxx (on this matter, see also the important contribution of Mann, op. cit., 96–98). A first-hand examination of the photocopy of his manuscript commentary on Samuel can ascertain beyond a doubt his Palestinian provenance or at least prolonged residence there.

98. He may have originated in Jerusalem; he was active in Egypt during the second half of the eleventh century; see my observations in "Hebrew in Arabic Characters: Qirqisānī's View," *Studies in Judaica, Karaitica and Islamica Presented to L. Nemoy*, ed. S. R. Brunswick (Ramat Gan, 1982), 122–23.

Jerusalem in the Late Middle Ages and Modern Era

32

Pilgrims, Politics and Holy Places: The Ethiopian Community in Jerusalem until ca. 1650

ANTHONY O'MAHONY

Introduction

The Ethiopian community in Jerusalem served at least from after the Crusader period onwards as an important point of contact between Ethiopia and the rest of the Christian world. The encounter which ensued took the form of a prolonged historical dialogue, a blend of religious, political, and cultural contacts, undertaken over many centuries by pilgrims, monks, and travelers passing through Jerusalem on their journey to Europe or Ethiopia. However, over time contacts became more difficult between these two parts of the Christian world as the forces of Islam sought to isolate and conquer the Ethiopian kingdom.[1]

The great Italian *Ethiopisant*, E. Cerulli, in his magisterial *Etiopi in Palestina*,[2] a comprehensive and meticulous historical survey of the Ethiopian community in Jerusalem, elaborates upon the above encounter in the following terms: knowledge regarding Ethiopia found its way to Europe through the itineraries of European pilgrims who had journeyed to the Holy Land. Their informants were members of the Ethiopian community or pilgrims in Jerusalem who, in their turn, on returning to Ethiopia brought back knowledge of Europe. The history of the Ethiopian presence in Jerusalem is also the history of the geographical, cultural and political knowledge regarding Ethiopia in medieval Europe and, at the same time, the history of the initial encounter between Europe and Ethiopia.[3] It was also in Jerusalem that the medieval European ideas regarding Ethiopia and its sovereign Prester John,[4] considered a potential ally in Christendom's war against Islam, were at least partly formed on the basis of the observations of the European pilgrims in the

467

Holy Land.[5] It was these ideas, both true and legendary, that stimulated the projects of the navigators of the great European discoveries towards the end of the fourteenth century,[6] and, as such, the Ethiopian presence in Palestine played an important role in the history of modern times.

Ethiopian communities were also established in Rome, and monks and pilgrims were also found in other parts of the Middle East, in the Coptic monasteries of Egypt,[7] as well as in Cyprus,[8] and in the second half of the fifteenth century a small Ethiopian community was discovered in Lebanon.[9] A polyglot Bible attests to an Ethiopian community of monks and pilgrims at a Coptic monastery in the desert around Scetis in the twelfth century.[10] Ethiopian monks were also found at the Church of St. George in the Christian quarter of Cairo and at Qusqam, an Egyptian monastery and pilgrimage site; this is evidenced by annotations to Ethiopic manuscripts.[11] From the fifteenth and sixteenth centuries onwards, a steady stream of Ethiopian pilgrims and diplomatic missions made their way to the Holy See.[12] Many of these pilgrims settled in Rome, where they provided Europe with knowledge regarding Ethiopia. In the pontifical archives there are a number of documents authorizing the payment of funds in support of these itinerant Ethiopians in Rome,[13] who were originally attached to the Church of St. Stephen. However, in 1539 the Holy See gave them a permanent house in "Santo Stefano dei Mori," situated behind St. Peter's. This would in time become the cradle of Ethiopian studies in Europe.[14]

Another point of possible contact between Ethiopia, Europe, and the Christian Orient was afforded by the ecclesiastical relations between Ethiopia and Egypt, as the only metropolitan or *abuna* in Ethiopia was a Coptic monk who would have been consecrated by the Coptic patriarch of Alexandria. This relationship required the dispatching of Ethiopian embassies to Cairo to secure the permission of the Muslim ruler and the cooperation of the patriarch. This brought the Ethiopian envoys into a place often frequented by Europeans and pilgrims on their way to or from Jerusalem.[15]

The importance of the Ethiopian presence in Jerusalem is, however, not limited to the growth of relations between Europe and Ethiopia, as Palestine also functioned for Ethiopia as a point of contact with Oriental Christians: Armenians,[16] Georgians,[17] Syrian Jacobites,[18] Nubians,[19] Copts,[20] and Maronites. The encounter between Ethiopians and these other Oriental Christians explains how cultural traditions and artistic influences[21] reached Ethiopia outside the close relationship between Ethiopia and Coptic Egypt.[22] Jerusalem widened the horizon of Ethiopia whose isolation from both Europe and the Christian Orient was thus much less hermetic than might have been supposed.[23]

The oldest testimony which has reached us about the presence of the Ethiopians in the Holy Land after the rise of Christianity is found in two letters from the circle of Saint Jerome who lived in Bethlehem between 386 and 412. His disciple Paula and her daughter Eustochium wrote to their friends in Rome, Lota and Marcella, mentioning the arrival of Ethiopian monks in the Holy Land. But it is difficult to know if the terms "Ethiopia," "Ethiopici," and "Ethiopes" are to be understood as pilgrims from the kingdom of Aksum or whether we should view these terms in these fourth-century texts as an expression for Africans and/or Black Africans in general.[24]

Over time, the Ethiopian pilgrims settled near the holy places in Palestine and came to form a more or less organized community. A variety of sources have preserved information on the presence of the Ethiopians in the Holy Land—letters and manuscripts sent to the Ethiopian community in Jerusalem from the Royal court in Ethiopia; travel accounts of European pilgrims to Jerusalem; chronicles of the other Christian communities in Jerusalem (Franciscans, Greeks, and Armenians); and, finally, historiographical works composed by Ethiopians living in the Holy Land.[25]

The Ethiopians in the Holy Land during the Middle Ages

Little is known about the life of the Ethiopians in Jerusalem from the fourth to thirteenth centuries. There is no certainty that there were Ethiopians amongst the "Surani" whom the Crusaders encountered when entering Jerusalem in July, 1099.[26] The Surani were Monophysite Christians in Palestine who were dependent on the jurisdiction of the Patriarch of Antioch. These included Syrians, Copts, Nubians, and possibly Ethiopians.[27] The Ethiopian monks and pilgrims would have worshiped and perhaps also lived with these other Oriental Christians, probably at the St. Mary Magdalen monastery in Jerusalem. These churches followed the teachings of the Alexandrian theologians who insisted on the union of the divine and human nature of Christ following the split in the Church at the Council of Chalcedon in 451.[28] The conquest of Jerusalem by Salah-ad-Din in September 1187 made a great impression on the Christians not only in Europe, but also in Ethiopia. One of the reasons given for Emperor Lalibella's construction of the rock churches in northern Ethiopia is said to have been the need felt by Ethiopians for a new Jerusalem.[29] Johann von Würzburg reports that Ethiopian pilgrims visited Jerusalem in the twelfth century, and refers to them as one of the nations who had a chapel in the Holy City.[30] In 1187, Salah ad-Din is said to have granted exemptions from a new communal tax to be paid to the Islamic rulers by the Greeks, Copts, Georgians, and Ethiopians. However, there is no evidence to prove that there were Ethiopians in Jerusalem during this period.[31]

The Syrian Jacobite historiographer Jacob Barhebraeus (1226–86) relates a story which throws some light on the presence of the Ethiopians in Jerusalem in the thirteenth century.[32] In 1237, a dispute broke out between the Coptic patriarch Cyril III ibn-Laqlaq (1235–43) and the Syrian Jacobite patriarch of Antioch, Ignatius II, when the former appointed and consecrated a Coptic bishop for Jerusalem. Barhebraeus tells us that an Ethiopian monk by the name of Thomas requested Ignatius, when visiting Jerusalem, to consecrate him Metropolitan of "Abyssinia." The normal procedure would be for the Ethiopian emperor to send a special embassy to the Coptic patriarch of Alexandria, not of Antioch, to obtain a new metropolitan or *abuna* for Ethiopia. The geographical boundary for ecclesiastical authority between the patriarchates of Antioch and Alexandria meant that Palestine and Jerusalem would be under the jurisdiction of Antioch. However, Cyril felt the need to consecrate a metropolitan to the Coptic community in Jerusalem due to the growing numbers of Egyptian Copts in Jerusalem and Syria, thus encroaching upon jurisdiction of the patriarchate of Antioch. The Ethiopian's request to be made metropolitan gave Ignatius the opportunity to repay Cyril since it was well known that Ethiopia depended on the patriarch of Alexandria. Barhebraeus remarks that this plan of Ignatius was considered illegal, as the metropolitan of Ethiopia was always an Egyptian Copt.[33] Ignatius, all too aware of the difficulties that the consecration of Thomas would pose, sought to consult the Dominican fathers.[34] The Dominicans made their opposition to the plan clear, but nevertheless offered their good services for an agreement to be reached between Cyril and Ignatius. However, the latter went ahead and consecrated the Ethiopian. The Dominicans, along with leaders of the Knights, Hospitalers, and Templars, protested the consecration before Ignatius. The patriarch decided to pass the incident off as a matter of linguistic misunderstanding and the affair was closed. There is no evidence that Thomas returned to Ethiopia.[35]

The reasons for the strong reaction of the Latins against Ignatius' actions are many. The position of the Latins in Palestine was relatively weak as against the growing power of the Ayyubid Sultan al-Malik al-Kamil (1180–1238) in Egypt. The Latins lived in Jerusalem on the Ayyubid's sufferance. The walls of the city had been demolished during the fifth Crusade and had not been rebuilt, and the Crusaders controlled very little of the hinterland. Furthermore, the action of the patriarch of Antioch could possibly have jeopardized the delicate negotiations which the Dominicans conducted with the patriarch of Alexandria for reunification between the Latin and Coptic churches.[36]

The presence of Ethiopians in Jerusalem in the thirteenth century is also explicitly attested in a Latin document, preserved in the Escorial, which can be dated to the end of that century.[37] In 1283, the Dominican friar Burchard of Mount Sion described the Ethiopians in his *Descriptio Terrae Sanctae* as "the most pious amongst the Orientals," a reference to their rigorous fasting and, in general, the characteristic features of their liturgical ceremonies which made such an impression on the European pilgrims to Jerusalem.[38]

It can be seen from various other sources that the Ethiopians were present in Jerusalem at the beginning of the thirteenth century. The first known letter addressed to the Ethiopian community in Jerusalem by the emperor dates from this period. The document is preserved in an Egyptian collection, a biography of the Sultan al-Malik al-Mansur Kalawan (1279–90). In 1290, Emperor Yagbe'ä Seyon (1285–94) sent an Ethiopian mission to Cairo with a letter and gifts for the Ethiopian community in Jerusalem, together with one hundred candles which were to be lighted in the churches there. The Ethiopian emperor also requested that the Ethiopians should be allowed to enter into the churches of Jerusalem without being subjected to a tax, especially since Ethiopian missions making their way to Cairo would often continue their journey in pilgrimage to the Holy City.[39]

We have no documentation that Ethiopians had direct knowledge of the Crusades. However, it seems unlikely that the kingdom was not aware of the military adventures of their fellow-Western Christians against Islam. It can only be assumed that the relative weakness of the Ethiopian kingdom in the thirteenth century, and the need to maintain good relations with the Ayyubid sultan in Egypt, precluded Christian Ethiopia from becoming more involved in this struggle in the eastern Mediterranean. After the fall of St. Jean d'Acre ('Akka) in 1291, which put an end to the Crusader domination in Palestine, voices were raised in the West for military action to reconquer the Holy Land. Various projects were conceived. One in particular was by Guillaume Adam, a Dominican friar who was later to become archbishop of Sultaniyyah and who had traveled to the island of Socotra in the Red Sea, where he had stayed for several months and from where he had made a number of unsuccessful attempts to travel to Ethiopia. In 1317, Adam submitted his plan for exterminating the Saracens, *De Modo Sarracenos Extirpandi*, which included the blockade of eastern trade in the Red Sea based on Socotra.[40] He also envisaged military cooperation between Europe and Ethiopia against the forces of Islam.[41]

The desire to establish contacts between Europe and Ethiopia was not just the preserve of the former but also of the latter. Niccolò da Poggibonsi, who had journeyed to Palestine between 1345–47, met a number of Ethiopians in Jerusalem who were also keen for an alliance with the Latins which would enable them to break the isolation imposed by the Islamic states.[42] We have details from the fourteenth century regarding the topography of the Ethiopian presence in Jerusalem and Palestine. Jacob of Verona states that in 1335 the Ethiopians possessed an altar in the Basilica of the Nativity in Bethlehem, and according to da Poggibonsi, writing in 1345, the Ethiopians had an altar in the apse of the Basilica of the Holy Sepulchre and in the chapel of the Virgin Mary of Golgotha. Da Poggibonsi further describes the Ethiopian liturgy and their participation in the procession on Palm Sunday. The Ethiopians were exempted from paying taxes to the sultan and from paying fees to enter the Holy Sepulchre; they were even permitted to carry the traditional Ethiopian handcross.[43]

In 1386, Johann von Bodmann visited the Holy Land and mentioned that two Ethiopian monks lived permanently as representatives of their community in the Church of the Holy Sepulchre in Jerusalem. By the time of Johann von Bodmann's visit, Muslim control over the Christian holy places was at times strictly enforced. He mentions that the door to the Holy Sepulchre was watched, permitting no one to enter the church except to replace one of the existing representatives or in the event of death.[44] This issue was to complicate relations between the Muslim ruler and their Christian subjects. It is recorded that when the Ethiopian Emperor Yeshaq (1414–27) learned that the door to the Holy Sepulchre remained closed and was only permitted to be opened on a few Christian feast days, this news led him to exact revenge on the Islamic communities surrounding his kingdom. However, it is probably more correct to say that Yeshaq's move against the Islamic states to the south was part of an expansionist policy being undertaken by the Ethiopian kingdom. Sultan Barsbay (1422–38) is supposed to have sought out the Coptic patriarch to kill him and to persecute the Christians in his territory in reaction to the Ethiopian emperor's plans, but for some unknown reason he refrained from carrying out this scheme.[45]

The Ethiopian Community in Fifteenth-
and Sixteenth-Century Jerusalem

Zar'a Ya'eqob's reign (1434–68) was a period of intense contact between Ethiopia and Jerusalem. The emperor sent an Ethiopian delegation to attend the Council of Florence in 1441, which was headed by Nicodemus, superior of the Ethiopian community in Jerusalem, and a year later sent an important pilgrimage from Ethiopia via Egypt to Jerusalem.

In 1441, Zar'a Ya'eqob commissioned monks from the Ethiopian community in Jerusalem to attend the Council of Florence (1438–45), which was called by Pope Eugene IV for the purpose of uniting the Eastern and Oriental churches with the papacy. Nicodemus, the head of the Ethiopian community in Jerusalem—and not the emperor—designated the four Ethiopians who would attend the Council of Florence.[46] In 1438, the Pope wished to issue a bull urging Prester John to expel the Muslims from Egypt and Palestine,[47] but a Franciscan friar, Alberto da Sarteano,[48] who had been appointed the apostolic commissioner *in partibus orientalibus Indie, Ethiopie, Egipti et Jerusalem* by the papal bull *Dum onus* (22 August, 1439), realized that the bull would have little effect and dissuaded the Pope from issuing it. However, the Pope entrusted a letter to friar Alberto da Sarteano to deliver to the head of the Ethiopian community, Nicodemus in Jerusalem. Four Ethiopian delegates from the community in Jerusalem were to travel to Egypt and, in the company of the Copts, embark for Europe; they arrived in Florence on 26 August, 1441. It has often been supposed that the Ethiopians were part of the same delegation as the Copts. In fact, even though they traveled together, and in spite of the relationship between the two churches, the delegations were separate and did not enjoy the same powers. The Copts had authority to accede to the bull of union, *Cantate domio,* whereas the Ethiopians could only observe and report back to the emperor, who was the effective head of the church. The Ethiopians did not have, and would not have had, authority on their own to subscribe to the union of the churches. No doubt the Pope hoped that, when notified of the outcome of the Council, the emperor would accede, but neither he nor his successors appear to have done so, and it is extremely improbable that Zarʿa Yaʿeqob would ever have consented to such a limitation of his own authority over religious matters.[49] A copy of the Latin text and Arabic translation of *Cantate domio* was sent to the Coptic patriarch of Alexandria, and attempts seem to have been made to send a copy to the Ethiopian court; there is some evidence that a copy of the bull was carefully studied by Zarʿa Yaʿeqob. Although the religious consequences of the Council of Florence were negligible for Ethiopia, it is quite possible that it exercised an important influence on cartographic information available in Europe regarding Ethiopian topography. The Ethiopian delegates sent from Jerusalem to the Council of Florence may have been responsible for much of the detail included in the map known as *Egyptus Novelo* and drawn in Florence under the supervision of the artist Pietro del Massajo.[50]

In 1481, a mission was sent to Egypt to ask the patriarch for a new *abuna.* On this occasion, the following requests were submitted to Sultan Qaʾitbay (1468–95):

1. when an Ethiopian mission makes its journey to Jerusalem, it should be exempt from paying taxes upon entering the Basilica of the Holy Sepulchre;

2. the basilica should remain open to all Christians for the duration of the Ethiopian mission's stay in Jerusalem;
3. during that stay, all Christians in Jerusalem should benefit from the same exemption from paying taxes, in honor of the Ethiopian mission.

In the fifteenth century, the Ethiopian emperors felt that they were in a position of strength vis-à-vis the Muslim rulers in Egypt to the north who held Palestine within their sphere of influence. As had become more or less customary, the mission of 1481 continued on to Jerusalem for pilgrimage purposes and to visit the Ethiopian community in the Holy City. They carried a decree permitting all Christians to enter the Holy Sepulchre without paying taxes. However, the local officials were said to have refused and would allow only members of the Ethiopian mission to enter the basilica; the members of the mission objected to this arrangement and insisted that the rights granted by the decree be honored. It is clear from the account by Mudir al-Din al-'Ulaymi, who recorded these events, that the Ethiopians were eventually allowed to enter the Holy Sepulchre along with members of the other Christian communities.[51] This event offers a concrete example of the origin of this tale brought to Europe by pilgrims regarding the privileged position of the Ethiopians in Jerusalem and the position of power that the Ethiopian emperor held against the sultan.[52]

Throughout the fifteenth century, the Ethiopian community consolidated its position in Jerusalem, and between 1460 and 1480 they acquired two more properties: the Chapel of Improperium inside the Basilica of the Holy Sepulchre and the Grotto of David on Mount Sion. In 1480, the Ethiopians owned the following in Jerusalem: (1) the chapel in the rotunda of the Basilica of the Holy Sepulchre; (2) the Chapel of Mary of Golgotha; (3) the Chapel of Improperium; and (4) the Grotto of David. By the beginning of the following century, the Ethiopian community was to have made two further acquisitions: an altar in the chapel of the Tomb of Mary in Gethsemane; and co-ownership with the Copts of a church near the Jordan River. In 1512, they acquired the Chapel of the Sacrifice of Abraham situated at the foot of Calvary. The principal center for the Ethiopian community in Jerusalem, however, was the monastery at the Grotto of David, which they lost when the Franciscans were expelled in 1559.

Even before the Ottoman conquest of Palestine in 1517, the power of the Egyptian rulers was in decline, which brought about a loosening of the restrictions on the position of the Christians in Jerusalem. In March 1513, under Sultan Qansuh al-Ghawri (1516–30), the Christians were granted exemption from paying taxes on arrival at Jaffa, Gaza, Ramallah, and Lydda, and on entering the Basilica of the Holy Sepulchre; the decree was issued in the form of an inscription at the left entrance of the basilica. However, these changes must be seen within a wider political context: the Mamluk sultan was threatened politically by expansion of the Ottomans to the east and economically by the growing maritime influence of the European powers to the south and west.

Barbone Morosini, a Venetian visiting Palestine in 1514, just prior to the Ottoman conquest, mentions in his itinerary all the sites traditionally associated with the Ethiopian presence in Jerusalem: the chapel in the Basilica of the Holy Sepulchre; the Chapel of Mary at Golgotha; the Chapel of Improperium; the Chapel of the Sacrifice of Abraham; and the Grotto of David. He also identifies the presence of Ethiopians in Bethlehem, where they celebrated at their own altar in the Basilica of the Nativity. This has been viewed as verifying the account of Jacob of Verona who places the Ethiopians there in 1335, which means that there could have been an Ethiopian presence in Bethlehem for nearly two centuries.[53]

The Arab historian Ibn Iyas describes probably the last Ethiopian embassy to Jerusalem before the change from Mamluk to Ottoman rule; it departed Cairo in 1516 on its way to Jerusalem and stayed there for a period of three days.[54] With regard to the Ethiopian pilgrims, they would have had to leave Ethiopia at Epiphany in order to be in Jerusalem for the celebrations of the Holy Week and Easter. Francesco Alvares, the chaplain of the Portuguese mission to Ethiopia, wrote that in 1520 another Ethiopian mission set out for Jerusalem, but this time the caravan included some 336 pilgrims. The caravan was attacked by Bedouins and almost completely annihilated, except for fifteen monks who escaped and continued their pilgrimage. After the destruction of the caravan, it is reported that the Ethiopian pilgrims did not set out on pilgrimage to the Holy Land for several years.[55]

The Ethiopian Community in Jerusalem after the Ottoman Conquest: 1517–1650

Cerulli has shown that the Ethiopian community in Jerusalem attained its greatest prosperity during the last years of the Mamluk rule, however this relatively good position was changed drastically for the worse by two events: the Ottoman conquest of Palestine in 1517 and the attack on Ethiopia by Ahmad Gran in the 1520s during which time he managed to invade most of the Christian kingdom, burning churches, monasteries, manuscripts, and icons, and killing those who refused to embrace Islam. These two events presaged hard times for the Ethiopian community in Jerusalem. Cut off from

Ethiopia, the community could no longer expect political and financial support and could not find means to pay the taxes and bribes demanded by the new Ottoman rulers. The result was a gradual lost of its rights and privileges in the holy places. Nevertheless, the Ethiopian community in Jerusalem did manage to survive the difficult period after the Ottoman conquest. The French pilgrim Denis Possot found Ethiopian monks living in Dair as-Sultan, and in his book *Le voyage de la Terre Sainte*, he describes how he and a small group of other French pilgrims visited that place where "Abraham fulfilled his duty of sacrificing Isaac, and the chapel is guarded by the black people called Abyssinians."[56]

The Portuguese Franciscan friar Pantaleão de Aveiro,[57] who spent a year and eight months in the Holy Land, from April 1563 till November 1564, describes in detail the position of the Ethiopian community in Jerusalem in his *Itinerário da Terra Santa, e suas particularidades*.[58] The whole of chapter XXXII, "*Abexins do preste Joaõ*" or "Prester John's Abyssinians," is an account of the Ethiopian community which the Portuguese Franciscan describes with great sympathy and admiration. He mentions Ethiopian participation in various ceremonies in Jerusalem: on the Mount of Olives during the feast of the Ascension—a privilege they have since lost—as well as participation in the ceremony of the Holy Fire. On the eve of Ascension Day, the Franciscan friars would go to the ceremonies on the Mount of Olives to sing vespers; they would remain during the night and sing high mass, and then take communion the following morning. This practice was adopted by the other Christians in Jerusalem. Pantaleão relates in his *Itinerário* how he saw Ethiopians, both men and women, among those taking communion, behaving with a devotion that edified him. He also mentions that it was their custom not to spit on the day on which they took communion and they did not eat anything like olives or plums which would necessitate taking stones out of their mouths. Pantaleão tells us that during the ceremony of the Holy Fire on Holy Saturday, the Ottoman authorities admitted only two Ethiopians into the chapel of the Holy Sepulchre, from which they emerged after some time with lighted candles.[59]

The five German pilgrim narratives from approximately the same time as Pantaleão's visit, which Cerulli examined for his *Etiopi in Palestina*, afford evidence that the Ethiopians possessed two chapels and refer ambiguously to two more. The first are the Chapel of Mocking and a chapel in the rotunda of the Church of the Holy Sepulchre. The *Itinerário* confirms their occupation of both (chapters XXVI and XXXV). Cerulli remarks that the Chapel of Abraham's Sacrifice, which about ten years earlier had been the principal center for the Ethiopians, is mentioned by only one of his five Germans, and even he does not state explicitly that it still belonged to them, while another passage might relate either to this chapel or to one in the forecourt, at one time called St. Mary of Golgotha and known to have been occupied by the Ethiopians by the mid-fourteenth century. The *Itinerário* establishes that both these were still in their possession, and Cerulli's suggestion that the second might have passed to the Franciscans by 1559 is not therefore tenable. Like the five German pilgrims, Pantaleão also makes no reference to the Ethiopians in connection with David's cave on Mount Sion, thus affording negative support to Cerulli's suggestion that the community had lost it when the Franciscans were deprived of their convent. In chapter XXII, Pantaleão also speaks of an Ethiopian martyr who was burnt by the Moors in the forecourt of the Church of the Holy Sepulchre, leaving a footprint in one of the stone slabs "as though on soft wax."

Pantaleão insists more than once that, although the Ethiopians had many elements not in conformity with what he considered to be proper Christian practice, they were yet obedient to the Holy See. Pantaleão describes the Ethiopians in Palestine as friends of the Latins who showed them deference and publicly took pride in their own subjection to the Holy See.

The Ethiopians were also said to be on good terms with the Ottomans. Pantaleão's explanation is the old story that the Prester John was able to divert the water of the Nile and so ruin Egypt; the sultan therefore paid something to the prester and treated his subjects well. It is interesting that the community should have been favorably regarded at this time, for it has been shown that the Ottoman conquest of Palestine in 1517 was, in fact, followed by a considerable decline in its prosperity.

After the Ottoman conquest of Palestine and Egypt in 1517, it is quite possible that many of those Ethiopian manuscripts from Jerusalem, which are today to be found in papal and Italian libraries, reached Europe with refugees leaving the Holy Land at that time. Some members of their community, but not all, left for Italy, Austria, and Spain. Between 1530 and 1550, dramatic years for the homeland, Ethiopians were back in Jerusalem, certainly out of devotion, but also to seek help from Christian Europe against the invasion of Ahmad Gran. By 1640, the Ethiopians came under the charge of the Armenians, and in 1654 their rights concerning property and religious ritual were given over to the Greeks. During the eighteenth century there were few Ethiopians in Jerusalem, while the nineteenth century saw their return to Dair as-Sultan.[60]

Notes

1. H. Erlich, *Ethiopia and the Middle East* (Boulder, 1994), 3–40. On the impact of Islam upon Ethiopia, see J. S. Trimingham, *Islam in Ethiopia* (Oxford, 1952); J. Cuoq, *L'Islam en Éthiopie des origines au XVIe siècle* (Paris, 1981); and E. Cerulli, *L'Islam de ieri e di oggi* (Rome, 1971).

2. Idem, *Etiopi in Palestina: Storia della Comunità Etiopica di Gerusalemme*, 2 vols. (Rome, 1943 and 1947); idem, "Tre nuovi documenti sugli in Palestina nel secolo XV," *Analecta Biblica* 12 (1959), 33–47. See the following studies on the Ethiopian community in Jerusalem: E. van Donzel: "The Ethiopian Presence in Jerusalem until 1517," *The Third International Conference on Bilad al-Sham: Palestine 19–24 April 1980* (Irbid, 1983), I, 93–104; K. Stoffregen-Pedersen, "The *Qeddusan*: The Ethiopian Christians in the Holy Land," *The Christian Heritage in the Holy Land*, eds. A. O'Mahony et al. (London, 1995), 129–48; idem, *The History of the Ethiopian Community in the Holy Land from the Time of Emperor Tewodros II till 1974* (Jerusalem, 1983); O. Meinardus: "The Ethiopians in Jerusalem," *Zeitschrift für Kirchengeschichte* 76 (1965), 112–47, 217–32.

3. On the relationship between Ethiopia and Europe, see the important studies by R. Lefèvre, "Riflessi Etiopici nella cultura Europea del Medioevo e des Rinascimento," *Annali Lateranensi* 8 (1944), 9–89; 9 (1945), 331–444; 11 (1947) 255–342.

4. C. F. Beckingham, " 'The Achievements of Prester John' and 'The Quest for Prester John'," *Between Islam and Christendom: Travellers, Facts and Legends in the Middle Ages and the Renaissance* (London, 1983), 3–24, 291–310). See further idem and Bernard Hamilton (eds.), *Prester John, the Mongols and the Ten Lost Tribes* (London, 1996).

5. European travelers to Palestine often reported exaggerated accounts of the decisive role which Ethiopia could play in a united Christian front against the Islamic powers in the eastern Mediterrranean. On the impact that the Ethiopians in Jerusalem had on various pilgrims from Europe to the Holy Land, see O. Meinardus, "Some Observations of Ethiopian Rituals by Mediaeval Pilgrims," *Publication de l'Institut des Études Orientales de la Bibliothèque Patriarcale d'Alexandrie* 13 (1964), 129–36. A constant theme in these accounts since the fourteenth century is the absolute control which the Ethiopians were believed to have over the flow of the Nile. On the association of Ethiopia and the origins of the Nile in European thought, see O. G. S. Crawford, "Some Medieval Theories about the Nile," *The Geographical Journal* 114 (1949), 6–29; E.-D. Hecht, "Ethiopia Threatens to Block the Nile," *Azania* 23 (1988), 1–10.

6. J. Thornton, *Africa and Africans in the Making of the Atlantic World, 1400–1680* (Cambridge, 1992), 25, 31–32; and see the important work by F. M. Rogers, *The Quest for Eastern Christians: Travels and Rumour in the Age of Discovery* (Minneapolis, 1962).

7. O. Meinardus, "Ethiopian Monks in Egypt," *Publication de l'Institut des Études Orientales de la Bibliothèque Patriarcale d'Alexandrie* 11 (1962), 61–70.

8. R. Lefèvre, "Roma e la Communità Etiopica di Cipro nei Secoli XV e XVI," *Rassegna di Studi Etiopica* 1 (1943), 71–86; E. Cerulli, "Two Ethiopian Tales on the Christians of Cyprus," *Abba Salama* 1 (1970), 178–85.

9. Idem, *Etiopi in Palestina* (above, note 2), I, 325–33.

10. The polyglot biblical texts are composed in parallel columns in Armenian, Arabic, Coptic, Syriac and Ge'ez. A note in Paris, Bib. Nat., éth. 46 indicates that the Ethiopian monks were still at Scetis in 1419; H. Zotenberg, *Catalogue des manuscrits éthiopiens (Ghe'ez et amharic) de la Bibliothèque Nationale* (Paris, 1877), 45. For further details, see M. Heldman, *The Marian Icons of the Painter Fre Seyon: A Study in Fifteenth-Century Ethiopian Art, Patronage and Spirituality* (Wiesbaden, 1994), 140–41.

11. Paris, Bib. Nat., éth. 35 was, according to a colophon, executed at the church of St.

George during the reign of Eskender (1478–94); Zotenberg (above, note 10), 32–6. The Four Gospels (Paris, Bib. Nat., éth. 32) was sent by the emperor Sayfa Ar'ad (1344–72) to the monastery of the Apostles at Qusqam; Zotenberg (above, note 10), 24–29. See Heldman (above, note 10), 140–41.

12. C. F. Beckingham, "An Ethiopian Embassy to Europe c. 1310," *Journal of Semitic Studies* 34 (1989), 337–46; idem, "Ethiopia and Europe 1200–1650," *The European Outthrust and Encounter: the First Phase c. 1400–c.1700*, eds. C. H. Clough and P. E. H. Hair (Liverpool, 1994), 77–95; P. Lachat: "Une ambassade éthiopienne auprès de Clement V, à Avignon, en 1310," *Annali Lateranensi* 31 (1967), 9–21.

13. R. Lefèvre, "Documenti Pontifici sui Rapporti con l'Etiopia nei Secoli XV e XVI," *Rassegna di Studi Etiopica* 5 (1946), 17–41; idem, "Note su alcuni pellegrini etiopi in Roma al tempo di Leone X," *Rassegna di Studi Etiopica* 21 (1965), 16–26.

14. M. Chaine, "Un monastère éthiopien à Rome au XVe et XVIe siècles, San Stefano dei Mori," *Mélanges de la Faculté Orientale* 5 (1911), 1–37; S. Euringer, "S. Stefano dei Mori in seiner Bedeutung für die abessinische Sprachwissenschaft und Missions Geschichte," *Oriens Christianus* 3, Series X (1935); P. Mauro da Leonessa, *Santo Stefano Maggiore degli Abissini e le Relazioni Romano-Etiopiche* (Vatican, 1929).

15. Abba Ayele' Taklahaymanot, "The Egyptian Metropolitan of the Ethiopian Church: a Study on a Chapter of History of the Ethiopian Church," *Orientalia Christiana Periodica* 54 (1988), 175–222.

16. K. Hintlian, *History of the Armenians in the Holy Land*[2] (Jerusalem, 1989); A. K. Sanjian, *The Armenian Communities in Syria under Ottoman Dominion* (Cambridge, MA, 1965).

17. G. Peradze, "An Account of the Georgian Monks and Monasteries in Palestine," *Georgica* 4–5 (1973), 181–246.

18. A. Palmer, "The History of the Syrian Orthodox in Jerusalem," *OC* 75 (1991), 16–43; 76 (1992), 74–94.

19. O. Meinardus, "The Christian Kingdoms of Nubia," *Cahier d'histoire égyptienne* 10 (1966), 133–64.

20. Idem, *The Copts in Jerusalem* (Cairo, 1960); idem, "The Copts in Jerusalem and the Question of the Holy Places," *Coptic Church Review* 16 (1995), 9–25; and idem, "The Copts in Jerusalem and the Question of the Holy Places," *Christian Heritage in the Holy Land* (above, note 2), 112–28.

21. Heldman (above, note 10), 139–62; T. Tamrat, *Church and State in Ethiopia 1270–1527* (Oxford, 1972), 248–67.

22. O. Meinardus, "A brief history of the Abunate of Ethiopia," *Wiener Zeitschrift für die Kunde des Morgenlandes* 58 (1962), 39–65.

23. For the important relationship between Ethiopia and Armenia, see in particular R. Pankhurst, "The History of Ethiopian-Armenian Relations," *REA* (NS) 12 (1977), 273–345; 13 (1978/79), 259–312; 15 (1981), 355–400.

24. Cerulli, *Etiopi in Palestina* (above, note 2), I, 1–7.

25. For a detailed discussion, see E. Issac, "Shelf List of Ethiopian Manuscripts in the Monasteries of the Ethiopian Patriarchate of Jerusalem," *Rassegna di Studi Etiopica* 30 (1984/86), 53–80; K. Stoffregen-Pedersen, "The Historiography of the Ethiopian Monastery in Jerusalem," *Ethiopian Studies: Proceedings of the Sixth International Conference, Tel Aviv, 14–17 April 1980*, ed. G. Goldenburg (Rotterdam and Boston, 1986), 419–26.

26. Cerulli, *Etiopi in Palestina* (above, note 2), I, 8–19.

27. R. Rose, "The Native Christians of Jerusalem, 1187–1260," *The Horns of Hattin*, ed. B. Z. Kedar (London, 1992), 239–49; B. Hamilton, *The Latin Church in the Crusader States: The Secular Church* (London, 1980), 188–211, 332–60.

28. W. H. C. Frend, *The Rise of the Monophysite Movement: Chapters in the History of the Church in the Fifth and Sixth Centuries* (Cambridge, 1972).

29. M. Heldman, "Architectural Symbolism, Sacred Geography and the Ethiopian Church," *Journal of Religion in Africa* 22 (1992), 222–41.

30. Cerulli, *Etiopi in Palestina* (above, note 2), I, 16.

31. Ibid., I, 31–37.

32. J. B. Abbeloos and Th. J. Lamy (eds.), *Gregorii Barhebraei, Chronicon Ecclesiasticum*, II (Louvain, 1872–77), 654–64; Cerulli, *Etiopi in Palestina* (above, note 2), I, 62–76.

33. The right of the Coptic church in Egypt to appoint the metropolitan or *abuna* of the Ethiopian church must be considered against the background of the apocryphal canon of the Council of Nicea; P. Mauro da Leonessa, "La versione etiopica dei canoni apocrifi del Concilio di Nicea," *Rassegna di Studi Etiopici* 2 (1942), 34–36.

34. J.-F. Friedenthal, "Dominican Involvement in the Crusader States," *New Blackfriars* 885 (1994), 429–37; F.-M. Abel, "Le Couvent des Frères Prêcheurs à Saint Jean d'Acre," *RB* 43 (1934), 265–84.

35. Tamrat (above, note 21), 70.

36. Hamilton (above, note 27), 350–51.

37. G. Antolín: *Catalogo de los códices latinos de la Real Biblioteca del Escorial*, III (Madrid, 1913), 44–45; Cerulli, *Etiopi in Palestina* (above, note 2), I, 77–79.

38. On Burchard of Mount Sion, see A. Grabois, "Christian Pilgrims in the Thirteenth Century and the Latin Kingdom of Jerusalem: Burchard of Mount Sion," *Outremer: Studies in the History of the Crusading Kingdom of Jerusalem*, eds. B. Z. Kedar et al. (Jerusalem, 1982), 285–95.

39. E. Quatremère: *Mémoires géographiques et historiques sur l'égypte et sur quelques contrées voisines*, II (Paris, 1811), 267–68; and Cerulli, *Etiopi in Palestina* (above, note 2), I, 88–90.

40. Beckingham, "Ethiopian Embassy" (above, note 12), 343–44; idem, "Some Notes on the History of Socotra," *Arabic and Islamic Studies*, eds. R. L. Bidwell and G. R. Smith (London, 1983), 172–81. For Guillaume Adam, see C. Kohler, "Documents relatifs à Guillaume Adam, Archevêque de Sultanieh, puis d'Antivari et son entourage (1318–46)," *Revue de l'Orient Latin* 10 (1903–04).

41. Cerulli, *Etiopi in Palestina* (above, note 2), I, 91–101.

42. Tamrat (above, note 21), 252–53. For Niccolò da Poggibonsi, see G. Golubovich, *Biblioteca Bio-Bibliografica della Terra Santa e dell'Oriente Francescano*, V: *Annali di Terra Santa dal 1346 al 1400* (Quaracchi, 1927); idem, *Fra Niccolò da Poggibonsi: A Voyage beyond the Seas (1346–1350)* (Jerusalem, 1945).

43. Cerulli, *Etiopi in Palestina* (above, note 2), I, 112–34.

44. Ibid., I, 162–73.

45. Ibid., I, 230–33.

46. See the following studies on Ethiopian participation at the Council of Florence: E. Cerulli: "L'Etiopia del secolo XV nel nuovi documenti storici," *Africa Italiana* 5 (1935) 58–80; idem, "Eugenio IV e gli Etiopi al Concilio di Firenze nel 1441," *Reale Accademia dei Lincei Rendiconti*, 7/IX (Rome, 1933), 347–68; G. Hoffman, "Le 'Chiese' Copta ed Etiopica nel Concilio di Firenze," *La civiltà cattolica* 2 (1942), 141–46, 228–35; R. Lefèvre, "Presenze etiopiche in Italia prima del Concilio di Firenze del 1439," *Rassegna di Studi Etiopica* 22 (1967–68), 5–26; and J. Gill, *The Council of Florence* (Cambridge, 1959), 321–27.

47. S. Tedeschi, "Etiopi e Copti al Concilio di Firenze," *Annuarium Historiae Conciliorum* 2 (1991), 380–407.

48. P. Santoni, "Albert da Sarteano, observant et humaniste, envoye pontifical à Jérusalem et au Caire," *Mélanges de l'École Française de Rome* 86 (1974), 189–97.

49. G. Haile, *The Mariology of Emperor Zar'a Ya'eqob of Ethiopia* (Rome, 1992); Tamrat (above, note 21), 206–47.

50. O. G. S. Crawford, *Ethiopian Itineraries circa 1400–1524* (Cambridge, 1958); C. F. Beckingham, "European Sources for Ethiopian History before 1634," *Paideuma* 33 (1987), 167–78.

51. 'Abd al-Rahman b. Muhammad Mujir al-Din al 'Ulaymi, *Kitab al-uns al-jalil bi-ta'rikh al-Quds wa al-Khalil,* II (Bulak, 1283), 657–58; Cerulli: *Etiopi in Palestina* (above, note 2), I, 283–84.

52. G. Wiet, "Les relations égypto–abyssines sous les sultans mamlouks," *Bulletin de la Societe d'Archeologie Copte* 4 (1938), 115–40, esp. p. 130.

53. The account of Barbone Morosini remains unpublished and is conserved in the Bibliotheca Marciana di Venezia; see also Cerulli, *Etiopi in Palestina* (above, note 2), I, 372–78.

54. Wiet (above, note 52), 136–39; Cerulli, *Etiopi in Palestina* (above, note 2), I, 381–94, where accounts of the mission from various Ethiopian and European documents are examined.

55. *The Prester John of the Indies. A True Relation of the Prester John, being the Narrative of the Portuguese Embassy to Ethiopia in 1520, written by Father Francesco Alvares,* trans. Lord Stanley of Alderly (1891), rev. and ed. with additional material by C. F. Beckingham and G. W. B. Huntingford (Cambridge, 1961).

56. D. Possot, *Le Voyage de la Terre Sainte,* annotated by Ch. Shefer (Paris, 1532; Paris [Leroux], 1890).

57. C. F. Beckingham, "Pantaleão de Aveiro and the Ethiopian Community in Jerusalem," *JSS* 7 (1962), 325–38; idem, "The Itinerário of Fr. Pantaleão de Aveiro," *Revista da Universidade de Coimbra* 27 (1979), 3–11.

58. The first-known edition was published in Lisbon in 1593 by Simão Lopes and reprinted in 1596, 1600, 1685, 1721 and 1732 in Lisbon, and in 1927 in Coimbra. This important account was one of the few sources which Cerulli did not use in his study *Etiopi in Palestina,* and awaits a critical edition based on the various editions.

59. There are also Armenian accounts which record Ethiopian participation at the Holy Fire: K. Hintlian, "Travellers and Pilgrims in the Holy Land: the Armenian Patriarchate of Jerusalem in the 17th and 18th Century," *Christian Heritage in the Holy Land* (above, note 2), 149–59.

60. S. Tedeschi, "Profilio storico di Dayr-as-Sultan," *Journal of Ethiopian Studies* 2 (1964), 92–130; K. Pedersen-Stoffregen, "Deir es-Sultan: The Ethiopian Monastery in Jerusalem," *Quaderni di Studi Etiopici* 8–9 (1987–88), 33–47.

33

The Greek Orthodox Community of Jerusalem in International Politics: International Solutions for Jerusalem and the Greek Orthodox Community in the Nineteenth and Twentieth Centuries

SOTIRIS ROUSSOS

Since the early eighteenth century, the diplomatic corps of countries such as France, Austria, and Russia had believed that Jerusalem should be handled as a special issue and that the Holy City should be "governed" under a special status separate from the political and social situation in the region. It was this very idea that led to Russo-Turkish agreements in the mid-eighteenth century and the great diplomatic effort regarding the protection of the Holy Places throughout the nineteenth century; it was this idea that also led to the abortive International Commission for the Holy Places in the early 1920s and propelled the proposals for internationalization in 1946–47.

The first part of the essay will cover the nineteenth century and the attitude of the Orthodox Patriarchate and community toward the interests and activities of England, Prussia, France, and the rejuvenated Catholic presence in Jerusalem as well as the increasing Russian influence. The period of post-World War I and of the British Mandate, with its attempts to find an international solution by setting up a special status for Jerusalem, will then be examined. In this respect, the International Commission for the Holy Places, and the British Commissions on the affairs of the Greek Orthodox Church in 1920s, will also be addressed. The third part of the paper will examine the attitude of the Greek Orthodox community and Church toward proposals for internationalization of the Holy City in the critical period of 1946–48.

✦ ✦ ✦

From the fifteenth century onward, the cornerstone of the Patriarchate's attitude and stance toward international intervention was its self-perception as the guardian of the Holy Places in the name of eastern Christianity. The Greek Orthodox patriarchs viewed themselves as heirs of Patriarch Sophronius who arranged the terms of Jerusalem's capitulation with the Caliph ʿUmar in 636. The rights and privileges of the Orthodox Church in the Holy Land were, according to the same view, secured by the *Akhdname* (Firman) of ʿUmar which was held by the Greek Orthodox Patriarchate.[1]

The Greek Orthodox Patriarchate saw also itself as the guardian of the Holy Places in the name of the Greek nation, το Γένος τῶν Ρωμαίων. For them, the Greek nation was the continuation of the later Byzantine period, the continuation of a Greek-speaking, Orthodox culture. Although the Greek Orthodox Church covered several races with different languages and cultures, it was this culture of the late Byzantine elite that prevailed. This elite became the leading group of the Greek Orthodox *millet*, effectively identifying the Greek Orthodox, *Rum*, with the Greeks.[2]

The Ottoman conquest of Jerusalem led to the subordination of the Patriarchates of Jerusalem, Antioch, and Alexandria to the Ecumenical Patriarchate of Constantinople. From the mid-sixteenth century onward, and for nearly three centuries, the Patriarch of Jerusalem resided in Istanbul. The *millet* system afforded the Ecumenical Patriarch a leading role in Orthodox Christian affairs—he was the leader of the *Rum millet* and of all the Orthodox regardless of language or race. The Greek Orthodox Patriarchate of Constantinople became the sole channel of communication between the *Porte* and the Greek Orthodox subjects. The Patriarch of Constantinople, therefore, could influence the election of the Patriarch of Jerusalem and consequently the administration of the Holy Places in the city.

The concentration of all this power transformed the Patriarchate into a center of intrigue and political maneuvering, including bribery for both removing and appointing patriarchs. During the seventeenth century, there were thirty-one patriarchs with an average tenure of no more than three years. During the same period, many of those patriarchs were deposed and reinstated, making a total of about sixty changes. This vacillation and instability weakened the patriarchs and strengthened the power of the Patriarchate's Greek-speaking apparatus, the *Phanariotes.*[3]

Members of that Greek-speaking elite also became part of high echelons of the Ottoman bureaucracy. The eighteenth century was marked by the domination of the *Phanariotes*, who had gained wealth and power and thus dictated their will to the ecclesiastics. Efforts by patriarchs to side with Greek Orthodox middle-class craftsmen guilds in order to counterbalance the *Phanariotes* did not bear any fruits.[4]

The arena of antagonism and maneuvering for the control of the Holy Places had now been transferred to the Ottoman court, the *Porte*, in Istanbul. During the eighteenth century, the influence of western powers, and particularly France, in the Ottoman empire reached unprecedented proportions.[5] Turkey had to grant certain privileges and Catholic influence reached its peak during the same period. The alliance between France and the Ottomans led to the Capitulation of 1740, a treaty which gave the French extensive trade and other privileges concerning the protection of French subjects and the building of churches. Among other provisions, the treaty gave the Franciscan Order a dominant position in the Holy Places at the expense of the Greek Orthodox Patriarchate. It was the first time since the crusades that a foreign, European power was in a position to regulate the status quo in the Holy Places and, as such, "internationalized" the issue.

At the beginning of the eighteenth century, the Patriarchate of Antioch, neglected as it was by Constantinople, turned to the French consuls and the Catholic Church. The Patriarchate of Alexandria followed suit. The shifting of loyalties from Constantinople to Rome concerning the Patriarchates of Antioch and Alexandria in 1721 increased the tension between the churches of Old and New Rome.[6] This French-Catholic interference was seen by the Orthodox as the greatest danger against the Greek Orthodox preeminence in the Holy Places. The official historian of the Patriarchate, Chrysostomos Papadopoulos, saw the reestablishment of Orthodox dominance in 1757 as an event of great importance.[7]

It was at that time that the parties of a centuries-long antagonism were crystallized. On one hand, the Catholics rested on the influence of foreign, western powers, namely France and Austria, and thus wished the "internationalization" of the issue. On the other, the Greek Orthodox Church and its apparatus, the *Phanar,* had to rely on the indigenous Greek Orthodox population and work in close connection with the Ottoman bureaucracy, central and local, and hence was always cautious toward foreign, "international" involvement.

The emergence of Russia as protector of the Orthodox of the Ottoman empire in the eighteenth century did not alter the attitude of the Greek Orthodox Church. During the Russo-Turkish war of 1787–91, the working relations between the Patriarchate, the *Porte,* and the local pasha helped the Confraternity of the Holy Sepulchre to overcome the disturbances of Muslims Arabs.[8] Similarly, at the beginning of the nineteenth century, the dispute between the Greek Orthodox and the Armenian Church over some of the Holy Places was settled through mediation by the Greek high-ranking member of the Ottoman bureaucracy, Georgios Karatzas, without involving Russia or any other European power.

The notion that the Holy Places were part of the international agenda, and indeed part of western diplomacy, became dominant during the Crimean crisis. In his endless search for prestige, Napoleon III decided to back the Catholics in the Holy Places (at the expense of the Greek Orthodox Patriarchate). Russian prestige was challenged and the issue became more perplexing due to secret concessions made by the Ottomans to both the Latins and the Orthodox. After laborious diplomatic efforts, at the end of 1852, the Ottomans decided to side with the Latins, believing that a Franco-Turkish alliance could thwart any Russian threat.[9]

The struggle for domination over the Holy Places, as well as Russian demands for further protection over Christian subjects of the Ottoman empire, led to the confrontation between Russia on the one hand, and France, England, and the Ottomans on the other. However, despite its Near Eastern pretext, the Crimean war was primarily fought for domination in central Europe and its main aim was to weaken the conservative alliance of Austria, Prussia, and Russia.[10]

As far as the Holy Places were concerned, the Paris Conference (1856) reestablished the status quo ante annulling the concessions given to the Latins by the Ottomans. Although the Greeks became the dominant church in the Holy Places, they had to share certain shrines with the Latins and the Armenians. The transfer of decision-making from Istanbul to Paris and other European capitals had been detrimental to Greek maneuvering and to its negotiating position.

Throughout the nineteenth century, it was deeply rooted in the Greek Orthodox conscience that the aim of all western diplomats in Istanbul, particularly of the French, was to protect and promote the Catholic interests in the Holy Places. According to a pamphlet of the Patriarchate published in Athens in 1919, every French ambassador in Istanbul was a staunch supporter of Catholicism and a fierce enemy of the Greek Orthodox.[11]

In the meantime, Palestine had become a common area of western interest and acquisition for both Protestant and Catholic groups. It was under the Prussian and English umbrella that the Protestant Bishopric of Jerusalem came into existence in 1841. Despite internal differences between the Anglicans and the Evangelicals, and their eventual failure, the bishopric gave impetus to Protestant activity in the Levant.[12]

For the Russians, these activities seemed to be the forerunners of Prussian and British political influence and penetration. Russian intervention and protection, though Orthodox, was not welcomed by the Greek Orthodox Patriarchate of Jerusalem. It was seen as an endeavor to dominate the Holy Places, playing the indigenous Arab Orthodox population against the Greek-speaking Patriarchate. It reminded them of the Slavonic Benevolent Society in Bulgaria which led to the emergence of Bulgarian "Church nationalism" and the subsequent creation of the Bulgarian Exarchate. It was another form of international intervention which reduced Ottoman rule over Orthodox matters and hence curtailed the influence of the *Phanariotes*, the Ecumenical Patriarchate apparatus, with respect to the election of the Patriarch of Jerusalem.

In 1845, Russian pressure led to the election of Cyrillos, who took up residence in Jerusalem and severed the close link with the *Phanar*. The second half of the eighteenth century was full of controversy and strife between the Russian Orthodox Ecclesiastical mission and Russian diplomats on the one hand, and the Greek Orthodox Patriarchate on the other. The Russian mission contributed a great deal to the education and welfare of the Arab Orthodox, who had been neglected by the Patriarchate.

Strong Arab Orthodox opposition, combined with Russian pressure, brought about a compromise with the Patriarchate in 1875 which gave some concessions to the Arabs without, however, losing the upper hand in the administration of the Holy Places. Working relations with the Ottoman *Porte* were not enough to preserve the position of the Greek Orthodox clergy in Palestine.

To the Greek Orthodox, the experience of the nineteenth century showed that no foreign intervention in the Holy Places could protect the interests of the Orthodox Church. On the contrary, foreign intervention was sometimes inimical toward the Patriarchate of Jerusalem and detrimental to the traditional links between the Patriarchate and the Ottoman central and local administrations. Even the emergence of the new Greek state in 1830 did not alter this basic idea of the Patriarchate. Athens became the second center of the Greek world, marking the beginning of an antagonism with the traditional center of the Greek Orthodox world, Constantinople.

✦ ✦ ✦

World War I brought new protagonists into the Middle East arena. The British were now the dominant power in Palestine and the Holy Places. The initiative of the Greek Orthodox in this completely new international and regional landscape was threefold: firstly, toward the Greek state, an emerging regional power; secondly, toward new international fora; and thirdly, and most importantly, toward the new masters of the region, the British.

Internal strife between the majority of the Holy Synod and Patriarch Damianos had weakened the Greek Orthodox Church in 1918. It was at that point that the majority of the Holy Synod openly asked for the moral and material help of a government beyond the region—the Greek government. This initiative had four possible motivations: firstly, the Greek national consciousness which prevailed among the members of the Patriarchate's hierarchy; secondly, the emergence of a strong Greek state on the "winners' " side, which was ready to undertake the role of a regional power in the eastern Mediterranean (the triumph of the irredentist policy of secular Athens had meant the end of the religious, communal power of Constantinople); thirdly, the collapse of protection resulting from the close connection between the Patriarchate and the Ottoman administration; and last, but not least, the loss of life-giving income from Rumania and Bessarabia due to the war and the situation in Russia. Nonetheless, the idea of seeking the protection of the Greek state was not shared by Patriarch Damianos and other members of the Confraternity. The complaints of the Greek consuls that the Patriarch was randomly ready to cooperate with them were a constant feature of their reports from Palestine.

On the international scene, the Patriarchate prepared and submitted to the Peace Conference in Paris a memorandum, which is a most vivid statement of Greek Orthodox reservations against the interference of European powers in the Holy Places. The memorandum came as an answer to the Latin one on the Holy Places, arguing that ". . . the Franciscans had settled down in the most important Holy Places since the fourteenth century through pecuniary means on the one hand, and on the other by the inter-mediation of Kings and Democracies."[13] In another paragraph, the memorandum stated that ". . . this struggle [for the Holy Places] used to end in favour of the Franciscans whenever the political influence of the West oppressed efficaciously the Sublime Porte leaving no outlet to it."

The views of the Greek Foreign Ministry, which was the channel of communication of the Patriarchate of Jerusalem with other governments and Orthodox churches, are of some interest. In 1918, the Second Directorate of the Foreign Ministry argued that the Holy Places were a sui generis land and should be handled as such. They therefore should be a *corpus separatum* administered by the local patriarchates and communities that had rights over the Holy Places, namely, the Greek Orthodox, the Latins, and the Armenians. Alternatively they saw a British protectorate as the preferable solution.[14] It is evident that the Greek Foreign Ministry wished to avoid the involvement of foreign powers and any kind of internationalization. The British solution reflected Greek reservations for a Catholic protectorate, either French or, less likely, Italian.

The reservations of the Greek Ministry were also shared by the Greek Orthodox Patriarchate in Jerusalem. The diplomatic struggle around the Commission for the Holy Places in the early 1920s clearly showed how weak the Greek Orthodox Church was in face of "internationalizing" the issue of Jerusalem and the Holy Places.

The idea of placing Jerusalem under a special international regime had already been conceived during secret British, French, and Russian talks in the winter of 1915–16 on the division of the Ottoman empire. The Sikes-Picot Agreement provided for a neutral entity including Jerusalem under international administration.[15]

As soon as the British troops entered the Holy City on the 9th December, 1917, Pasquale Baldi, a Catholic specialist on the Holy Places, outlined the Catholic plans and expectations regarding the Holy Places and made clear that the balance of power had been changed. Now it was the great powers and the international role of the Catholic Church, and not the Greek elites and the Ottoman bureaucracy, that played the decisive role in the matters of Jerusalem.[16] "Today," he argued, "it is not the question of counting how many Greeks are in the Ottoman empire but how many Catholics there are in the world. . . ."

In 1922, the Vatican increased its diplomatic effort in an attempt to secure a preponderant role for the Catholics in the Commission for the Holy Places. The views of the Vatican reflected its fears that a combination between Anglicanism, Zionism, and the Orthodox would harm the rights of the Catholics in the Holy Places.

The proposal of the Holy See was that only the state members of the League of Nations should participate in the Commission for the Holy Places, which was set by Article 14 of the Mandate. The other denominations, namely Greek Orthodox and Armenians, would have a consultative role. This provision meant that Catholics would decide over Orthodox and Armenian matters, let alone disputes between, for instance, Catholics and Greek Orthodox.[17]

The British proposed that the Commission for the Holy Places should have three subcommissions, one Christian, one Jewish, and one Muslim. The Christian subcommission would be composed of three Roman Catholics (Italian, Spanish, Belgian), three Orthodox (one of whom would be Greek and one Russian), one Armenian, and possibly one or two representatives of the Ethiopians and the Copts.

The British proposal met with strong French opposition, which maintained that a Christian commission should have a Catholic majority and, of course, the president of such a commission should be French, given the traditional role of France as protector of Catholicism. On the other hand, the preponderant role of France encountered a strong reaction by Italy in view of the fact that the Latin Patriarch of Jerusalem was Italian.

Facing this deadlock, the British stated in October, 1922 that they were not able to settle the disputes among the Catholic states and that they assumed the protection of the Orthodox rights since these were not represented by an

Orthodox power in the League of Nations. Thus, they would not accept a solution which would not be just for the Orthodox. The commission was never realized and the British Mandate undertook the obligation to preserve the status quo in the Holy Places.

✦ ✦ ✦

The diplomatic struggle over the Commission for the Holy Places revealed the weakness of the Greek Orthodox Patriarchate after the collapse of the Ottoman empire. The transfer of decision-making from Jerusalem and Istanbul to Paris, London, and Rome deprived the Greek Orthodox Church of any power and gave the Vatican the initiative. The arguments of European powers on the issue mirrored the same ideas and notions about the Holy Places which prevailed in the nineteenth century, especially after the Crimean War, whereby the Holy Places and Jerusalem were not part of the region and thus did not belong to the East and its tradition. They were in the East, but not quite eastern. They had an extraterritorial character and they could be thought of as part of Europe. If there was not a European power behind the Greek Orthodox Patriarchate, it had to be invented; otherwise, the Greek Orthodox could not have been represented. Tsarist Russia no longer existed and Greece was trying to heal the trauma of the Asia Minor disaster. The British undertook the task.

The Holy See saw the "internationalization" as an opportunity to redistribute the Holy Places and get the lion's share out of a Catholic-dominated Commission for the Holy Places. Dispute and antagonism among Catholic powers, as well as British reservations to accept French partnership in Palestine through a French-dominated Commission for the Holy Places, foiled the Vatican's plan.[18]

The Greek Orthodox Patriarchate of Jerusalem now had to change its attitude toward finding new allies, both regional and European. The British seemed to be reliable allies. The relations between the Anglican and the Orthodox Church had been long and amicable since the reign of the Patriarch of Constantinople, Cyrillos Loukaris, at the beginning of the seventeenth century. During the 1920s, high-ranking Greek Orthodox ecclesiastics participated in the Lambeth Conference; in the same period, the Anglo-Hellenic League of London included prominent members of both the Anglican and the Greek Orthodox Church.

Moreover, the Patriarchate did not oppose the Zionist plan for Palestine since this was the policy of the British Mandate. Patriarch Damianos adopted the line that Greek Orthodox Christians, like Jews, were a minority and that they should cooperate with each other. In general, the Patriarchate followed a path known since the Ottoman times. It coopted with the state's policies in order to preserve its internal autonomy and the control of the Holy Places. Tolerance for allegiance was a scheme known during the Ottoman era.

The policy of the Patriarchate was reinforced by British policy concerning the Holy Places. The British Mandate administration and the Foreign Office tried to avoid any international interference, mediation, or inquiry regarding either the Patriarchate of Jerusalem or the Holy Places in general. The handling of the two major crises in the Patriarchate in 1919–21 and in 1924–26 aimed at avoiding any international implications.

In 1919, the majority of the Holy Synod of the Patriarchate asked for the deposition of Patriarch Damianos, accusing him of being autocratic and corrupt, as well as responsible for mismanagement of the Patriarchate's revenues and for the abysmal debt of the Orthodox Church of Jerusalem. They also proposed the intervention and arbitration of the Patriarchates of Constantinople and Alexandria as well as the churches of Greece and Cyprus. The Bertram-Luke Commission was set up in order to avoid this interference or any other international implications concerning the preservation of the status quo in the Holy Places. The Commission ruled out any interference from abroad, either ecclesiastical or political, and reinstated the position of Patriarch Damianos.[19]

In 1925, the demands of the Arab Orthodox to play a decisive role in the Patriarchate's affairs and the refusal of the Greek hierarchy to accept such demands led to another crisis. The Arab Orthodox community constituted the vast majority of the Orthodox faithful in Palestine and felt that their rights and needs for education and social welfare were being ignored by the Patriarchate. They were excluded from the Church administration and the management of the Church revenues and lands.

The British administration responded by setting up of the Bertram-Young Commission, which aimed again at avoiding any international implications which could have transferred the matter from the jurisdiction of the Palestinian administration to the international fora, and indeed to the Council of the League of Nations. This primary aim of the Commission prevented proposals for radical alterations in the administration of the Jerusalem Patriarchate.

The Arab Orthodox community also opposed the notion of internationalization, though for different reasons. Although the Arab Orthodox community owed the emergence of its nationalism to the international, mainly Russian but also Protestant, educational mission in the Levant and the Holy Places, they did not espouse the idea of "internationalization" of the Holy City. On the contrary; they included the future of the Holy Places in their aspiration for the "nationalization" of the Orthodox Church in Palestine.[20]

In the late 1920s and the 1930s, many prominent Arab Orthodox individuals and newspapers were deeply involved in the Palestinian Arab national movement. The newspaper *Filastin* and its editor, 'Isa al-Isa, were among the strongest critics of the Patriarchate and advocates of greater Arab participation in the administration of the Church. From the 1920s onward, there were radical proposals for the establishment of an autonomous and autocephalous Palestinian Arab church following the example of the Bulgarian Exarchate

As K. Cragg has argued, the Arab Christians were and still are adversely affected by their minority status, their ambivalent relations with the West, and the complexity of their interreligious situation. For the Arab Christians, and the Arab Orthodox in particular, the basis of their Palestinian Arab nationalism and, at the same time, the greater issue is that of Palestine. The land of Palestine became one of the most important issues in the culture and history of the Palestinian Christians. This notion of Palestine could not exclude the Holy Places and, as such, any idea of *corpus separatum* for Jerusalem could not be accepted by the Arab Orthodox.[21]

In 1947, the extraterritorial character of the Holy Places would give way to *corpus separatum* of Jerusalem. The "internationalization," which was behind all European diplomatic initiatives from 1852 onward, was now presented unveiled. The Prussian suggestions of 1841 regarding an international agreement on Jerusalem, Bethlehem, and Nazareth were present and prevailed a century later.[22]

The General Assembly of the United Nations, in its resolution of 29th November, 1947, recommended the establishment of Jerusalem as *corpus separatum* under a special international regime to be administered by the United Nations. The Vatican saw the internationalization as an instrument to promote Catholic interests over the Holy Places. All relevant Encyclicals and Vatican broadcasting underscored the preservation of the Catholic rights in the Holy Places.

The Greek Orthodox Patriarchate reacted to the *corpus separatum* plan and tried to find allies in the region. Greece supported the United Nations plans since they had the blessing of London and Washington, and the Greek government could not afford to irritate its closest allies on a relatively minor issue in the midst of the civil war. Although the Greek government supported the plan, the Greek Orthodox Patriarchate was to come to an understanding with Israel against the *corpus separatum*. The reservations of the Patriarchate were deeply rooted in the mistrust toward the Catholics and the Vatican. In their view, every effort for internationalization was one more opportunity for the Catholics to dominate the Holy Places.

The recommendations and suggestions to the plan made by the Patriarchate of Jerusalem reflected these beliefs.[23] Regarding the nationality of the High

Commissioner, the Patriarchate regretted the fact that he could not be of either Israeli or Arab nationality, i.e., a member of the indigenous population. They feared that the possibility of a Catholic commissioner would harm the interests of the Greek Orthodox Patriarchate. Furthermore, the composition of the international court which would have the ultimate jurisdiction over disputes in the Holy Places excluded nationals of the region, both Arabs and Israelis. It was one more source of fear that Orthodox interests would not be given adequate consideration.

For the Greek Orthodox Church, in Jerusalem, Athens, and Constantinople, the plan for internationalization would transform Jerusalem into ". . . un centre d'intrigues internationales." In his letter to the United Nations, Patriarch Timotheos stressed that the Greek Orthodox Church should fully acquire adequate representation in accordance with the fourteen-century-long history of Orthodox presence. In the Patriarch's view, equity, justice, and a clear understanding of realities were the pillars of a practicable and lasting settlement in the Holy Places.[24] This clear understanding of the realities on the ground, the realities of the Orient, was always the criterion of Patriarchal policies.

In conclusion, throughout the nineteenth and early twentieth centuries, the notion of extraterritoriality and internationalization of the Holy Places was dominant in the policies of the European powers and the Holy See. In other words, Jerusalem was in Palestine but not quite Palestinian. The Vatican tried to use this notion in order to dominate the Holy Places. As Zander put it, ". . . in this struggle the Latins increasingly secured the support of external powers . . . whilst the Greeks had to rely on the indigenous Christian population and [indeed] their connections at the court in Constantinople."[25]

Every time the decision-making was transferred from Constantinople and Jerusalem to western capitals, the position of the Orthodox Church became precarious. Whenever the terrain of diplomatic effort was the East, the Greek Orthodox Church managed to preserve its position by coopting the state, whether it be Ottoman, British Mandate, Israeli, or Jordanian. The *millet* system shaped the attitude and perception of the Orthodox Church of Jerusalem. It was a status of autonomy and self-sufficiency which the Church, as a religious corporation, enjoyed together with extensive jurisdiction under the Ottoman rule.[26] Even the emergence of the Greek state did not alter the policy of the Patriarchate. It preferred to search for allies in the region rather than to rely on the external political aid of the Greek state. The fourteen-century-long history of the Patriarchate dictated that the only way for the preservation of its position would be to adjust itself to the realities of the region and to build its future with the living stones of the Holy Land.

Notes

1. L. G. A. Gust, *The Status Quo in the Holy Places* (Jerusalem, 1929), 5–6.

2. "Repudiation of Sir Anton Bertram's theories against the Patriarchate of Jerusalem," *Nea Sion* 32 (1937), 362–86 (Greek).

3. K. Cragg, *The Arab Christian. A History in the Middle East* (London, 1992), 118.

4. *History of the Greek Nation,* 15 vols. (Athens, 1975), XI, 126 (Greek).

5. W. Zander, *Israel and the Holy Places of Christendom* (London, 1971), 25.

6. Cragg (above, note 3), 125.

7. C. Papadopoulos, *History of the Church of Jerusalem* (Alexandria, 1910), 707 (Greek).

8. Ibid., 714–15.

9. A. J. P. Taylor, *The Struggle for Mastery in Europe 1848–1918* (Oxford, 1988), 49.

10. M. E. Yapp, *The Making of the Modern Middle East* (London, 1987), 74.

11. T. Themelis, *The Greeks in the Holy Places* (Athens, 1919), 48–50 (Greek).

12. T. Stavrou, "Russian Interest in the Levant 1843–1848," *The Middle East Journal* 17 (1963), 90–103.

13. Zander (above, note 5), 186–88.

14. Memorandum by K. Sakellaropoulos, Head of the Second Directorate, Archives of the Greek Ministry of Foreign Affairs (AYE), B/1918.

15. D. Neef, "Jerusalem in US Policy," *Journal of Palestine Studies* 23/89 (1993), 21.

16. R. Heacock, "Jerusalem and the Holy Places in European Diplomacy," *The Christian Heritage in the Holy Land,* eds. A. O'Mahoney, G. Gunner, and K. Hintlian (London, 1995), 208.

17. S. Minerbi, *The Vatican and Zionism. Conflict in the Holy Land 1895–1925* (Oxford, 1990), 70.

18. Ibid., 89–90.

19. S. Roussos, "Greece and the Arab Middle East: The Greek Orthodox Communities in Egypt, Syria and Palestine 1919–1940" (doctoral dissertation, University of London SOAS, 1994), 134–75.

20. S. Khuri and N. Khuri, *A Short History of the Orthodox Church of Jerusalem* (Jerusalem, 1925), 370–74 (Arabic).

21. Cragg (above, note 3), 235.

22. Zander (above, note 5), 72.

23. B. Papadopoulos, "A Brief Note on the Draft Statute of the Jerusalem District," *Nea Sion* 44 (1949), 199–212 (Greek).

24. A. Nachmani, *Israel, Turkey and Greece. Uneasy Relations in the Eastern Mediterranean* (London, 1987), 108–10.

25. Zander (above, note 5), 44.

26. N. J. Pantazopoulos, *Church and Law in the Balkan Peninsula during the Ottoman Rule* (Amsterdam, 1984), 6.

Index